The Global Transformations Reader

The Global Transformations Reader

An Introduction to the Globalization Debate

Edited by

David Held and Anthony McGrew

Polity

First published in 2000 by Polity Press
in association with Blackwell Publishers Ltd

Reprinted 2000

Editorial office:
Polity Press
65 Bridge Street
Cambridge CB2 1UR, UK

Marketing and production:
Blackwell Publishers Ltd
108 Cowley Road
Oxford OX4 1JF, UK

Published in the USA by
Blackwell Publishers Inc.
350 Main Street
Malden, MA 02148, USA

ISBN 0–7456–2199–6
ISBN 0–7456–2200–3 (pbk)

A catalogue record for this book is available from the British Library
Library of Congress Cataloguing-in-Publication Data

The global transformations reader: an introduction to the globalization debate / edited by David Held and Anthony McGrew.
     p. cm.
   Includes index.
   ISBN 0–7456–2199–6 -- ISBN 0–7456–2200–3 (pbk.)
      1. International relations. I. Held, David. II. McGrew, Anthony G.

JZ1318 .G56 2000
327.1'7--dc21
                                                                99-087851

Typeset in 10 on 12 pt Times Ten
by Graphicraft Limited, Hong Kong
Printed in Great Britain by T. J. International, Padstow, Cornwall

This book is printed on acid-free paper.

Contents

Preface   ix

Sources and Acknowledgements   xi

Acronyms   xiv

The Great Globalization Debate: An Introduction
David Held and Anthony McGrew   1

Part I   Conceptualizing Globalization

Introduction   47

1   Globalization
   George Modelski   49

2   Rethinking Globalization
   David Held and Anthony McGrew, David Goldblatt and Jonathan Perraton   54

3   World History in a Global Age
   Michael Geyer and Charles Bright   61

4   Globalization – a Necessary Myth?
   Paul Hirst and Grahame Thompson   68

5   The Network Society
   Manuel Castells   76

6   Time–Space Compression and the Postmodern Condition
   David Harvey   82

7   The Globalizing of Modernity
   Anthony Giddens   92

8   What is Globalization?
   Ulrich Beck   99

Part II   The Reconfiguration of Political Power?

Introduction   105

9   Sovereignty in International Society
   Robert O. Keohane   109

10   Compromising Westphalia
   Stephen D. Krasner   124

11 Has Globalization Ended the Rise and Rise of the Nation-State?
    Michael Mann   136

12 The Declining Authority of States
    Susan Strange   148

13 Global Market versus Regionalism
    Björn Hettne   156

14 International Law
    David Held   167

15 Globalization and Legal Certainty
    Volkmar Gessner   172

16 Governance in a Globalizing World
    James N. Rosenau   181

Part III   The Fate of National Culture

Introduction   191

17 Encountering Globalization
    Kevin Robins   195

18 The Globalization of Communication
    John B. Thompson   202

19 The Global Media
    Edward Herman and Robert McChesney   216

20 Disjuncture and Difference in the Global Cultural Economy
    Arjun Appadurai   230

21 Towards a Global Culture?
    Anthony D. Smith   239

Part IV   A Global Economy?

Introduction   249

22 A New Geo-economy
    Peter Dicken   251

23 The Global Economy
    Manuel Castells   259

24 Globalization and the History of the International Economy
    Paul Hirst and Grahame Thompson   274

25 Economic Activity in a Globalizing World
    Jonathan Perraton, David Goldblatt, David Held and Anthony McGrew 287

26 Global Markets and National Politics
    Geoffrey Garrett   301

27 The Woven World
    Daniel A. Yergin and Joseph Stanislaw   319

28 Has Globalization Gone Too Far?
    Dani Rodrik   323

29 The Passing of Social Democracy
    John Gray   328

30 Welfare State Limits to Globalization
    Elmar Rieger and Stephan Leibfried   332

Part V Divided Nations, Unruly World

Introduction   339

31 Globalization with a Human Face
    UNDP Report 1999   341

32 The Rise of the Fourth World
    Manuel Castells   348

33 Globalization and the Postcolonial World
    Ankie Hoogvelt   355

34 The West and the Third World
    D. K. Fieldhouse   361

35 The Gender Dimension
    Jill Steans   366

36 Environmental Issues and the Compression of the Globe
    Steven Yearley   374

37 Order, Globalization and Inequality in World Politics
    Ngaire Woods   387

Part VI World Orders, Normative Futures

Introduction   401

38 Democracy beyond Borders?
    Anthony McGrew   405

39 Regulating Globalization?
    David Held   420

40 Global Governance: Prospects and Problems
    Fred Halliday   431

41 Transnational Justice
    Onora O'Neill   442

42 The Idea of World Community
    Chris Brown   453

43 Beyond the States System?
    Hedley Bull   462

Index   468

Preface

Few contemporary phenomena elicit such political and academic controversy as globalization. Some consider it the fundamental dynamic of our epoch, a process of change which is to be promoted, managed or resisted; by contrast, others consider it the great myth of our times, a notion which misrepresents and misconstrues the real forces which shape our lives. In the public sphere especially, the idea of globalization is creating a new political faultline around which politicians and political parties of all persuasions seek to mobilize public opinion. From the 'globaphobia' of the radical right to the more adaptive strategies found in Third Way politics, globalization has become the rationale for diverse political projects. In the process, the idea of globalization has often become debased and confused.

In constructing this Reader, our central aim has been to bring clarity and enlightenment to the terms of the globalization debate. Because it is so important, it demands nothing less. The Introduction develops an intellectual framework for making sense of the controversy. It pursues an extended discussion between the sceptical account of globalization and those that defend its significance – the globalist position. In doing so, it identifies and examines the core areas of disagreement and convergence. Subsequent parts build on this by introducing the reader to the work of the main protagonists in the globalization discussion.

This Reader developed out of our earlier collaboration on *Global Transformations: Politics, Economics and Culture* (1999). As we contemplated designing and teaching courses on globalization, it readily became apparent that for most students the vast and diverse literature on globalization was an excessively daunting prospect. What was needed, we believed, was a collection which brought together the essential interventions in the globalization debate, from across the social sciences. The result is a Reader which, we hope, is the most comprehensive and up to date available.

Clearly, in preparing this volume, we have had to shorten many pieces in order to ensure both balance and coverage in the context of limited space. Where we have excised material this is annotated in the following way: cuts are marked by [...], and where more than a paragraph has been omitted, the ellipses appear on a line of their own; editorial additions or alterations are indicated by [additions or alterations]. Beyond that we have left the texts as far as possible unchanged. In exercising our editorial judgement, it was always our intention that students should, at some point, return to the originals to follow up specific arguments or evidential claims of special interest.

In preparing this volume, we have benefited enormously from the advice and assistance of many individuals. Brenda Martin provided research assistance; Pam Thomas and Sue Pope made the processing of the manuscript a much easier task; Connie Hallam dealt speedily with all the copyright matters; Ann Bone copy-edited the entire manuscript not only with great speed but also with incredible attention to detail;

and Serena Temperley helped at decisive stages of the production process. We are, in addition, very grateful to the many contributors who took time to comment on our proposed editorial changes and who approved the inclusion of their work in this volume.

David Held
Tony McGrew

Sources and Acknowledgements

The chapters are drawn from the following sources, and the editors and publishers are grateful for permission to use copyright material.

Chapter 1 is from George Modelski, *Principles of World Politics*, Free Press, New York, 1972, chapter 3; copyright © 1972 by The Free Press; reprinted by permission of the publishers, The Free Press, a division of Simon & Schuster, Inc.

Chapter 2 is from David Held and Anthony McGrew, David Goldblatt and Jonathan Perraton, *Global Transformations: Politics, Economics and Culture*, Polity Press, Cambridge, and Stanford University Press, Stanford, 1999, Introduction; reprinted by permission of the publishers.

Chapter 3 is from Michael Geyer and Charles Bright, 'World History in a Global Age', *American Historical Review*, vol. 100, no. 4 (October 1995), reprinted by permission of the American Historical Association.

Chapter 4 is from Paul Hirst and Grahame Thompson, *Globalization in Question*, 2nd edition, Polity Press, Cambridge, and Blackwell Publishers, New Malden, Mass., 1999, chapter 1; reprinted by permission of the authors and publishers.

Chapter 5 is from Manuel Castells, *The Information Age*, vol. 1: *The Rise of the Network Society*, Blackwell Publishers, Oxford and New Malden, Mass., 1996, Conclusion; reprinted by permission of the author and Blackwell Publishers.

Chapter 6 is from David Harvey, *The Condition of Postmodernity: An Enquiry into the Origins of Cultural Change*, Blackwell Publishers, Oxford and New Malden, Mass., 1989, chapter 17; reprinted by permission of the author and Blackwell Publishers.

Chapter 7 is from Anthony Giddens, *The Consequences of Modernity*, Polity Press, Cambridge, 1990; reprinted by permission of the author and publisher.

Chapter 8 is from Ulrich Beck, *What is Globalization?*, translated by Patrick Camiller, Polity Press, Cambridge, 1999, Introduction; reprinted by permission of Polity Press and Suhrkamp Verlag.

Chapter 9 is from Robert O. Keohane, 'Hobbes's Dilemma and Institutional Change in World Politics: Sovereignty in International Society', chapter 9 in Hans-Henrik Holm and Georg Sørensen (eds), *Whose World Order? Uneven Globalization and the End of the Cold War*, Westview Press, Boulder, Colo., 1995; copyright © 1995 by Westview Press, Inc., reprinted by permission of Westview Press, a member of Perseus Books, L.L.C.

Chapter 10 is reprinted in an abridged version from Stephen D. Krasner, 'Compromising Westphalia', *International Security*, vol. 20, no. 3 (Winter 1995), pp. 115–51; copyright © 1995 by the President and Fellows of Harvard College and the Massachusetts Institute of Technology; reprinted by permission of MIT Press Journals.

Chapter 11 is from Michael Mann, 'Has Globalization Ended the Rise and Rise of the Nation-State?', *Review of International Political Economy*, vol. 4, no. 3 (Autumn 1997), pp. 472–96; copyright © 1997 Routledge; reprinted by permission of Carfax Publishing, Taylor and Francis Ltd, P.O. Box 25, Abingdon, Oxon OX12 3UE.

Chapter 12 is from Susan Strange, *The Retreat of the State: The Diffusion of Power in the World Economy*, Cambridge University Press, Cambridge, 1996, chapter 1; reprinted by permission of the publisher and the Executors of the Estate of Susan Strange.

Chapter 13 is from Björn Hettne, 'The Double Movement: Global Market versus Regionalism', chapter 12 in R. W. Cox (ed.), *The New Realism: Perspectives on Multilateralism and World Order*,

United Nations University Press, Tokyo, 1998; copyright © 1998 by the United Nations University; reprinted by permission of the publishers; all rights reserved.

Chapter 14 is from David Held, *Democracy and the Global Order: From the Modern State to Cosmopolitan Governance*, Polity Press, Cambridge, and Stanford University Press, Stanford, 1995; copyright © 1995 David Held; reprinted by permission of the publishers.

Chapter 15 is from Volkmar Gessner, 'Globalization and Legal Certainty', chapter 12 in V. Gessner and A. C. Budak (eds), *Emerging Legal Certainty: Empirical Studies on the Globalization of Law*, Onati International Series in Law and Society, Ashgate, Aldershot, 1998; reprinted by permission of Ashgate Publishing Ltd.

Chapter 16 is from James N. Rosenau, 'Governance and Democracy in a Globalizing World', chapter 2 in Daniele Archibugi, David Held and Martin Köhler (eds), *Re-imagining Political Community: Studies in Cosmopolitan Democracy*, Polity Press, Cambridge, and Stanford University Press, Stanford, 1998; reprinted by permission of the author and publishers.

Chapter 17 is from Kevin Robins, 'What in the World's Going On?', chapter 1 in Paul du Gay (ed.), *Production of Culture/Cultures of Production*, Sage, London, in association with The Open University, 1997; © The Open University, 1997; reprinted by permission of the author and Sage Publications Ltd.

Chapter 18 is from John B. Thompson, *The Media and Modernity*, Polity Press, Cambridge, and Stanford University Press, Stanford, 1995, chapter 5; copyright © 1995 John B. Thompson; reprinted by permission of the author and publishers.

Chapter 19 is from Edward Herman and Robert McChesney, *The Global Media: The New Missionaries of Corporate Capitalism*, Cassell, London, 1997, chapter 2; reprinted by permission of the publisher, The Orion Publishing Group.

Chapter 20 is from Arjun Appadurai, 'Disjuncture and Difference in the Global Cultural Economy', *Theory, Culture & Society*, vol. 7 (1990), pp. 295–310; copyright © Theory, Culture & Society, 1990; reprinted by permission of the author and Sage Publications Ltd, London.

Chapter 21 is from Anthony D. Smith, 'Towards a Global Culture?', *Theory, Culture & Society*, vol. 7 (1990), pp. 171–91; reprinted by permission of the author and Sage Publications Ltd, London.

Chapter 22 is from Peter Dicken, *Global Shift: Transforming the World Economy*, 3rd edition, Paul Chapman, London, 1998, chapter 1; copyright © Peter Dicken 1998; reprinted by permission of the author and publisher.

Chapter 23 is from Manuel Castells, *The Information Age*, vol. 1: *The Rise of the Network Society*, Blackwell Publishers, Oxford and New Malden, Mass., 1996; reprinted by permission of the author and Blackwell Publishers.

Chapter 24 is from Paul Hirst and Grahame Thompson, *Globalization in Question*, 2nd edition, Polity Press, Cambridge, and Blackwell Publishers, New Malden, Mass., 1999, chapter 2; reprinted by permission of the authors and publishers.

Chapter 25 is from Jonathan Perraton, David Goldblatt, David Held and Anthony McGrew, 'The Globalization of Economic Activity', *New Political Economy*, vol. 2, no. 2 (1997), pp. 257–77; reprinted by permission of Carfax Publishing, Taylor and Francis Ltd, P.O. Box 25, Abingdon, Oxon OX12 3UE.

Chapter 26 is from Geoffrey Garrett, 'Global Markets and National Politics: Collision Course or Virtuous Circle?', *International Organization*, vol. 52, no. 4 (Autumn 1998), pp. 787–824; copyright © 1998 by The IO Foundation and the Massachusetts Institute of Technology; reprinted by permission of MIT Press Journals.

Chapter 27 is from Daniel A. Yergin and Joseph Stanislaw, *The Commanding Heights: The Battle between Government and the Marketplace that is Remaking the Modern World*, Simon & Schuster, New York, 1998, chapter 13; copyright © 1998 by Daniel A. Yergin and Joseph Stanislaw; reprinted by permission of the publisher.

Chapter 28 is from Dani Rodrik, *Has Globalization Gone Too Far?*, Institute of International Economics, Washington DC, 1997, chapter 1; reprinted by permission of the Institute of International Economics.

Chapter 29 is from John Gray, *False Dawn*, Granta Publications, London, and The New Press, New York, 1998, pp. 87–92; copyright © 1998 by John Gray, reprinted by permission of the publishers. US rights controlled by The New Press.

Chapter 30 is from Elmar Rieger and Stephan Leibfried, 'Welfare State Limits to Globalization', *Politics & Society*, vol. 26, no. 3 (September 1998), pp. 363–90; copyright © 1998 Sage Publications, Inc.; reprinted by permission of the publisher, Sage Publications, Inc., Thousand Oaks, Calif.

Chapter 31 is from UNDP, *Human Development Report 1999*, Oxford University Press, New York, 1999; copyright © 1999 by the United Nations Development Programme; reprinted by permission of Oxford University Press, Inc.

Chapter 32 is from Manuel Castells, *The Information Age*, vol. 3: *End of Millennium*, Blackwell Publishers, Oxford and New Malden, Mass., 1998, chapter 2; reprinted by permission of the author and Blackwell Publishers.

Chapter 33 is from Ankie Hoogvelt, *Globalisation and the Postcolonial World: The New Political Economy of Development*, Macmillan, London, and Johns Hopkins University Press, Baltimore, 1997, chapter 4 and Conclusion; copyright © 1998 Ankie Hoogvelt; reprinted by permission of the author and publishers.

Chapter 34 is from D. K. Fieldhouse, *The West and the Third World*, Blackwell Publishers, Oxford, and New Malden, Mass., 1999, chapter 12; reprinted by permission of the author and Blackwell Publishers.

Chapter 35 is from Jill Steans, *Gender and International Relations*, Polity Press, Cambridge, and Rutgers University Press, New Brunswick, 1998, chapter 6; copyright © Jill Steans 1998; reprinted by permission of the author and publishers.

Chapter 36 is from Steven Yearley, *Sociology, Environmentalism, Globalization*, Sage, 1996, chapters 2 and 3; copyright © Steven Yearley 1996; reprinted by permission of the author and Sage Publications Ltd.

Chapter 37 is from Ngaire Woods, 'Order, Globalization, and Inequality in World Politics', chapter 1 in A. Hurrell and N. Woods (eds), *Inequality, Globalization and World Politics*, Oxford University Press, Oxford, 1999, copyright © Andrew Hurrell and Ngaire Woods; reprinted by permission of Oxford University Press.

Chapter 38 is from Anthony McGrew, 'Democracy beyond Borders? Globalization and the Reconstruction of Democratic Theory and Politics', chapter 10 in A. G. McGrew (ed.), *The Transformation of Democracy? Globalization and Territorial Democracy*, Polity Press, Cambridge, 1997; reprinted by permission of the publisher.

Chapter 39 by David Held, 'Regulating Globalization? The Reinvention of Politics', is from a lecture given at the conference on Globalizations, Stockholm, 21–24 October 1998; copyright © 2000 David Held; by permission of the author.

Chapter 40 is from Fred Halliday, 'Global Governance: Prospects and Problems', first published in *Citizenship Studies*, vol. 4, no. 1 (2000); copyright © Fred Halliday 2000; reproduced here in shortened form by permission of the author.

Chapter 41 is from Onora O'Neill, 'Transnational Justice', chapter 11 in David Held (ed.), *Political Theory Today*, Polity Press, Cambridge, and Stanford University Press, Stanford, 1991; reprinted by permission of the author and publishers. A slightly revised version of the original essay is also appearing in Onora O'Neill, *Bounds of Justice*, Cambridge University Press, Cambridge, 2000.

Chapter 42 is from Chris Brown, 'International Political Theory and the Idea of World Community', chapter 4 in Ken Booth and Steve Smith (eds), *International Relations Theory Today*, Polity Press, Cambridge, and The Pennsylvania State University Press, University Park, 1995; reprinted by permission of the publishers.

Chapter 43 is from Hedley Bull, *The Anarchical Society: A Study of Order in World Politics*, Macmillan, London, and Columbia University Press, New York, 1977, pp. 248–56; copyright © 1977 Hedley Bull; reprinted by permission of the Macmillan Press Ltd and Columbia University Press.

Acronyms

ABC	American Broadcasting Company
AFP	Agence France-Presse
AIDS	acquired immune deficiency syndrome
AP	Associated Press
APEC	Asia-Pacific Economic Cooperation
ARF	ASEAN Regional Forum
ASEAN	Association of South East Asian Nations
BBC	British Broadcasting Corporation
BIS	Bank for International Settlements
BSE	bovine spongiform encephalopathy
CCTV	Central China Television
CENTO	Central Treaty Organization
CEO	chief executive officer
CFCs	chlorofluorocarbons
CIS	Commonwealth of Independent States
CNN	Cable News Network (US)
CO$_2$	carbon dioxide
COMECOM	Council for Mutual Economic Assistance
CSCE	Conference on Security and Cooperation in Europe (Helsinki)
EAEC	East Asian Economic Caucus
EC	European Community
ECE	Economic Commission for Europe (UN)
ECOSOC	Economic and Social Council (UN)
ECOWAS	Economic Organization of West African States
EEZ	Exclusive Economic Zone (for oceans)
EFTA	European Free Trade Association
EMS	European Monetary System
EMU	European Monetary Union
ERM	exchange rate mechanism (Europe)
EU	European Union
FAO	Food and Agriculture Organization
FDI	foreign direct investment
FLSAW	Forward Looking Strategies for the Advancement of Women to the Year 2000
FoE	Friends of the Earth
FTA	free trade area
G3	triad of Europe, Japan and North America

G5	Group of Five: France, Germany, Japan, UK, US
G7	Group of Seven: G5 plus Canada and Italy
GAD	Gender and Development
GATT	General Agreement on Tariffs and Trade
GDP	gross domestic product
GNP	gross national product
GONGOs	government-controlled NGOs
IBRD	International Bank for Reconstruction and Development (World Bank)
ICRC	International Committee of the Red Cross
IGO	intergovernmental organization
ILE	interlinked economy
ILO	International Labour Organization
IMF	International Monetary Fund
INCOTERMS	International Chamber of Commerce glossary defining terms used in international trade
INGO	international non-governmental organization
INSTRAW	International Institute for Training and Research for the Advancement of Women (UN)
IPCC	Intergovernmental Panel on Climate Change
ISI	import substitution industrialization
ITU	International Telecommunication Union
LDC	less developed country
MERCOSUR	Southern Cone Common Market (Latin America)
MITI	Ministry of International Trade and Industry (Japan)
MNC	multinational corporation/company
NAFTA	North American Free Trade Agreement
NATO	North Atlantic Treaty Organization
NBC	National Broadcasting Company (US)
NGO	non-governmental organization
NIC	newly industrializing country
NIE	newly industrializing economy
NWICO	New World Information and Communication Order
OAU	Organization of African Unity
OECD	Organization for Economic Cooperation and Development
PBEC	Pacific Basin Economic Council
R&D	research and development
SAARC	South Asian Association for Regional Cooperation
SADC	Southern African Development Community
SADCC	Southern Africa Development Coordinating Conference/Committee
SAP	structural adjustment programme
SEATO	South East Asia Treaty Organization
TNC	transnational corporation/company
TRIPS	trade in intellectual property rights
UN	United Nations
UNCITRAL	United Nations Commission on International Trade Law
UNCTAD	United Nations Conference on Trade and Development

UNDP	United Nations Development Programme
UNESCO	United Nations Educational, Scientific and Cultural Organization
UNIFEM	Voluntary Fund for the UN Decade for Women
UPA	United Press Association
UPI	United Press International
USAID	United States Agency for International Development
WID	Women in Development
WTO	World Trade Organization

The Great Globalization Debate: An Introduction

David Held and Anthony McGrew

Over the last decade the phenomenon of globalization – whether real or illusory – has captured the public imagination. In an epoch of profound and unsettling global change, in which traditional ideologies and grand theories appear to offer little purchase on the world, the idea of globalization has acquired the mantle of a new paradigm. Called upon to account for developments as diverse as the value of the euro, the worldwide popularity of *Star Wars*, the rise of Third Way politics and religious fundamentalism, the discourse of globalization seems to offer a convincing analysis of the contemporary human predicament. As with the idea of modernization, which acquired intellectual primacy within the social sciences during the 1960s, so today the notion of globalization has become the leitmotif of our age.

Although media references to globalization have become common over the last two decades, the concept itself can be traced back to a much earlier period. Its origins lie in the work of many nineteenth- and early twentieth-century intellectuals, from sociologists such as Saint-Simon to students of geopolitics such as MacKinder, who recognized how modernity was integrating the world. But it was not until the 1960s and early 1970s that the term 'globalization' was actually used. This 'golden age' of rapidly expanding political and economic interdependence – most especially between Western states – generated much reflection on the inadequacies of orthodox approaches to thinking about politics, economics and culture which presumed a strict separation between internal and external affairs, the domestic and international arenas, and the local and the global. For in a more interdependent world events abroad readily acquired impacts at home, while developments at home had consequences abroad. In the context of a debate about the growing interconnectedness of human affairs, world systems theory, theories of complex interdependence and the notion of globalization itself emerged as largely rival accounts of the processes through which the fate of states and peoples was becoming more intertwined (Modelski 1972; Wallerstein 1974; Keohane and Nye 1977). Following the collapse of state socialism and the consolidation of capitalism worldwide, academic and public discussion of globalization intensified dramatically. Coinciding with the rapid spread of the information revolution these developments appeared to confirm the belief that the world was fast becoming a shared social and economic space – at least for its most affluent inhabitants. However, whether the notion of globalization ultimately helps or hinders our understanding of the contemporary human condition, and strategies to improve it, is now a matter of intense intellectual and public dispute. For as the global babble has become more voluble it has invited greater critical scrutiny of these issues. In short, the great globalization debate has been joined.

Trying to make sense of this debate presents considerable difficulties since there are no definitive or fixed lines of contestation. Instead multiple conversations coexist (although few real dialogues), which together do not readily afford a coherent or simple characterization. Within shared traditions of social enquiry, whether neoclassical economics or world systems theory, no singular account of globalization has acquired the status of orthodoxy. On the contrary, competing assessments continue to order the discussion. Nor do the dominant ideological traditions of conservatism, liberalism or socialism offer coherent readings of, or responses to, a globalizing era. Just as some conservatives and socialists find common ground in dismissing the significance of globalization, others of similar political persuasion view it as a dramatic new threat to cherished values. Indeed, the very idea of globalization appears to disrupt established paradigms and political orthodoxies. Frequently little or no consistent correspondence is evident between the positions adopted by the protagonists in the globalization debate and their particular ideological or intellectual allegiances.

Accepting this heterogeneity, it is, nevertheless, feasible to identify a clustering of arguments around an emerging fissure between those who consider that contemporary globalization is a real and significant historical development – the globalists – and those who conceive it as a primarily ideological or mythical construction which has marginal explanatory value – the sceptics. Of course, this dualism is rather crude since it elevates two conflicting interpretations from among diverse arguments and opinions. But, as used here, the labels – globalists and sceptics – refer to ideal-type constructions. Ideal-types are heuristic devices which order a field of enquiry and identify the primary areas of consensus as well as contention. They assist in clarifying the primary lines of argument and, thus, in establishing the fundamental points of disagreement. They provide an accessible way into the mêlée of voices – rooted in the globalization literature but by definition corresponding to no single work, author or ideological position.

Neither the sceptical nor the globalist thesis, of course, exhausts the complexity or the subtleties of the interpretations of globalization to be found in the existing literature. Even within each position considerable differences of emphasis exist with respect to matters of historical interpretation as well as normative argument. Such differences will become apparent throughout the volume. For in selecting the contributions not only have we attempted to represent both extremes in the debate, but also the diversity of views within these dominant positions. A further editorial principle has been the desire to reflect the richness of the different disciplinary strands of social science in order that the essential interdisciplinarity of the debate is given proper attention. Accordingly, each of the following parts reflects a representative set of major contributions to the literatures on globalization while further embellishing, as well as carefully qualifying, the characterization of the globalization debate described below.

In organizing the contributions to the debate, we have constructed the volume around the critical themes which are addressed in the globalist and sceptical literatures alike. Part I (Conceptualizing Globalization) commences with an overview of the historical and conceptual issues surrounding the idea of globalization. Part II (The Reconfiguration of Political Power?) focuses on the controversy concerning the modern nation-state: its continued primacy versus its transformation. Building on this discussion, part III (The Fate of National Culture) illuminates the debate about the cultural ramifications of globalization, particularly in respect of the question of national culture and identity. Parts IV (A Global Economy?) and V (Divided Nations, Unruly World) introduce the major contributions to the discussion concerning the nature of the contemporary global economy and its consequences for patterns of global inequality. Finally, with critical issues of social justice and world order to the fore, part VI (World Orders, Normative Futures) considers the normative considerations raised in the globalization debate.

I Conceptualizing Globalization

No single universally agreed definition of globalization exists. As with all core concepts in the social sciences its precise meaning remains contested. Globalization has been variously conceived as action at a distance (whereby the actions of social agents in one locale can come to have significant consequences for 'distant others'); time–space compression (referring to the way in which instantaneous electronic communication erodes the constraints of distance and time on social organization and interaction); accelerating interdependence (understood as the intensification of enmeshment among national economies and societies such that events in one country impact directly on others); a shrinking world (the erosion of borders and geographical barriers to socio-economic activity); and, among other concepts, global integration, the reordering of interregional power relations, consciousness of the global condition and the intensification of interregional interconnectedness (Harvey 1989; Giddens 1990; Rosenau 1990; Jameson 1991; Robertson 1992; Scholte 1993; Nierop 1994; Geyer and Bright 1995; Johnston et al. 1995; Zürn 1995; Albrow 1996; Kofman and Youngs 1996; Held et al. 1999). What distinguishes these definitions is the differential emphasis given to the material, spatio-temporal and cognitive aspects of globalization. It is worth dwelling on this tripartite cluster of characteristics for a moment in order to establish a general conception of globalization before turning to the debate about its potential analytical and explanatory value.

A basic concept of globalization

Globalization has an undeniably material aspect in so far as it is possible to identify, for instance, flows of trade, capital and people across the globe. These are facilitated by different kinds of infrastructure – physical (such as transport or banking systems), normative (such as trade rules) and symbolic (such as English as a lingua franca) – which establish the preconditions for regularized and relatively enduring forms of global interconnectedness. Rather than mere random encounters, globalization refers to these entrenched and enduring patterns of worldwide interconnectedness. But the concept of globalization denotes much more than a stretching of social relations and activities across regions and frontiers. For it suggests a growing magnitude or intensity of global flows such that states and societies become increasingly enmeshed in worldwide systems and networks of interaction. As a consequence, distant occurrences and developments can come to have serious domestic impacts while local happenings can engender significant global repercussions. In other words, globalization represents a significant shift in the spatial reach of social action and organization towards the interregional or intercontinental scale. This does not mean that the global necessarily displaces or takes precedence over local, national or regional orders of social life. Rather, the latter can become embedded within more expansive sets of interregional relations and networks of power. Thus, the constraints of social time and geographical space, vital coordinates of modern social life, no longer appear to impose fixed barriers to many forms of social interaction or organization, as the existence of the World Wide Web and round-the-clock trading in global financial markets attests. As distance 'shrinks', the relative speed of social interaction increases too, such that crises and events in distant parts of the globe, exemplified by the East Asian economic crash of 1997, come to have an immediate worldwide impact involving diminishing response times for decision-makers.

Globalization engenders a certain cognitive shift expressed both in a growing public awareness of the ways in which distant events can affect local fortunes (and vice versa) as well as in public perceptions of shrinking time and geographical space.

Simply put, globalization denotes the expanding scale, growing magnitude, speeding up and deepening impact of interregional flows and patterns of social interaction. It refers to a shift or transformation in the scale of human social organization that links distant communities and expands the reach of power relations across the world's major regions and continents. But it should not be read as prefiguring the emergence of a harmonious world society or as a universal process of global integration in which there is a growing convergence of cultures and civilizations. For not only does the awareness of growing interconnectedness create new animosities and conflicts, it can fuel reactionary politics and deep-seated xenophobia. Since a significant segment of the world's population is either untouched directly by globalization or remains largely excluded from its benefits, it is a deeply divisive and, consequently, vigorously contested process. The unevenness of globalization ensures it is far from a universal process experienced uniformly across the entire planet.

The myth of globalization

For the sceptics it is precisely this kind of qualification that makes the very concept of globalization so deeply unsatisfactory. The question they pose is: what is the 'global' in globalization (Hirst 1997)? If the global cannot be interpreted literally, as a universal phenomenon, then the concept of globalization lacks clear specificity. Problematic too is a more relativist or subjectivist conception of the global which simply conceives it in terms of the apex of a hierarchy of spatial scales of social organization and interaction, from the local through to the national, regional and global. With no clear geographical referents, how is it possible to distinguish the international or the transnational from the global, or, for that matter, processes of regionalization from processes of globalization? It is precisely because much of the literature on globalization fails to specify the spatial referents for the global that, so the sceptics argue, the concept becomes so broad as to become impossible to operationalize empirically and, therefore, largely meaningless as a vehicle for understanding the contemporary world.

In interrogating the concept of globalization sceptics generally seek to establish a conclusive test of the globalization thesis. For the most part this involves constructing an abstract model of a global economy, global culture or world society and assessing how far contemporary trends match up to it (Sterling 1974; Perlmutter 1991; Dore 1995; Boyer and Drache 1996; Hirst and Thompson 1996). Embedded in many such models is a conception of a globalized economy or global society as akin to a national economy or society writ large. Others critical of the globalist thesis seek to assess how far contemporary trends compare with what several economic historians have argued was the *belle époque* of globalization, namely the period from 1890 to 1914 (Gordon 1988; Jones 1995; Hirst 1997). In both cases, there is a strong presumption that the statistical evidence by itself can establish the 'truth' about globalization. In this regard, the sceptical analysis is decidedly dismissive of the descriptive or explanatory value of the concept of globalization. Rather than globalization the sceptics conclude that a more valid conceptualization of current trends is captured by the terms 'internationalization' – that is, growing links between essentially discrete national economies or societies – and 'regionalization' or 'triadization' – the geographical clustering of cross-border economic and social exchanges (Ruigrok and Tulder 1995; G. Thompson 1998a; Weiss 1998; Hirst and Thompson 1999). This is an argument for the continuing primacy of territory, borders, place and national governments to the distribution and location of power, production and wealth in the contemporary world order. Yet a puzzle arises: namely, how to explain the disjuncture between the widespread discourse of globalization and the realities of a world in which, for the most part, the routines of everyday lives are dominated by national and local circumstances?

Instead of providing an insight into the forces shaping the contemporary world order, the concept of globalization, argue many sceptics, performs a rather different function. In essence, the discourse of globalization is understood as a primarily ideological construction; a convenient myth which, in part, helps justify and legitimize the neoliberal global project, that is, the creation of a global free market and the consolidation of Anglo-American capitalism within the world's major economic regions (Callinicos et al. 1994; Gordon 1988; Hirst 1997; Hoogvelt 1997). In this respect, the concept of globalization operates as a 'necessary myth', through which politicians and governments discipline their citizens to meet the requirements of the global marketplace. It is, thus, unsurprising that discussion of globalization became so widespread just at that juncture when the neoliberal project – the Washington consensus of deregulation, privatization, structural adjustment programmes (SAPs) and limited government – consolidated its hold within key Western capitals and global institutions such as the IMF.

Frequently associated with this sceptical position is a strong attachment either to an essentially Marxist or to a realist ontology. Traditional Marxist analysis considers that capitalism, as a social order, has a pathological expansionist logic, since to maintain profits capital constantly has to exploit new markets. To survive, national capitalism must continuously expand the geographical reach of capitalist social relations. The history of the modern world order is the history of Western capitalist powers dividing and redividing the world up into exclusive economic zones. Today, it is argued, imperialism has acquired a new form as formal empires have been replaced by new mechanisms of multilateral control and surveillance, such as the G7 and World Bank. As such, the present epoch is described by many Marxists not in terms of globalization, but instead as a new mode of Western imperialism dominated by the needs and requirements of finance capital within the world's major capitalist states (Van der Pijl 1999).

Realism too presents the existing international order as constituted primarily by and through the actions of the mightiest economically and militarily powerful states (and their agents). Accordingly, the internationalization of economic or social relations is argued to be contingent upon the policies and preferences of the great powers of the day since only they have sufficient military and economic muscle to create and maintain the conditions necessary for an open (liberal) international order (Waltz 1979). Without the exercise of American power, so the argument suggests, the existing liberal world order, which underpins the recent intensification of international interdependence, would eventually collapse (Gilpin 1987). This leads to a further critical point; namely, that liberal orders are historically unlikely to endure since, in a system in which states constantly struggle for dominance, the power of hegemonic states ultimately has a finite life. As many sceptics are wont to assert, without a hegemon to police a liberal system, as in the period 1919–39, a rush to autarky and the breakdown of world order will ensue (Gilpin 1981). International interdependence, according to this interpretation, is ultimately a temporary and contingent condition.

The globalist's response

The globalist account rejects the assertion that the concept of globalization can be simply dismissed either as a purely ideological construction or as a synonym for Western imperialism. While not denying that the discourse of globalization may well serve the interests of powerful social forces in the West, the globalist account also emphasizes that it reflects real structural changes in the scale of modern social organization. This is evident in, among other developments, the growth of MNCs, world financial markets, the diffusion of popular culture and the salience of global environmental degradation. Rather than conceiving globalization as a solely economic phenomenon, the globalist analysis gives equal status to other dimensions of social activity. This attachment to a differentiated or multidimensional conception of globalization reflects a Weberian and/or post-Marxist and post-structuralist understanding of social reality as constituted by a number of distinct institutional orders or networks of power: the economic, technological, political, cultural, natural, etc. (Mann 1986; Giddens 1990). To reduce globalization to a purely economic or technological logic is considered profoundly misleading since it ignores the inherent complexity of the forces that shape modern societies and world order. Thus, the globalist analysis commences from a conception of globalization as a set of interrelated processes operating across all the primary domains of social power, including the military, the political and the cultural. But there is no a priori assumption that the historical or spatial pattern of globalization within each of these domains is identical or even comparable. In this respect, patterns of cultural globalization, for instance, are not presumed necessarily to replicate patterns of economic globalization. The globalist account promotes a conception of globalization which recognizes this differentiation, allowing for the possibility that it proceeds at different tempos, with distinctive geographies, in different domains.

Central to this globalist conception is an emphasis on the particular spatial attributes of globalization. In seeking to differentiate global networks and systems from those operating at other spatial scales, such as the local or the national, the globalist analysis identifies globalization primarily with activities and relations which crystallize on an interregional or intercontinental scale (Geyer and Bright 1995; Castells 1996; Dicken 1998). This involves globalists in attempting to establish more precise analytical distinctions between the concept of globalization and the concepts of regionalization and localization, that is, the nexus of relations between geographically contiguous states, and the clustering of social relations within states, respectively (Dicken 1998). But, in so doing, the relationship between globalization and these other scales of social organization is not typically conceived in hierarchical or contradictory terms. On the contrary, the interrelations between these different scales are considered both fluid and dynamic.

The attempt to establish a more systematic specification of the concept of globalization is further complemented by the significance attached to its temporal or historical forms. Rather than trying to assess how contemporary global trends measure up to some abstract model of a globalized world, or simply comparing the magnitude of global flows between different epochs, the globalist account draws on socio-historical modes of analysis. This involves locating contemporary globalization within what the French historian Braudel refers to as the perspective of the 'longue durée' – that is, very long-term patterns of secular historical change (Helleiner 1997). As the existence of premodern world religions confirms, globalization is not only a phenomenon of the modern age.

Making sense of contemporary globalization requires placing it in the context of secular trends of world historical development (Modelski 1972; Hodgson 1993; Mazlish and Buultjens 1993; Bentley 1996; Frank and Gills 1996; Clark 1997; Frank 1998). But that development, as the globalist account also recognizes, is punctuated by distinctive phases – from the epoch of world discovery to the *belle époque* or the interwar years – when the pace of globalization appears to intensify or, alternatively, sometimes regress (Fernández-Armesto 1995; Geyer and Bright 1995). To understand contemporary globalization involves drawing on a knowledge of what differentiates these discrete phases, including how such systems and patterns of global interconnectedness are organized and reproduced, their different geographies and histories, and the changing configuration of interregional power relations. Accordingly, the globalist account stretches the concept of globalization to embrace the idea of its distinctive historical forms. This requires an examination of how patterns of globalization, both within and between different domains of activity, compare and contrast over time.

This particular tradition of socio-historical analysis encourages a conception of globalization as a somewhat indeterminate process; for globalization is not inscribed with a preordained logic which presumes a singular historical trajectory or end condition, that is, the emergence of a single world society or global civilization. In fact, teleological or determinist thinking is strongly resisted. Globalization, it is argued, is driven by a confluence of forces and embodies dynamic tensions. As noted earlier, the globalist analysis dismisses the presumption that globalization can be explained solely by reference to the imperatives of capitalism or technology (Axford 1995). Nor can it be understood as simply a projection of Western modernity across the globe (Giddens 1990). Rather, it is considered a product of multiple forces, including economic, political and technological imperatives, as well as specific conjunctural factors, such as, for instance, the creation of the ancient Silk Route or the collapse of state socialism. It harbours no fixed or given pattern of historical development. Moreover, since it pulls and pushes societies in different directions it simultaneously engenders cooperation as well as conflict, integration as well as fragmentation, exclusion and inclusion, convergence and divergence, order and disorder (Harvey 1989; Giddens 1990; Robertson 1992; Hurrell and Woods 1995; Rosenau 1997). Rejecting historicist or determinist interpretations of globalization, the globalist account invites an open-ended conception of global change rather than a fixed or singular vision of a globalized world.

Central to this globalist interpretation is, nonetheless, a conception of global change involving a significant reordering of the organizing principles of social life and world order. Three aspects of this tend to be identified in the globalist literature; namely, the transformation of dominant patterns of socio-economic organization, of the territorial principle, and of power. By eroding the constraints of space and time on patterns of social interaction, globalization creates the possibility of new modes of transnational social organization, for instance global production networks and regulatory regimes, while simultaneously making communities in particular locales vulnerable to global conditions or developments, as with the 1998 WTO ruling on the EU–US banana war and its fallout on the banana producers of the Windward Islands.

In transforming both the context of, and the conditions for, social interaction and organization, globalization also involves a reordering of the relationship between territory and socio-economic and political space. Put simply, as economic, social and political activities increasingly transcend regions and national frontiers this delivers a direct challenge to the territorial principle of modern social and political organization. That principle presumes a direct correspondence between society, economy and polity within an exclusive and bounded national territory. But globalization disrupts this correspondence in so far as social, economic and political activity can no longer be understood as coterminous with national territorial boundaries. This does not mean that territory and place are becoming irrelevant, but rather that, under conditions of contemporary globalization, they are reinvented and reconfigured, that is, cast in a global context and increasingly to be found in competition with one another (Castells 1996; Dicken 1998). The latter point connects with the third and final aspect of the transformations identified in the globalist literature; namely, the transformation of power relations.

At the core of the globalist account lies a concern with power: its instrumentalities, configuration, distribution, and impacts. Globalization is taken to express the expanding scale on which power is organized and exercised. In this respect, it involves the reordering of power relations between and across the world's major regions such that key sites of power and those who are subject to them are often oceans apart. To paraphrase Jameson, under conditions of contemporary globalization the truth of power no longer resides in the locales in which it is immediately experienced (Jameson 1991). Power relations are deeply inscribed in the dynamics of globalization, as the continuing disquisitions on its implications for the nation-state confirm.

II   The Reconfiguration of Political Power?

Contemporary social life is associated with the modern state which specifies the proper form of nearly all types of human activity. The state appears to be omnipresent, regulating the conditions of life from birth registration to death certification. From the policing of everyday activities to the provision of education and the promotion of health care, the steady expansion of state power appears beyond question. Quantitatively, the growth of the state, from the size of its budget to the scope of its jurisdiction, is one of the few really uncontested facts of the twentieth century. On many fundamental measures of political power (for example, the capacity to raise taxes and revenues, the ability to hurl concentrated force at enemies) states are, at least throughout most of the OECD world, as powerful if not more powerful than their predecessors (Mann 1997). The sceptics make a great deal of this, as they do of the rise and dominance of the modern state in general. It is useful to rehearse this position and its many implications for the form and distribution of political power, before examining the globalists' alternative account.

The formation and rule of the modern state

The claim of the modern state to an overarching role is a relatively novel one in human history, even in the place which gave birth to it – Western Europe. A thousand years ago, for example, an inhabitant of an English village knew little of life beyond it; the village was the beginning and practically the end of his or her world. She or he would have visited the nearest market town but would scarcely have ventured further; would have probably recognized the name of the king, although would rarely, if ever, have seen him; and may well have had more contact with representatives of the church than with any 'political' or military leaders (Lacey and Danziger 1999). And while five hundred years later two forms of political regime – absolute and constitutional monarchies – were beginning to crystallize across the European continent, Europe resembled more a mosaic of powers, with overlapping political claims and jurisdictions (Tilly 1975; Poggi 1978). No ruler or state was yet sovereign in the sense of being supreme over a bounded territory and population.

Modern states emerged in Western Europe and its colonial territories in the eighteenth and nineteenth centuries, although their origins date back to the late sixteenth century (Skinner 1978; Held 1995: chs 2–3). They distinguished themselves initially from earlier forms of political rule by claiming a distinctive symmetry and correspondence between sovereignty, territory and legitimacy. The distillation of the concept of sovereignty was pivotal to this development, for it lodged a special claim to the rightful exercise of political power over a circumscribed realm – an entitlement to rule over a bounded territory (see Skinner 1978). Modern states developed as nation-states – political bodies, separate from both ruler and ruled, with supreme jurisdiction over a demarcated territorial area, backed by a claim to a monopoly of coercive power, and enjoying legitimacy as a result of the loyalty or consent of their citizens. The major innovations of the modern nation-state – territoriality that fixes exact borders, monopolistic control of violence, an impersonal structure of political power and a distinctive claim to legitimacy based on representation and accountability – marked out its defining (and sometimes fragile) features. The regulatory power of such states expanded throughout the modern period creating – albeit with significant national differences – systems of unified rule across demarcated territories, centralized administration, concentrated and more effective mechanisms of fiscal management and resource distribution, new types of lawmaking and law enforcement, professional standing armies, a concentrated war-making capacity and, concomitantly, elaborate formal relations among states through the development of diplomacy and diplomatic institutions (P. Anderson 1974; Giddens 1985).

The consolidation of the power of leading European nation-states was part of a process in which an international society of states was created, first in Europe itself, and then, as Europe expanded across the globe, in diverse regions as Europe's demands on its colonies were pressed and resisted (Ferro 1997). This 'society of states' laid down the formal rules which all sovereign and autonomous states would, in principle, have to adopt if they were to become full and equal members of the international order of states. The origins of this order are often traced to the Peace Treaties of Westphalia of 1648, which concluded the Thirty Years' War (see Falk 1969; Krasner 1995; Keohane 1995). But the rule system codified at Westphalia is best understood as having created a *normative trajectory* in international law, which did not receive its fullest articulation until the late eighteenth and early nineteenth century. It was during this time that territorial sovereignty, the formal equality of states, non-intervention in the internal affairs of other recognized states, and state consent as the foundation stone of international legal agreement became the core principles of the modern international order (see Crawford and Marks 1998). Of course, the consolidation of this order across the world would, paradoxically, have to wait until the decline of its earliest protagonists – the European powers – and the formal initiation of decolonization after the Second World War. But it is perhaps fair to say that it was not until the late twentieth century that the modern international order of states became truly global; for it was only with the end of all the great empires – European, American and finally Soviet – that many peoples could finally join the society of states as independent political communities.

The number of internationally recognized states more than doubled between 1945 and the early 1990s (Union of International Associations 1996). The high point of the modern nation-state system was reached at the end of the twentieth century, buttressed and supported by the spread of new multilateral forms of international coordination and cooperation, in international organizations like the UN, and new international regulatory mechanisms, such as the universal human rights regime.

Not only has the modern nation-state become the principal type of political rule across the globe, but it has also increasingly assumed, since decolonization and the collapse of the Soviet empire, a particular political form; that is, it has crystallized as liberal or representative democracy (Potter et al. 1997). Several distinctive waves of democratization have brought particular countries in Europe, such as Portugal and Spain, into the democratic fold, while they have also brought numerous others closer to democracy in Latin America, Asia, Africa and Eastern Europe. Of course, there is no necessary evolutionary path to consolidated liberal democracy; the path is fragile and littered with obstacles – the hold of liberal democracy on diverse political communities is still tentative and open to challenge.

Surveying the political scene at the end of the twentieth century there are good reasons, argue the sceptics, for thinking of this period as the age of the modern nation-state. For states in many places have increasingly claimed a monopoly of the legitimate use of force and judicial regulation, established permanent military forces as a symbol of statehood as well as a means of ensuring national security, consolidated tax raising and redistributive mechanisms, established nation-wide communication infrastructures, sought to systematize a national or official language, raised literacy levels and created a national schooling system, promulgated a national identity, and built up a diverse array of national political, economic and cultural institutions. In addition, many states, west and east, have sought to create elaborate welfare institutions, partly as a means to promote and reinforce national solidarity, involving public health provision and social security (Ashford 1986). Moreover, OECD states have pursued macroeconomic management strategies, shifting from Keynesian demand management in the 1950s to 1970s to extensive supply-side measures in the 1980s and 1990s, in order to help sustain economic growth and widespread employment. Success in these domains has often remained elusive, but the Western nation-state's array of policy instruments and objectives have been emulated recently in many regions of the world.

It certainly can be argued that much of this 'emulation' has been more the result of necessity than of choice. Decolonization clearly did not create a world of equally free states. The influence of Western commerce, trade and political organization outlived direct rule. Powerful national economic interests have often been able to sustain hegemonic positions over former colonial territories through the replacement of 'a visible presence of rule' with the 'invisible government' of corporations, banks and international organizations (the IMF and the World Bank, for example) (Ferro 1997: 349–50). Furthermore, interlaced with this has been the sedimented interests and machinations of the major powers, jostling with each other for advantage, if not hegemonic status (Bull 1977; Buzan et al. 1993). The geopolitical roles of individual states may have changed (for example, the shifts in the relative position of the UK and France during the twentieth century from global empires to middle-ranking powers), but these changes have been accommodated within the prevailing structures of world order – the modern nation-state system and capitalist economic relations – which have governed the strategic choices open to political communities. The restricted nature of these choices has become even clearer with the collapse of Soviet communism and the bipolar division of the world established during the Cold War. Accordingly, the development programmes of states in sub-Saharan Africa, East Asia and Latin America appear to have acquired a uniform shape – market liberalization, welfare cut-backs, minimal regulation of private capital flows, deregulation of labour markets – and to be governed by political necessity rather than publicly sanctioned intervention.

Yet, however limited the actual control most states possess over their territories, they generally fiercely protect their sovereignty – their entitlement to rule – and their autonomy – their capacity to choose appropriate forms of political, economic and social development. The distinctive 'bargains' governments create with their citizens remain fundamental to their legitimacy. The choices, benefits and welfare policies of states vary dramatically according to their location in the hierarchy of states, but, in the age of nation-states, the independence bestowed by sovereignty, in principle, still matters greatly to all states. Modern nation-states are political communities which create the conditions for establishing national communities of fate; and few seem willing to give this up. Although national political choices are constrained, they still count and remain the focus of public deliberation and debate. According to the sceptics, national political traditions are still vibrant, distinctive political bargains can still be struck between governments and electorates, and states continue, given the political will, to rule. The business of national politics is as important as, if not more important than, it was during the period in which modern states were first formed.

Towards a global politics

Globalists would generally contest many aspects of the above account. Their argument runs as follows. The traditional conception of the state, in which it is posited as the fundamental unit of world order, presupposes its relative homogeneity, that is, that it is a unitary phenomenon with a set of singular purposes (Young 1972: 36). But the growth of international and transnational organizations and collectivities, from the UN and its specialized agencies to international pressure groups and social movements, has altered the form and dynamics of both state and civil society. The state has become a fragmented policy-making arena, permeated by transnational networks (governmental and non-governmental) as well as by domestic agencies and forces. Likewise, the extensive penetration of civil society by transnational forces has altered its form and dynamics.

The exclusive link between territory and political power has been broken. The contemporary era has witnessed layers of governance spreading within and across political boundaries. New international and transnational institutions have both linked sovereign states together and transformed sovereignty into the shared exercise of power. A body of regional and international law has developed which underpins an emerging system of global governance, both formal and informal.

This transformation can be illustrated by a number of developments, including the rapid emergence of international organizations and regimes. New forms of multilateral and global politics have been established involving governments, intergovernmental organizations (IGOs) and a wide variety of transnational pressure groups and international non-governmental organizations (INGOs). In 1909 there were 37 IGOs and 176 INGOs, while in the mid-1990s there were nearly 260 IGOs and nearly 5,500 INGOs. In addition, there has been an explosive development in the number of international treaties in force, as well as in the number of international regimes, such as the nuclear non-proliferation regime.

To this pattern of extensive political interconnectedness can be added the dense web of activity within and among the key international policy-making fora, including the UN, G7, IMF, WTO, EU, APEC, ARF and MERCOSUR summits and many other official and unofficial meetings. In the middle of the nineteenth century there were two or three interstate conferences or congresses per annum; today the number totals over four thousand annually. National government is increasingly locked into a multilayered system of governance – local, national, regional and global – and can barely monitor it, let alone stay in command.

At the regional level the EU, in remarkably little time, has taken Europe from the disarray of the post-Second World War era to a supranational polity in which sovereignty is pooled across a growing number of areas of common concern. Despite its contested nature, the EU represents a novel system of governance which institutionalizes intergovernmental collaboration to address collective and transborder issues. There has also been an acceleration in regionalization beyond Europe: in the Americas, Asia-Pacific and, to a lesser degree, in Africa. While the form taken by this type of regionalism is very different from the EU model, it has nonetheless had significant consequences for political power, particularly in the Asia-Pacific (ASEAN, APEC, ARF, PBEC and many other groupings). As regionalism has deepened so interregional diplomacy has intensified as old and new regional groupings seek to consolidate their relationships with each other. In this respect, regionalism has not been a barrier to contemporary political globalization – involving the shifting reach of political power, authority and forms of rule – but, on the contrary, has been largely compatible with it.

The momentum for international cooperation shows no sign of slowing, despite the many vociferous complaints often heard about it. The concerns of regional and global politics already go far beyond traditional geopolitics. Drug smugglers, capital flows, acid rain, the activities of paedophiles, terrorists and illegal immigrants do not recognize borders; neither can the policies for their effective management and resolution. International cooperation and coordination of national policies have become necessary requirements for managing the consequences of a globalizing world.

Fundamental changes have also occurred in the world military order. Few states now consider unilateralism or neutrality as a credible defence strategy. Global and regional security institutions have become more important. Most states today have chosen to sign up to a host of multilateral arrangements and institutions in order to enhance their security. But it is not just the institutions of defence which have become multinational. The way military hardware is manufactured has also changed. The age of 'national champions' has been superseded by a sharp increase in licensing, co-production agreements, joint ventures, corporate alliances and subcontracting. This means that few countries – not even the United States – can claim to have a wholly autonomous military production capacity. The latter can be highlighted also in connection with key civil technologies, such as electronics, which are vital to advanced weapons systems, and which are themselves the products of highly globalized industries.

The paradox and novelty of the globalization of organized violence today is that national security has become a multilateral affair. For the first time in history, the one thing that did most to give modern nation-states a focus and a purpose, and which has always been at the very heart of statehood, can now only be realized effectively if nation-states come together and pool resources, technology, intelligence, power and authority.

With the increase in global interconnectedness, the scope of strategic policy choices available to individual governments and the effectiveness of many traditional policy instruments tends to decline (see Keohane and Nye 1972: 392–5; Cooper 1986: 1–22). This tendency occurs, in the first instance, because of the growing irrelevance of many border controls – whether formal or informal – which traditionally served to restrict transactions in goods and services, production factors and technology, ideas and cultural interchange (see Morse 1976: chs 2–3). The result is a shift in the relative costs and benefits of pursuing different policy options. States suffer a further diminution in power because the expansion of transnational forces reduces the control individual governments can exercise over the activities of their citizens and other peoples. For example, the increased mobility of capital induced by the development of global financial markets shifts the balance of power between markets and states and generates powerful pressures on states to develop market-friendly policies, including low public deficits and expenditure, especially on social goods; internationally competitive (that is, low) levels of direct taxation; privatization and labour market deregulation. The decisions of private investors to move private capital across borders can threaten welfare budgets, taxation levels and other government policies. In effect, the autonomy of states is compromised as governments find it increasingly difficult to pursue their domestic agendas without cooperating with other agencies, political and economic.

In this context, many of the traditional domains of state activity and responsibility (defence, economic management, health and law and order) can no longer be served without institutionalizing multilateral forms of collaboration. As demands on the state have increased in the postwar years, the state has been faced with a whole series of policy problems which cannot be adequately resolved without cooperating with other states and non-state actors (Keohane 1984; McGrew 1992). Accordingly, individual states alone can no longer be conceived of as the appropriate political units for either resolving key policy problems or managing effectively a broad range of public functions.

These arguments suggest that the modern state is increasingly embedded in webs of regional and global interconnectedness permeated by quasi-supranational, intergovernmental and transnational forces, and unable to determine its own fate. Such developments, it is also contended, challenge both the sovereignty and legitimacy of states. Sovereignty is challenged because the political authority of states is displaced and compromised by regional and global power systems, political, economic and cultural. State legitimacy is at issue because with greater regional and global interdependence, states cannot deliver fundamental goods and services to their citizens without international cooperation, and even the latter can be quite inadequate in the face of global problems – from global warming to the volatile movements of the financial markets – which can escape political regulation altogether. To the extent that political legitimacy depends on competence and the ability to 'deliver the goods' to citizens, it is under increasing strain. Globalization, conclude the globalists, is eroding the capacity of nation-states to act independently in the articulation and pursuit of domestic and international policy objectives: the power and role of the territorial nation-state is in decline. Political power is being reconfigured.

III The Fate of National Culture

For long periods of human history most people have lived out their lives in a web of local cultures. While the formation and expansion of the great world religions and premodern empires carried ideas and beliefs across frontiers with decisive social impacts,

the most important vehicle for this, in the absence of direct military and political intervention, was the development of networks of ruling class culture (Mann 1986). At points
these bit deeply into the fragmented mosaic of local cultures, but for most people,
most of the time, their daily lives and routines persisted largely unchanged. Prior to the
emergence of nations and nation-states, most cultural communication and interaction
occurred either between elites or at very local and restricted levels. Little interaction
took place between the court and the village. It was not until the eighteenth century
that a new form of cultural identity coalesced between these two extremes.

The story of national culture: the sceptic's resource

The rise of the modern nation-state and nationalist movements altered the landscape
of political identity. The conditions involved in the creation of the modern state were
often also the conditions which generated a sense of nationhood. As state makers sought
to centralize and reorder political power in circumscribed territories, and to secure
and strengthen their power base, they came to depend on cooperative forms of social
relations with their subjects (Giddens 1985; Mann 1986). The centralization of power
spawned the dependence of rulers on the ruled for resources, human and financial. Greater
reciprocity was created between governors and governed and the terms of their
'exchange' became contested. In particular, the military and administrative requirements
of the modern state 'politicized' social relations and day-to-day activities. Gradually,
people became aware of their membership in a shared political community, with a common fate. Although the nature of this emergent identity was often initially vague, it
grew more definite and precise over time (Therborn 1977; Turner 1986; Mann 1987).

The consolidation of the ideas and narratives of the nation and nationhood has been
linked to many factors, including the attempt by ruling elites and governments to
create a new identity that would legitimize the enhancement of state power and the
coordination of policy (Breuilly 1992); the creation, via a mass education system, of
a common framework of understanding – ideas, meanings, practices – to enhance the
process of state-coordinated modernization (Gellner 1983); the emergence of new
communication systems – particularly new media (such as printing and the telegraph),
independent publishers and a free market for printed material – which facilitated inter-
class communication and the diffusion of national histories, myths and rituals, that is, a
new imagined community (B. Anderson 1983); and, building on a historic sense of homeland and deeply rooted memories, the consolidation of ethnic communities via a common public culture, shared legal rights and duties, and an economy creating mobility
for its members within a bounded territory (Smith 1986, 1995).

Even where the establishment of a national identity was an explicit political project
pursued by elites, it was rarely their complete invention. That nationalist elites actively
sought to generate a sense of nationality and a commitment to the nation – a 'national
community of fate' – is well documented. But 'it does not follow', as one observer aptly
noted, that such elites 'invented nations where none existed' (Smith 1990: 180–1). The
'nation-to-be' was not any large, social or cultural entity; rather, it was a 'community
of history and culture', occupying a particular territory, and often laying claim to a distinctive tradition of common rights and duties for its members. Accordingly, many nations
were 'built up on the basis of pre-modern "ethnic cores" whose myths and memories,
values and symbols shaped the culture and boundaries of the nation that modern elites

managed to forge' (Smith 1990: 180; and see Smith 1986). The identity that nationalists strove to uphold depended, in significant part, on uncovering and exploiting a community's 'ethno-history' and on highlighting its distinctiveness in the world of competing political and cultural values (cf. Hall 1992).

Of course, the construction of nations, national identities and nation-states has always been harshly contested and the conditions for the successful development of each never fully overlapped with that of the others (see Held et al. 1999: 48–9, 336–40). States are, as noted previously, complex webs of institutions, laws and practices, the spatial reach of which has been difficult to secure and stabilize over fixed territories. Nations involve cross-class collectivities which share a sense of identity and collective political fate. Their basis in real and imagined cultural, linguistic and historical commonalities is highly malleable and fluid, often giving rise to diverse expressions and ambiguous relationships to states. Nationalism is the force which links states to nations: it describes both the complex cultural and psychological allegiance of individuals to particular national identities and communities, and the project of establishing a state in which a given nation is dominant. The fixed borders of the modern state have generally embraced a diversity of ethnic, cultural and linguistic groups with mixed leanings and allegiances. The relationships between these groups, and between such groups and states, has been chequered and often a source of bitter conflict. In the late nineteenth and twentieth centuries, nationalism became a force which supported and buttressed state formation in certain places (for example, in France) and challenged or refashioned it elsewhere (for instance, in multi-ethnic states such as Spain or the United Kingdom) (see Held et al. 1999: 337–8).

However, despite the diversity of nationalisms and their political aims, and the fact that most national cultures are less than two hundred years old, these new political forces created fundamentally novel terms of political reference in the modern world – terms of reference which appear so well rooted today that many, if not the overwhelming majority of, peoples take them as given and practically natural (cf. Barry 1998). While earlier epochs witnessed cultural institutions that either stretched across many societies (world religions) or were highly localized in their form, the rise of nations, nationalism and nation-states led to the organization of cultural life along national and territorial lines. In Europe this assisted the consolidation of some older states, the creation of a plethora of new nation-states and, eventually, the fragmentation of multinational empires. The potency of the idea of the 'nation' was not lost on the rest of the world and notions of national culture and nationalism spread – partly as a result of the expansion of European empires themselves – to the Americas, Asia, Africa and the Middle East. This helped fuel independence movements, cementing once again a particular link between culture, geography and political freedom.

The struggle for national identity and nationhood has been so extensive that the sceptics doubt the latter can be eroded by transnational forces and, in particular, by the development of a so-called global mass culture. In fact, advocates of the primacy of national identity emphasize its enduring qualities and the deep appeal of national cultures compared to the ephemeral and ersatz qualities of the products of the transnational media corporations (see Smith 1990; and Brown 1995). Since national cultures have been centrally concerned with consolidating the relationships between political identity, self-determination and the powers of the state, they are, and will remain, the sceptics suggest, formidably important sources of ethical and political direction (see section VI below). Moreover, the new electronic networks of communication and

information technology which now straddle the world help intensify and rekindle traditional forms and sources of national life, reinforcing their influence and impact. These
networks, it has been aptly noted, 'make possible a denser, more intense interaction
between members of communities who share common cultural characteristics, notably
language'; and this provides a renewed impetus to the re-emergence of 'ethnic communities and their nationalisms' (Smith 1990: 175).

Furthermore, the sceptics argue, while new communication systems can create access
to distant others, they also generate an awareness of difference; that is, of the incredible diversity in lifestyles and value orientations (see Gilroy 1987; Robins 1991; Massey
and Jess 1995). Although this awareness may enhance cultural understanding, it often
leads to an accentuation of what is distinctive and idiosyncratic, further fragmenting
cultural life. Awareness of 'the other' by no means guarantees intersubjective agreement, as the Salman Rushdie affair only too clearly showed (see Parekh 1989). Moreover, although the new communication industries may generate a language of their own,
a particular set of values and consumption patterns, they confront a multiplicity of
languages and discourses through which people make sense of their lives and cultures
(J. B. Thompson 1990: 313ff.). The vast majority of the products of the mass-market
cultural corporations which flood across borders originate within the US and Western
societies. But the available evidence, according to the sceptics, suggests that national
(and local) cultures remain robust; national institutions continue in many states to have
a central impact on public life; national television and radio broadcasting continues
to enjoy substantial audiences; the organization of the press and news coverage retains
strong national roots; and foreign cultural products are constantly read and reinter-
preted in novel ways by national audiences (Miller 1992; Liebes and Katz 1993; J. B.
Thompson 1995).

Finally, defenders of national culture point out that there is no common global pool
of memories; no common global way of thinking; and no 'universal history' in and through
which people can unite. There is only a manifold set of political meanings and systems
through which any new global awareness must struggle for survival (see Bozeman 1984).
Given the deep roots of ethno-histories, and the many ways they are often refashioned,
this can hardly be a surprise. Despite the vast flows of information, imagery and people
around the world, there are few signs of a universal or global culture in the making,
and few signs of a decline in the political salience of nationalism.

Cultural globalization

Globalists take issue with most of the above, although they by no means dismiss
the significance of 'the national question'. Among the points they often stress are the
constructed nature of nationalist cultures; if these cultures were created more recently
than many are willing to recognize, and elaborated for a world in which nation-states
were being forged, then they are neither immutable nor inevitable in a global age.
Nationalism may have been functional, perhaps even essential, for the consolidation
and development of the modern state, but it is today at odds with a world in which
economic, social and many political forces escape the jurisdiction of the nation-state.

Given how slow many people's identities often are to change, and the strong desire
many people feel to (re)assert control over the forces which shape their lives, the complexities of national identity politics are, globalists concede, likely to persist. But such

politics will not deliver political control and accountability over regional and global phenomena unless a distinction is made between cultural nationalism – the conceptual, discursive and symbolic resources which are fundamental to people's lives – and political nationalism – the assertion of the exclusive political priority of national identity and national interests. The latter cannot deliver many sought-after public goods and values without regional and global collaboration. Only a global political outlook can ultimately accommodate itself to the political challenges of a more global era, marked by overlapping communities of fate and multilayered (local, national, regional and global) politics. Is there any reason to believe that such an outlook might emerge? Not only are there many sources for such an outlook in the present period but, globalists would argue, there are precedents to be found in the history of the modern state itself.

While the rise of nation-states and nationalist projects intensified cultural formation and interaction within circumscribed political terrains, the expansion of European powers overseas helped entrench new forms of cultural globalization with innovations in transport and communications, notably regularized mechanical transport and the telegraph. These technological advances helped the West to expand and enabled the secular philosophies which emerged in the late eighteenth and nineteenth centuries – especially science, liberalism and socialism – to diffuse and transform the cultural context of almost every society on the planet.

Contemporary popular cultures may not yet have had a social impact to match this but, globalists argue, the sheer scale, intensity, speed and volume of global cultural communications today is unsurpassed. For instance, the value of cultural exports and imports has increased many times over the last few decades; there has been a huge expansion in the trade of television, film and radio products; national broadcasting systems are subject to intensifying international competition and declining audience shares; and the figures for connections and users of the Internet are growing exponentially as communication patterns increasingly transcend national borders (UNESCO 1950, 1986, 1989; OECD 1997). The accelerating diffusion of radio, television, the Internet, satellite and digital technologies has made instant communication possible. Many national controls over information have become ineffective. People everywhere are exposed to the values of other cultures as never before. Nothing, not even the fact that we all speak different languages, can stop the flow of ideas and cultures. The English language is becoming so dominant that it provides a linguistic infrastructure as powerful as any technological system for transmitting ideas and cultures.

Beyond its scale, what is striking about today's cultural globalization is that it is driven by companies, not countries. Corporations, argue the globalists, have replaced states and theocracies as the central producers and distributors of cultural globalization. Private international institutions are not new but their mass impact is. News agencies and publishing houses in previous eras had a much more limited impact on local and national cultures than the consumer goods and cultural products of today's global corporations.

For the globalists the existence of new global communication systems is transforming relations between physical locales and social circumstances, and altering the 'situational geography' of political and social life (Meyrowitz 1985). In these circumstances, the traditional link between 'physical setting' and 'social situation' is broken. Geographical boundaries are overcome as individuals and collectivities experience events and developments far afield. Moreover, new understandings, commonalities and frames of meaning are elaborated without direct contact between people. As such, they can serve to detach, or disembed, identities from particular times, places and traditions, and can have a 'pluralizing impact' on identity formation, producing a variety of hyphenated identities which are 'less fixed or unified' (Hall 1992: 303, 309). While everyone has a local life, the ways people make sense of the world are now increasingly interpenetrated by developments and processes from diverse settings. Hybrid cultures and transnational media corporations have made significant inroads into national cultures and national identities. The cultural position of the modern state is transformed as a result (cf. McLuhan 1964; Rheingold 1995).

Those states which seek to pursue rigid closed-door policies on information and culture are certainly under threat from these new communication processes and technologies, and it is likely that the conduct of socio-economic life everywhere will be transformed by them as well. Cultural flows are transforming the politics of national identity and the politics of identity more generally. These developments have been interpreted, by some global theorists, as creating a new sense of global belonging and vulnerability which transcends loyalties to the nation-state, that is, to 'my country right or wrong' (see, for instance, Falk 1995b). The warrant for this latter claim can be found, it has been argued, in a number of processes and forces, including the development of transnational social movements with clear regional or global objectives, such as the protection of natural resources and the environment, and the alleviation of disease, ill-health and poverty (Ekins 1992). Groups like Friends of the Earth and Greenpeace have derived some of their success precisely from their ability to show the interconnectedness across nations and regions of the problems they seek to tackle. In addition, the constellation of actors, agencies and institutions – from regional political organizations to the UN – which are oriented towards international and transnational issues is cited as further evidence of a growing global political awareness. Finally, a commitment to human rights as indispensable to the dignity and integrity of all peoples – rights entrenched in international law and championed by transnational groups such as Amnesty International – is held as additional support of an emerging 'global consciousness'. These factors, it is also maintained, represent the cultural foundations of an incipient 'global civil society' (Falk 1995b; Kaldor 1998).

IV   A Global Economy?

Assessing competing claims about the fate of national cultures is complicated by the fact that, in part, it involves subjective questions of meaning for which systematic and reliable cross-cultural evidence is difficult to acquire. By contrast the debate about economic globalization suffers from almost exactly the opposite problem: namely, the existence of a multiplicity of data sources on diverse global trends, from merchandise trade and migration to foreign direct investment and child labour. At times, this tends to lend the debate a certain spurious objectivity as appeals to 'hard' evidence seek to establish the basis for conclusive judgements about competing claims. In practice, the discussion revolves as much around conflicting assessments of the validity of existing evidence and the value of different types of data as it does around issues of theoretical interpretation.

Although the debate about economic globalization has produced a voluminous literature, with contributions covering all the main traditions of economic and social analysis, the critical points of contention cluster around four fundamental questions. Put simply, these embrace:

- the extent to which economic activity is being globalized;
- whether a new form of capitalism, driven by 'the third industrial revolution', is taking hold across the globe;
- how far economic globalization remains subject to proper and effective national and international governance; and
- whether global competition spells the end of national economic strategy and the welfare state.

These four questions preoccupy both globalists and sceptics. A critical dialogue has opened up concerning the present form of the world economy; the dominant regime of capitalist accumulation; the modes and effectiveness of contemporary economic governance; and the robustness of national economic autonomy and sovereignty.

The persistence of national economies

The sceptical position reflects a cautious interpretation of contemporary global economic trends. Rather than a truly global economy the sceptics argue that, judged in historical terms, the present world economy remains far from closely integrated. By comparison with the *belle époque* of 1890–1914 both the magnitude and geographical scale of flows of trade, capital and migrants are currently of a much lower order (Gordon 1988; Weiss 1998; Hirst and Thompson 1999). Although today gross flows of capital between the world's major economies are largely unprecedented, the actual net flows between them are considerably less than at the start of the twentieth century (Zevin 1992). Many of these economies are less open to trade than in the past, and this is also the case for many developing countries (Hoogvelt 1997; Hirst and Thompson 1999). In addition, the scale of nineteenth-century migration across the globe dwarfs that of the present era by a significant magnitude (Hirst and Thompson 1999). In all these respects, the contemporary world economy is significantly less open and globalized than its nineteenth-century counterpart. It is also, argue the sceptics, significantly less integrated.

If economic globalization is associated with the integration of separate national economies, such that the actual organization of economic activity transcends national frontiers, then a global economy might be said to be emerging. Theoretically, in a globalized economy world market forces take precedence over national economic conditions as the real value of key economic variables (production, prices, wages and interest rates) respond to global competition. Just as local economies are submerged within national markets so, suggests the strong sceptical position, the real test of economic globalization is whether world trends confirm a pattern of global economic integration, that is, the existence of a single global economy (Hirst and Thompson 1999). In this respect the evidence, it is argued, falls far short of the exaggerated claims of many globalists. Even among the OECD states, undoubtedly the most interconnected of any economies, the contemporary trends suggest only a limited degree of economic and financial integration (Feldstein and Horioka 1980; Neal 1985; Zevin 1992; Jones 1995; Garrett 1998). Whether in respect of finance, technology, labour or production the evidence fails to confirm either the existence or the emergence of a single global economy (Hirst and Thompson 1999). Even multinational corporations, it is concluded, remain predominantly the captives of national or regional markets, contrary to their popular portrayal as 'footloose capital' (Tyson 1991; Ruigrok and Tulder 1995).

Rather than a global economy, the sceptics interpret current trends as evidence of a significant, but not historically unprecedented, internationalization of economic activity, that is, an intensification of linkages between separate national economies. Internationalization complements, rather than displaces, the predominantly national organization and regulation of contemporary economic and financial activity, conducted by national or local, public and private entities. To the sceptics all economics is principally national or local. But even the trend towards internationalization repays careful scrutiny; for it betrays a concentration of trade, capital and technological flows between the major OECD states to the exclusion of much of the rest of the world. The structure of world economic activity is dominated (and increasingly so) by the OECD economies and the growing links between them (Jones 1995). By far the largest proportion of humanity remains excluded from the so-called global market; there is a growing gap between North and South.

Far from an integrated global economy, what the sceptical analysis highlights is the increasing organization of world economic activity within three core blocs, each with its own centre and periphery; namely, Europe, Asia-Pacific and the Americas. This triadization of the world economy is associated with a growing tendency towards economic and financial interdependence *within* each of these three zones at the expense of integration between them (Lloyd 1992; Hirst and Thompson 1999). This process is further reinforced by the growing regionalization of economic activity, from the formal structures of APEC, NAFTA, MERCOSUR, ASEAN and the EU to the regional production and marketing strategies of multinational corporations and national firms (G. Thompson 1998a). Far from the present being an era of economic globalization, it is, especially by comparison with the *belle époque*, one defined by the growing fragmentation of the world economy into a multiplicity of regional economic zones dominated by powerful mercantilist forces of national economic competition and economic rivalry (Hart 1992; Sandholtz et al. 1992).

If the sceptical argument is dismissive of the notion of a global economy, it is equally critical of the proposition that the current era is defined by the existence of a nascent global capitalism. While not denying that capitalism, following the collapse of state socialism, is the 'only economic game in town' or that capital itself has become significantly more internationally mobile, such developments, it is argued, should not be read as evidence of a new globalized ('turbo') capitalism, transcending and subsuming national capitalisms (Callinicos et al. 1994; Ruigrok and Tulder 1995; Boyer and Drache 1996; Hirst and Thompson 1999). On the contrary, distinct capitalist social formations continue to flourish on the models of the European social-democratic mixed economy, the American neoliberal project and the developmental state of East Asia (Wade 1990). Despite the aspirations of its most powerful protagonists, the neoliberal tide of the 1990s has not forced a genuine or substantive convergence between these; nor can it claim a serious victory over its competitors (Scharpf 1991; Hart 1992). The 'end of history', in this respect, has turned out to be short-lived. The idea of global capitalism, personified by the business empires of figures such as George Soros and Bill Gates, may have great popular appeal but it is, ultimately, an unsatisfactory and misleading concept since it ignores the diversity of existing capitalist forms and the rootedness of all capital in discrete national capitalist structures.

Although the images of dealing rooms in New York or London, appearing almost daily on media news reports, reinforce the idea that capital is essentially 'footloose', the reality, suggest the sceptics, is that all economic and financial activity, from production, research and development to trading and consumption, has to take place some-where. To talk of the 'end of geography' is a serious exaggeration when place and space remain such vital determinants of the global distribution of wealth and economic power. Granted that, in a world of almost real-time communication, corporate capital and even small businesses may have the option of greater mobility, the fate of firms, large or small, is still primarily determined by local and national competitive advant-ages and economic conditions (Porter 1990; Ruigrok and Tulder 1995; G. Thompson 1998b). Even among the most substantial multinationals, competitive advantages are largely rooted in their respective national systems of innovation, while production and sales tend to be strongly regionally concentrated (Ruigrok and Tulder 1995; Thompson and Allen 1997). In effect, multinationals are little more than 'national corporations with international operations' since their home base is such a vital ingredient of their continued success and identity (Hu 1992) – a point British Airways learnt to its cost when its frequent flyers (predominantly of non-British origin) forced the airline to recon-sider its policy of replacing the Union Jack with global images on its aircraft tailplanes. Furthermore, a brief glance at the Fortune 500 list of the world's largest companies would confirm this since few are headquartered outside the US, UK, Germany or Japan. Indeed, closer inspection of the list would reveal the 'myth' of global capitalism as a convenient cover for the internationalization of American business above all else (Callinicos et al. 1994; Burbach et al. 1997). Governments, or at least the more pow-erful among them, thus retain considerable bargaining power with MNCs because they control access to vital national economic resources.

In dismissing the idea of 'footloose capital', the sceptical argument undermines the proposition that there is a new pattern of interdependence emerging between North and South. There is, the sceptics acknowledge, a popular belief that the deindustrial-ization of OECD economies is primarily a consequence of the export of manufactur-ing business and jobs to emerging economies and less developed economies, where wage rates are lower and regulatory requirements much less stringent. This interdependence between North and South is taken by some to define a new international division of labour in which developing economies are moving away from primary products to manu-facturing, while the OECD economies are shifting from manufacturing to services. But the actual evidence, the sceptics suggest, does not bear out such a dramatic shift, while the argument overgeneralizes from the East Asian experience (Callinicos et al. 1994; Hirst and Thompson 1996). The bulk of the world's poorest economies remain reliant on the export of primary products, while the OECD economies continue to dominate trade in manufactured goods (Hirst and Thompson 1999). Deindustrialization cannot be traced to the effects of foreign trade, especially cheap exports from the developing world, but rather is a consequence of technological change and changes in labour mar-ket conditions throughout the OECD economies (Rowthorn and Wells 1987; Krugman 1994, 1995). By exaggerating the changes in the international division of labour there is a serious risk of overlooking the deeper continuities in the world economy. Despite internationalization and regionalization, the role and position of most developing countries in the world economy have changed remarkably little over the entire course of the last century (Gordon 1988). The present international division of labour is one Marx would instantly recognize.

If the international division of labour has changed only marginally, so also has the governance of the world economy. Although the post-1945 era witnessed significant institutional innovations in international economic governance, especially with the creation of a multilateral system of economic surveillance and regulation – the Bretton Woods regime – the actions of the US, as the world's largest single economic agent, remain critical to the smooth functioning of the world economy. In effect, the governance of the world economy still remains reliant, especially in times of crisis, on the willingness of the most powerful state(s) to police the system – as the East Asian crash of 1997–8 demonstrated so dramatically. However, even in more stable times, it is the preferences and interests of the most economically powerful states, in practice the G7 governments, that take precedence. Economic multilateralism has not rewritten the basic principles of international economic governance, argue the sceptics, for it remains a realm in which might trumps right: where the clash of competing national interests is resolved ultimately through the exercise of national power and bargaining between governments (Gilpin 1987; Sandholtz et al. 1992; Kapstein 1994). In this respect, multilateral institutions have to be conceived as instruments of states – and the most powerful states at that.

Of course, it is not part of the sceptical argument that the governance of the world economy has not changed at all in response to growing internationalization and, especially, regionalization (Hirst and Thompson 1999). There is, on the contrary, a strong recognition that the most pressing issue confronting the guardians of the world economy, in the aftermath of the East Asian crash, is how to reform and strengthen the Bretton Woods system (Kapstein 1994; Hirst and Thompson 1999). Furthermore, there is an acknowledgement of growing tensions between the rule-making activities of multilateral bodies, such as the WTO, and regional bodies such as the EU. New issues, from the environment to food production, have found their way on to the governance agenda too. Many of these are highly politicized since they bite deep into the sovereign jurisdiction of states – the very core of modern statehood itself.

But national governments, the sceptics hold, remain central to the governance of the world economy, since they alone have the formal political authority to regulate economic activity. As most states today rely, to varying degrees, on international flows of trade and finance to ensure national economic growth, the limits to, and the constraints on, national economic autonomy and sovereignty have become more visible, especially in democratic states. Historically, however, these constraints are no greater than in previous epochs when, as noted previously, international interdependence was much more intense. Paradoxically, the *belle époque* was precisely the era during which nation-states and national economies were being forged (Gilpin 1981; Krasner 1993). Thus, contemporary conditions pose no real threat to national sovereignty or autonomy. Far from economic interdependence necessarily eroding national economic autonomy or sovereignty, it can be argued to have enhanced the national capabilities of many states. Openness to global markets, many economists argue, provides greater opportunities for sustained national economic growth. As the experience of the East Asian 'tigers' highlighted, global markets are entirely compatible with strong states (Weiss 1998). But even in those contexts where state sovereignty appears to be significantly compromised by internationalization, as in the case of the European Union, national governments, according to the sceptical interpretation, effectively pool sovereignty in order to enhance, through collective action, their control over external forces. Rather than conceiving national governments as simply responding to external economic forces, the sceptical position acknowledges their critical role (especially that of the most powerful) in creating the necessary national and international conditions for global markets to exist in the first place. In this respect, states are both the architects and the subjects of the world economy.

As subjects, however, states do not respond in identical ways to the dynamics of world markets or to external economic shocks. While international financial markets and international competition may well impose similar kinds of economic disciplines on all governments, this does not necessarily prefigure a convergence in national economic strategies or policies. Such pressures are mediated by domestic structures and institutional arrangements which produce enormous variations in the capacity of national governments to respond (Garrett and Lange 1996; Weiss 1998). States can and do make a difference, as the continuing diversity of capitalist forms indicates. This is especially the case in relation to macroeconomic and industrial policy, where significant national differences continue to exist even within the same regions of the world (Dore 1995; Boyer and Drache 1996; Garrett 1998). Nor is there much convincing evidence to suggest that international financial disciplines by themselves either preclude governments from pursuing progressive and redistributive economic strategies or, alternatively, prefigure the demise of the welfare state or robust policies of social protection (Garrett 1996, 1998; Rieger and Liebfried 1998; Hirst and Thompson 1999). The fact that levels of national welfare spending and social protection continue to differ considerably, even within the EU, points to the absurdity of such arguments. In the judgement of the sceptics, national governments remain, for the most part, the sole source of effective and legitimate authority in the governance of the world economy, while also being the principal agents of international economic coordination and regulation.

The new global economy

For the globalists this conclusion is hard to credit, for it completely overlooks the ways in which national governments are having to adjust constantly to the push and pull of global market conditions and forces. Contesting both the sceptics' evidence, and their interpretation of global economic trends, the globalist account points to the historically unprecedented scale and magnitude of contemporary global economic interaction (O'Brien 1992; Altvater and Mahnkopf 1997; Greider 1997; Rodrik 1997; Dicken 1998). Daily turnover on the world's foreign exchange markets, for instance, currently exceeds some sixty times the annual level of world exports, while the scale and intensity of world trade far exceeds that of the *belle époque*. Global production by multinational corporations is considerably greater than the level of world exports, and encompasses all the world's major economic regions. Migration, though perhaps slightly smaller in magnitude than in the nineteenth century, nevertheless has become increasingly globalized. National economies, with some exceptions, are presently much more deeply enmeshed in global systems of production and exchange than in previous historical eras, while few states, following the collapse of state socialism, remain excluded from global financial and economic markets. Patterns of contemporary economic globalization have woven strong and enduring webs across the world's major regions such that their economic fates are intimately connected.

Although the global economy as a single entity may not be as highly integrated as the most robust national economies, the trends, argue the globalists, point unambiguously towards intensifying integration within and across regions. The operation of global financial markets, for example, has produced a convergence in interest rates among the major economies (Fukao 1993; Gagnon and Unferth 1995). Financial integration also brings with it a contagion effect in that economic crisis in one region, as the East Asian crash of 1997–8 demonstrated, rapidly acquires global ramifications (Godement 1999). Alongside financial integration the operations of multinational corporations integrate national and local economies into global and regional production networks (Castells 1996; Gereffi and Korzeniewicz 1994; Dicken 1998). Under these conditions, national economies no longer function as autonomous systems of wealth creation since national borders are increasingly irrelevant to the conduct and organization of economic activity. In this 'borderless economy', as the more radical globalists conceive it, the distinction between domestic economic activity and global economic activity, as the range of products in any superstore will confirm, is becoming increasingly difficult to sustain (Ohmae 1990).

Accordingly, the contemporary phase of economic globalization, the globalists suggest, is distinguished from past phases by the existence of a single global economy transcending and integrating the world's major economic regions (Geyer and Bright 1995; Dickson 1997; Scholte 1997; Dicken 1998; Frank 1998). By comparison with the *belle époque*, an era distinguished by relatively high levels of trade protectionism and imperial economic zones, the present global economy is considerably more open and its operations impact upon all countries, even those nominally 'pariah' states such as Cuba or North Korea (Nierop 1994). Nor has the growth of regionalism produced a sharp division of the world into competing blocs; for the regionalization of economic activity has not been at the expense of economic globalization (Lloyd 1992; Anderson and Blackhurst 1993; Anderson and Norheim 1993). On the contrary, regionalism has largely facilitated and encouraged economic globalization since it offers a mechanism through which national economies can engage more strategically with global markets (Gamble and Payne 1991; Hanson 1998). Furthermore, there is little evidence to suggest, as do many sceptics, that a process of triadization is occurring in so far as economic interdependence between the three major centres of the global economy – the US, Japan and Europe – appears itself to be intensifying (Ohmae 1990; Dunning 1993; Greider 1997; Perraton et al. 1997; Dicken 1998; Haass and Liton 1998). Although the contemporary global economy is structured around three major centres of economic power – unlike the *belle époque* or the early postwar decades of US dominance – it is best described as a post-hegemonic order in so far as no single centre can dictate the rules of global trade and commerce (Gill 1992; Geyer and Bright 1995; Amin 1996). Of course, it remains a highly stratified order in that by far the largest share of global economic flows – such as trade and finance – are concentrated among the major OECD economies. But the dominance of OECD economies is being diluted as economic globalization significantly alters the geography of world economic activity and power.

Over the last few decades developing economies' shares of world exports and foreign investment flows (inwards and outwards) have increased considerably (Castells 1996; Dicken 1998; UNCTAD 1998a, 1998c). The NICs of East Asia and Latin America have become an increasingly important destination for OECD investment and an increasingly significant source of OECD imports – São Paulo, it is sometimes quipped, is Germany's largest industrial city (Dicken 1998). By the late 1990s almost 50 per cent of total world manufacturing jobs were located in developing economies, while over 60 per cent of developing country exports to the industrialized world were manufactured goods, a twelvefold increase in less than four decades (UNDP 1998). Contrary to the sceptical interpretation, contemporary economic globalization is neither solely, nor even primarily, an OECD phenomenon but, rather, embraces all continents and regions (UNCTAD 1998c).

By definition, the global economy is a capitalist global economy in that it is organized on the basis of market principles and production for profit. Historically, apart from the division of the world into capitalist and state socialist camps during the Cold War era, many would argue this has been the case since early modern times, if not since much before that (Wallerstein 1974; Braudel 1984; Fernández-Armesto 1995; Geyer and Bright 1995; Frank and Gills 1996; Frank 1998). However, what distinguishes the present global capitalist economy from that of prior epochs, argue the globalists, is its particular historical form. Over recent decades, the core economies in the global system have undergone a profound economic restructuring. In the process they have been transformed from essentially industrial to post-industrial economies (Piore and Sabel 1984; Castells 1996). Just as the twentieth century witnessed the global diffusion of industrial capitalism, so at the century's end post-industrial capitalism is taking its place.

With this restructuring has come a dramatic alteration in the form and organization of global capitalism. In variously referring to 'global informational capitalism', 'manic capitalism', 'turbo-capitalism', or 'supraterritorial capitalism', commentators seek to capture the qualitative shift occurring in the spatial organization and dynamics of this new global capitalist formation (Castells 1996; Greider 1997; Scholte 1997; Luttwak 1999). In the age of the Internet, to simplify the argument, capital – both productive and financial – has been liberated from national and territorial constraints, while markets have become globalized to the extent that the domestic economy constantly has to adapt to global competitive conditions. In a wired world, software engineers in Hyderabad can do the jobs of software engineers in London for a fraction of the cost. Inscribed in the dynamics of this new global capitalism is a powerful imperative towards the denationalization of strategic economic activities.

Central to the organization of this new global capitalist order is the multinational corporation. In 1997 there were 53,000 MNCs worldwide with 450,000 foreign subsidiaries selling $9.5 trillion of goods and services across the globe (UNCTAD 1998b). Today transnational production considerably exceeds the level of global exports and has become the primary means for selling goods and services abroad. Multinational corporations now account, according to some estimates, for at least 20 per cent of world production and 70 per cent of world trade (Perraton et al. 1997). They span every sector of the global economy from raw materials, to finance, to manufacturing, integrating and reordering economic activity within and across the world's major economic regions (Gill 1995; Castells 1996; Amin 1997). In the financial sector multinational banks are by far the major actors in global financial markets, playing a critical role in the management and organization of money and credit in the global economy (Walters 1993; Germain 1997). It is global corporate capital, rather than states, contend the globalists, that exercises decisive influence over the organization, location and distribution of economic power and resources in the contemporary global economy.

Contemporary patterns of economic globalization, the globalists also argue, have been accompanied by a new global division of labour brought about, in part, by the activities of multinationals themselves (Johnston et al. 1995; Hoogvelt 1997). The restructuring (deindustrialization) of OECD economies can be directly related to the outsourcing of manufacturing production by multinationals to the newly industrializing and transition economies of Asia, Latin America and Eastern Europe (Reich 1991; Wood 1994; Rodrik 1997). NICs now account for a significant proportion of global exports and, through integration into transnational production networks, have become extensions of, as well as competitors of, businesses in metropolitan economies. In this respect, globalization is reordering developing countries into clear winners and losers. Such restructuring is, moreover, replicated within countries, both North and South, as communities and particular locales closely integrated into global production networks reap significant rewards while the rest survive on the margins. Thus, contemporary economic globalization brings with it an increasingly unified world for elites – national, regional and global – but increasingly divided nations as the global workforce is segmented, within rich and poor countries alike, into winners and losers. The old North–South international division of labour is giving way, suggest the globalists, to a new global division of labour, which involves a reordering of interregional economic relations and a new pattern of wealth and inequality, transcending both post-industrial and industrializing economies (Reich 1991; Amin 1997; Hoogvelt 1997; Rodrik 1997; Castells 1998; Dicken 1998).

One of the central contradictions of this new order pertains to its governance. For the globalization of economic activity exceeds the regulatory reach of national governments while, at the same time, existing multilateral institutions of global economic governance have limited authority because states, jealously guarding their national sovereignty, refuse to cede them substantial power (Zürn 1995). Under these conditions, assert some of the more radical globalists, global markets effectively escape political regulation such that economic globalization is in danger of creating a 'runaway world' (Giddens 1999). Governments, therefore, have no real option other than to accommodate to the forces of economic globalization (Amin 1996; Cox 1997). Furthermore, the existing multilateral institutions of global economic governance, especially the IMF, World Bank and WTO, are conceived primarily, in so far as they advocate and pursue programmes which simply extend and deepen the hold of global market forces on national economic life, as the agents of global capital and the G7 states (Gill 1995; Korten 1995; Cox 1996). For the most part, the governance structures of the global economy operate principally to nurture and reproduce the forces of economic globalization, while also acting to discipline this nascent 'global market civilization' (Gill 1995; Korten 1995; Burbach et al. 1997; Hoogvelt 1997; Scholte 1997).

While accepting many of the precepts of this radical globalist position, others conceive the governance structures of the global economy as having considerable autonomy from the dictates of global capital and/or the G7 states (Rosenau 1990; Shaw 1994; Shell 1995; Cortell and Davies 1996; Castells 1997; Hasenclever et al. 1997; Milner 1997; Herod et al. 1998). According to these authors, multilateral institutions have become increasingly important sites through which economic globalization is contested, by weaker states and the agencies of transnational civil society, while the G7 states and global capital find themselves on many occasions at odds with their decisions or rules. Moreover, the political dynamics of multilateral institutions tend to mediate great power control, for instance through consensual modes of decision-making, such that they are never merely tools of dominant states and social forces (Keohane 1984, 1998; Ruggie 1993a; Hasenclever et al. 1997; Roberts 1998). Alongside these global institutions also exist a parallel set of regional bodies, from MERCOSUR to the EU, which constitute another dimension to what is an emerging system of multilayered economic governance (Rosenau 1990, 1997; Ruggie 1993b). Within the interstices of this system operate the social forces of an emerging transnational civil society, from the International Chamber of Commerce to the Jubilee 2000 campaign, seeking to promote, contest and bring to account the agencies of economic globalization (Falk 1987; Ekins 1992; Scholte 1993; Burbach et al. 1997; Castells 1997; Rosenau 1997). In this respect, the politics of global economic governance is much more pluralistic than the sceptics admit in so far as global and regional institutions exercise considerable independent authority. Economic globalization has been accompanied by a significant internationalization of political authority associated with a corresponding globalization of political activity.

Since national governments are deeply embedded in this system of multilayered economic governance, their role and power continues to be qualified decisively by economic globalization (Reich 1991; Ohmae 1995; Sassen 1996; Rosenau 1997). Some globalists regard nation-states as increasingly 'transitional modes of economic organization and regulation' since, in an age of global markets, it is believed they can no longer effectively manage or regulate their own national economies (Ohmae 1995). Sandwiched between the constraints of global financial markets and the exit options of mobile productive capital, national governments across the globe have been forced to adopt increasingly similar (neoliberal) economic strategies which promote financial discipline, limited government and sound economic management (Gill 1995; Strange 1996; Amin 1997; Greider 1997; Hoogvelt 1997; Scholte 1997; Yergin and Stanislaw 1998; Luttwak 1999). As global competition intensifies, governments are increasingly unable to maintain existing levels of social protection or welfare state programmes without undermining the competitive position of domestic business and deterring much-needed foreign investment (Reich 1991; Cox 1997; Greider 1997; Scholte 1997; Gray 1998). Borrowing to increase public expenditure or raising taxes to do so are both equally constrained by the dictates of global financial markets (Gourevitch 1986; Frieden 1991; Garrett and Lange 1991; Cox 1997; Germain 1997). Some globalists, moreover, argue that economic globalization spells the end of the welfare state and social democracy, while others point to a less dramatic convergence across the globe towards more limited welfare state regimes (Gourevitch 1986; Rodrik 1997; Gray 1998; Pieper and Taylor 1998). But about one matter they clearly concur: the economic autonomy, sovereignty and social solidarity of contemporary states are being eroded dramatically by contemporary processes of economic globalization (Zacher 1992; Ohmae 1995; Cable 1996; Sassen 1996; Strange 1996; Altvater and Mahnkopf 1997; Amin 1997; Castells 1997; Cox 1997; Greider 1997; Jessop 1997; Rosenau 1997; Scholte 1997; Shaw 1997).

V Divided Nations, Unruly World

Contemporary economic globalization, according to a recent UNDP report, is associated with an accelerating gap between rich and poor states as well as between peoples in the global economy (UNDP 1999). By determining the location and distribution of wealth and productive power in the world economy, globalization defines and reshapes global patterns of hierarchy and inequality. This has profound implications for human security and world order in so far as global inequalities condition the life chances of individuals and collectivities, not to mention creating the preconditions for a more unstable and unruly world (Herod et al. 1998; Hurrell 1999). Not surprisingly, the problem of global inequality has become one of the most pressing and contentious issues on the global agenda.

While there is much public and academic concern about global inequalities, the discussion does not readily crystallize into a neat dialogue between sceptics and globalists. In part, this is because the issues are so complex and, in part, because the scale of human tragedy involved is so overwhelming as to make the very idea of a debate about such matters something of an affront to moral sensitivities. While there is considerable disagreement among both sceptics and globalists about the consequences of, as well as the appropriate remedies for, global inequality, what tends to differentiate them above all are different diagnoses of the underlying causes of the problem and, in particular, its relationship to economic globalization.

Globalists tend, in analysing contemporary patterns of global inequality, to identify economic globalization as the primary culprit. In contrast, the sceptics tend to deny its significance, emphasizing instead the continuing reality of imperialism and/or the dynamics of geopolitics. Furthermore, these contrasting interpretations are usually associated with quite different ethical positions on the issue of global inequality and its remedies. They also lead to quite distinctive assessments of the consequences of economic globalization for both national and international solidarity and, ultimately, the governance and stability of the present world order.

Towards one world?

Among those globalists of a neoliberal persuasion contemporary economic globalization is taken to embody the creation of a single global market which, through the operation of free trade, capital mobility and global competition, is the harbinger of modernization and development (Ohmae 1990, 1995; Perlmutter 1991). Pointing to the East Asian economic miracle and the Latin American experience of the early to mid 1990s (and, indeed, to the quick recovery of many of these economies from the economic turmoil of 1997–8), neoliberals emphasize that the solution to global inequalities is to be found in pursuing policies of openness to global capital and global competition, and in seeking closer integration within the global economy. While there is a recognition that economic globalization generates losers as well as winners, neoliberals stress the growing diffusion of wealth and affluence throughout the world economy – the trickle-down effect. Global poverty, by historical standards, has fallen more in the last fifty years than in the past five hundred and the welfare of people in almost all regions has improved significantly over the last few decades (UNDP 1997). Rather than the old North–South fracture, a new worldwide division of labour is said to be replacing the traditional core–periphery model of global economic relations. As a result, the 'Third World' is becoming increasingly differentiated as more states, taking advantage of open global markets, become industrialized; South Korea, for instance, is now a member of the OECD, the Western club of 'rich' nations, while many other industrializing states aspire to membership. Recognizing both economic and moral limits to the pursuit of global equality, neoliberals remain willing to accept the 'natural' inequalities created by the global market when measured against the loss of liberty – and economic efficiency – entailed by multilateral intervention to redress the consequences of uneven economic globalization (Ohmae 1995).

To this extent, economic globalization is associated with growing global affluence: extreme poverty and global inequality are regarded as transitional conditions that will evaporate with market-led global modernization. Economic globalization, it is argued, establishes the preconditions for a more stable and peaceful world order since enduring economic interdependence, as relations between Western states confirm, makes the resort to military force or war increasingly irrational and, therefore, increasingly unlikely (Mitrany 1975; Howard 1981; Mueller 1989; Russett 1993).

Those globalists of a social democratic or radical persuasion offer a rather different interpretation of global inequalities. Economic globalization, they argue, is directly responsible for widening disparities in life chances across the globe – a deepening polarization of income and wealth (Beetham 1995; Commission on Global Governance 1995; Falk 1995a; Gill 1995; Bradshaw and Wallace 1996; Castells 1997; Greider 1997; Hoogvelt 1997; Gray 1998; UNDP 1999). Three related patterns are evident: the segmentation of the global workforce into those who gain and those who lose from economic globalization; the growing marginalization of the losers from the global economy; and the erosion of social solidarity within nations as welfare regimes are unable, or governments unwilling, to bear the costs of protecting the most vulnerable (Lawrence 1996; Castells 1997; Cox 1997; Dicken 1998; Gray 1998; Scharpf 1999). Economic globalization creates a more affluent world for some at the expense of growing poverty for others. That poverty, however, is no longer confined to the South, the developing world, but is on the rise in sectors of the affluent North as well (Birdsall 1998; UNDP 1999).

Economic globalization, argue these globalists, is responsible for the growing globalization of poverty. Within OECD economies inequality, unemployment and social exclusion have increased as many low-skilled and semi-skilled jobs have been relocated to more profitable ventures in developing countries (Rodrik 1997; Castells 1998). This global economic restructuring brings with it a horizontal segmentation of the workforce, within rich and poor countries alike, into winners and losers from global capitalism (Castells 1997). This divides nations and erodes the basis of social solidarity. In advanced economies global competition undermines the social and political coalitions necessary for strong welfare regimes and policies of social protection while, in the developing world, SAPs overseen by the IMF and World Bank severely limit government welfare spending. Today the globalization of poverty, it is suggested, is increasingly a matter of vital and shared global concern (Dickson 1997). By dividing states and peoples it engenders a deepening fragmentation of world order and societies, generating the conditions for a more unstable world. Unless economic globalization is tamed, so the argument goes, a new barbarism will prevail as poverty, social exclusion and social conflict envelop the world.

What is required is a new global ethic which recognizes 'a duty of care' beyond borders, as well as within them, and a global new deal between rich and poor states. This involves rethinking social democracy as a purely national project, recognizing that if it is to remain effective in a globalizing economy, it has to be embedded in a reformed and much stronger system of global governance which seeks to combine human security with economic efficiency (Held 1995; Giddens 1999; UNDP 1999). A reconstituted social democratic project requires the coordinated pursuit of national, regional and global programmes to regulate the forces of economic globalization – to ensure, in other words, that global markets begin to serve the world's peoples rather than vice versa. Extending social democracy beyond borders also depends on strengthening solidarities between those social forces, in different regions of the world, that seek to contest or resist the terms of contemporary economic globalization. Just as the Bretton Woods system established a world economic order conducive to the pursuit of national social democracy, a new global (social democratic) compact is required, argue many globalists, in order to tame the forces of economic globalization and to create a more just and humane world order.

The challenge of enduring inequality

To the sceptics, especially of a traditional Marxist disposition, the prospect of a global New Deal is decidedly utopian. While acknowledging that contemporary capitalism is creating a more divided and unruly world, it is, many would argue, sheer political naivety to assume that those states, corporations and social forces that benefit most from the present liberal world order are ever likely to consent to its effective reform, let alone its transformation (Callinicos et al. 1994; Burbach et al. 1997). In this account, core and periphery – First World and Third World – remain very much a fundamental feature of the current world order. Rather than international capital creating 'one world' it has been accompanied by deepening global inequality through the marginalization of most Third World economies, as trade and investment flows among OECD economies intensify to the exclusion of much of the rest of the globe. Rather than a new global division of labour, the radical account points to a deepening North–South fracture (Burbach et al. 1997).

Central to this account is a conception of contemporary economic internationalization as nothing more than a new mode of Western imperialism. Today 50 per cent of the world's population and two-thirds of its governments are bound by the disciplines of the IMF or the World Bank (Pieper and Taylor 1998). As the East Asian crisis demonstrated, even the most affluent industrializing states are subject to the rule of G7 governments, particularly the US. Economic internationalization reinforces, rather than replaces, historical patterns of dominance and dependence such that the possibilities for real development remain effectively blocked. As poverty increases, the conflict between North and South deepens, while the affluent West, through various mechanisms from NATO to the World Bank, resorts to a form of 'global riot control' to consolidate its power and secure its economic fortunes. The internationalization of capital is creating an increasingly unruly and violent world in which poverty, deprivation and conflict are the daily reality for most of the world's peoples. In this context, reforming the architecture of the present economic order is a futile gesture when what is required to end imperialism is national revolutionary change in both the metropoles and the periphery. Only a socialist international order, in which socialist states are the essential building blocks, can eradicate global poverty through the determined redistribution of wealth and privilege (Callinicos et al. 1994).

By contrast, those sceptics of a more realist disposition regard such prescriptions as pure idealism, if not fantasy, in a world that has recently witnessed the complete collapse of state socialism. The problem of global inequality, they suggest, is actually one of the more intractable international issues on the global agenda and one which denies effective resolution (Krasner 1985). In this respect, while they may concede that economic internationalization is associated with a growing polarization between rich and poor states, they do not consider it to be the sole, or even primary, cause of growing inequality. National factors, from resource endowments to economic policies, are just as, if not more, important as determinants of the pattern of global inequality (Gilpin 1987). To presume that it can be moderated, let alone eradicated, through coordinated international intervention, or the creation of a socialist world order, is a categorical mistake. For inequality is inscribed in the very structure of world order since a global hierarchy of power is a consequence of a system which ranks states according to their national economic and military endowments (Gilpin 1981; Krasner 1985; Clark 1989; Krasner 1993; K. W. Thompson 1994). Moreover, that hierarchy of power, realists argue, is essential to the maintenance of a stable international order, since in an anarchic – that is, self-help – states system peace and security ultimately depend on the willingness of the most powerful states to police the system. Hierarchy, and thereby inequality, is a vital ingredient of the realist conception of world order, and the basis for effective international governance (Woods 1999). Moderating global inequalities may be a moral aspiration but it is not necessarily a rational one if it undermines the principal basis of international order. Nor, in a system in which states constantly struggle to maintain their power and influence over others, is it a feasible aspiration. Multilateral attempts to redress global inequalities, by taming the power of global markets, are doomed necessarily to failure, since the weak have no effective means to coerce the strong into taking actions which by definition threaten their power and wealth (Krasner 1985). For these reasons, among others, sceptics express a certain antipathy towards, and reservations about, grand projects to establish a more equal and just world order (Woods 1999). Paradoxically, they reason, such a world order is likely to be neither more secure nor more peaceful than the present unjust one. This does not mean that those of a realist persuasion necessarily regard rising inequality as either morally acceptable or politically sustainable in the long run, but they consider that it remains a problem without any effective means of international resolution (Krasner 1985).

It is only within the borders of the nation-state – the nation as a moral community of fate – that legitimate and effective solutions to the problem of global inequality can be realized. Such solutions will always be partial and limited since governments cannot realistically aspire to redress all the external sources of domestic inequality. Although international cooperation between states may make it feasible to redress some of the worst excesses of the global market, in the end inequalities can only be confronted successfully and legitimately through the apparatus of national welfare regimes and the determined pursuit of national wealth and economic power. National governments, conclude the sceptics, remain the only proper and proven instruments for mediating and redressing the worst consequences of uneven economic internationalization and, thereby, realizing the 'good community' (Hirst and Thompson 1999).

VI World Orders, Normative Futures

Throughout the modern period concepts of the political good have generally been elaborated at the level of state institutions and practices; the state has been at the intersection of intellectually and morally ambitious conceptions of political life (Dunn 1990: 142–60). Political theory, by and large, has taken the nation-state as a fixed point of reference and has sought to place the state at the centre of interpretations of the nature and proper form of the political good. Relations among states have of course been analysed; but they have rarely been examined, especially in recent times, as a central element of political theory and political philosophy. The central element has been the territorial political community and its many possible relations to what is desirable or politically good.

Political communitarianism

The theory and practice of liberal democracy has added important nuances to this position. For within the framework of liberal democracy, while territorial boundaries and

the nation-state demarcate the proper spatial limits of the political good, the articulation of the latter is directly linked to the citizenry. Theories of the modern state tend
to draw a sharp contrast between the powers of the state and the power of the people
(Skinner 1989). For theorists of the state such as Hobbes, the state is the supreme political reference point within a specific community and territory; it is independent of subjects and rulers, with distinctive political properties (1968: chs 16–19). By contrast, theorists
of democracy tend to affirm the idea of the people as the active sovereign body with
the capacity, in principle, to make or break governments. As Locke bluntly put it, 'the
Community perpetually *retains a Supream Power*' over its lawmakers and legislature
(1963: 413; see also 1963: 477). The political good inheres in, and is to be specified by,
a process of political participation in which the collective will is determined through
the medium of elected representatives (Bobbio 1989: 144). Rightful power or authority,
that is, sovereignty, is vested in the people, subject to various entrenched rules, procedures and institutions which constitute national constitutional agreements and legal traditions. The democratic good unfolds in the context of these delimiting or self-binding
mechanisms (Holmes 1988; Dahl 1989).

The theory of the political good in the modern territorial polity rests on a number
of assumptions which repay an effort of clarification (see Miller 1999). These are that
a political community is properly constituted and bounded when:

1   Its members have a common socio-cultural identity; that is, they share an understand-
    ing, explicit or implicit, of a distinctive culture, tradition, language and homeland,
    which binds them together as a group and forms a (if not the) basis (acknowledged
    or unacknowledged) of their activities.
2   There is a common framework of 'prejudices', purposes and objectives that gener-
    ates a common political ethos; that is, an imagined 'community of fate' which con-
    nects them directly to a common political project – the notion that they form a people
    who should govern themselves.
3   An institutional structure exists – or is in the process of development – which pro-
    tects and represents the community, acts on its behalf and promotes the collective
    interest.
4   'Congruence' and 'symmetry' prevail between a community's 'governors' and
    'governed', between political decision-makers and decision-takers. That is to say,
    national communities exclusively 'programme' the actions, decisions and policies of
    their governments, and the latter determine what is right or appropriate for their
    citizens.
5   Members enjoy, because of the presence of conditions 1–4, a common structure of
    rights and duties, that is, they can lay claim to, and can reasonably expect, certain
    kinds of equal treatment, that is, certain types of egalitarian principles of justice and
    political participation.

According to this account, which in this context can be referred to as the sceptical
analysis of the political good, appropriate conceptions of what is right for the political community and its citizens follow from its cultural, political and institutional roots,
traditions and boundaries. These generate the resources – conceptual and organizational
– for the determination of its fate and fortunes. And the underlying principle of
justification is a communitarian one: ethical discourse cannot be detached from the 'form
of life' of a community; the categories of political discourse are integral to a particular

tradition; and the values of such a community take precedence over individual or global requirements (Walzer 1983; Miller 1988; MacIntyre 1981, 1988).

A global ethic

Globalists take issue with each of the above propositions, concluding that the political good today can only be disclosed by reflection on the diversity of the 'communities of fate' to which individuals and groups belong, and the way in which this diversity is reinforced by the political transformations globalization has brought in its wake. According to this globalist interpretation, the political good is entrenched in over-lapping communities, and in an emergent transnational civil society and global polity. Disputes about the political good should be disputes about the nature and proper form of the developing global order. The basis of this globalist view can be grasped from a critique of the above five points.

First, shared identity in political communities historically has been the result of intensive efforts of political construction; it has never been a given (see pp. 14–16; cf. Gellner 1983; B. Anderson 1983; Smith 1986, 1995). Even within the boundaries of old-established communities, cultural and political identity is often disputed by and across social classes, gender divisions, local allegiances, ethnic groupings and the generations. The existence of a shared political identity cannot simply be read off vociferously pro-claimed symbols of national identity. The meaning of such symbols is contested and the 'ethos' of a community frequently debated. The common values of a community may be subject to intense dispute. Justice, accountability, the rule of law and welfare are just a few terms around which there may appear to be a shared language, and yet fiercely different conceptions of these may be present (Held 1991: 11–21). In fact, if by a political consensus is meant normative integration within a community, then it is all too rare (Held 1996: part 2; and see below). Political identity is only by exception, for instance during wars, a singular, unitary phenomenon. Moreover, contemporary reflexive political agents, subject to an extraordinary diversity of information and communication, can be influenced by images, concepts, lifestyles and ideas from well beyond their immediate communities and can come to identify with groupings beyond their borders – ethnic, religious, social and political (J. B. Thompson 1995; Held et al. 1999: ch. 8; Keck and Sikkink 1998). And while there is no reason to suppose that they will uncritically identify with any one of these, self-chosen ideas, commitments or rela-tions may well be more important for some people's identity than 'membership in a community of birth' (J. Thompson 1998: 190; cf. Giddens 1991; Tamir 1993). Cultural and political identity today is constantly under review and reconstruction.

Second, the argument that locates the political good firmly within the terrain of the nation-state fails to consider or properly appreciate the diversity of political com-munities individuals can value; and the fact that individuals can involve themselves coherently in different associations or collectivities at different levels and for differ-ent purposes (J. Thompson 1998). It is perfectly possible, for example, to enjoy membership and voting rights in Scotland, the UK and Europe without necessarily threatening one's identification or allegiances to any one of these three political entities (see Archibugi et al. 1998). It is perfectly possible, in addition, to identify closely with the aims and ambitions of a transnational social movement – whether concerned with environmental, gender or human rights issues – without compromising other more local political commitments. Such a pluralization of political orientations and allegiances can be linked to the erosion of the state's capacity to sustain a singular political identity in the face of globalization. In the first instance, globalization is weakening the state's ability to deliver the goods to its citizens, thus eroding its legitimacy and the confidence of its citizens in its historic legacy. At the same time, the globalization of cultural processes and communications is stimulating new images of community, new avenues of political participation and new discourses of identity. Globalization is helping to create new communication and information patterns and a dense network of relations linking particular groups and cultures to one another, transforming the dynamics of political relations, above, below and alongside the state. Increasingly, successful political communities have to work with, not against, a multiplicity of identities, cultures and ethnic groupings. An overlapping consensus, which might underpin such communities, is often fragile and based purely on a commitment to common procedures – for instance, procedural mechanisms for the resolution of conflict – not a set of substantive, given values. A national political ethos may, at best, be skin-deep.

Third, globalization has 'hollowed out' states, undermining their sovereignty and autonomy. State institutions and political agents are increasingly like 'zombies', acting out the motions of politics but failing to determine any substantive, welfare-enhancing public good (Beck 1992, 1997). Contemporary political strategies involve easing adaptation to world markets and transnational economic flows. Adjustment to the international economy – above all, to global financial markets – becomes a fixed point of orientation in economic and social policy. The 'decision signals' of these markets, and of their leading agents and forces, become a, if not the, standard of rational decision-making. This position is linked, moreover, to the pursuit of distinctive supply-side measures – above all, to the use of education and training as tools of economic policy. Individual citizens must be empowered with cultural and educational capital to meet the challenges of increased (local, national, regional, global) competition and the greater mobility of industrial and financial capital. States no longer have the capacity and policy instruments they require to contest the imperatives of global economic change; instead, they must help individual citizens to go where they want to go via provision of social, cultural and educational resources. The terms of reference of public policy are set by global markets and corporate enterprise. The pursuit of the public good becomes synonymous with enhancing adaptation to this private end. Accordingly, the roles of the state as protector and representative of the territorial community, as a collector and (re)allocator of resources among its members, and as a promoter of an independent, deliberatively tested shared good are all in decline.

Fourth, the fate of a national community is no longer in its own hands. Regional and global economic, environmental and political processes profoundly redefine the content of national decision-making. In addition, decisions made by quasi-regional or quasi-supranational organizations such as the EU, WTO or the North Atlantic Treaty Organization (NATO) diminish the range of political options open to given national 'majorities'. In a similar vein, decisions by particular states – not just the most economically or militarily powerful nations – can ramify across borders, circumscribing and reshaping the political terrain. National governments by no means determine what is right or appropriate for their own citizens (Offe 1985). National policies with respect to interest rates, the harvesting of rainforests, the encouragement or restriction of the growing of genetically modified food, arms procurement and manufacture, incentive provisions to attract inward investment by multinational companies, along with decisions on a huge range of additional public matters from AIDS to the problems faced by a post-antibiotic culture, can have major consequences for those in neighbouring and distant lands. Political communities are thus embedded in a substantial range of processes which connect them in complex configurations.

Fifth, national communities are locked into webs of regional and global governance which alter and compromise their capacity to provide a common structure of rights, duties and welfare for their citizens. Regional and global processes, organizations and institutions undercut, circumscribe and delimit the kinds of entitlements and opportunities national states can offer and deliver. From human rights to trade regimes, political power is being rearticulated and reconfigured. Increasingly, contemporary patterns of globalization are associated with a multilayered system of governance, the diffusion of political power, and a widening gap between the influence of the richest and poorest communities. A complex constellation of 'winners' and 'losers' emerges. Locked into an array of geographically diverse forces, national governments are having to reconsider their roles and functions. Although the intensification of regional and global political relations has diminished the powers of national governments, it is recognized ever more that the nurturing and enhancement of the public good requires coordinated multilateral action, for instance, to prevent global recession and enhance sustainable growth, to protect human rights and intercede where they are grossly violated, to act to avoid environmental catastrophes such as ozone depletion or global warming. A shift is taking place from government to multilevel global governance. Accordingly, the institutional nexus of the political good is being reconfigured.

Each of the five propositions set forth by the sceptics – the theorists and advocates of the modern nation-state (see p. 32) – can be contrasted with positions held by the globalists. Thus, the political community and the political good need, on the globalists' account, to be understood as follows:

1 Individuals increasingly have complex loyalties and multilayered identities, corresponding to the globalization of economic and cultural forces and the reconfiguration of political power. The movements of cultural goods across borders, hybridization and the intermingling of cultures create the basis of a transnational civil society and overlapping identities – a common framework of understanding for human beings, which progressively finds expression in, and binds people together into, interlocking collectivities capable of constructing and sustaining transnational movements, agencies and legal and institutional structures.

2 The continuing development of regional, international and global flows of resources and networks of interaction, along with the recognition by growing numbers of people of the increasing interconnectedness of political communities in diverse domains – including the social, cultural, economic and environmental – generate an awareness of overlapping 'collective fortunes' which require collective solutions. Political community begins to be reimagined in both regional and global terms.

3 An institutional structure exists comprising elements of local, national, regional and global governance. At different levels, individual communities (albeit often imperfectly) are protected and represented; their collective interests require both multilateral advancement and domestic (local and national) adjustment if they are to be sustained and promoted.

4 Complex economic, social and environmental processes, shifting networks of regional and international agencies, and the decisions of many states and private

organizations cut across spatially delimited, national locales with determinate consequences for their political agendas and strategic choices. Globalization decisively
alters what it is that a national community can ask of its government, what politicians can promise and effectively deliver, and the range of people(s) affected by
governmental actions. Political communities are 'reprogrammed'.

5   The rights, duties and welfare of individuals can only be adequately entrenched if,
in addition to their proper articulation in national constitutions, they are underwritten
by regional and global regimes, laws and institutions. The promotion of the political
good and of egalitarian principles of justice and political participation are rightly
pursued at regional and global levels. Their conditions of possibility are inextricably linked to the establishment and development of robust transnational organizations and institutions of regional and global governance. In a global age, the latter
are the necessary basis of cooperative relations and just conduct.

In contradistinction to the conception of the political good promulgated by advocates
of the modern nation-state, what is right for the individual political community and its
citizens, in the globalists' account, must follow from reflection on the processes which
generate an intermingling of national fortunes and fates. The growing fusion of worldwide economic, social, cultural and environmental forces requires a rethinking of the politically and philosophically 'isolationist' position of the communitarians and sceptics.
For the contemporary world 'is not a world of closed communities with mutually impenetrable ways of thought, self-sufficient economies and ideally sovereign states' (O'Neill
1991: 282). Not only is ethical discourse separable from forms of life in a national community, but it is developing today at the intersection and interstices of overlapping
communities, traditions and languages. Its categories are increasingly the result of the
mediation of different cultures, communication processes and modes of understanding.
There are not enough good reasons for allowing, in principle, the values of individual
political communities to trump or take precedence over global principles of justice and
political participation. Of course, the globalists, like the sceptics, often have very different
conceptions of what exactly is at stake here, that is, they hold very different views of
what the global order should be like and the moral principles which might inform it.
But they draw a clear-cut distinction between their conception of where the political
good inheres and that of the sceptics. While for the latter ethical discourse is, and remains,
firmly rooted in the bounded political community, for the former it belongs squarely
to the world of 'breached boundaries' – the 'world community' or 'global village'.

Conclusion

The great globalization debate, summarized in table 1, identifies some of the most fundamental issues of our time. Despite a propensity for hyperbole on both sides, the protagonists have generally elaborated highly important and carefully considered arguments.
These pose key questions about the organization of human affairs and the trajectory
of global social change. They also raise matters which go to the centre of political discussion, illuminating some of the strategic choices societies confront and the constraints
which define the possibilities of effective political action.

Are the two main positions fundamentally at odds and contradictory in all respects,
or is a productive synthesis possible? It is not the purpose of this Introduction, or of

Table 1 The great globalization debate: in sum

	Sceptics	Globalists
1 Concepts	Internationalization not globalization Regionalization	One world, shaped by highly extensive, intensive and rapid flows, movements and networks across regions and continents
2 Power	The nation-state rules Intergovernmentalism	Erosion of state sovereignty, autonomy and legitimacy Decline of nation-state Rise of multilateralism
3 Culture	Resurgence of nationalism and national identity	Emergence of global popular culture Erosion of fixed political identities Hybridization
4 Economy	Development of regional blocs Triadization New imperialism	Global informational capitalism The transnational economy A new global division of labour
5 Inequality	Growing North–South divide Irreconcilable conflicts of interest	Growing inequality within and across societies Erosion of old hierarchies
6 Order	International society of states Political conflict between states inevitably persists International governance and geopolitics Communitarianism	Multilayered global governance Global civil society Global polity Cosmopolitanism

the volume for that matter, to answer this question. Indeed, we have sought to do this at length elsewhere and it would take us far beyond the scope of this volume to map out this terrain here (see Held et al. 1999). A number of points, however, are worth emphasizing by way of a conclusion.

In the first instance, the debate raises profound questions of interpretation. But while it highlights that facts certainly do not speak for themselves, and depend for their meaning on complex interpretative frameworks, it would be wrong to conclude that the marshalled evidence is of secondary importance. There are clashes involving the conceptualization and interpretation of some of the most critical evidence. However, often the kind of evidence proffered by both sides differs markedly. For example, sceptics put primary emphasis on the organization of production and trade (stressing the geo-graphical rootedness of MNCs and the marginal changes in trade–GDP ratios over the twentieth century), while globalists focus on financial deregulation and the explos-ive growth of global financial markets over the last twenty-five years. Sceptics stress the continuing primacy of the national interest and the cultural traditions of national communities which sustain their distinct identity, while globalists point to the growing significance of global political problems – such as worldwide pollution, global warming and financial crises – which create a growing sense of the common fate of humankind. A considered response to the debate would have to weigh all these considerations before coming to a settled view.

Secondly, although there are, of course, very significant differences between (and within) each camp, there is some common ground. The debate does not simply comprise ships passing in the night. Indeed, both sides would accept that:

1 There has been some growth in recent decades in economic interconnectedness within and among regions, albeit with multifaceted and uneven consequences across dif-ferent communities.
2 Interregional and global (political, economic and cultural) competition challenges old hierarchies and generates new inequalities of wealth, power, privilege and knowledge.
3 Transnational and transborder problems, such as the spread of genetically modified foodstuffs and money laundering, have become increasingly salient, calling into question the traditional role, functions and institutions of accountability of national government.
4 There has been an expansion of international governance at regional and global levels – from the EU to the WTO – which poses significant normative questions about the kind of world order being constructed and whose interests it serves.
5 These developments require new modes of thinking about politics, economics and cultural change. They also require imaginative responses from politicians and policy-makers about the future possibilities and forms of effective political regulation and democratic accountability.

Thirdly, we believe that the debate highlights that there is much to be learned from both sides; it would be implausible to maintain that either side comprises mere rhetoric and ideology. The sceptical case has significant historical depth and needs to be carefully dissected if a globalist's position is to be adequately defended. Many of the empirical claims raised by the sceptics' arguments, for example, concerning the historical significance of contemporary trade and direct investment flows, require detailed and rigorous examination. But having said that, globalism, in its various forms, does illu-minate important transformations going on in the spatial organization of power – the changing nature of communication, the diffusion and speed-up of technical change, the spread of capitalist economic development, and so on – even if its understanding of these matters sometimes exaggerates their scale and impact. Finally, the political chal-lenges raised by the debate are profound and merit the most serious consideration. For at stake are questions about the ethical and institutional principles which might or should inform the proper organization of human affairs and the future form of world order.

The volume ahead elaborates on these issues and positions, drawing on the most soph-isticated arguments from both sides of the debate. The quality and originality of the contributions are of the highest order and they offer, together, a comprehensive introduction to the globalization literature.

References

Albrow, M. (1996) *The Global Age*. Cambridge: Polity Press.

Altvater, E. and Mahnkopf, B. (1997) The world market unbound. *Review of International Political Economy* 4(3).

Amin, S. (1996) The challenge of globalization. *Review of International Political Economy* 2.

Amin, S. (1997) *Capitalism in the Age of Globalization*. London: Zed Press.

Anderson, B. (1983) *Imagined Communities: Reflections on the Origins and Spread of Nationalism*. London: Verso.

Anderson, K. and Blackhurst, R. (eds) (1993) *Regional Integration and the Global Trading System*. Brighton: Harvester.

Anderson, K. and Norheim, H. (1993) Is world trade becoming more regionalized? *Review of International Economics* 1.

Anderson, P. (1974) *Lineages of the Absolutist State*. London: New Left Books.

Archibugi, D., Held, D. and Köhler, M. (eds) (1998) *Re-imagining Political Community: Studies in Cosmopolitan Democracy*. Cambridge: Polity Press.

Ashford, D. (1986) *The Emergence of the Welfare State*. Oxford: Blackwell.

Axford, B. (1995) *The Global System*. Cambridge: Polity Press.

Barry, B. (1998) The limits of cultural politics. *Review of International Studies* 24(3).

Beck, U. (1992) *Risk Society: Towards a New Modernity*. London: Sage.

Beck, U. (1997) *The Reinvention of Politics*. Cambridge: Polity Press.

Beck, U. (1999) *What is Globalization?* Cambridge: Polity Press.

Beetham, D. (1995) What future for economic and social rights? *Political Studies* 48 (special issue).

Bentley, J. H. (1996) Cross-cultural interaction and periodization in World History. *American Historical Review* 101 (June).

Birdsall, N. (1998) Life is unfair: inequality in the world. *Foreign Policy* 111.

Bobbio, N. (1989) *Democracy and Dictatorship*. Cambridge: Polity Press.

Boyer, R. and Drache, D. (eds) (1996) *States against Markets*. London: Routledge.

Bozeman, A. B. (1984) The international order in a multicultural world. In H. Bull and A. Watson (eds), *The Expansion of International Society*, Oxford: Oxford University Press.

Bradshaw, Y. W. and Wallace, M. (1996) *Global Inequalities*. London: Pine Forge Press/Sage.

Braudel, F. (1984) *The Perspective of the World*. New York: Harper and Row.

Breuilly, J. (1992) *Nationalism and the State*. Manchester: Manchester University Press.

Brown, C. (1995) International political theory and the idea of world community. In K. Booth and S. Smith (eds), *International Relations Theory Today*, Cambridge: Polity Press.

Bull, H. (1977) *The Anarchical Society*. London: Macmillan.

Burbach, R., Núñez, O. and Kagarlitsky, B. (1997) *Globalization and its Discontents*. London: Pluto Press.

Buzan, B., Little, R. and Jones, C. (1993) *The Logic of Anarchy*. New York: Columbia University Press.

Cable, V. (1996) Globalization: can the state strike back? *The World Today* (May).

Callinicos, A. et al. (1994) *Marxism and the New Imperialism*. London: Bookmarks.

Castells, M. (1996) *The Rise of the Network Society*. Oxford: Blackwell.

Castells, M. (1997) *The Power of Identity*. Oxford: Blackwell.

Castells, M. (1998) *End of Millennium*. Oxford: Blackwell.

Clark, I. (1989) *The Hierarchy of States: Reform and Resistance in the International Order*. Cambridge: Cambridge University Press.

Clark, R. P. (1997) *The Global Imperative*. Boulder: Westview Press.

Commission on Global Governance (1995) *Our Global Neighbourhood*. Oxford: Oxford University Press.

Cooper, R. N. (1986) *Economic Policy in an Interdependent World*. Cambridge, Mass.: MIT Press.

Cortell, A. P. and Davies, J. W. (1996) How do international institutions matter? The domestic impact of international rules and norms. *International Studies Quarterly* 40.

Cox, R. (1996) Globalization, multilateralism and democracy. In R. Cox (ed.), *Approaches to World Order*, Cambridge: Cambridge University Press.

Cox, R. (1997) Economic globalization and the limits to liberal democracy. In A. McGrew (ed.), *The Transformation of Democracy? Globalization and Territorial Democracy*, Cambridge: Polity Press.

Crawford, J. and Marks, S. (1998) The global democracy deficit: an essay on international law and its limits. In Archibugi et al. 1998.

Dahl, R. A. (1989) *Democracy and its Critics*. New Haven: Yale University Press.

Dicken, P. (1998) *Global Shift*. London: Paul Chapman.

Dickson, A. (1997) *Development and International Relations*. Cambridge: Polity Press.

Dore, R. (ed.) (1995) *Convergence or Diversity? National Models of Production in a Global Economy*. New York: Cornell University Press.

Dunn, J. (1990) *Interpreting Political Responsibility*. Cambridge: Polity Press.

Dunning, J. (1993) *Multinational Enterprises and the Global Economy*. Wokingham: Addison-Wesley.

Ekins, P. (1992) *A New World Order: Grassroots Movements for Global Change*. London: Routledge.

Falk, R. (1969) The interplay of Westphalian and Charter conceptions of the international legal order. In R. Falk and C. Black (eds), *The Future of the International Legal Order*, vol. 1, Princeton: Princeton University Press.

Falk, R. (1987) The global promise of social movements: explorations at the edge of time. *Alternatives* 12.

Falk, R. (1995a) Liberalism at the global level: the last of the independent commissions? *Millennium* 24(3).

Falk, R. (1995b) *On Humane Governance: Toward a New Global Politics*. Cambridge: Polity Press.

Feldstein, M. and Horioka, C. (1980) Domestic savings and international capital flows. *Economic Journal* 90.

Fernández-Armesto, F. (1995) *Millennium*. London: Bantam.

Ferro, M. (1997) *Colonization: A Global History*. London: Routledge.

Frank, A. G. (1998) *Re-Orient: Global Economy in the Asian Age*. New York: University of California Press.

Frank, A. G. and Gills, B. K. (eds) (1996) *The World System*. London: Routledge.

Frieden, J. (1991) Invested interests: the politics of national economic policies in a world of global finance. *International Organization* 45(4).

Frost, M. (1986) *Towards a Normative Theory of International Relations*. Cambridge: Cambridge University Press.

Fukao, M. (1993) International integration of financial markets and the costs of capital. *Journal of International Securities Markets* 7.

Gagnon, J. and Unferth, M. (1995) Is there a world real interest rate? *Journal of International Money and Finance* 14.

Gamble, A. and Payne, A. (1991) Conclusion: the new regionalism. In A. Gamble and A. Payne (eds), *Regionalism and World Order*, London: Macmillan.

Garrett, G. (1996) Capital mobility, trade and the domestic politics of economic policy. In R. O. Keohane and H. V. Milner (eds), *Internationalization and Domestic Politics*, Cambridge: Cambridge University Press.

Garrett, G. (1998) Global markets and national politics. *International Organization* 52.

Garrett, G. and Lange, P. (1991) Political responses to interdependence: what's 'left' for the left? *International Organization* 45(4).

Garrett, G. and Lange, P. (1996) Internationalization, institutions and political change. In R. O. Keohane and H. V. Milner (eds), *Internationalization and Domestic Politics*, Cambridge: Cambridge University Press.

Gellner, E. (1983) *Nations and Nationalism*. Oxford: Blackwell.

Gereffi, G. and Korzeniewicz, M. (eds) (1994) *Commodity Chains and Global Capitalism*. Westport: Praeger.

Germain, R. (1997) *The International Organization of Credit*. Cambridge: Cambridge University Press.

Geyer, M. and Bright, C. (1995) World history in a global age. *American Historical Review* 100(4).

Giddens, A. (1985) *The Nation-State and Violence*, vol. 2 of *A Contemporary Critique of Historical Materialism*. Cambridge: Polity Press.

Giddens, A. (1990) *The Consequences of Modernity*. Cambridge: Polity Press.

Giddens, A. (1991) *Modernity and Self-Identity*. Cambridge: Polity Press.

Giddens, A. (1999) *The Third Way*. Cambridge: Polity Press.

Gill, S. (1992) Economic globalization and the internationalization of authority: limits and contradictions. *GeoForum* 23(3).

Gill, S. (1995) Globalization, market civilization and disciplinary neoliberalism. *Millennium* 24(3).

Gilpin, R. (1981) *War and Change in World Politics*. Cambridge: Cambridge University Press.

Gilpin, R. (1987) *The Political Economy of International Relations*. Princeton: Princeton University Press.

Gilroy, P. (1987) *There Ain't No Black in the Union Jack*. London: Hutchinson.

Godement, F. (1999) *The Downsizing of Asia*. London: Routledge.

Gordon, D. (1988) The global economy: new edifice or crumbling foundations? *New Left Review* 168.

Gourevitch, P. (1986) *Politics in Hard Times*. New York: Cornell University Press.

Graham, G. (1997) *Ethics and International Relations*. Oxford: Blackwell.

Gray, J. (1998) *False Dawn*. London: Granta.

Greider, W. (1997) *One World, Ready or Not: The Manic Logic of Global Capitalism*. New York: Simon and Schuster.

Haass, R. N. and Liton, R. E. (1998) Globalization and its discontents. *Foreign Affairs* (May–June).

Hall, S. (1992) The question of cultural identity. In S. Hall, D. Held and A. McGrew (eds), *Modernity and its Futures*, Cambridge: Polity Press.

Hanson, B. T. (1998) What happened to Fortress Europe? External trade policy liberalization in the European Union. *International Organization* 52(1) (Winter).

Hart, J. (1992) *Rival Capitalists: International Competitiveness in USA, Japan and Western Europe*. Princeton: Princeton University Press.

Harvey, D. (1989) *The Condition of Postmodernity*. Oxford: Blackwell.

Hasenclever, A., Mayer, P. and Rittberger, V. (1997) *Theories of International Regimes*. Cambridge: Cambridge University Press.

Held, D. (ed.) (1991) *Political Theory Today*. Cambridge: Polity Press.

Held, D. (1995) *Democracy and the Global Order: From the Modern State to Cosmopolitan Governance*. Cambridge: Polity Press.

Held, D. (1996) *Models of Democracy*, 2nd edn. Cambridge: Polity Press.

Held, D. and McGrew, A., Goldblatt, D. and Perraton, J. (1999) *Global Transformations: Politics, Economics and Culture*. Cambridge: Polity Press.

Helleiner, E. (1997) Braudelian reflections on economic globalization: the historian as pioneer. In S. Gill and J. Mittleman (eds), *Innovation and Transformation in International Studies*, Cambridge: Cambridge University Press.

Herod, A., Tuathail, G. O. and Roberts, S. M. (eds) (1998) *Unruly World? Globalization, Governance and Geography*. London: Routledge.

Hirst, P. (1997) The global economy: myths and realities. *International Affairs* 73(3) (July).

Hirst, P. and Thompson, G. (1996) *Globalization in Question*. Cambridge: Polity Press.

Hirst, P. and Thompson, G. (1999) *Globalization in Question*, 2nd edn. Cambridge: Polity Press.

Hobbes, T. (1968) *Leviathan*. Harmondsworth: Penguin.

Hodgson, M. G. S. (1993) The interrelations of societies in history. In E. Burke (ed.), *Rethinking World History: Essays on Europe, Islam and World History*, Cambridge: Cambridge University Press.

Holmes, S. (1988) Precommitment and the paradox of democracy. In J. Elster and R. Stagstad (eds), *Constitutionalism and Democracy*, Cambridge: Cambridge University Press.

Hoogvelt, A. (1997) *Globalization and the Postcolonial World: The New Political Economy of Development*. London: Macmillan.

Howard, M. (1981) *War and the Liberal Conscience*. Oxford: Oxford University Press.

Hu, W. (1992) Global corporations are national firms with international operations. *California Management Review* 34.

Hurrell, A. (1999) Security and inequality. In A. Hurrell and N. Woods, *Inequality, Globalization and World Politics*, Oxford: Oxford University Press.

Hurrell, A. and Woods, N. (1995) Globalization and inequality. *Millennium* 2.

Jameson, F. (1991) *Postmodernism: The Cultural Logic of Late Capitalism*. London: Verso.

Jessop, B. (1997) Capitalism and its future: remarks on regulation, government and governance. *Review of International Political Economy* 4(3).

Johnston, R. J., Taylor, P. J. and Watts, M. J. (eds) (1995) *Geographies of Global Change*. Oxford: Blackwell.

Jones, R. J. B. (1995) *Globalization and Interdependence in the International Political Economy*. London: Frances Pinter.

Kaldor, M. (1998) *New and Old Wars*. Cambridge: Polity Press.

Kapstein, E. B. (1994) *Governing the Global Economy: International Finance and the State*. Cambridge, Mass.: Harvard University Press.

Keck, M. and Sikkink, K. (1998) *Activists beyond Borders*. New York: Cornell University Press.

Keohane, R. O. (1984) *After Hegemony*. Princeton: Princeton University Press.

Keohane, R. O. (1995) Hobbes's dilemma and institutional change in world politics: sovereignty in international society. In H.-H. Holm and G. Sørensen (eds), *Whose World Order?* Boulder: Westview Press.

Keohane, R. O. (1998) International institutions: can interdependence work? *Foreign Policy* (Spring).

Keohane, R. O. and Nye, J. S. (1972) *Transnational Relations and World Politics*. Cambridge, Mass.: Harvard University Press.

Keohane, R. and Nye, J. (1977) *Power and Interdependence*. Boston: Little, Brown.

Kofman, E. and Youngs, G. (eds) (1996) *Globalization: Theory and Practice*. London: Pinter.

Korten, D. C. (1995) *When Corporations Ruled the World*. Hartford: Kumerian Press.

Krasner, S. D. (1985) *Structural Conflict: The Third World against Global Liberalism*. Los Angeles: University of California Press.

Krasner, S. D. (1993) Economic interdependence and independent statehood. In R. H. Jackson and A. James (eds), *States in a Changing World*. Oxford: Oxford University Press.

Krasner, S. D. (1995) Compromising Westphalia. *International Security* 20(3).

Krugman, P. (1994) Does third world growth hurt first world prosperity? *Harvard Business Review* (July).

Krugman, P. (1995) Growing world trade: causes and consequences. *Brookings Papers on Economic Activity*.

Lacey, R. and Danziger, D. (1999) *The Year 1000*. London: Little, Brown.

Lawrence. R. (1996) *Single World, Divided Nations? International Trade and OECD Labor Markets*. Washington DC: Brookings Institution.

Liebes, T. and Katz, E. (1993) *The Export of Meaning: Cross-Cultural Readings of Dallas*. Cambridge: Polity Press.

Linklater, A. (1998) *The Transformation of Political Community*. Cambridge: Polity Press.

Lloyd, P. J. (1992) Regionalization and world trade. *OECD Economics Studies* 18 (Spring).

Locke, J. (1963) *Two Treatises of Government*. Cambridge: Cambridge University Press.

Luttwak, E. (1999) *Turbo-Capitalism*. New York: Basic Books.

McGrew, A. G. (1992) Conceptualizing global politics. In McGrew and Lewis et al. 1992.

McGrew, A. G. and Lewis, P. G. et al. (1992) *Global Politics*. Cambridge: Polity Press.

MacIntyre, A. (1981) *After Virtue*. London: Duckworth.

MacIntyre, A. (1988) *Whose Justice? Which Rationality?* London: Duckworth.

McLuhan, M. (1964) *Understanding Media: The Extension of Man*. London: Routledge and Kegan Paul.

Mann, M. (1986) *The Sources of Social Power*, vol. 1: *A History of Power from the Beginning to AD 1760*. Cambridge: Cambridge University Press.

Mann, M. (1987) Ruling strategies and citizenship. *Sociology* 21(3).

Mann, M. (1997) Has globalization ended the rise and rise of the nation-state? *Review of International Political Economy* 4.

Massey, D. and Jess, P. (eds) (1995) *A Place in the World? Culture, Places and Globalization*. Oxford: Oxford University Press.

Mazlish, B. and Buultjens, R. (eds) (1993) *Conceptualizing Global History*. Boulder: Westview Press.

Meyrowitz, J. (1985) *No Sense of Place*. Oxford: Oxford University Press.

Miller, D. (1988) The ethical significance of nationality. *Ethics* 98.

Miller, D. (1992) The young and the restless in Trinidad: a case of the local and the global in mass consumption. In R. Silverstone and E. Hirsch (eds), *Consuming Technology*, London: Routledge.

Miller, D. (1999) Justice and inequality. In A. Hurrell and N. Woods (eds), *Inequality, Globalization and World Politics*, Oxford: Oxford University Press.

Milner, H. V. (1997) *Interests, Institutions and Information: Domestic Politics and International Relations*. Princeton: Princeton University Press.

Mitrany, D. (1975) The progress of international government (1932). In P. Taylor (ed.), *The Functional Theory of Politics*, London: LSE/Martin Robertson.

Modelski, G. (1972) *Principles of World Politics*. New York: Free Press.

Morse, E. (1976) *Modernization and the Transformation of International Relations*. New York: Free Press.

Mueller, J. (1989) *Retreat from Doomsday: The Obsolescence of Major War*. New York: Basic Books.

Neal, L. (1985) Integration of international capital markets. *Journal of Economic History* 45 (June).

Nierop, T. (1994) *Systems and Regions in Global Politics*. London: John Wiley.

O'Brien, R. (1992) *The End of Geography: Global Financial Integration*. London: Pinter.

OECD (1997) *Communications Outlook*. Paris: Organization for Economic Cooperation and Development.

Offe, C. (1985) *Disorganized Capitalism*. Cambridge: Polity Press.

Ohmae, K. (1990) *The Borderless World*. London: Collins.

Ohmae, K. (1995) *The End of the Nation State*. New York: Free Press.

O'Neill, O. (1991) Transnational justice. In D. Held (ed.), *Political Theory Today*, Cambridge: Polity Press.

Parekh, B. (1989) Between holy text and moral word. *New Statesman* 23 Mar.

Perlmutter, H. V. (1991) On the rocky road to the first global civilization. *Human Relations* 44(9).

Perraton, J., Goldblatt, D., Held, D. and McGrew, A. (1997) The globalization of economic activity. *New Political Economy* 2 (Spring).

Pieper, U. and Taylor, L. (1998) The revival of the liberal creed: the IMF, the World Bank and inequality in a globalized economy. In D. Baker, G. Epstein and R. Podin (eds), *Globalization and Progressive Economic Policy*, Cambridge: Cambridge University Press.

Piore, M. and Sabel, C. (1984) *The Second Industrial Divide*. New York: Basic Books.

Poggi, G. (1978) *The Development of the Modern State*. London: Hutchinson.

Porter, M. (1990) *The Competitive Advantage of Nations*. London: Macmillan.

Potter, D., Goldblatt, D., Kiloh, M. and Lewis, P. (eds) (1997) *Democratization*. Cambridge: Polity Press.

Reich, R. (1991) *The Work of Nations*. New York: Simon and Schuster.

Rheingold, H. (1995) *The Virtual Community*. London: Mandarin.

Rieger, E. and Liebfried, S. (1998) Welfare limits to globalization. *Politics and Society* 26(3).

Roberts, S. M. (1998) Geo-governance in trade and finance and political geographies of dissent. In Herod et al. 1998.

Robertson, R. (1992) *Globalization: Social Theory and Global Culture*. London: Sage.

Robins, K. (1991) Tradition and translation. In J. Corner and S. Harvey (eds), *Enterprise and Heritage: Crosscurrents of National Politics*. London: Routledge.

Rodrik, D. (1997) *Has Globalization Gone Too Far?* Washington DC: Institute for International Economics.

Rosenau, J. N. (1990) *Turbulence in World Politics*. Brighton: Harvester Wheatsheaf.

Rosenau, J. N. (1997) *Along the Domestic-Foreign Frontier*. Cambridge: Cambridge University Press.

Rowthorn, R. and Wells, J. (1987) *De-industrialization and Foreign Trade*. Cambridge: Cambridge University Press.

Ruggie, J. (1993a) Territoriality and beyond. *International Organization* 41(1).

Ruggie, J. (ed.) (1993b) *Multilateralism Matters*. New York: Columbia University Press.

Ruigrok, W. and Tulder, R. V. (1995) *The Logic of International Restructuring*. London: Routledge.

Russett, B. (1993) *Grasping the Democratic Peace: Principles for a Post–Cold War World*. Princeton: Princeton University Press.

Sandholtz, W. et al. (1992) *The Highest Stakes*. Oxford: Oxford University Press.

Sassen, S. (1996) *Losing Control? Sovereignty in an Age of Globalization*. New York: Columbia University Press.

Scharpf, F. (1991) *Crisis and Choice in European Social Democracy*. New York: Cornell University Press.

Scharpf, F. (1999) *Governing in Europe: Effective and Democratic?* Oxford: Oxford University Press.

Scholte, J. A. (1993) *International Relations of Social Change*. Buckingham: Open University Press.

Scholte, J. A. (1997) Global capitalism and the state. *International Affairs* 73(3) (July).

Shaw, M. (1994) *Global Society and International Relations*. Cambridge: Polity Press.

Shaw, M. (1997) The state of globalization: towards a theory of state transformation. *Review of International Political Economy* 4(3).

Shell, G. R. (1995) Trade legalism and international relations theory: an analysis of the WTO. *Duke Law Journal* 44(5).

Skinner, Q. (1978) *The Foundations of Modern Political Thought*, vol. 2. Cambridge: Cambridge University Press.

Skinner, Q. (1989) The state. In T. Ball, J. Farr and R. L. Hanson (eds), *Political Innovation and Conceptual Change*, Cambridge: Cambridge University Press.

Slater, D. (1995) Challenging western visions of the global: the geopolitics of theory and north–south relations. *European Journal of Development Research* 7(2).

Smith, A. D. (1986) *The Ethnic Origins of Nations*. Oxford: Blackwell.

Smith, A. D. (1990) Towards a global culture? In M. Featherstone (ed.), *Global Culture: Nationalism, Globalization and Modernity*, London: Sage.

Smith, A. D. (1995) *Nations and Nationalism in a Global Era*. Cambridge: Polity Press.

Sterling, R. W. (1974) *Macropolitics: International Relations in a Global Society*. New York: Knopf.

Strange, S. (1996) *The Retreat of the State*. Cambridge: Cambridge University Press.

Tamir, Y. (1993) *Liberal Nationalism*. Princeton: Princeton University Press.

Therborn, G. (1977) The rule of capital and the rise of democracy. *New Left Review* 13.

Thompson, G. (1998a) Globalization versus regionalism? *Journal of North African Studies*.

Thompson, G. (1998b) International competitiveness and globalization. In T. Baker and J. Köhler (eds), *International Competitiveness and Environmental Policies*, Brighton: Edward Elgar.

Thompson, G. and Allen J. (1997) Think global and then think again: economic globalization in context. *Area* 29(3).

Thompson, J. (1998) Community identity and world citizenship. In Archibugi et al. 1998.

Thompson, J. B. (1990) *Ideology and Modern Culture*. Cambridge: Polity Press.

Thompson, J. B. (1995) *The Media and Modernity*. Cambridge: Polity Press.

Thompson, K. W. (1994) *Fathers of International Thought: The Legacy of Political Theory*. Baton Rouge: Louisiana State University Press.

Tilly, C. (ed.) (1975) *The Formation of National States in Western Europe*. Princeton: Princeton University Press.

Turner, B. S. (1986) *Citizenship and Capitalism*. London: Allen and Unwin.

Tyson, L. (1991) They are not us: why American ownership still matters. *American Prospect* (Winter).

UNCTAD (1998a) *The Least Developed Countries 1998*. Geneva: UN Conference on Trade and Development.

UNCTAD (1998b) *Trade and Development Report 1998*. Geneva: UN Conference on Trade and Development.

UNCTAD (1998c) *World Investment Report 1998*. Geneva: UN Conference on Trade and Development.

UNDP (1997) *Human Development Report 1997*. New York: Oxford University Press.

UNDP (1998) *Globalization and Liberalization*. New York: Oxford University Press.

UNDP (1999) *Globalization with a Human Face: Human Development Report 1999*. New York: Oxford University Press.

UNESCO (1950) *World Communications Report*. Paris: United Nations Educational, Scientific and Cultural Organization.

UNESCO (1986) *International Flows of Selected Cultural Goods*. Paris: United Nations Educational, Scientific and Cultural Organization.

UNESCO (1989) *World Communications Report*. Paris: United Nations Educational, Scientific and Cultural Organization.

Union of International Associations (1996) *Yearbook of International Organizations 1996–1997*. Munich: K. G. Saur.

Van der Pijl, K. (1999) *Transnational Classes and International Relations*. London: Routledge.

Wade, R. (1990) *Governing the Market: Economic Theory and the Role of Government in East Asian Industrialization*. Princeton: Princeton University Press.

Wallerstein, I. (1974) *The Modern World System*. New York: Academic Press.

Walters, A. (1993) *World Power and World Money*. Brighton: Harvester.

Waltz, K. (1979) *The Theory of International Politics*. New York: Addison-Wesley.

Walzer, M. (1983) *Spheres of Justice: A Defence of Pluralism and Equality*. Oxford: Martin Robertson.

Weiss, L. (1998) *State Capacity: Governing the Economy in a Global Era*. Cambridge: Polity Press.

Wood, A. (1994) *North–South Trade, Employment and Inequality*. Oxford: Oxford University Press.

Woods, N. (1999) Order, globalization and inequality in world politics. In A. Hurrell and N. Woods (eds), *Inequality, Globalization and World Politics*, Oxford: Oxford University Press.

Yergin, D. A. and Stanislaw, J. (1998) *The Commanding Heights*. New York: Simon and Schuster.

Young, O. (1972) The actors in world politics. In J. Rosenau, V. Davis and M. East (eds), *The Analysis of International Politics*, New York: Cornell University Press.

Zacher, M. (1992) The decaying pillars of the Westphalian temple. In J. N. Rosenau and O. E. Czempiel (eds), *Governance without Government*, Cambridge: Cambridge University Press.

Zevin, R. (1992) Are world financial markets more open? In T. Banuri and J. B. Schor (eds), *Financial Openness and National Autonomy*, Oxford: Oxford University Press.

Zürn, M. (1995) The challenge of globalization and individualization. In H.-H. Holm and G. Sorensen (eds), *Whose World Order?* Boulder: Westview Press.

Part I
Conceptualizing Globalization

Globalization, writes Modelski, is the history of growing engagement between the world's major civilizations. It is not so much a phenomenon of the modern age as one which begins with the sporadic encounters amongst the earliest civilizations and, as the third millennium dawns, finds its expression in enduring webs of worldwide economic, cultural, political and technological interconnectedness. What, if anything, distinguishes this contemporary phase of globalization from earlier epochs? How should globalization be conceived? Is globalization the myth of our age or does it proffer a convincing narrative for the present period? These questions, among others, dominate the contributions to this part.

Beginning with the problem of conceptualization, the contributions by Modelski and by Held, McGrew, Goldblatt and Perraton seek to establish a simple but precise definition of globalization, and a methodology for making sense of it in historical terms. Both contributions advance an understanding of globalization which recognizes the possibility of its distinctive historical forms and which avoids a determinist view; that is, globalization understood as the progressive unification of humanity. This leaves open the issue of what is distinctive about contemporary patterns of globalization; a question to which the contributions of both Geyer and Bright and Hirst and Thompson deliver fundamentally different answers. Geyer and Bright take seriously the long history of globalization; they seek to identify what is historically unique about its contemporary expression and configuration, most especially by comparison with the age of global empires. By contrast, Hirst and Thompson consider the present era as exhibiting much weaker and less intense forms of global integration than the high point of the *belle époque* (1890–1914). In so doing, they call into question the very concept of globalization as a valid term for understanding what is new about the current epoch.

Both Castells and Harvey take issue with the proposition that globalization is an unhelpful and misleading notion, offering, from distinctive perspectives, a counter to the sceptical position. From a broadly neo-Marxist standpoint they both consider that the present period reflects profound changes in the dynamics of the capitalist order. But whereas Castells identifies the emergence of a 'new global informational capitalism' – the network society – Harvey argues the same developments define a much more profound break with the project of capitalist modernity. A new, postmodern, more fragmented global capitalism is acquiring hegemony across the planet, as time and space are re-organized by the dictates of multinational capital.

While accepting some of the central arguments of globalists, Giddens and Beck hold that the present era of globalization has to be understood as embodying much more than simply a capitalist logic. The driving forces of globalization are also to be found in the dynamics of technology, communication, international relations, and the global diffusion of risks – from the ecological to the financial. Rather than globalization defining a new postmodern age, in which the local is superseded by the global, they point to the growing tensions between a world still primarily organized by the 'modern container' of social life – nation-states – and new patterns of socio-economic organization which transcend them. Such tensions produce an ongoing dialectic of change and uncertainty – a global risk society – in which the global and the local intersect in complex ways, reshaping the conditions of contemporary social life with many unintended consequences. Globalization, in this view, defines a process of global social change but one which is still anchored in the institutions of the modern era.

1

Globalization

George Modelski

In clear contrast with all other historical societies, the contemporary world society is global. The process by which a number of historical world societies were brought together into one global system might be referred to as globalization. The nature and the shape assumed as a result of that process remain even today one of the basic factors of world politics.

Throughout recorded history, a trend can be observed toward the enlargement of the geographical scope of human communities; it has been one aspect of the increasing scale of social organization. Six thousand years ago, when a Great Society began to take form among the city states of Mesopotamia, the effective radius of its area may have been two or three hundred miles; two thousand years ago, when the Roman Empire dominated the Mediterranean basin, the radius of its control may have been one thousand miles or more (for a time it included Mesopotamia). The spread and enlargement of areas of civilization were at the same time occurring in the Chinese and Indian realms, so much so that what McNeill calls the "closure of the Eurasian ecumene" occurred between 500 BC and 200 AD,[1] some two millennia ago. Within that timespan, Hellenic culture reached India, while the Han Empire established a degree of contact with India and its missions established the existence of the Roman Empire. The epidemics that swept the ancient world around that time may have been the first practical consequence of the establishment of some pattern of interaction in the Old World. Generally, however, these interactions remained for a long time intermittent, indirect, nonpolitical, and not yet truly global.

The Moslem World

At the opening of the period of globalization, at about 1000 AD, the nearest approximation to a worldwide political order was the Moslem world. Its origins lay in the Arab conquests of the seventh century, and its binding force was Islam. At that time it ranged from Spain and Morocco, through Damascus, Cairo and Baghdad, to Persia and the North of India; in the centuries that followed, it reached as far as the Indonesian islands, and Central and East Africa. Even by comparison with medieval Europe, it was a prosperous, productive and culturally rich world. Its cities, Baghdad and Cairo, were cosmopolitan and populous (Cairo had more than one million inhabitants during the medieval period), as well as being centers of artistic and literary creation. Its scholars and scientists were the true successors of Greek learning, while its universities predated Europe's by at least a century.

[...]

For several hundred years, the Moslem world was the true seat of civilization. In relation to it medieval Europe was for a long time not only politically on the defensive, but also economically and culturally inferior. Indeed, by occupying a central position in the Eurasian-African landmass and using it for their far-flung trade, the Moslems had already brought together the major centers of world civilization. Only the New World eluded them, and interoceanic shipping.

[...]

After 1500, the Moslem world was strategically outflanked by European naval operations, and its vitality continued to decline. While Islam continued to gain adherents in Asia and Africa, the brilliance of the medieval period did not return.

The Expansion of Europe

The work of political unification of the world now fell to Europe. In one sense, the drive that produced it was a response to the prosperity of the Islamic world and the threat that was perceived to emanate from it. Leading that drive were the Portuguese and Spaniards, who had learned to respect and fear the Moslems during the centuries of the *Reconquista*. It was a genuine explosion of energy and vitality, of a breadth and scope hitherto unknown. Within a short space of time, soon after Copernicus reordered the heavens, men not only circumnavigated the globe, but followed up this feat with the establishment and maintenance of a permanent network of worldwide contacts.

The process of globalization was set in motion by people who lived in a small corner of the earth, not in the centers of world civilization. For the five hundred years that followed, it was they who determined the speed and the character of globalization; they also thereby shaped the structure of world politics.

By 1500, the characteristic features of modern world politics could already be discerned in embryo in Europe; in the course of globalization these features became characteristics of the entire global system.

[...]

Some Other Features

One striking feature of the process of globalization has been the quality of arrogance and violence that fueled it. William McNeill notes the "deeprooted pugnacity and recklessness" which, in combination with advanced military technology and acquired immunity to a variety of diseases within a brief space of time, gave the Europeans of the Atlantic Seaboard the command of the oceans.[2] European warlikeness (even of the merchants who on the high seas easily assumed the role of pirates) was most pronounced when compared with the attitudes and aptitudes of all the other major world civilizations (except for the Moslems, another "community of will"). None of them could match the naked, if well-organized, force of their ruthless opponents. In the process of globalization, European warlikeness might well have become a dominant feature of the entire system of world politics.

[...]

A great expansion in state activity and efficiency may well have been the most profound influence of globalization. Royal governments in Portugal, Spain, England and France organized and reaped the fruits of discovery and exploitation. In this, they learnt much from the Italian city states, Venice, Genoa and Florence: during the late medieval period, these were models of administrative organization and efficiency. But they soon had to expand their organization greatly in order to govern their newly acquired posts and territories – that is, efficiently to conduct higher-level administration at a distance. The Spanish Crown was the first to develop an elaborate machinery for the government of its American possessions; it thus gave employment to the rising number of graduates of law schools and universities. In turn, strong bureaucracies undermined tendencies toward popular rule, created a steady flow of revenue, and made the rulers independent of the control of assemblies, which had been so prominent in the earlier period. "Bureaucracy, like absolutism, strengthened its grip upon the kingdoms of Europe, in part at least as the consequence of the needs experienced and experiments conducted overseas."[3]

In military governmental operations, globalization was peculiarly favorable to, as well as dependent upon, the development of the navy. Effective naval operations over long distances require not only technology, but above all a sound political organization: a steady tax base, because they are expensive; a shipbuilding and supplies industry, geared to governmental demand; a manpower base that might be relatively small, but had to be loyal and well trained; and a governmental system that would be capable of coordinating these elements toward long-term goals. Governments that were capable of equipping fleets for sailing the world would also, as a rule, be efficient and strong governments, and it was they who set the tone of political organization.

Good navies were, for their part, closely dependent on the organization of commerce. The first Portuguese explorations were organized and financed by the Royal government; the monopoly of the spice trade that flowed from them was conducted entirely for the benefit of the King. This fusion of political and commercial activities probably contributed to the early decline of the trade. Spanish trade with the Americas was conducted by a monopoly of the merchants of Seville, with the financial backing of Italian and German houses, but it was less lucrative. It was the injection of Dutch and English enterprise, based on the long commercial experience of the cities of the Netherlands, that led to the development of specialized, corporate trade enterprises. The Dutch and English East Indies Companies became particularly famous, but there were many others. They all began as devices for pooling efforts to equip and supply fleets that sailed long distances. Voyages to the East, for instance, could last several years, and their profits were far from certain, although they could be spectacular. The organization, forethought, trust and care that were required for launching such expeditions were of a high order. Practices evolved in the organization and management of long-distance, hence higher-layered, trade and production activities became the bases of modern corporate organization.[4]

[. . .]

An Appraisal

The way in which the world has been brought together was a spectacular enterprise, with a magnificence all its own. Its role in shaping human destiny has not often enough been appreciated, even though the tales of exploration and adventure have long held the fascination of European audiences. But the spectacle and the splendor also had their shadows, and some of these have been dark and long.

A most important characteristic of globalization was its marvelously uncontrolled character. Despite the force and impetus of the process, this was not an organized expansion of a centralized system, as were the contemporaneous Chinese expeditions to Africa. This was not an expansion of one entity, called Europe, seizing overseas territory; it was rather the spilling over of a multitude of enterprises from Europe onto the world. In turn, the impact of the process also changed Europe. No one empire emerged but rather a series of imperial domains, each in competition with the others. Despite attempts at monopolization, no one rule attained overwhelming superiority; conversely, no single empire gave its ruler sufficient power to establish dominion over the whole of Europe.

[. . .]

Globalization helped to consolidate the system of independent states for Europe, and ultimately also for the world, by fostering the growth of a diversity of organizations, each one of which served as the seedbed of new autonomy and diversity. But above all, this process strengthened the state, and by doing so it markedly affected the course of future political development.

Who benefited from globalization? In a broad sense, the Western community did. During the past few centuries, the share of the European stock in the world's population has risen substantially.[5] In part, this is attributable to an earlier burst of population growth in Europe; but this early growth had also made possible large-scale migrations and the settlement of some of the world's most fertile and productive lands, in the attractive temperate zones, by people of European descent. The abundant lands and waters of North America, southern South America, South Africa and Australia became extensions of Europe, and their exploitation significantly altered the distribution of global wealth in favor of the European groups. As the result of globalization, the Europeans and their descendants today control the major part of cultivable land and the most productive sources of food, and they could also control the resources of the seas.[6]

Within Europe, those who benefited the most were those governments and states, and their subjects, that led and controlled the process. At first, the Iberian monarchies grew powerful on its proceeds, then the Dutch, the English and the French. Globalization altered the distribution of power away from Central Europe – including the cities of Northern Italy, the German lands and the Baltic area – to the coastlands of the North Atlantic. The process of growth redounded in the first place to the benefit of those who organized it.

Side by side with the benefits of globalization must be put its considerable costs and its range of adverse, indeed disintegrative effects. With regard to a number of human societies, its impact has been deadly, both in terms of social organization and for individual members of such societies, for whom the prospects of life declined tragically as the result of European impact. The societies of Mexico and Peru disintegrated, and in the century following the conquest the population of Central America declined catastrophically, through violence, disease and depression.[7] Similar disasters befell the Indian populations of North America, the inhabitants of many Pacific islands and the aboriginal populations of Australia.

[. . .]

Most of the time globalization was a process of incorporating external parts into the ongoing fabric of Western-centered world politics. Those governments, societies, individuals that proved adept and adaptable enough were brought within the mainstream by means of cooptation. The great majority were either dominated, controlled, ignored or isolated. An alternative mode of adaptation – that of adjusting Western-type life patterns to the requirements of the rest of the world – has not been adequately considered. Cooptation certainly has been neither deep, rapid nor sufficiently extensive. Complementary adaptation is yet to be explored – for instance, through the selective slowing down of growth rates. The work of globalization could yet be carried to completion in unsuspected ways.

Globalization ultimately raises the problem of whether the large community, indeed the community of mankind, can be a good community. Renowned political thinkers have consistently opted for an ideal community that is small and intimate. By and large, contemporary political thought points to the lack of community in large-scale organizations.

The historical experience of globalization does not permit us to make any optimistic or easy conclusion. It offers no grounds for the opinion that the large community must, of necessity, create wide benefits; indeed, there are reasons for thinking that it may instead create opportunities for great dangers. But it also discloses no theoretical or practical considerations that show that the large community is inherently unable to be good. The large community is here and can no longer be avoided; perhaps it can be made better.

Notes

1   W. H. McNeill, *The Rise of the West* (Chicago: Chicago University Press, 1963), ch. 7.
2   Ibid., pp. 623–4.
3   J. H. Parry, *The Age of Reconnaissance* (New York: New America Library, 1964), p. 320.
4   The prominence of corporate organization in the economic development of the United States may have had its origins in the early influence of such commercial corporations. Virginia was founded by an English chartered company; New York was a trading post of the Dutch West India Company; the Hudson Bay Company had been prominent in Canadian history for centuries.
5   C. M. Cipolla, *The Economic History of World Population* (Harmondsworth: Penguin, 1964), pp. 102–4, quoting Kuczynski, according to whom the white population of the earth was about 22 percent of the human species in 1800 and about 35 percent in 1930; more recently, this proportion may have been declining.
6   According to G. Borgstrom, *The Hungry Planet* (New York: Collier, 1965), "the privileged nations of the world" – which include the United States and account for some 450 million people – dispose of as many food calories per year as 1,300 million people at the bottom of the scale, who live in the least developed countries. "We like to think that we owe our abundance to our greater skill and ingenuity, completely forgetting that we owe it equally or maybe even to a greater extent to our good fortune in the great lottery of mankind, which has given us a disproportionate share of the world's agricultural resources" (p. 29).
7   Central Mexico had a population of 11 million in 1519 and one of 2.5 million in 1597 (quoted by Parry, *Age of Reconnaissance*, p. 246).

2

Rethinking Globalization

David Held and Anthony McGrew,
David Goldblatt and Jonathan Perraton

[. . .]
Rethinking Globalization: an Analytical Framework

What is globalization? Although in its simplest sense globalization refers to the widening, deepening and speeding up of global interconnectedness, such a definition begs further elaboration. Despite a proliferation of definitions in contemporary discussion – among them 'accelerating interdependence', 'action at a distance' and 'time-space compression'[1] (see, respectively, Ohmae 1990; Giddens 1990; Harvey 1989) – there is scant evidence in the existing literature of any attempt to specify precisely what is 'global' about globalization. For instance, all the above definitions are quite compatible with far more spatially confined processes such as the spread of national or regional interconnections. In seeking to remedy this conceptual difficulty, this study commences from an understanding of globalization which acknowledges its distinctive spatial attributes and the way these unfold over time.

Globalization can be located on a continuum with the local, national and regional.[2] At the one end of the continuum lie social and economic relations and networks which are organized on a local and/or national basis: at the other end lie social and economic relations and networks which crystallize on the wider scale of regional and global interactions. Globalization can be taken to refer to those spatio-temporal processes of change which underpin a transformation in the organization of human affairs by linking together and expanding human activity across regions and continents. Without reference to such expansive spatial connections, there can be no clear or coherent formulation of this term.

Accordingly, the concept of globalization implies, first and foremost, a *stretching* of social, political and economic activities across frontiers such that events, decisions and activities in one region of the world can come to have significance for individuals and communities in distant regions of the globe. In this sense, it embodies transregional interconnectedness, the widening reach of networks of social activity and power, and the possibility of action at a distance. Beyond this, globalization implies that connections across frontiers are not just occasional or random, but rather are regularized such that there is a detectable *intensification*, or growing magnitude, of interconnectedness, patterns of interaction and flows which transcend the constituent societies and states of the world order. Furthermore, growing extensity and intensity of global interconnectedness may also imply a *speeding up* of global interactions and processes as the development of worldwide systems of transport and communication increases the potential velocity of the global diffusion of ideas, goods, information, capital and people. And the growing *extensity*, *intensity* and *velocity* of global interactions may also be associated with a deepening enmeshment of the local and global such that the *impact* of distant events is magnified while even the most local developments may come to have enormous global consequences. In this sense, the boundaries between domestic matters and global affairs may be blurred. A satisfactory definition of globalization must capture each of these elements: extensity (stretching), intensity, velocity and impact. And a satisfactory account of globalization must examine them thoroughly. We shall refer to these four elements henceforth as the 'spatio-temporal' dimensions of globalization.

By acknowledging these dimensions a more precise definition of globalization can be offered. Accordingly, globalization can be thought of as

> *a process (or set of processes) which embodies a transformation in the spatial organ-ization of social relations and transactions – assessed in terms of their extensity, intensity, velocity and impact – generating transcontinental or interregional flows and networks of activity, interaction, and the exercise of power.*

In this context, flows refer to the movements of physical artefacts, people, symbols, tokens and information across space and time, while networks refer to regularized or patterned interactions between independent agents, nodes of activity, or sites of power (Modelski 1972; Mann 1993; Castells 1996).

This formulation helps address the failure of existing approaches to differentiate globalization from more spatially delimited processes – what we can call 'localization', 'nationalization', 'regionalization' and 'internationalization'. For as it is defined above, globalization can be distinguished from more restricted social developments. Localization simply refers to the consolidation of flows and networks within a specific locale. Nationalization is the process whereby social relations and transactions are developed within the framework of fixed territorial borders. Regionalization can be denoted by a clustering of transactions, flows, networks and interactions between functional or geographical groupings of states or societies, while internationalization can be taken to refer to patterns of interaction and interconnectedness between two or more nation-states irrespective of their specific geographical location (see Nierop 1994; Buzan 1998). Thus contemporary globalization describes, for example, the flows of trade and finance between the major regions in the world economy, while equivalent flows within them can be differentiated in terms of local, national and regional clusters.

In offering a more precise definition of these concepts it is crucial to signal that globalization is not conceived here in opposition to more spatially delimited processes but, on the contrary, as standing in a complex and dynamic relationship with them. On the one hand, processes such as regionalization can create the necessary kinds of economic, social and physical infrastructures which facilitate and complement the deepening of globalization. In this regard, for example, economic regionalization (for instance, the European Union) has not been a barrier to the globalization of trade and production but a spur. On the other hand, such processes can impose limits to globalization, if not encouraging a process of deglobalization. However, there is no a priori reason to assume that localization or regionalization exist in an oppositional or contradictory relationship to globalization. Precisely how these processes interrelate in economic and other domains is more an empirical matter [. . .].

Historical forms of globalization

Sceptics of the globalization thesis alert us to the fact that international or global inter-connectedness is by no means a novel phenomenon; yet they overlook the possibility that the particular form taken by globalization may differ between historical eras. To distinguish the novel features of globalization in any epoch requires some kind of analytical framework for organizing such comparative historical enquiry. For without such a framework it would be difficult to identify the most significant features, continuities or differences between epochs. Thus the approach developed here centres on the idea of *historical forms of globalization* as the basis for constructing a systematic comparative analysis of globalization over time. Utilizing this notion helps provide a mechanism for capturing and systematizing relevant differences and similarities. In this context, historical forms of globalization refer to

the spatio-temporal and organizational attributes of global interconnectedness in discrete historical epochs.

To say anything meaningful about either the unique attributes or the dominant features of contemporary globalization requires clear analytical categories from which such descriptions can be constructed. Building directly on our earlier distinctions, historical forms of globalization can be described and compared initially in respect of the four spatio-temporal dimensions:

- the extensity of global networks
- the intensity of global interconnectedness
- the velocity of global flows
- the impact propensity of global interconnectedness.

Such a framework provides the basis for both a *quantitative* and a *qualitative* assessment of historical patterns of globalization. For it is possible to analyse (1) the extensiveness of networks of relations and connections; (2) the intensity of flows and levels of activity within these networks; (3) the velocity or speed of interchanges; and (4) the impact of these phenomena on particular communities. A systematic assessment of how these phenomena have evolved provides insights into the changing historical forms of globalization; and it offers the possibility of a sharper identification and comparison of the key attributes of, and the major disjunctures between, distinctive forms of globalization in different epochs. Such a historical approach to globalization avoids the current tendency to presume either that globalization is fundamentally new, or that there is nothing novel about contemporary levels of global economic and social interconnectedness since they appear to resemble those of prior periods.

Of course, the very notion of historical forms of globalization assumes that it is feasible to map, in an empirical sense, the extensity, intensity, velocity and impact propensity of global flows, networks and transactions across time. [. . .] But one particular dimension of globalization is especially difficult to operationalize: the impact propensity of global flows, networks and transactions. Yet without some clear understanding of the nature of impact, the notion of globalization would remain imprecise. How should impact propensity be conceived?

For the purpose of this study, we distinguish between four analytically distinct types of impacts: *decisional*, *institutional*, *distributive* and *structural*. Decisional impacts refer to the degree to which the relative costs and benefits of the policy choices confronting governments, corporations, collectivities and households are influenced by global forces and conditions. Thus globalization may make some policy options or courses of action more or less costly and, in so doing, condition the outcome of individual or organizational decision-making. Depending on decision-makers' and collectivities' sensitivity or vulnerability to global conditions, their policy choices will be constrained or facilitated to a greater or lesser degree.[3] Decisional impacts can be assessed in terms of high impact (where globalization fundamentally alters policy preferences by transforming the costs and benefits of different courses of action) and low impact (where policy preferences are only marginally affected).

But the impact of globalization may not always be best understood in terms of decisions taken or forgone, since it may operate less transparently by reconfiguring the agenda of decision-making itself and, consequently, the available choices which agents may or may not realistically make. In other words, globalization may be associated with what Schattschneider referred to as the 'mobilization of bias' in so far as the agenda and choices which governments, households and corporations confront are set by global conditions (1960: 71). Thus, while the notion of decisional impacts focuses attention on how globalization directly influences the preferences and choices of decision-makers, the notion of institutional impact highlights the ways in which organizational and collective agendas reflect the effective choices or range of choices available as a result of globalization. In this respect, it offers insights into why certain choices may never even be considered as options at all.

Beyond such considerations, globalization may have considerable consequences for the distribution of power and wealth within and between countries. Distributional impacts refer to the ways in which globalization shapes the configuration of social forces (groups, classes, collectivities) within societies and across them. Thus, for instance, trade may undermine the prosperity of some workers while enhancing that of others. In this context, some groups and societies may be more vulnerable to globalization than others.

Finally, globalization may have discernible structural impacts in so far as it conditions patterns of domestic social, economic and political organization and behaviour. Accordingly, globalization may be inscribed within the institutions and everyday functioning of societies (Axford 1995). For instance, the spread of Western conceptions of the modern state and capitalist markets has conditioned the development of the majority of societies and civilizations across the globe. They have forced or stimulated the adaptation of traditional patterns of power and authority, generating new forms of rule and resource allocation. The structural consequences of globalization may be visible over both the short and the long term in the ways in which states and societies accommodate themselves to global forces. But such accommodation is, of course, far from automatic. For globalization is mediated, managed, contested and resisted by governments, agencies and peoples. States and societies may display varying degrees of sensitivity or vulnerability to global processes such that patterns of domestic structural adjustment will vary in terms of their degree and duration.

In assessing the impact of globalization on states and communities, it is useful to emphasize that the four types of impact can have a direct bearing on them, altering their form and modus operandi, or an indirect bearing, changing the context and balance of forces with which states have to contend. Decisional and institutional impacts tend to be direct in this regard, although they can have consequences for the economic and social circumstances in which states operate. Distributional and structural impacts tend to be indirect but, of course, none the less significant for that.

There are other important features of historical forms of globalization which should be distinguished. In addition to the spatio-temporal dimensions which sketch the broad shape of globalization, there are four dimensions which map its specific organizational profile: *infrastructures, institutionalization, stratification* and *modes of interaction*. Mapping the extensity, intensity, velocity and impact propensity of networks of global interconnectedness necessarily involves mapping the *infrastructures* which facilitate or carry global flows, networks and relations. Networks cannot exist without some kind of infrastructural support. Infrastructures may be physical, regulative/legal, or symbolic, for instance, a transportation infrastructure, the law governing war, or mathematics as the common language of science. But in most domains infrastructures are constituted by some combination of all these types of facility. For example, in the financial realm there is a worldwide information system for banking settlements, regulated by a regime of common rules, norms and procedures, and working through its own technical language via which its members communicate.

Infrastructures may facilitate or constrain the extensity and intensity of global connectedness in any single domain. This is because they mediate flows and connectivity: infrastructures influence the overall level of interaction capacity in every sector and thus the potential magnitude of global interconnectedness. Interaction capacity, understood as the potential scale of interaction defined by existing technical capabilities, is determined primarily, but not exclusively, by technological capacity and communications technology (see Buzan et al. 1993: 86). For instance, the interaction capacity of the medieval world system, constrained as it was by limited means of communication, among other things, was considerably less than that of the contemporary era, in which satellites and the Internet facilitate instant and almost real-time global communication (Deibert 1997). Thus changes in infrastructure have important consequences for the development and evolution of global interaction capacity.

Infrastructural conditions also facilitate the *institutionalization* of global networks, flows and relations. Institutionalization comprises the regularization of patterns of interaction and, consequently, their reproduction across space and time. To think in terms of the institutionalization of patterns of global connections (trade, alliances, etc.) is to acknowledge the ways in which global networks and relations become regularized and embedded in the practices and operations of the agencies (states, collectivities, households, individuals) in each social domain, from the cultural to the criminal (see Giddens 1979: 80). [. . .]

Discussion of infrastructures and institutionalization links directly to the issue of power. By power is meant the capacity of social agents, agencies and institutions to maintain or transform their circumstances, social or physical; and it concerns the resources which underpin this capacity and the forces that shape and influence its exercise. Accordingly, power is a phenomenon found in and between all groups, institutions and societies, cutting across public and private life. While 'power', thus understood, raises a number of complicated issues, it usefully highlights the nature of power as a universal dimension of human life, independent of any specific site or set of institutions (see Held 1989, 1995).

But the power of an agent or agency or institution, wherever it is located, never exists in isolation. Power is always exercised, and political outcomes are always determined, in the context of the relative capabilities of parties. Power has to be understood as a relational phenomenon (Giddens 1979: ch. 2; Rosenau 1980: ch. 3). Hence, power expresses at one and the same time the intentions and purposes of agencies and institutions and the relative balance of resources they can deploy with respect to each other. However, power cannot simply be conceived in terms of what agents or agencies do or do not do. For power is also a structural phenomenon, shaped by and in turn shaping the socially structured and culturally patterned behaviour of groups and the practices of organizations (Lukes 1974: 22). Any organization or institution can condition and limit the behaviour of its members. The rules and resources which such organizations and institutions embody rarely constitute a neutral framework for action, for they establish patterns of power and authority and confer the right to take decisions on some and not on others; in effect, they institutionalize a power relationship between 'rulers' and 'ruled', 'subjects' and 'governors' (McGrew 1988: 18–19).

Globalization transforms the organization, distribution and exercise of power. In this respect, globalization in different epochs may be associated with distinctive patterns of global *stratification*. In mapping historical forms of globalization, specific attention needs to be paid to patterns of stratification. In this context, stratification has both a social and a spatial dimension: hierarchy and unevenness, respectively (see Falk 1990: 2–12). Hierarchy refers to asymmetries in the control of, access to and enmeshment in global networks and infrastructures, while unevenness denotes the asymmetrical effects of processes of globalization on the life chances and well-being of peoples, classes, ethnic groupings and the sexes. These categories provide a mechanism for identifying the distinctive relations of global domination and control in different historical periods.

There are important differences too in the dominant *modes of interaction* within each epoch of globalization. It is possible to distinguish crudely between the dominant types of interaction – imperial or coercive, cooperative, competitive, conflictual – and the primary instruments of power, for example, military vs economic instruments. Thus, arguably, in the late nineteenth-century era of Western expansion, imperialism and military power were the dominant modes and instruments of globalization, whereas in the late twentieth century economic instruments, competition and cooperation appear to take precedence over military force (Morse 1976).

All in all, historical forms of globalization can be analysed in terms of eight dimensions: see box 1. Collectively, they determine the shape of globalization in each epoch.

Box 1 Historical forms of globalization: key dimensions

Spatio-temporal dimensions
1 the extensity of global networks
2 the intensity of global interconnectedness
3 the velocity of global flows
4 the impact propensity of global interconnectedness

Organizational dimensions
5 the infrastructure of globalization
6 the institutionalization of global networks and the exercise of power
7 the pattern of global stratification
8 the dominant modes of global interaction

Notes

1 By 'accelerating interdependence' is understood the growing intensity of international enmeshment among national economies and societies such that developments in one country impact directly on other countries. 'Action at a distance' refers to the way in which, under conditions of contemporary globalization, the actions of social agents (individuals, collectivities, corporations, etc.) in one locale can come to have significant intended or unintended consequences for the behaviour of 'distant others'. Finally, 'time-space compression' refers to the manner in which globalization appears to shrink geographical distance and time; in a world of instantaneous communication, distance and time no longer seem to be a major constraint on patterns of human social organization or interaction.
2 Regions refer here to the geographical or functional clustering of states or societies. Such regional clusters can be identified in terms of their shared characteristics (cultural, religious, ideological, economic, etc.) and high level of patterned interaction relative to the outside world (Buzan 1998).
3 'Sensitivity involves degrees of responsiveness within a policy-framework – how quickly do changes in one country bring costly changes in another and how great are the costly effects ... Vulnerability can be defined as an actor's liability to suffer costs imposed by external events even after policies have been altered' (Keohane and Nye 1977: 12).

References

Axford, B. (1995) *The Global System*. Cambridge: Polity Press.
Buzan, B. (1998) The Asia-Pacific: what sort of region, in what sort of order? In McGrew and Brook 1998.
Buzan, B., Little, R. and Jones, C. (1993) *The Logic of Anarchy*. New York: Columbia University Press.
Castells, M. (1996) *The Rise of the Network Society*. Oxford: Blackwell.
Deibert, R. (1997) *Parchment, Printing and Hypermedia*. New York: Columbia University Press.
Falk, R. (1990) Economic dimensions of global civilization. Working paper prepared for the Cairo meeting of the Global Civilization Project, Center for International Studies, Princeton University.
Giddens, A. (1979) *Central Problems in Social Theory: Action, Structure and Contradiction in Social Analysis*. London: Macmillan.
Giddens, A. (1990) *The Consequences of Modernity*. Cambridge: Polity Press.
Harvey, D. (1989) *The Condition of Postmodernity*. Oxford: Blackwell.
Held, D. (1989) *Political Theory and the Modern State*. Cambridge: Polity Press.
Held, D. (1995) *Democracy and the Global Order: From the Modern State to Cosmopolitan Governance*. Cambridge: Polity Press.
Keohane, R. O. and Nye, J. (1977) *Power and Interdependence*. Boston: Little, Brown.
Lukes, S. (1974) *Power: A Radical View*. London: Macmillan.
McGrew, A. G. (1988) Conceptualising Global Politics. Unit 1 in A. G. McGrew (ed.), *Global Politics*, Milton Keynes: Open University.
McGrew, A. G. and Brook, C. (eds) (1998) *Asia-Pacific in the New World Order*. London: Routledge.
Mann, M. (1993) *The Sources of Social Power*, vol. 2: *The Rise of Classes and Nation-States, 1760–1914*. Cambridge: Cambridge University Press.
Modelski, G. (1972) *Principles of World Politics*. New York: Free Press.
Morse, E. (1976) *Modernization and the Transformation of International Relations*. New York: Free Press.
Nierop, T. (1994) *Systems and Regions in Global Politics: An Empirical Study of Diplomacy, International Organization and Trade 1950–1991*. Chichester: John Wiley.
Ohmae, K. (1990) *The Borderless World*. London: Collins.
Rosenau, J. (1980) *The Study of Global Interdependence*. London: Frances Pinter.
Schattschneider, E. F. (1960) *The Semi-Sovereign People: A Realist View of Democracy in America*. New York: Rinehart and Winston.

3

World History in a Global Age

Michael Geyer and Charles Bright

[...]

The process of globalization was not simply an acceleration along a continuum of European expansion but a new ordering of relations of domination and subordination among all regions of the world. This fact captures the revolutionizing quality of the European departure at [the mid-nineteenth century]. Unlike other regions in crisis at the mid-century passage, Europe alone resolved its regional crisis by turning outward, externalizing its quest for solutions in projections of power overseas, and it did so not by conquests in the old manner of empire building, through spatial expansion and occupation, but in a new effort, with new capabilities, to synchronize global time and coordinate interactions *within* the world.[1] This development – the metaphors matter here: this was no longer quite a "thrust" or "projection" of force but an exercise in "webbing" or "enveloping" – was sustained by new technologies, especially the telegraph and, later on, radio and telephones, but it was fully articulated in transnational regimes of power made possible by the formation of communications-based systems of control (the gold standard, the global deployment of maritime force, or the futures markets) that began to envelop the world in global circuits of power by the end of the century.[2] These systems of control, which proliferated throughout the long twentieth century, were the key that enabled a "new" European imperialism to exploit the self-improving strategies of all other regions, adapting the dynamics of competitive inter-action among regions to move beyond mere extensions of power "over" others to the direct, sustained organization "of" others in global regimes of control. In this way, the European-Atlantic world became "the West" and gained its status as the centering axis of an integrating world.

As the dynamics of regional crisis drove Europe outward along externalizing paths, European initiatives collided, overlapped, and interacted with the dynamics of parallel crises in other regions and with strategies of competitive self-improvement that were devised to shore up regional power and to fend off or contain external pressures. Historiographic attention focuses on East Asia, but elements of these struggles can be observed in the Indian, Persian, Arab, African, and Latin American worlds as well. As regional power centers moved to defend autonomy, Europeans found in these self-improvement efforts the pathways and the allies for further and deeper intervention. This was a profoundly disruptive, extremely violent, and often callous process, but it was never simply the plunder of compradors. Instead, Western expansionism picked up and amplified regional and local processes of self-mobilization, permeating and trans-forming them in the course of using them. The projections of Western power were thus locally articulated as self-mobilizations and absorbed into the very fabric of local affairs – causing wider ramifications of change, much of it beyond the view, let alone the control, of European powers, but also beginning processes of utterly dependent integration that deepened as self-improvement strategies took hold.[3]

Global integration was thus not a set of procedures devised in the West and super-imposed on the rest as if a compliant world waited for its victimization, but, for this very reason, neither was global integration flatly or consistently rejected. Rather, integration was carried forward, asymmetrically and unevenly, on a global scale. India and Egypt, as well as Argentina, China, Persia, and Africa, became victims of Western expansionism and of outright aggression. But imperialism was also able to exist because Indians, Egyptians, Argentines, Chinese, Persians, and Africans helped make it happen, and not simply as lackeys and dupes but pursuing strategies of renewal that synchronized in the web of European-dominated global regimes. Running at full tilt themselves, they engaged Western power in complex patterns of collaboration and resistance, accommodation and cooptation, as they tried (often against great odds but also, we may add, with remarkable success) to reproduce and renew local worlds, using imperialists to shore up or to create positions of power, using sites of indigenous power to make deals, using the European and American positions as interlopers in order to selectively appropriate the ways of the conquerors to local ends. In this way, *they* were the ones to produce the resources for global integration, creating in the process a more integrated world, albeit not exactly as Western imperialists had intended.[4] Global integration was built with this kind of labor.

The surpluses of this labor forged an ever tighter (if always competitive and contested) concentration of power within the West. That is, military power was projected everywhere, but nowhere was it more concentrated and lethal than within the European region. State power was extended as colonial regimes throughout Asia and Africa, even as state power became concentrated and coordinated in Europe. Western communication and transportation systems reached into every corner of the world, yet nowhere were the linkages denser or their impact more far-reaching than in the European-Atlantic region. Industrial goods were available and traded everywhere, but both trade and production were most heavily concentrated and grew most rapidly in the core region. The intensification and concentration of capitalist production went hand in hand with its global extension, binding the world together in tighter, if always uneven and unequal, global circuits of power, capital, and culture.[5]

Within this integrating world, Europeans and Americans increasingly drew the lines of demarcation that defined an emergent global center over and against the rest. Global integration entailed a spatial reorganization of human and capital mobility that came to the fore in a rush of imperial imaginings by travelers, expatriates, civil servants, and armchair enthusiasts. These were elaborated into universal knowledge in a set of new imperial sciences: geography, ethnology, and biology being pioneer disciplines of the day. It was also toward the end of the nineteenth century that barriers were erected to control the movements of non-European peoples and a more rigid racial segregation was devised to define white privilege and to ensure control over racial "others," not only in colonial and semi-colonial environments but very much at the centers of power as well. Racism became deeply entrenched in legal, social, and cultural practices.[6] This division of people underwrote a new global division of labor that separated, world-wide, capital-intensive industrial production from handicrafts and extraction, agriculture from industry, and was further reinforced by new procedures for allocating and controlling the movement of wealth, grounded in the international acceptance of the gold standard and of financial rules enforced, primarily, by the Bank of England. Across an integrating world, new lines of segregation and distinction were thus drawn and powerfully imagined in racialist world views that set the white European-Atlantic region and its dispersed settlements around the world apart from the rest and ensured their privilege.

The deepening chasms that divided an increasingly integrated world, together with the proliferating distinctions between "us" and "them" that were handed down as social sciences (modern/traditional, advanced/backward) and constituted Western discourse about the rest, swallowed up the older, enlightened imagination of "humanity" that had previously informed world history narratives. As difference and distinction grew within an integrating world, the overarching simplicities of universal history were supplanted by naturalized histories of the "rest" – studied as the grand traditions of world civilizations in the humanities – and by a specialized and instrumental knowledge about progress – pursued as development and modernization theories in the social sciences. The West (in fact, a few core European states, subsequently enlarged to a European–North Atlantic world and only belatedly extended to the Pacific rim) *gained* in this process a new intellectual identity as a discrete region. Europe was constituted as the West in the context of forging a unified, scientific narrative for an integrating world.[7] This was, one might add, a secular West that in the science of modernizing the world found a counter to and a strategy for surpassing its older religious identity as the site of (Latin) Christianity in juxtaposition, internally, to Judaism and, externally, to Islam.[8] That Islam became a powerful and modernizing global imagination in its own right during the course of the long twentieth century (and not merely in the last two decades or so) is commonly forgotten.

The paradigm of global modernization was powerful knowledge with an unequivocal vision of the world to come. It underwrote a new narrative of world history, which left behind the pieties of Enlightenment thought. This history of a world being integrated predicted, first, that in dominating the world through its mastery of the technical and material means of global integration, the West would actually control the world and be able to shape the course of global development, and, second, that in shaping the world, the West held secure knowledge, positive empirical proof in its own development, of the direction and outcome of world history. The world would become more like the West in a protracted process of modernization, and, as the rest of the world moved toward uplift and progress, the division between "the West" and "the rest" would diminish.

It did not happen this way. First, efforts to establish global order proved notoriously unstable and short-lived. The two most powerful ventures, the *pax britannica* in the first half and the *pax americana* in the second half of the long twentieth century, came and went quickly as world-ordering efforts. Neither was able to transform a staggering superiority in force into lasting political order – that is, into a consensual global politics as opposed to domination and the threat of violence. This proved to be the single most abiding limitation on the West's ability to realize global control. Second, it did not happen this way because Western mastery of the powers of production and destruction (and of the scientific knowledge that underwrote it) never imparted a sure capacity to shape and mold the world into a homogeneous global civilization.[9] What Western exertions produced instead was a disorderly world of proliferating difference, a world in which the very production of difference was lodged in the processes of globalization that the West had presumed to control. Even where difference was partially overcome by non-Western efforts to emulate and surpass Western productivity – a path taken by Japan and, later, others in the northeast Asian region, for example[10] – the power of the Western narrative, with its presumption of control and its racist exclusions, masked emergent dynamics of integration.

[...]

Throughout the long twentieth century, the world-wide mobilizations of peoples and resources and their channeling into transnational networks of exchange were effected by, and contained within, emergent state structures. States flourished in the context of globalization, a fact that must qualify much of the commonplace concern about global integration and transnational regimes threatening the integrity or autonomy of the state.[11] They did so because the condition of globality has always been organized locally, in one place after the other, according to particular circumstances and conditions that happen to obtain. No matter how powerful or abstract the networks of global exchange or how remote their nodes of control, each transaction needs articulation in some particular place, in some meaningful idiom, under specific circumstances; processes of globalization must come to ground in concrete social, cultural, and political contexts that move people to purposive ends and thus allow them, in some fashion, to represent themselves. In the twentieth century, states have sought, in their own interests and in the promotion of national development, to negotiate these connections; indeed, it was the (relative) success of the state in managing the linkages with an integrating world that allowed "national" politics to flourish. This is why states have grown in tandem with globalization,[12] but it is also where powerful questions arise: for the process of global integration, while not destroying states, has had a tendency to bypass politics, short-circuit the formation of national agendas, and challenge the capacity of the state for political self-organization, that is, to constitute the nation and organize complex social relations.[13] The result of this development is not only growing disillusionment with politics, world-wide, but the proliferation and strengthening of family and kinship networks and, more generally, of identity-based (ethnic or religious) communities as substitutes for national politics in much of the world.[14] These go together with the proliferation of export platforms, para-states, "private" (family-based) states, and state satrapies. Here we find the key questions requiring closer examination for the whole of the long twentieth century – not in the collapse of the state but in the uncertainties of nations and in the crises of politics as popular representation.

[...]

Increasingly over the course of the twentieth century, struggles for autonomy have turned into contestations over the *terms* of global integration – not over whether the world should move together but by whom and under what terms the identities of individuals, social groups, and entire societies should be defined. As this point is reached and passed again and again, the former center loses particularity; the more globalization proceeds, the less any region or society can pretend to control the struggle over the terms of integration. Thus we arrive at the end of the twentieth century in a global age, losing our capacity for narrating our histories in conventional ways, outward from one region, but gaining the ability to think world history, pragmatically and realistically, at the interstices of integrating circuits of globalizing networks of power and proliferating sites of localizing politics. This is the new condition of globality.

[...]

Notes

1   As general texts: David Harvey, *The Condition of Postmodernity: An Enquiry into the Origins of Cultural Change* (Oxford, 1989); James Carey, *Communications as Culture: Essays on Media and Society* (Boston, 1989); Roger Friedland and Deirdre Boden (eds), *NowHere: Space, Time*

and Modernity (Berkeley, 1994). As historical introduction: Daniel R. Headrick, *The Tools of Empire: Technology and European Imperialism in the Nineteenth Century* (New York, 1981); and Headrick, *The Invisible Weapon: Telecommunications and International Politics, 1851–1945* (New York, 1991). See also Catherine Bertho-Lavenir, *L'état et les télécommunications en France et à l'étranger 1837–1987* (Geneva, 1991). The most detailed case studies are on the United States: Edwin N. Asmann, *The Telegraph and the Telephone: Their Development and Role in the Economic History of the United States; The First Century, 1844–1944* (n.p., 1980); Menaham Blondheim, *News over the Wires: The Telegraph and the Flow of Public Information in America, 1844–1897* (Cambridge, Mass., 1994).

2   A good starting point for discussion is Susan Strange, *States and Markets* (New York, 1988). While these circuits of power are not generally well researched, there has been a great deal of study on the workings of the gold standard. Arthur I. Bloomfield, *Monetary Policy under the International Gold Standard, 1880–1914* (1959; New York, 1978), remains valuable. More recent treatments are Marcello De Cecco, *Money and Empire: The International Gold Standard, 1890–1914* (Oxford, 1974); Barry Eichengreen (ed.), *The Gold Standard in Theory and History* (New York, 1985); Ian Drummond, *The Gold Standard and the International Monetary System, 1900–1939* (Basingstoke, 1987); Giulio Gallarotti, *The Anatomy of an International Monetary Regime: The Classical Gold Standard, 1880–1914* (New York, 1995). A recent study of the British managers of the system that focuses on personalities and players is now in its second volume: David Kynaston, *The City of London*, vol. 2: *Golden Years, 1890–1914* (London, 1995).

3   The comparison between Canada and Argentina is most instructive for this development. D. C. M. Platt and Guido Di Tella, *Argentina, Australia, and Canada: Studies in Comparative Development, 1870–1965* (New York, 1985); Jeremy Adelman, *Frontier Development: Land, Labour, and Capital on the Wheatlands of Argentina and Canada, 1890–1914* (Oxford, 1994); Carl E. Solberg, *The Prairies and the Pampas: Agrarian Policy in Canada and Argentina, 1880–1930* (Stanford, 1987); Roberto Cortes Conde, *Some Notes on the Industrial Development of Argentina and Canada in the 1920s* (Buenos Aires, 1985). The debate on Argentina is first of all significant for intrinsic reasons, the conjunctures of the Argentine economy, and their consequences for national identity. See the debate between Andrew Thompson, " 'Informal Empire': An Explanation in the History of Anglo-Argentine Relations, 1810–1914," *Journal of Latin American Studies* 24 (1992): 419–36; and A. G. Hopkins, "Informal Empire in Argentina: An Alternative View," *Journal of Latin American Studies* 26 (1994): 469–84; Tulio Halperín-Donghi, "Un cuarto de siglo de historiografia argentina (1960–1985)," *Desarrollo económico* 25 (1986): 487–520; Juan C. Korol and Hilda Sabato, "Incomplete Industrialization: An Argentine Obsession," *Latin American Research Review* 25 (1990): 7–30, with the pertinent literature. On the political consequences, see José Carlos Chiaramonte, *Nacionalismo y Liberalismo económicos en la Argentina, 1860–1880* (Buenos Aires, 1971); and Nicolas Shumway, *The Invention of Argentina* (Berkeley, 1991). But this debate is perhaps even more important for its paradigmatic character in the controversy about development/underdevelopment and export-led growth versus import substitution and theories of dependency. For the latter, see the key studies of the Comisión Económica para América Latina (CEPAL), *Análisis y proyecciones del desarrollo económico* (2 vols, Mexico City, 1958); Aldo Ferrer, *La económica argentina* (Buenos Aires, 1963); and Raul Prebisch, "El desarrollo económico de la America Latina y algunos de sus principales problemas," *Desarrollo económico* 26 (1986): 479–502. See the assessment by Kathryn Sikkink, "The Influence of Raul Prebisch on Economic Policy Making in Argentina, 1950–1962," *Latin American Research Review* 23 (1988): 91–114, and the subsequent commentaries and debate: 115–31.

4   The debate on the practices of domination and subordination is currently one of the more exciting historiographic debates, with a stake for every part of the world, including Europe and the United States. This debate developed out of "resistance" studies on the one hand and the critique of the discourse of national liberation on the other. Its current main opponent is world-systems theory (see Frederick Cooper et al. (eds), *Confronting Historical Paradigms* (Madison, 1993)), and its often unacknowledged crossover in literary studies is

postcolonial literary theory: Bill Ashcroft, Gareth Griffiths, and Helen Tiffin (eds), *The Post-colonial Studies Reader* (London, 1995). The finer points of debate are represented by John Comaroff, "Images of Empire, Contests of Conscience: Models of Colonial Domination in South Africa," *American Ethnologist* 16 (1989): 609–21; Jean Comaroff, *Body of Power, Spirit of Resistance: The Culture and History of a South African People* (Chicago, 1985); John Comaroff and Jean Comaroff, *Ethnicity, Nationalism, and the Politics of Identity in an Age of Revolution* (Chicago, 1994), on the one hand, and on the other, Frederick Cooper and Ann L. Stoler, "Tensions of Empire: Colonial Control and Visions of Rule," *American Ethnologist* 16 (1989): 609–84; Ann Stoler, "Sexual Affronts and Racial Frontiers: European Identities and the Cultural Politics of Exclusion in South East Asia," *Comparative Studies in Society and History* 34 (1992): 514–51; Nicholas B. Dirks (ed.), *Colonialism and Culture* (Ann Arbor, 1992). Sexual politics have long been a central concern: Anne McClintock, *Imperial Leather: Race, Gender and Sexuality in the Colonial Context* (London, 1995). Achille Mbembe, "The Banality of Power and the Aesthetics of Vulgarity in the Postcolony," *Public Culture* 4 (1992): 1–30, has raised a storm (*Public Culture* 5 (1992): 47–145), putting sexual *politics* right back into the state. Religious practices as a site of opposition have also emerged as a central area of study. See Jean-Pierre Chrétien, *L'invention religieuse en Afrique. Histoire et religion en Afrique noire* (Paris, 1993); Jean Comaroff and John Comaroff, *Of Revelation and Revolution: Christianity, Colonialism, and Consciousness in South Africa* (Chicago, 1991). Finally, on the powers of nationalism and socialism: Frederick Cooper, *The Dialectics of Decolonization: Nationalism and Labor Movements in Postwar Africa* (Ann Arbor, 1992).

5   This, at last, is an operating "world system" whose outlines just barely come into view – and whose polemical as well as scientific literature on the very phenomenon of world systems is part and parcel of its working. Both are discussed in Eric Hobsbawm, *Age of Extremes* (London, 1994). We have sketched out the operations of this hegemonic period in Michael Geyer and Charles Bright, "For a Unified History of the World in the Twentieth Century," *Radical History Review* 39 (1987): 69–91, and will return to the subject.

6   Hannah Arendt, *The Origins of Totalitarianism*, new edn (New York, 1966), is one of the most powerful reminders of this universality of (Western) racism. However, her argument about South Africa is also one of the most troubling of the book, suggesting persistent difficulties of a powerful strand of Western political thought to address the subject of race and race-making (as Thomas Holt has called it). In Arendt's case, this may well be not a matter of getting the facts wrong or of having incomplete information, as historians might suggest, but of getting the wrong "canon" in approaching the issue. Bonnie Honig, "Arendt, Identity, and Difference," *Political Theory* 16 (1988): 77–98. In any case, the new separations were deftly captured by E. M. Forster in his novel *A Passage to India* (1924) and have been studied closely for South Africa by Charles van Onselen, "Race and Class in the South African Countryside: Cultural Osmosis and Social Relations in the Sharecropping Economy of the South-Western Transvaal, 1900–1950," *American Historical Review* 95 (Feb. 1990): 99–123; and for Indonesia by Ann Stoler, "Rethinking Colonial Categories: European Communities and the Boundaries of Rule," *Comparative Studies in Society and History* 31 (1989). George M. Fredrickson drew important distinctions between Jim Crow in the United States and the developing system of racial separation in South Africa, in *White Supremacy: A Comparative Study in American and South African History* (New York, 1981), but the centrality of racial demarcations in both systems between the 1890s and the 1940s remains salient. Joel Williamson explored the nexus of sexual imagery and racism in white imaginings in *The Crucible of Race: Black/White Relations in the American South since Emancipation* (New York, 1984).

7   Dorothy Ross, *The Origins of American Social Science* (Cambridge, 1991); Daniel Lerner, James S. Coleman, and Ronald P. Dore, "Modernization," *International Encyclopedia of the Social Sciences* (New York, 1968), vol. 10, pp. 386–409; Robert A. Nisbet, *Social Change and History: Aspects of the Western Theory of Development* (New York, 1969); Carl E. Pletsch, "The Three Worlds, or the Division of Social Scientific Labor, circa 1950–1975,"

Comparative Studies in Society and History 23 (1981): 565–90; Leonard Binder, "The Natural History of Development Theory," *Comparative Studies in Society and History* 28 (1986): 3–23. For Europe: Hans-Ulrich Wehler, *Modernisierungstheorie und Geschichte* (Göttingen, 1975).

8 Vassilis Lambropoulos, *The Rise of Eurocentrism: Anatomy of Interpretation* (Princeton, 1993).

9 Dieter Senghaas, *The European Experience: A Historical Critique of Development Theory*, trans. K. H. Kimmig (Leamington Spa, 1985). Frédérique A. Marglin and Stephen A. Marglin, *Dominating Knowledge: Development, Culture, and Resistance* (Oxford, 1990); Immanuel Wallerstein, *Unthinking Social Science: The Limits of Nineteenth-Century Paradigms* (Cambridge, 1991).

10 Akira Iriye, *Across the Pacific: An Inner History of American–East Asian Relations* (New York, 1967); and Iriye, *China and Japan in the Global Setting* (Cambridge, Mass., 1992); see also the panoramic view by Walter A. McDougall, *Let the Sea Make a Noise: A History of the North Pacific from Magellan to MacArthur* (New York, 1993).

11 Francis H. Hinsley, *Sovereignty*, 2nd edn (Cambridge, 1986); Theodor Schieder, *Der Nationalstaat in Europa als historisches Phänomen* (Cologne, 1964); Leonard Tivey (ed.), *The Nation-State: The Formation of Modern Politics* (Oxford, 1981); Michael Mann (ed.), *The Rise and Decline of the Nation State* (Oxford, 1990), provide solid background for a discussion of the issue. The "crisis" of the nation-state is discussed in David Held, "The Decline of the Nation State," in Stuart Hall and Martin Jacques (eds), *New Times: The Changing Face of Politics in the 1990s* (London, 1989); Joseph A. Camilleri and Jim Falk, *The End of Sovereignty? The Politics of a Shrinking and Fragmenting World* (Aldershot, 1992); Michael Zürn, "Jenseits der Staatlichkeit: Über die Folgen der ungleichen Denationalisierung," *Leviathan* 20 (1992): 490–513; Kenichi Ohmae, *The Borderless World: Power and Strategy in the Interlinked Economy* (New York, 1990).

12 Craig Calhoun, "Imagined Communities and Indirect Relationships: Large-Scale Social Integration and the Transformation of Everyday Life," in Pierre Bourdieu and James S. Coleman (eds), *Social Theory for a Changing Society* (Boulder, 1991), pp. 95–120; and "Indirect Relationships, Information Technology, and the Transformation of Everyday Life," in Neil J. Smelser and Hans Haferkamp (eds), *Social Change and Modernity* (Berkeley, 1992), pp. 205–36.

13 Robert H. Jackson, *Quasi-States: Sovereignty, International Relations and the Third World* (Cambridge, 1990); Ronald M. Grant and E. Spencer Wellhofer (eds), *Ethno-Nationalism, Multinational Corporations, and the Modern State* (Denver, 1979); Mathew Horsman, *After the Nation-State: Citizens, Tribalism, and the New World Disorder* (London, 1994); Anthony G. McGrew et al., *Global Politics: Globalization and the Nation-State* (Cambridge, 1992). The discussion on (West) Africa is rather different in that it raises the problem of states, as territorial and political organizations, being unsuited to organize society and a threat to survival. Michael Bratton, "Beyond the State: Civil Society and Associational Life in Africa," *World Politics* 41 (1989): 407–30; Jean-François Bayart, *L'état en Afrique. La politique du ventre* (Paris, 1989); Basil Davidson, *The Black Man's Burden: Africa and the Curse of the Nation-State* (New York, 1990).

14 This has been the crux of the issue of "multiculturalism" everywhere. See Charles Taylor, *The Ethics of Authenticity* (Cambridge, Mass., 1991); and Taylor, *Multiculturalism and "The Politics of Recognition": An Essay*, with commentary by Amy Gutmann (ed.) et al. (Princeton, 1992). For reopening the debate on national history, see Partha Chatterjee, *Nationalist Thought and the Colonial World* (London, 1986) and *The Nation and its Fragments* (Princeton, 1993) for India and Prasenjit Duara, *Rescuing History from the Nation: Questioning Narratives of Modern China* (Chicago, 1995), for China.

4

Globalization – a Necessary Myth?

Paul Hirst and Grahame Thompson

Globalization has become a fashionable concept in the social sciences, a core dictum in the prescriptions of management gurus, and a catch-phrase for journalists and politicians of every stripe. It is widely asserted that we live in an era in which the greater part of social life is determined by global processes, in which national cultures, national economies and national borders are dissolving. Central to this perception is the notion of a rapid and recent process of economic globalization. A truly global economy is claimed to have emerged or to be in the process of emerging, in which distinct national economies and, therefore, domestic strategies of national economic management are increasingly irrelevant. The world economy has internationalized in its basic dynamics, it is dominated by uncontrollable market forces, and it has as its principal economic actors and major agents of change truly transnational corporations that owe allegiance to no nation-state and locate wherever on the globe market advantage dictates.

This image is so powerful that it has mesmerized analysts and captured political imaginations. But is it the case? [...]

We began this investigation with an attitude of moderate scepticism. It was clear that much had changed since the 1960s, but we were cautious about the more extreme claims of the most enthusiastic globalization theorists. In particular it was obvious that radical expansionary and redistributive strategies of national economic management were no longer possible in the face of a variety of domestic and international constraints. However, the closer we looked the shallower and more unfounded became the claims of the more radical advocates of economic globalization. In particular we began to be disturbed by three facts. First, the absence of a commonly accepted model of the new global economy and how it differs from previous states of the international economy. Second, in the absence of a clear model against which to measure trends, the tendency to casually cite examples of the internationalization of sectors and processes as if they were evidence of the growth of an economy dominated by autonomous global market forces. Third, the lack of historical depth, the tendency to portray current changes as unique and without precedent and firmly set to persist long into the future.

To anticipate, as we proceeded our scepticism deepened until we became convinced that globalization, as conceived by the more extreme globalizers, is largely a myth. Thus we argue that:

1   The present highly internationalized economy is not unprecedented: it is one of a number of distinct conjunctures or states of the international economy that have existed since an economy based on modern industrial technology began to be generalized from the 1860s. In some respects, the current international economy is *less* open and integrated than the regime that prevailed from 1870 to 1914.

2 Genuinely transnational companies appear to be relatively rare. Most companies are based nationally and trade multinationally on the strength of a major national location of assets, production and sales, and there seems to be no major tendency towards the growth of truly international companies.

3 Capital mobility is not producing a massive shift of investment and employment from the advanced to the developing countries. Rather foreign direct investment (FDI) is highly concentrated among the advanced industrial economies and the Third World remains marginal in both investment and trade, a small minority of newly industrializing countries apart.

4 As some of the extreme advocates of globalization recognize, the world economy is far from being genuinely 'global'. Rather trade, investment and financial flows are concentrated in the Triad of Europe, Japan and North America and this dominance seems set to continue.

5 These major economic powers, the G3, thus have the capacity, especially if they coordinate policy, to exert powerful governance pressures over financial markets and other economic tendencies. Global markets are thus by no means beyond regulation and control, even though the current scope and objectives of economic governance are limited by the divergent interests of the great powers and the economic doctrines prevalent among their elites.

We should emphasize that this [article] challenges the strong version of the thesis of *economic* globalization, because we believe that without the notion of a truly globalized economy many of the other consequences adduced in the domains of culture and politics would either cease to be sustainable or become less threatening. Hence most of the discussion here is centred on the international economy and the evidence for and against the process of globalization.

[. . .]

Models of the International Economy

We can only begin to assess the issue of globalization if we have some relatively clear and rigorous model of what a global economy would be like and how it represents both a new phase in the international economy and an entirely changed environment for national economic actors. Globalization in its radical sense should be taken to mean the development of a new economic structure, and not just conjunctural change towards greater international trade and investment within an existing set of economic relations. An extreme and one-sided ideal type of this kind enables us to differentiate *degrees* of internationalization, to eliminate some possibilities and to avoid confusion between claims. Given such a model it becomes possible to assess it against evidence of international trends and thus enables us more or less plausibly to determine whether or not this phenomenon of the development of a new supranational economic system is occurring. In order to do this we have developed two basic contrasting ideal types of international economy, one that is fully globalized, and an open international economy that is still fundamentally characterized by exchange between relatively distinct national economies and in which many outcomes, such as the competitive performance of firms and sectors, are substantially determined by processes occurring at the national level. These ideal types are valuable in so far as they are useful in enabling us to clarify the issues conceptually, that is, in specifying the difference between a new global economy and merely extensive and intensifying international economic relations. Too often evidence compatible with the latter is used as though it substantiated the former. With a few honourable exceptions, the more enthusiastic advocates of globalization have failed to specify that difference, or to specify what evidence would be decisive in pointing to a structural change towards a global economy. Increasing salience of foreign trade and considerable and growing international flows of capital are not *per se* evidence of a new and distinct phenomenon called 'globalization'. [...]

Type 1: An inter-national economy

We shall first develop a simple and extreme version of this type. An *inter-national economy* is one in which the principal entities are national economies. Trade and investment produce growing interconnection between these still national economies. Such a process involves the increasing integration of more and more nations and economic actors into world market relationships. Trade relations, as a result, tend to take on the form of national specializations and the international division of labour. The importance of trade is, however, progressively replaced by the centrality of investment relations between nations, which increasingly act as the organizing principle of the system. The form of interdependence between nations remains, however, of the 'strategic' kind. That is, it implies the continued relative separation of the domestic and the international frameworks for policy-making and the management of economic affairs, and also a relative separation in terms of economic effects. Interactions are of the 'billiard ball' type; international events do not directly or necessarily penetrate or permeate the domestic economy but are refracted through national policies and processes. The international and the domestic policy fields either remain relatively separate as distinct levels of governance, or they work 'automatically'. In the latter case adjustments are not thought to be the subject of policy by public bodies or authorities, but are a consequence of 'unorganized' or 'spontaneous' market forces.

Perhaps the classic case of such an 'automatic' adjustment mechanism remains the Gold Standard, which operated at the height of the Pax Britannica system from mid-nineteenth century to 1914. Automatic is put in inverted commas here to signal the fact that this is a popular caricature. The actual system of adjustment took place very much in terms of overt domestic policy interventions. [...]

Great Britain acted as the political and economic hegemon and the guarantor of this system. But it is important to recognize that the Gold Standard and the Pax Britannica system was merely one of several structures of the international economy in this century. Such structures were highly conditional on major sociopolitical conjunctures. Thus the First World War wrecked British hegemony, accelerating a process that would have occurred far more slowly merely as a consequence of British industrial decline. It resulted in a period of protectionism and national autarchic competition in the 1930s, followed by the establishment of American hegemony after the Second World War and by the reopened international economy of the Bretton Woods system. This indicates the danger of assuming that current major changes in the international economy are unprecedented and that they are inevitable or irreversible. The lifetime of a prevailing system of international economic relations in this century has been no more than thirty to forty years. Indeed, given that most European currencies did not become fully convertible until the late 1950s, the full Bretton Woods system after the Second World War only lasted upwards of thirteen to fourteen years. Such systems have been transformed by major changes in the politico-economic balance of power and the conjunctures that have effected these shifts have been large-scale conflicts between the major powers. In that sense, the international economy has been determined as to its structure and the distribution of power within it by the major nation-states.

[. . .]

The point of this ideal type drawing on the institutions of the *belle époque* is not, however, a historical analogy: for a simple and automatically governed international economic system *like* that before 1914 is unlikely to reproduce itself now. The current international economy is relatively open, but it has real differences from that prevailing before the First World War: it has more generalized and institutionalized free trade through the WTO, foreign investment is different in its modalities and destinations – although a high degree of capital mobility is once again a possibility – the scale of short-term financial flows is greater, the international monetary system is quite different and freedom of labour migration is drastically curtailed. The pre-1914 system was, nevertheless, genuinely international, tied by efficient long-distance communications and industrialized means of transport.

The communications and information technology revolution of the late twentieth century has further developed a trading system that could make day-to-day world prices: it did not create it. In the second half of the nineteenth century the submarine intercontinental telegraph cables enabled the integration of world markets (Standage 1998). Modern systems dramatically increase the possible volume and complexity of transactions, but we have had information media capable of sustaining a genuine international trading system for over a century. The difference between a trading system in which goods and information moved by sailing ship and one in which they moved by steam ships and electricity is qualitative. If the theorists of globalization mean that we have an economy in which each part of the world is linked by markets sharing close to real-time information, then that began not in the 1970s but in the 1870s.

Type 2: A globalized economy

A *globalized economy* is a distinct ideal type from that of the inter-national economy and can be developed by contrast with it. In such a global system distinct national economies are subsumed and rearticulated into the system by international processes and transactions. The inter-national economy, on the contrary, is one in which processes that are determined at the level of national economies still dominate and international phenomena are outcomes that emerge from the distinct and differential performance of the national economies. The inter-national economy is an aggregate of nationally located functions. Thus while there is in such an economy a wide and increasing range of international economic interactions (financial markets and trade in manufactured goods, for example), these tend to function as opportunities or constraints for nationally located economic actors and their public regulators.

The global economy raises these nationally based interactions to a new power. The international economic system becomes autonomized and socially disembedded, as markets and production become truly global. Domestic policies, whether of private corporations or public regulators, now have routinely to take account of the predominantly international determinants of their sphere of operations. As systemic interdependence grows, the national level is permeated by and transformed by the international.

In such a globalized economy the problem this poses for public authorities of different countries is how to construct policies that coordinate and integrate their regulatory efforts in order to cope with the systematic interdependence between their economic actors.

The first major consequence of a globalized economy would thus be that its governance is fundamentally problematic. Socially decontextualized global markets would be difficult to regulate, even supposing effective cooperation by the regulators and a coincidence of their interests. The principal difficulty is to construct both effective and integrated patterns of national and international public policy to cope with global market forces. The systematic economic interdependence of countries and markets would by no means necessarily result in a harmonious integration enabling world consumers to benefit from truly independent, allocatively efficient market mechanisms. On the contrary, it is more than plausible that the populations of even successful and advanced states and regions would be at the mercy of autonomized and uncontrollable (because global) market forces. Interdependence would then readily promote *dis-integration* – that is, competition and conflict – between regulatory agencies at different levels. Such conflict would further weaken effective public governance at the global level. Enthusiasts for the efficiency of free markets and the superiority of corporate control compared with that of public agencies would see this as a rational world order freed from the shackles of obsolete and ineffective national public interventions. Others, less sanguine but convinced globalization *is* occurring, like Cerny (1998), see it as a world system in which there can be no generalized or sustained public reinsurance against the costs imposed on localities by unfavourable competitive outcomes or market failures.

Even if one does not accept that the full process of globalization is taking place, this ideal type can help to highlight some aspects of the importance of greater economic integration within the major regional trade blocs. Both the European Union (EU) and the North American Free Trade Area (NAFTA) will soon be highly integrated markets of continental scale. Already in the case of the EU it is clear that there are fundamental problems of the integration and coordination of regulatory policies between the different public authorities at Union, national and regional level.

It is also clear that this ideal type highlights the problem of weak public governance for the major corporations. Even if such companies were truly global, they would not be able to operate in all markets equally effectively and, like governments, would lack the capacity to reinsure against unexpected shocks relying on their own resources alone. Governments would no longer be available to assist as they have been for 'national champions'. Firms would therefore seek to share risks and opportunities through inter-corporate investments, partnerships, joint ventures, etc. Even in the current internationalized economy we can recognize such processes emerging.

A second major consequence of the notion of a globalizing international economy would be the transformation of multinational companies (MNCs) into transnational companies (TNCs) as the major players in the world economy.[1] The TNC would be genuine footloose capital, without specific national identification and with an internationalized management, and at least potentially willing to locate and relocate anywhere in the globe to obtain either the most secure or the highest returns. In the financial sector this could be achieved at the touch of a button and in a truly globalized economy would be wholly dictated by market forces, without deference to national monetary policies. In the case of primarily manufacturing companies, they would source, produce and market at the global level as strategy and opportunities dictated. The company would no longer be based on one predominant national location (as with the MNC) but would service global markets through global operations. Thus the TNC, unlike the MNC, could no longer be controlled or even constrained by the policies of particular national states. Rather it could escape all but the commonly agreed and enforced international regulatory standards. National governments could not adopt particular and effective regulatory policies that diverged from these standards to the detriment of TNCs operating within their borders. The TNC would be the main manifestation of a truly globalized economy.

Julius (1990) and Ohmae (1990, 1993), for example, both consider this trend towards true TNCs to be well established. Ohmae argues that such 'stateless' corporations are now the prime movers in an interlinked economy (ILE) centred on North America, Europe and Japan. He contends that macroeconomic and industrial policy intervention by national governments can only distort and impede the rational process of resource allocation by corporate decisions and consumer choices on a global scale. Like Akio Morita of Sony, Ohmae argues that such corporations will pursue strategies of 'global localization' in responding on a worldwide scale to specific regionalized markets and locating effectively to meet the varying demands of distinct localized groups of consumers. The assumption here is that TNCs will rely primarily on foreign direct investment and the full domestication of production to meet such specific market demands. This is in contrast to the strategy of flexibly specialized core production in the company's main location and the building of branch assembly plants where needed or where dictated by national public policies. The latter strategy is compatible with nationally based companies. The evidence from Japanese corporations which are the most effective operators in world markets favours the view that the latter strategy is predominant (Williams et al. 1992). Japanese companies appear to have been reluctant to locate core functions like R&D or high value-added parts of the production process abroad. Thus national companies with an international scope of operations currently and for the foreseeable future seem more likely to be the pattern than the true TNCs. Of course, such multinational companies, although they are nationally based, are internationally orientated. Foreign markets influence their domestic strategies and foreign competitors their production processes. Although MNCs continue to trade substantially *within* their national economies, significant percentages of foreign sales influence their actions. The point, however, is that this is not new; companies in the long boom period after 1945 were influenced in this way too, and were successful only if they met the standards of international competition.

A third consequence of globalization would be the further decline in the political influence and economic bargaining power of organized labour. Globalized markets and TNCs would tend to be mirrored by an open world market in labour. Thus while companies requiring highly skilled and productive labour might well continue to locate in the advanced countries, with all their advantages, rather than merely seek areas where wages are low, the trend towards the global mobility of capital and the relative national fixity of labour would favour those advanced countries with the most tractable labour forces and the lowest social overheads relative to the benefits of labour competence and motivation. 'Social democratic' strategies of enhancement of working conditions would thus be viable only if they assured the competitive advantage of the labour force, without constraining management prerogatives, and at no more overall cost in taxation than the average for the advanced world. Such strategies would clearly be a tall order and the tendency of globalization would be to favour management at the expense of even strongly organized labour, and, therefore, public policies sympathetic to the former rather than the latter. This would be the 'disorganized capitalism' of Lash and Urry (1987) with a vengeance, or it could be seen as placing a premium on moderate and defensive strategies where organized labour remains locally strong (Scharpf 1991, 1997).

A final and inevitable consequence of globalization is the growth in fundamental multi-polarity in the international political system. In the end, the hitherto hegemonic national power would no longer be able to impose its own distinct regulatory objectives in either its own territories or elsewhere, and lesser agencies (whether public or private) would thus enjoy enhanced powers of denial and evasion *vis-à-vis* any aspirant 'hegemon'. A variety of bodies from international voluntary agencies to TNCs would thus gain in relative power at the expense of national governments and, using global markets and media, could appeal to and obtain legitimacy from consumers/citizens across national boundaries. Thus the distinct disciplinary powers of national states would decline, even though the bulk of their citizens, especially in the advanced countries, remained nationally bound. In such a world, national military power would become less effect-ive. It would no longer be used to pursue economic objectives because 'national' state control in respect of the economy would have largely disappeared. The use of military force would be increasingly tied to non-economic issues, such as nationality and reli-gion. A variety of more specific powers of sanction and veto in the economic sphere by different kinds of bodies (both public and private) would thus begin to compete with national states and begin to change the nature of international politics. As economics and nationhood pulled apart, the international economy would become even more 'indus-trial' and less 'militant' than it is today. War would be increasingly localized; wherever it threatened powerful global economic interests the warring parties would be subject to devastating economic sanction.

The Argument in Outline

[. . .]

The strong concept of a globalized economy outlined above acts as an ideal type which we can compare to the actual trends within the international economy. This globalized economy has been contrasted to the notion of an inter-national economy in the above analysis in order to distinguish its particular and novel features. The opposition of these two types for conceptual clarity conceals the possibly messy combination of the two in reality. This makes it difficult to determine major trends on the basis of the available evidence. These two types of economy are not inherently mutually exclusive; rather in certain conditions the globalized economy would *encompass and subsume* the inter-national economy. The globalized economy would rearticulate many of the features of the inter-national economy, transforming them as it reinforced them. If this phenom-enon occurred there would thus be a complex combination of features of both types of economy present within the present conjuncture. The problem in determining what is happening is to identify the dominant trends: either the growth of globalization or the continuation of the existing inter-national patterns.

It is our view that such a process of hybridization is not taking place, but it would be cavalier not to consider and raise the possibility. Central in this respect is the evid-ence [. . .] for the weak development of TNCs and the continued salience of MNCs, and also the ongoing dominance of the advanced countries in both trade and FDI. Such evidence is consistent with a continuing inter-national economy, but much less so with a rapidly globalizing hybrid system. Moreover, we should remember that an inter-national economy is one in which the major nationally based manufacturers and the major financial trading and service centres are strongly externally oriented, emphasizing international trading performance. The opposite of a globalized economy is not thus a nationally inward-looking one, but an open world market based on trading nations and regulated to a greater or lesser degree by both the public policies of nation-states and supranational agencies [...]. Such an economy has existed in some form or another since the 1870s, and has continued to re-emerge despite major setbacks, the most serious being the crisis of the 1930s. The point is that it should not be confused with a global economy. [...]

Note

1   This distinction between MNCs and TNCs is not usual. There is a tendency to use them inter-changeably, increasingly with the use of TNC as a generally accepted term for both types. Where we use the term TNC it should be clear that we are referring to a *true* TNC in the context of discussing the strong globalizers' view.

References

Cerny, P. (1998) Neomedievalism, civil war and the new security dilemma: globalization as a durable disorder. *Civil Wars* 1(1): 36–64.

Julius, D. (1990) *Global Companies and Public Policy*. London: RIIA, Pinter.

Lash, S. and Urry, J. (1987) *The End of Organized Capitalism*. Cambridge: Polity Press.

Ohmae, K. (1990) *The Borderless World*. London and New York: Collins.

Ohmae, K. (1993) The rise of the region state. *Foreign Affairs* (Spring): 78–88.

Scharpf, F. (1991) *Crisis and Choice in European Social Democracy*. Ithaca: Cornell University Press.

Scharpf, F. (1997) Negative and positive integration in the political economy of European welfare states. In G. Marks (ed.), *Governance in the European Union*, London: Sage.

Standage, T. (1998) *The Victorian Internet: The Remarkable Story of the Telegraph and the Nineteenth Century Online Pioneers*. London: Weidenfeld and Nicolson.

Williams, K., Haslem, C., Williams, J. and Adcroft, A. (1992) Factories as warehouses: Japanese manufacturing, foreign direct investment in Britain and the United States. University of East London Occasional Paper on Business, Economy and Society, no. 6.

5

The Network Society

Manuel Castells

Our exploration of emergent social structures across domains of human activity and experience leads to an overarching conclusion: as a historical trend, dominant functions and processes in the information age are increasingly organized around networks. Networks constitute the new social morphology of our societies, and the diffusion of networking logic substantially modifies the operation and outcomes in processes of production, experience, power, and culture. While the networking form of social organization has existed in other times and spaces, the new information technology paradigm provides the material basis for its pervasive expansion throughout the entire social structure. Furthermore, I would argue that this networking logic induces a social determination of a higher level than that of the specific social interests expressed through the networks: the power of flows takes precedence over the flows of power. Presence or absence in the network and the dynamics of each network *vis-à-vis* others are critical sources of domination and change in our society: a society that, therefore, we may properly call the network society, characterized by the preeminence of social morphology over social action.

[. . .]

A network-based social structure is a highly dynamic, open system, susceptible to innovating without threatening its balance. Networks are appropriate instruments for a capitalist economy based on innovation, globalization, and decentralized concentration; for work, workers, and firms based on flexibility, and adaptability; for a culture of endless deconstruction and reconstruction; for a polity geared towards the instant processing of new values and public moods; and for a social organization aiming at the supersession of space and the annihilation of time. Yet the network morphology is also a source of dramatic reorganization of power relationships. Switches connecting the networks (for example, financial flows taking control of media empires that influence political processes) are the privileged instruments of power. Thus, the switchers are the power holders. Since networks are multiple, the interoperating codes and switches between networks become the fundamental sources in shaping, guiding, and misguiding societies. The convergence of social evolution and information technologies has created a new material basis for the performance of activities throughout the social structure. This material basis, built in networks, earmarks dominant social processes, thus shaping social structure itself.

So observations and analyses [. . .] seem to indicate that the new economy is organized around global networks of capital, management, and information, whose access to technological know-how is at the roots of productivity and competitiveness. Business firms and, increasingly, organizations and institutions are organized in networks of variable geometry whose intertwining supersedes the traditional distinction between corporations and small business, cutting across sectors, and spreading along different geographic clusters of economic units. Accordingly, the work process is increasingly individualized, labor is disaggregated in its performance, and reintegrated in its outcome through a multiplicity of interconnected tasks in different sites, ushering in a new division of labor based on the attributes/capacities of each worker rather than on the organization of the task.

However, this evolution towards networking forms of management and production does not imply the demise of capitalism. The network society, in its various institutional expressions, is, for the time being, a capitalist society. Furthermore, for the first time in history, the capitalist mode of production shapes social relationships over the entire planet. But this brand of capitalism is profoundly different from its historical predecessors. It has two fundamental distinctive features: it is global, and it is structured, to a large extent, around a network of financial flows. Capital works globally as a unit in real time; and it is realized, invested, and accumulated mainly in the sphere of circulation, that is as finance capital. While finance capital has generally been among the dominant fractions of capital, we are witnessing the emergence of something different: capital accumulation proceeds, and its value-making is generated, increasingly, in the global financial markets enacted by information networks in the timeless space of financial flows. From these networks, capital is invested, globally, in all sectors of activity: information industries, media business, advanced services, agricultural production, health, education, technology, old and new manufacturing, transportation, trade, tourism, culture, environmental management, real estate, war-making and peace-selling, religion, entertainment, and sports. Some activities are more profitable than others, as they go through cycles, market upswings and downturns, and segmented global competition. Yet whatever is extracted as profit (from producers, consumers, technology, nature, and institutions) is reverted to the meta-network of financial flows, where all capital is equalized in the commodified democracy of profit-making. In this electronically operated global casino specific capitals boom or bust, settling the fate of corporations, household savings, national currencies, and regional economies. The net result sums to zero: the losers pay for the winners. But who are the winners and the losers changes by the year, the month, the day, the second, and permeates down to the world of firms, jobs, salaries, taxes, and public services. To the world of what is sometimes called "the real economy," and of what I would be tempted to call the "unreal economy," since in the age of networked capitalism the fundamental reality, where money is made and lost, invested or saved, is in the financial sphere. All other activities (except those of the dwindling public sector) are primarily the basis to generate the necessary surplus to invest in global flows, or the result of investment originated in these financial networks.

Financial capital needs, however, to rely for its operation and competition on knowledge and information generated and enhanced by information technology. This is the concrete meaning of the articulation between the capitalist mode of production and the informational mode of development. Thus, capital that would remain purely speculative is submitted to excessive risk, and ultimately washed out by simple statistical probability in the random movements of the financial markets. It is in the interaction between investment in profitable firms and using accumulated profits to make them fructify in the global financial networks that the process of accumulation lies. So it depends on productivity, on competitiveness, and on adequate information on investment and long-term planning in every sector. High-technology firms depend on financial resources to go on with their endless drive toward innovation, productivity, and competitiveness. Financial capital, acting directly through financial institutions or indirectly through the dynamics of stock exchange markets, conditions the fate of high-technology industries. On the other hand, technology and information are decisive tools in generating profits and in appropriating market shares. Thus, financial capital and high-technology, industrial capital are increasingly interdependent, even if their modes of operation are specific to each industry. Hilferding and Schumpeter were both right, but their historical coupling had to wait until it was dreamed of in Palo Alto and consummated in Ginza.

Thus, capital is either global or becomes global to enter the accumulation process in the electronically networked economy. Firms [. . .] are increasingly organized in networks, both internally and in their relationship. So capital flows, and their induced production/management/distribution activities, are spread in interconnected networks of variable geometry. Under these new technological, organizational, and economic conditions, who are the capitalists? They are certainly not the legal owners of the means of production, who range from your/my pension fund to a passer-by at a Singapore ATM suddenly deciding to buy stock in Buenos Aires' emergent market. But this has been to some extent true since the 1930s, as shown by Berle and Means' classic study on control and ownership in United States corporations. Yet neither are [they] the corporate managers, as suggested in their study, and, thereafter, by other analysts. For managers control specific corporations, and specific segments of the global economy, but do not control, and do not even know about, the actual, systemic movements of capital in the networks of financial flows, of knowledge in the information networks, of strategies in the multifaceted set of network enterprises. Some actors at the top of this global capitalist system are indeed managers, as in the case of Japanese corporations. Others could still be identified under the traditional category of bourgeoisie, as in the overseas Chinese business networks, who are culturally bonded, often family or personally related, share values and, sometimes, political connections. In the United States, a mixture of historical layers provides to the capitalist characters a colorful array of traditional bankers, nouveau riche speculators, self-made geniuses-turned-entrepreneurs, global tycoons, and multinational managers. In other cases, public corporations (as in French banking or electronics firms) are the capitalist actors. In Russia, survivors of communist *nomenklatura* compete with wild young capitalists in recycling state property in the constitution of the newest capitalist province. And all over the world, money-laundering from miscellaneous criminal businesses flows toward this mother of all accumulations that is the global financial network.

So all these are capitalists, presiding over all sorts of economies, and people's lives. But a capitalist class? There is not, sociologically and economically, such a thing as a global capitalist class. But there is an integrated, global capital network, whose movements and variable logic ultimately determine economies and influence societies. Thus, above a diversity of human-flesh capitalists and capitalist groups there is a faceless collective capitalist, made up of financial flows operated by electronic networks. This is not simply the expression of the abstract logic of the market, because it does not truly follow the law of supply and demand: it responds to the turbulences, and unpredictable movements, of noncalculable anticipations, induced by psychology and society, as much as by economic processes. This network of networks of capital both unifies and commands specific centers of capitalist accumulation, structuring the behavior of capitalists around their submission to the global network. They play their competing, or converging, strategies by and through the circuits of this global network, and so they are ultimately dependent upon the nonhuman capitalist logic of an electronically operated, random processing of information. It is indeed capitalism in its pure expression of the endless search for money by money through the production of commodities by commodities. But money has become almost entirely independent from production, including production of services, by escaping into the networks of higher-order electronic interactions barely understood by its managers. While capitalism still rules, capitalists are randomly incarnated, and the capitalist classes are restricted to specific areas of the world where they prosper as appendixes to a mighty whirlwind which manifests its will by spread points and futures options ratings in the global flashes of computer screens.

What happens to labor, and to the social relationships of production, in this brave new world of informational, global capitalism? Workers do not disappear in the space of flows, and, down to earth, work is plentiful. Indeed, belying apocalyptic prophecies of simplistic analyses, there are more jobs and a higher proportion of working-age people employed than at any time in history. This is mainly because of the massive incorporation of women in paid work in all industrialized societies, an incorporation that has generally been absorbed, and to a large extent induced, by the labor market without major disruptions. So the diffusion of information technologies, while certainly displacing workers and eliminating some jobs, has not resulted, and it does not seem that it will result in the foreseeable future, in mass unemployment. This in spite of the rise of unemployment in European economies, a trend that is related to social institutions rather than to the new production system. But, if work, workers, and working classes exist, and even expand, around the world, the social relationships between capital and labor are profoundly transformed. At its core, capital is global. As a rule, labor is local. Informationalism, in its historical reality, leads to the concentration and globalization of capital, precisely by using the decentralizing power of networks. Labor is disaggregated in its performance, fragmented in its organization, diversified in its existence, divided in its collective action. Networks converge toward a meta-network of capital that integrates capitalist interests at the global level and across sectors and realms of activity: not without conflict, but under the same overarching logic. Labor loses its collective identity, becomes increasingly individualized in its capacities, in its working conditions, and in its interests and projects. Who are the owners, who the producers, who the managers, and who the servants, becomes increasingly blurred in a production system of variable geometry, of teamwork, of networking, outsourcing, and subcontracting. [...] Who is contributing to value creation in the electronics industry: the Silicon Valley chip designer, or the young woman on the assembly line of a South-East Asian factory? Certainly both, albeit in quite substantially different proportions. Thus, are they jointly the new working class? Why not include in it the Bombay computer consultant subcontracted to program this particular design? Or the flying manager who commutes or telecommutes between California and Singapore customizing chip production and electronics consumption? There is unity of the work process throughout the complex, global networks of interaction. But there is at the same time differentiation of work, segmentation of workers, and disaggregation of labor on a global scale. So while capitalist relationships of production still persist (indeed, in many economies the dominant logic is more strictly capitalist than ever before), capital and labor increasingly tend to exist in different spaces and times: the space of flows and the space of places, instant time of computerized networks versus clock time of everyday life. Thus, they live by each other, but do not relate to each other, as the life of global capital depends less and less on specific labor, and more and more on accumulated, generic labor, operated by a small brains trust inhabiting the virtual palaces of global networks. Beyond this fundamental dichotomy a great deal of social diversity still exists, made up of investors' bids, workers' efforts, human ingenuity, human suffering, hirings and layoffs, promotions and demotions, conflicts and negotiations, competition and alliances: working life goes on. Yet, at a deeper level of the new social reality, social relationships of production have been disconnected in their actual existence. Capital tends to escape in its hyperspace of pure circulation, while labor dissolves its collective entity into an infinite variation of individual existences. Under the conditions of the network society, capital is globally coordinated, labor is individualized. The struggle between diverse capitalists and miscellaneous working classes is subsumed into the more fundamental opposition between the bare logic of capital flows and the cultural values of human experience.

Processes of social transformation summarized under the ideal type of the network society go beyond the sphere of social and technical relationships of production: they deeply affect culture and power as well. Cultural expressions are abstracted from history and geography, and become predominantly mediated by electronic communication networks that interact with the audience and by the audience in a diversity of codes and values, ultimately subsumed in a digitized, audiovisual hypertext. Because information and communication circulate primarily through the diversified, yet comprehensive media system, politics becomes increasingly played out in the space of media. Leadership is personalized, and image-making is power-making. Not that all politics can be reduced to media effects, or that values and interests are indifferent to political outcomes. But whoever the political actors and whatever their orientations, they exist in the power game through and by the media, in the whole variety of an increasingly diverse media system, that includes computer-mediated communication networks. The fact that politics has to be framed in the language of electronically based media has profound consequences on the characteristics, organization, and goals of political processes, political actors, and political institutions. Ultimately, the powers that are in the media networks take second place to the power of flows embodied in the structure and language of these networks.

At a deeper level, the material foundations of society, space and time are being transformed, organized around the space of flows and timeless time. Beyond the metaphorical value of these expressions [...] a major hypothesis is put forward: dominant functions are organized in networks pertaining to a space of flows that links them up around the world, while fragmenting subordinate functions, and people, in the multiple space of places, made of locales increasingly segregated and disconnected from each other. Timeless time appears to be the result of the negation of time, past and future, in the networks of the space of flows. Meanwhile clock time, measured and valued differentially for each process according to its position in the network, continues to characterize subordinate functions and specific locales. The end of history, enacted in the circularity of computerized financial flows or in the instantaneity of surgical wars, overpowers the biological time of poverty or the mechanical time of industrial work. The social construction of new dominant forms of space and time develops a meta-network that switches off nonessential functions, subordinate social groups, and devalued territories. By so doing, infinite social distance is created between this meta-network and most individuals, activities, and locales around the world. Not that people, locales, or activities disappear. But their structural meaning does, subsumed in the unseen logic of the meta-network where value is produced, cultural codes are created, and power is decided. The new social order, the network society, increasingly appears to most people as a meta-social disorder. Namely, as an automated, random sequence of events, derived from the uncontrollable logic of markets, technology, geopolitical order, or biological determination.

[...]

6

Time–Space Compression and the Postmodern Condition

David Harvey

[. . .] I want to suggest that we have been experiencing, these last two decades, an intense phase of time–space compression that has had a disorienting and disruptive impact upon political-economic practices, the balance of class power, as well as upon cultural and social life. While historical analogies are always dangerous, I think it no accident that postmodern sensibility evidences strong sympathies for certain of the confused political, cultural, and philosophical movements that occurred at the beginning of this century (in Vienna for example) when the sense of time–space compression was also peculiarly strong. I also note the revival of interest in geopolitical theory since around 1970, the aesthetics of place, and a revived willingness (even in social theory) to open the problem of spatiality to a general reconsideration (see, e.g., Gregory and Urry 1985, and Soja 1988).

The transition to flexible accumulation was in part accomplished through the rapid deployment of new organizational forms and new technologies in production. Though the latter may have originated in the pursuit of military superiority, their application had everything to do with bypassing the rigidities of Fordism and accelerating turnover time as a solution to the grumbling problems of Fordism–Keynesianism that erupted into open crisis in 1973. Speed-up was achieved in production by organizational shifts towards vertical disintegration – sub-contracting, outsourcing, etc. – that reversed the Fordist tendency towards vertical integration and produced an increasing roundaboutness in production even in the face of increasing financial centralization. Other organizational shifts – such as the 'just-in-time' delivery system that reduces stock inventories – when coupled with the new technologies of electronic control, small-batch production, etc., all reduced turnover times in many sectors of production (electronics, machine tools, automobiles, construction, clothing etc.). For the labourers this all implied an intensification (speed-up) in labour processes and an acceleration in the de-skilling and re-skilling required to meet new labour needs [. . .].

Accelerating turnover time in production entails parallel accelerations in exchange and consumption. Improved systems of communication and information flow, coupled with rationalizations in techniques of distribution (packaging, inventory control, containerization, market feed-back, etc.), made it possible to circulate commodities through the market system with greater speed. Electronic banking and plastic money were some of the innovations that improved the speed of the inverse flow of money. Financial services and markets (aided by computerized trading) likewise speeded up, so as to make, as the saying has it, 'twenty-four hours a very long time' in global stock markets.

Of the many developments in the arena of consumption, two stand out as being of particular importance. The mobilization of fashion in mass (as opposed to elite) markets provided a means to accelerate the pace of consumption not only in clothing, ornament, and decoration but also across a wide swathe of life-styles and recreational activities (leisure and sporting habits, pop music styles, video and children's games, and the like). A second trend was a shift away from the consumption of goods and into the consumption of services – not only personal, business, educational, and health services, but also into entertainments, spectacles, happenings, and distractions. The 'lifetime' of such services (a visit to a museum, going to a rock concert or movie, attending lectures or health clubs), though hard to estimate, is far shorter than that of an automobile or washing machine. If there are limits to the accumulation and turnover of physical goods (even counting the famous six thousand pairs of shoes of Imelda Marcos), then it makes sense for capitalists to turn to the provision of very ephemeral services in consumption. This quest may lie at the root of the rapid capitalist penetration [. . .] of many sectors of cultural production from the mid-1960s onwards.

Of the innumerable consequences that have flowed from this general speed-up in the turnover times of capital, I shall focus on those that have particular bearing on postmodern ways of thinking, feeling, and doing.

The first major consequence has been to accentuate volatility and ephemerality of fashions, products, production techniques, labour processes, ideas and ideologies, values and established practices. The sense that 'all that is solid melts into air' has rarely been more pervasive (which probably accounts for the volume of writing on that theme in recent years). [. . .]

In the realm of commodity production, the primary effect has been to emphasize the values and virtues of instantaneity (instant and fast foods, meals, and other satisfactions) and of disposability (cups, plates, cutlery, packaging, napkins, clothing, etc.). [. . .] 'Compared to the life in a less rapidly changing society, more situations now flow through the channel in any given interval of time – and this implies profound changes in human psychology' [Toffler 1970]. This transience, Toffler goes on to suggest, creates 'a temporariness in the structure of both public and personal value systems' which in turn provides a context for the 'crack-up of consensus' and the diversification of values within a fragmenting society. [. . .] In this regard, it is instructive to see how Toffler (pp. 326–9), at a much later moment of time–space compression, echoes the thinking of Simmel, whose ideas were shaped at a moment of similar trauma more than seventy years before.

[. . .]

But, as so often happens, the plunge into the maelstrom of ephemerality has provoked an explosion of opposed sentiments and tendencies. To begin with, all sorts of technical means arise to guard against future shocks. Firms sub-contract or resort to flexible hiring practices to discount the potential unemployment costs of future market shifts. Futures markets in everything, from corn and pork bellies to currencies and government debt, coupled with the 'securitization' of all kinds of temporary and floating debts, illustrate techniques for discounting the future into the present. Insurance hedges of all kinds against future volatility become much more widely available.

Deeper questions of meaning and interpretation also arise. The greater the ephemerality, the more pressing the need to discover or manufacture some kind of eternal truth that might lie therein. The religious revival, that has become much stronger since the late sixties, and the search for authenticity and authority in politics (with all of its accoutrements of nationalism and localism and of admiration for those charismatic and 'protean' individuals with their Nietzschian 'will to power') are cases in point. The revival of interest in basic institutions (such as the family and community), and the search for historical roots are all signs of a search for more secure moorings and longer-lasting values in a shifting world.

[...]

The spatial adjustments have been no less traumatic. The satellite communications systems deployed since the early 1970s have rendered the unit cost and time of communication invariant with respect to distance. It costs the same to communicate over 500 miles as it does over 5,000 via satellite. Air freight rates on commodities have likewise come down dramatically, while containerization has reduced the cost of bulk sea and road transport. It is now possible for a large multinational corporation like Texas Instruments to operate plants with simultaneous decision-making with respect to financial, market, input costs, quality control, and labour process conditions in more than fifty different locations across the globe (Dicken 1986: 110–13). Mass television ownership coupled with satellite communication makes it possible to experience a rush of images from different spaces almost simultaneously, collapsing the world's spaces into a series of images on a television screen. The whole world can watch the Olympic Games, the World Cup, the fall of a dictator, a political summit, a deadly tragedy . . . while mass tourism, films made in spectacular locations, make a wide range of simulated or vicarious experiences of what the world contains available to many people. The image of places and spaces becomes as open to production and ephemeral use as any other.

We have, in short, witnessed another fierce round in that process of annihilation of space through time that has always lain at the centre of capitalism's dynamic [...]. Marshall McLuhan described how he thought the 'global village' had now become a communications reality in the mid-1960s:

> After three thousand years of explosion, by means of fragmentary and mechanical technologies, the Western World is imploding. During the mechanical ages we had extended our bodies in space. Today, after more than a century of electronic technology, we have extended our central nervous system itself in a global embrace, abolishing both space and time as far as our planet is concerned.

In recent years a whole spate of writing has taken this idea on board and tried to explore, as for example Virilio (1980) does in his *Esthétique de la disparition*, the cultural consequences of the supposed disappearance of time and space as materialized and tangible dimensions to social life.

But the collapse of spatial barriers does not mean that the significance of space is decreasing. Not for the first time in capitalism's history, we find the evidence pointing to the converse thesis. Heightened competition under conditions of crisis has coerced capitalists into paying much closer attention to relative locational advantages, precisely because diminishing spatial barriers give capitalists the power to exploit minute spatial differentiations to good effect. Small differences in what the space contains in the way of labour supplies, resources, infrastructures, and the like become of increased significance. Superior command over space becomes an even more important weapon in class struggle. It becomes one of the means to enforce speed-up and the redefinition of skills on recalcitrant work forces. Geographical mobility and decentralization are used

against a union power which traditionally concentrated in the factories of mass production. Capital flight, deindustrialization of some regions, and the industrialization of
others, the destruction of traditional working-class communities as power bases in class
struggle, become leitmotifs of spatial transformation under more flexible conditions of
accumulation (Martin and Rowthorn 1986; Bluestone and Harrison 1982; Harrison and
Bluestone 1988).

As spatial barriers diminish so we become much more sensitized to what the world's
spaces contain. Flexible accumulation typically exploits a wide range of seemingly contingent geographical circumstances, and reconstitutes them as structured internal elements of its own encompassing logic. For example, geographical differentiations in the
mode and strengths of labour control together with variations in the quality as well as
the quantity of labour power assume a much greater significance in corporate locational
strategies. New industrial ensembles arise, sometimes out of almost nothing (as the various silicon valleys and glens) but more often on the basis of some pre-existing mix of
skills and resources. The 'Third Italy' (Emilia-Romagna) builds upon a peculiar mix of
co-operative entrepreneurialism, artisan labour, and local communist administrations
anxious to generate employment, and inserts its clothing products with incredible success into a highly competitive world economy. Flanders attracts outside capital on the
basis of a dispersed, flexible, and reasonably skilled labour supply with a deep hostility to unionism and socialism. Los Angeles imports the highly successful patriarchal labour
systems of South-East Asia through mass immigration, while the celebrated paternal-
istic labour control system of the Japanese and Taiwanese is imported into California
and South Wales. The story in each case is different, making it appear as if the unique-
ness of this or that geographical circumstance matters more than ever before. Yet it
does so, ironically, only because of the collapse of spatial barriers.

While labour control is always central, there are many other aspects of geographical
organization that have risen to a new prominence under conditions of more flexible
accumulation. The need for accurate information and speedy communication has emphasized the role of so-called 'world cities' in the financial and corporate system (centres
equipped with teleports, airports, fixed communication links, as well as a wide array of
financial, legal, business, and infrastructural services). The diminution of spatial barriers
results in the reaffirmation and realignment of hierarchy within what is now a global
urban system. The local availability of material resources of special qualities, or even
at marginally lower costs, starts to be ever more important, as do local variations in
market taste that are today more easily exploited under conditions of small-batch production and flexible design. Local differences in entrepreneurial ability, venture capital,
scientific and technical know-how, social attitudes, also enter in, while the local networks of influence and power, the accumulation strategies of local ruling elites (as opposed
to nation-state policies), also become more deeply implicated in the regime of flexible
accumulation.

But this then raises another dimension to the changing role of spatiality in contemporary society. If capitalists become increasingly sensitive to the spatially differentiated
qualities of which the world's geography is composed, then it is possible for the peoples
and powers that command those spaces to alter them in such a way as to be more rather
than less attractive to highly mobile capital. Local ruling elites can, for example, implement strategies of local labour control, of skill enhancement, of infrastructural provision, of tax policy, state regulation, and so on, in order to attract development within
their particular space. The qualities of place stand thereby to be emphasized in the midst

of the increasing abstractions of space. The active production of places with special qualities becomes an important stake in spatial competition between localities, cities, regions, and nations. Corporatist forms of governance can flourish in such spaces, and themselves take on entrepreneurial roles in the production of favourable business climates and other special qualities. And it is in this context that we can better situate the striving [...] for cities to forge a distinctive image and to create an atmosphere of place and tradition that will act as a lure to both capital and people 'of the right sort' (i.e. wealthy and influential). Heightened inter-place competition should lead to the production of more variegated spaces within the increasing homogeneity of international exchange. But to the degree that this competition opens up cities to systems of accumulation, it ends up producing what Boyer (1988) calls a 'recursive' and 'serial' monotony, 'producing from already known patterns or molds places almost identical in ambience from city to city: New York's South Street Seaport, Boston's Quincy Market, Baltimore's Harbor Place'.

We thus approach the central paradox: the less important the spatial barriers, the greater the sensitivity of capital to the variations of place within space, and the greater the incentive for places to be differentiated in ways attractive to capital. The result has been the production of fragmentation, insecurity, and ephemeral uneven development within a highly unified global space economy of capital flows. The historic tension within capitalism between centralization and decentralization is now being worked out in new ways. Extraordinary decentralization and proliferation of industrial production ends up putting Benetton or Laura Ashley products in almost every serially produced shopping mall in the advanced capitalist world. Plainly, the new round of time–space compression is fraught with as many dangers as it offers possibilities for survival of particular places or for a solution to the overaccumulation problem.

[...]

None of these shifts in the experience of space and time would make the sense or have the impact they do without a radical shift in the manner in which value gets represented as money. Though long dominant, money has never been a clear or unambiguous representation of value, and on occasion it becomes so muddled as to become itself a major source of insecurity and uncertainty. Under the terms of the postwar settlement, the question of world money was put on a fairly stable basis. The US dollar became the medium of world trade, technically backed by a fixed convertibility into gold, and backed politically and economically by the overwhelming power of the US productive apparatus. The space of the US production system became, in effect, the guarantor of international value. But [...] one of the signals of the breakdown of the Fordist–Keynesian system was the breakdown of the Bretton Woods agreement, of convertibility of US dollars to gold, and the shift to a global system of floating exchange rates. The breakdown in part occurred because of the shifting dimensionalities of space and time generated out of capital accumulation. Rising indebtedness (particularly within the United States), and fiercer international competition from the reconstructed spaces of the world economy under conditions of growing accumulation, had much to do with undermining the power of the US economy to operate as an exclusive guarantor of world money.

The effects have been legion. The question of how value should now get represented, what form money should take, and the meaning that can be put upon the various forms of money available to us, has never been far from the surface of recent concerns. Since 1973, money has been 'de-materialized' in the sense that it no longer has a formal or

tangible link to precious metals (though the latter have continued to play a role as one potential form of money among many others), or for that matter to any other tangible commodity. Nor does it rely exclusively upon productive activity within a particular space. The world has come to rely, for the first time in its history, upon immaterial forms of money – i.e. money of account assessed quantitatively in numbers of some designated currency (dollars, yen, Deutschmarks, sterling, etc.). Exchange rates between the different currencies of the world have also been extremely volatile. Fortunes could be lost or made simply by holding the right currency during the right phases. The question of which currency I hold is directly linked to which place I put my faith in. That may have something to do with the competitive economic position and power of different national systems. That power, given the flexibility of accumulation over space, is itself a rapidly shifting magnitude. The effect is to render the spaces that underpin the determination of value as unstable as value itself. This problem is compounded by the way that speculative shifts bypass actual economic power and performance, and then trigger self-fulfilling expectations. The de-linking of the financial system from active production and from any material monetary base calls into question the reliability of the basic mechanism whereby value is supposed to be represented.
[. . .]
The breakdown of money as a secure means of representing value has itself created a crisis of representation in advanced capitalism. It has also been reinforced by, and added its very considerable weight to, the problems of time–space compression which we earlier identified. The rapidity with which currency markets fluctuate across the world's spaces, the extraordinary power of money capital flow in what is now a global stock and financial market, and the volatility of what the purchasing power of money might represent, define, as it were, a high point of that highly problematic intersection of money, time, and space as interlocking elements of social power in the political economy of postmodernity.

It is, furthermore, not hard to see how all of this might create a more general crisis of representation. The central value system, to which capitalism has always appealed to validate and gauge its actions, is dematerialized and shifting, time horizons are collapsing, and it is hard to tell exactly what space we are in when it comes to assessing causes and effects, meanings or values. The intriguing exhibition at the Pompidou Centre in 1985 on 'The Immaterial' (an exhibition for which none other than Lyotard acted as one of the consultants) was perhaps a mirror image of the dissolution of the material representations of value under conditions of more flexible accumulation, and of the confusions as to what it might mean to say, with Paul Virilio, that time and space have disappeared as meaningful dimensions to human thought and action.

There are, I would submit, more tangible and material ways than this to go about assessing the significance of space and time for the condition of postmodernity. It should be possible to consider how, for example, the changing experience of space, time, and money has formed a distinctive material basis for the rise of distinctive systems of interpretation and representation [. . .]. If we view culture as that complex of signs and significations (including language) that mesh into codes of transmission of social values and meanings, then we can at least begin upon the task of unravelling its complexities under present-day conditions by recognizing that money and commodities are themselves the primary bearers of cultural codes. Since money and commodities are entirely bound up with the circulation of capital, it follows that cultural forms are firmly rooted in the daily circulation process of capital. [. . .]

The annihilation of space through time has radically changed the commodity mix that enters into daily reproduction. Innumerable local food systems have been reorganized through their incorporation into global commodity exchange. French cheeses, for example, virtually unavailable except in a few gourmet stores in large cities in 1970, are now widely sold across the United States. And if this is thought a somewhat elite example, the case of beer consumption suggests that the internationalization of a product, that traditional location theory always taught should be highly market-oriented, is now complete. Baltimore was essentially a one-beer town (locally brewed) in 1970, but first the regional beers from places like Milwaukee and Denver, and then Canadian and Mexican beers followed by European, Australian, Chinese, Polish, etc. beers became cheaper. Formerly exotic foods became commonplace while popular local delicacies (in the Baltimore case, blue crabs and oysters) that were once relatively inexpensive jumped in price as they too became integrated into long-distance trading.

The market place has always been an 'emporium of styles' (to quote Raban's phrase) but the food market, just to take one example, now looks very different from what it was twenty years ago. Kenyan haricot beans, Californian celery and avocados, North African potatoes, Canadian apples, and Chilean grapes all sit side by side in a British supermarket. This variety also makes for a proliferation of culinary styles, even among the relatively poor. Such styles have always migrated, of course, usually following the migration streams of different groups before diffusing slowly through urban cultures. The new waves of immigrants (such as the Vietnamese, Koreans, Filipinos, Central Americans, etc. that have added to the older groups of Japanese, Chinese, Chicanos, and all the European ethnic groups that have also found their culinary heritage can be revived for fun and profit) make a typical United States city such as New York, Los Angeles, or San Francisco (where the last census showed the majority of the population to be made up of minorities) as much an emporium of culinary styles as it is an emporium of the world's commodities. But here, too, there has been an acceleration, because culinary styles have moved faster than the immigration streams. It did not take a large French immigration to the United States to send the croissant rapidly spreading across America to challenge the traditional doughnut, nor did it take a large immigration of Americans to Europe to bring fast-food hamburgers to nearly all medium-sized European cities. Chinese takeaways, Italian pizza-parlours (run by a US chain), Middle Eastern felafel stalls, Japanese sushi bars . . . the list is now endless in the Western world.

The whole world's cuisine is now assembled in one place in almost exactly the same way that the world's geographical complexity is nightly reduced to a series of images on a static television screen. This same phenomenon is exploited in entertainment palaces like Epcott and Disneyworld; it becomes possible, as the US commercials put it, 'to experience the Old World for a day without actually having to go there'. The general implication is that through the experience of everything from food, to culinary habits, music, television, entertainment, and cinema, it is now possible to experience the world's geography vicariously, as a simulacrum. The interweaving of simulacra in daily life brings together different worlds (of commodities) in the same space and time. But it does so in such a way as to conceal almost perfectly any trace of origin, of the labour processes that produced them, or of the social relations implicated in their production. [. . .]

There seem to be two divergent sociological effects of all of this in daily thought and action. The first suggests taking advantage of all of the divergent possibilities [. . .] and cultivating a whole series of simulacra as milieux of escape, fantasy, and distraction:

All around us – on advertisement hoardings, bookshelves, record covers, television screens – these miniature escape fantasies present themselves. This, it seems, is how we are destined to live, as split personalities in which the private life is disturbed by the promise of escape routes to another reality. (Cohen and Taylor 1978, quoted in McHale 1987: 38)

[...]

But it is exactly at this point that we encounter the opposite reaction that can best be summed up as the search for personal or collective identity, the search for secure moorings in a shifting world. Place-identity, in this collage of superimposed spatial images that implode in upon us, becomes an important issue, because everyone occupies a space of individuation (a body, a room, a home, a shaping community, a nation), and how we individuate ourselves shapes identity. Furthermore, if no one 'knows their place' in this shifting collage world, then how can a secure social order be fashioned or sustained?

There are two elements within this problem that deserve close consideration. First, the capacity of most social movements to command place better than space puts a strong emphasis upon the potential connection between place and social identity. This is manifest in political action. The defensiveness of municipal socialism, the insistence on working-class community, the localization of the fight against capital, become central features of working-class struggle within an overall patterning of uneven geographical development. The consequent dilemmas of socialist or working-class movements in the face of a universalizing capitalism are shared by other oppositional groups – racial minorities, colonized peoples, women, etc. – who are relatively empowered to organize in place but disempowered when it comes to organizing over space. In clinging, often of necessity, to a place-bound identity, however, such oppositional movements become a part of the very fragmentation which a mobile capitalism and flexible accumulation can feed upon. 'Regional resistances', the struggle for local autonomy, place-bound organization, may be excellent bases for political action, but they cannot bear the burden of radical historical change alone. 'Think globally and act locally' was the revolutionary slogan of the 1960s. It bears repeating.

The assertion of any place-bound identity has to rest at some point on the motivational power of tradition. It is difficult, however, to maintain any sense of historical continuity in the face of all the flux and ephemerality of flexible accumulation. The irony is that tradition is now often preserved by being commodified and marketed as such. The search for roots ends up at worst being produced and marketed as an image, as a simulacrum or pastiche (imitation communities constructed to evoke images of some folksy past, the fabric of traditional working-class communities being taken over by an urban gentry). The photograph, the document, the view, and the reproduction become history precisely because they are so overwhelmingly present. The problem, of course, is that none of these are immune from tampering or downright faking for present purposes. At best, historical tradition is reorganized as a museum culture, not necessarily of high modernist art, but of local history, of local production, of how things once upon a time were made, sold, consumed, and integrated into a long-lost and often romanticized daily life (one from which all trace of oppressive social relations may be expunged). Through the presentation of a partially illusory past it becomes possible to signify something of local identity and perhaps to do it profitably.

The second reaction to the internationalism of modernism lies in the search to construct place and its meanings qualitatively. Capitalist hegemony over space puts the aesthetics of place very much back on the agenda. But this, as we have seen, meshes only too well with the idea of spatial differentiations as lures for a peripatetic capital that values the option of mobility very highly. Isn't this place better than that place, not only for the operations of capital but also for living in, consuming well, and feeling secure in a shifting world? The construction of such places, the fashioning of some localized aesthetic image, allows the construction of some limited and limiting sense of identity in the midst of a collage of imploding spatialities.

The tension in these oppositions is clear enough but it is hard to appreciate their intellectual and political ramifications.

[. . .]

This should alert us to the acute geopolitical dangers that attach to the rapidity of time–space compression in recent years. The transition from Fordism to flexible accumulation, such as it has been, ought to imply a transition in our mental maps, political attitudes, and political institutions. But political thinking does not necessarily undergo such easy transformations, and is in any case subject to the contradictory pressures that derive from spatial integration and differentiation. There is an omnipresent danger that our mental maps will not match current realities. The serious diminution of the power of individual nation states over fiscal and monetary policies, for example, has not been matched by any parallel shift towards an internationalization of politics. Indeed, there are abundant signs that localism and nationalism have become stronger precisely because of the quest for the security that place always offers in the midst of all the shifting that flexible accumulation implies. The resurgence of geopolitics and of faith in charismatic politics (Thatcher's Falklands War, Reagan's invasion of Grenada) fits only too well with a world that is increasingly nourished intellectually and politically by a vast flux of ephemeral images.

Time–space compression always exacts its toll on our capacity to grapple with the realities unfolding around us. Under stress, for example, it becomes harder and harder to react accurately to events. [. . .] If 'seasoned negotiators cracked under the pressure of tense confrontations and sleepless nights, agonizing over the probable disastrous consequences of their snap judgements and hasty actions', then how much more difficult must decision-making now be? The difference this time is that there is not even time to agonize. And the problems are not confined to the realms of political and military decision-making, for the world's financial markets are on the boil in ways that make a snap judgement here, an unconsidered word there, and a gut reaction somewhere else the slip that can unravel the whole skein of fictitious capital formation and of interdependency.

The conditions of postmodern time–space compression exaggerate in many respects the dilemmas that have from time to time beset capitalist procedures of modernization in the past (1848 and the phase just before the First World War spring particularly to mind). While the economic, cultural, and political responses may not be exactly new, the range of those reponses differs in certain important respects from those which have occurred before. The intensity of time–space compression in Western capitalism since the 1960s, with all of its congruent features of excessive ephemerality and fragmentation in the political and private as well as in the social realm, does seem to indicate an experiential context that makes the condition of postmodernity somewhat special. But by putting this condition into its historical context, as part of a history of successive waves of time–space compression generated out of the pressures of capital accumulation with its perpetual search to annihilate space through time and reduce turnover time, we can at least pull the condition of postmodernity into the range of a condition accessible to historical materialist analysis and interpretation. [. . .]

References

Bluestone, B. and Harrison, B. (1982) *The Deindustrialisation of America*. New York.

Cohen, S. and Taylor, L. (1978) *Escape Attempts: The Theory and Practice of Resistance to Everyday Life*. Harmondsworth.

Boyer, R. and Mistral, J. (1988) Le bout du tunnel? Stratégies conservatrices et nouveau régime d'accumulation. Paper delivered at the International Conference on the Theory of Regulation, Barcelona, 16–18 June.

Dicken, P. (1986) *Global Shift: Industrial Change in a Turbulent World*. London.

Gregory, D. and Urry, J. (eds) (1985) *Social Relations and Spatial Structures*. London.

Harrison, B. and Bluestone, B. (1988) *The Great U-turn: Capital Restructuring and the Polarizing of America*. New York.

McHale, B. (1987) *Postmodernist Fiction*. London.

McLuhan, M. (1966) *Understanding Media: The Extensions of Man*. New York.

Martin, R. and Rowthorn, B. (eds) (1986) *The Geography of Deindustrialisation*. London.

Soja, E. (1988) *Postmodern Geographies: The Reassertion of Space in Critical Social Theory*. London.

Toffler, A. (1970) *Future Shock*. New York.

Virilio, P. (1980) *L'esthétique de la disparition*. London.

7

The Globalizing of Modernity

Anthony Giddens

Modernity is inherently globalizing – this is evident in some of the most basic characteristics of modern institutions, including particularly their disembeddedness and reflexivity. But what exactly is globalization, and how might we best conceptualize the phenomenon? I shall consider these questions at some length [. . .] since the central importance of globalizing processes today has scarcely been matched by extended discussions of the concept in the sociological literature. [. . .] The undue reliance which sociologists have placed upon the idea of 'society', where this means a bounded system, should be replaced by a starting point that concentrates upon analysing how social life is ordered across time and space – the problematic of time-space distanciation. The conceptual framework of time-space distanciation directs our attention to the complex relations between *local involvements* (circumstances of co-presence) and *interaction across distance* (the connections of presence and absence). In the modern era, the level of time-space distanciation is much higher than in any previous period, and the relations between local and distant social forms and events become correspondingly 'stretched'. Globalization refers essentially to that stretching process, in so far as the modes of connection between different social contexts or regions become networked across the earth's surface as a whole.

Globalization can thus be defined as the intensification of worldwide social relations which link distant localities in such a way that local happenings are shaped by events occurring many miles away and vice versa. This is a dialectical process because such local happenings may move in an obverse direction from the very distanciated relations that shape them. *Local transformation* is as much a part of globalization as the lateral extension of social connections across time and space. Thus whoever studies cities today, in any part of the world, is aware that what happens in a local neighbourhood is likely to be influenced by factors – such as world money and commodity markets – operating at an indefinite distance away from that neighbourhood itself. The outcome is not necessarily, or even usually, a generalized set of changes acting in a uniform direction, but consists in mutually opposed tendencies. The increasing prosperity of an urban area in Singapore might be causally related, via a complicated network of global economic ties, to the impoverishment of a neighbourhood in Pittsburgh whose local products are uncompetitive in world markets.

Another example from the very many that could be offered is the rise of local nationalisms in Europe and elsewhere. The development of globalized social relations probably serves to diminish some aspects of nationalist feeling linked to nation-states (or some states) but may be causally involved with the intensifying of more localized nationalist sentiments. In circumstances of accelerating globalization, the nation-state has become 'too small for the big problems of life, and too big for the small problems of life'.[1] At the same time as social relations become laterally stretched and as part of the same process, we see the strengthening of pressures for local autonomy and regional cultural identity.

Two Theoretical Perspectives

Apart from the work of Marshall McLuhan and a few other individual authors, discussions of globalization tend to appear in two bodies of literature, which are largely distinct from one another. One is the literature of international relations, the other that of 'world-system theory', particularly as associated with Immanuel Wallerstein, which stands fairly close to a Marxist position.

Theorists of international relations characteristically focus upon the development of the nation-state system, analysing its origins in Europe and its subsequent worldwide spread. Nation-states are treated as actors, engaging with one another in the international arena – and with other organizations of a transnational kind (intergovernmental organizations or non-state actors). Although various theoretical positions are represented in this literature, most authors paint a rather similar picture in analysing the growth of globalization.[2] [. . .] Nation-states, it is held, are becoming progressively less sovereign than they used to be in terms of control over their own affairs – although few today anticipate in the near future the emergence of the 'world-state' which many in the early part of this century foresaw as a real prospect.

While this view is not altogether wrong, some major reservations have to be expressed. For one thing, it again covers only one overall dimension of globalization as I wish to utilize the concept here – the international coordination of states. Regarding states as actors has its uses and makes sense in some contexts. However [. . .] treating states as actors having connections with each other and with other organizations in the international arena makes it difficult to deal with social relations that are not between or outside states, but simply cross-cut state divisions.

A further shortcoming of this type of approach concerns its portrayal of the increasing unification of the nation-state system. The sovereign power of modern states was not formed prior to their involvement in the nation-state system, even in the European state system, but developed in conjunction with it. Indeed, the sovereignty of the modern state was from the first *dependent upon the relations between states*, in terms of which each state (in principle if by no means always in practice) recognized the autonomy of others within their own borders. No state, however powerful, held as much sovereign control in practice as was enshrined in legal principle. The history of the past two centuries is thus not one of the progressive loss of sovereignty on the part of the nation-state. Here again we must recognize the dialectical character of globalization and also the influence of processes of uneven development. Loss of autonomy on the part of some states or groups of states has often gone along with an *increase* in that of others, as a result of alliances, wars, or political and economic changes of various sorts. [. . .]

Since the stance of world-system theory differs so much from international relations, it is not surprising to find that the two literatures are at arm's distance from one another. Wallerstein's account of the world system makes many contributions, in both theory and empirical analysis.[3] Not least important is the fact that he skirts the sociologists' usual preoccupation with 'societies' in favour of a much more embracing conception of globalized relationships. He also makes a clear differentiation between the modern era and preceding ages in terms of the phenomena with which he is concerned. What he refers to as 'world economies' – networks of economic connections of a geographically extensive sort – have existed prior to modern times, but these were notably different from the world system that has developed over the past three or four centuries. Earlier world economies were usually centred upon large imperial states and never covered more than certain regions in which the power of these states was concentrated. The emergence of capitalism, as Wallerstein analyses it, ushers in a quite different type of order, for the first time genuinely global in its span and based more on economic than political power – the 'world capitalist economy'. The world capitalist economy, which has its origins in the sixteenth and seventeenth centuries, is integrated through commercial and manufacturing connections, not by a political centre. Indeed, there exists a multiplicity of political centres, the nation-states. The modern world system is divided into three components, the core, the semi-periphery, and the periphery, although where these are located regionally shifts over time.

[. . .]

Wallerstein successfully breaks away from some of the limitations of much orthodox sociological thought, most notably the strongly defined tendency to focus upon 'endogenous models' of social change. But his work has its own shortcomings. He continues to see only one dominant institutional nexus (capitalism) as responsible for modern transformations. World-system theory thus concentrates heavily upon economic influences and finds it difficult satisfactorily to account for just those phenomena made central by the theorists of international relations: the rise of the nation-state and the nation-state system. Moreover, the distinctions between core, semi-periphery, and periphery (themselves perhaps of questionable value), based upon economic criteria, do not allow us to illuminate political or military concentrations of power, which do not align in an exact way to economic differentiations.

Dimensions of Globalization

I shall, in contrast, regard the world capitalist economy as one of four dimensions of globalization (see figure [1]).[4] The nation-state system is a second dimension; as the discussion above indicated, although these are connected in various ways, neither can be explained exhaustively in terms of the other.

If we consider the present day, in what sense can world economic organization be said to be dominated by capitalistic economic mechanisms? A number of considerations are relevant to answering this question. The main centres of power in the world economy are capitalist states – states in which capitalist economic enterprise (with the class relations that this implies) is the chief form of production. The domestic and international economic policies of these states involve many forms of regulation of economic activity, but, as noted, their institutional organization maintains an 'insulation' of the economic from the political. This allows wide scope for the global activities of business corporations, which always have a home base within a particular state but may develop many other regional involvements elsewhere.

Business firms, especially the transnational corporations, may wield immense economic power, and have the capacity to influence political policies in their home bases and elsewhere. The biggest transnational companies today have budgets larger than those of

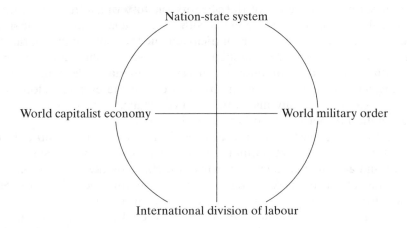

Figure [1] The dimensions of globalization

all but a few nations. But there are some key respects in which their power cannot rival that of states – especially important here are the factors of territoriality and control of the means of violence. There is no area on the earth's surface, with the partial exception of the polar regions, which is not claimed as the legitimate sphere of control of one state or another. All modern states have a more or less successful monopoly of control of the means of violence within their own territories. No matter how great their economic power, industrial corporations are not military organizations (as some of them were during the colonial period), and they cannot establish themselves as political/legal entities which rule a given territorial area.

If nation-states are the principal 'actors' within the global political order, corporations are the dominant agents within the world economy. In their trading relations with one another, and with states and consumers, companies (manufacturing corporations, financial firms, and banks) depend upon production for profit. Hence the spread of their influence brings in its train a global extension of commodity markets, including money markets. However, even in its beginnings, the capitalist world economy was never just a market for the trading of goods and services. It involved, and involves today, the commodifying of labour power in class relations which separate workers from control of their means of production. This process, of course, is fraught with implications for global inequalities.

All nation-states, capitalist and state socialist, within the 'developed' sectors of the world, are primarily reliant upon industrial production for the generation of the wealth upon which their tax revenues are based. [. . .] The pursuit of growth by both Western and East European societies inevitably pushes economic interests to the forefront of the policies which states pursue in the international arena. But it is surely plain to all, save those under the sway of historical materialism, that the material involvements of nation-states are not governed purely by economic considerations, real or perceived. The influence of any particular state within the global political order is strongly conditioned by the level of its wealth (and the connection between this and military strength). However, states derive their power from their sovereign capabilities, as Hans J. Morgenthau emphasizes.[5] They do not operate as economic machines, but as 'actors' jealous of their territorial rights, concerned with the fostering of national cultures, and having strategic geopolitical involvements with other states or alliances of states.

The nation-state system has long participated in that reflexivity characteristic of modernity as a whole. The very existence of sovereignty should be understood as something that is reflexively monitored, for reasons already indicated. Sovereignty is linked to the replacement of 'frontiers' by 'borders' in the early development of the nation-state system: autonomy inside the territory claimed by the state is sanctioned by the recognition of borders by other states. [...]

One aspect of the dialectical nature of globalization is the 'push and pull' between tendencies towards centralization inherent in the reflexivity of the system of states on the one hand and the sovereignty of particular states on the other. Thus, concerted action between countries in some respects diminishes the individual sovereignty of the nations involved, yet by combining their power in other ways, it increases their influence within the state system. The same is true of the early congresses which, in conjunction with war, defined and redefined states' borders – and of truly global agencies such as the United Nations. [...]

The third dimension of globalization is the world military order. In specifying its nature, we have to analyse the connections between the industrialization of war, the flow of weaponry and techniques of military organization from some parts of the world to others, and the alliances which states build with one another. Military alliances do not necessarily compromise the monopoly over the means of violence held by a state within its territories, although in some circumstances they certainly can do so.

In tracing the overlaps between military power and the sovereignty of states, we find the same push-and-pull between opposing tendencies noted previously. [...] [A]s a result of the massive destructive power of modern weaponry, almost all states possess military strength far in excess of that of even the largest of pre-modern civilizations. Many economically weak Third World countries are militarily powerful. In an important sense there is no 'Third World' in respect of weaponry, only a 'First World', since most countries maintain stocks of technologically advanced armaments and have modernized the military in a thoroughgoing way. Even the possession of nuclear weaponry is not confined to the economically advanced states.

The globalizing of military power obviously is not confined to weaponry and alliances between the armed forces of different states – it also concerns war itself. Two world wars attest to the way in which local conflicts became matters of global involvement. In both wars, the participants were drawn from virtually all regions (although the Second World War was a more truly worldwide phenomenon). In an era of nuclear weaponry, the industrialization of war has proceeded to a point at which [...] the obsolescence of Clausewitz's main doctrine has become apparent to everyone.[6] The only point of holding nuclear weapons – apart from their possible symbolic value in world politics – is to deter others from using them.

While this situation may lead to a suspension of war between the nuclear powers (or so we all must hope), it scarcely prevents them from engaging in military adventures outside their own territorial domains. [...]

The fourth dimension of globalization concerns industrial development. The most obvious aspect of this is the expansion of the global division of labour, which includes the differentiations between more and less industrialized areas in the world. Modern industry is intrinsically based on divisions of labour, not only on the level of job tasks but on that of regional specialization in terms of type of industry, skills, and the production of raw materials. There has undoubtedly taken place a major expansion of global interdependence in the division of labour since the Second World War. This has helped to bring about shifts in the worldwide distribution of production, including the deindustrialization of some regions in the developed countries and the emergence of the 'Newly Industrializing Countries' in the Third World. It has also undoubtedly served to reduce the internal economic hegemony of many states, particularly those with a high level of industrialization. It is more difficult for the capitalist countries to manage their economies than formerly was the case, given accelerating global economic interdependence. This is almost certainly one of the major reasons for the declining impact of Keynesian economic policies, as applied at the level of the national economy, in current times.

One of the main features of the globalizing implications of industrialism is the worldwide diffusion of machine technologies. The impact of industrialism is plainly not limited to the sphere of production, but affects many aspects of day-to-day life, as well as influencing the generic character of human interaction with the material environment.

Even in states which remain primarily agricultural, modern technology is often applied in such a way as to alter substantially pre-existing relations between human social organization and the environment. This is true, for example, of the use of fertilizers or other artificial farming methods, the introduction of modern farming machinery, and so forth. The diffusion of industrialism has created 'one world' in a more negative and threatening sense than that just mentioned – a world in which there are actual or potential ecological changes of a harmful sort that affect everyone on the planet. Yet industrialism has also decisively conditioned our very sense of living in 'one world'. For one of the most important effects of industrialism has been the transformation of technologies of communication.

This comment leads on to a further and quite fundamental aspect of globalization, which lies behind each of the various institutional dimensions that have been mentioned and which might be referred to as cultural globalization. Mechanized technologies of communication have dramatically influenced all aspects of globalization since the first introduction of mechanical printing into Europe. They form an essential element of the reflexivity of modernity and of the discontinuities which have torn the modern away from the traditional.

The globalizing impact of media was noted by numerous authors during the period of the early growth of mass circulation newspapers. Thus one commentator in 1892 wrote that, as a result of modern newspapers, the inhabitant of a local village has a broader understanding of contemporary events than the prime minister of a hundred years before. The villager who reads a paper 'interests himself simultaneously in the issue of a revolution in Chile, a bush-war in East Africa, a massacre in North China, a famine in Russia'.[7]

The point here is not that people are contingently aware of many events, from all over the world, of which previously they would have remained ignorant. It is that the global extension of the institutions of modernity would be impossible were it not for the pooling of knowledge which is represented by the 'news'. This is perhaps less obvious on the level of general cultural awareness than in more specific contexts. For example, the global money markets of today involve direct and simultaneous access to pooled information on the part of individuals spatially widely separated from one another.

Notes

1 Daniel Bell, 'The world and the United States in 2013', *Daedalus* 116 (1987).
2 See for example James N. Rosenau, *The Study of Global Interdependence* (London: Pinter, 1980).
3 Immanuel Wallerstein, *The Modern World System* (New York: Academic, 1974).
4 This figure (and the discussion which accompanies it) supersedes that which appears on p. 277 of Giddens, *Nation-State and Violence* (Cambridge: Polity Press, 1985).
5 H. J. Morgenthau, *Politics among Nations* (New York: Knopf, 1960).
6 Clausewitz was a subtle thinker, however, and there are interpretations of his ideas which continue to insist upon their relevance to the present day.
7 Max Nordau, *Degeneration* (1892; New York: Fertig, 1968), p. 39.

8

What is Globalization?

Ulrich Beck

[...]
With the peaceful fall of the Berlin Wall and the collapse of the Soviet empire, many thought that the end of politics was nigh as we entered an age beyond socialism and capitalism, utopia and emancipation. In the years since then, however, the ceremonial farewells to politics have become rather more subdued. The current scare-word 'globalization', seemingly unavoidable in any public statement, points not to an end of politics but to its *escape* from the categories of the national state, and even from the schema defining what is 'political' and 'non-political' action. For whatever the referent of the new globalization rhetoric (economy, markets, job competition, production, goods and services, financial flows, information, lifestyles), the political consequences of the stage-managed *economic* globalization risk stand out in sharp relief. Institutions of industrial society which seemed shut tight can be 'cracked' and opened up to political intervention. The premises of the welfare state and pension system, of income support, local government and infrastructural policies, the power of organized labour, industry-wide free collective bargaining, state expenditure, the fiscal system and 'fair taxation' – all this melts under the withering sun of globalization and becomes susceptible to (demands for) political moulding. Every social actor must respond in one way or another; and the typical responses do *not* fit into the old left–right schema of political action.[1]
[...]
The global operation of the economy is sapping the foundations of national economics and national states, unleashing sub-politics on a quite novel scale and with incalculable consequences. The next objective will be to shunt the old adversary, 'labour', out of harm's way, but above all to serve notice on the 'ideal aggregate capitalist' (as Marx called the *state*) so that it is freed from the entanglement with labour that developed in the course of the nineteenth and twentieth centuries.

'All fixed, fast-frozen relations, with their train of ancient and venerable prejudices and opinions, are swept away' – Marx, already in the *Communist Manifesto*, hardly kept secret his celebration of the revolutionary potential of capital. Today the 'fixed and fast-frozen' is the welfare-state and trade-union organization of labour, while the 'ancient and venerable' are the bureaucratic prescriptions and fiscal exactions of the (national) state. Efficiency and neatness, then, will supposedly result from a novel politics based upon the 'material constraints' of globalization.
[...]
The downward pressure on the welfare state, then, results not only from a combination of dwindling resources and rocketing expenditure, but also from the fact that it lacks the means to satisfy demands upon it at a time when the gulf between rich and poor is growing ever wider. As the national framework loses its binding force, the

winners and the losers of globalization cease to sit at the same table. The new rich no longer 'need' the new poor. And so it becomes increasingly difficult to even out the differences between them, because there is no framework in which this overarching conflict could be represented and regulated.

It is not hard to see what this entails. The conflictual logic of the capitalist zero-sum game has been re-emerging and growing sharper, while the state has been losing its customary means to pacify and conciliate by increasing the size of the economic cake available for distribution.

A question mark thus appears over the model of the first, national modernity, which was conceived and organized within a particular cultural identity (a 'people'), a territory and a state. At the same time, however, no new unity of humanity, planet earth and world state has become visible or even desirable to large numbers of people.
[. . .]

In this pitch-dark view of things, economic globalization merely completes what has been driven forward intellectually by postmodernism and politically by individualization: namely, the collapse of modernity. The diagnosis points towards a *capitalism without work* that will *create unemployment on a huge scale*; the historical association between market economy, welfare state and democracy, the Western model that integrated and legitimated the nation-state project of modernity, is thus destined to break down. According to this scenario, neoliberals are the liquidators of the West – even if they set themselves up as its reformers. As far as the welfare state, democracy and a public sphere are concerned, they are pursuing a course of modernization to the death.

But decline begins in the head. Fatalism is also a language disorder. And before jumping off the Eiffel Tower, one really ought to consult a language therapist. 'Concepts are empty: they no longer grip, illuminate or inflame. The greyness lying over the world [. . .] may also come from a kind of verbal mildew.'[2] What appears as collapse might, if it succeeds in overcoming the fatal orthodoxies of the first modernity, open out into a second modernity.[3]
[. . .]

[It] is difficult to speak out against the world power of the world market. This is possible only by destroying the image of an all-powerful world market that rules in people's heads and cripples all action. In this [article] I would like to oppose that mega-spectre haunting Europe, and to do so with the slingshot of a distinction between *globalism* on the one hand, and *globality* and *globalization* on the other. This distinction is designed to break up the *territorial orthodoxy of the political and the social*, posed in absolute institutional categories, which arose with the national-state project of the first modernity.

By *globalism* I mean the view that the world market eliminates or supplants political action – that is, the ideology of rule by the world market, the ideology of neoliberalism. It proceeds monocausally and economistically, reducing the multi-dimensionality of globalization to a single, economic dimension that is itself conceived in a linear fashion. If it mentions at all the other dimensions of globalization – ecology, culture, politics, civil society – it does so only by placing them under the sway of the world-market system. Of course, there can be no denying the central importance of economic globalization, also as an option and perception of corporate players. But the ideological core of globalism is that a basic difference of the first modernity is hereby liquidated, that is, the difference between politics and economics. The central task of politics, which is to define the basic legal, social and ecological conditions under which economic activity first becomes socially possible and legitimate, drops out of view or is suppressed. Globalism implies that a complex structure such as Germany – its state, its society, its culture, its foreign policy – can be run in the way that a company is run. But this involves a veritable imperialism of economics, where companies demand the basic conditions under which they can optimize their goals.

The striking thing is that globalism, understood in this way, casts its spell even over its opponents. Along with affirmative globalism, there is also a 'negative' globalism which, having been convinced of the inescapable dominance of the world market, takes refuge in various forms of protectionism.

Conservative protectionists bewail the collapse of values and the declining signific-ance of the national dimension, but rather contradictorily also pursue the neoliberal destruction of the national state.

Green protectionists see the national state as a political biotope threatened with extinc-tion, which upholds environmental standards against world market forces and is thus as deserving of protection as nature itself.

Red protectionists don for every case the dusted-down costume of class struggle; glob-alization is another word for 'right after all' as they celebrate their Marxist feast of the resurrection. However, it is a 'being right' that is afflicted with utopian blindness.

These pitfalls of globalism should be distinguished from what I would like to call – in tune with Anglo-American discussion – globality and globalization.

Globality means that *we have been living for a long time in a world society*, in the sense that the notion of closed spaces has become illusory. No country or group can shut itself off from others. Various economic, cultural and political forms therefore collide with one another, and things that used to be taken for granted (including in the Western model) will have to be justified anew. 'World society', then, denotes the totality of social relationships which are *not* integrated into or determined (or deter-minable) by national-state politics. Self-perceptions, as staged by the national mass media, here play a crucial role, so that world society in the narrower sense – to propose a still politically relevant operational criterion – means *perceived* or *reflexive* world society. The question of how far it exists may therefore (in accordance with the Thomas theorem that what people believe to be real becomes real in its consequences) be empir-ically turned into the question of how, and to what extent, people and cultures around the world relate to one another in their differences, and to what extent this self-perception of world society is relevant to how they behave.

'World' in the combination 'world society' thus means *difference* or *multiplicity*, and 'society' means *non*-integration, so that we may [. . .] conceive world society as *multi-plicity without unity*. As we shall see, this presupposes a number of very different things: transnational forms of production and labour market competition, global reporting in the media, transnational consumer boycotts, transnational ways of life, as well as 'glob-ally' perceived crises and wars, military and peaceful use of atomic energy, destruction of nature, and so on.

Globalization, on the other hand, denotes the *processes* through which sovereign national states are criss-crossed and undermined by transnational actors with varying prospects of power, orientations, identities and networks.

One essential feature distinguishing the second from the first modernity is the fact that *the new globality cannot be reversed*. This means that the various autonomous logics of globalization – the logics of ecology, culture, economics, politics and civil society – exist side by side and cannot be reduced or collapsed into one another. Rather, each must be independently decoded and grasped in its interdependences. The guiding supposition is that only in this way can the perspective and the space for political action be opened up. Why? Because only then can the depoliticizing spell of globalism be broken; only with a multidimensional view of globality can the globalist ideology of 'material compulsion' be broken down. But what is it that makes globality irreversible? Eight reasons may be given under the following headings:

1   The geographical expansion and ever greater density of international trade, as well as the global networking of finance markets and the growing power of transnational corporations.
2   The ongoing revolution of information and communications technology.
3   The universal *demands* for human rights – the (lip service paid to the) principle of democracy.
4   The stream of images from the global culture industries.
5   The emergence of a postnational, polycentric world politics, in which transnational actors (corporations, non-governmental organizations, United Nations) are growing in power and number alongside governments.
6   The question of world poverty.
7   The issue of environmental destruction.
8   Transcultural conflicts in one and the same place.

[. . .] Globality means that from now on nothing which happens on our planet is only a limited local event; all inventions, victories and catastrophes affect the whole world, and we must reorient and reorganize our lives and actions, our organizations and institutions, along a 'localglobal' axis. Globality, understood in this way, denotes the new situation of the second modernity. This concept also concentrates elementary reasons why [. . .] politics will have to be refounded or reinvented.

This concept of globality may be distinguished from the concept of a *globalization process* (a dialectical process, one would say in old-fashioned language), which creates transnational social links and spaces, revalues local cultures, and promotes third cultures ('a little of this, a little of that, is the way new things come into the world' – Salman Rushdie). Within this complex framework, the question of the *extent* of successful globalization as well as of its *limits* may be posed anew in relation to three parameters: (a) extension in *space*; (b) stability over *time*; and (c) social *density* of the transnational networks, relationships and image-flows.

This conceptual horizon makes it possible to answer a further question: namely, what is historically specific about contemporary globalization and its paradoxes at a particular place (for example, in comparison with the 'capitalist world-system' that was already under construction in the age of colonialism)?

The peculiarity of the present, and future, globalization process lies in the empirically ascertainable *scale, density and stability of regional–global relationship networks and their self-definition through the mass media, as well as of social spaces and of image-flows at a cultural, political, economic and military level*. World society is thus not a mega-national society containing and dissolving all national societies within itself, but a world horizon characterized by multiplicity and non-integration which opens out when it is produced and preserved in communication and action.

Sceptics will ask what is new about this, and answer: nothing really important. But they are wrong: historically, empirically and theoretically. What is new is not only the everyday life and interaction across national frontiers, in dense networks with a high degree of mutual dependence and obligation. New, too, is the self-perception of this transnationality (in the mass media, consumption or tourism); new is the 'placelessness' of community, labour and capital; new are the awareness of global ecological dangers and the corresponding arenas of action; new is the inescapable perception of trans-cultural Others in one's own life, with all the contradictory certainties resulting from it; new is the level at which 'global culture industries' circulate [. . .]; new are the rise of a European structure of states, and the number and power of transnational actors, institutions and agreements; and new, finally, is the degree of economic concentration, which is nevertheless slowed down by cross-frontier competition in the world market.

Globalization, then, also means *no* world state – or, to be more precise, world society *without a world state* and *without world government*. A globally *disorganized* capitalism is continually spreading out. For there is no hegemonic power and no inter-national regime, either economic or political.

[. . .]

Notes

1   See A. Giddens, *Beyond Left and Right* (Cambridge, 1994).
2   U. Beck, 'Väter der Freiheit', in Beck (ed.), *Kinder der Freiheit* (Frankfurt, 1997), pp. 377ff.
3   *Pater semper incertus*. An unforgiving dispute has broken out in the press over the paternity of the term 'second modernity'. Not to have read and not to be able to quote are not, however, sufficient grounds for originality – and suspicions. 'Auf dem Weg in die Zweite Moderne' (Towards the Second Modernity) is the title of a series edited by myself. And 'Auf dem Weg in eine andere Moderne' (Towards a New Modernity) was the subtitle of my book *Risk Society* (London, 1992), which first appeared in German in 1986. Already a distinction is drawn there between 'simple' and 'reflexive' modernization, a 'first' and a 'second' modernity – as in each of my books that came after it. *The Reinvention of Politics* (Cambridge, 1997), which first appeared in German in 1993, was originally intended to have the title *Jenseits von Links und Recht* (Beyond Left and Right), and then *Zweite Moderne* (Second Modernity); both were subsequently rejected for various reasons. Now, it may be true that the meaning one gives to a concept plays only a marginal role, but even in terms of content there is a great similarity between *second modernity* and *new* or *different modernity*. The themes of the book series I have been editing – individualization, ecological crisis, society without work, even glob-alization itself – were already central themes of *Risk Society*. (I know that the next complaint will be: 'Aha, so there's nothing new!') If there is a conceptual elective affinity, then it is with the expression coined by Jürgen Habermas, 'uncompleted modernity'. See also J. Habermas, 'Jenseits des Nationalstaats?', in U. Beck (ed.), *Politik der Globalisierung* (Frankfurt, 1997).

Part II

The Reconfiguration of Political Power?

One thousand years ago, a modern political map of the world would have been incomprehensible. This is not just because much of the world was still to be 'discovered'. People simply did not think of political power as something divided by clear-cut boundaries and unambiguous territorial domains. Modern politics emerged with and was shaped by the development of political communities tied to specific pieces of land, and formed into a nation-state. This saw political power centralized within Europe, state structures created and eventually the emergence of a new order among states. Forms of democracy were developed within certain political communities, while at the same time the creation of empires prevented democratic accountability from developing in many other places. Today, questions arise as to whether we are living through another political transformation which might be as important as the creation of the nation-state. Is the exclusive link between territory and political power being broken by globalization?

The modern nation-state is the principal form of political rule across the globe, and is likely to remain so, the sceptics argue. The seventeenth century marked the beginning of the contemporary international system – the key parts of which are sovereign states claiming exclusive authority within their own geographic boundaries. This system is characterized by territorial states which settle their differences privately and sometimes by force; which seek to place their own national interest above all others; and which recognize no superior authority to themselves. Changes in international law, regional associations and global institutions in the twentieth century have not altered the fundamental form and shape of this state system. For the division of the globe into nation-states, with distinctive sets of geopolitical interests, was built into institutions of regional and global governance, for instance, the veto powers granted to leading states (the US, Russia, Britain, France and China) in the Security Council of the United Nations. Furthermore, the new challenges of growing internationalism do not diminish the state-centric world. Sceptics discount the presumption that internationalization prefigures the emergence of a new, less state-centric world order. Far from considering national governments as becoming immobilized by international imperatives, they point to their growing centrality in the active promotion and regulation of cross-border activity.

Globalists take issue with these contentions. At the heart of the globalist thesis is the conviction that globalization is transforming the nature and form of political power today. Globalists argue that the right of most states to rule within circumscribed territories – their sovereignty – is on the edge of transformation, as is the practical nature of this entitlement – the actual capacity of states to rule. According to these authors, contemporary processes of globalization are historically unprecedented; and governments and societies across the globe are having to adjust to a world in which there is no longer a clear distinction between international and domestic, external and internal affairs. Globalization involves a 'massive shake-out' of societies, economies, institutions of governance and world order. For some globalists, contemporary globalization is reconstituting the power, functions and authority of national government. In this world, national governments are relegated to little more than transmission belts for global economic change, or, at best, intermediate institutions and mechanisms sandwiched between increasingly powerful local, regional and global mechanisms of power and authority. Other globalists take a less radical view. They talk less in terms of 'the end of the state', and more in terms of a new spectrum of political developments and adjustment strategies in which the state finds itself relocated in multiple regional and global political networks.

The extracts which follow reflect this complex debate and offer important refinements of the arguments on both sides. Keohane begins by examining what he calls 'Hobbes's dilemma'. Hobbes thought that since people are egotistical and self-interested, and always seek more intensive pleasure and gain, no security is possible in the political and social worlds. Moreover, since there is no good reason to suppose that rulers will behave any differently from the ruled, there is a high risk that states will be predatory and oppressive. While accepting fundamental elements of this 'realist' characterization of the nature of humankind and state activity, Keohane argues that institutions can shape and alter the nature of this dilemma and its outcomes; and that, historically, the sovereign constitutional state has in fact done this. But what interests him above all is the place of sovereignty under contemporary conditions of 'complex interdependence'; that is, areas where there are 'multiple channels of contact existing among pluralistic societies' and where war is excluded as a primary means of resolving policy and political outcomes. In these circumstances, Keohane argues, neither states nor transnational relations will replace one another; for sovereignty neither remains intact under existing forms of complex interdependence nor is wholly eroded. Rather, sovereignty today is increasingly transformed as it has become 'less a territorially defined barrier' and more 'a bargaining resource for a politics characterized by complex transnational networks'. Keohane traces out this development taking into account different developmental levels of complex interdependence around the world. He concludes that, while the institution of sovereign statehood is being modified, it is not likely to be superseded, and that Hobbes's dilemma will never be resolved entirely. Nevertheless, in the context of an intensification of economic globalization, the end of the Cold War, and the emergence of marked domains of peace as well as conflict, one thing is certain; we are entering a period of increasing diversity which will require the further development of international institutions to facilitate cooperation across economic, political and cultural domains.

The article by Krasner takes a view which complements Keohane's in many respects. The peace of Westphalia (1648) is generally taken by international relations scholars to mark the beginning of the modern states system, the beginning of a universe composed of sovereign states based on the principles of state autonomy and territorial integrity. Krasner argues that the Westphalian model of the international order has never, in fact, been an accurate description of many of the entities called states. Moreover, he contends that compromises to the model are nothing new: 'breaches of the Westphalian model have been an enduring characteristic of the international environment.' What this argument suggests is that there has never been a 'golden age' of Westphalian states, now in decline. The historical reality has been much more complex. Compromises of the Westphalian order have been a characteristic of the international system and, what is more, they have often been essential to peace and stability. Krasner concludes: 'Compromising Westphalia is not only inevitable, it can also be good'; it has introduced an element of flexibility into the behaviour of states and the states system – a flexibility which has allowed for new circumstances to be accommodated and for transformations to take place creating the possibility of a durable, peaceful international system.

Assessing directly globalist arguments about the end of the nation-state, Mann analyses four supposed 'threats' – global capitalism, environmental danger, identity politics and post-nuclear geopolitics. He sets out how all four impact differently on nation-states in different regions, and contain both 'state weakening and strengthening tendencies, and increase the significance of inter-national as well transnational networks'. In this highly differentiated analysis Mann points to the diverse impacts of these threats, and their variable outcomes. He suggests that the patterns are too varied to allow one simply to argue that the nation-state and the nation-state system are strengthening or weakening. And he concludes that while 'human interaction networks are now penetrating the globe', they are doing so in 'multiple, variable and uneven ways'.

The position taken by Susan Strange contests such a standpoint. Her view is that politicians and governments have lost the authority they used to have and that their command over outcomes has diminished. Her argument is that 'the impersonal forces of world markets, integrated over the postwar period more by private enterprise in finance, industry and trade than by cooperative decisions of governments, are now more powerful than states.' Both the authority and legitimacy of states are in decline and, as a consequence, a serious vacuum is opening up in the international order; 'a yawning hole of non-authority, ungovernance it might be called'.

Hettne accepts that there has been a major expansion of market forces, creating the need for new institutions of political accountability and control. But he would take issue with Strange's conclusions. For Hettne world regions can and do complement the expanding scope and reach of global forces. He seeks to show that the concept of region has assumed a new importance in the organization of world affairs. In addition, he argues that political and economic trends point towards further regionalization. In his judgement, the processes of globalization and of regionalization are complementary. Seeking to unpack the changing relationship between the 'forces of globalization' and the 'forces of regionalization', Hettne explores a growing shift from the territorial logic of state control to the emergence of regional systems of states and territories preoccupied with regulation and accountability in a wider context. It is in this that he sees good grounds for believing that regionalization and globalization may well prove to be mutually reinforcing processes.

What has been the role of international law in these developments? Held's chapter explores the way the development of international law has placed individuals, governments and non-governmental organizations under new systems of legal regulation. He sets out how international law has become a vast changing corpus of rules, quasi-rules and precedents which set out new and changing bases of coexistence and cooperation in the international order. He detects at the heart of this an emerging conflict between claims made on behalf of the states system and those made on behalf of an alternative organizing principle of world order. While this conflict is far from settled, new directions in international law are, he believes, clearly discernible. Although Gessner would not wholly dispute this position, he takes a more pessimistic view of international legal development. In his account, international legal developments can be seen, at best, as 'a colourful patchwork of structures', creating little in the way of new legal certainties.

Finally, Rosenau examines many new forms of collaboration in world politics, and seeks to assess which steering or control mechanisms actually regulate the actions of transnational political and economic subjects. He provides a map of the changing forms – nascent and institutionalized – of global governance. Examples of the different dimensions and types of global governance are elaborated. But while clear trends in the development of global governance can be detected, there is still considerable room for debate as to how these developments will eventually crystallize. As Rosenau puts it: 'in this time of continuing and profound transformations too much remains murky to project beyond the immediate present and anticipate long-term trajectories.' One cannot conclude with any confidence what precisely these developmental paths will be in the century ahead.

9

Sovereignty in International Society

Robert O. Keohane

[...] [A]ny coherent attempt to understand contemporary international relations must include an analysis of the impact of two factors: long-term tendencies toward globalization – the intensification of transnational as well as interstate relations – and the more immediate effects of the end of the Cold War and the collapse of the Soviet Union. For the United States, accustomed to being both relatively autonomous and a leader of a "free world" coalition, both of these changes have immediate impact. Indeed, the very concept of world leadership is up for grabs as it has not been since World War II. [...] I do not expect the end of the Cold War to lead to a new world order, which President George Bush sought to celebrate in 1991. Voltaire is reputed to have said that the Holy Roman Empire was neither holy, nor Roman, nor an empire, and one could say about the new world order that it is neither new, nor global in scope, nor an order. A focus on the effects of the end of the Cold War, and of globalization [...] is more fruitful.

As a result of the end of the Cold War, the United States is likely to reduce its global ambitions and be disinclined to enter into new alliances, although US policymakers will continue to seek to enhance the role of NATO and US leadership in it. US economic rivalry with former Cold War allies will no longer be muted by the need to remain united in the face of a Soviet threat, as Joanne Gowa anticipated on theoretical grounds before the end of the Cold War.[1] Severe competitive pressures on major US corporations, resulting both from the rapidity of technological change and from globalization, are combining with anxiety about rapid increases in Japanese (and more generally, East Asian) economic capabilities relative to those of the United States to increase policymakers' concern about the competitive position of the United States in the world economy. Economic strength is ultimately the basis for economic and military power, and the United States can no longer take its economic preponderance for granted. US domestic policies will increasingly be oriented toward maintaining competitiveness in the world economy, which in turn requires technological leadership and may also involve further attempts to organize a trade and investment bloc, as in the North American Free Trade Agreement (NAFTA). Increasing concern in the United States about its commercial competitiveness was evident before the end of the Cold War but has been accentuated by the collapse of the Soviet Union. The Soviet collapse reduces both the US need for allies against another superpower and the incentive for US commercial rivals to defer to US leadership.

During the early years of the Cold War, world politics was unusually hierarchical in structure. The United States was to a remarkable degree economically and militarily self-sufficient: At least for some time, it could have managed to be quite autarchic. However, US policymakers viewed autarchy as unattractive, since it would have forced the United States to forgo the economic benefits of foreign trade and investment, and it could have led to the creation of a coalition against the United States that included the potential power centers of China, Japan, and Western Europe. The impact of autarchy on US political institutions, Assistant Secretary of State Dean Acheson told Congress in 1945, would be severe: "If you wish to control the entire trade and income of the United States, which means the life of the people, you could probably fix it so that everything produced here would be consumed here, but that would completely change our Constitution, our relations to property, human liberty, our very conception of law."[2]

The decision by the United States in 1945 to maintain a capitalist economy with increasing openness (measured by such indicators as trade and investment as shares of gross domestic product) has been a crucial source of the globalization – the increasingly global character of social, economic, and political transactions – that we now experience. And the outward orientation of US policy clearly owes a great deal to the Soviet challenge and the Cold War. Now that the Cold War is over, globalization continues apace and has implications for sovereignty that affect the United States as well as other capitalist democracies.

Yet globalization coexists with an older feature of world politics: States are independent entities with diverse interests and have no guarantees that other states will act benignly toward them or even keep their commitments. World politics is a "self-help system," as Kenneth N. Waltz has expressed it, in which states seek to maintain and insofar as feasible expand their power and in which they are concerned about their power relative to others as well as about their own welfare.[3] One of the earliest and most powerful expressions of these assumptions about human nature and human interactions was enunciated by Thomas Hobbes in the seventeenth century. Hobbes, who was thinking principally about domestic politics and civil strife but who referred also to international relations, developed an argument for unified sovereignty and authoritarian rule that led to what I will refer to as Hobbes's dilemma. Hobbes's dilemma encapsulates the existential tragedy that results when human institutions collapse and people expect the worst from each other, whether this occurs in Somalia, Bosnia, or the Corcyrean Revolution described by Thucydides: "Death thus ranged in every shape. . . . There was no length to which violence did not go. . . . Reckless audacity came to be considered as the courage of a loyal ally; prudent hesitation, specious cowardice; moderation was seen to be a cloak for unmanliness; ability to see all sides of a question, inaptness to act on any. . . . The cause of all these evils was the lust for power arising from greed and ambition."[4]

However, Hobbes's dilemma is not a statement of immutable fact, since it can be avoided; indeed, it can be seen as an expression of the dead end to which Hobbesian assumptions can lead. Properly appreciated, it is less an insightful key to world politics than a metaphor of the "realist trap."[5] Adopting an institutionalist perspective, I suggest that one way out of the realist trap is to explore further the concept of *sovereignty*. Sovereignty is often associated with realist thinking; and globalist writers sometimes argue that its usefulness and clarity have been diminished in the modern world.[6] In contrast, I will argue that sovereign statehood is an *institution* – a set of persistent and connected rules prescribing behavioral roles, constraining activity, and shaping expectations[7] – whose rules significantly modify the Hobbesian notion of anarchy. We can understand this institution by using a rationalistic argument: Its evolution can be understood in terms of the rational interests of the elites that run powerful states, in view of the institutional constraints that they face. Our prospects for understanding the present conjuncture – globalization, the end of the Cold War, the dubious prospects for a new world order – will be enhanced if we understand the nature of sovereignty.

The first section covers Hobbes's dilemma and the failure of Hobbes's solution to it and includes a brief summary of institutionalist responses at the domestic and international levels of analysis. In the section on sovereignty under conditions of high interdependence I develop an argument about how sovereignty is changing in those areas of the world characterized by "complex interdependence," areas within which multiple channels of contact exist among pluralistic societies and between which war is excluded as a means of policy.[8] In the section on zones of peace and conflict I introduce a cautionary note by arguing that we are entering a period of great diversity in world politics, with zones of conflict as well as a zone of peace, and therefore emphasizing the limits to institutionalist solutions to Hobbes's dilemma. [...]

In this chapter I do not sketch a vision of what the world should be like – if I were to do so, I would outline a Rawlsian utopia or offer a political strategy for change. Rather, as a social scientist I seek to analyze some of the actual changes in the international system from the standpoint of the United States and the institutionalist international relations theory that I have sought to develop. Rather than speculate on current events, I have sought to identify a major institution, that of sovereign statehood, and ask in light of past experience how it is changing. Hence I do not try to survey recent changes but to focus on sovereignty both as a lens through which to view the contemporary world and as a concept with implications for international relations theory. My hope is that what may appear idiosyncratic in my account will lead to some insights even if it does not command universal acceptance.

Hobbes's Dilemma and the Institutionalist Response

We can summarize Hobbes's dilemma in two propositions:

1 *Since people are rational calculators, self-interested, seeking gain and glory, and fearful of one another, there is no security in anarchy.* Concentrated power is necessary to create order; otherwise, "the life of man [is] solitary, poor, nasty, brutish and short."[9]

2 *But precisely because people are self-interested and power-loving, unlimited power for the ruler implies a predatory, oppressive state.* Its leaders will have ex post incentives to renege on commitments; ex ante, therefore, they will find it difficult to persuade their subjects to invest for the long term, lend the state money, and otherwise create the basis for wealth and power. This is what Martin Wight calls "the Hobbesian paradox": "The classic Realist solution to the problem of anarchy is to concentrate power in the hands of a single authority and to hope that this despot will prove a partial exception to the rule that men are bad and should be regarded with distrust."[10]

Hobbes firmly grasped the authoritarian-predatory state horn of his dilemma. Partly because he regarded reason as the servant of the passions, he was pessimistic about prospects for cooperation among people not controlled by a centralized power. His solution is to establish "Leviathan," a centralized, unified state enabled "by terror . . . to form the wills of them all to peace at home and mutual aid against their enemies abroad."[11]

Yet Hobbes's solution to the problem of domestic anarchy reproduces his dilemma at the international level: *The Hobbesian solution creates a "war of all against all."* Sovereigns, "because of their independency, are in continual jealousies and in the state and posture of gladiators."[12] Under neither general anarchy nor the Hobbesian solution to it can international trade or other forms of economic exchange flourish: Property rights are in both circumstances too precarious.

For Hobbes, the fact that war is reproduced at the international level is not debilitating, since by fighting each other the sovereigns "uphold the industry of their subjects." That is, the gains from international economic exchange that are blocked by warfare are dwarfed by the gains from internal economic exchange; and the "hard shell" of the nation-state, described over 30 years ago by John Herz, protects subjects from most direct depredations of international war.[13] Since it is not necessary to overcome anarchy at the international level, the contradiction inherent in the Hobbesian paradox does not pose the problems for Hobbes's approach to international relations that it poses for his solution to problems of domestic anarchy.

In much realist thought Hobbes's international solution has been reified as if it were an essential quality of the world. Yet by his own argument about the consequences of anarchy, its implications seem morally unacceptable. Only the ad hoc assumption that rulers can protect their subjects appears superficially to save his solution from condemnation by his own argument. Even in the seventeenth century, the Hobbesian external solution – anarchy tempered by the ability to defend territory – only worked for island countries such as England. The Thirty Years' War devastated much of Germany, killing a large portion of the population; the population of the state of Württemberg fell from 450,000 in 1620 to under 100,000 in 1639, and the great powers are estimated to have suffered 2,000,000 battle deaths.[14] If the result of accepting realist pessimism is inevitable military conflict among the great powers, locked into a mutually destructive competition from which they cannot escape, then rather than celebrating our awareness of tragedy, we had better look for a way out of the realist trap.

Both of Hobbes's solutions to his dilemma are deficient. Indeed, their deficiencies stem from the same cause: the lack of attention to how institutions can profoundly affect self-interested action by changing constraints and incentives. Institutions are not a substitute for self-interest, but they shape self-interest, both domestically and internationally.[15]

[...]

Institutions: Constitutional Government and Sovereignty

The historically successful answer to Hobbes's dilemma at the internal level – constitutional government – is very different from that proposed by Hobbes. Liberal thinkers have sought to resolve Hobbes's dilemma by building reliable representative institutions, with checks on the power of rulers, hence avoiding the dilemma of accepting either anarchy or a "predatory state."[16] These institutions presuppose the establishment of a monopoly of force within a given territory; hence the emphasis of realist international relations theory on the role of state power helps to explain their existence. However, regardless of institutions' dependence on state power, liberal insights are in my view important for understanding contemporary world politics. Changes in the nature of states profoundly affect international relations, and although world politics falls short of the normative standards of liberalism, it is more highly institutionalized than realists think.

For liberals, constitutional government must be combined with a framework of stable property rights that permit markets to operate in which individual incentives and social welfare are aligned with one another.

> Individuals must be lured by incentives to undertake the socially desirable activities [that constitute economic growth]. Some mechanism must be devised to bring social and private rates of return into closer parity. . . . A discrepancy between private and social benefits or costs means that some third party or parties, without their consent, will receive some of the benefits or incur some of the costs. Such a difference occurs when property rights are poorly defined, or are not enforced. If the private costs exceed the private benefits, individuals ordinarily will not be willing to undertake the activity even though it is socially profitable.[17]

The political argument of constitutionalism is familiar: Constitutionalism is to constrain the ruler, thus creating order without arbitrariness or predation. Economically, constitutional government created institutions that could make sovereigns' promises credible, thereby reducing uncertainty, facilitating the operation of markets, and lowering interest rates for loans to sovereigns, thus directly creating power resources for states with constitutional governments.[18] Constitutionalism involved a modification of the traditional conception of sovereignty, dating to the thought of Jean Bodin and reflected in that of Hobbes. This conception linked sovereignty to will, "the idea that there is a final and absolute authority in the political community."[19] This notion, however, was challenged by theorists such as Locke and Montesquieu, whose ideas were developed and applied by the American revolutionaries. The debates between 1763 and 1775 in the American colonies over relations with Britain "brought into question the entire concept of a unitary, concentrated, and absolute governmental sovereignty."[20] As James Madison put it in a letter of 1787 to Thomas Jefferson: "The great desideratum of Government is, so to modify the sovereignty as that it may be sufficiently neutral between different parts of the Society to control one part from invading the rights of another, and at the same time sufficiently controuled itself, from setting up an interest adverse to that of the entire Society."[21] Thus internal sovereignty became pluralized and constitutionalized in liberal polities.

Externally, Hobbes's dilemma of internal anarchy versus international anarchy was traditionally dealt with, if not resolved, by the institution of sovereignty. Internationally, formal sovereignty can be defined, as Hans J. Morgenthau did, as "the supreme legal authority of the nation to give and enforce the law within a certain territory and, in consequence, independence from the authority of any other nation and equality with it under international law."[22] This doctrine is traditionally seen as an outcome of the Peace of Westphalia, although Stephen Krasner has recently argued convincingly that this "Westphalian system" was not inherent in the treaties signed in 1648.[23] As Martin Wight and the English school of international relations have shown, the function of the concept of sovereignty changed over time: "It began as a theory to justify the king being master in his new modern kingdom, absolute internally. Only subsequently was it turned outward to become the justification of equality of such sovereigns in the international community."[24] By the eighteenth and nineteenth centuries, as Hedley Bull explains, the conception of sovereignty as reflecting equality and reciprocity had become the core principle of international society. The exchange of recognition of sovereignty had become "a basic rule of coexistence within the states system," from which could be derived corollaries such as the rule of nonintervention and the rights of states to domestic jurisdiction.[25]

This is not to imply that rulers were either altruistic or that they followed norms of international society that were in conflict with their conceptions of self-interest. On the contrary, I assume that self-interest, defined in the traditional terms of maintenance of rule, extension of power, and appropriation of wealth, constitutes the best explanatory principle for rulers' behavior. However, the institution of sovereignty served their interests by restraining intervention. Intervention naturally led to attempts to foster disunion and civil war and therefore reduced the power of monarchs vis-à-vis civil society. Hence, agreement on principles of nonintervention represented a cartel-type solution to a problem of collective action: In specific situations, the dominant strategy was to intervene, but it made sense to refrain *conditional on others' restraint*. With respect to intervention, as well as logically, sovereignty and reciprocity were closely linked. Traditional sovereign statehood was an international institution prescribing fairly clear rules of behavior. Indeed, between the late seventeenth and the mid-twentieth centuries it was the central institution of international society, and it continues to be so in much of the world. It is true that world politics was "anarchic" in the specific sense that it lacked common government and states had to rely on their own strategies and resources, rather than outside authority, to maintain their status and even, in extreme situations, their existence. But this "anarchy" was institutionalized by general acceptance of the norm of sovereignty. To infer from the lack of common government that the classical Western state system lacked accepted norms and practices is to caricature reality and to ignore what Bull and Wight referred to as international society.[26]

International institutions include organizations, formal rules (regimes), and informal conventions. The broad institutional issue to which traditional sovereignty was an appropriate response is how to preserve and extend order without having such severe demands placed on the institutions that they either collapse or produce more disorder. The key question is how well a set of institutions is adapted to underlying conditions, especially the nature and interests of the interacting units. The Westphalian system was well adapted, since the essential principle of sovereignty was consistent with the demand for freedom of action by states, relatively low levels of interdependence, and the desire of rulers to limit intervention that could jeopardize their control over their populations. As reductions in the cost of transportation increased the potential benefits from international trade, adaptations in the institution of sovereign statehood were made to permit powerful states to capture these gains. Colonialism enabled European states to capture such gains in the nineteenth century, but it was premised on the assumptions that intraimperial gains from trade would outweigh losses from interimperial barriers; that resistance by colonized peoples would be minimal; and that colonialism would retain legitimacy in the metropoles. By 1945 all of these premises were being challenged, not least in the United States. Oceanic hegemony, established first by Britain, then by the United States, constituted another response to the need for a set of enforceable rules to control opportunism, but it proved to be vulnerable to the consequences of its own success: the rapid growth of other countries and their resistance to hegemonic dominance. Yet as noted earlier, the restoration of traditional sovereignty would not create the basis for large-scale economic exchange under conditions of high interdependence. Fundamental contracting problems among sovereign states therefore generate a demand for international regimes: sets of formal and informal rules that facilitate cooperation among states.[27] Such regimes can facilitate mutually beneficial agreements – even though they fall far short of instituting rules that can guarantee the ex ante credibility of commitments.

Sovereignty under Conditions of High Interdependence

To judge from renewed debates about the concept, traditional notions of sovereignty seem to be undergoing quite dramatic change. On issues as diverse as ratification of the Maastricht Treaty for European integration and the role of the United Nations in Iraq, sovereignty has once again become a contested concept.

One way of thinking about this process has been articulated eloquently by Alexander Wendt, who puts forward the hypothesis that interactions among states are changing their concepts of identity and their fundamental interests. States will "internalize sovereignty norms," and this process of socialization will teach them that "they can afford to rely more on the institutional fabric of international society and less on individual national means" to achieve their objectives.[28] Georg Sørensen sees this process of socialization as breaking the neorealists' automatic link between anarchy and self-help.[29]

Wendt himself has modestly and perceptively acknowledged that the force of his argument depends on "how important interaction among states is for the constitution of their identities and interests."[30] Furthermore, for rational leaders to rely more on international institutions to maintain their interests, these institutions need to be relatively autonomous – that is, not easily manipulated by other states. Yet evidence seems plentiful that in contemporary pluralistic democracies, state interests reflect the views of dominant *domestic* coalitions, which are constituted increasingly on the basis of common interests with respect to the world political economy.[31] And the history of the European Community – the most fully elaborated and authoritative multilateral institution in modern history – demonstrates that states continue to use international institutions to achieve their own interests, even at the expense of their partners.

At a more basic theoretical level, no one has yet convincingly traced the microfoundations of a socialization argument: how and why those individuals with influence over state policy would eschew the use of the state as agent for their specific interests in order to enable it to conform to norms that some self-constituted authorities proclaimed to be valid. The only major attempt in recent centuries to found an international institution on untested belief – the League of Nations – was a tragic failure. The League could only have succeeded if governments had genuinely believed that peace was indivisible and that this belief was shared sufficiently by others that it would be safe to rely "on the institutional fabric of international society." But in fact, that belief was not shared by key elites, and in light of long experience with the weakness of international institutions, it is hard to blame them.[32] Idealists hope to transmute positive beliefs into reality; but the conditions for the success of this strategy are daunting indeed.

Despite the wishful thinking that seems to creep into idealistic institutionalism, its proponents usefully remind us that sovereign statehood is an institution whose meaning is not fixed but has indeed changed over time. And they have shown convincingly that sovereignty has never been simply a reflection, at the level of the state, of international anarchy, despite Kenneth Waltz's definition, which equates sovereignty with autonomy.[33] If idealistic institutionalism does not provide an answer to questions about the evolution of sovereignty, it certainly helps open the door to a discussion of these issues.

I propose a rational-institutionalist interpretation of changes in sovereignty. Just as cooperation sometimes emerges from discord, so may intensified conflict under conditions of interdependence fundamentally affect the concept of sovereignty and its functions. The concept of sovereignty that emerges, however, may be very different in different parts of the world: no linear notion of progress seems applicable here. In this section I will just sketch the argument for changes in sovereignty under conditions of complex interdependence.

Sovereignty has been most thoroughly transformed in the European Community (EC). The legal supremacy of community over national law makes the EC fundamentally different, in juridical terms, from other international organizations. Although national governments dominate the decisionmaking process in Europe, they do so within an institutional context involving the pooling and sharing of sovereignty, and in conjunction with a commission that has a certain degree of independence. As in the United States, it is difficult to identify "the sovereign institution" in the European Community: There is no single institutional expression of the EC's will. Yet unlike in the United States, the constituent parts retain the right to veto amendments to the constitutional document (in the EC case the Treaty of Rome), and there is little doubt that secession from the community would not be resisted by force. So the European Community is not by any means a sovereign state, although it is an unprecedented hybrid, for which the traditional conception of sovereignty is no longer applicable.[34]

Interdependence is characterized by continual discord within and between countries, since the interests of individuals, groups, and firms are often at odds with one another. As global economic competition among sectors continues to increase, so will policy contention. Indeed, such discord reflects the responsiveness of democracies to constituency interests. A stateless competitive world market economy, in which people as well as factors of production could move freely, would be extremely painful for many residents of rich countries: the quasi-rents they now receive as a result of their geographical location would disappear. Matters would be even worse for people not protected by powerful governments who had to face economic agents wielding concentrated power or supported by state policy. It is not surprising, therefore, that people around the world expect protective action from their governments – and in Europe from the European Community and its institutions – and that free trade is more a liberal aspiration than a reality. In a bargaining situation, concentrating resources is valuable, and only the state can solve the collective-action problem for millions of individuals. Hence as global competition intensifies with technological change and the decline of natural barriers to exchange, public institutions are likely to be used in an increasing variety of ways to provide advantages for their constituents. In most of the world, the state is the key institution: The state is by no means dead. In Europe, supranational and intergovernmental institutions play a significant role, along with states. Economic conflict between the EC and other major states, and among states (within and outside the EC) is likely to be accentuated by the end of the Cold War, which has reduced incentives to cooperate on economic issues for the sake of political solidarity.[35]

The mixture to be expected of multilateral cooperation and tough interstate bargaining is exemplified by recent patterns in international trade. During the 1980s the GATT dispute-settlement procedure was more actively employed than ever in the past; and it frequently led to the settlement of trade issues.[36] Furthermore, the Uruguay Round of GATT will subject many service sectors and agriculture to multilateral regulation to which they have not been subject previously and should thus lead to substantial liberalization of world trade. However, bilateralism appears to have grown during the 1980s with the negotiation of formal bilateral agreements by the United States as well as the maintenance of so-called voluntary export restraints and the use of bilateral agreements to resolve issues on which major countries such as the United States have taken aggressive unilateral action. Between 10 and 20 percent of OECD imports are subject to nontariff measures; in some sectors such as textiles the figures approach 50 percent. In December 1993 the Uruguay Round GATT negotiations were brought to a successful conclusion after having continued for almost three years beyond their original deadline of December 1990. But we simultaneously observe increases in globalization and in mercantilist policy.[37] Yet I expect that the OECD democracies will continue to have sufficient interest in securing the benefits of the international division of labor such that full-scale economic warfare, much less military conflict, will remain unlikely.

Under these conditions of complex interdependence, and even outside of the institutions of the EC, the meaning of sovereignty changes. Sovereignty no longer enables states to exert effective supremacy over what occurs within their territories: Decisions are made by firms on a global basis, and other states' policies have major impacts within one's own boundaries. Reversing this process would be catastrophic for investment, economic growth, and electoral success. What sovereignty does confer on states under conditions of complex interdependence is legal authority that can either be exercised to the detriment of other states' interests or be bargained away in return for influence over others' policies and therefore greater gains from exchange. Rather than connoting the exercise of supremacy within a given territory, sovereignty provides the state with a legal grip on an aspect of a transnational process, whether involving multinational investment, the world's ecology, or the movement of migrants, drug dealers, and terrorists. *Sovereignty is less a territorially defined barrier than a bargaining resource for a politics characterized by complex transnational networks.* Although this shift in the function of sovereignty is a result of interdependence, it does not necessarily reduce discord, since there are more bargaining issues between states that are linked by multiple channels of contact than between those with barriers between them. Such discord takes place within a context from which military threats are excluded as a policy option, but distributional bargaining is tough and continuous.

I suggest, therefore, that within the OECD area the principle and practice of sovereignty are being modified quite dramatically in response to changes in international interdependence and the character of international institutions. In the European Community the relevant changes in international institutions have a juridical dimension; indeed, one implication of European Community law is that bargaining away sovereignty to the EC may be effectively irreversible, since the EC takes over the authority formerly reserved to states. In other parts of the OECD area, states accept limits on their formerly sovereign authority as a result of agreeing to multilateral regimes with less organizational or legal authority than the EC; and sovereignty may therefore be easier to recapture, albeit at a cost, in the future. In the aspiring democracies of Eastern Europe, some of my colleagues have recently observed a pattern of "anticipatory adaptation," by which one of these countries unilaterally adopts "norms associated with membership in an [international] organization prior to its actually being accorded full status in that organization."[38] We can understand the pattern of often conflictual cooperation among the economically advanced democracies as one of "cooperation under anarchy" if we are very careful about what anarchy means, but it may be more useful to see it as a question of institutional change.[39] The institution of sovereign statehood, which was well adapted for the Westphalian system, is being modified, although not superseded, in response to the interests of participants in a rapidly internationalizing political economy.

Zones of Peace and Conflict: a Partially Hobbesian World

Unfortunately, the institutionalist solution to Hobbes's dilemma is difficult to implement both domestically and internationally.

[...]

What seems [...] likely is that domestic and international political institutions will remain highly varied in form, strength, and function in different parts of the world. The OECD area, or much of it, will remain characterized by complex interdependence. Nationalism may be strengthened in some countries but will not threaten the status of the OECD area as a zone of peace in which pluralistic conflict management is successfully institutionalized. International regimes will continue to provide networks of rules for the management of both interstate and transnational relationships, although increased economic competition is likely to both limit the growth of these regimes and provide grounds for sharp disagreements about how their rules should be applied. The domestic institutional basis for these regimes will be provided by the maintenance of pluralist, constitutional democracies that will not fight each other, whose governments are not monolithic, and between which there is sufficient confidence that agreements can be made.[40] As argued in the previous section, sovereignty is likely, in these areas, to serve less as a justification of centralized territorial control and a barrier to intervention and more as a bargaining tool for influence over transnational networks. It will be bargained away in somewhat different ways within different contexts involving security, economic issues, arrangements for political authority, and cultural linkages among countries.[41]

In other parts of the world complex interdependence will not necessarily prevail. Some of these areas may be moving toward a situation in which force is not employed and in which the domestic conditions for democracy are emerging: This seems to be true in much of East Asia and Latin America. In others relatively stable patterns of authoritarian rule may emerge or persist. For much of the developing world, therefore, some shift toward sovereignty as a bargaining resource in transnational networks will be observable. For instance, the developing countries were able to use their ability to withhold consent to the Montreal Protocol on depletion of the ozone layer to secure a small fund to facilitate the transition to production of less harmful substitutes for chlorofluorocarbons (CFCs).[42]

In much of the former Soviet Union and in parts of Africa, the Middle East, and Asia, however, neither domestic institutions nor prospects of economic gain are likely to provide sufficient incentives for international cooperation. In these zones of conflict, military conflict will be common. The loyalties of populations of states may be divided, as in Bosnia, along ethnic or national lines, and no state may command legitimacy. Secessionist movements may prompt intervention from abroad, as in Georgia. Governments of neighboring countries may regard shifts of power in nearby states as threatening to them and be prompted therefore to intervene to prevent these changes. New balances of power and alliances, offensive as well as defensive, may emerge in a classic and often bloody search for power and order. Since traditional security risks – involving fears of cross-border attacks, civil wars, and intervention – will remain paramount, sovereignty will remain highly territorial and the evolution toward sovereignty as a bargaining resource in transnational relations that is taking place in the OECD area will be retarded. Intervention and chaos may even ensue.[43]

We do not know precisely which regions, much less countries, will be characterized by endemic strife. On the basis of past conflict or ethnic division, the Middle East, much of Africa, the southern tier of the former Soviet Union, and parts of South Asia would seem to be in the greatest danger.

[...]

Conclusion

Globalization and the end of the Cold War have created a new situation in world politics. In some ways, the new world is more like traditional world politics than was the world from 1945 to the mid-1980s: Political alignments will become more fragmented and fluid, and economic competition will not be muted by alliance cooperation. In other respects, however, the new world will be very different from the world before World War II. Globalization seems irreversible with all its implications for the permeability of borders and the transformation of sovereignty among the economically advanced democracies; and international institutions have become central to the political and military as well as the economic policies of the major states.[44]

Yet Hobbes's dilemma cannot be ignored. Without well-developed constitutional institutions, the alternatives in many countries lie between anarchy and predation, neither of which is attractive. The extensive patterns of agreement characteristic of complex interdependence depend on pluralist democratic institutions. Less ambitious forms of world order, relatively peaceful but not necessarily so cooperative, depend on stable domestic institutions, although whether they depend on democracy is not yet entirely clear. At any rate, predatory authoritarian states are likely to become involved in international conflict, and intensely divided states are particularly prone to do so. The latter are likely targets for intervention by the former. It seems unlikely not only that democracy will sweep the world but also that all states will be governed by stable institutions, even authoritarian ones. Hence "world order" does not seem to be impending: A global security community is unlikely soon to come into existence.

[...]

The key problem of world order now is to seek to devise institutional arrangements that are consistent both with key features of international relations and the new shape of domestic politics in key countries. It will be very difficult to construct such institutions. They must be built not only by governments but by international civil society under conditions of globalization. They must be constructed not by a single hegemonic power but by several countries whose interests conflict in multiple ways. Nevertheless, among advanced democracies appropriate institutions could facilitate political and economic exchange by reducing transaction costs, providing information, and making commitments credible. The resulting benefits will accrue not only to governments but to transnational corporations and professional societies, and to some workers as well, in both developing and developed countries. But adjustment costs will be high, hence there will be losers in the short run; there may also be long-run losers, since globalization will continue to put downward pressure on wages for those workers in developed countries who can be replaced by workers in poorer parts of the world or who compete in national labor markets with such workers. Hence domestic institutions that provide retraining, that spread the costs of adjustment, and perhaps that redistribute income on a continuing basis to globally disadvantaged groups will be essential corollaries to maintaining and strengthening international institutions in an age of globalization.

[...]

Social scientists viewing the new world order should be humble on two dimensions. Our failure to foresee the end of the Cold War should make us diffident about our ability to predict the future. And the weakness of our knowledge of the conditions for constitutional democracy and for peace should make us reluctant to propose radical new plans for global democratization or peacekeeping. Nevertheless, we can go beyond the Hobbesian solution to Hobbes's dilemma of anarchy and order: We can focus on how institutions embodying the proper incentives can create order without predation within societies, and how even much weaker international institutions can moderate violence and facilitate cooperation in international relations. Strong institutions cannot be suddenly created: Both constitutional democracy and a reciprocity-laden conception of sovereignty emerged over a period of centuries. Nevertheless, it is imperative to avoid the magnitude of violence and dysfunction that occurred in the West. We should encourage the creation and maintenance of institutions, domestic and international, that provide incentives for the moderation of conflict, coherent decisionmaking to provide collective goods, and the promotion of economic growth. It is in such lasting institutions that our hopes for the future lie.

Notes

1   Joanne Gowa, "Bipolarity, Multipolarity and Free Trade," *American Political Science Review* 83(4) (Dec. 1989): 1245–56.
2   US House, Special Committee on Post-War Economic Policy and Planning, *Hearings* (Washington DC: GPO, 1945), p. 1082. Cited in Gabriel Kolko, *The Politics of War: The World and United States Foreign Policy, 1943–1945* (New York: Vintage Books of Random House, 1968), p. 254.
3   Kenneth N. Waltz, *Theory of International Politics* (Reading, Mass.: Addison Wesley, 1979).
4   Thucydides, *The Peloponnesian War*, Book 3, paras 81–2.
5   On the "realist trap," see Robert O. Keohane, "Theory of World Politics: Structural Realism and Beyond," in Keohane, *International Institutions and State Power: Essays in International Relations Theory* (Boulder: Westview Press, 1989), pp. 35–73, esp. pp. 65–6.
6   Hans-Henrik Holm and Georg Sørensen, "A New World Order: The Withering Away of Anarchy and the Triumph of Individualism? Consequences for IR-Theory," *Cooperation and Conflict* 28(3) (1993): 265–301.
7   For this definition, see Keohane, *International Institutions and State Power*, pp. 3–7 and ch. 7.
8   Robert O. Keohane and Joseph S. Nye, Jr, *Power and Interdependence: World Politics in Transition* (Boston: Little, Brown, 1977 and 1989).
9   Thomas Hobbes, *Leviathan* (Paris, 1651), Book 1, ch. 13.
10 Martin Wight, *International Theory: The Three Traditions* (New York: Holmes & Meier, 1992), p. 35.
11 *Leviathan*, part 2, ch. 17.
12 *Leviathan*, part 1, ch. 13.
13 John M. Herz, *International Politics in the Atomic Age* (New York: Columbia University Press, 1959).

14 Evan Luard, *War in International Society* (New Haven: Yale University Press, 1987), p. 247, says that perhaps 40 percent of the rural and town population of Germany may have died, although this estimate may be too high. On battle deaths, see Charles Tilly, *Coercion, Capital and European States, AD 990–1990* (Oxford: Blackwell, 1990), p. 165.

15 Sovereign statehood in my view has helped shape states' conceptions of self-interest. For instance, great-power intervention in Africa during the Cold War was focused on helping the great power's clients gain power within unified states, rather than on promoting fragmentation. The one major attempt to change boundaries by war – Somalia's invasion of Ethiopia in the late 1970s – led to withdrawal of US support for Somalian military actions and a resounding defeat. For an astute analysis, see Robert H. Jackson and Carl G. Rosberg, "Why Africa's Weak States Persist: The Empirical and the Juridical in Statehood," *World Politics* 35(1) (Oct. 1982): 1–24.

16 See Margaret Levi, *Of Rule and Revenue* (Berkeley: University of California Press, 1988), esp. ch. 1.

17 Douglass C. North and Robert Paul Thomas, *The Rise of the Western World* (Cambridge: Cambridge University Press, 1973), pp. 2–3.

18 Charles P. Kindleberger, *A Financial History of Western Europe* (London: Allen and Unwin, 1984); Douglass C. North and Barry R. Weingast, "Constitutions and Commitment: The Evolution of Institutions Governing Public Choice in Seventeenth-Century England," *Journal of Economic History* 49(4) (Dec. 1989): 803–32.

19 F. H. Hinsley, *Sovereignty*, 2nd edn (Cambridge: Cambridge University Press, 1986), p. 1.

20 Bernard Bailyn, *The Ideological Origins of the American Revolution* (Cambridge: Belknap Press of Harvard University Press, 1967), pp. 201–29.

21 Madison to Jefferson, October 24, 1787, J. P. Boyd (ed.), *The Papers of Thomas Jefferson* (Princeton: Princeton University Press, 1955), pp. 278–9.

22 Hans J. Morgenthau, *Politics among Nations*, 4th edn (New York: Knopf, 1967), p. 305.

23 Stephen D. Krasner, "Westphalia and All That," draft chapter (Oct. 1992) for Judith Goldstein and Robert O. Keohane (eds), *Ideas and Foreign Policy: Beliefs, Institutions and Political Change* (Ithaca: Cornell University Press, 1993).

24 Wight, *International Theory*, pp. 2–3.

25 Hedley Bull, *The Anarchical Society* (New York: Columbia University Press, 1977), pp. 34–7. Martin Wight makes this connection between sovereignty and reciprocity explicit by saying that "reciprocity was inherent in the Western conception of sovereignty." *Systems of States* (Leicester: Leicester University Press, 1977), p. 135.

26 One difficulty with realist characterizations of anarchy is that they conflate three different meanings of the terms: (1) lack of common government; (2) insignificance of institutions; and (3) chaos, or Hobbes's "war of all against all." Only the first meaning can be shown to be true in general of international relations. For a good discussion of anarchy in international relations, see Helen V. Milner, "The Assumption of Anarchy in International Relations Theory: A Critique," *Review of International Studies* 17(1) (Jan. 1991): 67–86.

27 Robert O. Keohane, *After Hegemony: Cooperation and Discord in the World Political Economy* (Princeton: Princeton University Press, 1984); Stephen D. Krasner (ed.), *International Regimes* (Ithaca: Cornell University Press, 1982). Note that a demand for international regimes does not create its own supply; hence a functional theory does not imply, incorrectly, that efficient institutions always emerge or that we live in the (institutionally) best of all possible worlds.

28 Alexander Wendt, "Anarchy Is What States Make of It," *International Organization* 46(2) (Spring 1992): 414–15.

29 Georg Sørensen, "The Limits of Neorealism: Western Europe after the Cold War," paper presented at the Nordic International Studies Association (NISA) Inaugural Conference, Oslo, Aug. 18–19, 1993, p. 9.

30 Wendt, "Anarchy Is What States Make of It," p. 423.

31 Peter J. Katzenstein, *Small States in World Markets* (Ithaca: Cornell University Press, 1984); Peter Gourevitch, *Politics in Hard Times* (Ithaca: Cornell University Press, 1986); Helen V. Milner, *Resisting Protectionism* (Princeton: Princeton University Press, 1988); Ronald

Rogowski, *Commerce and Coalitions* (Princeton: Princeton University Press, 1989); Jeffry A. Frieden, "National Economic Policies in a World of Global Finance," *International Organization* 45(4) (Autumn 1991): 425–52; Andrew Moravcsik, "Liberalism and International Relations Theory," Working Paper, no. 92–6, Center for International Affairs, Harvard University, Oct. 1992.

32   See Inis L. Claude, *Power and International Relations* (New York: Random House, 1962).

33   For Waltz a sovereign state "decides for itself how it will cope with its internal and external problems." That is, sovereignty is the equivalent of self-help, which derives from anarchy. Waltz, *Theory of International Politics*, p. 96. A brilliant critique of Waltz's failure to incorporate a historical dimension in his theory is by John Gerard Ruggie, "Continuity and Transformation in the World Polity: Toward a Neorealist Synthesis," *World Politics* 35 (Jan. 1983): 261–85. For Ruggie's chapter, other commentaries, and a reply by Waltz, see Robert O. Keohane (ed.), *Neorealism and its Critics* (New York: Columbia University Press, 1986).

34   For general discussions see Robert O. Keohane and Stanley Hoffmann, *The New European Community: Decisionmaking and Institutional Change* (Boulder: Westview Press, 1991); and Alberta M. Sbragia (ed.), *Europolitics: Institutions and Policymaking in the "New" European Community* (Washington DC: Brookings, 1992). On the European Court of Justice and neofunctional theory, see Anne-Marie Burley and Walter Mattli, "Europe Before the Court: A Political Theory of Legal Integration," *International Organization* 47(1) (Winter 1993): 41–76. It is not clear that the Maastricht Treaty, even if ratified, will fundamentally alter practices relating to sovereignty in the EC. On Maastricht, see Wayne Sandholtz, "Choosing Union: Monetary Politics and Maastricht," *International Organization* 47(1) (Winter 1993): 1–40.

35   For a general argument about the "security externalities" of agreements to open borders to free trade, see Gowa, "Bipolarity, Multipolarity and Free Trade."

36   Robert E. Hudec, Daniel L. M. Kennedy, and Mark Sgarabossa, "A Statistical Profile of GATT Dispute Settlement Cases: 1948–1990," MS, University of Minnesota Law School, 1992.

37   See Helge Hveem, "Hegemonic Rivalry and Antagonistic Interdependence: Bilateralism and the Management of International Trade," paper presented at the First Pan-European Conference in International Studies, Heidelberg, Sept. 16–20, 1992. His figures come from the UNCTAD database on trade control measures. On p. 16 Hveem quotes Robert Gilpin about the "complementary development" of globalization and mercantilism, citing "The Transformation of the International Political Economy," *Jean Monnet Chair Papers* (European Policy Unit at the European University Institute, Firenze).

38   Stephan Haggard, Marc A. Levy, Andrew Moravcsik, and Kalypso Nicolaides, "Integrating the Two Halves of Europe: Theories of Interests, Bargaining and Institutions," in Robert O. Keohane, Joseph S. Nye, and Stanley Hoffmann (eds), *After the Cold War: International Institutions and State Strategies in Europe, 1989–1991* (Cambridge, Mass.: Harvard University Press, 1993), p. 182.

39   Kenneth A. Oye (ed.), *Cooperation under Anarchy* (Princeton: Princeton University Press, 1986).

40   Democratic pluralism is necessary for the multiple channels of contact between societies characteristic of complex interdependence. With respect to restraints on the use of force, it seems clear from the large literature on democracy and war that democracies have rarely, if ever (depending on one's definition), fought one another, although they vigorously fight nondemocracies. However, nondemocracies have often been at peace with one another, so democracy is certainly not necessary to peace. Furthermore, until recently democracies have been relatively few and either scattered or allied against a common enemy (or both); so the empirical evidence for the causal impact of mutual democracy is weak. Among the OECD countries peace seems ensured by a combination of mutual economic and political interests, lack of territorial conflict, and mutual democracy. On theoretical grounds, however, no one has yet succeeded in showing that mutual democracy is sufficient: to do so, one would have to develop and test a convincing theory of why democracies should not fight one another. For

some of this literature, see Michael Doyle, "Kant, Liberal Legacies and Foreign Affairs," *Philosophy and Public Affairs* 12 (1983): 205–35 and 323–53 (two-part article); Zeev Maos and Nasrin Abdolali, "Regime Types and International Conflict," *Journal of Conflict Resolution* 33 (1989): 3–35; and Georg Sørensen, "Kant and Processes of Democratization: Consequences for Neorealist Thought," *Journal of Peace Research* 29 (1992): 397–414. My thinking on this issue has been affected by a stimulating talk given at the Harvard Center for International Affairs by Professor Joanne Gowa of Princeton University on May 6, 1993, and by a just-completed Ph.D. dissertation at Harvard University by John Owen on sources of "democratic peace."

41 My characterization of emerging patterns of world politics has much in common with the stimulating discussion of "plurilateralism" offered by Philip G. Cerny in "Plurilateralism: Structural Differentiation and Functional Conflict in the Post–Cold War World Order," *Millennium: Journal of International Studies* 22 (Spring 1993): 27–52.

42 Edward A. Parson, "Protecting the Ozone Layer," in Peter M. Haas, Robert O. Keohane, and Marc A. Levy (eds), *Institutions for the Earth: Sources of Effective International Environmental Protection* (Cambridge, Mass.: MIT Press, 1993), pp. 49–50.

43 For a similar argument, contrasting a liberal core and a realist periphery, see James M. Goldgeier and Michael McFaul, "A Tale of Two Worlds: Core and Periphery in the Post–Cold War Era," *International Organization* 46(1) (Spring 1992): 467–92.

44 On international institutions, see Keohane, Nye, and Hoffmann, *After the Cold War*.

10

Compromising Westphalia

Stephen D. Krasner

The Peace of Westphalia, which ended the Thirty Years' War in 1648, is taken to mark the beginning of the modern international system as a universe composed of sovereign states, each with exclusive authority within its own geographic boundaries. The Westphalian model, based on the principles of autonomy and territory, offers a simple, arresting, and elegant image. It orders the minds of policymakers. It is an analytic assumption for neo-realism and neo-liberal institutionalism, both of which posit that states can be treated as if they were autonomous, unified, rational actors. It is an empirical regularity for various sociological and constructivist theories of international politics. Moreover, it is a benchmark for observers who discern a basic erosion of sovereignty in the contemporary world.

This article demonstrates, however, that the Westphalian model has never been an accurate description of many of the entities that have been called states. The assumption that states are independent rational actors can be misleading because it marginalizes many situations in which rulers have, in fact, not been autonomous. Moreover, the conclusion that sovereignty is now being altered because the principles of Westphalia are being transgressed is historically myopic. Breaches of the Westphalian model have been an enduring characteristic of the international environment because there is nothing to prevent them. Rulers have chosen or been forced to accept other principles, including human rights, minority rights, democracy, communism, and fiscal responsibility. There has never been some golden age of the Westphalian state. The Westphalian model has never been more than a reference point or a convention; it has never been some deeply confining structure from which actors could not escape.

The Westphalian state is a system of political authority based on territory and autonomy. Territoriality means that political authority is exercised over a defined geographic space rather than, for instance, over people, as would be the case in a tribal form of political order. Autonomy means that no external actor enjoys authority within the borders of the state. Territorial violations of the Westphalian model involve the creation of authority structures that are not coterminous with geographic borders. Examples include the British Commonwealth (but not colonial empires in which authority and territory are coterminous, even if tracts of land are not contiguous), the European Union, Antarctica, Andorra, and the Exclusive Economic Zone (EEZ) for the oceans. Some authoritative actions within a given territory are decided by actors within that territory, but others are decided by extra-territorial entities, such as the European Court. Most of these efforts to create authority structures that transcend territory have failed, but that has not deterred statesmen from inventing new institutional forms: the Westphalian model has not constrained the imagination.

Violations of the principle of autonomy, in which an external actor is able to exercise some authoritative control within the territory of a state, have been more frequent than those of territoriality, but not always as obvious. The most modest way in which autonomy can be compromised is if some external actor alters conceptions of legitimate action that are held by groups within a given polity.[1] Autonomy can also be transgressed if rulers agree to governance structures that are controlled by external actors, or if more powerful actors impose institutions, policies, or personnel on weaker states. Examples of transgressions of autonomy include the influence of the Catholic Church on attitudes about the legitimacy of birth control and abortion, bondholders' committees that regulated financial activities in some Balkan states and elsewhere in the nineteenth century, International Monetary Fund (IMF) conditionality accepted by some developing countries since the 1960s, protectorates in which major powers control foreign but not domestic policy, provisions for the treatment of minorities imposed on central and eastern European states after the first Balkan Wars and World War I, and the constitutional structure of regimes in Soviet satellites during the Cold War.

Compromises of Westphalia have occurred in four ways – through conventions, contracting, coercion, and imposition. These four modalities are distinguished by whether the behavior of one actor depends on that of another and by whether at least one of the actors is better off and none worse off. In conventions, rulers enter into agreements, such as human rights accords, from which they expect some gain, but their behavior is not contingent on what others do. In contracting, rulers agree to violate Westphalian principles, but only if they are provided some benefit, such as a foreign loan. In coercion, the rulers of stronger states make weaker ones worse off by engaging in credible threats to which the target might or might not acquiesce. In imposition, the target is so weak that it has no option but to comply with the preferences of the stronger.

Conventions, contracts, coercion, and imposition have all been enduring patterns of behavior in the international system, and thus many states have not conformed to the Westphalian model. Every major peace treaty since 1648 – Westphalia, Utrecht, Vienna, Versailles, and Helsinki – has violated the Westphalian model in one way or another. Compromising the Westphalian model is always available as a policy option because there is no authority structure to prevent it: nothing can preclude rulers from transgressing against the domestic autonomy of other states or creating authority structures that transcend territory.

In the international system, institutions are less constraining and more fluid, more subject to challenge and change than in more settled circumstances. The mechanisms for locking in particular institutional forms, such as socialization, positive reinforcement between structures and agents, or path-dependent processes, are weaker at the international level than in well-established domestic polities. This is even true for the Westphalian state which is taken to be the core institutional form of the modern international system. In international politics, nothing is ever off the table.

Rather than being regarded as an empirical regularity in which territoriality and autonomy are accurate descriptions of most if not all states, or as an analytic assumption that regards central decision-makers as capable of independently formulating policies subject only to constraints imposed by the international system, the Westphalian model is better conceptualized as a convention or reference point that might or might not determine the behavior of policymakers who are also motivated by material interests, security, and national ideals, and whose ability to influence outcomes depends upon their power. All states are not the same. Some have closely approximated the Westphalian model. Others have not. Some non-Westphalian forms of political organization, such as empires, tribes, and trading leagues, have disappeared, but at the same time the principles of Westphalia are frequently ignored.[2]

The following section of this article traces some of the confusion about the nature of sovereignty to the fact that the term has been used in several different ways. Then the mechanisms through which the principles of territoriality and autonomy have been violated – conventions, contracting, coercion, and imposition – are explicated. This is followed by a discussion of why the Westphalian model has both persisted and been frequently violated. In the conclusion, I argue that it would be constructive to recognize how fragile the Westphalian model has been, not only because violations of the principles of territoriality and autonomy will take place in any event, but also because compromising Westphalia is sometimes the best way to achieve peace and stability.

The Westphalian Model and Other Versions of Sovereignty

One of the reasons that observers have been so quick to point to changes in the nature of sovereignty is that the term has been used in at least three different ways in addition to the Westphalian model. First, students of comparative politics have focused on both the degree of control exercised by public entities and the organization of authority within territorial boundaries. For instance, the inability of the central institutions to regulate economic activities or to maintain order has been described as a loss of sovereignty. The site of public authority – for instance, with the populace, a hereditary monarch, or an oligarchy – has been defined as the location of sovereignty.

Second, sovereignty has been comprehended as if it were synonymous with the degree of control exercised by public authorities over transborder movements. This is a meaning frequently employed by scholars working from a liberal interdependence perspective.[3] The inability to regulate the flow of goods, persons, and ideas across territorial boundaries has been described as a loss of sovereignty.

Third, sovereignty has been understood as the right of certain actors to enter into international agreements. This is the concept used in international legal scholarship. Sovereign states can make treaties.[4]

Finally, sovereignty has been understood as the Westphalian model: an institutional arrangement for organizing political life that is based on territoriality and autonomy. States exist in specific territories. Within these territories, domestic political authorities are the only arbiters of legitimate behavior. A Westphalian state system is different from an empire, in which there is only one authority structure; it is different from tribes, in which authority is claimed over groups of individuals but not necessarily over specific geographic areas; it is different from European feudalism, where the Catholic Church claimed authority over some kinds of activities regardless of their location; and it is different from a system in which authority structures over different issue areas are not geographically coterminous, one possible description of the European Union.

These four conceptions of sovereignty are distinct, but changes in the parameters of one can lead to changes in the parameters of others. For instance, if central authorities in a state have lost control over activities within their boundaries (a loss of sovereignty as understood by some students of comparative politics), it is more likely that external actors would be able to compromise the autonomy of the state (a loss of sovereignty according to the Westphalian model). Actors in other states could influence the expectations and sense of legitimacy of groups within the civil society of the weaker state. Rulers could surrender legitimate control in exchange for external support. Rulers in more powerful states could coerce or impose changes on rulers who were no longer able to extract resources from their domestic population.

In another example, an inability to control transborder flows (a loss of sovereignty as understood from a liberal interdependence perspective) could lead to contractual arrangements that compromise the autonomy of the state (a violation of the Westphalian model). Changes in technology, especially reductions in the cost of transportation and communication, have created a more integrated global economy and made it more difficult for states to regulate the international movement of goods, capital, ideas, and labor. To enhance their regulatory capacity, rulers may enter into contractual agreements in which they assent to constraints on their own behavior in exchange for similar obligations being accepted by others.[5] Autonomy (one principle of Westphalian sovereignty) may or may not be transgressed by such constraints, depending on whether attitudes about legitimate behavior are changed or whether institutions, personnel, and policy become subject to external authority. For instance, the Basle agreement of 1987, which specified the ways in which capital would be calculated within the banking systems of the major industrialized countries, did not compromise autonomy, even though it did alter domestic policy.[6] In contrast, arrangements within the European Union such as mutual recognition, which allows entities operating in one state to be governed by the laws of another, have violated the Westphalian model.[7] Individual states retain the formal right to renounce the Union (thus there is no breach of the international legal understanding of sovereignty), but the costs would be very high.

More generally, agreements that are voluntarily entered into by rulers, what I have termed contracts and conventions, would never violate the international law definition of sovereignty, but could violate the Westphalian model if they compromised the autonomy of the state, whether in modest ways by altering domestic views of legitimate behavior, as did the Helsinki accords in eastern Europe, or in more decisive ways by subjecting domestic institutional arrangements, personnel, or policies to the scrutiny of or control by external actors, as has been the case for some IMF stand-by agreements.[8] Whether or not a voluntary agreement, a contract, or a convention violates the Westphalian model is an empirical question.

Finally, situations in which rulers in one country have been compelled by coercion or imposition to alter their domestic institutions, personnel, or policies would violate both international law conceptions of sovereignty and the Westphalian model. For example, the would-be rulers of eastern Europe after World War I had no choice but to accept the conditions for the treatment of minorities that were imposed on them by the victorious powers. Latin American countries subjected to gunboat diplomacy around the turn of the century had no choice but to dedicate some of their state revenues to refunding international obligations.

Whether sovereignty is understood as the organization and efficacy of domestic authority structures, the ability to exercise control over transborder movements, the right to enter into international agreements, or an institutional structure characterized by territoriality and autonomy depends upon the analytic constructs and empirical concerns of particular analysts. There is no single definition of sovereignty because the meaning of the term depends on the theoretical context within which it is being used.

The Westphalian model is a basic concept for some of the major theoretical approaches to international relations, including neo-realism and neo-liberal institutionalism, for both of which it is an analytic assumption, as well as international society perspectives, for which it is an empirical regularity. For neo-realism, the ontological givens in the international system are Westphalian states, understood as unitary rational actors operating in an anarchic setting and striving to enhance their well-being and security. These states are constrained only by the external environment, that is, by the power of other states. Realism does not suppose that all states can guarantee their autonomy. If, however, a state loses its autonomy – if, for instance, its political structures and personnel are chosen by others – then neo-realism has nothing to say about how such penetrated non-Westphalian states might act. The relations between Czechoslovakia and the Soviet Union after the Prague Spring of 1968, for instance, are not amenable to realist analysis. Czechoslovakia was not responding to external constraints, as an autonomous or Westphalian state might. Its policies were dictated by externally imposed constitutional structures and personnel.

Similarly, the Westphalian model is an analytic assumption for neo-liberal institutionalism.[9] The actors are assumed to be Westphalian states, unified rational autonomous entities striving to maximize their utility in the face of constraints that emanate from an anarchic although interdependent international environment. What distinguishes neo-liberalism from neo-realism is its different understanding of the characteristic problem for these Westphalian states: for neo-liberal institutionalism, the problem is the resolution of market failures, whereas for neo-realism it is security and distributional conflicts.[10]

The Westphalian model is also a core concept for international society approaches, most notably the English school and various constructivist approaches.[11] Here the Westphalian model is understood as a behavioral regularity based on shared understandings rather than as an analytic assumption. All participants in international society – public officials, diplomats, statesmen, political leaders – hold the same fundamental views about the nature of the system, the actors, and how they behave. Modern international society is composed of territorial units within which public institutions exercise exclusive authority. Actions follow particular patterns not because they are dictated by some higher authority, or coerced by the threat of force, or constrained by the power of other states, but because players have a shared intersubjective understanding. The consequences of anarchy itself are socially constructed. The role of sovereign states permits some kinds of activities but not others. The rules of sovereignty give states full autonomy over activities within their own borders and prohibit intervention in the internal affairs of other states.

The Westphalian model is an excellent starting point for analyzing (neo-realism or neo-liberal institutionalism) or understanding (international society perspectives) much of what goes on in the international environment. A great deal of what takes place is completely consistent with the Westphalian model, whether it is treated as an analytic assumption or behavioral regularity generated by intersubjective shared understanding: the claims of external actors are rebuffed; authoritative decision-makers declare war, form alliances, enter into trade agreements, and regulate migration.

As this article demonstrates, however, there are many other situations in which territoriality or autonomy has been violated. Some are the result of an inability to control either transborder flows or domestic behavior, leading rulers to conclude contractual arrangements that are consistent with international legal understandings of sovereignty, but which violate the Westphalian model by compromising domestic autonomy or establishing new institutional arrangements that transcend territoriality. Some are the result of major powers imposing personnel, policies, or institutions on weaker states, a situation that violates both the Westphalian model and the view of states as entities capable of entering into voluntary accords.

Rulers have always had the option of violating Westphalian principles. The assertion that the contemporary system represents a basic transformation because sovereignty seems to be so much at risk is not well-founded: it ignores the fact that violations of the principles of territoriality and autonomy have been an enduring characteristic of the international system both before and after the Peace of Westphalia.

Compromising Territoriality and Autonomy

The principles of autonomy or territoriality can be breached through conventions, contracts, coercion, or imposition. The four modalities through which autonomy and territoriality can be compromised are distinguished by whether they are pareto-improving or not, and contingent or not. Conventions and contracts are pareto-improving, that is, they make at least one party better off without making anyone worse off. Rulers are not forced into such arrangements. They enter them voluntarily because compromising Westphalian principles is more attractive than honoring them. Coercion and imposition leave at least one of the actors worse off; they are thus not pareto-improving. Contracts and coercion involve contingent behavior; the actions of one ruler depend upon what the other does. Conventions and imposition do not involve contingent behavior. Given the many opportunities and incentives to violate Westphalian principles, it is not surprising that many states have existed with either their territoriality or autonomy compromised.

Conventions

Conventions are agreements in which rulers make commitments that expose their own policies to some kind of external scrutiny by agreeing to follow certain domestic practices.[12] Signatories might, for instance, endorse liberal conceptions of human rights, or agree to hold regular elections, or stipulate that religious or ethnic identity would not affect the franchise or opportunities for employment, or that refugees would be entitled to specific social security benefits and educational opportunities.

Conventions are entered into voluntarily. They make at least one actor better off without making any worse off; if they did not, rulers would not sign them, since the status quo would still be available. The signatories do not usually secure any direct gain except the pledge from other parties to the agreement that they will behave in the same way. The willingness of a particular state to abide by a convention is not contingent on the behavior of others. Some rulers can violate a convention without prompting any change in the domestic policies or institutions of others.

In the contemporary world, the most obvious class of conventions is that of human rights accords. Human rights agreements cover relations between rulers and ruled, including both citizens and non-citizens. They involve pledges by national authorities to treat individuals within their territory in a certain way. As of 1993 the United Nations listed twenty-five such instruments.[13] Another compendium records forty-seven compacts including those associated with regional organizations and specialized agencies.[14]

[...]

Contracts

A contract is an agreement between the legitimate authorities in two or more states or state authorities and another international actor, such as an international financial institution, that is mutually acceptable, pareto-improving, and contingent. A contract can violate the Westphalian model if it alters domestic conceptions of legitimate behavior, subjects domestic institutions and personnel to external influence, or creates institutional arrangements that transcend national boundaries. Obviously, many contracts between states do not transgress the Westphalian model. An international agreement that obligates a state only to change some specific aspect of its foreign policy would not be a violation of autonomy, nor would a treaty that involved only a change in domestic policy but had no other consequences.

Rulers must believe that a contract makes them better off; otherwise they would not enter into it in the first place, since the status quo remains available. The behavior of one of the actors is contingent on the behavior of the others. In contractual arrangements, rulers would not compromise the autonomy or territorial authority of their state unless the behavior of others also changed: if one actor abrogates the contract the other would prefer to do so as well.

Compromising autonomy: sovereign lending

Historically, sovereign lending, especially to weaker states, has frequently involved contractual arrangements that compromise the autonomy although not the territoriality of the borrower. Borrowers have not simply agreed to repay their obligations, an arrangement that would have no impact on autonomy. Rather they have frequently agreed to dedicate specific revenues, or to accept oversight of domestic policies, or to permit revenues to be collected by foreign entities, or to change their domestic institutional structures.

[. . .]

Coercion and imposition

Coercion and imposition exist along a continuum determined by the costs of refusal for the target state. Coercion occurs when rulers in one state threaten to impose sanctions unless their counterparts in another compromise their domestic autonomy. The target can acquiesce or resist. Imposition occurs when the rulers or would-be rulers of a target state have no choice; they are so weak that they must accept domestic structures, policies, or personnel preferred by more powerful actors or else be eliminated. The higher the cost, the more a particular situation moves toward the pole of imposition. When applied against already established states, coercion and imposition are violations of the international law, as well as the Westphalian, conception of sovereignty. When applied against the would-be rulers of not yet created states, coercion and imposition are violations of the Westphalian model because the autonomy of any state that does emerge has been constrained by external actors, but are not violations of international law concepts of sovereignty, which only apply once a state has secured international recognition allowing it to enter into agreements with other states.

Unlike either conventions or contracts, coercion and imposition leave at least one actor worse off. The status quo, which the target prefers, is eliminated as an option by the initiating actor.

If one state successfully coerces or imposes on another changes in the latter's institutions, policies, or personnel, then the target is no longer a Westphalian state: its policy is constrained not simply by the external power of other states, but also by the ability of others to change the nature of the target's internal politics. (It is empirically unlikely that coercive activity would lead to changes in concepts of legitimacy held by domestic groups, something that does happen in the case of contracts and conventions.) Political leaders in the target state are not free to consider all possible policies because some options are precluded by externally imposed domestic structures, policies, or personnel. Indeed the rulers themselves might simply be the quislings of the dominant state.

Coercion and imposition, unlike conventions and contracts, always involve power asymmetry. Imposition entails forcing the target to do something that it would not otherwise do. Coercion requires threats of sanctions. The initiator must be better off if the target resists and the sanctions are imposed than if no threats were made at all, or else the threat would not be credible. Obviously, it is even more attractive for the sender if the target capitulates. The initiator has the ability to remove the status quo from the set of options available to the target.

[...]

Weakness and Persistence

The Westphalian model has persisted for a long period of time but has been frequently defeated. It has been both enduring and flimsy. In some instances, actors have merely given it lip service, sometimes not even that; in others, it has guided and constrained behavior. Yet it has not been replaced by some alternative conception of how the international system might be organized.

The Westphalian model is not a stable equilibrium: actors have frequently had both the incentive and power to deviate from it. It is not a generative grammar, producing individual entities (states) that replicate and reinforce the general model. It is not a constitutive rule like the rules of chess (if two players agree that bishops will move in a straight line, they are not playing chess): if a ruler agrees that domestic ethnic minorities will be given specific rights and that behavior will be monitored by external actors, or that financial affairs will be managed by a committee appointed by foreign bond-holders, or that external groups can oversee elections, this has not been viewed as an indication that some new form of political order has been developed.

[...]

Rather than being treated as an empirical regularity or as an analytic assumption, the Westphalian model can be more usefully understood as a reference point or convention. The Westphalian model has become common knowledge, but it has never been taken for granted in the sense of precluding the exploration or implementation of alternative arrangements. The autonomy of states has been compromised in a wide variety of ways because there is no structure of authority in the international system that can prevent stronger actors from engaging in imposition or coercion, or rulers in general from transgressing their own autonomy, as well as that of others, by entering into contracts and conventions. These violations of Westphalian principles are not a reflection of a breakdown of order; they are not like widespread criminality in the face of official impotence and corruption. Rather, transgressions against Westphalia have reflected the attraction of alternative principles as well as asymmetries of power. Violations of the Westphalian model, as well as the model itself, have been an enduring characteristic of international relations.

In practice, the strong have been better able to maintain their territorial integrity and autonomy than the weak. The United States, a powerful state almost from its inception, has closely conformed with the Westphalian model. The institutional structures and policies that emerged from the Revolutionary War were indigenously determined. The United States was too powerful to be subject to gunboat diplomacy during the nineteenth century, even though some of its public entities defaulted on their international obligations. Minority rights protections imposed on eastern Europe at the conclusion of World War I were not reciprocally accepted by US policymakers. The United States has signed relatively few human rights conventions, even though the highly individualistic conceptions of human rights developed after World War II reflected US values.

In contrast, weaker states have been more subject to external imposition and coercion and have been more likely to enter into contractual arrangements that violate their autonomy but not that of the other parties. All of the states that emerged from the Ottoman and Habsburg empires in the nineteenth and twentieth centuries were subject to some constraints on their institutional structures or policies. Whether forced to accept the minorities' protections of the Treaty of Berlin of 1878 or the Versailles settlement after World War I, the imposition of communist rule, or the political conditionality of the European Bank, not one of the states of eastern Europe created since the Napoleonic Wars has ever conformed with the Westphalian model.
[. . .]
Nevertheless, the model has persisted because it does serve some of the interests of some actors. It has traditionally been most vigorously championed by weaker states since they are the ones that are most subject to imposition, coercion, or limited contractual opportunities.[15] It has also been attractive for rulers in more powerful states because mutual recognition of the rule of non-intervention among the strong (but not necessarily with regard to the weak) has made it easier for them to maintain their domestic control.[16]

Given the anarchic nature of the international system, violations of the Westphalian model, or any other institutional form for that matter, ought not to be surprising, even if the form persists over a long period of time. Territory and autonomy are part of common knowledge, but they have never been able to exclude alternative principles and practices. The Westphalian model has never been taken for granted; it has not generated identical actors all of which enjoy exclusive authority within their boundaries; it has not prevented the powerful from violating its precepts; but it has been a point of common reference that rulers have honored or supplanted depending upon their interests, values, and power.

Conclusions

In the contemporary world, peace and stability would be better served by explicitly recognizing that the Westphalian model has, in fact and in theory, always been contested. It is historically myopic to take the Westphalian model as a benchmark that accurately describes some golden age when all states exercised exclusive authority within their own borders. Weaker states have frequently been subject to coercion and imposition and been unable to defend their autonomy. Stronger ones have entered into conventions and contracts that violate their autonomy and even territoriality.

Some analysts have suggested that the basic nature of the international system is changing: sovereignty is dramatically eroding; domestic and international politics cannot be distinguished; rulers cannot unilaterally govern critical state functions such as monetary policy; multilateralism is coming to dominate other forms of diplomacy.[17]

Violations of Westphalia, however, are an old problem, not a new one, even though contractual arrangements prompted by greater globalization have become more prominent. The activities of contemporary international financial institutions have their analogs in foreign controlled committees that governed finance in some weaker states in the nineteenth century. Concerns about minority rights generated by the Balkan war of the 1990s resemble similar issues that arose after earlier Balkan wars and World War I. Coercion and imposition have almost always involved a multilateral component, because great powers have recognized that mutually antagonistic attempts to force others to act in specific ways can be costly. The gold exchange standard operated by Britain in the late nineteenth century arguably imposed more rigid constraints on the domestic monetary autonomy of states than do contemporary financial flows and agreements.

Given the asymmetries of power, diversity of interests, and the weakness of institutionalizing mechanisms in the international system, it would be more productive to stop thinking of the Westphalian model as some ideal or historical reality and to treat it as a reference point or convention that is useful in some circumstances but not others. Some states have the power to preserve their territory and autonomy; others do not.[18] Some of the weak are incapable of governing their own populations, and are threats to international stability as well. The populations of these states, if not their rulers, would be better off if Westphalia were compromised. Many Third World states are incapable of independently implementing reasonable economic policies. For them conditionality is a good thing, even if it is inconsistent with the Westphalian model. Given the configuration of power in the Middle East – the existence of a number of large Arab states that will always be in one way or another a potential threat to Israel – the Palestinian question cannot be resolved by the creation of a Westphalian state: the autonomy of any Palestinian state will have to be compromised in one way or another.

At the same time, relations among the major powers – entities that are capable of defending their territory and autonomy – are stabilized by recognizing the Westphalian model unless, as is the case in Europe, they have contracted otherwise. Russia may be able to compromise the autonomy of the members of the Commonwealth of Independent States, but other countries are unlikely to be able to compromise the autonomy of Russia. A Panamanian military force will not invade the United States, arrest its president, and return him or her to Panama for trial regardless of how perverse US drug policies might be. Manuel Noriega, however, suffered exactly this fate.

The entities that are now called states vary enormously in their capabilities. Calling an entity a sovereign state is no guarantee that it will be able to defend its autonomy. Compromising Westphalia is not only inevitable, it can also be good. Explicitly recognizing that different principles ought to vary with the capacity and behavior of states would not only make normative discourse more consistent with empirical reality, it would also contribute to the more imaginative construction of institutional forms – forms that compromise Westphalia – that could create a more stable and peaceful international system.

Notes

1   For example, the influence of the Catholic Church, Amnesty International, pan-Islamic move-
    ments, or ethnic groups is sometimes described as compromising the sovereignty of states.
    However, I would not want to push this particular point because such influence does not
    involve authoritative control.
2   Charles Tilly, *Coercion, Capital and European States, AD 990–1990* (Cambridge, Mass.:
    Blackwell, 1990); Hendrik Spruyt, *The Sovereign State and its Competitors: An Analysis of
    Systems Change* (Princeton: Princeton University Press, 1994); and David Strang, "Anomaly
    and Commonplace in European Political Expansion: Realist and Institutional Accounts,"
    International Organization 45(2) (Spring 1991), pp. 143–62.
3   See, for instance, Richard Cooper, *The Economics of Interdependence: Economic Policy in
    the Atlantic Community* (New York: McGraw-Hill, 1968).
4   For a similar discussion of sovereignty, see Daniel Deudney, "The Philadelphian System:
    Sovereignty, Arms Control, and Balance of Power in the American States-union circa
    1787–1861," *International Organization* 49(2) (Spring 1995), p. 198.
5   The ability to conclude such contractual agreements could, however, depend on the domestic
    organization of the polity. It is easier for policymakers in liberal democratic states to make
    credible commitments because they are constrained by domestic constituencies than for auto-
    cratic states whose policies are more subject to the capricious and arbitrary goals of their
    rulers. See Robert O. Keohane, "Hobbes's Dilemma and Institutional Change in World Politics:
    Sovereignty in International Society," in Hans-Henrik Holm and Georg Sørensen (eds), *Whose
    World Order? Uneven Globalization and the End of the Cold War* (Boulder: Westview, 1995),
    pp. 170–2.
6   For a discussion of the Basle accord, see Ethan Kapstein, "Resolving the Regulator's
    Dilemma: International Coordination of Banking Regulations," *International Organization*
    43(2) (Spring 1989), pp. 323–47.
7   See Kalypso Nicolaides, "Mutual Recognition and the Meaning of Sovereignty," paper,
    Kennedy School of Government, Harvard University, Feb. 18, 1994, for an insightful dis-
    cussion of the way in which mutual recognition compromises conventional notions of
    sovereignty, termed here the Westphalian model.
8   For a discussion of the impact of the Helsinki accords, see Daniel Thomas, "Social
    Movements and International Institutions: A Preliminary Framework," paper presented at
    the American Political Science Association Annual Convention, Washington DC, 1991; for
    one example of how IMF accords changed domestic institutions and personnel, see Robin
    Broad, *Unequal Alliance: The World Bank, The International Monetary Fund, and the
    Philippines* (Berkeley: University of California Press, 1988), pp. 61–75.
9   Robert O. Keohane, *After Hegemony: Cooperation and Discord in the World Political
    Economy* (Princeton: Princeton University Press, 1984), is the seminal exposition of this
    perspective.
10 For the classic exposition of the problems caused by interdependence, see Cooper, *The
    Economics of Interdependence*. For a discussion of the distinction between market failure
    and distributional issues, see Stephen D. Krasner, "Global Communications and National
    Power: Life on the Pareto Frontier," *World Politics* 43(3) (April 1991), pp. 336–67.
11 Hedley Bull, *The Anarchical Society* (London: Macmillan, 1977); John G. Ruggie, "Territoriality
    and Beyond: Problematizing Modernity in International Relations," *International Organiza-
    tion* 47(1) (Winter 1993), pp. 139–74; Alexander Wendt, "Anarchy Is What States Make of
    It: The Social Construction of State Politics," *International Organization* 46(2) (Spring
    1992), pp. 391–425; Alexander Wendt, "Constructing International Politics," *International
    Security* 20(1) (Summer 1995), pp. 71–81; J. Samuel Barkin and Bruce Cronin, "The State
    and the Nation: Changing Norms and the Rules of Sovereignty in International Relations,"
    International Organization 48(1) (Winter 1994), pp. 107–30; Hedley Bull and Adam Watson
    (eds), *The Expansion of International Society* (Oxford: Oxford University Press, 1984);
    Adam Watson, *The Evolution of International Society* (London: Routledge, 1992). See

Barry Buzan, "From International Realism to International Society: Structural Realism and Regime Theory Meet the English School," *International Organization* 47(3) (Summer 1993), pp. 327–52, for a comparison of US and British approaches to international relations.

12 I am indebted to Jay Smith for suggesting the term "conventions."

13 United Nations, *Human Rights: International Instruments: Chart of Ratifications as of 31 December 1993*, ST/HR/4/Rev. 9 (New York, 1994).

14 Ian Brownlie, *Basic Documents on Human Rights*, 3rd edn (Oxford: Clarendon Press, 1992).

15 Even here there are exceptions. The Third World strongly supported international sanctions designed to end apartheid in South Africa because the elimination of a racist regime was more compelling than universally adhering to the norm of non-intervention in the internal affairs of states.

16 Keohane, "Hobbes's Dilemma," p. 172. The extent to which even strong states have been willing to honor each other's autonomy has depended on the resources they have had for intervention. The United States and especially the Soviet Union, which could employ the attraction of communist ideology, attempted to undermine each other's domestic autonomy.

17 See for instance, James Rosenau, *Turbulence in World Politics: A Theory of Change and Continuity* (Princeton: Princeton University Press, 1990); Hans-Henrik Holm and Georg Sørensen, "Introduction: What Has Changed?" in Holm and Sørensen, *Whose World Order?*, pp. 5–6; John G. Ruggie (ed.), *Multilateralism Matters: The Theory and Praxis of an Institutional Form* (New York: Columbia University Press, 1993).

18 Robert Jackson has pointed out that the nineteenth-century rule of basing international recognition on the ability to maintain internal control was abandoned after World War II. See Jackson, *Quasi-States: Sovereignty, International Relations and the Third World* (Cambridge: Cambridge University Press, 1990).

11

Has Globalization Ended the Rise and Rise of the Nation-State?

Michael Mann

Introduction

The human sciences seem full of enthusiasts claiming that a new form of human society is emerging.
[...]
But is it [...]? To suggest that it is, various groups of enthusiasts advance four main theses.

1   Capitalism, now become global, transnational, post-industrial, 'informational', consumerist, neoliberal and 'restructured', is undermining the nation-state – its macroeconomic planning, its collectivist welfare state, its citizens' sense of collective identity, its general caging of social life.
2   New 'global limits', especially environmental and population threats, producing perhaps a new 'risk society', have become too broad and too menacing to be handled by the nation-state alone.
3   'Identity politics' and 'new social movements', using new technology, increase the salience of diverse local and transnational identities at the expense of both national identities and those broad class identities which were traditionally handled by the nation-state. For this and for the previous reason we are witnessing the stirrings of a new transnational 'civil society', social movements for peace, human rights and environmental and social reform which are becoming truly global.
4   Post-nuclearism undermines state sovereignty and 'hard geopolitics', since mass mobilization warfare underpinned much of modern state expansion yet is now irrational. [...]

So the empirical part of this article will investigate whether these four nation-state-weakening theses are correct. Since they downplay political power relations, it also considers two political counter-theses.

A   State institutions, both domestic and geopolitical, still have causal efficacy because they too (like economic, ideological and military institutions) provide necessary conditions for social existence: the regulation of aspects of social life which are distinctively 'territorially centred' (see Mann 1986: ch. 1). Thus they cannot be the mere consequence of other sources of social power.

B   Since states vary greatly, if (A) is true, these variations will cause variations in other spheres of social life. Even within Europe states differ in size, power, geography and degree of centralization. Across the globe, variations dramatically increase: in degree of democracy, level of development, infrastructural power, geopolitical power, national indebtedness, etc. They also inhabit very different regional settings. Can contemporary capitalism, even if reinforced by environmental limits, 'cultural postmodernity' and demilitarization, render all this variation irrelevant, and have the *same* effects on all countries? Or will these variations cause variation among these forces, and so limit globalization?

Only the most breathless of enthusiasts would deny all validity to these counter-theses – or to the survival of the nation-state as wielder of some economic, ideological, military and political resources. The task is to establish *degrees* of relative causality: to what extent is the nation-state being transformed, to what extent is it declining – or even perhaps still growing?

But to establish this we must also make some conceptual distinctions. We can roughly distinguish five socio-spatial networks of social interaction in the world today:

1   *local* networks – which for present purposes just means subnational networks of interaction;
2   *national* networks, structured or (more neutrally) bounded by the nation-state;
3   *inter-national* networks, that is relations between nationally constituted networks. Most obviously, these include the 'hard geopolitics' of inter-state relations which centre on war, peace and alliances. But they also include 'soft geopolitics' between states – negotiations about more peaceable and particular matters like air transport communications, tax treaties, air pollution, etc. And they include relations between networks that are more nationally than state-constituted: for example, the emergence of 'national champions' playing on a broader playing-field – whether these are football teams or giant corporations;
4   *transnational* networks, passing right through national boundaries, being unaffected by them. These might not be very extensive – perhaps a religious sect organized across two neighbouring countries – or they might be continent-wide or even worldwide. Many transnational arguments about contemporary society rest on a 'macroregional' base. Examples are the frequent distinctions between 'Liberal/Anglo-Saxon', 'Nordic/ Social Democratic' or 'Christian Democratic/corporatist' forms of contemporary social organization;
5   *global* networks cover the world as a whole – or, perhaps more realistically, they cover most of it. But we should distinguish between networks which radiate universalistically or particularistically across the globe. The feminist movement may spread through almost all countries, but usually only among rather particular, smallish groups. The Catholic Church has some presence in all continents but only has quite a narrow base across Asia, while being near-universal across Latin America. The capitalism evoked by many of the enthusiasts is a universal global network, evenly diffusing through economic and social life just about everywhere. Thus global networks might be formed by either a single universal network or by a more segmented series of networks between which existed rather particularistic relations.

Over the last centuries local interaction networks have clearly diminished in relative weight; while longer-distance networks – national, inter-national and transnational – have become denser, structuring more of people's lives. Genuinely global networks have emerged relatively recently. Note that global networks need not be the same as transnational networks, though many enthusiasts equate them. Nor are they necessarily economic in nature. Global networks may be constituted by geopolitics [...] or by ideological movements like a religion or socialism or feminism or neoliberalism – the combination amounting perhaps to a new transnational civil society.

Since national and inter-national networks are constituted or fundamentally constrained by the nation-state, the future of the nation-state thus turns critically upon the answer to two questions: *Is the social significance of national and inter-national networks declining relative to some combination of local and transnational networks? And to the extent that global networks are emerging, what is the relative contribution to them of national/inter-national versus local/transnational networks?*

The 'Modest Nation-State' of the North

I start with the most familiar and dominant form of state in the world today. In the 'west', or more precisely the 'northwest' of western Europe and its white colonies, arose a state claiming formal political sovereignty over 'its' territories and a legitimacy based on the 'people' or 'nation' inhabiting them. This is what we mean by the nation-state.

The regulatory powers of such states expanded through several centuries. First, from the end of the Middle Ages they increasingly plausibly claimed a monopoly of judicial regulation and military force. Then, in the eighteenth and especially the nineteenth centuries they sponsored integrating communications infrastructures and basic control of the poor. The twentieth century saw welfare states, macroeconomic planning and the mobilization of mass citizen nationalism. All the while more states legitimated themselves in terms of 'the people', either 'representing' the people (liberal democracies) or 'organically embodying' it (authoritarian regimes), with varying degrees of civil, political and social citizenship. To a degree, therefore, northwesterners became 'caged' into national interaction networks, and these became supplemented by the inter-national relations between nation-states which we know by the term 'geopolitics'.

This is the now familiar story of 'the rise and rise' of the nation-state and the nation-state system – to which I have contributed myself (Mann 1986, 1993).
[...]

Since 1945 the [nation-state] further diffused across almost all the rest of 'the north', i.e. the whole European continent and increasing regions of East and South Asia. Its formal trappings have also dominated 'the south', while all states meet in a forum called 'The United Nations'. The [...] nation-state might seem to dominate the entire globe. In some limited senses it actually does. Only a few states do not base their legitimacy on the nation, or lack a monopoly of domestic coercion or real territorial boundedness. Almost all manage to implement policies oriented towards basic population control, health and education. Plunging mortality and rising literacy have multiple causes but some lie in the realm of effective public policy. For these reasons I will go ahead and describe contemporary states as nation-states. Yet most of them actually possess rather limited control over their territories and boundaries, while their claims to represent the nation are often specious. For much of the world a *true* nation-state remains more aspiration for the future than present reality. The nation-state's rise has been global, but modest and very uneven. The modest nation-state came to dominate the 'north', has been part of its expansion and represents a desired future for the bulk of the world's people. Is all this now threatened?

The Capitalist Threat

The enthusiasts have correctly identified many important transformations of capitalism. It is not necessary here to document capitalism's use of new 'informational' and 'post-industrial' technology to expand through much of the world and penetrate more of social life. But how great is its threat to the nation-state? And just how 'global' and/or 'transnational' is it?

In a formal geographic sense capitalism *is* now more or less global. Two great geo-political events permitted massive extension. First, decolonization largely ended the segmentation of the world economy into separate imperial zones. Second, the collapse of Soviet autarchy opened up most of Eurasia to capitalist penetration. Only Iran, China and a handful of smaller communist countries now maintain partial blockages, and these are declining or may be expected to start declining soon. China retains distinct property forms (mixing private with varieties of public ownership and control), and there still also remain (declining) areas of subsistence economy scattered through the world. Yet capitalist commodity exchange clearly dominates. With no confident adversary in sight, capitalism is becoming – at least minimally – global. That was not so in 1940, or even in 1980. It is obviously a major transformation.

But are its global networks 'pure' in the sense of being singularly universal, or do other more particularistic principles of social organization also help constitute them? An economy may be global, but this may be conferred by help from national and international networks of interaction.

[. . .]

[M]ost 'transnational' economic relations cannot be necessarily equated with a global universalism. The bulk of capitalist activity is more 'trilateral' than global, being concentrated in the three regions of the advanced 'north': Europe, North America and East Asia. These contain over 85 per cent of world trade, over 90 per cent of production in advanced sectors like electronics, plus the headquarters of all but a handful of the top 100 multinationals (including banks). This does not necessarily mean capitalism is not global. It may only indicate that the north is rich, the south is poor – and that both are locked together in a global network of interaction. But it does suggest that capitalism retains a geo-economic order, dominated by the economies of the advanced nation-states. Clusters of nation-states provide the stratification order of globalism. Among other consequences, this protects the citizens of the north: the poorly educated child of an unskilled worker in Britain or the United States will enjoy far better material conditions of existence (including twenty more years of life) than will his/her counterpart in Brazil or India. True, inequalities within all these nation-states are widening, yet it is almost inconceivable that the bulk of the privileges of national citizens in northern countries could be removed. That would cause such social disorder as to be incommensurate with a stable and profitable capitalism. The nation-state provides some of the structure, and some of the stratification structure, of the global networks of capitalism. If the commodity rules, it only does so entwined with the rule of – especially northern – citizenship.

The global economy is also subject to loose and predominantly 'soft' inter-national regulation in the shape of organizations like G7, GATT, the World Bank or the IMF. These are also northern-dominated. Some of these are involved in seemingly endless negotiations of trade liberalization – and these are likely to drag on a lot longer since national governments have been recently raising non-tariff barriers. We are nowhere near global free trade, but we may be moving a little closer and this is at present ideologically dominant. But is this just another liberalization phase in the normal historical oscillation around the middle zone between the free trade and protectionist poles? That depends on the resolution of other tendencies discussed in this article.

So, at the moment and probably also for the near future, a rapidly globalizing economy does not only acquire its character from transnational networks of interaction. What adds up to the global is a very complex mix of the local, the national, the international (represented in my discussion mostly by northern trilateralism) – and the truly transnational. The *transnational* commodity does not rule the globe.

Over time some of these national and inter-national structurings may decline. Northern domination of the world economy may diminish because of the pressures of comparative advantage. Apart from very high-tech activities, much productive enterprise may migrate to the lower costs of the south, producing more globalization (though not necessarily much reducing inequality). But so far migration has operated not by some 'transnational' logic (of random walk?) but by some combination of four other principles: the possession of useful natural resources, geographical propinquity (neighbouring countries), geopolitical alliances (friendly countries), and state and civil society stability (predictable countries). Whereas the first factor is found fairly randomly through the world – and so oil alone can develop rather backward, distant countries – the last three factors are generally interconnected. The historical development of the major northern economies emerged amid broader regional settings, from which neighbouring states and societies also benefited. Thus expansion has mostly been to the Koreas and the Mexicos, friendly neighbours with relatively developed nations and states, rather than, say, to most African countries. Nor does most growth take a regional, 'enclave' pattern within states (except where raw materials matter, or where extension is over a border and the neighbouring government sponsors 'enterprise zones'). Development then tends to diffuse across the core territories of these states, aiding the development of their overall civil societies and their drift towards becoming nation-states. Thus extension of the north – and so globalization – has depended upon, and in turn reinforced, the nation-states benefiting from it. This form of globalization reinforces national networks of interaction.

Since finance capital seems more transnational than industrial capital, its constraints upon the nation-state are usually those most emphasized by the enthusiasts. Its mobility and velocity produce financial movements which dwarf the fiscal resources of states and which constrain two of the three props of post-war state fiscal policy – interest rates and currency valuation (taxation being less affected). Yet it is difficult to assess the overall significance of this, for two reasons. First, the numbers do not offer real precision about power relations. Since currencies, shares, futures, etc. can be traded many times over in a single day, the paper value of 'financial flows' vastly exceeds that of world trade, and continues to grow. But power cannot be simply read off such sums. What are being traded are property rights to raw materials, manufactured goods and (increasingly) services, almost all of which have much greater fixity of location and therefore presumably a degree of national identity.

Second, it is not clear how effective macroeconomic planning ever was in the north-west. It *seemed* effective while massive growth was occurring and governments had access to surpluses. Many were able to be mildly interventionist (though selective incentives were generally more effective than physical controls). But since then we have seen the collapse not only of Keynesian economics but also of economic theory in general. Economists now more or less admit they have no explanation of any of the great booms or slumps of the twentieth century (or at least one that does not depend on singular events like great world wars). Macroeconomic planning was a general ideology surrounding some highly abstract concepts, from which were precariously derived some technical tools (including, most fundamentally, national accounting) and policies (which in fact also depended on contingencies). Macroeconomic planning still contains such a mixture, though its emphasis has changed. The ideological pretensions and the ability to expand spending have certainly declined. Thus we may expect looser and fiscally more cautious national/inter-national (i.e. trilateral) macroeconomic policies: a proliferation of G7 and GATT guidelines and piecemeal liberalizing agreements; MITI-style [the highly interventionist Japanese Ministry of Trade and Industry] collaboration and incentive programmes more than nationalization or direct state investment; central banks more than politicians; less the pretence of controlling markets than of signalling intentions to them; and, above all, no increases in taxation masquerading as grandiose economic theory.

Nor are the reasons for these less than dramatic power reductions easy to interpret. [...]

[N]ational economies [...] vary considerably – in their prosperity, their cohesion and their power. Consider [...] the three main regions of the north. North America is dominated by its superpower, the USA. This has an unusual state, dominated by its unique war machine and (rather meagre) social security system. Most other governmental activities which in most other northern countries are mainly the province of the central state (criminal justice, education and most welfare programmes) are the concern of fifty separate 'states' or local governments in the USA. Three major industries are closely entwined with the federal government, agriculture, the military-industrial complex and health care, and may be said to be somewhat (if particularistically) planned. They are likely to remain so – though the current plan is to downsize the military by just under a quarter over two decades. Many other industries have closer relations with 'state' and local governments, for example property development and construction. Federal legislation has been traditionally tight in the area of labour relations and monopolies, especially restraining the growth of US unions and banks. But there has been little macroeconomic planning by any level of government. The principal 'planning' agency (over interest rates) is the Federal Reserve Bank, which is largely autonomous of government. There is no serious American industrial policy; this is left to the post-war powerhouses of the US economy, the large corporations. Much of this is due to the radical separation of powers enshrined by the US constitution. A coordinated political economy cannot easily be run by a President and his cabinet, two Houses of Congress, a Supreme Court and fifty 'states' (which are also fragmented by the same separation of powers) – especially when they belong to different political parties. Thus it is difficult to see much of a weakening of US government powers, since these were never exercised very actively.

[...]

East Asia is at present also dominated by a single nation-state, though Japan is not a military superpower. Japanese political economy differs from both North American and European, with far more coordination between the state and capitalist corporations (and, in a more dependent role, the labour unions): 'Governing the market', Wade (1990) calls it; 'Governed interdependence', say Weiss and Hobson (1995). Such national coordination has been adapted in varying forms across the smaller economies of East Asia. These include active industrial policies centring on selective tax rates or conditional subsidies for key or export sectors, public absorbing of risk for innovation and government coordination of inter-firm collaboration for technology upgrading (Weiss 1995). These countries also have political stability and an advanced civil, i.e. 'national', society which is stable, literate and broadly honest. They have also experienced phenomenal growth[, t]hough growth is stuttering [. . .].

[. . .]

East Asia offers different combinations of capitalist transformation and nation-states.

Europe is the only one of the three regions to have experienced significant political transformation. [. . .]

The original impetus for [. . .] this was mainly geopolitical and military: to prevent a third devastating war in the continent, more specifically to bind Germany into a peaceful concert of nation-states. The United States had its own, primarily geopolitical, reasons for encouraging it. Thus the 'Six' and the 'Nine' were being bound together before much of the capitalist transformation had occurred. But since the chosen mechanisms of binding were [to begin with] primarily economic, they were then intensified by this transformation. The economy of Europe has thus been substantially transnationalized.

Yet the European Union also remains an association between nation-states, an international network of interaction. Specific geopolitical agreements between Germany and France, with the support of their client Benelux states, have always been its motor of growth. Germany and France, like the other states, have lost many particularistic autonomies. But, when allied, they remain the masters on most big issues. [. . .] The minor and economically weaker states may seem to have lost more, but their sovereignty on the big issues was more limited in the past. Britain has stood to lose most, because of its historic geopolitical independence from the rest of Europe. And they vote and acquire ministries based on a combination of their population size and economic muscle. 'They' are states and national economies, represented by statesmen (and women) and national technocrats and business leaders. This is not traditional 'hard' geopolitics, since the agenda is primarily economic and the participants believe war between them is unthinkable. It is 'soft' geopolitics structured by much denser inter-national (plus the remaining national) networks of interaction.

[. . .]

But suppose that the drift of the economy is towards more and more transnational globalism, that free trade is largely achieved as the EU, NAFTA, the Asian and Pacific Conference countries and other trade groups merge under the loose umbrella of GATT, that multinationals become more cosmopolitan, that development of the south becomes more diffuse, less nation-state-centric. Would this amount to a single transnational/ global economy in which the commodity and the single market ruled universally?

The answer is both yes and no. All goods and services would then have a price on a single market and capitalist enterprises would organize their financing, production and exchange. 'Consumerism' already dominates, some of the enthusiasts say; business accountancy practices spread through previously insulated institutions like civil services or universities; and athletes sell their skills to the highest bidder on free and relatively new markets. Such commodity penetration would broaden.

But even so, the rules of those markets might still have their particularities, some being the effects of national and inter-national networks of interaction. Though a far broader range of goods are now bought and sold, many of the most important ones are not actually sold as commodities on free markets. None of the three biggest industries in the US economy, defence, health care and (probably) illicit drugs, are simply dominated by commodity production, though all involve considerable transnational networks. In defence [for example] the government is a monopolistic customer for hi-tech weapons systems and it decides what other states (friendly ones) will be allowed as customers; supply is not very competitive (sometimes only one manufacturer will 'tender' and sometimes profit is calculated on a cost-plus basis). The weapons embody more 'use' than 'exchange' value – the USA *must* have them, almost regardless of cost, and the corporation can produce them without much thought of market risk. [. . .]

Though the capitalist economy is now significantly global, its globalism is 'impure', a combination of both the transnational and the inter-national. The potential universalism of the former is undercut by the particularisms of nation-states – and indeed also by the particularisms of human social practices at large.

Environmental Limits, New Social Movements and a New Transnational Civil Society

Through population growth, soil and plant erosion, water shortages, atmospheric pollution and climate change, we encounter a second form of globalism – reinforced by the dangers of biological, chemical and nuclear warfare alluded to later. We are indeed living in Beck's 'risk society' (though this is not the only society we are living in) and have only done so in the second half of the twentieth century. On some of these issues the traditional 'solution' of letting the south or the poor starve can endure. But on others, humanity together faces severe risks. These are not identical to the risks of capitalism, though the two are deeply entwined (since capitalism is now the dominant form of economic production). The 'mastery' and 'exploitation' of nature, and the enormous increase in human potentiality to do so throughout the globe, are also attributable to industrialism and to the other modes of production developed in the modern period. State socialism (and fascism too) was even more destructive of the environment, while the petty commodity production of small peasants has also been forced into many destructive practices. Nation-states, scientific establishments and (until the last few years) virtually all modern institutions contributed their piece of destruction. And rampant population growth also has sources other than capitalism, for example military, religious and patriarchal practices. To deal with these risks responses must go beyond the nation-state and capitalism alike.

Present responses on environmental issues seem mainly two-fold. First, organizations are already in action embodying variant forms of the famous environmental maxim 'Think globally, act locally'. These are mainly mixed local-transnational presssure groups and NGOs, some of them formal pressure groups (like Greenpeace), others carried by professional and scientific networks (of soil scientists, ornithologists, demographers, etc.). They are more 'modern' than 'postmodern', since they reject scientific-material exploitation of nature on primarily scientific and social-scientific grounds. Though their elites originated in the north, they have increasingly spread globally, among both highly educated southern elites and among diverse, and rather particular, groups threatened by real material problems. Such networks use the most modern and global means of communication. In exploiting these, they sometimes outflank national government and international capital alike – as consumers mobilized through western Europe to boycott Shell, humiliate the British government, and force the towing back of the Brent Spar oil platform in 1995. We may expect more of this.

Is this a 'global civil society'? Its structure is not entirely new: in the early twentieth century socialists (and, to a lesser extent, anarchists, pacifists and fascists) also generated extensive transnational networks covering much of the globe, using similarly advanced technology (printing presses, immediate translation, dictaphones, etc. – see Trotsky's remarkable study in Mexico City). The socialists launched a wave of revolutions, some successful, most unsuccessful. Many of the more idealistic proponents of the notion of a new civil society expect its scale eventually to dwarf such historical analogies.

Second, however, there is also increasing deployment of intergovernmental agencies: macroregional and continental agencies, UN conferences, etc. Their key participants, those who could implement coordinated policy decisions, are representatives of nation-states. 'Soft geopolitics' is becoming denser in this arena too. The other main delegates are the 'experts' mentioned two paragraphs above, who lead a double life. Though nurtured in transnational professional associations, they must adopt the perspective of the nation-state, persuading governments that global concerns are actually in the national interest. Some hit on excellent wheezes. Some American ornithologist managed to persuade the State Department to insert into its aid programme to Belize a requirement to protect a rare bird of which the Belize planners had not previously heard. More significantly, feminists involved in development agencies are pressuring reactionary dictators in the south to put more resources into the education of women since this will reduce the birth rate (one of the primary goals of almost all southern governments).

Thus environmental issues mainly encourage dual networks of interaction, one a potentially local/transnational civil society, the other inter-national, in the form of 'soft' geopolitics. The former may transcend the nation-state, the latter coordinate states more tightly together, though perhaps in partly consensual terms which are not incompatible with a gradual spread of a civil society. Again it is a mixed story.

And this is also the case with others among the 'new social movements'. It is usually argued that those concerned with the 'new politics' of identity – of gender, sexuality, lifestyle, age cohort, religion and ethnicity – weaken national (and nationally regulated class) identities, replacing or supplementing them with local-cum-transnational sources of identity. Ethnic politics are too variable to be dealt with in a few paragraphs (and I am writing about them at length elsewhere). So one sentence will do here: ethnic politics may fragment existing states, but – given the defeat of alternative multinational and socialist states – they fragment them into more, supposedly more authentic, nation-states. But for other social movements based on identity politics, I wish to argue that on balance they strengthen existing nation-states.

[...]

Feminists, gays, religious fundamentalists, etc. use emerging global networks of communication and NGOs, and they focus energies on the UN as well as their own state. However, most contending actors demand *more* regulation by their own nation-state through its legal or welfare agencies: to restrict or liberalize abortion, pre-marital conception and single parenting; to clarify harassment, child abuse and rape and the evidence needed to prosecute them; to guarantee or restrict the rights of those with unorthodox sexual preferences or lifestyles. Since authoritative social regulation remains overwhelmingly the province of the nation-state, the emergence of new identities may ultimately reinvigorate its politics and broaden its scope. New social movements claim to be turned off by class politics. Perhaps class politics will decline – but not national politics in general.

Post-militarism and a New World Order

As Martin Shaw argues, it is in the realm of hard geopolitics that the northern nation-states have experienced the most radical transformation – because this is where they learned the bitterest lessons [Shaw 1997]. In the two great northern wars (more commonly called the world wars) they suffered perhaps 70–80 million dead – as a direct consequence of the nation-state system. Through those wars they also pioneered weapons so devastating that they could no longer be actually used for any rational 'hard geopolitical' purpose. Northern states are now less willing to engage themselves in whole-sale war than almost any states in history. The original backbone of the nation-state is turning to jelly.

But again our three regions vary. None are more reluctant militarists than the Europeans, the guilty perpetrators of both wars, reliant for their defence for the last fifty years on the USA and presently faced by no serious threat to their security. Though the EU contains two nuclear powers, has its Franco-German brigade and its curious Western European [Defence] Union, all this is less significant than the unprecedented virtual absence of serious 'hard geopolitics' within Europe. Germans remain the most constrained of all by anti-militarism. The determination to break with the terrible character of European history is probably the most causally determining modern trans-formation of all, and the one which is most encroaching upon traditional national sovereignties. But to make European history the general pattern of the world would be ethnocentric in the extreme. And if it was, then the analogy would require more than just a restructuring of capitalism reinforced by a 'cultural turn'. The analogy would require future wars killing many millions of people in other regions of the world, before they too cried 'enough'.

Yet most Japanese may also have cried 'enough'. They are at present reluctant militarists. Some Japanese politicians are bolder than their German counterparts in expressing nationalism, but they still get slapped down. Yet East Asia is potentially an insecure region. The United States differs again. It suffered little during the two great northern wars – indeed its economy greatly benefited. It is a military superpower, still projects a standing armed force of 1,200,000 into the next century, and still modernizes its hardware. It remains the global policeman, a role which European and Japanese governments are keen to see continue and may even help finance. But even in the USA defence cuts have been sizeable and it is doubtful that the American electorate has the stomach for warfare in which many American lives would be lost. In any case these northern regions dominate the world without war.

The world nonetheless remains conflict-ridden, with a substantial place for 'hard' geopol-itics. Consider this list: rising ethnic separatism, conflict between potentially nuclear states like India and Pakistan or the two Chinas, China's geopolitical role incommensurate with its real strength, the instability of Russia and some smaller well-armed powers, the prevalence of military regimes in the world, the likely proliferation of nuclear weapons and the largely uncontrolled current spread of chemical and biological weapons

through the world. Who knows what eco-tensions, resulting from water shortages, foreign-dominated exploitation of a country's habitat, etc. might lurk around the corner? It is unlikely militarism or war will just go away. All these threats constitute serious obstacles to the diffusion of transnational and universal global networks.
[...]

Conclusion

This article has analysed four supposed 'threats' to contemporary nation-states: capitalist transformation, environmental limits, identity politics and post-militarism. We must beware the more enthusiastic of the globalists and transnationalists. With little sense of history, they exaggerate the former strength of nation-states; with little sense of global variety, they exaggerate their current decline; with little sense of their plurality, they downplay inter-national relations. In all four spheres of 'threat' we must distinguish: (a) differential impacts on different types of state in different regions; (b) trends weakening *and* some trends strengthening nation-states; (c) trends displacing national regulation to inter-national as well as to transnational networks; (d) trends simultaneously strengthening nation-states *and* transnationalism.

I have hazarded some generalizations. Capitalist transformation seems to be somewhat weakening the most advanced nation-states of the north yet successful economic development would strengthen nation-states elsewhere. The decline of militarism and 'hard geopolitics' in the north weakens its traditional nation-state core there. Yet the first three supposed 'threats' should actually intensify and make more dense the international networks of 'soft geopolitics'. And identity politics may (contrary to most views) actually strengthen nation-states. These patterns are too varied and contradictory, and the future too murky, to permit us to argue simply that the nation-state and the nation-state system are *either* strengthening *or* weakening. It seems rather that (despite some postmodernists), as the world becomes more integrated, it is *local* interaction networks that continue to decline – though the fragmentation of some presently existing states into smaller ethnically defined states would be something of a counter-trend, i.e. the reduction of the nation-state to a more local level.

Global interaction networks are indeed strengthening. But they entwine three main elements. First, part of their force derives from the more global scale of transnational relations originating principally from the technology and social relations of capitalism. But these do not have the power to impose a singular universalism on global networks. Thus, second, global networks are also modestly segmented by the particularities of nation-states, especially the more powerful ones of the north. Third, that segmentation is mediated by inter-national relations. These include some 'hard' politics, and if these turned again to major wars or international tensions, then segmentation would actually increase. Yet at present the expansion of 'soft' geopolitics is more striking, and this is rather more congenial to transnationalism. Is this a single 'global society'? Not in the strongest sense often implied by the more enthusiastic theorists. These global networks contain no singular, relatively systemic principle of interaction or integration. My own view of 'society' is less demanding, since I conceive of human societies as always formed of multiple, overlapping and intersecting networks of interaction. Globalism is unlikely to change this. Human interaction networks are now penetrating the globe, but in multiple, variable and uneven fashion.

References

Mann, M. (1986) *From the Beginning to* AD *1760*, vol. 1 of *The Sources of Social Power*. Cambridge: Cambridge University Press.

Mann, M. (1993) *The Rise of Classes and Nation-States*, vol. 2 of *The Sources of Social Power*. Cambridge: Cambridge University Press.

Shaw, M. (1997) The state of globalization: towards a theory of state transformation. *Review of International Political Economy* 4(3) (Autumn).

Wade, R. (1990) *Governing the Market: Economic Theory and the Rise of the Market in East Asian Industrialization*. Princeton: Princeton University Press.

Weiss, L. (1995) Governed interdependence: rethinking the government–business relationship in East Asia. *Pacific Review* 8.

Weiss, L. and Hobson, J. (1995) *States and Economic Development: A Comparative Historical Analysis*. Cambridge: Polity Press.

12

The Declining Authority of States

Susan Strange

Today it seems that the heads of governments may be the last to recognise that they and their ministers have lost the authority over national societies and economies that they used to have. Their command over outcomes is not what it used to be. Politicians everywhere talk as though they have the answers to economic and social problems, as if they really are in charge of their country's destiny. People no longer believe them. Disillusion with national leaders brought down the leaders of the Soviet Union and the states of central Europe. But the disillusion is by no means confined to socialist systems. Popular contempt for ministers and for the head of state has grown in most of the capitalist countries – Italy, Britain, France and the United States are leading examples. Nor is the lack of confidence confined to those in office; opposition parties and their leaders are often no better thought of than those they wish to replace. In the last few years, the cartoonists and the tabloid press have been more bitter, less restrained critics of those in authority in government than at any other time this century. Although there are exceptions – mostly small countries – this seems to be a worldwide phenomenon of the closing years of the twentieth century, more evident in some places than others, but palpable enough to suggest that some common causes lie behind it.

This [. . .] is written in the firm belief that the perceptions of ordinary citizens are more to be trusted than the pretensions of national leaders and of the bureaucracies who serve them; that the commonsense of common people is a better guide to understanding than most of the academic theories being taught in universities. The social scientists, in politics and economics especially, cling to obsolete concepts and inappropriate theories. These theories belong to a more stable and orderly world than the one we live in. It was one in which the territorial borders of states really meant something. But it has been swept away by a pace of change more rapid than human society had ever before experienced.

For this reason I believe the time has come to reconsider a few of the entrenched ideas of some academic colleagues in economics, politics, sociology and international relations. The study of international political economy has convinced me that we have to rethink some of the assumptions of conventional social science, and especially of the study of international relations. These concern: firstly, the limits of politics as a social activity; secondly, the nature and sources of power in society; thirdly, the necessity and also the indivisibility of authority in a market economy; and fourthly, the anarchic nature of international society and the rational conduct of states as the unitary actors within that society. The first and second are assumptions commonly taken for granted in political science. The third is an assumption of much liberal, or neo-classical economic science. And the last is an assumption of much so-called realist or neo-realist thinking in international relations. Each of these assumptions will be examined more closely later [. . .].

But first it may help to outline briefly the argument [. . .] as a whole. That will show the context in which these more fundamental questions about politics and power arise and have to be reconsidered. The argument put forward is that the impersonal forces of world markets, integrated over the postwar period more by private enterprise in finance, industry and trade than by the cooperative decisions of governments, are now more powerful than the states to whom ultimate political authority over society and economy is supposed to belong.

Where states were once the masters of markets, now it is the markets which, on many crucial issues, are the masters over the governments of states. And the declining authority of states is reflected in a growing diffusion of authority to other institutions and associations, and to local and regional bodies, and in a growing asymmetry between the larger states with structural power and weaker ones without it.

There are, to be sure, some striking paradoxes about this reversal of the state–market balance of power. One, which disguises from many people the overall decline of state power, is that the *intervention* of state authority and of the agencies of the state in the daily lives of the citizen appears to be growing. Where once it was left to the individual to look for work, to buy goods or services with caution in case they were unsafe or not what they seemed to be, to build or to pull down houses, to manage family relationships and so on, now governments pass laws, set up inspectorates and planning authorities, provide employment services, enforce customer protection against unclean water, unsafe food, faulty buildings or transport systems. The impression is conveyed that less and less of daily life is immune from the activities and decisions of government bureaucracies.

That is not necessarily inconsistent with my contention that state *power* is declining. It is less effective on those basic matters that the market, left to itself, has never been able to provide – security against violence, stable money for trade and investment, a clear system of law and the means to enforce it, and a sufficiency of public goods like drains, water supplies, infrastructures for transport and communications. Little wonder that it is less respected and lacks its erstwhile legitimacy. The need for a political authority of some kind, legitimated either by coercive force or by popular consent, or more often by a combination of the two, is the fundamental reason for the state's existence. But many states are coming to be deficient in these fundamentals. Their deficiency is not made good by greater activity in marginal matters, matters that are optional for society, and which are not absolutely necessary for the functioning of the market and the maintenance of social order. Trivialising government does not make its authority more respected; often, the contrary is true.

The second paradox is that while the governments of established states, most notably in North America and western Europe, are suffering this progressive loss of real authority, the queue of societies that want to have their own state is lengthening. This is true not only of ethnic groups that were forcibly suppressed by the single-party government of the former Soviet Union. It is true of literally hundreds of minorities and aboriginal peoples in every part of the world – in Canada and Australia, in India and Africa, even in the old so-called nation-states of Europe. Many – perhaps the majority – are suppressed by force, like the Kurds or the Basques. Others – like the Scots or the Corsicans – are just not strong enough or angry enough to offer a serious challenge to the existing state. Still others such as the native Americans, the Aboriginals, the Samis or the Flemish are pacified by resource transfers or by half-measures that go some way to meet their perceived need for an independent identity. Only a few, such as the Greenlanders, the Slovaks or Slovenes or the unwanted, unviable Pacific island-states, have succeeded in getting what they wanted – statehood. But once achieved, it does not seem to give them any real control over the kind of society or the nature of their economy that they might have preferred. In short, the desire for ethnic or cultural autonomy is universal; the political means to satisfy that desire within an integrated world market economy is not. Many, perhaps most, societies have to be content with the mere appearance of autonomy, with a facade of statehood. The struggle for independence has often proved a pyrrhic victory.

The final paradox which can be brought as evidence against my basic contention about the hollowness of state authority at the end of this century is that this is a western, or even an Anglo-Saxon phenomenon, and is refuted by the Asian experience of the state. The Asian state, it is argued, has in fact been the means to achieve economic growth, industrialisation, a modernised infrastructure and rising living standards for the people. Singapore might be the prime example of a strong state achieving economic success. But Japan, Korea, Taiwan are all states which have had strong governments, governments which have successfully used the means to restrict and control foreign trade and foreign investment, and to allocate credit and to guide corporate development in the private sector. Is it not premature – just another instance of Eurocentrism therefore – to assume the declining authority of the state?

There are two answers to this third paradox. One is that all these Asian states were exceptionally fortunate. They profited in three ways from their geographical position on the western frontier of the United States during the Cold War. Their strategic importance in the 1950s and after was such that they could count on generous military and economic aid from the Americans, aid which was combined with their exceptionally high domestic savings and low patterns of consumption. The combination gave a head start to rapid economic development. Secondly, and also for strategic reasons, they could be – almost had to be – exempted from the pressure to conform to the norms of the open liberal economy. They were allowed, first formally and then informally, to limit foreign imports and also to restrict the entry of the foreign firms that might have proved too strong competitors for their local enterprises. At the same time, they were given relatively open access first to the large, rich US market for manufactures, and later, under some protest, to the European one. And thirdly, the technology necessary to their industrialisation was available to be bought on the market, either in the form of patents, or in the person of technical advisors from Europe and America or through corporate alliances which brought them the technology without the loss of managerial control.

Now, I would argue, these special dispensations are on the way out, and not only because the Cold War is over. The Asian governments will be under increasing pressure from Washington to adopt more liberal non-discriminatory policies on trade and investment. And they will also be under pressure from within to liberalise and to allow more competition, including foreign competition, for the benefit of consumers and of other producers. In short, the exceptionalism of the Asian state during the Cold War has already been substantially eroded, and will continue to be so. As it has been at other times, and in other places, there will be contests for control over the institutions and agencies of government in most of the Asian countries. There will be contests between factions of political parties, between vested interests both in the private sectors and in the public sector. There will be power struggles between branches of the state bureaucracy. Both the unity and the authority of government are bound to suffer.

The Neglected Factor – Technology

The argument [I want to make] depends a good deal on the accelerating pace of technological change as a prime cause of the shift in the state–market balance of power. Since social scientists are not, by definition, natural scientists, they have a strong tendency to overlook the importance of technology which rests, ultimately, on advances in physics, in chemistry and related sciences like nuclear physics or industrial chemistry. In the last 100 years, there has been more rapid technological change than ever before in human history. On this the scientists themselves are generally agreed. It took hundreds – in some places, thousands – of years to domesticate animals so that horses could be used for transport and oxen (later heavy horses) could be used to replace manpower to plough and sow ground for the production of crops in agriculture. It has taken less than 100 years for the car and truck to replace the horse and for aircraft to partly take over from road and rail transport. The electric telegraph as a means of communication was invented in the 1840s and remained the dominant system in Europe until the 1920s. But in the next eighty years, the telegraph gave way to the telephone, the telephone gave way to radio, radio to television and cables to satellites and optic fibres linking computers to other computers. No one under the age of thirty or thirty-five today needs convincing that, just in their own lifetime, the pace of technological change has been getting faster and faster. The technically unsophisticated worlds of business, government and education of even the 1960s would be unrecognisable to them. No fax, no personal computers, no accessible copiers, no mobile phones, no video shops, no DNA tests, no cable TV, no satellite networks connecting distant markets, twenty-four hours a day. The world in which their grandparents grew up in the 1930s or 1940s is as alien to them as that of the Middle Ages. There is no reason to suppose that technological change in products and processes, driven by profit, will not continue to accelerate in future.

This simple, everyday, commonsense fact of modern life is important because it goes a long way to explaining both political and economic change. It illuminates the changes both in the power of states and in the power of markets. Its dynamism, in fact, is basic to my argument, because it is a continuing factor, not a once-for-all change.

For the sake of clarity, consider first the military aspects of technical change, and then the civilian aspects – although in reality each spills over into the other. In what are known as strategic studies circles, no one doubts that the development of the atom bomb in the middle of the twentieth century, and later of nuclear weapons carried by intercontinental missiles, has brought about a major change in the nature of warfare between states. Mutual assured destruction was a powerful reason for having nuclear weapons – but equally it was a good reason for not using them. After the paradoxical long peace of the Cold War, two things began to change. The expectation that, sooner or later, nuclear war would destroy life on the planet began to moderate. And confidence began to wane that the state could, by a defensive strategy, prevent this happening. Either it would or it wouldn't, and governments could do little to alter the probabilities. Thus, technology had undermined one of the primary reasons for the existence of the state – its capacity to repel attack by others, its responsibility for what Adam Smith called 'the defence of the realm'.

At the same time technology has had its effect on civilian life. Medical technology has made human life both longer and more comfortable. Electrical technology has liberated millions of women from the drudgery that imprisoned previous generations in the day-long labour of preparing food, keeping the family's clothes clean and mended, and houses clean and warm. As washing machines, vacuum cleaners, dishwashers, central heating and refrigerators and freezers spread down the income levels, more people had more to lose from inter-state conflict. Comfort bred conservatism in politics. Moreover, the new wealth was being acquired by the Germans and the Japanese, who had actually been defeated in World War II. Acquiring territory was no longer seen as a means to increase wealth. Losing territory did not mean the state became poorer or weaker. Gaining market shares in the world outside the territorial borders of the state, however, did enable formerly poor countries like Japan, Taiwan or Hong Kong to earn the foreign exchange with which to buy capital goods, foreign technology and the necessary resources of energy and raw materials. As John Stopford and I have argued, competition for world market shares has replaced competition for territory, or for control over the natural resources of territory, as the 'name of the game' between states (Stopford and Strange 1991; Strange in Rizopoulos 1990). In this new game, the search for allies among other states goes on, but not for their added military capabilities. It is for the added bargaining power conferred by a larger economic area.

Moreover, the search for allies is not confined to other states or inter-governmental organizations. It is supplemented by a search for allies among foreign-owned firms. These firms may be persuaded, in exchange for access to the national market, to raise the finance, apply their technology, provide the management and the access to export markets – in short, to take all the steps necessary to locate production of goods or services within the territory of the host state. In most developing or ex-socialist countries, the prospect of new jobs and extra export earnings brought by such investments have become powerful reasons for a change of attitude toward the so-called 'multinationals'.

The Second Neglect – Finance

Not the least of the TNC's attractions to host states is its ability to raise finance both for the investment itself and – even more important – for the development of new technology. Another key part of the argument [. . .] is that, besides the accelerating pace of technological change, there has been an escalation in the capital cost of most technological innovations – in agriculture, in manufacturing and the provision of services, and in new products and in new processes. In all of these, the input of capital has risen while the relative input of labour has fallen. It is this increased cost which has raised the stakes, as it were, in the game of staying up with the competition. This is so whether we look at competition from other firms who are also striving for larger market shares, or whether we look at governments trying to make sure that the economies for whose performance they are held responsible stay up with the competition in wealth-creation coming from other economies. Thus, to the extent that a government can benefit from a TNC's past and future investments without itself bearing the main cost of it, there are strong reasons for forging such alliances.

But the escalating costs of technological change are also important for a more fundamental reason, and not just because it explains the changing policies of host states to TNCs. It has to do with change in the world system. The cost of new technology in the production structure has added to the salience of money in the international political economy. It is no exaggeration to say that, with a few notable exceptions, scholars in international relations for the past half-century have grossly neglected the political aspects of credit-creation, and of changes in the global financial structure.[1] In much theorising about international relations or even international political economy there is no mention at all of the financial structure (as distinct from the international monetary order governing the exchange relations of national currencies). Briefly, the escalating capital costs of new technologies could not have been covered at all without, firstly, some very fundamental changes in the volume and nature of credit created by the capitalist market economy; and secondly, without the added mobility that in recent years has characterised that created credit. The *supply* of capital to finance technological innovation (and for other purposes) has been as important in the international political economy as the *demand* from the innovators for more money to produce ever more sophisticated products by ever more capital-intensive processes of production.

These supply and demand changes take place, and take effect, in the market. And it is markets, rather than state–state relations, that many leading texts in international political economy tend to overlook. Much more emphasis is put on international monetary relations between governments and their national currencies. To the extent that attention is paid at all to the institutions creating and marketing credit in the world economy, they are held to be important chiefly for the increased volatility they may cause to exchange rates, or to the impact they may have on the ability of governments to borrow abroad to finance development or the shortfall between revenue and spending, or between export earnings and import bills.

More significant in the long run, however, when it comes to evolving better theories to explain change in the international political economy is the accompanying neglect of the three-way connections between the supply side of international finance (credit), the demand side from firms, and the political intervention of governments as regulators of banking and financial markets and as borrowers or lenders, at home and abroad. There are theories to explain each of the three, but no unifying theory to explain their mutual connections.

[. . .]

Awareness of this failure of inter-connection between bodies of theory relating to political and economic change customarily treated by social scientists in isolation from each other has powerfully motivated [this work]. My exploration of the phenomenon of diffuse authority over the global political economy is necessarily sketchy and incomplete. Yet by drawing attention to both the theoretical lacunae in social science and to the empirical evidence of the increasing exercise of non-state authority, my hope is that further work will be inspired to develop at both the theoretical and the empirical level.

Politics, Power and Legitimacy

There are three premises underlying the argument [here]. Each relates directly to – indeed, challenges – some of the conventional assumptions of economics, social and political science and international relations. The first premise is that politics is a common activity; it is not confined to politicians and their officials. The second is that power over outcomes is exercised impersonally by markets and often unintentionally by those who buy and sell and deal in markets. The third is that authority in society and over economic transactions is legitimately exercised by agents other than states, and has come to be freely acknowledged by those who are subject to it.

[. . .]

[T]hree general propositions about the patterns of legitimate authority now developing in the international political economy towards the end of the twentieth century [can be established]. One is that there is growing asymmetry among allegedly sovereign states in the authority they exercise in society and economy. In international relations, back to Thucydides, there has always been some recognition of a difference between small states and great powers, in the way each behaves to others and in the options available to them in their relations with other states. But there has been a tendency all along to assume a certain uniformity in the nature and effectiveness of the control which each state has over social and economic relations within their respective territorial boundaries. The attributes of domestic sovereignty, in other words, were assumed automatically to go with the regulation accorded each state by its peers. Now, I shall argue, that assumption can no longer be sustained. What was regarded as an exceptional anomaly when in 1945 the United States conceded two extra votes in the UN General Assembly for the Soviet Union – one for the 'sovereign' republic of the Ukraine and one for Byelorussia – now hardly attracts comment. The micro-states of Vanuatu and the Republic of San Marino are admitted to the select circle of member-states of the United Nations. But no one really believes that recognition of their 'sovereignty' is more than a courteous pretence. It is understood that there is only a difference of degree between these and many of the smaller and poorer members of the international society of states who are established occupants of seats in the UN.

The second proposition is that the authority of the governments of all states, large and small, strong and weak, has been weakened as a result of technological and financial change and of the accelerated integration of national economies into one single global market economy. Their failure to manage the national economy, to maintain employment and sustain economic growth, to avoid imbalances of payments with other states, to control the rate of interest and the exchange rate is not a matter of technical incompetence, nor moral turpitude nor political maladroitness. It is neither in any direct sense their fault, nor the fault of others. None of these failures can be blamed on other countries or on other governments. They are, simply, the victims of the market economy.

The third proposition complements the second. It is that some of the fundamental responsibilities of the state in a market economy – responsibilities first recognised, described and discussed at considerable length by Adam Smith over 200 years ago – are not now being adequately discharged by anyone. At the heart of the international political economy, there is a vacuum, a vacuum not adequately filled by intergovernmental institutions or by a hegemonic power exercising leadership in the common interest. The polarisation of states between those who retain some control over their destinies and those who are effectively incapable of exercising any such control does not add up to a zero-sum game. What some have lost, others have not gained. The diffusion of authority away from national governments has left a yawning hole of non-authority, ungovernance it might be called.
[. . .]

Note

1   The notable exceptions include Veseth 1990; Wachtel 1986; Frieden 1987; Moffitt 1984; Calleo 1982. I should add that we all owe big debts to the economic historians such as Kindleberger, Cipolla, Feis and de Cecco, and more recently Cain and Hopkin; to the practitioners such as Volcker and Gyoten; and not least to journalists such as the late Fred Hirsch and Yoichi Funabashi.

References

Calleo, D. (1982) *The Imperious Economy*, Cambridge, Mass.: Harvard University Press.

Frieden, Jeffry (1987) *Banking on the World: The Politics of American International Finance*. New York: Harper and Row.

Moffitt, M. (1984) *The World's Money: International Banking from Bretton Woods to the Brink of Insolvency*. London: Joseph.

Rizopoulos, N. (ed.) (1990) *Sea-Changes: American Foreign Policy in a World Transformed*. New York: Council on Foreign Relations.

Stopford, John and Strange, Susan (1991) *Sterling and British Policy: A Political Study of an International Currency in Decline*. Oxford: Oxford University Press.

Veseth, Michael (1990) *Mountains of Debt: Crisis and Change in Renaissance Florence, Victorian Britain and Post-war America*. Oxford: Oxford University Press.

Wachtel, Howard (1986) *The Money Mandarins: The Making of a New Supranational Economic Order*. New York: Pantheon Books.

13

Global Market versus Regionalism

Björn Hettne

An economic system presupposes some kind of social order. A social order is a coherent system of rules which is accepted by the actors constituting the system. The concept can contain both coercive and consensual dimensions. The market system of exchange is not in itself an order, but is confined by a particular order that expresses its underlying value system, or normative content. Therefore, market systems differ to the extent that their underlying social orders differ. If, as in the case of the post-communist world, there is a transition between different orders, the market can only reflect the confusion and turbulence of this transition, but it will not by itself create order.

In Europe the concept of 'social market' is commonly used to designate a market system which is mildly regulated to maintain a reasonable degree of social justice in society. In the context of the EC/EU, the so called 'social dimension' of the integration process fulfils a similar role, although it is uncertain how to implement it in a transnational context where states differ in their commitments to the goal of social justice.

The problem of social order and what is often called 'economic freedom', meaning non-regulation of economic activities and flows, has been thoroughly analysed and discussed primarily in national contexts. This essay deals with the problem of how, on a world scale and in a context where no formal political authority exists, 'economic freedom' can be made compatible with social order. The basic issue is the relationship between forces of globalisation and forces of regionalisation. Regionalism is one possible approach to 'a new multilateralism'.

[. . .]

[The material below] explores the potentials and possibilities of a regionalised world order; that is the territorial logic of the state applied to the emerging regional systems (neo-mercantilism). It should be remembered, however, that real developments depend on the dialectical relationship between the two logics, the forces of market expansion and the need for political control. Globalisation and regionalisation can be seen as complementary processes, modifying each other, in the formation of a new world order. World regions rather than nation-states may in fact constitute basic units in a future multilateral world order.

Regionalism: Some Conceptual Clarifications

Regionalism is looked upon as a threat by some and as a promise by others. Since various meanings are attached to it, some conceptual clarifications may be in order.

First of all, what is a region? It is not a very homogeneous phenomenon, even if we limit ourselves to world regions (macroregions) and forget about different subnational regions or microregions. Three contrasting, although not necessarily contradicting, models should be underlined: trading blocs or 'megamarkets' resulting from the possible breaking up of the free trade regime; the geo-political division of the world into sometimes competing, sometimes aligned military-political power blocs; and the process of regionalisation from below resulting largely from internal transformations within emerging regions. Here we are mainly concerned with regions in the third sense, that is transnational formations which express a regional identity rather similar to nationalism. This 'extended nationalism'[1] is the 'new' regionalism.

Second, one has to make a distinction between a *normative* and a *positive* understanding of regionalism. In what follows, I suggest a normative meaning: regional integration as a political project. I use substitutes such as 'regional cooperation' or 'regional initiatives' in a more positive or descriptive context.

Third, one should also distinguish *hegemonic regionalism*, brought about by pressure from a hegemonic power, exemplified by SEATO (South East Asia Treaty Organization), CENTO (Central Treaty Organization) and so on, from *autonomous regionalism*, which essentially is regionalism from below.[2] It is the latter which is relevant in discussing the new regionalism. The hegemonic regional arrangements led to few if any links among its members and were of little use in intra-regional and intra-state conflict resolution.

Fourth, regionalism can refer exclusively to a particular region, or it can be a world order concept. One can argue in favour of or against, for instance, ASEAN (Association of South East Asian Nations) regionalism without bothering about other regions. One can even deplore the formation of rival regions. However, one can also be primarily concerned with advantages or disadvantages of a regionalised world, that is a world order consisting of regional groupings as the defining element. The first meaning of regionalism, as a form of 'extended nationalism' with a potential aggressiveness towards other regions, can perhaps be called *particularistic regionalism*, the second meaning, as a potential world order, *universalistic regionalism*. The positive and normative approaches apply in both cases. As far as universalistic regionalism is concerned, the normative approach would indicate a preferred world order, characterised by a 'concertation' of distinct regional cultures.

It must, finally, be emphasised that world regions as distinct political actors are evolving through a dialectical historical process, and that they, consequently, differ a lot in their *capacity as actor*. We could perhaps speak of degrees of *regionness* in analogy with concepts such as 'stateness' and 'nationness'. A higher degree of regionness implies a higher degree of economic independence, communication, cultural homogeneity, coherence, capacity to act and, in particular, capacity to resolve conflicts. Regionalisation is the process of increasing regionness, and the concept can refer to a single region as well as to the world system.

We can distinguish *five levels of regional complexity, of 'regionness'*. They express a certain evolutionary logic, but the idea is not to suggest a stage theory but rather a framework for comparative analysis.

The first level is region as a *geographical and ecological unit*, delimited by natural geographical barriers: 'Europe from the Atlantic to the Urals', 'Africa south of the Sahara', or 'the Indian subcontinent'. In order to further regionalise, this particular territory must, necessarily, be inhabited by human beings.

The second level is, thus, region as *social system*, which implies translocal relations of social, political, cultural and economic nature between human groups. These relations may be positive or negative, but, either way, they constitute some kind of regional complex. For instance, they can form a security complex, in which the constituent units (normally states) are dependent on each other as well as the overall political stability of the regional system, as far as their own security is concerned.[3] The region, like the international system of which it forms part, is anarchic. The classic case is nineteenth-century Europe. At this low level of organisation, power balance or some kind of 'concert' is the sole security guarantee. From a regionalist perspective (in the normative sense) this is a rather primitive security mechanism.

The third level is region as *organised cooperation* in any of the cultural, economic, political or military fields. In this case, region is defined by the membership of the regional organisation in question. The point to be stressed here is the unidimensionality which characterises this stage of regional cooperation. The creation of a regional organisation is a crucial step towards multilateralism in a regional context. In the absence of any organised regional cooperation, the concept of regionalism does not make much sense. But it is also important that the organised cooperation covers the whole relevant region. It should not be any group of countries in more or less temporary coalitions pursuing purely national interests. It should be possible to relate the 'formal region' (defined by organisational membership) to the 'real region' (which has to be defined through less precise criteria) in order to assess the relevance and future potential of a particular regional organisation.

Regional cooperation through a formal organisation is sometimes rather superficial, but at least a framework for cooperation is created. This can be of great value, if and when an objective need for cooperation should arise. An example is the South Asian Association for Regional Cooperation (SAARC). Of particular importance in this case is that the 'organisational region' corresponds to the regional security complex. This is, for instance, not the case with ASEAN, which organised the capitalist community of countries in the South East Asian region, in contradistinction to the communist or post-communist grouping. As this particular division is losing its relevance, prerequisites for a more authentic regionalism are emerging.

The fourth level is region as *regional civil society*, which takes shape when the organisational framework promotes social communication and convergence of values throughout the region. Of course the pre-existence of a shared cultural tradition throughout the region is of crucial importance here, but culture is not only a given but continuously created and recreated. However, the defining element here is the multidimensional quality of regional cooperation.

The fifth level of regionness is region as *acting subject* with a distinct identity, actor capability, legitimacy, and structure of decision-making. Crucial areas for regional intervention are conflict resolution (between and within former 'states') and welfare (in terms of social security and regional balance). The organisational expression of this level of complexity naturally also tends to become more complex, as the current transformation of the European Community into a European Union shows. The ultimate outcome of this comprehensive level of regionalism (which is something for the future) could be a 'region-state', which in terms of scope can be compared to the classical empires, but in terms of political order constitutes a voluntary evolution of sovereign national political units into a supranational community to which certain functions are transferred.

The higher degrees of regionness define what I mean by *the new regionalism*. It differs from the 'old' regionalism in the following respects:

(a) Whereas the old regionalism was formed in a bipolar Cold War context, the new is taking shape in a more multipolar world order.

(b) Whereas the old regionalism was created 'from above' (that is by the super-powers), the new is a more spontaneous process 'from within' (in the sense that the constituent states themselves are main actors).

(c) Whereas the old regionalism was specific with regard to objectives, the new is a more comprehensive, multidimensional process.

Europe represents the most advanced regional arrangement the world has seen, and it will consequently serve as our paradigm for the new regionalism in the sense that its conceptualisation draws on empirical observations of the European process. Further-more, Europe is also a concrete model often referred to as an example to follow by other regional organisations. In more negative terms, the integration process in Europe is seen as a threat to the global trade system, the so-called Fortress Europe, and there-fore a pretext for organising regional trade systems, such as NAFTA or the East Asian Economic Caucus (EAEC). Thus, the emphasis on the new regionalism as a process 'from within' does not mean that it is purely endogenous to the respective region. Even if the initiatives are taken within the region, the factors which make these initiatives necessary are global.

The Dimensions of Regionalisation

The process of regionalisation implies a change from relative heterogeneity to increased homogeneity with regard to different dimensions, the most important being *culture, security, economic policies and political regime.*

Cultural homogeneity is formed very slowly. Normally, regionalisation necessitates a certain degree of cultural homogeneity to start with, what we can call an 'inherent regional civil society'. The Nordic countries, for instance, are and have always been culturally very similar, and this made it possible for them to adopt very different solutions to their security problems and yet constitute what has been called a security community. In con-trast, the fundamental cultural similarity among South Asian states has not prevented inter-state hostilities which are due to differences in other dimensions, made manifest especially by the break-up of European empires into a number of more or less real-istic nation-state projects. Cultural homogenisation also has its limits and in order not to become conflictive it must be countered by cultural pluralism.

Security is a crucial dimension, and security divisions therefore imply economic divi-sions, as was very clearly shown in the pattern of regional economic cooperation in Europe during the Cold War. Consequently, a fundamental change of the security order paves the way for a new pattern of regional economic cooperation as well.[4] It should there-fore be expected that the dismantling of the Cold War system dramatically changes the preconditions for regional cooperation globally. A greater South East Asian region (ASEAN plus the Indochina region) and a reunification of the two Koreas are such possibilities. The Indo-Pakistan conflict, although largely indigenous to the region, also had its Cold War dimension, which further complicated the issue. Similarly, post-apartheid Southern Africa will be a quite different political entity compared with the situation that prevailed before.

A common security order is a necessary, albeit not sufficient, precondition for regional integration. Of equal importance is the compatibility of economic policies. An autarkic ambition of a certain state, particularly if it happens to be the regional power (like India in South Asia), will effectively prevent a process of regionalisation from taking place to the extent that the rest of the states are outward-oriented. Regional integration based on a shared commitment to the market principle is the normal case, but history has shown that free trade areas, in which unequal countries participate, regularly generate tensions which ultimately erode the regional arrangement. The new regionalism could avoid this trap by a commitment to 'developmental regionalism', which would imply regional economic regulation without going to the extent of delinking from the world economy. There is, however, so far very little empirical experience of this strategy.

The homogenisation of *economic policies* may pave the way for further regionalisation, as when similar regimes are voted to power simultaneously, but it may also be a conscious political decision, as when the economic and political union was decided in Maastricht. This decision was obviously premature in view of the real differences among the twelve, not to speak of some of the candidates for future membership. Nevertheless, the decision should lead to a further harmonisation of economic policies in order to avoid or not to prolong two or more camps within the European union.

On the global level, the IMF and the World Bank exercise a near-monopoly over credit, as far as weaker clients are concerned. The conditions of access to this credit system, the economic conditionalities, are such as to homogenise the rules of the economic game throughout the world. Similarly, there are strong global forces favouring democratisation of national political regimes. In 1991 the number of democratic states for the first time in world history exceeded the number of non-democratic states.[5] To some extent this is the result of new political conditionalities in development aid. It goes without saying that the democratic reforms 'imposed' by these measures are in harmony with Western conceptions of democracy, whereas, as the Algerian aborted election showed, radical popular influences in Third World societies are not necessarily welcomed by the guardians of the world order.

The Dynamics of Regionalisation

Regionalisation is a complex process of change taking place simultaneously at three levels: the structures of the world system as a whole, the level of interregional relations, and the internal pattern of the single region. Changes on the three levels interact, and the relative importance of them differs from one region to another.

What I call the '*new regionalism*' was not consistent with the bipolar Cold War system, since the 'quasi-regions' in this system tended to reproduce the global division within their own respective regions. This pattern of hegemonic regionalism was of course evident in Europe, but it was more or less discernible in all world regions at the height of the Cold War. The end of it could lead either to a multipolar system or to a reinforcement of US hegemony.

Moving to the level of interregional relations, European regionalism is the trigger of global regionalisation, at least in two different ways: one positive (promoting regionalism), the other negative (provoking regionalism). In the *positive* way, the European Community has been seen as the model to emulate. This was explicitly stated in the Colombo meeting of the SAARC (December 1991). Similarly the Abuja summit (July

1991) of the OAU called for an African Economic Community on the lines of the EC, and the SADCC (renaming itself SADC) upgraded its supranational competence. The EC is, furthermore, actively encouraging regional formations in the Third World through its 'regional dialogue' or 'group-to-group diplomacy'. This is quite different from the entrenched US bilateralism with the more or less explicit purpose of discouraging regionalism.

The *negative* aspect referred to is of course the infamous European Fortress – the threat of regional protectionism which will provoke rather than promote other regional bloc formations. After the break-down in the GATT negotiations in late 1991, for which European agricultural protectionism was blamed, the Malaysian prime minister referred to the European Fortress as an established fact. He consequently invited Japan to act as a leader of an East Asian Economic Grouping – later to be called Caucus – which implied an East and South East Asian superbloc with a Sino-Japanese core. This would be a formidable response to potential European and North American fortresses. The Japanese response was silence, but there are reasons to believe that the option is kept open. Thus, even in regions where there is a strong commitment to multilateralism, pre-parations for regional groupings are being made, perhaps in secret.

Will the EU become a Fortress Europe? No one knows, and the point to be made here is that the future pattern of interregional relations depends on which of several possible scenarios for internal change and external relations will come about. What could be more unpredictable than the fall of the Berlin Wall in 1989? And the consequences are still hard to grasp. Will the Commonwealth of Independent States (CIS) become a region? Or will Ukraine and Belorus turn to the West, while Russia 'goes Pacific'? Where will Central Asia belong? Will it remain in the CIS or will it be 'divided' between Turkey and Iran?

Finally, on the level of 'the region in the process of taking shape', the basic dimen-sion is homogenisation, and the elimination of extremes, in terms of culture, security, economic policies and political systems.

Some further comments on the dynamics of regionalisation must be made. The pro-cess of regionalisation is itself multidimensional at least at higher levels of 'regionness'. For instance, the security system influences the pattern of economic relations between the states of the region. In Europe, the EC, EFTA, and COMECON were clearly reflections of the Cold War order. The end of this order created a completely new situ-ation, as far as regional economic cooperation was concerned. In South Asia, the secur-ity order has created a very strange situation with an introverted India – while all other states maximise their external economic relations in order to minimise their dependence on the regional great power. Again, a transformation of the South Asian regional secur-ity complex into a regional security community would also completely change the basis for regional economic cooperation. Another example, which few would consider a likely candidate for a coherent region, is the post-Soviet region organised in the CIS. The formation of a regional political structure, more or less like the formation of nation-states, implies a major transformation of power structures on different levels of society, and this is hardly conceivable without a major crisis.

The 'Black-Hole Syndrome'

The actual process of regionalisation is triggered by events, the importance of which can be understood only in retrospect. However, one type of event, relevant for region-alisation, which seems to turn up frequently is the 'black-hole syndrome'.

'Black hole' (a metaphor coined by Richard Falk) is a 'pretheoretic' way of account-ing for the disintegration of nation-states, or rather 'nation-state projects', in the con-text of global change. The earlier examples of break-down of states are few, and tended rather to confirm the basic persistence of the inter-state, or Westphalian, system. The division of Pakistan was explained by the geopolitical peculiarity of that particular state-formation. Biafra proved the impossibility of separatism, and Lebanon did revert to a generalised state of conflict rather than breaking up.

Today, the situation is different, and the reason is that the structure of the world order is changing, thus lifting the 'overlay' of stabilising controls which formed part of the old order, that is the Cold War. The peripheral tendencies characterising a num-ber of state-formations that contain great socio-economic and cultural differences will likely take the upper hand as the geopolitical environment becomes transformed and creates new possible alignments and a direct approach to the world economy for emerging microregions.

Yugoslavia provides the paradigm, now more or less repeated all over the post-Soviet region. The collapse of political authority at one level opens up a previously latent power struggle at a lower level, and the process may go on almost indefinitely in a complex multi-ethnic polity. If there is not even an embryonic regional structure the process of disintegration may go on until the 'international community' is forced to take action. Somalia provides one example. To the extent that there is a regional institutional frame-work which can be used for purposes of conflict resolution, the tendency is for the region to intervene.[6] Thus, the eruption of 'black holes' under certain conditions promotes the process of regionalisation.

'Black holes', or the threat of them, lead to regional security crises, as we can see: Yugoslavia in Europe, Sri Lanka in South Asia, Afghanistan in Central Asia, Lebanon in the Middle East, Liberia in West Africa, Somalia and Ethiopia in East Africa, Cambodia in South East Asia, and Nagorno-Karabakh and Moldova in the latest 'region': the CIS. These security crises form part of regionalisation processes – but there is of course no uniform outcome. Rather, one could say that 'black holes' can make or break regions, depending on the viability of the regional arrangement.

For obvious reasons, 'black holes' are seen as critical problems within the concerned region, while they look less threatening at a long distance, particularly if there are sev-eral of them erupting at the same time. Europeans worry more about Yugoslavia than about Liberia, Japanese more about Cambodia than Somalia. Thus one has reasons to believe that a regional engagement in regional conflict resolution is preferable to a global [one]. Even the small steps which have been taken towards humanitarian intervention, overruling state sovereignty, are quite dramatic in terms of yesterday's praxis of inter-national law.[7]

Hegemonism and Regionalism

As was noted in my opening paragraph, a market, in order to function, presupposes some kind of social order. The premise holds for the past as well as for the present. It was the historical function of mercantilism to create 'national economies' out of localised 'natural economies'. The nation-state was then the protector and promoter of the economy situated within the boundaries of the state. This meant a dramatic expan-sion of the market system.

The crucial issue now is how economic exchange and even cooperation can take place under the conditions of anarchy supposedly characterising the international system or, differently put, how the 'anarchy' becomes orderly enough to permit 'free', that is largely unregulated, economic transactions of different types.

Theoretically at least, this problem can be solved in more than one way. Recent debate, however, has focused on the importance of hegemonic stability for the functioning of the international economy and thus also on the implications of hegemonic decline. These are, on the economic level, a fragmentation of the world economy, and, on the political level, an increased rivalry between leading capitalist countries, or possibly between carriers of the predominant model and a project to replace it with some qualitatively different model.

The theory of hegemonic stability, which explains the persistence of a global liberal trade regime by the backing from a hegemonic power, assumes a free-trade orientation of the hegemon, as well as a willingness to pay the necessary costs for keeping the world economy open. The hegemon guarantees the liberal world economy. Deviation from required hegemonic behaviour implied in the definition (for instance exploiting its position for short-run benefits) already by itself indicates hegemonic decline. Thus, it is necessary to distinguish between being *dominant* in the international system and performing a *functional* role for its orderly functioning.

Hegemony is a special kind of power, based on different but mutually supportive dimensions, fulfilling certain functions (providing international collective goods) in a larger system which lacks a formal authority structure and, consequently, is more or less voluntarily accepted by other actors. A hegemony is primarily a consensual order, such as was analysed by Gramsci in a national (Italian) context.[8] This implies that hegemony can decline simply as a consequence of a legitimacy deficit, even if the coercive power resources as such should remain intact. It also implies that a reduction in military capability is compatible with the maintenance of a hegemonic position – to the extent that the leadership role of the hegemon for various pragmatic reasons continues to be accepted. Since a social order is necessary, any order is preferable to anarchy, or what Polanyi called the utopian project of the rule of the market.[9]

Theorising about hegemony is highly abstract, since there is little empirical evidence to draw on. A specific hegemony is a historical structure. A historical structure is *sui generis*. British hegemony developed in a power vacuum, and the resources devoted to military power were therefore marginal.[10] In contrast, the US hegemony evolved in the context of a superpower conflict which involved competing socio-economic systems, engaged in a Cold War and planning for an 'imaginary war'.[11] This added a radically new dimension to the post-war hegemonic rivalry, a systemic conflict.

Thus, the Cold War order was dualistic, in the sense that a socialist subsystem existed as a challenge to the capitalist world order, providing rebellious states with a safe haven. Regionalism was subsumed under the Cold-War logic, which implied a linkage between regional organisations and the fundamental cleavage of the system (hegemonic regionalism). The New World Order proclaimed by US President George Bush during the Gulf War can be seen as a counter strategy of the declining hegemon against the challenges of 'regional hegemonism', the Iraqs to come. Regional hegemonism is the 'malign' form of neo-mercantilism. The New Regionalism is the 'benign' form. The great task in creating a post-hegemonic future is to promote 'benign' rather than 'malign' neo-mercantilism.

[...]

The Neo-mercantilist Position

Let us now try to draw the threads together. The 'new regionalism' can be defined as a multidimensional process of regional integration which includes economic, political, social and cultural aspects. It is both a positive concept, summarising certain tendencies in the world system, and a normative position, arguing in favour of such tendencies as a potential new world order. Here I am particularly concerned with the second meaning, which I have called the neo-mercantilist position.[12] It is a package rather than a single policy, whether concerned with economics or foreign policy. The concept thus goes beyond the free trade idea, that is the interlinking of several previously more or less secluded national markets into one functional economic unit. Rather, the political ambition of creating territorial identity and regional coherence is the primary neo-mercantilist goal. In this observation other differences between 'old' and 'new' regionalism are implied. New regionalism is spontaneous and 'from below', or rather 'from within', whereas the old type often was imposed on a group of countries in the interest of superpower strategy. The new regionalism belongs to a new global situation characterised by multipolarity.

What we could call neo-mercantilism is thus a transnational phenomenon. Its spokesmen do not believe in the viability of closed national economies in the present stage of the development of the world economy. On the other hand, neither do they believe in the viability of an unregulated world economy. Nor do they – in contrast with the Trilateralists – put much faith in the possibility of managing such a world economy. Rather, neo-mercantilists believe in the regionalisation of the world into more or less self-sufficient blocs, where political stability and social welfare are major concerns. Ultimately, this will lead to region-states, replacing nation-states and thereby restoring stability and control.

This is the 'benign' view of mercantilism, contrasted to a 'malevolent' view by Barry Buzan as follows:

> The benign view sees a mercantilist system of large, inward-looking blocs, where protectionism is predominantly motivated by considerations of domestic welfare and internal political stability. Such a system potentially avoids many of the organizational problems of trying to run a global or quasi-global liberal economy in the absence of political institutions on a similar scale. The malevolent view sees a rerun of the mercantilist dynamic of the past, in which protectionism is motivated primarily by considerations of state power.[13]

Karl Polanyi, critic of the market utopia and early neo-mercantilist, warned against the 'hazards of planetary interdependence' associated with global market expansion.[14] This sceptical view corresponds to the one taken by contemporary neo-mercantilists who conceive a market system as a fragile arrangement. The post-war world economy is seen as a historic compromise between international economic *laissez-faire* and a certain level of domestic control.

This essentially Keynesian approach was gradually abandoned during the crisis of the 1970s, and in the subsequent decade purist liberal principles were becoming increasingly dominant, a trend that culminated when the socialist world began to disintegrate towards the end of the decade. The conclusion of the Cold War led to a hegemonic position for the market, which would indicate that the stage is set for the second phase of Polanyi's double movement, that is when the self-protection of society is activated.

This leads up to the argument for a regionalised world system as the form that today's protectionism could take. It is different from the classical Listian argument in favour of a coherent national economy. Keynes essentially repeated List's argument when he, in a now classic article written before the war, questioned the value of free trade.[15] He saw a certain degree of national self-sufficiency as a precondition for international political stability, denouncing the 'decadent international capitalism' of his time.

A decade later, when international peace had been fundamentally disturbed, Karl Polanyi developed a regionalist scenario, posed against what he at the time feared was going to be a new fruitless attempt to reshape the hegemonic world order or 'universal capitalism', this time under the leadership of the United States. Like Keynes earlier, he was concerned with the crucial question in international political economy: what kind of international economic structure and pattern of development was most conducive to peace and long term stability. Both warned against an unregulated liberal world order, but while Keynes emphasised the need for national self-sufficiency, Polanyi saw the solution to the world order problem in an emerging pattern of regionalism.[16] Polanyi, however, underestimated the post-war hegemonic potential of the United States, calling it 'an attempt doomed to failure'.

The post-war hegemonic world order is now in a process of transformation towards some kind of 'post-hegemonic', or 'post-Cold-War' world order. Hence the concept of region again assumes a new importance as a possible mode of organising the world. The world system logic is pointing towards further regionalisation, at least in the shorter perspective. Ultimately, the two processes of globalisation and regionalisation may prove complementary.

There is a difference between this new form of protectionism and the traditional mercantilist concern with state-building and national power. Neo-mercantilists argue in favour of the regionalisation of the world into more or less self-sufficient blocs. These blocs would be introverted and maintain symmetric relations among themselves. This is the 'benign' type. The 'malign' type is offensive and aggressive, an 'extended economic nationalism'. The 'benign view' of mercantilism coincides with what I call 'the new regionalism'.

[. . .]

Notes

1   D. Seers, *The Political Economy of Nationalism* (Oxford: Oxford University Press, 1983).

2   A. Acharya, 'Regional military-security cooperation in the Third World: a conceptual analysis of the relevance and limitations of ASEAN', *Journal of Peace Research* 29(1) (1992); and S. D. Muni, 'Changing global order and cooperative regionalism: the case of southern Asia', in Helena Lindolm (ed.), *Approaches to the Study of International Political Economy* (Göteborg: Padrigu, 1992).

3   B. Buzan, *People, States and Fear: An Agenda for International Security Studies in the Post-Cold War Era* (Brighton: Harvester Wheatsheaf, 1991).

4   Björn Hettne, 'The concept of mercantilism', in L. Magnusson (ed.), *Mercantilist Economies* (Boston: Kluwer, 1993).

5   H.-H. Holm and G. Sørensen, 'A new world order: the withering away of anarchy and the triumph of individualism? Consequences for IR theory', IPRA General Conference, Kyoto, 1992.

6   In the summer of 1990, in the shadow of the Kuwait crisis, ECOWAS (Economic Organization of West African States) intervened in the Liberian civil war. Although not fully backed

by the whole region, it was unprecedented in the history of African regional cooperation. The Liberian crisis can be said to have speeded up the process of regional cooperation. The shared view in the region was that 'the ECOWAS states cannot stand idly by and watch a member state slide into anarchy' (WA, 1–7 July 1991).

7 The point is well taken by Flora Lewis (*International Herald Tribune*, Friday, 17 July 1992): The words of Helsinki do represent a striking advance in formal international relations. They assert the 'collective conscience of our community' that insistence on human and democratic rights does not 'belong exclusively to the internal affairs of the state concerned. This propounds both a serious limitation on the thesis of absolute national sovereignty and a new responsibility as my brother's keeper.'

8 R. W. Cox, 'Gramsci, hegemony and international relations: an essay in method', *Millennium: Journal of International Studies* 12(2) (1983).

9 'To allow the market mechanism to be the sole director of the fate of human beings and their natural environment . . . would result in the demolition of society' (K. Polanyi, *The Great Transformation* (Boston: Beacon Press, 1957), pp. 71–3).

10 P. Kennedy, *The Rise and Fall of the Great Powers* (New York: Random House, 1987), p. 151.

11 M. Kaldor, *The Baroque Arsenal* (London: Deutsch, 1982).

12 Hettne, 'The concept of mercantilism'.

13 B. Buzan, 'Economic structure and international security: the limits of the liberal case', *International Organization* 38(4) (1984), p. 608.

14 Polanyi, *The Great Transformation*, p. 181.

15 J. M. Keynes, 'National self-sufficiency', *Yale Review* 22(4) (1933), pp. 755–69.

16 Karl Polanyi, 'Universal capitalism or regional planning', *London Quarterly of World Affairs* (Jan. 1945).

14

International Law

David Held

The development of international law has placed individuals, governments and non-governmental organizations under new systems of legal regulation. International law has recognized powers and constraints, and rights and duties, which transcend the claims of nation-states and which, while they may not be backed by institutions with coercive powers of enforcement, nonetheless have far-reaching consequences.

Throughout the nineteenth century, international law was conceived [. . .] as a law between states; states were its subjects and individuals its objects. The exclusion of the individual from the provisions of international law has been challenged and undermined in the twentieth century. From the minorities treaties, associated with the establishment of the League of Nations after the First World War, to the UN's Universal Declaration of Human Rights (1948) and subsequent Covenants on Rights (1966), it has been recognized that individuals have rights and obligations over and above those set down in their own judicial and authority systems (see Vincent 1992: 269–92). Not only have some states conceded that individuals may legitimately refuse to serve in national armies (for instance, by recognizing legally the status of conscientious objection), but they have also accepted that there are clear occasions when an individual has a moral obligation beyond that of his or her obligation as a citizen of a state – opening up a gap between the rights and duties bestowed by citizenship, and the creation in international law of new forms of liberties and obligations.

This gap is exemplified by the results of the International Tribunal at Nuremberg (and the parallel Tribunal in Tokyo). The Tribunal laid down, for the first time in history, that when *international rules* that protect basic humanitarian values are in conflict with *state laws*, every individual must transgress the state laws (except where there is no room for 'moral choice') (Cassese 1988: 132). The legal framework of the Nuremberg Tribunal marked a highly significant change in the legal direction of the modern state, for the new rules challenged the principle of military discipline and subverted national sovereignty at one of its most sensitive points: the hierarchical relations within the military. Contemporary international law has generally endorsed the position taken by the Tribunal, and has affirmed its rejection of the defence of obedience to superior orders in matters of responsibility for crimes against peace and humanity.[1]

Of all the international declarations of rights which were made in the post-war years, the European Convention for the Protection of Human Rights and Fundamental Freedoms (1950) is especially noteworthy. In marked contrast to the Universal Declaration of Human Rights and the subsequent UN Covenants of Rights, the European Convention was concerned, as its preamble indicates, 'to take the first steps for the *collective enforcement* of certain of the rights stated in the Universal Declaration' (emphasis added). The European initiative was committed to a most remarkable and radical legal innovation: an innovation which in principle would allow individual citizens to initiate proceedings against their own governments. European countries have now accepted an (optional) clause of the Convention which permits citizens to petition directly the European Commission on Human Rights, which can take cases to the Committee of Ministers of the Council of Europe and then (given a two-thirds majority on the Council) to the European Court of Human Rights. While the system is far from straightforward and is problematic in many respects, it has been claimed that, along-side the other legal changes introduced by the European Community, it no longer leaves the state 'free to treat its own citizens as it thinks fit' (Capotorti 1983: 977; cf. Coote 1992). It is interesting, in addition, to note that the Treaty of European Union (the Maastricht Treaty) makes provision, in principle, for the establishment of a European Union citizenship and an ombudsman to whom citizens may directly appeal.

Human rights have also been promoted in other regions of the world, partly in response to United Nations encouragement that such rights should be entrenched in institutions at regional levels. Notable developments have occurred in America and Africa. The American Convention on Human Rights, which came into force in 1978, has both a commission and a court, although they are as yet far less well used than their West European counterparts. The Organization of African Unity adopted the African (Banjul) Charter of Human and People's Rights in 1981; it too has a commission concerned to promote human rights. While citizens in many African countries have established organizations to seek compliance with this agreement, many of its leading provisions remain substantially unenforced. Nonetheless, what all these charters highlight is further evidence of a gradual shift from the principle that state sovereignty must be safeguarded irrespective of its consequences for individuals, groups and organizations. Respect for the autonomy of the subject, and for an extensive range of human rights, creates a new set of ordering principles in political affairs which, where effectively entrenched, can delimit and curtail the principle of state sovereignty itself.

There are two legal rules which, since the very beginnings of the international community, have been taken to uphold national sovereignty: 'immunity from jurisdiction' and 'immunity of state agencies'. The former prescribes that 'no state can be sued in the courts of another state for acts performed in its sovereign capacity'; and the latter stipulates that 'should an individual break the law of another state while acting as an agent for his country of origin and be brought before that state's courts, he is not held "guilty" because he did not act as a private individual but as the representative of the state' (Cassese 1988: 150–1). The underlying purpose of these rules is to protect a government's autonomy in all matters of foreign policy and to prevent domestic courts from ruling on the behaviour of foreign states (on the understanding that all domestic courts everywhere will be so prevented). And the upshot has traditionally been that governments have been left free to pursue their interests subject only to the constraints of the 'art of politics'.

It is notable, however, that these internationally recognized legal mainstays of sovereignty have been progressively questioned by Western courts. Efforts have been made, for instance, to increase the accountability of political leaders for wrongdoing while in office. A recent step in this direction has been the attempt to make leaders of foreign states vulnerable to civil claims in relation to acts of law-breaking by them. A well-known case involves claims for compensation against Imelda Marcos and the estate of Ferdinand Marcos, pursued in the US by the estates of two young labour leaders, murdered in Seattle some years ago, in what was allegedly a covert operation by a

Philippines intelligence unit (Falk 1991: 17). Although national sovereignty has most often protected foreign leaders against charges of wrongdoing, civil or criminal, the tension between national sovereignty and international law is now marked – in the Marcoses' case, $15 million was awarded to the plaintiffs – and it is by no means clear how it will be resolved.

There is a further tendency in contemporary international law no longer to regard a state as legitimate simply by virtue of the effectiveness of its claim to public power; that is to say, there is a tendency to reject a principle of legitimacy which is indifferent to the nature, form and operation of political power. Entrenched in certain legal instruments is the view that a legitimate state must be a democratic state that upholds certain common values.[2] The full status of this tendency is ambiguous, but it is noteworthy. For instance, the Universal Declaration of Human Rights asserts the democratic principle along with enumerated rights as a 'common standard of achievement for all peoples and nations' in Article 21 (see United Nations 1988: 2 and 5). However, the word 'democracy' does not itself appear in the Declaration and the adjective 'democratic' appears only once (in Article 29). The UN International Covenant on Civil and Political Rights (1966) (which came into force in 1976), by contrast, elaborates this principle in Article 25 as a legal obligation, although it only loosely specifies its meaning (see United Nations 1988: 28).

The European Convention on Human Rights is explicit in its connection of democracy and state legitimacy, as is the statute of the Council of Europe which makes a commitment to democracy a condition of membership. But one of the most significant indicators of the erosion of an unqualified endorsement of state sovereignty in international law comes from the challenge to the principle and practice of non-interference in the internal affairs of a state. The clearest statement of this challenge in recent times can be found in the 1992 declaration of the Helsinki Conference on Security and Co-operation in Europe (CSCE), involving over fifty states including the US and Canada. In the declaration the states recognize their accountability to each other and underline the rights of citizens to demand from their governments respect for democratic values and standards:

> We emphasise that the commitments undertaken in the field of the human dimension of the CSCE [that is, human rights] are matters of direct and legitimate concern to all participating States and do not belong exclusively to the internal affairs of the State concerned. The protection and promotion of human rights and fundamental freedoms and the strengthening of democratic institutions continue to be a vital basis for our comprehensive security. (CSCE 1992: para. 8, p. 2)

While these commitments remain fragile and far from universal, they signal the beginnings of a new approach to the concept of legitimate political power in international law.

The decline in the efficacy of state sovereignty is evidenced further in recent questioning of the traditional principles regulating the appropriation of territory and resources. At the heart of classical international law (the Westphalian model), the earth, sea and air were recognized as phenomena legitimately falling under the sovereign authority of states on the condition that 'whoever possessed a territory and exercised actual control over it successfully secured a legal title' [. . .]. While the principle of state sovereignty has been extended in recent times to cover the control of resources in a variety of domains, including the continental shelf and 'economic zones' (areas which stretch up to 200 nautical miles from coastal states), a new concept was propounded in 1967 as a potential vehicle for rethinking the legal basis of the appropriation and exploitation of resources: the 'common heritage of mankind'. Although the principle was subject to intensive discussion in the United Nations and elsewhere, it was eventually enshrined in two important treaties, the Convention on the Moon and Other Celestial Bodies (1979) and the Convention on the Law of the Sea (1982). First introduced as a way of thinking about the impact of new technologies, which opened up the possibility of the exploitation of resources (on the sea-bed or on stars and other planets) which were beyond national jurisdiction, its early champions saw it as a basis for arguing that the vast domains of hitherto untapped resources should be developed for the benefit of all, particularly the poor and the developing nations. There are five elements to the concept of the common heritage, namely, '(1) the exclusion of a right of appropriation; (2) the duty to exploit . . . resources in the interest of mankind . . . ; (3) the duty to explore and exploit for peaceful purposes only; (4) the duty to pay due regard to scientific research; and (5) the duty duly to protect the environment' (Cassese 1986: 390).

The introduction of the concept of the common heritage points to the possibility of a legal order based on equity and cooperation. Although there is still a great deal of argument as to exactly where and how this principle should be applied, and how the benefits which accrue from the exploitation of new resources should be distributed, the introduction of the concept was a turning point in international legal thinking. Furthermore, it has been taken up in debates about the environment and, in particular, in discussions about the management of the 'global commons' and their shared ecosystems (see World Commission on Environment and Development 1987: 18–19). Moreover, elements of the concept can be traced in the Rio Declaration on Environment and Development and in Agenda 21, both adopted at the Earth Summit in Brazil in 1992.

The Rio Declaration takes as its primary goal the creation of 'a new and equitable global partnership through the creation of new levels of cooperation among states, key sectors of societies and people' (United Nations 1993: 3). Principle 7 of the Declaration demands that 'states shall cooperate in a spirit of global partnership to conserve, protect and restore the health and integrity of the Earth's ecosystem'; and Principle 12 calls for 'environmental measures addressing transboundary or global environmental problems' which should, 'as far as possible, be based on an international consensus' (pp. 4 and 5). Setting out what this new global partnership might mean, Agenda 21 specifies that

> This partnership commits all States to engage in a continuous and constructive dialogue, inspired by the need to achieve a more efficient and equitable world economy, keeping in view the increasing interdependence of the community of nations and that sustainable development should become a priority item on the agenda of the international community. It is recognized that, for the success of this new partnership, it is important to overcome confrontation and to foster a climate of genuine cooperation and solidarity. (United Nations 1993: 14; and see ibid.: 111, 238)[3]

International law is a vast and changing corpus of rules, quasi-rules and precedents which set out the basis of coexistence and cooperation in the international order. Traditionally, international law has identified and upheld the idea of a society of sovereign states as 'the supreme normative principle' of the political organization of humankind (Bull 1977: 140ff.). In recent decades, the subject, scope and source of international law have all been contested; and opinion has shifted against the doctrine that international law is and should be a 'law between states only and exclusively' (see

Oppenheim 1905: ch. 1). At the heart of this shift lies a conflict between claims made on behalf of the states system and those made on behalf of alternative organizing principles of world order. While the recent political resurgence of Islam, and the renewed intensity of many nationalist struggles, indicate that this conflict is far from settled, new directions in international law are clearly discernible.

Notes

1 However, moves to apply the Nuremberg principles consistently and impartially across diverse geopolitical circumstances have been unsuccessful, although there remains [...] support for the development of an International Criminal Court with legal competence to apprehend and try those who initiate and perpetrate 'crimes of state', even when the accused are *in absentia* (see below).

2 I would like to thank Kevin Boyle for drawing my attention to this cluster of issues. For a thorough treatment see James Crawford (1994).

3 The Rio Declaration and Agenda 21 also embody remarkable tensions between the declared (and reaffirmed) 'sovereign rights of states' and the prerogatives of the new global partnership, although even in those sections affirming the former there is a concern to ensure that activities which fall within the jurisdiction or control of particular states do not cause damage to the environment of other states or to areas beyond the limits of national jurisdiction (see Principle 2). On principles of accountability and enforcement, however, there is little precision.

References

Bull, H. (1977) *The Anarchical Society*. London: Macmillan.

Capotorti, F. (1983) Human rights: the hard road towards universality. In R. St. J. Macdonald and D. M. Johnson (eds), *The Structure and Process of International Law*, The Hague: Martinus Nijhoff.

Cassese, A. (1986) *International Law in a Divided World*. Oxford: Clarendon Press.

Cassese, A. (1988) *Violence and Law in the Modern Age*. Cambridge: Polity Press.

Coote, A. (ed.) (1992) *The Welfare of Citizens: Developing New Social Rights*. London: IPPR/ Rivers Oram Press.

Crawford, J. (1994) *Democracy in International Law*. Inaugural Lecture. Cambridge: Cambridge University Press.

CSCE (1992) *Helsinki Declaration*. Conference on Security and Cooperation in Europe 1992. Helsinki: CSCE.

Falk, R. (1991) Positive prescriptions for the near future. World Order Studies Program Occasional Paper, no. 20, Center for International Studies, Princeton University.

Oppenheim, L. (1905) *International Law*, vol. 1. London: Longmans.

United Nations (1988) *Human Rights: A Compilation of International Instruments*. New York: UN Publications.

United Nations (1993) *Report of the United Nations Conference on Environment and Development*, vol. 1. 3 vols, New York: UN Publications.

Vincent, J. (1992) Modernity and universal human rights. In A. G. McGrew and P. G. Lewis et al., *Global Politics*, Cambridge: Polity Press.

World Commission on Environment and Development (1987) *Our Common Future*. Oxford: Oxford University Press.

15

Globalization and Legal Certainty

Volkmar Gessner

[...]
The following discussion on global institutions as support structures for cross-border interactions attempts to relate some [...] empirical observations to the problem of legal (un)certainty in the global arena.

Institutions Providing Global Legal Certainty

The social institutions providing (or not) stable action patterns in legally relevant situations [...] are rules, courts, legal professions and support structures. Institutions created in order to foster legal certainty for cross-border legal interaction can then be distinguished as those located on the programme level and those on the role level (see table 1).

Legal rules

In our previous study[1] the role of state law (private international law and international conventions) and of state courts in reducing insecurity of cross-border exchanges has been discussed and – as regards international cases in domestic courts – made the object

Table 1 Social institutions for cross-border legal interaction

	Programmes	Roles
State	International private law International conventions	Judges in international cases Central authorities in the fields of international legal assistance Consulates
Non-state	Law merchant Rules of third cultures	Institutions of third cultures Chambers of commerce Commercial associations Non-commercial institutions Law firms Arbitrators Brokers Debt collection agencies

of empirical research. The system of state conventions appeared to be very weak in guiding global legal interactions because of its lacking universality and its being frequently disregarded in legal practice. It was found that courts handled international cases like domestic cases, unable to consider foreign elements of the cases and uninformed as regards foreign law. Legal certainty may only be provided to those parties whose law is applied. Owing to the fact that domestic courts do not take much notice of court opinions in other countries, we also observed hardly any international legal developments initiated by case law. The globalization of law is still mainly an exercise of legal science and international organizations and has not as yet reached far into judicial practice.

This is also true of the *lex mercatoria*. The law merchant is spoken of under a number of names, including international, transnational or supranational commercial law; international customs or usages; general principles of international commercial law; and *lex mercatoria*. Regardless of the label, the same phenomenon, a set of rules encompassing the trading practices of the international merchant community, is being described. The ambit of the *lex mercatoria* is determined by the object of its constituent elements, but also by its origin and its customary, and thus spontaneous, nature.[2] Elements of this legal order are the following:

- general principles of law recognized by the commercial nations;
- universal rules like the Uniform Customs and Practices for Documentary Credits;
- universally used contract clauses like the INCOTERMS;
- universally used standard form contracts;
- codes of conduct;
- arbitral awards.

This normative order is far from being comprehensive and may therefore in many cases lead to insecurity and uncertainty about the legal situation. One must often seek guidance from sources other than the law merchant, in particular from state law, or must invent a new solution. In addition, most state courts refuse to apply the *lex mercatoria* and even refuse to enforce arbitration awards based on these autonomous rules. Hence arbitrators are also reluctant to refer to this set of rules.

It appears from these discussions that legal certainty cannot be achieved globally on the level of programmes. Programmes are a relatively abstract form of integrating expectations which requires a minimum of homogeneity of its legal subjects. Because of differences in their economic position, highly industrialized and developing societies will not integrate their expectations easily. Negative examples of unified (civil) law conventions which were signed and ratified by only a few countries are abundant. The positive exceptions of numerous ratifications are to be found mainly in procedural law (such as the UNCITRAL Arbitration Conventions and the Hague Conventions) and – as regards substantive law – in transport law. Ole Lando perceives many situations in which the application of the *lex mercatoria* provides legal certainty. This is certainly true for some of the *lex mercatoria* rules which are universally recognized and applied in legal practice, such as the Uniform Customs and Practices for Documentary Credit and the INCOTERMS. Equally, a number of trade norms and standard conditions help to secure cross-border commercial transactions. Export trade could not be imagined without these autonomously created legal instruments. But even these *lex mercatoria* rules are universal only in part because some areas of commercial activities are far from being homogeneous globally. In particular, Third World legal actors complain of a bias in favour of the interests of industrialized nations.

Other failures of integration on the level of programmes are based on cultural differences which already hinder the ratification of many international conventions and certainly influence the implementation of global legal programmes. Unlike the European Union, where the European Court of Justice effectively directs the application and interpretation of European law, there is no such court with a global jurisdiction. The implementation of international conventions is left to the judicial styles of courts and the claim consciousness of parties of different legal cultures in the world. Last but not least, geographical aspects are responsible for insurmountable differences. For example, standards for environmental protection are more relevant for some parts of the world because of their geographical location and relative economic wealth and therefore do not lead to universal integration of expectations.

Our empirical studies observed the weaknesses of programmes like the (Brussels) Convention on the Recognition and Enforcement of Foreign Judgments, the (Vienna) Convention on the International Sale of Goods, the (Hague) Legal Assistance Conventions and domestic international private law as regards state programmes. *Lex mercatoria* rules were hardly found at all in fields of legal practice observed in the course of our empirical and comparative research.

Legal science and international institutions active in the production of globalized law are very aware of the weakness of their programmes but generally do not question the programme level of global regulation as such. Notwithstanding this programme optimism, they have also been active at the roles level, creating and fostering the autonomous creation of global legal institutions.

Professions

Expectations which are integrated by roles are placed on a lower level of abstraction and may therefore be more suited to the global type of interaction. They are more specific to areas of action such as those of the customs officer, the stewardess or the hotel receptionist. Travellers know their expectations and expect them to be realized in quite a similar way all around the world. Some legal roles like those of lawyers, brokers, notaries, arbitrators and law professors are likewise relatively well defined globally and are able to create and support universal legal orientations. These orientations are legal not because they are supported by law (which is the programme level) but by legal roles. As regards arbitrators, this was well demonstrated by Dezalay and Garth: members of the international arbitration 'club' have a common understanding of legal principles and legal procedures. Parties who opt for arbitration know perfectly well the (international commercial) principles for the decisions and the basic ideas of the arbitrators. The circle of international arbitrators consists of only some 200–300 people from whom the parties choose those they know from previous arbitration procedures or published awards or legal practice.[3] In this highly personalized situation, their expectations as to the outcome of the dispute seem to be more secure than when anonymous state courts decide the cases.

This view is strongly supported by Ole Lando, who asserts that 'arbitrators of different nationalities who have applied the *lex mercatoria* in collegiate arbitral tribunals have not experienced great difficulties in reaching consensus . . . Most arbitrators have common ethics and common notions of how business should be conducted that lead them in the same direction.'[4]

As regards the legal professions all around the world, first one has to state that, in general, lawyers get little to no training in international or foreign aspects of law and are mostly unable to handle cross-border cases. Private individuals therefore get no legal advice on the international matters with which they are more and more confronted: in family affairs, consumer affairs and tourism.[5] Only larger business actors find legal advice in international law firms (mostly of US-American provenance) who draft their contracts in such a way as to protect them against any state law influence. These complex contracts are indeed able to provide a high degree of legal certainty. The lawyers' role is to provide legal information on domestic and on foreign law, to develop new financial instruments and sophisticated drafting, negotiating and deal-making techniques, to resolve disputes out of court[6] and to bridge the gap between legal cultures.[7] To that extent, their situation is comparable to that of the 'arbitration club': because the number of players is limited, their role is defined by a set of global behavioural patterns which is often maintained by frequent contacts (there exist only a few centres in the world where most of these law firms are located) and exchanges in networks, journals and the Internet mailboxes. International lawyers may not yet have formed an autonomous community comparable to the 'arbitration club', but, as legal representatives in negotiations, litigators or in-house counsels, they are of considerable economic and legal influence and have the power to create a certain degree of legal certainty simply by the fact that they monopolize legal interactions of all important global actors. It seems to be a common situation that Chinese, Egyptian, German and Malaysian firms are internationally represented in contract negotiations by US-American law firms just like their US commercial partners. There is no 'third culture' of law firms around the world, but US law firms clearly have been able to define the roles an international lawyer has to play if he or she wishes to succeed in the global market of legal services.

It is true that even experienced US-American law firms report frequent interaction problems in their global dealings, in contract negotiation and conflict resolution.[8] But they are in the process of creating a surprising variety of networks, training centres and courses, international libraries and international associations which will enable them soon to feel almost at home in the global legal market – at least as long as the US and common law domination prevails.

Rather than focusing on arbitrators and international law firms (an area in which we have not carried out much empirical research) we will proceed with a discussion on the possible contribution to legal certainty of other types of support structures which can be observed in the world society: institutions of the law merchant, in particular institutions of global 'third cultures', as well as other support structures whether created by state initiative or by non-state actors.

Third cultures

These structures, like the aforementioned professional communities, do have a set of rules common to all members but in the main integrate expectations on a much lower level than the programme level. They develop well-defined roles and expect their 'clients' also to observe very specific behavioural patterns. Global differentiation of social fields, rather than creating anomic situations, shapes secure expectation structures, the only problem being how to get into the subsystem.

Third cultures as conceived above are regular phenomena of the *lex mercatoria* as well as of global non-business communities. They develop in the world society just as semi-autonomous fields develop in national societies, are defined by a limited number of actors who share (economic or idealist) interests, have common ethics and follow the same patterns and customs. Worldwide third cultures are the scientific communities, the mafias, the religious communities and above all those commercial branches which were able to a large degree to monopolize the area of their activities. The example of the diamond industry as well as those studies elaborated in the course of our own project (the banking sector and the London reinsurance market) may illustrate their characteristic way of creating autonomous behavioural patterns and the high degree of 'legal' certainty all members can rely on.

The diamond industry, that internationally active and economically important branch of business, has been carefully studied by Lisa Bernstein.[9] In the market of rough diamonds, 80–85 per cent of the world's supply is controlled by the De Beers cartel, which distributes the rough diamonds through four brokers. The brokers sell presorted boxes of diamonds to some 150–200 dealers, known as sight-holders, during ten viewing sessions, held in London each year. Sight-holders, together with manufacturers, wholesalers and brokers, are members of the worldwide 20 diamond dealers' clubs which secure the steady supply of goods. Although it is possible to buy stones on the 'open market', a dealer who does not have access to the trading clubs – essential links with the worldwide diamond distribution network, the 'World Federation of Diamond Bourses' – will be at a competitive disadvantage. The clubs or bourses therefore can exercise a strict control over their local or foreign members and impose their own rules and dispute resolution mechanism. Non-compliance means loss of reputation (the name of the rule-breaker is circulated to all of the bourses in the world federation) and in practice exclusion from the diamond business. The system remains completely apart from state penal law, contract law and bankruptcy law, and state courts are replaced by arbitration or on occasion by proceedings in Jewish rabbinical courts.

The diamond cartel is not so much integrated on the programme level but has developed specific roles like sight-holders, brokers, club members, arbitrators and the rabbi within which expectations are defined and implemented. It seems irrelevant to which legal culture the actors belong, because the diamond dealers' culture is a global culture independent of national legal or legal cultural influences.

Recent information in the media seems to indicate that the De Beers cartel will come under pressure from diamond producers so far not active in the cartel (such as the countries of the former Soviet Union). New global actors might destroy cultural patterns of global interaction and quickly reduce successful structures of legal certainty.

In Klaus Frick's research project,[10] the international activities of the banks are in a similar way described as a 'third culture' where all actors have 'opted out of the legal system'. As in the diamond trade, there is only a limited number of actors and strong control over compliance with usages, contracts, verbal commitments and standard forms. Despite the enormous number of transactions and the gigantic amounts of money transferred worldwide, disputes hardly ever arise. Some few cases go to arbitration and hardly any to state courts. The system has been rationalized for centuries and has recently been computerized in order to avoid errors and misunderstandings. The personnel have well-defined roles and are trained carefully to comply with global behavioural standards. No elaborated programme is integrating mutual expectations all over the world, but roles are clearly defined up to the pinstripe suit of higher-ranking executives. And the institutions do everything to negotiate problems that arise and will rather write losses off than go to third party dispute resolution – to say nothing of litigation.

As far as state law exists (letters of credit, documentary credit, cheques) it has been prepared with the strong participation of the banking sector. Recent attempts of the European Union to gain some control (for example, over the costs of money transfer in the Union or over money laundering) have so far been successfully held back in order to allow for autonomous solutions of the problems. Regulatory interventions might in this specific case be successful on the programme level owing to the homogeneous structure of the European banking sector. But this is true only for the European Union, where the programme level is used frequently and with not completely unrealistic chances of implementation. Universally, the banking sector is integrated on the role level rather than on the programme level.

Christine Stammel's research project concerns the 'third culture' of the reinsurance business.[11] This business is to a very high degree dominated by international actors who participate in global exchange. A major market-place is the City of London, where a number of brokers bring the reinsurers and their clients, the ceding offices (the primary insurers who are seeking insurance cover), together. The contractual practices in use are extremely informal. The broker drafts a 'slip' which is nothing but a paper which documents the contract conditions in a short form. He will also collect the premium from the ceding office and deduct his share before he passes the money on to the reinsurer. His task is, furthermore, to collect the claims arising under the reinsurance contract and he will sustain the communication between reinsurer and ceding office. This picture of informal contracts and relationships based on trust rather than on law is very much akin to Stanley's description of the subcultural code of ethics in the City of London.[12] Disputes until recently were resolved only by arbitration. In the last few years a series of catastrophes started which hit the market hard. The fact that documentation of reinsurance contracts had been treated as a 'stepchild' in the past was an invitation at least to try to avoid payments under the policy. Under economic pressure and the growing number of actors, the autonomy of this 'third culture' apparently breaks down. Disputes lead more frequently to litigation before the London Commercial Court where highly specialized judges (possibly experienced in the reinsurance business in their previous role as barristers) seem to have gained the confidence of the reinsurance business. This is probably not a shift to the programme level but rather a development on the level of roles: insiders are replaced by external experts who are able to deal with the rising complexity of reinsurance issues. The community of experts involved in these issues remains small: it consists of some 30 London City law firms and a handful of High Court judges.

Support structures

Most state support structures for cross-border legal interaction work on the basis of a programme, a municipal law or an international convention. Consulates execute the consular law, central authorities mostly execute a legal assistance convention, domestic judges are guided by private international law or some unified law. But there is empirical evidence that, if these structures offer legal certainty at all, this is due to specific roles: a judge specializing in commercial cases or a member of a chamber for international matters,[13] a civil servant experienced in cross-border matters such as social security of migrants,[14] a consul with a legal background able to understand the law and the legal culture of the host country.[15] If the programmes determined the practice of these support structures, the latter would show similar patterns of behaviour. This is not the case, either in an international comparison (for example, German and New York and Spanish judges) or even in a national comparison (German consuls in the Netherlands and German consuls in Kuala Lumpur).

The focus on roles is equally justified in regard to non-state support structures. Lawyers and arbitrators have already been mentioned in their well-defined international business for well-defined groups of global actors. Whereas most lawyers and most arbitrators are unfamiliar with international matters, a small number of those professionals are highly experienced but only accessible to important business enterprises who act in the main outside state-provided patterns. Neither commercial institutions (like the national chambers of commerce, the foreign chambers of commerce or the International Chamber of Commerce in Paris) nor the headquarters of commercial branches or commercial services (like the debt collection agencies[16] or the brokers in insurance business[17]) nor non-commercial institutions (like those supporting child support claims[18]) are executing a universal or in some way general programme. They render (or not) legal certainty to very specific clients by complying (or not) with very specific expectations, making use of complex devices of which an international convention might be a part. A good example is the Milan Chamber of Commerce,[19] which serves the local industry by providing assistance in its domestic and international dealings without referring to programmes or state rules and even without using *lex mercatoria* rules or arbitration.

Winners and Losers of Global Legal Uncertainty

Legal certainty is a complex phenomenon which consists of shared normative expectations and of trust in compliance. Studies in comparative law show the different ways this goal can be achieved in national legal systems. A sociolegal comparison in addition demonstrates that not only legal structures but also social structures with autonomous rules and sanction mechanisms succeed in providing legal certainty. Globally, legal and social structures compete in offering better solutions. Our brief overview has compared the contributions of state law (including international conventions), law merchant and third cultures to securing stable expectations and predictable behaviour. All in all, the picture we have offered suggests little success in achieving legal certainty on the programme level. Legal certainty increases from transactions governed by state law, over transactions governed by the law merchant, to transactions governed by third cultural mechanisms. The non-state mechanisms, in spite of the relative security which they offer to their 'clients', seem fragile and may break down whenever the number of actors increases (this may be the case already in some international transactions, such as consumer transactions), whenever the transaction costs of third party decision-making surpass the transaction costs avoided by the creation of third party intervention (this may be the case with arbitration) or whenever economic interests prevail over group solidarity (this is the situation in the reinsurance market). In spite of interesting global developments in favour of securing economic exchanges, legal certainty is accomplished successfully and in a stable way neither by state legal devices nor by *lex mercatoria*, nor by norms and behavioural patterns created autonomously within third cultures. Some specific roles create legal certainty for some specific groups, but most global actors, such as small and medium-sized enterprises, consumers, members of binational families, migrants and victims of accidents in foreign countries, gain no access to these groups and cannot make use of qualified support structures.

[. . .]

Notes

1   Volkmar Gessner (ed.), *Foreign Courts: Civil Litigation in Foreign Legal Cultures* (Aldershot: Dartmouth, 1996).

2   Michael T. Medwig, 'The new law merchant: legal rhetoric and commercial reality', *Law and Policy in International Business* 24 (1993): 589–616.

3   Yves Dezalay and Bryant Garth, *Dealing in Virtue: International Commercial Arbitration and the Construction of a Transnational Legal Order* (Chicago: University of Chicago Press, 1996).

4   Ole Lando, 'The lex mercatoria in international commercial arbitration', *International and Comparative Law Quarterly* 34 (1985): 747–68.

5   Cf. Hanno von Freyhold, Volkmar Gessner, Enzo Vial and Helmut Wagner (eds), *The Cost of Civil Litigation for Consumers in the Single Market*, Report to the EU-Kommission (Bremen, 1995).

6   Our court file analyses in Bremen, Hamburg, Milan and New York support the assumption that disputes over complex contracts are never taken to court. Cf. Gessner, *Foreign Courts*.

7   Roger J. Goebel, 'Professional qualification and educational requirements for law practice in a foreign country: bridging the cultural gap', *Tulane Law Review* 63 (1989): 443–523.

8   Sunwolf, 'Communication between legal cultures: strategies, perceptions and beliefs of American lawyers who practice international litigation', in Johannes Feest and Volkmar Gessner (eds), *Interaction of Legal Cultures* (Onati: Onati Pre-Publications, 1998).

9   Lisa Bernstein, 'Opting out of the legal system: extralegal contractual relations in the diamond industry', *Journal of Legal Studies* 21 (1992): 115–57.

10 K. Frick, 'Third cultures versus regulators: cross-border legal relations of banks', in V. Gessner and Ali Cem Budak (eds), *Emerging Legal Certainty: Empirical Studies on the Globalization of Law*, Onati International Series in Law and Society (Aldershot: Ashgate, Dartmouth, 1988).

11 C. Stammel, 'Back to the courtroom? Developments in the London reinsurance market', in Gessner and Budak, *Emerging Legal Certainty*. See also her doctoral dissertation on the same subject, published as Christine Stammel, *Waving the Gentlemen's Business Good-Bye* (Frankfurt: Peter Lang Verlag, 1998).

12 Christopher Stanley, 'Serious money: legitimation of deviancy in the financial markets', *International Journal of the Sociology of Law* 20 (1992): 43–60.

13 Cf. Stammel, 'Back to the courtroom?', regarding the judges in the London Commercial Court; and Volkmar Gessner, 'International cases in German first instance courts', in Gessner, *Foreign Courts*, pp. 181–5, with regard to the judges in the Hamburg international chambers.

14 Cf. Pierre Guibentif ('Cross-border legal issues arising from international migration: the case of Portugal', in Gessner and Budak, *Emerging Legal Certainty*) who found that cross-border social security rights are protected in Portugal thanks only to an administrative network of contacts otherwise atypical in the context of Portuguese administrative culture. This network creates a special relationship between officials all of whom are particularly concerned with the problems of Portuguese emigrants abroad.

15 Cf. Andreas Petzold, 'Obtaining information on foreign legal systems', in Gessner and Budak, *Emerging Legal Certainty*. The overall picture of the quality of legal advice given by consulates is one of a few thoughtful, creative responses, and a few dreadfully ignorant and useless replies. The great majority provide some of the information that is required and obtainable, but remain below the potential the existing sources allow.

16 Ali Cem Budak, 'Cross-border debt collection: examples of Turkey and Germany', in Gessner and Budak, *Emerging Legal Certainty*. According to this study, debt collection

agencies have developed a bundle of strategies for collecting foreign debts and are highly successful whenever they use renegotiation instead of law enforcement.

17 Stammel, 'Back to the courtroom?' Brokers handle reinsurance contracts in a surprisingly informal way and often only write down on a 'slip' what seem to be the essentials of the insurance cover. Neither legal nor law merchant rules define this situation. Recently, more and more lawyers are becoming involved in contract drafting and conflict resolution, which may lead to some reinsurance contract law; that is, to the development of expectations on the level of programmes.

18 Cf. Kirstin Grotheer, 'Cross-border maintenance claims of children', in Gessner and Budak, *Emerging Legal Certainty*. This study gives the impression of a legal 'overkill' of legal assistance and law enforcement conventions, leading to extraordinary bureaucratic efforts, costs and delays. Some small institutions with a modest budget seem to handle cross-border maintenance claims much better. As Grotheer suggests, they provide on the basis of experience and contacts a feeling of legal certainty in an otherwise rather anomic situation.

19 Cf. Vittorio Olgiati on the Milan Chamber of Commerce: 'The political economy of the Chamber of Commerce of Milan: towards a new "universitas mercatorium"', in Gessner and Budak, *Emerging Legal Certainty*. He describes this institution as being based in the Mussolini era on Fascist corporatism. During that period the chambers of commerce in Italy were conceived in legal terms as a sort of economic prefecture. Since 1993, they have constituted a system of autonomous institutions performing functions of general interest as well as providing private support, assistance and advice.

16

Governance in a Globalizing World

James N. Rosenau

[...]

Conceptual Nuances

In order to grasp the complexities that pervade world politics, we need to start by drawing a nuanced set of distinctions among the numerous processes and structures that fall within the purview of global governance. Perhaps most importantly, it is necessary to clarify that global governance does not refer only to the formal institutions and organizations through which the management of international affairs is or is not sustained. The United Nations system and national governments are surely central to the conduct of global governance, but they are only part of the full picture. Consequently, in the ensuing analysis global governance is conceived to include systems of rule at all levels of human activity – from the family to the international organization – in which the pursuit of goals through the exercise of control has transnational repercussions. The reason for this broad formulation is simple: in an ever more interdependent world where what happens in one corner or at one level may have consequences for what occurs at every other corner and level, it seems a mistake to adhere to a narrow definition in which only formal institutions at the national and international levels are considered relevant. In the words of the Council of Rome,

> We use the term governance to denote the *command* mechanism of a social system and its actions that endeavor to provide security, prosperity, coherence, order and continuity to the system . . . Taken broadly, the concept of governance should not be restricted to the national and international systems but should be used in relation to regional, provincial and local governments as well as to other social systems such as education and the military, to private enterprises and even to the microcosm of the family.[1]

Governance, in other words, encompasses the activities of governments, but it also includes the many other channels through which 'commands' flow in the form of goals framed, directives issued and policies pursued.

Command and control

But the concept of commands can be misleading. It implies that hierarchy, and perhaps even authoritarian rule, characterize governance systems. Such an implication may be descriptive of many forms of governance, but hierarchy is certainly not a necessary prerequisite to the framing of goals, the issuing of directives and the pursuit of policies. Indeed, a central theme of the ensuing analysis is that often the practices and institutions of governance can and do evolve in such a way as to be minimally dependent on hierarchical, command-based arrangements. Accordingly, while preserving the core of the Council of Rome formulation, here we shall replace the notion of command mechanisms with the concept of *control* or *steering* mechanisms, terms that highlight the purposeful nature of governance without presuming the presence of hierarchy. These terms, moreover, are informed by the etymological roots of 'governance': the term 'derives from the Greek "kybernan" and "kybernetes" which means "to steer" and "pilot or helmsman" respectively (the same Greek root from which "cybernetics" is derived). The process of governance is the process whereby an organization or society steers itself, and the dynamics of communication and control are central to that process.'[2]

To grasp the concept of control one has to appreciate that it consists of relational phenomena which, taken holistically, comprise systems of rule. Some actors, the controllers, seek to modify the behaviour and/or orientations of other actors, the controllees, and the resulting patterns of interaction between the former and the latter can properly be viewed as a system of rule sustained by one or another form of control. It does not matter whether the controllees resist or comply with the efforts of controllers; in either event, attempts at control have been undertaken. But it is not until the attempts become increasingly successful and compliance with them increasingly patterned that a system of rule founded on mechanisms of control can be said to have evolved. Rule systems and control mechanisms, in other words, are founded on a modicum of regularity, a form of recurrent behaviour that systematically links the efforts of controllers to the compliance of controllees through either formal or informal channels.[3]

It follows that systems of rule can be maintained and their controls successfully and consistently exerted even in the absence of established legal or political authority. The evolution of intersubjective consensuses based on shared fates and common histories, the possession of information and knowledge, the pressure of active or mobilizable publics, and/or the use of careful planning, good timing, clever manipulation and hard bargaining can – either separately or in combination – foster control mechanisms that sustain governance without government.[4]

Interdependence and proliferation

Implicit in the broad conception of governance as control mechanisms is a premise that interdependence not only involves flows of control, consequence and causation within systems, but that it also sustains flows across systems. These micro-macro processes – the dynamics whereby values and behaviours at one level get converted into outcomes at more encompassing levels, outcomes which in turn get converted into still other consequences at still more encompassing levels – suggest that global governance knows no boundaries, geographic, social, cultural, economic or political. If major changes occur in the structure of families, if individual greed proliferates at the expense of social consciences, if people become more analytically skilful, if crime grips neighbourhoods, if schools fail to provoke the curiosity of children, if racial or religious prejudices become pervasive, if the drug trade starts distributing its illicit goods through licit channels, if defiance comes to vie with compliance as characteristic responses to authority, if new trading partners are established, if labour and environmental groups in different countries form cross-border coalitions, if cities begin to conduct their own foreign commercial policies – to mention only some of the more conspicuous present-day dynamics – then the consequences of such developments will ripple across and fan out at provincial, regional, national and international levels as well as across and within local communities. Such is the crazy-quilt nature of modern interdependence. And such is the staggering challenge of global governance.

And the challenge continues to intensify as control mechanisms proliferate at a breathtaking rate. For not only has the number of UN members risen from 51 in 1945 to 185 a half-century later, but the density of non-governmental organizations (NGOs) has increased at a comparable pace. More accurately, it has increased at a rate comparable to the continuing growth of the world's population beyond 5 billion and a projected 8 billion in 2025. More and more people, that is, need to concert their actions to cope with the challenges and opportunities of daily life, thus giving rise to more and more organizations to satisfy their needs and wants. Indeed, since the needs and wants of people are most effectively expressed through organized action, the organizational explosion of our time is no less consequential than the population explosion. Hastened by dynamic technologies that have shrunk social, economic, political and geographic distances and thereby rendered the world ever more interdependent, expanded by the advent of new global challenges such as those posed by a deteriorating environment, an AIDS epidemic and drug trafficking, and further stimulated by widespread authority crises within existing governance mechanisms,[5] the proliferation of organizations is pervasive at and across all levels of human activity – from neighbourhood organizations, community groups, regional networks, national states and transnational regimes to international systems.[6]

Not only is global life marked by a density of populations, in other words; it is also dense with organized activities, thereby complicating and extending the processes of global governance. For while organizations provide decision points through which the steering mechanisms of governance can be carried forward, so may they operate as sources of opposition to any institutions and policies designed to facilitate governance. Put in still another way, if it is the case, as many (and this author) argue,[7] that global life late in the twentieth century is more complex than ever before in history, it is partly because the world is host to ever greater numbers of organizations in all walks of life and in every corner of every continent. And it is this complexity, along with the competitive impulses which lead some organizations to defy steerage and resort to violence, that make the tasks of governance at once so difficult and so daunting.

Disaggregation and innovation

An obvious but major conceptual premise follows from the foregoing: namely, there is no single organizing principle on which global governance rests, no emergent order around which communities and nations are likely to converge. Global governance is the sum of myriad – literally millions – of control mechanisms driven by different histories, goals, structures and processes. Perhaps every mechanism shares a history, culture and structure with a few others, but there are no characteristics or attributes common to all mechanisms. This means that any attempt to assess the dynamics of global governance will perforce have multiple dimensions, that any effort to trace a hierarchical structure of authority which loosely links disparate sources of governance to each other is bound to fail. In terms of governance, the world is too disaggregated for grand logics that postulate a measure of global coherence.

Put differently, the continuing disaggregation that has followed the end of the Cold War suggests a further extension of the anarchic structures that have long pervaded world politics. If it was possible to presume that the absence of hierarchy and an ultimate authority signified the presence of anarchy during the era of hegemonic leadership and superpower competition, such a characterization of global governance is all the more pertinent today. Indeed, it might well be observed that a new form of anarchy has evolved in the current period – one that involves not only the absence of a highest authority, but that also encompasses such an extensive disaggregation of authority as to allow for much greater flexibility, innovation and experimentation in the development and application of new control mechanisms.

Stated in terms of a rough quantitative measure, it is perhaps suggestive of the scale of disaggregative dynamics and the shift of authority away from governments that in the United States even the police function is in relative decline: whereas people once relied on public authorities to protect them from crime, in recent years they have turned to hiring their own police. The number of publicly authorized police on duty throughout the country has remained roughly at half a million since 1980, but during the same period the number of private security guards has risen more than 600,000 (to 1.6 million)[8] and expenditures to maintain them are roughly double the amount spent on public police protection.[9] In sum, while politicians and pundits may speak confidently or longingly about establishing a new world order, such a concept is only meaningful as it relates to the prevention or containment of large-scale violence and war. It is not a concept that can be used synonymously with global governance if by the latter is meant the vast numbers of rule systems that have been caught up in the proliferating networks of an ever more interdependent world.

Emergence and evolution

Underlying the growing complexity and continuing disaggregation of modern governance are the obvious but often ignored dynamics of change wherein control mechanisms emerge out of path-dependent conditions and then pass through lengthy processes of either evolution and maturation or decline and demise. In order to acquire the legitimacy and support they need to endure, successful mechanisms of governance are more likely to evolve out of bottom-up than top-down processes. As such, as mechanisms that manage to evoke the consent of the governed, they are self-organizing systems, steering arrangements that develop through the shared needs of groups and the presence of developments that conduce to the generation and acceptance of shared instruments of control.

But there is no magic in the dynamics of self-organization. Governance does not just suddenly happen. Circumstances have to be suitable, people have to be amenable to collective decisions being made, tendencies towards organization have to develop, habits of cooperation have to evolve, and a readiness not to impede the processes of emergence and evolution has to persist. The proliferation of organizations and their ever greater interdependence may stimulate felt needs for new forms of governance, but the transformation of these needs into established and institutionalized control mechanisms is never automatic and can be marked by a volatility that consumes long stretches of time. Yet, at each stage of the transformation, some form of governance can be said to exist, with a preponderance of the control mechanisms at any moment in time evolving somewhere in the middle of a continuum that runs from nascent to fully institutionalized mechanisms, from informal modes of framing goals, issuing directives and pursuing policies to formal instruments of decision-making, conflict resolution and resource allocation.

No matter how institutionalized rule systems may be, in other words, governance is not a constant in these turbulent and disaggregated times. It is, rather, in a continuous process of evolution, a becoming that fluctuates between order and disorder as conditions change and emergent properties consolidate and solidify. To analyse governance by freezing it in time is to ensure failure in comprehending its nature and vagaries.

The Relocation of Authority

Notwithstanding the evolutionary dynamics of control mechanisms and the absence of an overall structural order, it is possible to identify pockets of coherence operating at different levels and in different parts of the world that can serve as bases for assessing the contours of global governance in the future. It may be the case that 'processes of governance at the global level are inherently more fragile, contingent, and unevenly experienced than is the case within most national political systems',[10] but this is not to deny the presence of central tendencies. One such tendency involves an 'upsurge in the collective capacity to govern': despite the rapid pace of ever greater complexity and decentralization – and to some extent because of their exponential dynamics – the world is undergoing 'a remarkable expansion of collective power', an expansion that is highly disaggregated and unfolds unevenly but that nevertheless amounts to a development of rule systems 'that have become (1) more intensive in their permeation of daily life, (2) more permanent over time, (3) more extensive over space, (4) larger in size, (5) wider in functional scope, (6) more constitutionally differentiated, and (7) more bureaucratic'.[11] Global governance in the coming decades may not take the form of a single world order, but it will not be lacking in activities designed to bring a measure of coherence to the multitude of jurisdictions that are proliferating on the world stage.

Perhaps even more important, a pervasive tendency can be identified in which major shifts in the location of authority and the site of control mechanisms are underway on every continent and in every country, shifts that are as pronounced in economic and social systems as they are in political systems. Indeed, in some cases the shifts have transferred authority away from the political realm and into the economic and social realms even as in still other instances the shift occurs in the opposite direction.

Partly these shifts have been facilitated by the end of the Cold War and the lifting of the constraints inherent in its bipolar global structure of superpower competition. Partly they have been driven by a search for new, more effective forms of political organization better suited to the turbulent circumstances that have evolved with the shrinking of the world by dynamic technologies.[12] Partly they have been driven by the skill revolution that has enabled citizens to identify their needs and wants more clearly as well as to be more thoroughly empowered to engage in collective action.[13] Partly they have been stimulated and sustained by subgroupism – the fragmenting and coalescing of groups into new organizational entities – that has created innumerable new sites from which authority can emerge and towards which it can gravitate.[14] Partly they have been driven by the continuing globalization of national and local economies that has undermined long-established ways of sustaining commercial and financial relations.[15] And, no less, the shifts have been accelerated by the advent of interdependence issues – such as environmental pollution, AIDS, monetary crises and the drug trade – that have fostered new and intensified forms of transnational collaboration as well as new social movements that are serving as transnational voices for change.[16]

In short, the numerous shifts in the loci of governance stem from interactive tensions whereby processes of globalization and localization are simultaneously unfolding on a worldwide scale. In some situations the foregoing dynamics are fostering control mechanisms that extend beyond national boundaries and in others the need for the psychic comfort of neighbourhood or ethnic attachments is leading to the diminution of national entities and the formation or extension of local mechanisms. The combined effect of the simultaneity of these contradictory trends is that of lessening the capacities for governance located at the level of sovereign states and national societies.[17] Much governance will doubtless continue to be sustained by states and their governments initiating and implementing policies in the context of their legal frameworks – and in some instances national governments are likely to work out arrangements for joint governance with rule systems at other levels – but the effectiveness of their policies is likely to be undermined by the proliferation of emergent control mechanisms both within and outside their jurisdictions.[18] In the words of one analyst, 'the very high levels of interdependence and vulnerability stimulated by technological change now necessitate new forms of global political authority and even governance.'[19]

Put more emphatically, perhaps the most significant pattern discernible in the criss-crossing flow of transformed authority involves processes of bifurcation whereby control mechanisms at national levels are, in varying degrees, yielding space both to more encompassing forms of governance and to narrower, less comprehensive forms. For analytic purposes, we shall refer to the former as transnational governance mechanisms and the latter as subnational governance mechanisms, terms that do not preclude institutionalized governmental mechanisms but that allow for the large degree to which our concern is with dynamic and evolving processes rather than with the routinized procedures of national governments.

While transnational and subnational mechanisms differ in the extent of their links across national boundaries – all the former are by definition boundary-spanning forms of control, while some of the latter may not extend beyond the jurisdiction of their states – both types must face the same challenges to governance. Both must deal with a rapidly changing, ever more complex world in which people, information, goods and ideas are in continuous motion and, thus, endlessly reconfiguring social, economic and political horizons. Both are confronted with the instabilities and disorder that derive from resources shortages, budgetary constraints, ethnic rivalries, unemployment and incipient or real inflation. Both need to contend with the ever greater relevance of scientific findings and the epistemic communities that form around the findings. Both are subject to the continuous tensions that spring from the inroads of corrupt practices, organized crime and restless publics that have little use for politics and politicians. Both must cope with pressures for further fragmentation of subgroups on the one hand and for more extensive transnational links on the other. Both types of mechanisms, in short, have severe adaptive problems and, given the fragility of their legal status and the lack of long-standing habits of support for them, many of both types may fail to maintain their essential structures intact.[20] Global governance, it seems reasonable to anticipate, is likely to consist of proliferating mechanisms that fluctuate between bare survival and increasing institutionalization, between considerable chaos and widening degrees of order.

Mechanisms of Global Governance

Steering mechanisms are spurred into existence through several channels: through the sponsorship of states, through the efforts of actors other than states at the transnational or subnational levels, or through states and other types of actors jointly sponsoring the formation of rule systems. They can also be differentiated by their location on the aforementioned continuum that ranges from full institutionalization on the one hand to nascent processes of rule-making and compliance on the other. Although extremes on a continuum, the institutionalized and nascent types of control mechanisms can be causally linked through evolutionary processes. It is possible to trace at least two generic routes that link the degree to which transnational governance mechanisms are institutionalized and the sources that sponsor these developments. One route is the direct, top-down process wherein states create new institutional structures and impose them on the course of events. A second is much more circuitous and involves an indirect, bottom-up process of evolutionary stages wherein nascent dynamics of rule-making are sponsored by publics or economies that experience a need for repeated interactions that foster habits and attitudes of cooperation which, in turn, generate organizational activities that eventually get transformed into institutionalized control mechanisms.[21] Stated more generally, whatever their sponsorship, the institutionalized mechanisms tend to be marked by explicit hierarchical structures, whereas those at the nascent end of the continuum develop more subtly as a consequence of emergent interaction patterns which, unintentionally and without prior planning, culminate in fledgling control mechanisms for newly formed or transformed systems.

Table 1 offers examples of the rule systems derivable from a combination of the several types of sponsors and the two extremes on the continuum, a matrix that suggests the considerable variety and complexity out of which the processes of global governance evolve. In the table, moreover, there are hints of the developmental processes whereby nascent mechanisms become institutionalized: as indicated by the arrows, some of the control mechanisms located in the right-hand cells have their origins in left-hand cells as interdependence issues that generate pressures from the non-governmental world for intergovernmental cooperation which, in turn, leads to the formation of issue-based transnational institutions. The history of more than a few control mechanisms charged with addressing environmental problems exemplifies how this subtle evolutionary path can be traversed.

However they originate, and at whatever pace they evolve, transnational governance mechanisms tend to be essentially forward looking. They may be propelled by dissatisfactions over existing (national or subnational) arrangements, but their evolution is likely to be marked less by despair over the past and present and more by hope for the future, by expectations that an expansion beyond existing boundaries will draw on cooperative impulses which may serve to meet challenges and fill lacunae that would otherwise be left unattended. To be sure, globalizing dynamics tend to create resistance and opposition, since any expansion of governance is bound to be detrimental to those who have a stake in the status quo. Whether they are explicitly and formally designed or subtly and informally constructed, however, on balance transnational systems of governance tend to evolve in a context of hope and progress, a sense of breakthrough, an appreciation that old problems can be circumvented and moved towards either the verge of resolution or the edge of obsolescence.

Table 1 The sponsorship and institutionalization of control mechanisms

		Nascent	Institutionalized
Not state-sponsored	Transnational	• non-governmental organizations • social movements • epistemic communities • multinational corporations	• Internet • European Environmental Bureau • credit-rating agencies
	Subnational	• ethnic minorities • micro regions • cities	• American Jewish Congress • the Greek lobby • crime syndicates
State-sponsored		• macro regions • European community • GATT	• United Nations system • European Union • World Trade Organization
Jointly sponsored		• cross-border coalitions • issue regimes	• election monitoring • human rights regime

Relatively speaking, on the other hand, subnational mechanisms are usually (though not always) energized by despair, by frustration with existing systems that seems best offset by contracting the scope of governance, by a sense that large-scale cooperation has not worked and that new subgroup arrangements are bound to be more satisfying. This distinction between transnational and subnational governance mechanisms can, of course, be overstated, but it does suggest that the delicacies of global governance at subnational levels may be greater than those at transnational levels.
[. . .]

Notes

Parts of this essay have been adapted from J. N. Rosenau, 'Governance in the twenty-first century', *Global Governance: a Review of Multilateralism and International Organizations* 1(1) (Winter 1995): 23–38, © 1995 by Lynne Rienner Publishers Inc., used with permission, and J. N. Rosenau, *Along the Domestic-Foreign Frontier: Exploring Governance in a Turbulent World* (Cambridge: Cambridge University Press, 1997), ch. 21.

1 A. King and B. Schneider, *The First Global Revolution: A Report of the Council of Rome* (New York: Pantheon, 1991), pp. 181–2 (emphasis added). For other inquiries that support the inclusion of small, seemingly local systems of rule in a broad analytic framework, see J. Friedmann, *Empowerment: The Politics of Alternative Development* (Oxford: Blackwell, 1992); and R. Huckfeldt, E. Plutzer and J. Sprague, 'Alternative contexts of political behavior: churches, neighborhoods, and individuals', *Journal of Politics* 55 (May 1993): 365–81.

2 S. A. Rosell et al., *Governing in an Information Society* (Montreal: Institute for Research on Public Policy, 1992), p. 21.

3 Rule systems have much in common with what has come to be called the 'new institutionalism'. See, for example, R. O. Keohane, 'International institutions: two approaches', *International Studies Quarterly* 32 (Dec. 1988): 379–96; J. G. March and J. P. Olsen, 'The new institutionalism: organizational factors in political life', *American Political Science Review* 78 (Sept. 1984): 734–49; and O. R. Young, 'International regimes: toward a new theory of institutions', *World Politics* 39 (Oct. 1986): 104–22. For an extended discussion of how the concept of control is especially suitable to the analysis of both formal and informal political phenomena, see J. N. Rosenau, *Calculated Control as a Unifying Concept in the Study of International Politics and Foreign Policy*, Research Monograph 15, Center of International Studies (Princeton: Princeton University, 1963).

4 Cf. J. N. Rosenau and E.-O. Czempiel (eds), *Governance without Government: Order and Change in World Politics* (Cambridge: Cambridge University Press, 1992). Also see the formulations in P. Mayer, V. Rittberger and M. Zurn, 'Regime theory: state of the art and perspectives', in V. Rittberger (ed.), *Regime Theory and International Relations* (Oxford: Oxford University Press, 1993); and T. J. Sinclair, 'Financial knowledge as governance', paper presented at the annual meeting of the International Studies Association, Acapulco, 23–7 Mar. 1993.

5 For a discussion of the breadth and depth of the world's authority crises, see J. N. Rosenau, 'The relocation of authority in a shrinking world', *Comparative Politics* 24 (Apr. 1992): 253–72.

6 A vivid picture of the organizational explosion in the non-governmental world is presented in L. M. Salamon, 'The global associational revolution: the rise of the third sector on the world scene', *Foreign Affairs* (July–Aug. 1994): 109. As for the world of governments, in addition to the new states that have recently swollen the ranks of the international system, a measure of the extraordinary organizational density that has evolved can be extrapolated – assuming the pattern is global in scale – from the following description of the United States some three decades ago:

> It has been estimated that there are over 8,000 multifunctional and autonomous local governments, including over 3,000 counties and more than that number of urban governments for the thousands of incorporated municipalities which speckle the map. The mesh is made still finer by the number of special-purpose districts which have been mushrooming over the past decades, particularly in the major metropolitan regions. From 1942 to 1962 the number of special districts (excluding school districts) grew from 8,300 to over 18,000. When school districts are added, the result in 1962 was an astonishing total of over 63,000 local governments with some autonomous authority over specific parcels of U.S. space.... Emerging from this complex geopolitical web are thousands of discrete units of territorial identity and exclusion – cities and suburbs, townships and countries, school districts and whole metropolitan regions – which instill a sense of community and apartness usually surpassed only at the national and family levels.

See E. W. Soja, *The Political Organization of Space*, Resource Paper 8 (Washington DC: Association of American Geographers, 1971), p. 45.

7 For an extended discussion of why the changes at work in the world today involve differences in kind rather than degree, see J. N. Rosenau, *Along the Domestic-Foreign Frontier: Exploring Governance in a Turbulent World* (Cambridge: Cambridge University Press, 1997), ch. 2.

8 J. P. Pinkerton, *What Comes Next: The End of Big Government – and the New Paradigm Ahead* (New York: Hyperion, 1995), p. 43.

9 K. Phillips, *Boiling Point: Republicans, Democrats, and the Decline of Middle-Class Prosperity* (New York: Random House, 1993), p. 141.

10 A. G. McGrew, 'Global politics in a transitional era', in A. G. McGrew, P. G. Lewis et al., *Global Politics: Globalization and the Nation-State* (Cambridge: Polity Press, 1992), p. 318.

11 M. Hewson, 'The media of political globalization', paper presented at the annual meeting of the International Studies Association, Washington DC, Mar. 1994, p. 2.

12   For cogent analyses of the bases of political organization, see E. Adler, 'Imagined (security) communities', paper presented at the annual meeting of the American Political Science Association, New York, 1–4 Sept. 1994; D. Ronfeldt, 'Tribes, institutions, markets, networks: a framework about societal evolution', Rand Corporation, Santa Monica, 1996; and Soja, *The Political Organization of Space*.

13   The skill revolution is outlined in J. N. Rosenau, *Turbulence in World Politics: a Theory of Change and Continuity* (Princeton: Princeton University Press, 1990), ch. 13. An analysis of how the skill revolution has empowered people to engage more effectively in collective action can be found in Rosenau, 'The relocation of authority in a shrinking world'. Systematic data tracing skills across sixty years and supporting the proposition that they have expanded, at least among diverse types of elites, are presented in J. N. Rosenau and W. M. Fagen, 'Increasingly skillful citizens: a new dynamism in world politics?', *International Studies Quarterly* 41 (Dec. 1997): 655–86.

14   The dynamics of subgroupism are set forth in Rosenau, *Turbulence in World Politics*, pp. 133–6, 396–8.

15   See, for example, P. F. Drucker, *Post-Capitalist Society* (New York: HarperCollins, 1993).

16   A discussion of the impact of new interdependence issues is offered in Rosenau, *Turbulence in World Politics*, pp. 429–30. The emergent role of new social movements is assessed in R. B. J. Walker, *One World, Many Worlds: Struggles for a Just World Peace* (Boulder: Lynne Rienner, 1988); and L. P. Thiele, 'Making democracy safe for the world: social movements and global politics', *Alternatives*, 18 (1993), pp. 273–305.

17   For analyses of these contradictory trends, see J. N. Rosenau, 'The person, the household, the community, and the globe: notes for a theory of multilateralism in a turbulent world', in Robert W. Cox (ed.), *The New Realism: Perspectives on Multilateralism and World Order* (Houndsmills: Macmillan, 1997), pp. 57–80.

18   None of this is to imply, of course, that the shifts in the loci of authority occur easily, with a minimum of commotion and a maximum of clarity. Far from it: the shifts derive from delicate bargaining, and usually they must overcome extensive opposition. As a result:

> Transfer of authority is a complicated process and it seems there no longer is one single identifiable sovereign, but a multitude of authorities at different levels of aggregation and several centres with differing degrees of coercive power (not all of them public and governmental!) . . . it becomes increasingly difficult to differentiate between public and private institutions, the State and Civil Society, domestic and international.

See K. Lahteenmaki and J. Kakonen, 'Regionalization and its impact on the theory of international relations', paper presented at the annual meeting of the International Studies Association, Washington DC, Mar. 1994, pp. 32–3.

19   J. Vogler, 'Regimes and the global commons: space, atmosphere and oceans', in McGrew and Lewis et al., *Global Politics*, p. 118.

20   For a conception of political adaptation in which adaptive systems are posited as being able to keep fluctuations in their essential structures within acceptable limits, see J. N. Rosenau, *The Study of Political Adaptation* (London: Frances Pinter, 1981).

21   For a cogent analysis in which this bottom-up process is posited as passing through five distinct stages, see B. Hettne, 'The new regionalism: implications for development and peace', in B. Hettne and A. Inotai, *The New Regionalism: Implications for Global Development and International Security* (Helsinki: UNU World Institute for Development Economics Research, 1994), pp. 7–8.

Part III
The Fate of National Culture

The movement of cultures is linked with the movement of people. The earliest movements of people took their cultures with them across regions and continents. The globalization of culture has, accordingly, a long history. The great world religions showed how ideas and beliefs can cross the continents and transform societies. No less important were the great premodern empires which, in the absence of direct military and political control, held their domains together through a common culture of ruling elites.

However, there is something quite distinctive, globalists argue, about the sheer scale, intensity and speed of global cultural communications today. This can be linked to many factors. First, the twentieth century has witnessed a wave of new technological innovations in communications and transportation, along with the transformation of older technologies, which together have generated functioning global infrastructures. These have opened up a massive series of communication channels that cross national borders, increasing the range and type of communications to and from all the world's regions. Second, contemporary patterns of cultural globalization have created a far greater intensity of images and practices, moving with far greater extensity and at a far greater velocity than in earlier periods. At both the domestic and the international level, cultures, societies and economies are becoming more information dense. This process is compounded by the fact that new global communication systems are used for business and commercial purposes. While there remain significant differences in information density and velocity in different parts of the globe, it is becoming increasingly difficult for people to live in any place culturally isolated from the wider world.

Against such propositions the sceptics argue that there is little sign as yet that national cultures are in terminal decline. They point out that the key supposed agents of cultural globalization – Coca-Cola, McDonald's, Microsoft and so on – are in the business of making profits and pursuing commerce, not in the business of creating alternative centres of political identity and legitimacy. The world remains a place of competing cultures, all investing in their own symbolic resources, and seeking to enlarge their spheres of influence. There is little basis for global cultural projects to flourish. Just as the territorial state is far more resilient than globalists suggest, so too are national cultures. In fact, the resilience of national cultures is an important part of the explanation of why territorial states persist and continue to play such a key part in the determination of the shape of international order.

The contours of the debate about cultural globalization are set out and explained in the section below. In the first paper, by Robins, the growing mobility of goods and commodities, information and communication products and services across borders is introduced. The complexity of this phenomenon and of its diverse impacts is emphasized. Robins seeks to set out how and why it is that cultural globalization involves an unequal and uneven set of processes which call into question old certainties and hierarchies of identity. In such a world, the cultural meaning of boundaries is transformed and cultural continuities are disrupted. Examining these processes further, Thompson retraces the emergence of globalization in the sphere of communication. When did it begin? How did it develop? In seeking to answer these questions Thompson provides a systematic survey of the emergence of global communication networks. After dwelling on some of the structural characteristics of globalized processes of communication, he investigates 'the creative interface between the globalized diffusion of media products and their localized appropriation'. Thompson concludes by arguing that while the globalization of communication has altered the nature of symbolic exchange and transformed certain aspects of the life conditions of people throughout the world, it has not done so straightforwardly at the expense of local and national cultural life. The importance which media messages have for individuals depends crucially 'on the contexts of reception and on the resources that recipients bring to bear on the reception process'. But he emphasizes as well that the localized appropriation of global media products can also be a source of tension and conflict. Global media products may expand people's horizons of understanding and interpretation; but they can also lead to antagonism between local, national and global forces.

The chapter which follows by Herman and McChesney provides a detailed overview of media globalization, focusing on the global trend to deregulation, global corporate media consolidation, and its uneven development. The positive and negative effects of a globalizing of the media are examined and the risks assessed of the growing consolidation of 'a commercial model of communication'. This type of communication tends to erode the public sphere and to create a 'culture of entertainment' that might well be incompatible, or at least in some tension, with a democratic order. Herman and McChesney conclude by examining the ways in which 'media outputs are commodified and are designed to serve market ends, not citizenship needs'.

Appadurai examines the interplay between forces of cultural homogenization and cultural heterogenization. He expresses scepticism about arguments which emphasize the significance of cultural globalization either as a form of Americanization or as a form of commodification. What these arguments fail to consider, he contends, is that 'at least as rapidly as forces from various metropolises are brought into new societies they tend to become indigenized in one or [an]other way.' This gives rise to highly complex forms of cultural community and shifting patterns of cultural understanding. In Appadurai's view, the shifting balance between cultural homogenization and cultural heterogenization creates a highly complex, overlapping, disjunctive cultural order. The critical point is that global cultural processes today are meshed in a highly varied mutual contest 'of sameness and difference on a stage characterized by radical disjunctures between different sorts of global flows and the uncertain landscapes created in and through these disjunctures'.

Finally, for all those who hold the view that a global culture is emerging, Smith's article provides a most telling challenge. Not only is the idea of a global culture vague and imprecise, but there is very little evidence, he suggests, that national cultures are being swept aside. The latter remain the obstinate bases of collective cultural identity. National sentiments and values in respect of a sense of continuity, shared memories and a common destiny still pervade many given collectivities which have had a common experience and distinctive history. As Smith puts it, 'vernacular mobilization; the politicization of cultures; the role of intelligentsia and other strata; and the intensification of cultural wars . . . are some of the reasons . . . why national cultures . . . continue to divide our world into discrete cultural blocks, which show little sign of homogenization, let alone amalgamation.' Despite global shifts in the technical and linguistic infrastructures of communication, it is highly unlikely that any kind of global culture or cosmopolitan ideal will truly supersede the world of nations.

17

Encountering Globalization

Kevin Robins

[. . .]
Globalization is about growing mobility across frontiers – mobility of goods and commodities, mobility of information and communications products and services, and mobility of people. Walk down your local high street and you will be aware of global chains such as McDonald's or Benetton. You may buy the global products of Sony, Procter and Gamble or the Coca-Cola Corporation. In your local supermarkets you will buy more or less exotic fruits and vegetables from almost anywhere in the world, along with ingredients for curries, stir-fries, pizzas, and other 'world foods'. If you go out to eat you can choose from restaurants providing a whole range of 'ethnic' cuisines (Italian, Chinese, Indian, Korean, Thai, etc.). Go to the off-licence and you cannot but be aware of the increasing globalization of the market for wines (not just French or Spanish, but now South African, Chilean, Australian, and even Crimean varieties) and beers (Italian, American, Indian, Brazilian, Japanese, and more). Your coat might be produced in Turkey, your hi-fi in Japan, and your car in Korea. And, of course, we could push this analysis back one stage further, for the various inputs into the production of these commodities (raw materials, labour, components, finance) are also likely to come from a range of geographical sources.

Through the development of satellite and cable services, and on the basis of more liberal media regulation, the television market is moving from national to transnational scale. CNN can bring you 'real-time' access to news stories across the world, as we clearly saw at the time of the Gulf War in 1991. The Disney Channel is targeted at a global audience. 'It's an MTV World' is the cover story of a recent issue of *Newsweek* magazine (24 April 1995) [. . .] – itself now a global media enterprise. The main headline: 'Rock around the clock and around the world with the ultimate New Age multinational'. Through the new telecommunications networks – from voice through to fax and e-mail – we can now enter into global communications 'at the touch of a button' (though paying for them is, of course, another matter). And if you have access to the Internet and the World Wide Web, you may gain access to global databases, and you can choose to become a member of a global user group. Instantaneous and ubiquitous communication is giving substance to the Canadian philosopher Marshall McLuhan's idea, first put forward in the 1960s, that the world is now becoming a 'global village'.

There are gathering flows of people, too, not just of physical and information products and goods. Members of the international business elite now undertake international travel on a routine and regular basis, constituting themselves as a global community of frequent-flier cosmopolitans. Far more numerous are those whose mobility and movement are precipitated by need or by despair, the migrants who take advantage of a cheap plane or train to seek work in the world's more affluent centres, establishing themselves there as minority communities in exile. Leisure pursuits, too, like the pursuit of employment, are associated with accelerating flows. If where you live is a tourist resort, you will be familiar with visitors from Europe or from the United States, increasingly from Japan and the Far East, and now, too, from Eastern Europe and Russia. And you will doubtless be aware of the relative ease with which you can undertake holiday travel, not just to the South of France, or the Costa Brava, but now to Florida Disneyland, or to Goa or the Caribbean. [. . .] Mobility has become ordinary in the emerging global order. But it is also possible to see the world without having to move. For now 'the world' is able to come to where we are. As the writer Simon Winchester puts it in his introduction to Martin Parr's collection of photographs, *Small World*:

> A whole new industry has been born from the manufacturing of . . . foreign-theme entertainment parks, the world brought to your doorstep by, first, the Americans (with both the outer world, and outer space, tucked into the more exotic corners of Disneyland) and then by the Japanese – who went on to develop the idea to a fine art, settling outside Tokyo an English village that is more brimming with thatch and swimming in bitter beer than anywhere in the Cotswolds. Soon the Europeans are to have such a *parc internationale*, with little great walls of China and petit Taj Mahals constructed in fields convenient for the fun-filled charabancs that converge on Cherbourg. (Parr 1995)

[. . .]

With mobility, comes encounter. In many respects, this may be stimulating and productive. Global encounters and interactions are producing inventive new cultural forms and repertoires. Musical culture provides an excellent example: Salma and Sabine are Pakistani sisters who sing Abba songs in Hindi; Rasta-Cymru is a Welsh-speaking reggae band; El Vez is a Latino Elvis impersonator with attitude; Cartel is a Turkish–German group appropriating US West-coast rap music and style. The anthropologist Jan Nederveen Pieterse reflects on the significance of such musical and other cultural intermixtures:

> How do we come to terms with phenomena such as Thai boxing by Moroccan girls in Amsterdam, Asian rap in London, Irish bagels, Chinese tacos and Mardi Gras Indians in the United States, or Mexican schoolgirls dressed in Greek togas dancing in the style of Isadora Duncan? How do we interpret Peter Brook directing the Mahabharata, or Ariane Mnouchkine staging a Shakespeare play in Japanese Kabuki style for a Paris audience in the Théâtre du Soleil? (Nederveen Pieterse 1995: 53)

Nederveen Pieterse describes these phenomena in terms of the origination of 'third cultures', the 'creolization of global culture', the development of an 'intercontinental crossover culture'. Globalization, from this perspective, is conceived in terms of a process of creative and conjoining *hybridization*.

Of course, this is only one aspect of the logic of globalization. The encounter between cultures can produce tension and friction. The globalization process can equally be associated with confrontation and the collision of cultures. At the present time, we can see some of the stresses of global change in the difficult relations between Western and Islamic worlds. It is there in the conflict between French people and Algerian migrants, or in the divisions between Germans and their Turkish 'guest workers'. The building of Europe's largest mosque in Rome, the historical centre of Christendom, has had some problematical repercussions. In Britain, the 'Rushdie affair' has testified to the difficulty of intercultural understanding. The Iranian government has sought to block American satellite broadcasting to prevent the 'Westoxification' of Iranian society (while many Iranians have been actively seeking to acquire satellite dishes in order to see Western programmes such as *Baywatch* and *Beavis and Butthead*). In August 1995, the socialist mayor of Courcouronnes, south of Paris, put a ban on satellite dishes to prevent the reception of programmes from North Africa. 'Integration', he maintained, 'does not mean transforming France into a nation of the Maghreb' (*Observer*, 17 Sept. 1995).

But there are also cultural confrontations within the Western world itself. It is apparent in the ambivalence and anxiety felt in Europe towards American cultural exports: in 1995, the Uruguay Round of GATT (General Agreement on Tariffs and Trade) negotiations almost broke down on account of French intransigence about maintaining restrictive quotas on US film and television products. 'Are we all Americans now?' Andrew Billen wondered (*Observer*, 17 Sept. 1995), as the Disney Channel arrived in Britain. There is the clear sense in some quarters that 'Americanization' – from Hollywood to Coke and McDonald's – is a threat to the integrity of European cultural life (see Tomlinson 1997). In these defensive and protective responses to cultural encounter, we are a long way from the celebration of cultural hybridization.

Complexities of Globalization

Having argued that globalization and global encounter constitute a new logic of economic and cultural development, I want now to make two important qualifications to what would otherwise risk being too facile an argument. [. . .]

The first point of qualification [. . .] is that globalization does not supersede and displace everything that preceded it. As well as recognizing social innovation, we must have regard to the evident continuities in social and cultural life. Globalization may be seen in terms of an accumulation of cultural phenomena, where new global elements coexist alongside existing and established local or national cultural forms. [. . .]

[Second] I want to emphasize [globalization's] complexity and diversity (which make it particularly unamenable to ideal-type categorizations). The processes of global change are multifarious, and they are also experienced differentially by all those who confront them. [. . .]

There are more and less benign encounters with the forces of globalization. The geographer Doreen Massey captures this inequality well in relation to the experience of human mobility and movement. [. . .] At one end of the spectrum, she argues, there are those 'at the forefront' of what is going on: 'the jet-setters, the ones sending and receiving the faxes and the e-mail, holding the international conference calls, the ones distributing the films, controlling the news, organizing the investments and the international currency transactions'. At the other end are those who are out of control:

> The refugees from El Salvador or Guatemala and the undocumented migrant workers from Michoacán in Mexico crowding into Tijuana to make perhaps a fatal dash for it across the border into the USA to grab a chance of a new life. Here the experience of movement, and indeed of a confusing plurality of cultures, is very different. And there are those from India, Pakistan, Bangladesh and the Caribbean, who come halfway round the world only to get held up in an interrogation room at Heathrow. (Massey 1993: 61–2)

'Some initiate flows and movement,' Massey observes, 'others don't; some are more on the receiving end of it than others; some are effectively imprisoned by it' (1993: 61). Globalization is an uneven and an unequal process.
[...]

A World of Difference

[...] I want [...] to look at some broader aspects of globalization in relation to culture and identity. For it is surely clear that the global shift – associated with the creation of world markets, with international communication and media flows, and with international travel – has profound implications for the way we make sense of our lives and of the changing world we live in. For some, the proliferation of shared or common cultural references across the world evokes cosmopolitan ideals. There is the sense that cultural encounters across frontiers can create new and productive kinds of cultural fusion and hybridity. But, where some envisage and enjoy cosmopolitan complexities, others perceive, and often oppose, what they see as cultural homogenization and the erosion of cultural specificity. Globalization is also linked to the revalidation of particular cultures and identities. Globalization is, then, transforming our apprehension of the world in sharply contrasting ways. It is provoking new senses of disorientation and of orientation, giving rise to new experiences of both placeless and placed identity.

Old certainties and hierarchies of identity are called into question in a world of dissolving boundaries and disrupted continuities. Thus, in a country that is now a container of African and Asian cultures, can the meaning of what it is to be British ever again have the old confidence and surety it might once have had? And what does it mean now to be European in a continent coloured not only by the cultures of its former colonies, but also by American and Japanese cultures? Is not the very category of identity itself problematical? Is it at all possible, in global times, to sustain a coherent and unified sense of identity? Continuity and historicity of identity are challenged by the immediacy and intensity of global cultural confrontations. Of course, we should not believe that these developments are entirely unprecedented [...] a great many cultures have historical experience of global intrusion [...]. Nonetheless we should have regard to what is without precedent at the end of the twentieth century: the scale, the extent, the comprehensive nature, of global integration. We should consider [...] the particular complexities of global encounter at this century's end.

One very powerful dimension of global cultural change has been that which has sought to dissolve the frontiers and divisions between different cultures. It has been actively promoted by global corporate interests [...] – it is an ideal that is particularly sympathetic to those members of the class of symbolic analysts working in the creative areas of media, advertising, and so on. We could consider it in terms of the global culture and philosophy associated with 'McDonaldization' or 'Coca-colonization'. But a particularly good example – because it is so explicit and self-aware about its objectives – is that of Benetton advertising. Through its 'United Colors of Benetton' slogan, the company has actively promoted the idea of the 'global village', associated with global consumer citizenship. What is advocated is the ideal of a new, 'universal' identity that transcends old, particularistic attachments. But transcendence is through incorporation, rather than through dissolution. Michael Shapiro describes it as 'a globalizing, ecumenical impulse':

Ever since [Oliviero] Toscanini [the artistic creator of the campaigns] produced the
slogan, *The United Colors of Benetton*, the Benetton company has made explicit its desire
to dominate the mediascape with a symbolism that comprehends nationalities, ethnicities,
religions, and even tribal affiliations. The world of geopolitical boundaries – boundaries
transversed by Benetton's enterprises – is no impediment to the production of media-
carried global symbolism. (Shapiro 1994: 442)

This global corporate philosophy is further refined in Benetton's most recent campaign,
concerned with global threats and disasters:

In this case, the interpretative work locates the observer in a global community, trying
to make sense of the violent clashes of ethno-nationalists. This global self-identification is
precisely the difference-effacing stance that Benetton is trying to achieve. The interpretative contemplation of global threats and catastrophes cuts across ethnicities, nationalities,
and tribalisms, allowing Benetton to position its products in a universalizing thematic that
transcends cultural inhibitions. (1994: 448)

What the example of Benetton makes clear is the resourcefulness of global advertising,
both incorporating and effacing cultural difference in its endeavours to put in place the
new global acumen.

A second dimension of cultural globalization that we should consider is that which
promotes cultural encounter and interaction. Here, in stark contrast with the first dimension that we have just looked at, we are concerned with the active interpenetration,
combination and mixture of cultural elements. These processes are, as Akbar Ahmed
makes clear, a consequence of both communication flows and human flows:

The mixing of images, interlocking of cultures, juxtaposition of different peoples, availability
of information are partly explained because populations are mobile as never before. The
mobility continues in spite of increasingly rigid immigration controls. Filipino maids in
Dubai, Pakistani workers in Bradford, the Japanese buying Hollywood studios, Hong Kong
Chinese entrepreneurs acquiring prime property in Vancouver testify to this. The swirling
and eddying of humanity mingles ideas, cultures and values as never before in history.
(Ahmed 1992: 26)

Cultures are transformed by the incorporations they make from other cultures in the
world. Salman Rushdie (1991: 394) has famously written of 'the transformation that comes
of new and unexpected combinations of human beings, cultures, ideas, politics, movies,
songs'; '*Mélange*, hotchpotch,' he declares, 'a bit of this and a bit of that is *how new-
ness enters the world*.' This process of hybridization is particularly apparent now in developments within popular culture. The sociologist Les Back (1994: 14) describes the
bhangramuffin music of the singer/songwriter Apache Indian as 'a meeting place where
the languages and rhythms of the Caribbean, North America and India mingle, producing a new and vibrant culture'. 'Artists like Apache Indian are expressing and defining
cultural modes that are simultaneously local and global,' Back observes. 'The music manifests itself in a connective supplementarity – raga plus bhangra plus England plus India
plus Kingston plus Birmingham' (p. 15). Places too can be characterized in terms of
hybridity: places of encounter, meeting places, crucibles in which cultural elements are
turned into new cultural compounds. Doreen Massey (1993: 66) argues for the recognition of 'a sense of place which is extraverted, which includes a consciousness of its

links with the wider world, which integrates in a positive way the global and the local'. A 'global sense of place' involves openness to global dynamics and also an acceptance of cultural diversity and the possibilities of cultural encounter within.

The third dimension of cultural globalization that I want to [emphasize] concerns developments that apparently involve a rejection or turning away from the turbulent changes associated with global integration. These developments express themselves in a turn, or return, to what are seen as traditional and more fundamental loyalties. In the recent period, we have become increasingly aware of the resurgence of national, regional, ethnic and territorial attachments. In Eastern Europe, particularly in the former Yugoslavia, we have witnessed the growth of neo-nationalism in its most milit-ant form, but it has also been a feature of Western Europe, with the assertion of Basque, Breton or Scottish identities. It has now become a journalistic commonplace to describe such regionalist or nationalist reassertion in terms of a reversion or regression to tribal loyalties. These loyalties and attachments seem to go against the grain of glob-alization; they appear to articulate the desire and need for stability and order, as a refuge from the turbulence and upheaval of global transformation. And, of course, there is a great deal of truth in this theory of resistance through roots. But we might, at the same time, also see this as itself an expression of the globalization process – Anthony Smith (1991: 143) writes of the 'globalization of nationalism'. Resurgent nations are also seek-ing to position themselves in the new global space.

We may see the same contradictory relation to the globalization process in the case of resurgent religious cultures and identities. While there has been a return to funda-mentals within Hinduism, Judaism and Christianity, it is the case of Islamic fundamentalism that has been made to stand out for its opposition to global times. The attempts by some Islamic countries to ban satellite television have seemed to symbolize resistance to global information and communication flows [. . .]. A *Guardian* headline (5 Aug. 1994) expressed it perfectly: 'As satellite television shrinks the world, traditionalists from Tehran to Bollywood [India] take on the dishes in a war of the heavens.' At one level, of course, this does indeed represent a defensive and protective response to the disruptions of global modernity. As Akbar Ahmed (himself a Muslim) makes clear in his book *Post-modernism and Islam*, we must see such actions in the context of the struggle by tradi-tional cultures, and particularly Islam, to come to terms with Western globalization:

> The West, though the dominant global civilization, will continue to expand its boundaries to encompass the world; traditional civilizations will resist in some areas, accommodate to change in others. In the main, only one, Islam, will stand firm in its path. Islam, therefore, appears to be set on a collision course with the West. (Ahmed 1992: 264)

But we must see this as far more than just closure and retreat from global culture. What we must also recognize is the aspiration to create a space within global culture. For many Muslims, Ahmed argues, the objective is 'to participate in the global civil-ization without their identity being obliterated' (ibid.). As Peter Beyer (1994) argues, the 'revitalization of religion is a way of asserting a particular (group) identity, which in turn is a prime method of competing for power and influence in the global system' (p. 4); the 'central thrust is to make Islam and Muslims more determinative in the world system, not to reverse globalization. The intent is to shape global reality, not to negate it' (p. 3). The point is to create a global civilization on a different basis from that which is being elaborated by the symbolic analysts of the West.

What I am trying to bring out in all of this is the factor of diversity and difference in the cultural experience of global modernity: new forms of universal culture, new kinds of particularism, new hybrid developments, all of them gaining their significance from their new global context. We should not think of globalization in terms of homogenization, then, in line with what is commonly believed and feared.

But nor should we see it just in terms of diversity and differentiation, which is the opposite temptation that many more critical spirits have succumbed to. What globalization in fact brings into existence is a new basis for thinking about the relation between cultural convergence and cultural difference.

[. . .]

The globalization process must be seen in terms of the complex interplay of economic and cultural dynamics, involving confrontation, contestation and negotiation. The global future is therefore sure to have surprises in store for us.

References

Ahmed, A. (1992) *Postmodernism and Islam*. London: Routledge.

Back, L. (1994) The sounds of the city. *Anthropology in Action* 1(1): 11–16.

Beyer, P. (1994) *Religion and Globalization*. London: Sage.

Massey, D. (1993) Power-geometry and a progressive sense of place. In J. Bird et al. (eds), *Mapping the Future: Local Cultures, Global Change*, London: Routledge.

Nederveen Pieterse, J. (1995) Globalization as hybridization. In M. Featherstone, S. Lash and R. Robertson (eds), *Global Modernities*, London: Sage.

Parr, M. (1995) *Small World*. Stockport: Dewi Lewis.

Rushdie, S. (1991) *Imaginary Homelands*. London: Granta/Penguin.

Shapiro, M. (1994) Images of planetary danger: Luciano Benetton's ecumenical fantasy. *Alternatives* 19(4): 433–54.

Smith, A. D. (1991) *National Identity*. Harmondsworth: Penguin.

Tomlinson, J. (1997) Internationalization, globalization and media imperialism. In K. Thompson (ed.), *Media and Cultural Regulation*, London: Sage/The Open University.

18

The Globalization of Communication

John B. Thompson

One of the salient features of communication in the modern world is that it takes place on a scale that is increasingly global. Messages are transmitted across large distances with relative ease, so that individuals have access to information and communication which originates from distant sources. Moreover, with the uncoupling of space and time brought about by electronic media, the access to messages stemming from spatially remote sources can be instantaneous (or virtually so). Distance has been eclipsed by proliferating networks of electronic communication. Individuals can interact with one another, or can act within frameworks of mediated quasi-interaction, even though they are situated, in terms of the practical contexts of their day-to-day lives, in different parts of the world.

The reordering of space and time brought about by the development of the media is part of a broader set of processes which have transformed (and are still transforming) the modern world. These processes are commonly described today as 'globalization'. The term is not a precise one, and it is used in differing ways in the literature.[1] In the most general sense, it refers to the growing interconnectedness of different parts of the world, a process which gives rise to complex forms of interaction and interdependency. Defined in this way, 'globalization' may seem indistinguishable from related terms such as 'internationalization' and 'transnationalization', and these terms are often used interchangeably in the literature. But while these various notions refer to phenomena that are closely connected, the process of globalization, as I shall understand it here, involves more than the expansion of activities beyond the boundaries of particular nation-states. Globalization arises only when (a) activities take place in an arena which is global or nearly so (rather than merely regional, for example); (b) activities are organized, planned or coordinated on a global scale; and (c) activities involve some degree of reciprocity and interdependency, such that localized activities situated in different parts of the world are shaped by one another. One can speak of globalization in this sense only when the growing interconnectedness of different regions and locales becomes systematic and reciprocal to some degree, and only when the scope of interconnectedness is effectively global.

[. . .]

There can be no doubt that the organization of economic activity and concentrations of economic power have played a crucial role in the process of globalization. But all forms of power – economic, political, coercive and symbolic – have both contributed to and been affected by this process. If one retraces the process of globalization, one finds that these various forms of power overlap with one another in complex ways, sometimes reinforcing and sometimes conflicting with one another, creating a shifting interplay of forms of power. In this chapter I shall focus primarily on the social organization of symbolic power and the ways in which it has contributed to and been transformed by the process of globalization. But this will necessarily involve some discussion of economic, political and coercive power as well.

[...]

The Emergence of Global Communication Networks

The practice of transmitting messages across extended stretches of space is not new. [...] Elaborate networks of postal communication were established by political authorities in the Roman Empire and by political, ecclesiastical and commercial elites in medieval Europe. With the development of printing in the late fifteenth century, books, pamphlets and other printed materials were circulated well beyond the locales of their production, frequently crossing the frontiers of the emerging nation-states. Moreover, as European powers developed trading relations with other parts of the world, communication channels were established between Europe and those regions of the world that were drawn increasingly into the spheres of European colonial expansion.

It was only in the nineteenth century, however, that communication networks were systematically organized on a global scale. It was in the nineteenth century, therefore, that the globalization of communication took hold. This was partly due to the development of new technologies which enabled communication to be dissociated from physical transportation. But it was also linked directly to economic, political and military considerations. I shall examine the beginnings of the globalization of communication by focusing on three key developments of the late nineteenth and early twentieth centuries: (1) the development of underwater cable systems by the European imperial powers; (2) the establishment of international news agencies and their division of the world into exclusive spheres of operation; and (3) the formation of international organizations concerned with the allocation of the electromagnetic spectrum.

(1) The telegraph was the first medium of communication which successfully exploited the communication potential of electricity. Experiments with early forms of telegraphy took place in the late eighteenth and early nineteenth centuries, but the first electromagnetic telegraphs were developed in the 1830s. In 1831 Joseph Henry of Albany, New York, succeeded in transmitting signals over a mile-long circuit, and by 1837 usable systems had been developed by Cooke and Wheatstone in England and Morse in the United States. The system devised by Cooke and Wheatstone, which used needles that could be read visually, was initially installed along the railway between Paddington and West Drayton in July 1839. But Morse's system, which used a dot–dash code for the transmission of messages, eventually proved to be the most successful. In 1843 Morse built his first practical telegraph line between Washington and Baltimore with funds provided by the US Congress. Subsequently the telegraph industry developed rapidly in the United States and in Europe, stimulated by demand from the railways, the press, and the business and financial sectors.

The early telegraph systems were land-based and therefore restricted in terms of their geographical scope. It was not until the 1850s that reliable methods of underwater telegraphy were developed. The early submarine cables were generally made of copper wire coated with gutta percha, a natural insulating material made from the sap of a Malayan tree.[2] In 1851–2 submarine cables were successfully laid across the English Channel and between England and Ireland. In 1857–8 the first attempt was made to lay a cable across the Atlantic Ocean, though it ended in failure. The first attempts to link Britain with India were similarly unsuccessful. In 1864, however, a submarine cable was successfully laid between Karachi and the Persian Gulf; the line was then connected by land-based cables to Constantinople and Europe. By 1865 a telegraph link between Britain and India was complete. A year later, a transatlantic cable was successfully laid.

Following these early successes, the submarine cable industry developed rapidly. In the early 1870s, cables were laid throughout South-East Asia, so that Europe was linked to China and Australia. Cables were also laid between Europe and South America, and along the coasts of Africa. Most of the cables were produced, laid and operated by private companies, although these companies often received substantial financial assistance from governments. London was the centre of this expanding communication network and was the principal source of finance for the international submarine cable business. By 1900, approximately 190,000 miles of submarine cable had been laid throughout the world. British firms owned 72 per cent of these cables, and a substantial proportion were owned by one firm – the Eastern and Associated Companies founded by the Manchester merchant John Pender, who had been involved in the submarine cable industry since the 1860s.

The early submarine cable networks were used primarily for commercial and business purposes, although political and military concerns also played an important role in their development. As leaders of the most extensive empire of the late nineteenth century, British officials were well aware of the strategic value of rapid communications. The British Admiralty and the Colonial, War and Foreign Offices placed pressure on the government to construct additional submarine cables which did not cross non-British territories, and which would therefore be less vulnerable in times of crisis. One such cable was laid between Britain and the Cape of Good Hope in 1899–1901, and was used during the Boer War. This line was subsequently extended to Mauritius, Ceylon, Singapore and Australia, thereby connecting Britain to South-East Asia and Australia via a route which avoided the Middle East.

The submarine cable networks developed in the second half of the nineteenth century thus constituted the first global system of communication in which the capacity to transmit messages was clearly separated from the time-consuming processes of transportation. Individuals located in the major urban centres of Europe and North America acquired the means to communicate almost instantaneously with other parts of the world. The contrast with earlier forms of transport-based communication was dramatic. Up to the 1830s, a letter posted in England took five to eight months to reach India; and due to monsoons in the Indian Ocean, it could take two years for a reply to be received.[3] In the 1870s, a telegram could reach Bombay in five hours, and the answer could be back on the same day. And in 1924, at the British Empire Exhibition, King George V sent himself a telegram which circled the globe on all-British lines in 80 seconds. Rapid communication on a global scale – albeit along routes that reflected the organization of economic and political power – was a reality.

(2) A second development of the nineteenth century which was of considerable significance for the formation of global communication networks was the establishment of international news agencies. The significance of news agencies in this context was

threefold. First, the agencies were concerned with the systematic gathering and dissemination of news and other information over large territories – primarily in Europe to begin with, but soon extending to other parts of the world. Second, after an initial period of competitive rivalry, the major news agencies eventually agreed to divide up the world into mutually exclusive spheres of operation, thus creating a multilateral ordering of communication networks which was effectively global in scope. Third, the news agencies worked closely with the press, providing newspapers with stories, extracts and information which could be printed and diffused to a wide audience. Hence the news agencies were tied into networks of communication which, via print (and later radio and television), would reach a significant and growing proportion of the population.

The first news agency was established in Paris by Charles Havas in 1835.[4] A wealthy entrepreneur, Havas acquired what was primarily a translating office, the *Correspondance Garnier*, and turned it into an agency which collected extracts from various European papers and delivered them daily to the French press. By 1840 the agency catered for clients in London and Brussels as well, supplying news by coach and by means of a regular pigeon service. In the late 1840s, rival news-gathering services were set up in London by Paul Julius Reuter and in Berlin by Bernard Wolff. The agencies took advantage of the development of telegraph cable systems, which made it possible to transmit information over ever-greater distances at great speed. Competition among the three agencies intensified in the 1850s, as each agency sought to secure new clients and to expand its sphere of operation. However, in order to avoid damaging conflicts, the agencies eventually decided to cooperate by dividing the world up into mutually exclusive territories. By virtue of the Agency Alliance Treaty of 1869, Reuter obtained the territories of the British Empire and the Far East; Havas acquired the French Empire, Italy, Spain and Portugal; and Wolff was granted the exclusive right to operate in German, Austrian, Scandinavian and Russian territories. While the agencies were independent commercial organizations, their domains of operation corresponded to the spheres of economic and political influence of the major European imperial powers. Each agency worked closely with the political and commercial elites of the country which served as its home base, enjoying some degree of political patronage and providing information which was valuable for the conduct of trade and diplomacy.

The triple agency cartel dominated the international collection and dissemination of news until the outbreak of the First World War. Other news agencies were established in the late nineteenth and early twentieth centuries, but most had aligned themselves with one of the three principals. In the wake of the First World War, however, the triple agency cartel was broken by the expansion of two American agencies, Associated Press (AP) and the United Press Association (UPA, subsequently transformed into United Press International or UPI). Associated Press was a cooperative established in 1848 by six New York daily newspapers. AP joined the European cartel in 1893, agreeing to supply the European agencies with news from America in return for the exclusive right to distribute news in the United States. The United Press Association was founded by E. W. Scripps in 1907, partly in order to break the hold of AP in the domestic US news market. In addition to serving the US market, UPA set up offices in South America and sold news to South American and Japanese newspapers. During the First World War and its aftermath, both AP and UPA expanded their activities worldwide, placing increasing pressure on the cartel arrangements. By the early 1930s the triple agency cartel was effectively at an end; in 1934 Reuters signed a new agreement with AP which gave the American agencies a free hand to collect and distribute news throughout the world. While the American agencies expanded rapidly and Reuters maintained a strong position in the global market, the other European agencies underwent major changes. The capitulation of France in 1940 brought about the dissolution of Havas, although it was eventually replaced by a new agency, the Agence France-Presse (AFP), which took over many of the assets and connections of its predecessor. With the rise of Nazism and the subsequent defeat and partition of Germany following the Second World War, the Wolff agency lost its position of influence in the international domain and eventually disappeared.

Since the Second World War, the four major agencies – Reuters, AP, UPI and AFP – have maintained their positions of dominance in the international system for the collection and dissemination of news and other information. Many other agencies have been established and expanded their spheres of operation; and some agencies, such as TASS and the Deutsche Presse Agentur, acquired (at least temporarily) a prominent international role. But the four majors remain the key actors in the global information order. Many newspapers and broadcasting organizations throughout the world depend heavily on them for international news, as well as for news of their own geopolitical region, and many of the smaller agencies are affiliated to them. The major news agencies have also expanded and diversified their activities, taking advantage of new developments in information and communication technology and emerging as central players in the new global market for information and data of various kinds, including information relating to financial and commercial transactions.[5]

The dominance of the major news agencies, combined with other inequalities in the international flow of information and communication, has led to calls from various quarters for a reorganization of the global information order. A series of conferences and commissions sponsored by UNESCO in the 1970s and early 1980s generated a wide-ranging debate on the theme of a 'New World Information and Communication Order' (NWICO). The proponents of NWICO were seeking a more equitable balance in the international flow and content of information, as well as a strengthening of the technological infrastructures and productive capacities of less developed countries in the sphere of communication. But the UNESCO initiatives met with considerable resistance from certain governments and interest groups in the West. In 1984 the United States withdrew from UNESCO, followed by the United Kingdom in 1985; together this deprived UNESCO of around 30 per cent of its budget and greatly limited the effectiveness of any policy recommendations.[6] Nevertheless, the NWICO debate helped to increase awareness of the issues raised by the dominance of the major news agencies and, more generally, by the inequalities associated with the globalization of communication. It also helped to stimulate the development of various forms of cooperation among so-called Third World countries, including the expansion of regional and non-aligned news agencies in Africa and elsewhere.[7]

(3) A third development which played an important role in the globalization of communication also stems from the late nineteenth century: it concerns the development of new means of transmitting information via electromagnetic waves and the succession of attempts to regulate the allocation of the electromagnetic spectrum. [. . .] The use of electromagnetic waves for the purposes of communication greatly expanded the capacity to transmit information across large distances in a flexible and cost-efficient way, dispensing with the need to lay fixed cables over land or under sea. But the increasing

use of electromagnetic waves also created a growing need to regulate the allocation of spectrum space both within and between countries. Each country developed its own legislative framework for spectrum allocation and selective licensing. Initially one of the key concerns of the authorities entrusted with the task of allocating spectrum space was to set aside a segment of the spectrum for military and security purposes, thereby minimizing interference from amateur radio users. But as the commercial potential of the new medium became increasingly clear, political authorities became directly involved in the selective licensing of broadcasting organizations, which were granted exclusive rights to broadcast at designated frequencies in particular regions. The practices of selective licensing were shaped not only by the technical constraints of spectrum scarcity but also by a broader set of political considerations concerning the proper nature and role of broadcasting organizations, considerations which varied greatly from one country to another.[8]

The international frameworks for the management of spectrum space were less effective. The key organization in this regard was the International Telegraph Union, subsequently transformed into the International Telecommunication Union (ITU). Originally formed in 1865 under a convention signed by 20 European states, the union was concerned primarily with the establishment of international standards and the resolution of technical problems.[9] At its 1906 Berlin conference, it dealt with radio for the first time and agreed to allocate certain sections of the spectrum to specific services, such as the frequencies used by ships at sea. Subsequently the ITU convened a regular conference – the World Administrative Radio Conference or WARC – to address problems of spectrum allocation and related issues. In the early phase of these international activities, frequencies were generally allocated on a first come, first served basis.[10] Users simply notified the ITU of the frequencies they were using or wished to use, and they thereby acquired a 'squatter's right'. But as demands on the radio spectrum increased, the ITU gradually adopted a more active stance. Sections of the spectrum were allocated to particular services, and the world was divided into three broad regions – Europe and Africa, the Americas, and Asia and the South Pacific – which could each be planned in more detail. The systems developed by the ITU have none the less come under increasing pressure in recent years, partly as a result of rising demands by existing users and partly due to new demands by countries hitherto largely excluded from the domain of international telecommunications.

The development of technologies capable of transmitting messages via electromagnetic waves, together with the emergence of national and international organizations concerned with the management of spectrum space, marked a decisive advance in the globalization of communication. It was now possible to transmit increasing quantities of information over large distances in an efficient and virtually instantaneous way. Moreover, the messages transmitted by electromagnetic waves were potentially accessible to anyone who was within range of the signals and who had the equipment to receive them – a fact which was of enormous significance for the commercial exploitation of the medium. However, during the first half of the twentieth century most communication by electromagnetic transmission remained confined to specific geographical locales, such as particular urban areas, nation-states or the regions between land and ships at sea. It was not until the 1960s, with the launching of the first successful geo-stationary communication satellites, that communication by electromagnetic transmission became fully global in scope. I shall return to this development shortly.

Patterns of Global Communication Today: An Overview

While the origins of the globalization of communication can be traced back to the mid-nineteenth century, this process is primarily a phenomenon of the twentieth. For it is during the twentieth century that the flow of information and communication on a global scale has become a regularized and pervasive feature of social life. There are, of course, many dimensions to this process; the twentieth century has witnessed an unparalleled proliferation of the channels of communication and information diffusion. The rapid development of systems of radio and television broadcasting throughout the world has been an important but by no means the only aspect of this process. The globalization of communication has also been a structured and uneven process which has benefited some more than others, and which has drawn some parts of the world into networks of global communication more quickly than other parts. Since the late 1960s, the characteristics of global communication flows have been studied in some detail by researchers in international communication – well before the term 'globalization' gained currency in the social sciences.[11] In this section I shall draw on this literature for the purpose of analysing some of the main patterns of global communication today. I shall not attempt to analyse these patterns in a detailed and comprehensive fashion, but merely to identify some of the main dimensions of globalized communication processes; and I shall be concerned above all to highlight their structured and uneven character. While the range of relevant issues is potentially very wide, I shall restrict my attention to four themes: (1) the emergence of transnational communication conglomerates as key players in the global system of communication and information diffusion; (2) the social impact of new technologies, especially those associated with satellite communication; (3) the asymmetrical flow of information and communication products within the global system; and (4) the variations and inequalities in terms of access to the global networks of communication.

(1) The globalization of communication in the twentieth century is a process that has been driven primarily by the activities of large-scale communication conglomerates. The origins of these conglomerates can be traced back to the transformation of the press in the nineteenth century [. . .]. The change in the economic basis of newspapers, precipitated and promoted by the introduction of new methods of production, set in motion a long-term process of accumulation and concentration in the media industries. In the course of the twentieth century, this process has increasingly assumed a transnational character. Communication conglomerates have expanded their operations in regions other than their countries of origin; and some of the large industrial and financial concerns have, as part of explicit policies of global expansion and diversification, acquired substantial interests in the information and communication sector. Through mergers, acquisitions and other forms of corporate growth, the large conglomerates have assumed an ever-greater presence in the global arena of the information and communication trade.

The names of some of the largest communication conglomerates are well known: Time Warner, formed by the merger of Time, Inc., and Warner Communications in 1989 and now the largest media enterprise in the world, has subsidiaries in Australia, Asia, Europe and Latin America. The German-based Bertelsmann group, with strong interests in publishing, television, music and high-tech information systems, has operations in Europe, the United States and Latin America. Rupert Murdoch's News Corporation, which has substantial interests in publishing, television and film, probably has the most extensive reach, with subsidiaries in Europe, the United States, Australia and Asia. These and other large communication conglomerates operate increasingly in a worldwide market and organize their activities on the basis of strategies which are effectively global in design. But nearly all of the large conglomerates are based in North America, Western Europe, Australia or Japan; very few are based in Third World countries, although the latter provide important markets for their goods and services.[12] Hence the development of communication conglomerates has led to the formation of large concentrations of economic and symbolic power which are privately controlled and unevenly distributed, and which can deploy massive resources to pursue corporate objectives in a global arena. It has also led to the formation of extensive, privately controlled networks of communication through which information and symbolic content can flow.

The nature and activities of some of the large communication conglomerates have been documented in the literature and I shall not examine them further here.[13] There is a need, however, for more up-to-date comparative research on the activities of these conglomerates, on the ways in which they are adapting to the changing economic and political circumstances of the 1990s, and on their exploitation of new technological developments.

(2) The development of new technologies has played an important role in the globalization of communication in the late twentieth century, both in conjunction with the activities of communication conglomerates and independently of them. Three interrelated developments have been particularly important. One is the deployment of more extensive and sophisticated cable systems which provide much greater capacity for the transmission of electronically encoded information. A second development is the increasing use of satellites for the purposes of long-distance communication, often in conjunction with land-based cable systems. The third development – in many ways the most fundamental – is the increasing use of digital methods of information processing, storage and retrieval. The digitalization of information, combined with the development of related electronic technologies (microprocessors, etc.), has greatly increased the capacity to store and transmit information and has created the basis for a convergence of information and communication technologies, so that information can be converted relatively easily between different communication media.

All three of these technological developments have contributed in fundamental ways to the globalization of communication. Most obviously, the use of telecommunications satellites, positioned in geosynchronous orbits and interlinked, has created a system of global communication which is virtually instantaneous and which dispenses with the need for terrestrial relays and transmission wires. Since their development in the early 1960s, telecommunications satellites have been used for a variety of purposes.[14] The needs of the military and of large commercial organizations have always played an important role, and many multinational corporations make extensive use of satellite communication. Satellites have also been increasingly integrated into the normal telecommunications networks, carrying a growing proportion of the international traffic in telephone, telex, fax, electronic mail and related communication services.

From the outset, telecommunications satellites were also used as relay stations and distribution points for television broadcasting. They formed an integral part of national network systems in the USA, the former USSR and elsewhere, and they were used as distribution points to supply cable systems on a national and international basis. In recent years, however, the development of more sophisticated satellites, capable of transmitting stronger, well-targeted signals, has made possible the introduction of direct broadcasting by satellite (or DBS). The first DBS systems began transmitting programmes in the USA in 1975, and the first European systems began operating in 1986; by the early 1990s, a variety of DBS systems were operating or planned in other parts of the world. Part of the significance of DBS is that it creates new distribution systems outside of the established terrestrially based networks of broadcasting – systems which are often privately owned and controlled and in which the large communication conglomerates may have a substantial stake. Moreover, these new distribution systems are inherently transnational since, from a technical point of view, there is no reason why the reception area (or 'footprint') of a DBS satellite should correspond even roughly to the territorial boundaries of a particular nation-state.

In addition to creating new transnational distribution networks, the development of DBS and other technologies (including cable and videocassette recorders) has expanded the global market for media products. The international flow of films, TV programmes and other materials has increased as producers and distributors seek to exploit the lucrative markets created by satellite and cable channels and by videocassette rentals and sales. This expansion of the global market should be viewed against the backcloth of earlier trends in the international flow of media products.

(3) A central feature of the globalization of communication is the fact that media products circulate in an international arena. Material produced in one country is distributed not only in the domestic market but also – and increasingly – in a global market. It has long been recognized, however, that the international flow of media products is a structured process in which certain organizations have a dominant role, and in which some regions of the world are heavily dependent on others for the supply of symbolic goods. Studies carried out in the early 1970s by Nordenstreng and Varis showed a clear asymmetry in the international flow of television programmes: there was, to a large extent, a one-way traffic in news and entertainment programmes from the major exporting countries to the rest of the world.[15] The United States was (and remains) the leading exporter in television programming, selling far more material to other countries (especially to Latin America, Europe, Canada, Australia and Japan) than it imports from abroad. Some European countries, such as Britain and France, were also major exporters (and remain so); but, unlike the United States, they also imported a significant quantity of programming from abroad (mainly from the US). Subsequent studies by Varis and others have tended to confirm the unevenness of flow, although they have also produced a more complex picture and have highlighted the growing importance of intraregional trade (for instance, countries like Mexico and Brazil have emerged as major producers and exporters of programming material to other parts of Latin America).[16]

The structured character of the international flow of symbolic goods is the outcome of various historical and economic factors. In the domain of news, the patterns of dependence reflect the legacy of the international news agencies established in London, Paris and New York (although the precise significance of Western-based news agencies remains a matter of some dispute[17]). In the sphere of entertainment, the economic power of Hollywood continues to exert a major influence on the international flow of films and TV programmes. Many television stations in less developed countries do not have the resources to produce extensive programming of their own. The import of American serials, at prices negotiated on a country-by-country basis, is a relatively inexpensive (and financially very attractive) way to fill broadcasting schedules.

While some of the broad patterns of international flow have been documented over the years, the research remains fragmentary. There are many sectors of the information and communication industries which have yet to be studied in detail from this point of view. And the ways in which existing patterns of international flow will be affected by new technological developments – such as those associated with satellite and cable systems, or those linked more generally to the digitalization of information – is a question which demands a good deal more research. Given the complexity of global networks of transmission and trade and the huge volume of material which passes through them, it is unlikely that our understanding of patterns of international flow will ever be more than partial. But further research could help to shed light on some of the more significant trends.

(4) In addition to analysing the patterns of international flow, it is essential to consider the patterns of access to and uptake of material transmitted through global networks. Much of the research on patterns of international flow has been based on the content analysis of television broadcasting schedules in different countries. But in some parts of the world, access to television broadcasting services was restricted for many years to the relatively small proportion of the population which lived in the major urban areas. For the rural population, which comprises 70–90 per cent of the population in many Third World countries, radio has probably been a more important medium of communication than television.[18] Of course, this situation is changing continuously as more resources are devoted to the development of television services and as more individuals and families are able to gain access to them. But significant inequalities remain in terms of the capacity of individuals in different parts of the world, and in different parts and social strata of the same country, to gain access to the materials which are diffused through global networks.

Quite apart from these inequalities of access, globalized symbolic materials are subjected to different patterns of uptake. Taken on its own, the content analysis of programming schedules tells us relatively little about who watches which programmes, how long they watch them for, etc., and hence tells us relatively little about the extent of uptake of globally distributed material.[19] Moreover, if we wish to explore the impact of the globalization of communication, we must consider not only the patterns of uptake but also the *uses* of globalized symbolic materials – that is, what recipients do with them, how they understand them, and how they incorporate them into the routines and practices of their everyday lives.

[. . .]

Globalized Diffusion, Localized Appropriation: Towards a Theory of Media Globalization

[. . .]

We have already shed some light on the global–local axis by examining some of the patterns of global diffusion. I now want to develop this analysis further by focusing on the process of appropriation and pursuing three interrelated themes. The first theme is this: given the hermeneutical character of appropriation, it follows that the significance which media messages have for individuals and the uses to which mediated symbolic materials are put by recipients depend crucially on the contexts of reception and on the resources that recipients bring to bear on the reception process. This is well illustrated by the Liebes and Katz study of the reception of *Dallas*. It is also vividly demonstrated by the perceptive account by Sreberny-Mohammadi and Mohammadi of the role of communication media in the Iranian Revolution.[20] During the 1970s, traditional religious language and imagery were used in Iran as symbolic weapons in the struggle against the Shah, who was associated with the corrupting importation of Western culture. Although Khomeini was in exile, his speeches and sermons were recorded and smuggled into Iran on audiocassettes, which were easily reproduced and widely diffused. But with the development of an Islamic regime in the post-revolutionary period, Western cultural products began to assume a very different significance for many Iranians. Videos of Western films and tapes of Western pop music circulated as part of a popular cultural underground, taking on a subversive character; they helped to create an alternative cultural space in which individuals could take some distance from a regime experienced by many as oppressive.[21] Examples such as these illustrate well the contextually bounded character of the process of appropriation. As symbolic materials circulate on an ever-greater scale, locales become sites where, to an ever-increasing extent, globalized media products are received, interpreted and incorporated into the daily lives of individuals. Through the localized process of appropriation, media products are embedded in sets of practices which shape and alter their significance.

Let us now consider a second theme: how should we understand the social impact of the localized appropriation of globalized media products? Here I want to emphasize one key feature of this process. I want to suggest that the appropriation of globalized symbolic materials involves what I shall describe as *the accentuation of symbolic distancing from the spatial-temporal contexts of everyday life*. The appropriation of symbolic materials enables individuals to take some distance from the conditions of their day-to-day lives – not literally but symbolically, imaginatively, vicariously. Individuals are able to gain some conception, however partial, of ways of life and life conditions which differ significantly from their own. They are able to gain some conception of regions of the world which are far removed from their own locales.

The phenomenon of symbolic distancing is brought out well by James Lull in his study of the impact of television in China.[22] Television became a widespread medium in China only in the course of the 1980s. In the 1960s and 1970s relatively few television sets were sold in China; they were very expensive relative to normal wages and were generally restricted to the more privileged urban elites. In the 1980s, however, domestic television production increased dramatically; by 1990 most urban families owned at least one TV set, and there was about one set for every eight people nationwide.[23] Broadcasting is dominated by the national network, Central China Television (CCTV), which supplies a large proportion of the programming material to the various regional and local stations operating throughout the country.

What sense do Chinese viewers make of the programmes they watch? Lull pursues this question through a series of extended interviews with families in Shanghai, Beijing, Guangzhou and Xian. Among other things, he shows that, while many Chinese viewers are critical of the programmes available to them, they value television for the way that it offers new vistas, new lifestyles and new ways of thinking. 'In our daily lives we just go to work and come home, so we want to see something that is different from our own life. TV gives us a model of the rest of the world':[24] this comment by a 58-year-old accountant from Shanghai captures well the effect of symbolic distancing in the age of global communication. Chinese viewers are drawn to programmes imported from

Japan, Taiwan, Europe and the United States not only for their information and enter-tainment value, but also because they give a glimpse – albeit a fleeting and partial one – of what life is like elsewhere. When people watch international news, for instance, they may pay as much attention to street scenes, housing and clothing as to the com-mentary which accompanies the pictures from foreign lands.

[...]

In emphasizing the phenomenon of symbolic distancing, I do not want to suggest, of course, that this is the *only* aspect of the process of appropriation which is worthy of consideration. On the contrary, in the actual circumstances of day-to-day life, it is likely that the appropriation of globalized media products will interact with localized prac-tices in complex ways and may, in some respects, serve to consolidate established rela-tions of power or, indeed, to create new forms of dependency. [...]

This brings us to a third theme that I want briefly to consider: the localized appro-priation of globalized media products is also a source of tension and potential conflict. It is a source of tension partly because media products can convey images and mess-ages which clash with, or do not entirely support, the values associated with a tradi-tional way of life. In some contexts this discordance may be part of the very appeal of media products: they help individuals to take a distance, to imagine alternatives, and thereby to question traditional practices. So, for instance, it seems that Egyptian soap operas are of interest to young Bedouin women in the Western Desert precisely because they present a set of lifestyles – such as the possibility of marrying for love and living separately from the extended family – which diverge from the set of options tradition-ally available to them.[25]

[...]

It would be imprudent to claim that the localized appropriation of globalized media products has been a major factor in stimulating broader forms of social conflict and social change in the modern world; most forms of social conflict are extremely com-plex and involve many diverse factors. But it could be plausibly argued that the increasingly globalized diffusion of media products has played a role in triggering off some of the more dramatic conflicts of recent years. Lull contends that the stream of domestic and international television programmes transmitted throughout China in the 1980s created a cultural reservoir of alternative visions, encouraging people to question traditional values and official interpretations and helping them to imagine alternative ways of living. By itself, this certainly did not bring about the audacious demonstration in Tiananmen Square, nor did it determine the course of the subsequent confrontation. But in the absence of television it seems unlikely that the events of Tiananmen Square would have unfolded in the way they did, nor would they have been witnessed by millions of individuals in China and throughout the world.

[...]

Notes

1 For a review of different usages, see Roland Robertson, *Globalization: Social Theory and Global Culture* (London: Sage, 1992), esp. ch. 1.

2 See Daniel R. Headrick, *The Tools of Empire: Technology and European Imperialism in the Nineteenth Century* (Oxford: Oxford University Press, 1981), ch. 11; Bernard S. Finn, *Submarine Telegraphy: The Grand Victorian Technology* (Margate: Thanet Press, 1973).

3 Headrick, *The Tools of Empire*, p. 130.

4   For more detailed accounts of the development of the major news agencies, see Graham
    Storey, *Reuters' Century 1851–1951* (London: Max Parrish, 1951); Oliver Boyd-Barrett, *The
    International News Agencies* (London: Constable, 1980); Anthony Smith, *The Geopolitics of
    Information: How Western Culture Dominates the World* (London: Faber, 1980).
5   The growth and diversification of Reuters in the 1970s and 1980s was particularly pronounced.
    In 1963, two-thirds of Reuters' revenue of £3 million came from media subscribers. In 1989,
    the media accounted for only 7 per cent of Reuters' revenue; 55 per cent was derived from
    the money market, 19 per cent from securities, 8 per cent from commodities and 11 per cent
    from client services. By 1990 Reuters' overall revenue had risen to £1,369 million, of which
    82.5 per cent was earned overseas. (See Jeremy Tunstall and Michael Palmer, *Media Moguls*
    (London and New York: Routledge, 1991), p. 56.)
6   For a detailed account of the NWICO debate and the role of UNESCO, see Thomas L.
    McPhail, *Electronic Colonialism: The Future of International Broadcasting and Communica-
    tion*, 2nd edn (Newbury Park, Calif.: Sage, 1987).
7   On the development of news agencies and other mechanisms of information exchange in
    Third World countries, see Oliver Boyd-Barrett and Daya Kishan Thussu, *Contra-Flow in
    Global News: International and Regional News Exchange Mechanisms* (London: John
    Libbey, 1992).
8   For further discussion of the institutional frameworks of broadcasting, see John B. Thompson,
    Ideology and Modern Culture: Critical Social Theory in the Era of Mass Communication
    (Cambridge: Polity Press, 1991), pp. 183–92.
9   See McPhail, *Electronic Colonialism*, ch. 5; John Howkins, 'The management of the spec-
    trum', *InterMedia* 7(5) (Sept. 1979): 10–22.
10 Howkins, 'The management of the spectrum', p. 14.
11 Among the most important and influential of the early studies were the UNESCO-
    sponsored surveys carried out by Nordenstreng and Varis in 1971–3 and by Varis in 1983.
    See Kaarle Nordenstreng and Tapio Varis, *Television Traffic – A One-Way Street? A Survey
    and Analysis of the International Flow of Television Programme Material*, Reports and Papers
    on Mass Communication, no. 70 (Paris: UNESCO, 1974); Tapio Varis, *International Flow
    of Television Programmes*, Reports and Papers on Mass Communication, no. 100 (Paris:
    UNESCO, 1986). Numerous other studies have been carried out. For useful discussions of
    the relevant literature, see Jeremy Tunstall, *The Media Are American: Anglo-American Media
    in the World* (London: Constable, 1977); Elihu Katz and George Wedell, *Broadcasting in
    the Third World: Promise and Performance* (Cambridge, Mass.: Harvard University Press,
    1977); Smith, *The Geopolitics of Information*; Ralph Negrine and S. Papathanassopoulos, *The
    Internationalization of Television* (London: Pinter, 1990); Preben Sepstrup, *Transnationaliza-
    tion of Television in Europe* (London: John Libbey, 1990); Annabelle Sreberny-Mohammadi,
    'The global and the local in international communications', in James Curran and Michael
    Gurevitch (eds), *Mass Media and Society* (London: Edward Arnold, 1991); Geoffrey
    Reeves, *Communications and the 'Third World'* (London: Routledge, 1993).
12 A recent UNESCO report on world communications showed that, of the 78 largest com-
    munication conglomerates ranked according to total media turnover, 39 were based in the
    United States, 25 in Western Europe, 8 in Japan, 5 in Canada and 1 in Australia; none were
    based in the Third World. (See *World Communication Report* (Paris: UNESCO, 1989),
    pp. 104–5.)
13 See, for example, Ben H. Bagdikian, *The Media Monopoly*, 4th edn (Boston: Beacon Press,
    1992); Anthony Smith, *The Age of Behemoths: The Globalization of Mass Media Firms* (New
    York: Priority Press, 1991); Tunstall and Palmer, *Media Moguls*.
14 For further discussion of historical and technical aspects of satellite communications, see Abram
    Chayes, James Fawcett, Masami Ito, Alexandre-Charles Kiss et al., *Satellite Broadcasting*
    (London: Oxford University Press, 1973); Jonathan F. Galloway, *The Politics and Techno-
    logy of Satellite Communications* (Lexington: D. C. Heath, 1972).
15 Nordenstreng and Varis, *Television Traffic*; see also Tapio Varis, 'Global traffic in tele-
    vision', *Journal of Communication* 24 (1974): 102–9.

16 See Varis, *International Flow of Television Programmes*; Annabelle Sreberny-Mohammadi, 'The "World of the News" study: results of international cooperation', *Journal of Communications* 34 (1984): 121–34; Sepstrup, *Transnationalization of Television in Europe.*

17 Some commentators have argued that the influence of Western-based news agencies has been exaggerated. See, for example, Robert L. Stevenson, 'The "World of the News" study: pseudo debate', *Journal of Communications* 34 (1984): 134–8; Michael Tracey, 'The poisoned chalice? International television and the idea of dominance', *Daedalus* 114 (1985): 17–55.

18 See Katz and Wedell, *Broadcasting in the Third World*, ch. 1.

19 For a discussion of some of the issues involved in studying patterns of consumption in relation to the globalization of communication, see Sepstrup, *Transnationalization of Television in Western Europe*, ch. 4.

20 See Annabelle Sreberny-Mohammadi and Ali Mohammadi, *Small Media, Big Revolution: Communication, Culture, and the Iranian Revolution* (Minneapolis: University of Minnesota Press, 1994).

21 Ibid., pp. 186–8.

22 See James Lull, *China Turned On: Television, Reform, and Resistance* (London: Routledge, 1991).

23 Ibid., p. 23.

24 Quoted in ibid., p. 171.

25 See Lila Abu-Lughod, 'Bedouins, cassettes and technologies of public culture', *Middle East Report* 159(4) (1989): 7–11, 47.

19

The Global Media

Edward Herman and Robert McChesney

In the 1990s, while media systems are still primarily national and local, the media that operate across borders continue to strengthen and have a steadily greater impact on indigenous systems. The dominant players treat the media markets as a single global market with local subdivisions. The rapidity of their global expansion is explained in part by equally rapid reduction or elimination of many of the traditional institutional and legal barriers to cross-border transactions. They have also been facilitated by technological changes such as the growth of satellite broadcasting, videocassette recorders, fiber optic cable and phone systems. Also critically important has been the rapid growth of cross-border advertising, trade and investment, and thus the demand for media and other communication services. [. . .]

Overview of Media Globalization

Media and entertainment outlays are growing at a faster rate than GDP almost everywhere in the world and significantly faster in the Far East and Central Europe.[1] A 1996 survey of teenagers in television-owning households in forty-one nations finds that they watch on average six hours of television per day, and nowhere in the survey is the figure under five hours.[2] This has been a boon for the US entertainment industry, as it dominates the global market for the production of television programming as well as film. Employment in the entertainment industry in Los Angeles alone has more than doubled from 53,000 in 1988 to 112,000 in 1995.[3] In Germany, for example, the twenty-one most heavily viewed films and nine of the top ten video rentals for 1995 were produced by US film studios.[4] 'The overseas market is a lot like the domestic market was 15 years ago,' one media executive states. 'It's wide open.'[5] As the US market is the most mature in media and entertainment consumption, it is the global market that is drawing industry attention. One media industry analyst concludes that 'the long-term growth opportunities overseas dwarf what we think is likely to occur in the United States.'[6]

This growth trend is not without its interruptions; for example, in 1996, after a decade of increased output, the film studios reduced production in the face of a saturated market and some short-term losses.[7] The global music industry too had a sharp fall in its rate of growth in 1996, after years of double digit rates. The dominance of the United States should also not be exaggerated. Some of the key firms producing media and entertainment fare in the United States itself have significant foreign ownership. Non-US media conglomerates, including the Japanese Sony (no. 5), Canadian Seagram (no. 15), Dutch Philips (no. 18), and Australian News Corporation (no. 27) all rank on the top thirty list of the non-US firms with the largest US investments.[8] Many other non-US firms are participating fully in the media and entertainment boom around the world, particularly though not exclusively through the control of TV stations, cable systems, and other distribution channels.

Moreover, a major lesson of the 1990s has been that although Hollywood fare in film, television, and music has considerable appeal worldwide, this appeal has its limits. In Western Europe, the top-rated TV programs are nearly always domestically produced, and there is widespread recognition that audiences often prefer home-grown programs, if these have the resources to compete with Hollywood productions.[9] There has also been an increase in the export of cultural products by nations other than the United States in the 1990s, not only from Europe but from the developing nations.[10] Yet this only qualifies the mainly US domination of the global media market; it does not challenge it. A 1996 advertising industry survey of 20,000 consumers in nineteen nations revealed that 41.5 percent of the respondents considered US cultural fare to be excellent or very good, more than twice the figure for any other nation.[11] The United States enjoyed a trade surplus with Europe in media fare of $6.3 billion in 1995, more than tripling the media trade surplus between the US and Europe for 1988.[12] 'In Europe,' one leading Italian film producer acknowledged, with the slight exception of France, 'we've been 90 percent colonized [by Hollywood] in terms of quantity of product on the market.'[13]

The leading global media firms are producing fare in languages other than English. For example, MTV, the global music television service, has begun to differentiate its content around the world and incorporate local music.[14] After the initial campaign to establish a pan-Asian television service faltered for lack of cultural specificity, its format was changed to incorporate local programming and languages.[15] 'We soon learned that one just can't pour Western programs down people's throats,' an executive of News Corporation's Asian Star Television Ltd acknowledged.[16] A Disney executive states that 'For all children, the Disney characters are local characters and this is very important. They always speak local languages . . . The Disney strategy is to "think global, act local".'[17] As US-based media giants earn a larger share of revenues abroad, they increasingly target different regions and nations of the world, and they enter joint ventures with local producers. Partially as a result, much of the domestically produced media content around the world increasingly has the flavor of Hollywood.[18]

The three media industries that entered the 1990s with the most developed global markets – book publishing, recorded music, and film production – have continued their growth in sometimes booming global oligopolistic markets. Book publishing is less concentrated than film or music, primarily due to language differences, yet the ten largest firms accounted for 25 percent of 1995's global sales of $80 billion. The world's three largest book publishers are owned by Bertelsmann, Time Warner, and Viacom, respectively the world's third, first, and fourth largest media conglomerates. Most of the other global book publishing giants are also affiliated with global media powers like News Corporation, Hachette, and Pearson. The top three book publishers alone accounted for over $10 billion in 1995 sales. The 1990s have been a period of rapid corporate consolidation both globally and in national markets. In Spain, France, and Germany, for example, the three largest book publishers command over 50 percent of the market. Industry analysts expect further consolidation, with the largest global publishers accounting for an increasing share of the market.[19]

Recorded music is the most concentrated global media market. The leading five firms, in order of global market share, are PolyGram (19 percent), Time Warner (18 percent),

Sony (17 percent), EMI (15 percent), and Bertelsmann (13 percent). The only other player of any note is Universal (formerly MCA) (9 percent).[20] All but EMI are part of larger global media conglomerates. Some estimates show these six firms' combined sales as accounting for over 90 percent of the global market, while others place it closer to 80 percent.[21] The market boomed in the early and mid-1990s with a 10 percent increase in sales in 1995 to raise global revenues to $40 billion. Recorded music has successfully shifted to digital format as compact discs now account for 70 percent of revenues.[22] Global sales grew by 38 percent from 1992 to 1995. With western markets relatively mature, sales in the developing world are growing more rapidly.[23] A music industry trade publication forecasts that China's market for recorded music will increase by 900 percent between 1994 and 2001, to over $2.1 billion. In anticipation of this shift in demand, the 'big five' music firms and Universal are increasing their number of recording artists in the developing world.[24]

Global film production in the 1990s is dominated by the studios owned by Disney, Time Warner, Viacom, Universal (owned by Seagram), Sony, PolyGram (owned by Philips), MGM, and News Corporation. All but MGM are parts of large global media conglomerates. There are large and sometimes subsidized national film industries, but with only a few exceptions the commercial export market is effectively the province of these eight firms, several of which are not owned by Americans but all of which are part of 'Hollywood.' After the burst of US expansion in the early 1980s, the percentage of non-US revenue for the film industry increased from 33 percent in 1984 to over 50 percent in 1993, where it has remained.[25] 'The international business is exploding,' a Hollywood distributor stated in 1995, predicting that by 2000 non-US revenues will account for 60–70 percent of studio income.[26]

Several factors suggest that global growth rates for the film studios will remain high for the foreseeable future. First, there is the construction of thousands of US-inspired (often US-owned) multiscreen theater complexes across the planet. 'Most of the world is severely underscreened,' one multiplex builder observed, and multiscreen theaters 'provide an environment that attracts audiences like magnets.' Some of the construction is being carried out by companies like Viacom, Universal, and Time Warner, which also produce films. 'Building theaters is kind of like drilling oil wells, only you get more gushers,' a film industry analyst concludes.[27] In Asia, where much of the construction is taking place, Time Warner forecasts annual growth rates of over 20 percent for the coming decade.[28] Second, the widespread diffusion of videocassette players has spurred the home video market, which brought in $8.8 billion, or over half of the film studios' 1995 global income.[29] Some expect the launching of digital video disks in the late 1990s to have the same stimulative effect on film sales in the late 1990s that the launching of CDs had for music sales in the late 1980s and early 1990s.[30] Third, the rise of multichannel commercial television broadcasting has created enormous demand for Hollywood fare. Several multibillion dollar deals signed in 1996 provided nothing short 'of a windfall for major Hollywood studios.'[31] The future may even be brighter; Universal's president states that 'Television in Europe is poised for extraordinary growth.'[32] Indeed, by 1997 Hollywood was in the midst of its greatest expansion in the number of 'sound stages,' or production studios for film, television, and video production, in its history.[33]

The vast surge in demand may well have laid the foundation for an increase in worldwide film production, At the same time, however, the global film market rewards the largest budgeted films disproportionately. A 1996 *Variety* survey of 164 Hollywood releases concluded that films with budgets greater than $60 million tended to be far more profitable than less expensive films.[34] In 1996 just 13 of the 417 films released by Hollywood studios accounted for nearly 30 percent of total box office.[35] While the main studios are increasing their output to meet demand, they are concentrating upon the production of 'blockbusters.'[36] With the financial stakes so high, the implications for filmmaking tend to be 'homogenization of content and less risk taking,' as one Hollywood producer acknowledges.[37]

One entertainment genre that needs little differentiation for global commercial success is violence, and Hollywood has established itself as the preeminent producer of 'action' fare. 'Kicking butt,' one US media executive states, 'plays everywhere.' The major US studios find violent fare as close to risk-free as anything they produce, and they have little trouble locating non-US interests willing to cover a share of production costs in return for distribution or broadcasting rights in their nation or region. 'For the US studio it's an excellent deal,' the same executive concludes. 'Even if the show bombs, the production cost is not drastic. If it hits, it's all upside.' And with non-US sales playing a larger role in studio planning, violent fare for film and television looks set to command a larger segment of Hollywood output.[38]

[. . .]

The Global Trend to Deregulation

[. . .] Rapid changes in the global media system have been based on a 'new information order' of market freedom, and they have strengthened market rule. In the United States, for example, the First Amendment to the constitution has been increasingly interpreted as a statute that protects commercial speech from government interference.[39] Even the limited regulatory standards and enforcement of antitrust statutes to prevent media concentration that existed in the past have lessened to the point of irrelevance.[40] The 1996 US Telecommunications Act, as one observer noted, opened up a 'Pandora's box of consolidation in the media industry,' as deregulation was the order of the day.[41] Encouraged by powerful media lobbies, this commercial spirit permeates all national debates concerning media. It also is true for regional bodies like the European Union, the home of outstanding public broadcasting systems but now devoted to establishing a single European market for commercial media. As a rule of thumb, the only basis for substantive media policy debates at the national level is when there are conflicts between powerful media interests. So it is that domestic media interests have been able to get some statutory protection from global media encroachment in the form of quotas and the like. But these campaigns for domestic protection have met with considerable resistance; in every nation there are powerful forces pressing the case for full integration into the global media market.[42]

At the international level, the dominant institutions and trade agreements continue to work toward the elimination of all barriers to the market. When the United States and Mexico signed a pact in 1996 to open up their respective satellite TV markets to the other, Federal Communications Commission Chair Reed Hundt termed the deal 'consistent with the spirit of NAFTA,' the regional free trade deal.[43] As the media have become increasingly central to the world economy, media policy matters have become the province of organizations like the IMF and the WTO. The IMF is committed to encouraging the establishment of commercial media globally to better serve the needs of a market economy. The WTO's mission is to encourage a single global market for commercial media, and to oppose barriers to this, however noble the intent.[44] In what may be a precedent-setting case, in January 1997 the WTO ruled that Canada could not impose special taxes or tariffs on US magazine publishers to protect Canadian periodicals. This was interpreted as strengthening 'Washington's case against cultural protection trade policies used by many other countries.'[45] In view of the global nature of the communication industries and technologies, there is an increasing acceptance of reduced national government control over vital areas of communication.[46]

[. . .]

Global Corporate Media Consolidation

US-based firms – though not necessarily owned by Americans – continue to dominate the global media market, and by all accounts they will do so for a long time to come.[47] In global media markets, US firms can capitalize upon their historic competitive advantage of having by far the largest and most lucrative indigenous market to use as a testing ground and to yield economies of scale. Insofar as Hollywood and Madison Avenue have determined the formats for global commercial entertainment, this also accentuates the US advantage.[48] US-based firms can also take advantage of the widespread and growing international use of the English language, especially among the middle and upper classes.[49] Most of the large US-based media firms are in the process of moving from a 'US-centric production and an international distribution network' model to a more transnational production and distribution model.[50] The increasing need for the media giants to 'localize' their content is encouraging them to 'establish wider international bases.'[51] Another factor in globalizing production is to take advantage of lower costs outside of the United States.[52]

The 1990s has seen an unprecedented wave of mergers and acquisitions among global media giants. What is emerging is a tiered global media market. In the first tier are around ten colossal vertically integrated media conglomerates. Six firms that already fit that description are News Corporation, Time Warner, Disney, Bertelsmann, Viacom and TCI. These firms are major producers of entertainment and media software and have global distribution networks. Although the firms in the first tier are quite large – with annual sales in the $10–25 billion range – they are a notch or two below the largest global corporate giants, although all of them rank among the 500 largest global firms in annual sales. Four other firms that round out this first group include PolyGram (owned by Philips), NBC (owned by General Electric), Universal (owned by Seagram), and Sony. All four of these firms are conglomerates with non-media interests, and three of them (Sony, GE, and Philips) are huge electronics concerns that at least double the annual sales of any first-tier media firm. None of them is as fully integrated as the first six firms, but they have the resources to do so if they wish.

There is a second tier of approximately three dozen quite large media firms – with annual sales generally in the $2–10 billion range – that fill regional or niche markets within the global system.[53] Most of these firms rank among the 1,000 largest global firms in terms of market valuation. These second-tier firms tend to have working agreements and/or joint ventures with one or more of the giants in the first tier and with each other; none attempt to 'go it alone.' As the head of Norway's largest media company stated, 'We want to position ourselves so if Kirch or Murdoch want to sell in Scandinavia, they'll come to us first.'[54] Finally, there are thousands of relatively small national and local firms that provide services to the large firms or fill small niches, and their prosperity is dependent in part upon the choices of the large firms.

In this period of flux all media firms are responding to a general market situation that is *forcing* them to move toward being much larger, global, vertically integrated conglomerates. One media industry observer characterizes the late 1990s as 'an all-out rush to claim global turf,' and 'a slugfest the likes of which have never been seen.'[55] A Wall Street media analyst states that 'the name of the game is critical mass. You need buying power and distribution. The ante has been upped. It's a global arena.'[56] 'The minimum hurdle for the size that you have to be has gone up,' a media consulting firm executive comments. 'Look, a couple of years ago, a $2 billion to $3 billion company was a well-sized company. Now there is really a concern from the executives of a lot of these companies that they are going to get left behind.'[57] Indeed, even in the current period of high growth it is just as likely that the number of major film and music producers for the global market will decrease rather than increase.

It is when the effects of horizontal and vertical integration, conglomeration, and globalization are combined that a sense of the profit potential emerges. First, there are often distinct cost savings. The media consultant who advised Viacom when it purchased Paramount in 1994 estimated that merely combining the two firms would immediately generate $105 million in cost savings.[58] This comes from fuller utilization of existing personnel, facilities, and 'content' resources. When a giant wishes to launch a new enterprise, it can draw upon its existing staff and resources. NBC or News Corporation, for example, are capable of launching global television news channels because they will use their journalists from their present staffs and other news resources. The marginal cost is quite low.[59] A second source of profitability deriving from conglomeration and vertical integration is the exploitation of new opportunities for cross-selling, cross-promotion, and privileged access. These benefits were given great emphasis in corporate explanations of the benefits of the Disney–ABC and Time Warner–Turner mergers, where they were regularly referred to as 'synergies.' It should be noted, however, that these gains are based on monopoly power, and are not gains to society any more than a firm's greater ability to levy higher prices would be. They are private and 'pecuniary' gains, not social and 'real' gains. The other side of the coin of effective cross-selling (etc.) is the exclusion of others, a reduction of competition, and pressure on rivals to follow the same exclusionary path.

When Disney, for example, produces a film, it can also guarantee the film showings on pay cable television and commercial network television, and it can produce and sell soundtracks based on the film, it can create spin-off television series, it can produce related amusement park rides, CD-Roms, books, comics and merchandise to be sold in Disney retail stores. Moreover, Disney can promote the film and related material incessantly across all its media properties. Even films which do poorly at the box office can become profitable in this climate. Disney's 1996 *Hunchback of Notre Dame* generated a disappointing $99 million at the US and Canadian box offices. According to *Adweek* magazine, however, it is expected to generate $500 million in *profit* (not just revenues), after the other revenue streams are taken into account. And films that are hits can become spectacularly successful. Disney's 1994 *The Lion King* earned over $300 million at the US box office, yet generated over $1 billion in profit for Disney.[60] In sum, the profit whole for the vertically integrated firm can be significantly greater than the profit potential of the individual parts in isolation. Firms without this cross-selling and cross-promotional potential are at a serious disadvantage in competing in the global marketplace. This is the context for the wave of huge media mergers in the 1990s.

As the Disney example suggested, the 'synergies' do not end with media. Time Warner, Universal, and Disney all have theme parks and, likewise, Time Warner, Disney, and Viacom all have chains of retail stores to capitalize upon their media 'brands.'[61] Universal captures the spirit of the times in developing a five-year marketing plan for the 1995 film character 'Babe' to turn it into a 'mass-market cash cow.'[62] There will be a *Babe* film sequel in 1998, an animated *Babe* television series, along with *Babe* toys and books.[63] Universal is also launching 'brand galleries,' retail outlets based on its most well-known Universal Studios films and characters, at its Florida and California theme parks. It is also designing plans for two other chains of retail stores, one to stand alone and another to be a 'boutique' inside existing chain retailers such as Toys 'Я' Us.[64] Viacom is part of a joint venture to launch a chain of 'Bubba Gump' seafood restaurants to capitalize upon the popularity of its *Forrest Gump* motion picture.[65] Turner Broadcasting aggressively markets its 'brands' from its huge movie and cartoon library to advertisers for use in commercials.[66] Both TCI and Disney are moving into the production of educational material, regarded as a lucrative market as the privatization and commercialization of US schools gathers momentum.[67] Moreover, in view of their experience with commercial programming, media firms may be positioned to profit from the drive to bring advertising-supported fare into schools. The largest US commercial education firm, Channel One, only blossomed after being purchased by media firm K-III.[68] By 1997 Channel One was being 'broadcast' to some 40 percent of all US middle schools and high schools. Reebok, for example, has brought Channel One advertising into the heart of its marketing, using its school advertisements to promote the programs it sponsors over commercial television networks.[69]

The size and market power of the media giants also make it possible to engineer exclusive strategic alliances for cross-promotion with other marketing and retailing powerhouses. In 1996 Disney signed a ten-year deal with McDonald's, giving the fast food chain exclusive global rights to promote Disney products in its restaurants. Disney can use McDonald's 18,700 outlets to promote its global sales, while McDonald's can use Disney to assist it in its unabashed campaign to 'dominate every market' in the world.[70] PepsiCo. signed a similar promotional deal for a 1996 re-release of the *Star Wars* film trilogy, in which all of PepsiCo.'s global properties – including Pepsi-Cola, Frito-Lay snacks, Pizza Hut, and Taco Bell – were committed to the promotion.[71] Universal has taken this process the furthest, by keeping it in-house. In 1997 it began heavily promoting its media fare on parent corporation Seagram's beverage products, including Tropicana orange juice.[72] These link-ups between global marketers and media firms are becoming standard operating procedure, and they do much to enhance the profitability and competitive position of the very largest global firms.

It is important to note that these giant mergers, while enlarging profit opportunities in some respects, can run into difficulties, sometimes quite immense ones at that. The prices paid for the properties may be excessive and/or the interest payments on the debt incurred may prevent necessary capital expenditures and make the firm vulnerable to recession or other unexpected difficulties. Major mergers or acquisitions are often accompanied by the sale of assets to retire debt and refocus the firm's activities in areas where the firm has a large stake. In the late 1990s this process is being encouraged by Wall Street. Many corporate media stock prices have floundered during a bull market, putting severe pressure on corporate media managers to generate earnings growth in the short term. One investment banker observed that the largest media conglomerates will likely 'trim down to focus on businesses that are strong cash flow and high-growth, and get out of the businesses that aren't.'[73] In some cases the anticipated 'synergies' do not materialize or may be more than offset by difficulties in meshing with previously independent operations. Several global electronics giants, including General Electric and Sony, purchased major media firms thinking they could expand their profit potential through the complementary nature of media 'hardware' and 'software.' This has not yet proved to be the case. Matsushita found this route notably unrewarding, unloading (then) MCA to Seagram in 1995 after painful losses.

Firms grow and compete in the global marketplace by internal processes, reinvesting earnings to create new facilities, as well as by mergers and acquisitions. In establishing new ventures, media firms frequently participate in joint ventures with one or more of their rivals on specific media projects. Joint ventures are attractive because they reduce the capital requirements and risk of the participants and permit them to spread their resources more widely. Joint ventures also provide a more flexible weapon than formal mergers or acquisitions, which often require years for negotiation and approval and then getting the new parts assimilated. The ten largest global media firms have, on average, joint ventures with five of the other nine giants. They each also average six joint ventures with second-tier media firms. [. . .] Media giants also use joint ventures as a means of easing entry into new international markets, teaming up with 'local international partners who best understand their own turf.'[74] This is a major route through which the largest national and regional media firms around the world are brought into the global market system. Joint ventures are not without their problems, as media partners can develop differing visions for the joint enterprise; along these lines Universal and Viacom had a dispute over their USA cable television network, and US West has been dissatisfied with its shared operations with Time Warner.[75]

Beyond joint ventures, there is also overlapping direct ownership of these firms. Seagram, for example, owner of Universal, also owns 15 percent of Time Warner and has other media equity holdings.[76] TCI is a major shareholder in Time Warner and has holdings in numerous other media firms.[77] The Capital Group Companies' mutual funds, valued at $250 billion, are among the very largest shareholders in TCI, News Corporation, Seagram, Time Warner, Viacom, Disney, Westinghouse, and several other smaller media firms.[78] The head of Capital Group's media investments, Gordon Crawford, is a trusted adviser to the CEOs of nearly all of these firms. He plays an important role in engineering mergers and joint ventures across the media industry.[79] In particular, through Capital Group's holdings in Seagram and TCI as well as its direct holdings in Time Warner, Crawford is one of the most influential shareholders in Time Warner.[80] More generally, in view of their great merger activity and rapid expansion, the media giants find themselves increasingly reliant on the largest Wall Street commercial and investment banks for strategic counsel and capital. A handful of global institutions like Chase Manhattan, Morgan Stanley, and Salomon Brothers have been key advisers in the major mergers of the mid-1990s.[81]

Competition in media markets is quite different from the notion of competition that dominates popular usage of the term. When politicians, business executives, and academics invoke the term 'competition,' they almost invariably refer to the kind found in economics textbooks, based upon competitive markets where there are innumerable players, price competition, and easy entry. This notion of competition has never had much applicability in communication markets. As noted, the 'synergies' of recent mergers rest on and enhance monopoly power. Reigning oligopolistic markets are dominated by a handful of firms that compete – often quite ferociously within the oligopolistic framework – on a non-price basis and are protected by severe barriers to entry. No start-up studio, for example, has successfully joined the Hollywood oligopoly in 60 years.[82] Whether the new studio Dream Works, formed by Stephen Spielberg, David Geffen, and Jeffrey Katzenbach, succeeds, this is obviously an exceptional case, drawing upon the unique wealth and connections of its founders. If successful, Dream Works will probably become a second-tier player specializing in providing content to media giants through joint ventures and working agreements.

Rupert Murdoch of News Corporation poses the rational issue for an oligopolistic firm when pondering the shakeout in the global media market: 'We can join forces now, or we can kill each other and then join forces.'[83] In this spirit, in 1997 Murdoch contacted Viacom CEO Sumner Redstone, informing him it was time they stopped 'being perceived as adversaries,' and that they should 'see what we can do together.'[84] Time Warner CEO Gerald Levin claims that with rapidly expanding economic opportunities 'there is enough new business, both domestically and internationally, that there won't be a war of attrition.'[85] And if the giants are pursuing this new business in joint ventures with major rivals in many local and national markets, the likelihood of cut-throat competition recedes markedly. John Malone, the CEO of TCI, whose entrepreneurial drive is often noted, states that 'Nobody can really afford to get mad with their competitors, because they are partners in one area and competitors in another.'[86] The *Wall Street Journal* observes that media 'competitors wind up switching between the roles of adversaries, prized customers and key partners.'[87] In this sense the global media and communication market exhibits tendencies not only of an oligopoly, but of a cartel or at least a 'gentleman's club.' Paine Webber's media analyst terms it the global 'communications kereitsu,' in reference to the Japanese corporate system of interlocking ownership and management.[88]

[...]

Uneven Development of the Global Media Market

Even if the market is becoming the worldwide method for organizing communication, and nonmarket principles and values are playing a much smaller role in determining the nature of media systems, the globalization–commercialization process does not operate at the same pace and to the same extent around the world. Each nation's indigenous commercial and/or noncommercial media system responds somewhat differently to the encroachment of global market forces, leading to continued variation in local markets. Moreover, nation states remain the most important political forces in communication and much else; the pace and course of media market liberalization varies from nation to nation and region to region, though the general trend toward deregulation is clear. In short, each country will have to be understood on its own terms as well as in the context of the global media market for the foreseeable future.

The core tendencies of the global market itself will also tend to produce a highly uneven worldwide media system. Commercial media markets are attracted to people with the money to purchase their products (and the necessary media hardware to use them), and to people with enough money to purchase the products that program sponsors wish to advertise. If global advertisers are interested in a sector of the population or a region, global media firms will move quickly to accommodate them. A nation like India provides a case in point. Over half of its 900 million population is entirely irrelevant to the global media market and, at present rates of change, will continue to be irrelevant for generations. But the prospering middle classes are another matter. 'There are 250 million people in the middle-class in India alone,' Disney's Michael Eisner observes, 'which is an enormous opportunity.'[89] And it has only begun to be incorporated into the global media market in any appreciable way in the past decade. The same can be said of upper and middle classes across Asia, the Middle East, and Latin America. [...]

Media Globalization Effects

The central features of the media globalization of the past decade or so have been larger cross-border flows of media outputs, the growth of media TNCs and the tendency toward centralization of media control, and the spread and intensification of commercialization. The short-term effects of this process at the local and national level have been complex, variable, and by no means entirely negative. Among the positive effects, we may note first the global media's competitive pressure on, and threat to, state-controlled broadcasting systems that are sometimes complacent, stodgy, and performing poorly, and energized into extending and deepening their services.

Another positive effect of media globalization and commercialization is the rapid dissemination of the popular culture developed in the dominant commercial centers to the far corners of the earth. Its universal acceptance indicates that a widely felt need and demand are being met, and its global reach makes for a greater connectedness and linkage among peoples and the emergence of some kind of global culture. There is also some flow *toward* the cultural centers, and horizontal flows within regions as well, that may open new vistas and enhance understanding of different cultures within dominant and subordinate states.

[...]

These positive effects of a globalizing media suggest the possibility of continued change, and net positive benefits – with a slowly globalizing media widening audience options, new technologies and channels maintaining or increasing diversity and offsetting centralizing tendencies, local and national media preserving their local character as they pick and choose among global media offerings, and public broadcasting systems declining only slowly and maintaining in substantial degree their public service character and quality.

Our view, on the other hand, is less optimistic. We regard the primary effect of the globalization process – the crucial feature of globalization, and manifestation of the strength of the great powers and TNCs whose interests they serve – to be the implantation of the commercial model of communication, its extension to broadcasting and the 'new media,' and its gradual intensification under the force of competition and bottom-line pressures. The commercial model has its own internal logic and, being privately owned and relying on advertiser support, tends to erode the public sphere and to create a 'culture of entertainment' that is incompatible with a democratic order. Media outputs are commodified and are designed to serve market ends, not citizenship needs.

Furthermore, by their essential nature the commercial media will integrate well into the global market system and tend to serve its needs. This means greater openness to foreign commerce in media products, channels, and ownership. As the media are commercialized and centralized their self-protective power within each country increases from their growing command over information flows, political influence, and ability to set the media–political agenda (which comports well with that of advertisers and the corporate community at large).

Although the global media continue their growth and consolidation, and the tide of commercialization and centralization remains strong, this process has met local and national resistance, which has sometimes slowed it down and helped to preserve indigenous cultural-political media space. Within any specific nation, domestic media, traditions, language, and regulation still play key, often predominant, roles in determining the media culture. The development of a global commercial media system is not a linear process but, rather, a complex one characterized by fits and starts; and while the trendline seems clear its future remains uncertain. [. . .]

Notes

1 *Media and Entertainment*, Schroder Wertheim & Co. report, Oct. 4, 1995, p. 3.
2 Jane L. Levere, "Advertising," *New York Times*, June 11, 1996, p. C6.
3 Ted Johnson, "The Upsizing of Hollywood," *Variety*, Mar. 18–24, 1996, p. 65.
4 "A Week in the Life of German Showbiz," *Variety Global Media Report*, May 27 to June 2, 1996, pp. 16, 41.
5 Comment of Ed Wilson, President of Eyemark Entertainment. In Greg Spring, "Cable, Overseas Deals Beckon," *Electronic Media*, May 20, 1996, p. 12.
6 "Interview with Melissa T. Cook," *Wall Street Transcript*, Mar. 18, 1996, p. 2.
7 Ronald Grover, "Lights, Camera, Less Action," *Business Week*, July 1, 1996, pp. 50, 52.
8 Gustavo Lombo, "The Land of Opportunity," *Forbes*, July 15, 1996, pp. 292–4.
9 "European Ratings Snapshot," *Variety*, Oct. 14, 1996, p. 22.
10 *Our Creative Diversity: Report of the World Commission on Culture and Development* (Paris: World Commission on Culture and Development, 1995), p. 27.
11 Richard Tomkins, "US Tops Poll on Cultural Exports," *Financial Times*, Dec. 4, 1996, p. 9.
12 "Trade Imbalance Tops $6bn," *Television Business International*, Dec. 1996, p. 16.
13 David Rooney, "Filmauro Firing up Exhib, Distrib Arms," *Variety*, Nov. 25–Dec. 1, 1996, p. 29.
14 Mark Landler, "MTV Finds Increasing Competition for Foreign Viewers," *New York Times*, Mar. 25, 1996, p. C7.
15 Andrew Geddes, "TV Finds No Pan-Asian Panacea," *Advertising Age*, July 18, 1994.
16 Neel Chowdhury, "STAR-TV Shines in India," *International Herald Tribune*, July 16, 1996, p. 15.
17 Comment of D. Bourse. Cited in Doug Wilson, *Strategies of the Media Giants* (London: Pearson Professional, 1996), p. 40.
18 John Tagliabue, "Local Flavor Rules European TV," *New York Times*, Oct. 14, 1996, pp. C1, C3; Alice Rawsthorn, "Hollywood Goes Global," *Financial Times*, Sept. 27, 1996, special section, p. x.
19 Alice Rawsthorn, "World Book Market 'Faces Further Consolidation'," *Financial Times*, Oct. 2, 1996, p. 16.
20 Alice Rawsthorn, "Out of Tune with the Times," *Financial Times*, June 25, 1996, p. 15.
21 Alice Rawsthorn, "PolyGram is Biggest Music Group," *Financial Times*, May 9, 1996, p. 6; "Musical Chairs," *The Economist*, Dec. 23, 1995–Jan. 5, 1996, p. 78.
22 "Music Sales," *Variety*, Apr. 22–8, 1996, p. 7.
23 Alice Rawsthorn, "Recorded Music Sales Bound towards $40bn," *Financial Times*, Apr. 17, 1996, p. 5.

24 The trade publication is *Music Business International* magazine. Cited in Alice Rawsthorn, "China to Lead Global Music Sales Growth," *Financial Times*, Jan. 24, 1996, p. 7.

25 Harold L. Vogel, *Entertainment Industry Economics: A Guide for Financial Analysis*, 3rd edn (New York and Cambridge: Cambridge University Press, 1994), p. 40.

26 Comment of Ted Shugrue of Columbia TriStar Films (owned by Sony). Cited in Antonia Zerbisias, "The World at their Feet," *Toronto Star*, Aug. 27, 1995, p. C1; see also Cäcilie Rohwedder, Lisa Bannon, and Eben Shapiro, "Spending Spree by German Kirch Group Spells Bonanza for Hollywood Studios," *Wall Street Journal*, Aug. 1, 1996, p. B1.

27 Quotations of Greg Coote of Village Roadshow and David Davis of Houlihan, Lokey, Howard & Zukin. Cited in Leonard Klady, "US Exhibs Discover the Joy of Plex O'Seas," *Variety*, Apr. 8–14, 1996, pp. 9, 14.

28 Andrew Tanzer and Robert La Franco, "Luring Asians from their TV Sets," *Forbes*, June 3, 1996, p. 41.

29 "Global Fast Forward," *Variety*, Apr. 22–8, 1996, p. 13.

30 Neil Weinberg, "The Fourth Wave," *Forbes*, Nov. 20, 1996, p. 114; Peter M. Nichols, "A New CD Marvel Awaits, But the Horizon Recedes," *New York Times*, Aug. 25, 1996, sec. 2, pp. 1, 20.

31 Rohwedder, Bannon, and Shapiro, "Spending Spree."

32 Bernard Weinraub, "MCA in $2.5 Billion Sale of Shows to German TV," *New York Times*, July 31, 1996, p. C1.

33 Linda Lee, "Film and TV Output Soars, Spurring Demand for Studio Space," *New York Times*, Jan. 20, 1997 pp. C1, C7.

34 Leonard Klady, "Why Mega-flicks Click," *Variety*, Nov. 25–Dec. 1, 1996, p. 1.

35 John Lippman, "Hollywood Reeled Record $5.8 Billion Last Year, Boosted by Blockbuster Films," *Wall Street Journal*, Jan. 3, 1997, p. B2.

36 Bernard Weinraub, "Media," *New York Times*, Jan. 6, 1997, p. C7.

37 Barbara Maltsby, "The Homogenization of Hollywood," *Media Studies Journal*, 10(2–3) (Spring/Summer 1996): 115.

38 Bill Carter, "Pow! Thwack! Bam! No Dubbing Needed," *New York Times*, Week in Review section, Nov. 3, 1996, p. 6.

39 Ira Teinowicz, "Court Further Bolsters Commercial Speech," *Advertising Age*, May 27, 1996, p. 47.

40 Edward S. Herman, "The Media Mega-mergers," *Dollars and Sense*, no. 205 (May–June 1996): 8–13.

41 Mark Landler, "In Cable TV, More is Less," *New York Times*, Week in Review section, Nov. 10, 1996, p. 4.

42 Andy Stern, "Eurocrats Set to Clash on Quota Battleground," *Variety*, Feb. 12–18, 1996, p. 35.

43 Anthony DePalma, "US and Mexico Reach Accord over Satellite TV Transmission," *New York Times*, Nov. 9, 1996, p. 20.

44 Ira Teinowicz and Don Angus, "US Joins the Canada Ad Fight," *Advertising Age*, Mar. 18, 1996, p. 44.

45 Anthony DePalma, "World Trade Body Opposes Canadian Magazine Tariffs," *New York Times*, Jan. 20, 1997, p. C8.

46 "Digital Dilemmas," *The Economist*, Mar. 23, 1996, p. 82; "The Revolution that Could Bring Viewers 1,800 New Channels," *Financial Times*, Apr. 25, 1996, p. 8.

47 Wilson, *Strategies of the Media Giants*, p. 5.

48 Frank Biondi, "A Media Tycoon's Take on the 21st Century," *Business Week*, Nov. 18, 1994, p. 190.

49 Helen Bunting, *US Media Markets: Leading the World?* (London: Pearson Professional, 1995), p. 98.

50 Mark Landler, "Think Globally, Program Locally," *Business Week*, Nov. 18, 1994, pp. 186–9.

51 Bunting, *US Media Markets*, pp. 99, 3.

52 "Warner Opens Animation Studio," *Financial Times*, June 22–3, 1996, p. 4; Julia Flynn and Katherine Ann Miller, "Tinseltown on the Thames," *Business Week*, Aug. 5, 1996, pp. 47–8.

53   Diane Mermigas, "Still to Come: Smaller Media Alliances," *Electronic Media*, Feb. 5, 1996, p. 38.

54   Marlene Edmunds, "Vertically Integrated Schibsted Rises to Top," *Variety*, Oct. 14–20, 1996, p. 52.

55   Diane Mermigas, "Media Players Mining for Global Gold," *Electronic Media*, Dec. 11, 1995, p. 18.

56   Comment of Porter Bibb, analyst for Ladenburg Thalmann & Co. Cited in Keith J. Kelly, "Time Warner Temblor Topples Structure," *Advertising Age*, Nov. 20, 1995, p. 6.

57   Comments of Michael J. Wolf, lead partner at Booz, Allen & Hamilton. Cited in Rita Koselka, "Mergermania in Medialand," *Forbes*, Oct. 23, 1995, p. 254.

58   Koselka, "Mergermania in Medialand," p. 258.

59   Christopher Dixon, presentation to Association of Investment Management and Research, New York City, Jan. 31, 1996, p. 4.

60   Marla Matzer, "Contented Kingdoms," in supplement to *Adweek*, Oct. 7, 1996, pp. 30, 33.

61   Jeff Jensen, "Viacom Eyes Venues for Merchandising," *Advertising Age*, Apr. 6, 1996, p. 3.

62   Jeff Jensen, "MCA/Universal Grooms 'Babe' for a New Career as Mass-Market Brand," *Advertising Age*, Apr. 29, 1996, p. 16.

63   Diane Mermigas, "New Day Dawns for Universal Television," *Electronic Media*, Jan. 6, 1997, p. 24.

64   Jeff Jensen, "Universal to Present New Image," *Advertising Age*, July 1, 1996, p. 28.

65   Matzer, "Contented Kingdoms," p. 34.

66   Sally Goll Beatty, "Turner Lets Some of its Treasures Moonlight for Other Marketers," *Wall Street Journal*, May 22, 1996, p. B8; Chuck Ross, "Heyer Steering Turner into Marketing Alliances," *Advertising Age*, Apr. 22, 1996, p. 53.

67   Larry Dum, "Pressure Builds when a Giant Enters a Niche," *New York Times*, Sept. 16, 1996, p. C4.

68   Joshua Levine, "TV in the Classroom," *Forbes*, Jan. 27, 1997, p. 98.

69   *Wall Street Journal*, Jan. 29, 1997, p. B2.

70   "Macworld," *The Economist*, June 29, 1996, p. 62.

71   Alice Rawsthorn, "PepsiCo. to Feel Force of Star Wars," *Financial Times*, May 17, 1996, p. 21.

72   Diane Mermigas, "Seagram Eyes Global Arena for Universal," *Electronic Media*, Jan. 13, 1997, p. 94.

73   Laura Landro, "Entertainment Giants Face Pressure to Cut Costs, Get into Focus," *Wall Street Journal*, Feb. 11, 1997, pp. A1, A17.

74   Diane Mermigas, "Liberty Sees Sports as Key to Global Kingdom," *Electronic Media*, May 13, 1996, p. 4.

75   Both the Viacom–Universal conflict over the US cable network and the Time Warner–US West conflict over Time Warner Entertainment are being negotiated and also considered by the court system as the book goes to press in March 1997. It is probable that both conflicts will be resolved by the end of the calendar year, with the joint ventures formally terminated.

76   Bernard Simon, "Seagram to Hold On to 15 percent Stake in Time Warner," *Financial Times*, June 1, 1995, p. 18.

77   Raymond Snoddy, "Master of Bits at Home in the Hub," *Financial Times*, May 28, 1996, p. 17.

78   Catherine E. Celebrezze, "The Man who Bought the Media," *EXTRA!* 9(2) (Mar.–Apr. 1996): 21–2.

79   Mark Robichaux, "Tim Robertson Turns TV's Family Channel into a Major Business," *Wall Street Journal*, Aug. 29, 1996, p. A6.

80   Linda Grant, "Moneyman to the Moguls," *Fortune*, Sept. 9, 1996, pp. 37–8.

81   Martin Peers, "Wall Street Looks Overseas," *Variety*, Oct. 14–20, 1996, pp. 41–2.

82   Ronald Grover, "Plenty of Dreams, Not Enough Work?" *Business Week*, July 22, 1996, p. 65.

83   Paula Dwyer, "Can Rupert Conquer Europe?" *Business Week*, Mar. 25. 1996 p. 169.

84 Elizabeth Lesly, Gail DeGeorge and Ronald Grover, "Sumner's Last Stand," *Business Week*, Mar. 3, 1997, p. 67.
85 Quoted in *Wisconsin State Journal*, Feb. 9. 1996, p. A2.
86 Snoddy, "Master of Bits at Home in the Hub."
87 Elizabeth Jensen and Eben Shapiro, "Time Warner's Fight with News Corp. Belies Mutual Dependence," *Wall Street Journal*, Oct. 28, 1996, p. A1.
88 Dixon, presentation, p. 2.
89 Bill Carter and Richard Sandomir, "The Trophy in Eisner's Deal," *New York Times*, Aug. 6, 1996, sec. 3, p. 11.

20

Disjuncture and Difference in the Global Cultural Economy

Arjun Appadurai

The central problem of today's global interactions is the tension between cultural homogenization and cultural heterogenization. A vast array of empirical facts could be brought to bear on the side of the 'homogenization' argument, and much of it has come from the left end of the spectrum of media studies (Hamelink 1983; Mattelart 1983; Schiller 1976), and some from other, less appealing, perspectives (Gans 1985; Iyer 1988). Most often, the homogenization argument subspeciates into either an argument about Americanization, or an argument about 'commoditization', and very often the two arguments are closely linked. What these arguments fail to consider is that at least as rapidly as forces from various metropolises are brought into new societies they tend to become indigenized in one or other way: this is true of music and housing styles as much as it is true of science and terrorism, spectacles and constitutions. The dynamics of such indigenization have just begun to be explored in a sophisticated manner (Barber 1987; Feld 1988; Hannerz 1987, 1989; Ivy 1988; Nicoll 1989; Yoshimoto 1989), and much more needs to be done. But it is worth noticing that for the people of Irian Jaya, Indonesianization may be more worrisome than Americanization, as Japanization may be for Koreans, Indianization for Sri Lankans, Vietnamization for the Cambodians, Russianization for the people of Soviet Armenia and the Baltic Republics. Such a list of alternative fears to Americanization could be greatly expanded, but it is not a shapeless inventory: for polities of smaller scale, there is always a fear of cultural absorption by polities of larger scale, especially those that are near by. One man's imagined community (Anderson 1983) is another man's political prison.

This scalar dynamic, which has widespread global manifestations, is also tied to the relationship between nations and states, to which I shall return later in this essay. For the moment let us note that the simplification of these many forces (and fears) of homogenization can also be exploited by nation-states in relation to their own minorities, by posing global commoditization (or capitalism, or some other such external enemy) as more 'real' than the threat of its own hegemonic strategies.

The new global cultural economy has to be understood as a complex, overlapping, disjunctive order, which cannot any longer be understood in terms of existing center-periphery models (even those that might account for multiple centers and peripheries). Nor is it susceptible to simple models of push and pull (in terms of migration theory) or of surpluses and deficits (as in traditional models of balance of trade), or of consumers and producers (as in most neo-Marxist theories of development). Even the most complex and flexible theories of global development which have come out of the Marxist tradition (Amin 1980; Mandel 1978; Wallerstein 1974; Wolf 1982) are inadequately quirky, and they have not come to terms with what Lash and Urry (1987) have recently called 'disorganized capitalism'. The complexity of the current global economy has to do with certain fundamental disjunctures between economy, culture and politics which we have barely begun to theorize. [. . .]

I propose that an elementary framework for exploring such disjunctures is to look at the relationship between five dimensions of global cultural flow which can be termed: (a) ethnoscapes; (b) mediascapes; (c) technoscapes; (d) finanscapes; and (e) ideo-scapes. [. . .] I use terms with the common suffix scape to indicate first of all that these are not objectively given relations which look the same from every angle of vision, but rather that they are deeply perspectival constructs, inflected very much by the historical, linguistic and political situatedness of different sorts of actors: nation-states, multinationals, diasporic communities, as well as sub-national groupings and movements (whether religious, political or economic), and even intimate face-to-face groups, such as villages, neighborhoods and families. Indeed, the individual actor is the last locus of this perspectival set of landscapes, for these landscapes are eventually navigated by agents who both experience and constitute larger formations, in part by their own sense of what these landscapes offer. These landscapes, thus, are the building blocks of what, extending Benedict Anderson, I would like to call 'imagined worlds', that is, the mul-tiple worlds which are constituted by the historically situated imaginations of persons and groups spread around the globe (Appadurai 1989). An important fact of the world we live in today is that many persons on the globe live in such imagined 'worlds' and not just in imagined communities, and thus are able to contest and sometimes even sub-vert the 'imagined worlds' of the official mind and of the entrepreneurial mentality that surround them. The suffix scape also allows us to point to the fluid, irregular shapes of these landscapes, shapes which characterize international capital as deeply as they do international clothing styles.

By 'ethnoscape', I mean the landscape of persons who constitute the shifting world in which we live: tourists, immigrants, refugees, exiles, guestworkers and other moving groups and persons constitute an essential feature of the world, and appear to affect the politics of and between nations to a hitherto unprecedented degree. This is not to say that there are not anywhere relatively stable communities and networks, of kinship, of friendship, of work and of leisure, as well as of birth, residence and other filiative forms. But it is to say that the warp of these stabilities is everywhere shot through with the woof of human motion, as more persons and groups deal with the realities of having to move, or the fantasies of wanting to move. What is more, both these real-ities as well as these fantasies now function on larger scales, as men and women from villages in India think not just of moving to Poona or Madras, but of moving to Dubai and Houston, and refugees from Sri Lanka find themselves in South India as well as in Canada, just as the Hmong are driven to London as well as to Philadelphia. And as international capital shifts its needs, as production and technology generate different needs, as nation-states shift their policies on refugee populations, these moving groups can never afford to let their imaginations rest too long, even if they wished to.

By 'technoscape', I mean the global configuration, also ever fluid, of technology, and of the fact that technology, both high and low, both mechanical and informational, now moves at high speeds across various kinds of previously impervious boundaries. Many countries now are the roots of multinational enterprise: a huge steel complex in Libya may involve interests from India, China, Russia and Japan, providing different com-ponents of new technological configurations. The odd distribution of technologies, and thus the peculiarities of these technoscapes, are increasingly driven not by any obvious economies of scale, of political control, or of market rationality, but of increasingly complex relationships between money flows, political possibilities and the availability of both low and highly skilled labor. So, while India exports waiters and chauffeurs to Dubai and Sharjah, it also exports software engineers to the United States (indentured briefly to Tata-Burroughs or the World Bank), then laundered through the State Department to become wealthy 'resident aliens', who are in turn objects of seductive messages to invest their money and know-how in federal and state projects in India. The global economy can still be described in terms of traditional 'indicators' (as the World Bank continues to do) and studied in terms of traditional comparisons (as in Project Link at the University of Pennsylvania), but the complicated technoscapes (and the shifting ethnoscapes) which underlie these 'indicators' and 'comparisons' are further out of the reach of the 'queen of the social sciences' than ever before. How is one to make a meaningful comparison of wages in Japan and the United States, or of real estate costs in New York and Tokyo, without taking sophisticated account of the very complex fiscal and investment flows that link the two economies through a global grid of currency speculation and capital transfer?

Thus it is useful to speak as well of 'finanscapes', since the disposition of global capital is now a more mysterious, rapid and difficult landscape to follow than ever before, as currency markets, national stock exchanges, and commodity speculations move megamonies through national turnstiles at blinding speed, with vast absolute implications for small differences in percentage points and time units. But the critical point is that the global relationship between ethnoscapes, technoscapes and finanscapes is deeply disjunctive and profoundly unpredictable, since each of these landscapes is subject to its own constraints and incentives (some political, some informational and some techno-environmental), at the same time as each acts as a constraint and a parameter for movements in the other. Thus, even an elementary model of global political economy must take into account the shifting relationship between perspectives on human movement, technological flow, and financial transfers, which can accommodate their deeply disjunctive relationships with one another.

Built upon these disjunctures (which hardly form a simple, mechanical global 'infrastructure' in any case) are what I have called 'mediascapes' and 'ideoscapes', though the latter two are closely related landscapes of images. 'Mediascapes' refer both to the distribution of the electronic capabilities to produce and disseminate information (newspapers, magazines, television stations, film production studios, etc.), which are now available to a growing number of private and public interests throughout the world; and to the images of the world created by these media. These images of the world involve many complicated inflections, depending on their mode (documentary or entertainment), their hardware (electronic or pre-electronic), their audiences (local, national or transnational) and the interests of those who own and control them. What is most important about these mediascapes is that they provide (especially in their television, film and cassette forms) large and complex repertoires of images, narratives and 'ethnoscapes' to viewers throughout the world, in which the world of commodities and the world of 'news' and politics are profoundly mixed. What this means is that many audiences throughout the world experience the media themselves as a complicated and interconnected repertoire of print, celluloid, electronic screens and billboards. The lines between the 'realistic' and the fictional landscapes they see are blurred, so that the further away these audiences are from the direct experiences of metropolitan life, the more likely they are to construct 'imagined worlds' which are chimerical, aesthetic, even fantastic objects, particularly if assessed by the criteria of some other perspective, some other 'imagined world'.

'Mediascapes', whether produced by private or state interests, tend to be image-centered, narrative-based accounts of strips of reality, and what they offer to those who experience and transform them is a series of elements (such as characters, plots and textual forms) out of which scripts can be formed of imagined lives, their own as well as those of others living in other places. These scripts can and do get disaggregated into complex sets of metaphors by which people live (Lakoff and Johnson 1980) as they help to constitute narratives of the 'other' and proto-narratives of possible lives, fantasies which could become prolegomena to the desire for acquisition and movement.

'Ideoscapes' are also concatenations of images, but they are often directly political and frequently have to do with the ideologies of states and the counter-ideologies of movements explicitly oriented to capturing state power or a piece of it. These ideoscapes are composed of elements of the Enlightenment world-view, which consists of a concatenation of ideas, terms and images, including 'freedom', 'welfare', 'rights', 'sovereignty', 'representation' and the master-term 'democracy'. The master-narrative of the Enlightenment (and its many variants in England, France and the United States) was constructed with a certain internal logic and presupposed a certain relationship between reading, representation and the public sphere (for the dynamics of this process in the early history of the United States, see Warner 1990). But their diaspora across the world, especially since the nineteenth century, has loosened the internal coherence which held these terms and images together in a Euro-American master-narrative, and provided instead a loosely structured synopticon of politics, in which different nation-states, as part of their evolution, have organized their political cultures around different 'keywords' (Williams 1976).

As a result of the differential diaspora of these keywords, the political narratives that govern communication between elites and followings in different parts of the world involve problems of both a semantic and a pragmatic nature: semantic to the extent that words (and their lexical equivalents) require careful translation from context to context in their global movements; and pragmatic to the extent that the use of these words by political actors and their audiences may be subject to very different sets of contextual conventions that mediate their translation into public politics. Such conventions are not only matters of the nature of political rhetoric (viz. what does the aging Chinese leadership mean when it refers to the dangers of hooliganism? What does the South Korean leadership mean when it speaks of 'discipline' as the key to democratic industrial growth?).

These conventions also involve the far more subtle question of what sets of communicative genres are valued in what way (newspapers versus cinema for example) and what sorts of pragmatic genre conventions govern the collective 'readings' of different kinds of text. So, while an Indian audience may be attentive to the resonances of a political speech in terms of some key words and phrases reminiscent of Hindi cinema, a Korean audience may respond to the subtle codings of Buddhist or neo-Confucian rhetorical strategy encoded in a political document. The very relationship of reading to hearing and seeing may vary in important ways that determine the morphology of these different 'ideoscapes' as they shape themselves in different national and trans-national contexts. This globally variable synaesthesia has hardly even been noted, but it demands urgent analysis. Thus 'democracy' has clearly become a master-term, with powerful echoes from Haiti and Poland to the Soviet Union and China, but it sits at the center of a variety of ideoscapes (composed of distinctive pragmatic configurations of rough 'translations' of other central terms from the vocabulary of the Enlightenment). This creates ever new terminological kaleidoscopes, as states (and the groups that seek to capture them) seek to pacify populations whose own ethnoscapes are in motion, and whose mediascapes may create severe problems for the ideoscapes with which they are presented. The fluidity of ideoscapes is complicated in particular by the growing diasporas (both voluntary and involuntary) of intellectuals who continuously inject new meaning-streams into the discourse of democracy in different parts of the world.

This extended terminological discussion of the five terms I have coined sets the basis for a tentative formulation about the conditions under which current global flows occur: *they occur in and through the growing disjunctures between ethnoscapes, technoscapes, finanscapes, mediascapes and ideoscapes.* This formulation, the core of my model of global cultural flow, needs some explanation. First, people, machinery, money, images, and ideas now follow increasingly non-isomorphic paths: of course, at all periods in human history, there have been some disjunctures between the flows of these things, but the sheer speed, scale and volume of each of these flows is now so great that the disjunctures have become central to the politics of global culture. The Japanese are notoriously hospitable to ideas and are stereotyped as inclined to export (all) and import (some) goods, but they are also notoriously closed to immigration, like the Swiss, the Swedes and the Saudis. Yet the Swiss and Saudis accept populations of guestworkers, thus creating labor diasporas of Turks, Italians and other circum-mediterranean groups. Some such guestworker groups maintain continuous contact with their home-nations, like the Turks, but others, like high-level South Asian migrants, tend to desire lives in their new homes, raising anew the problem of reproduction in a deterritorialized context.

Deterritorialization, in general, is one of the central forces of the modern world, since it brings laboring populations into the lower class sectors and spaces of relatively wealthy societies, while sometimes creating exaggerated and intensified senses of criticism or attachment to politics in the home-state. Deterritorialization, whether of Hindus, Sikhs, Palestinians or Ukrainians, is now at the core of a variety of global fundamentalisms, including Islamic and Hindu fundamentalism. In the Hindu case for example (Appadurai and Breckenridge, forthcoming) it is clear that the overseas movement of Indians has been exploited by a variety of interests both within and outside India to create a complicated network of finances and religious identifications, in which the problems of cultural reproduction for Hindus abroad have become tied to the politics of Hindu fundamentalism at home.

At the same time, deterritorialization creates new markets for film companies, art impresarios and travel agencies, who thrive on the need of the deterritorialized population for contact with its homeland. Naturally, these invented homelands, which constitute the mediascapes of deterritorialized groups, can often become sufficiently fantastic and one-sided that they provide the material for new ideoscapes in which ethnic conflicts can begin to erupt. The creation of 'Khalistan', an invented homeland of the deterritorialized Sikh population of England, Canada and the United States, is one example of the bloody potential in such mediascapes, as they interact with the 'internal colonialisms' (Hechter 1974) of the nation-state. The West Bank, Namibia and Eritrea are other theaters for the enactment of the bloody negotiation between existing nation-states and various deterritorialized groupings.

The idea of deterritorialization may also be applied to money and finance, as money managers seek the best markets for their investments, independent of national boundaries. In turn, these movements of monies are the basis of new kinds of conflict, as Los Angelenos worry about the Japanese buying up their city, and people in Bombay worry about the rich Arabs from the Gulf States who have not only trans-formed the prices of mangoes in Bombay, but have also substantially altered the profile of hotels, restaurants and other services in the eyes of the local population, just as they continue to do in London. Yet, most residents of Bombay are ambivalent about the Arab presence there, for the flip side of their presence is the absence of friends and kinsmen earning big money in the Middle East and bringing back both money and luxury commodities to Bombay and other cities in India. Such commodities transform consumer taste in these cities, and also often end up smuggled through air and sea ports and peddled in the gray markets of Bombay's streets. In these gray markets, some mem-bers of Bombay's middle-classes and of its lumpenproletariat can buy some of these goods, ranging from cartons of Marlboro cigarettes, to Old Spice shaving cream and tapes of Madonna. Similarly gray routes, often subsidized by the moonlighting activities of sailors, diplomats, and airline stewardesses who get to move in and out of the country regularly, keep the gray markets of Bombay, Madras and Calcutta filled with goods not only from the West, but also from the Middle East, Hong Kong and Singapore.

It is this fertile ground of deterritorialization, in which money, commodities and persons are involved in ceaselessly chasing each other around the world, that the mediascapes and ideoscapes of the modern world find their fractured and frag-mented counterpart. For the ideas and images produced by mass media often are only partial guides to the goods and experiences that deterritorialized populations transfer to one another. In Mira Nair's brilliant film, *India Cabaret*, we see the multiple loops of this fractured deterritorialization as young women, barely competent in Bombay's metropolitan glitz, come to seek their fortunes as cabaret dancers and prostitutes in Bombay, entertaining men in clubs with dance formats derived wholly from the prurient dance sequences of Hindi films. These scenes cater in turn to ideas about Western and foreign women and their 'looseness', while they provide tawdry career alibis for these women. Some of these women come from Kerala, where cabaret clubs and the porno-graphic film industry have blossomed, partly in response to the purses and tastes of Keralites returned from the Middle East, where their diasporic lives away from women distort their very sense of what the relations between men and women might be. These tragedies of displacement could certainly be replayed in a more detailed analysis of the relations between the Japanese and German sex tours to Thailand and the tragedies of the sex trade in Bangkok, and in other similar loops which tie together fantasies about the other, the conveniences and seductions of travel, the economics of global trade and the brutal mobility fantasies that dominate gender politics in many parts of Asia and the world at large.

While far more could be said about the cultural politics of deterritorialization and the larger sociology of displacement that it expresses, it is appropriate at this juncture to bring in the role of the nation-state in the disjunctive global economy of culture today. The relationship between states and nations is everywhere an embattled one. It is pos-sible to say that in many societies, the nation and the state have become one another's projects. That is, while nations (or more properly groups with ideas about nationhood) seek to capture or co-opt states and state power, states simultaneously seek to capture and monopolize ideas about nationhood (Baruah 1986; Chatterjee 1986; Nandy 1989). In general, separatist, transnational movements, including those which have included terror in their methods, exemplify nations in search of states: Sikhs, Tamil Sri Lankans,

Basques, Moros, Quebecois, each of these represent imagined communities which seek to create states of their own or carve pieces out of existing states. States, on the other hand, are everywhere seeking to monopolize the moral resources of community, either by flatly claiming perfect coevality between nation and state, or by systematically museumizing and representing all the groups within them in a variety of heritage politics that seems remarkably uniform throughout the world (Handler 1988; Herzfeld 1982; McQueen 1988). Here, national and international mediascapes are exploited by nation-states to pacify separatists or even the potential fissiparousness of all ideas of difference. Typically, contemporary nation-states do this by exercising taxonomical control over difference; by creating various kinds of international spectacle to domesticate difference; and by seducing small groups with the fantasy of self-display on some sort of global or cosmopolitan stage. One important new feature of global cultural politics, tied to the disjunctive relationships between the various landscapes discussed earlier, is that state and nation are at each other's throats, and the hyphen that links them is now less an icon of conjuncture than an index of disjuncture. This disjunctive relationship between nation and state has two levels: at the level of any given nation-state, it means that there is a battle of the imagination, with state and nation seeking to cannibalize one another. Here is the seedbed of brutal separatisms, majoritarianisms that seem to have appeared from nowhere, and micro-identities that have become political projects within the nation-state. At another level, this disjunctive relationship is deeply entangled with the global disjunctures discussed throughout this essay: ideas of nationhood appear to be steadily increasing in scale and regularly crossing existing state boundaries: sometimes, as with the Kurds, because previous identities stretched across vast national spaces, or, as with the Tamils in Sri Lanka, the dormant threads of a transnational diaspora have been activated to ignite the micro-politics of a nation-state.

In discussing the cultural politics that have subverted the hyphen that links the nation to the state, it is especially important not to forget its mooring in the irregularities that now characterize 'disorganized capital' (Lash and Urry 1987; Kothari 1989). It is because labor, finance and technology are now so widely separated that the volatilities that underlie movements for nationhood (as large as transnational Islam on the one hand, or as small as the movement of the Gurkhas for a separate state in the North-East of India) grind against the vulnerabilities which characterize the relationships between states. States find themselves pressed to stay 'open' by the forces of media, technology, and travel which had fueled consumerism throughout the world and have increased the craving, even in the non-Western world, for new commodities and spectacles. On the other hand, these very cravings can become caught up in new ethnoscapes, mediascapes, and eventually, ideoscapes, such as 'democracy' in China, that the state cannot tolerate as threats to its own control over ideas of nationhood and 'peoplehood'. States throughout the world are under siege, especially where contests over the ideoscapes of democracy are fierce and fundamental, and where there are radical disjunctures between ideoscapes and technoscapes (as in the case of very small countries that lack contemporary technologies of production and information); or between ideoscapes and finanscapes (as in countries, such as Mexico or Brazil, where international lending influences national politics to a very large degree); or between ideoscapes and ethnoscapes (as in Beirut, where diasporic, local and translocal filiations are suicidally at battle); or between ideoscapes and mediascapes (as in many countries in the Middle East and Asia) where the lifestyles represented on both national and international TV and cinema completely overwhelm and undermine the rhetoric of national politics: in the Indian case, the myth of the law-breaking hero has emerged to mediate this naked struggle between the pieties and the realities of Indian politics, which has grown increasingly brutalized and corrupt (Vachani 1989).

[. . .]

The globalization of culture is not the same as its homogenization, but globalization involves the use of a variety of instruments of homogenization (armaments, advertising techniques, language hegemonies, clothing styles and the like), which are absorbed into local political and cultural economies, only to be repatriated as heterogeneous dialogues of national sovereignty, free enterprise, fundamentalism, etc. in which the state plays an increasingly delicate role: too much openness to global flows and the nation-state is threatened by revolt – the China syndrome; too little, and the state exits the international stage, as Burma, Albania and North Korea, in various ways have done. In general, the state has become the arbiter of this *repatriation of difference* (in the form of goods, signs, slogans, styles, etc.). But this repatriation or export of the designs and commodities of difference continuously exacerbates the 'internal' politics of majoritarianism and homogenization, which is most frequently played out in debates over heritage.

Thus the central feature of global culture today is the politics of the mutual effort of sameness and difference to cannibalize one another and thus to proclaim their successful hijacking of the twin Enlightenment ideas of the triumphantly universal and the resiliently particular. This mutual cannibalization shows its ugly face in riots, in refugee-flows, in state-sponsored torture and in ethnocide (with or without state support). Its brighter side is in the expansion of many individual horizons of hope and fantasy, in the global spread of oral rehydration therapy and other low-tech instruments of well-being, in the susceptibility even of South Africa to the force of global opinion, in the inability of the Polish state to repress its own working-classes, and in the growth of a wide range of progressive, transnational alliances. Examples of both sorts could be multiplied. The critical point is that both sides of the coin of global cultural process today are products of the infinitely varied mutual contest of sameness and difference on a stage characterized by radical disjunctures between different sorts of global flows and the uncertain landscapes created in and through these disjunctures.

Note

A longer version of this essay appears in *Public Culture*, vol. 2, no. 2 (Spring 1990): 1–24, and also as chapter 2 of Arjun Appadurai, *Modernity at Large*, University of Minnesota Press, 1996.

References

Amin, S. (1980) *Class and Nation: Historically and in the Current Crisis*. New York and London: Monthly Review.

Anderson, B. (1983) *Imagined Communities: Reflections on the Origin and Spread of Nationalism*. London: Verso.

Appadurai, A. (1989) Global ethnoscapes: notes and queries for a transnational anthropology. In R. G. Fox (ed.), *Interventions: Anthropology of the Present*.

Appadurai, A. and Breckenridge, C. A. (forthcoming) *A Transnational Culture in the Making: The Asian Indian Diaspora in the United States*. London: Berg.

Barber, K. (1987) Popular arts in Africa. *African Studies Review* 30(3).

Baruah, S. (1986) Immigration, ethnic conflict and political turmoil, Assam 1979–85. *Asian Survey* 26(11).

Chatterjee, P. (1986) *Nationalist Thought and the Colonial World: A Derivative Discourse.* London: Zed Books.

Feld, S. (1988) Notes on world beat. *Public Culture* 1(1): 31–7.

Gans, Eric (1985) *The End of Culture: Toward a Generative Anthropology.* Berkeley: University of California Press.

Hamelink, C. (1983) *Cultural Autonomy in Global Communications.* New York: Longman.

Handler, R. (1988) *Nationalism and the Politics of Culture in Quebec.* Madison: University of Wisconsin Press.

Hannerz, U. (1987) The world in Creolization. *Africa* 57(4): 546–59.

Hannerz, U. (1989) Notes on the global ecumene. *Public Culture* 1(2): 66–75.

Hechter, M. (1974) *Internal Colonialism: The Celtic Fringe in British National Development, 1536–1966.* Berkeley and Los Angeles: University of California Press.

Herzfeld, M. (1982) *Ours Once More: Folklore, Ideology and the Making of Modern Greece.* Austin: University of Texas Press.

Ivy, M. (1988) Tradition and difference in the Japanese mass media. *Public Culture* 1(1): 21–9.

Iyer, P. (1988) *Video Night in Kathmandu.* New York: Knopf.

Kothari, R. (1989) *State against Democracy: In Search of Humane Governance.* New York: New Horizons.

Lakoff, G. and Johnson, M. (1980) *Metaphors We Live By.* Chicago and London: University of Chicago Press.

Lash, S. and Urry, J. (1987) *The End of Organized Capitalism.* Madison: University of Wisconsin Press.

McQueen, H. (1988) The Australian stamp: image, design and ideology. *Arena* 84 (Spring): 78–96.

Mandel, E. (1978) *Late Capitalism.* London: Verso.

Mattelart, A. (1983) *Transnationals and Third World: The Struggle for Culture.* South Hadley, Mass.: Bergin and Garvey.

Nandy, A. (1989) The political culture of the Indian state. *Daedalus* 118(4): 1–26.

Nicoll, F. (1989) My trip to Alice. *Criticism, Heresy and Interpretation (CHAI)* 3: 21–32.

Schiller, H. (1976) *Communication and Cultural Domination.* White Plains: International Arts and Sciences.

Vachani, L. (1989) Narrative, pleasure and ideology in the Hindi film: an analysis of the outsider formula. M.A. thesis, Annenberg School of Communication, University of Pennsylvania.

Wallerstein, I. (1974) *The Modern World-System.* 2 vols, New York and London: Academic Press.

Warner, M. (1990) *The Letters of the Republic: Publication and the Public Sphere.* Cambridge, Mass.: Harvard University Press.

Williams, R. (1976) *Keywords.* New York: Oxford University Press.

Wolf, E. (1982) *Europe and the People without History.* Berkeley: University of California Press.

Yoshimoto, M. (1989) The postmodern and mass images in Japan. *Public Culture* 1(2): 8–25.

21

Towards a Global Culture?

Anthony D. Smith

The initial problem with the concept of a 'global culture' is one of the meaning of terms. Can we speak of 'culture' in the singular? If by 'culture' is meant a collective mode of life, or a repertoire of beliefs, styles, values and symbols, then we can only speak of cultur*es*, never just culture; for a collective mode of life, or a repertoire of beliefs, etc., presupposes different modes and repertoires in a universe of modes and repertoires. Hence, the idea of a 'global culture' is a practical impossibility, except in inter-planetary terms. Even if the concept is predicated of *homo sapiens*, as opposed to other species, the differences between segments of humanity in terms of lifestyle and belief-repertoire are too great, and the common elements too generalized, to permit us to even conceive of a globalized culture.

Or are they? Can we not at last discern the lineaments of exactly that world culture which liberals and socialists alike had dreamed of and hoped for since the last century? [...]

What is the content of such a [...] 'global culture'? How shall we picture its oper-ations? Answers to such questions usually take the form of extrapolation from recent western cultural experiences of 'postmodernism'. Beneath a modernist veneer, we find in practice a pastiche of cultural motifs and styles, underpinned by a universal scientific and technical discourse. A global culture, so the argument runs, will be eclectic like its western or European progenitor, but will wear a uniformly streamlined packaging. Standardized, commercialized mass commodities will nevertheless draw for their con-tents upon revivals of traditional, folk or national motifs and styles in fashions, furnishings, music and the arts, lifted out of their original contexts and anaesthetized. So that a global culture would operate at several levels simultaneously: as a cornucopia of standardized commodities, as a patchwork of denationalized ethnic or folk motifs, as a series of gen-eralized 'human values and interests', as a uniform 'scientific' discourse of meaning, and finally as the interdependent system of communications which forms the material base for all the other components and levels.[1]

It might be argued that there is nothing especially new about a 'global culture', that earlier cultural imperialisms were every whit as eclectic and simultaneously standard-ized. After all, the hellenization that Alexander's armies carried throughout the ancient Near East drew on a variety of local motifs as well as giving them expres-sion in the Greco-Macedonian forms of theatre, assembly, marketplace and gymnasium. And the same was true of the pax Romana throughout the Mediterranean world (see Tcherikover 1970; Balsdon 1979).

Yet, those pre-modern cultural imperialisms were neither global nor universal. They were ultimately tied to their places of origin, and carried with them their special myths and symbols for all to recognize and emulate. Today's emerging global culture is tied to no place or period. It is context-less, a true melange of disparate components drawn from everywhere and nowhere, borne upon the modern chariots of global telecommunications systems.

There is something equally timeless about the concept of a global culture. Widely diffused in space, a global culture is cut off from any past. As the perennial pursuit of an elusive present or imagined future, it has no history. A global culture is here and now and everywhere, and for its purposes the past only serves to offer some decontextualized example or element for its cosmopolitan patchwork.

This sense of timelessness is powerfully underlined by the pre-eminently technical nature of its discourse. A global culture is essentially calculated and artificial, posing technical problems with technical solutions and using its folk motifs in a spirit of detached playfulness. Affectively neutral, a cosmopolitan culture reflects a technological base made up of many overlapping systems of communications bound by a common quantitative and technical discourse, manned by an increasingly technical intelligentsia, whose 'culture of critical discourse' replaces the social critique of its earlier humanistic counterparts (see Gouldner 1979).

Memory, Identity and Cultures

Eclectic, universal, timeless and technical, a global culture is seen as pre-eminently a 'constructed' culture, the final and most imposing of a whole series of human constructs in the era of human liberation and mastery over nature. In a sense, the nation too was just such a construct, a sovereign but finite 'imagined community'.

Nations were 'built' and 'forged' by state elites or intelligentsias or capitalists; like the Scots kilt or the British Coronation ceremony, they are composed of so many 'invented traditions', whose symbols we need to read through a process of 'deconstruction', if we are to grasp the hidden meanings beneath the 'text' of their discourse. The fact, therefore, that a global culture would need to be constructed, along with global economic and political institutions, should occasion no surprise; nor should we cavil at the eclecticism with which such a cosmopolitan culture is likely to make use of bits and pieces of pre-existing national and folk cultures.[2]

Let us concede for the moment that nations are, in some sense, social 'constructs' and 'imagined' communities. Is it because of this 'constructed' quality that they have managed to survive and flourish so well? Are we therefore justified in predicting the same bright future for an equally well crafted 'global culture'?

To answer affirmatively would require us to place the whole weight of demonstration on the common characteristic of human construction and imagination, at the expense of those characteristics in which nations and national cultures differ markedly from our description of the qualities of a global culture. The obstinate fact is that national cultures, like all cultures before the modern epoch, are *particular*, *timebound* and *expressive*, and their eclecticism operates within strict cultural constraints. As we said at the outset, there can in practice be no such thing as 'culture', only specific, historical cultures possessing strong emotional connotations for those who share in the particular culture. It is, of course, possible to 'invent', even manufacture, traditions as commodities to serve particular class or ethnic interests. But they will only survive and flourish as part of the repertoire of national culture if they can be made continuous with a much longer past that members of that community presume to constitute their 'heritage'. In other words, 'grafting' extraneous elements must always be a delicate operation; the new traditions must evoke a popular response if they are to survive, and that means hewing close to vernacular motifs and styles. That was the instinct which guided most nationalists and helped to ensure their lasting successes. The success of the nineteenth-century British Coronation ceremony or the Welsh Eisteddfodau owed much to the ability of those who revived them to draw on much older cultural motifs and traditions, memories of which were still alive; though in one sense 'new', these revivals were only able to flourish because they could be presented, and were accepted, as continuous with a valued past (see Hobsbawm and Ranger 1983).

If cultures are historically specific and spatially limited, so are those images and symbols that have obtained a hold on human imagination. Even the most imperialist of those images – emperor, Pope or Tsar – have drawn their power from the heritage of Roman and Byzantine symbolism. It is one thing to be able to package imagery and diffuse it through world-wide telecommunications networks. It is quite another to ensure that such images retain their power to move and inspire populations, who have for so long been divided by particular histories and cultures, which have mirrored and crystallized the experiences of historically separated social groups, whether classes or regions, religious congregations or ethnic communities. The meanings of even the most universal of imagery for a particular population derive as much from the historical experiences and social status of that group as from the intentions of purveyors, as recent research on the national reception of popular television serials suggests (see Schlesinger 1987). [...]

In other words, images and cultural traditions do not derive from, or descend upon, mute and passive populations on whose *tabula rasa* they inscribe themselves. Instead, they invariably express the identities which historical circumstances have formed, often over long periods. The concept of 'identity' is here used, not of a common denominator of patterns of life and activity, much less some average, but rather of the subjective feelings and valuations of any population which possesses common experiences and one or more shared cultural characteristics (usually customs, language or religion). These feelings and values refer to three components of their shared experiences:

1   a sense of continuity between the experiences of succeeding generations of the unit of population;
2   shared memories of specific events and personages which have been turning-points of a collective history; and
3   a sense of common destiny on the part of the collectivity sharing those experiences.

By a collective cultural identity, therefore, is meant those feelings and values in respect of a sense of continuity, shared memories and a sense of common destiny of a given unit of population which has had common experiences and cultural attributes. [...]

It is in just these senses that 'nations' can be understood as historic identities, or at least deriving closely from them, while a global and cosmopolitan culture fails to relate to any such historic identity. Unlike national cultures, a global culture is essentially memoryless. Where the 'nation' can be constructed so as to draw upon and revive latent popular experiences and needs, a 'global culture' answers to no living needs, no identity-in-the-making. It has to be painfully put together, artificially, out of the many existing folk and national identities into which humanity has been so long divided. There are no 'world memories' that can be used to *unite* humanity; the most global experiences to date – colonialism and the World Wars – can only serve to remind us of our historic cleavages. (If it is argued that nationalists suffered selective amnesia in order to construct their nations, the creators of a global culture would have to suffer total amnesia, to have any chance of success!)

The central difficulty in any project to construct a global identity, and hence a global culture, is that collective identity, like imagery and culture, is always historically specific because it is based on shared memories and a sense of continuity between generations.

To believe that 'culture follows structure', that the techno-economic sphere will provide the conditions and therefore the impetus and content of a global culture, is to be misled once again by the same economic determinism that dogged the debate about 'industrial convergence', and to overlook the vital role of common historical experiences and memories in shaping identity and culture. Given the plurality of such experiences and identities, and given the historical depth of such memories, the project of a global culture, as opposed to global communications, must appear premature for some time to come.

'Ethno-history' and Posterity

If it proves difficult to envisage a point of departure for this project in common human experiences and memories, the universal stumbling-block to its construction is not far to seek. That ubiquitous obstacle is embodied in the continued presence of pre-modern ties and sentiments in the modern epoch. Indeed, just as a 'postmodern' era awaits its liberation from the modern industrial world, so the latter is still weighed down by the burden of pre-modern traditions, myths and boundaries. I have argued elsewhere that many of today's nations are built up on the basis of pre-modern 'ethnic cores' whose myths and memories, values and symbols shaped the culture and boundaries of the nation that modern elites managed to forge. Such a view, if conceded, must qualify our earlier acceptance of the largely 'constructed' quality of modern nations. That nationalist elites were active in inculcating a sense of nationality in large sections of 'their' populations who were ignorant of any national affiliations, is well documented (see Kedourie 1960; Breuilly 1982). It does not follow that they 'invented nations where none existed', as Gellner had once claimed, even where they used pre-existing materials and even when nations are defined as large, anonymous, unmediated, co-cultural units (see Gellner 1964: ch. 7; also Gellner 1983: ch. 5).

Nationalists, like others, found themselves constrained by accepted cultural traditions, from which they might select, and by popular responses, which they hoped to channel, if not manipulate. But their room for cultural manoeuvre was always limited by those cultural traditions and popular, vernacular repertoires of myth, memory, symbol and value. For nationalists, the 'nation-to-be' was not any large, anonymous, co-cultural unit. It was a community of history and culture, possessing a compact territory, unified economy and common legal rights and duties for all members. If 'nationalism creates nations' in its own image, then its definition of the nation was of a piece with its aspirations for collective autonomy, fraternal unity and distinctive identity. The identity and unity that was sought was of and for an existing historic culture-community, which the nationalists thought they were reviving and returning to a 'world of nations'. It depended, therefore, in large measure on the rediscovery of the community's 'ethno-history', its peculiar and distinctive cultural contribution to the worldwide fund of what Weber called 'irreplaceable culture values'. This was the nationalist project, and it is one that has by no means run its course, even as signs of its supersession by wider projects are on the horizon. In fact, it can be argued that nationalist and post-nationalist projects feed off each other, and are likely to do so for some time to come.

In fact, the success of the nationalist project depended not only on the creative skills and organizational ability of the intelligentsia, but on the persistence, antiquity and resonance of the community's ethno-history. The more salient, pervasive and enduring that history, the firmer the cultural base it afforded for the formation of a modern nation. Once again, these are largely subjective aspects. It is the salience of that history in the eyes of the community's members, and the *felt* antiquity of their ethnic ties and sentiments, which give an ethno-history its power and resonance among wide strata. It matters little whether the communal events recounted happened in the manner purveyed, or if heroes acted nobly as tradition would have us believe; the Exodus, William Tell, Great Zimbabwe, derive their power not from a sober historical assessment, but from the way events, heroes and landscapes have been woven by myth, memory and symbol into the popular consciousness. For the participants in this drama, ethnohistory has a 'primordial' quality, or it is powerless (Smith 1988).[3]

Why do such myths and memories retain their hold, even today, to fuel the nationalist project? There is no single answer; but two considerations must take priority. The first is the role of ethno-history, its myths, values, memories and symbols, in assuring collective dignity (and through that some measure of dignity for the individual) for populations which have come to feel excluded, neglected or suppressed in the distribution of values and opportunities. By establishing the unity of a submerged or excluded population around an ancient and preferably illustrious pedigree, not only is the sense of bonding intensified, but a reversal of collective status is achieved, at least on the cognitive and moral levels. [...]

The second consideration is even more important. With the attenuation of the hold of traditional cosmic images of another, unseen existence beyond the everyday world, the problem of individual oblivion and collective disintegration becomes more pressing and less easily answered. Loss of social cohesion feeding off an increasing sense of individual meaninglessness, in a century when the old 'problem of evil' has been posed in unparalleled ways, drives more and more people to discover new ways of understanding and preserving 'identity' in the face of annihilation. For many, the only guarantee of preservation of some form of identity is in the appeal to 'posterity', to the future generations that are 'ours', because they think and feel as 'we' do, just as our children are supposed to feel and think like each of us individually. With the dissolution of all traditional theodicies, only the appeal to a collective posterity offers hope of deliverance from oblivion (see Smith 1970; Anderson 1983: ch. 1).

[...]

Vernacular Mobilization and Cultural Competition

There are also more specific reasons for the continuing hold of national cultures with their ethnic myths and memories in an increasingly interdependent world.

Perhaps the most common way in which nations have been, and are being, formed is through processes of 'vernacular mobilization' and 'cultural politicization'. Where ethnic communities (or *ethnie*) lack states of their own, having usually been incorporated in wider polities in an earlier epoch, they risk dissolution in the transition to modernity, unless an indigenous intelligentsia emerges, strong enough to mobilize wider sections of 'their' community on the basis of a rediscovered ethno-history and vernacular culture. The success of the intelligentsia largely hinges on their ability to discover a convincing cultural base, one that can find a popular response, at least among educated strata. The intelligentsia are populist to the extent that they make use of (some) popular culture and a living communal history, even where they stop short of mobilizing actual peasants. The important task is to convince immediate followers, and enemies outside, of the cultural viability of the nation-to-be. The richer, more fully documented the ethno-history, the more widely spoken the vernacular tongue and the more widely practised the native customs and religion, the less difficult will it be to convince others, friends and enemies, of the actuality of the 'nation'; for it can be made to 'flow' coterminously with the demotic *ethnie* and seem its reincarnation after a long period of presumed death. Conversely, the scantier the records of ethno-history and less widely spoken the vernacular and practised the customs, the harder will it be to convince others of the viability of the national project, and the more it will be necessary to find new ways of overcoming doubt and hostility. Hence the appeal to lost epics and forgotten heroes – an Oisin or Lemminkainen – to furnish a noble pedigree and sacred landscape for submerged or neglected communities (see Hutchinson 1987; Branch 1985: Introduction).

To create the nation, therefore, it is not enough simply to mobilize compatriots. They must be taught who they are, where they came from and whither they are going. They must be turned into co-nationals through a process of mobilization into the vernacular culture, albeit one adapted to modern social and political conditions. Only then can the old-new culture become a political base and furnish political weapons in the much more intense cultural competition of a world of nations. Old religious sages and saints can now be turned into national heroes, ancient chronicles and epics become examples of the creative national genius, while great ages of achievement in the community's past are presented as the nation's 'golden age' of pristine purity and nobility. The former culture of a community, which had no other end beyond itself, now becomes the talisman and legitimation for all manner of 'national' policies and purposes, from agricultural villagization to militarism and aggrandisement. Ethnicity is nationalized (see Seton-Watson 1977: chs 2–4; Smith 1986: ch. 8).

Though the intelligentsia tend to be the prime beneficiaries of the politicization of culture, other strata share in the realization of the national project. Peasants and workers are not immune, even if they are rarely prime movers, particularly where a marxisant 'national communism' holds sway. On the whole, it is the nationalist motifs which tap peasant energies most effectively, particularly where a foreign threat can be convincingly portrayed, as when China was invaded by Japan (see Johnson 1969; Smith 1979: ch. 5). Because of this 'multi-class' character, the national project retains a popularity that is the envy of other ideological movements; for it appears to offer each class not just a tangible benefit, but the promise of dignity and unity in the 'super-family' of the nation (see Nairn 1977: ch. 9; Horowitz 1985: ch. 2).

One other reason for the continuing power of the national idea today needs to be remembered. This is the accentuation of that idea and of the several national cultures across the globe by their competition for adherents and prestige. I am not simply referring here to the way in which such cultures have become interwoven with the rivalry of states in the international arena. The cultures themselves have been thrown into conflict, as communities in their struggle for political rights and recognition have drawn upon their cultural resources – music, literature, the arts and crafts, dress, food and so on – to make their mark in the wider political arena, regionally and internationally, and continue to do so by the use of comparative statistics, prestige projects, tourism and the like. These are veritable 'cultural wars', which underline the polycentric nature of our interdependent world, as each community discovers afresh its 'national essence' in its 'irreplaceable culture values' (Weber 1968: ch. 5).

Vernacular mobilization; the politicization of cultures; the role of intelligentsia and other strata; and the intensification of cultural wars: here are some of the reasons, briefly sketched, why national cultures inspired by rediscovered ethno-histories continue to divide our world into discrete cultural blocks, which show little sign of harmonization, let alone amalgamation. When we add the sharply uneven nature of the distributions of both a 'rich' ethno-history and economic and political resources between nations and *ethnie* today, the likelihood of an early 'supersession' of nationalism appears remote. Feeding on each other, ethnic nationalisms seem set to multiply and accentuate national and ethnic boundaries and the uneven distribution of cultural and economic resources, at least in those areas where there remain a multitude of unsatisfied ethno-national claims. If the various regional inter-state systems appear strong enough (for how long?) to contain conflicting ethno-nationalist movements, even in Africa and Asia, the number and intensity of current and potential ethnic conflicts hardly suggests a global diminution of the power of nationalism or the hold of national cultures in the next few decades. [. . .]

Conclusion

From the standpoint of both global security and cosmopolitan culture, this is a bleak conclusion. There is, however, another side to the overall picture, which may over the longer term help to mitigate some of the worst effects of intensified and proliferating ethno-national conflicts. I refer to the growing importance of the lingua franca and of various 'culture areas'.
[. . .]

Such culture areas are, of course, a far cry from the ideal of a global culture which will supersede the many national cultures that still divide the world so resoundingly. Their loose patchwork quality and mixture of cultures do not as yet offer a serious challenge to the still fairly compact, and frequently revived, national cultures. [. . .]

[. . .] We are still far from even mapping out the kind of global culture and cosmopolitan ideal that can truly supersede a world of nations, each cultivating its distinctive historical character and rediscovering its national myths, memories and symbols in past golden ages and sacred landscapes. A world of competing cultures, seeking to improve their comparative status rankings and enlarge their cultural resources, affords little basis for global projects, despite the technical and linguistic infrastructural possibilities.

At the same time, the partial mixing of cultures, the rise of lingua franca and of wider 'Pan' nationalisms, though sometimes working in opposed directions, have created the possibility of 'families of culture' which portend wider regional patchwork culture-areas.

Such culture-areas may perhaps serve as models in the more long-term future for even broader inter-continental versions. Even in such distant scenarios, it is hard to envisage the absorption of ethno-national cultures, only a diminution in their political relevance. So attenuated a cosmopolitanism is unlikely to entail the supersession of national cultures.

Notes

1 I have brought together different phases of twentieth-century western culture in this sketch, in particular, the modernist trends of the 1960s, the 'postmodern' reactions of the 1960s and 1970s, and the technical 'neutrality' of the mass computer revolution of the 1980s. Of course, these trends and phases overlap: Stravinsky's pastiche dates from the early 1920s, while 'modernism' still exerts profound influences till today. The main point is that this Western image of 'things to come' is composed of several contradictory layers.

2 For the idea that nations should be conceived as sovereign but limited 'imagined communities', see Anderson (1983). His analysis, which gives pride of place to the 'technology of print capitalism' and the 'administrative pilgrimages' of provincial (read 'national' today) elites (to Washington, Moscow, Brussels?), could indeed shed light on the chances, and obstacles, to the rise of wider 'regional' cultures today.

3 This should not be construed as an argument for 'primordialism', the view that ethnicity and nationality are somehow 'givens' of human existence and/or history. For a discussion of the issues involved, see the essays by Brass and Robinson in Taylor and Yapp (1979); cf. also A. D. Smith (1984).

References

Anderson, Benedict (1983) *Imagined Communities: Reflections on the Origins and Spread of Nationalism*. London: Verso and New Left Books.

Balsdon, J. V. (1979) *Romans and Aliens*. London: Duckworth.

Branch, Michael (ed.) (1985) *Kalevala: The Land of Heroes*, trans. W. F. Kirby. London: Athlone.

Breuilly, John (1982) *Nationalism and the State*. Manchester: Manchester University Press.

Gellner, Ernest (1964) *Thought and Change*. London: Weidenfeld and Nicolson.

Gellner, Ernest (1983) *Nations and Nationalism*. Oxford: Blackwell.

Gouldner, Alvin (1979) *The Rise of the Intellectuals and the Future of the New Class*. London: Macmillan.

Hobsbawm, Eric and Ranger, Terence (eds) (1983) *The Invention of Tradition*. Cambridge: Cambridge University Press.

Horowitz, Donald (1985) *Ethnic Groups in Conflict*. Berkeley: University of California Press.

Hutchinson, John (1987) *The Dynamics of Cultural Nationalism; The Gaelic Revival and the Creation of the Irish Nation State*. London: Allen and Unwin.

Johnson, Chalmers (1969) Building a communist nation in China. In R. A. Scalapino (ed.), *The Communist Revolution in Asia*, Englewood Cliffs: Prentice Hall.

Kedourie, Elie (1960) *Nationalism*. London: Hutchinson.

Nairn, Tom (1977) *The Break-up of Britain*. London: New Left Books.

Schlesinger, Philip (1987) On national identity: some conceptions and misconceptions criticised. *Social Science Information* 26(2): 219–64.

Seton-Watson, Hugh (1977) *Nations and States: An Inquiry into the Origins of Nations and the Politics of Nationalism*. London: Methuen.

Smith, Anthony D. (1970) Modernity and evil: some sociological reflections on the problem of meaning. *Diogenes* 71: 65–80.

Smith, Anthony D. (1979) *Nationalism in the Twentieth Century*. Oxford: Martin Robertson.

Smith, Anthony D. (1984) Ethnic myths and ethnic revivals. *European Journal of Sociology* 25: 283–305.

Smith, Anthony D. (1986) *The Ethnic Origins of Nations*. Oxford: Blackwell.

Smith, Anthony D. (1988) The myth of the 'modern nation' and the myths of nations. *Ethnic and Racial Studies* 11(1): 1–26.

Taylor, David and Yapp, Malcolm (eds) (1979) *Political Identity in South Asia*. London and Dublin: Centre of South Asian Studies, SOAS, Curzon Press.

Tcherikover, Victor (1970) *Hellenistic Civilisation and the Jews*. New York: Athenaeum.

Weber, Max (1968) *Economy and Society*, vol. 1, ed. G. Roth and C. Wittich. New York: Bedminster Press.

Part IV
A Global Economy?

The debate about economic globalization revolves around four fundamental issues: whether a single borderless global economy exists today; the driving forces behind global economic integration; the extent to which states or global markets are in control of socio-economic life; and the limits to progressive economic policy and the welfare state under conditions of economic globalization.

In general the globalists consider that the pattern and intensity of contemporary economic globalization is historically unprecedented; a single global economy can be said to be in the making. Driven by the third industrial revolution – the new electronic, information order – and a neoliberal economic agenda, the shifting organization of economic power and activity now outstrips the regulatory capacity of states, even the most powerful. While global markets do not entail the end of the state as an economic unit (few think that they do), they nevertheless severely erode national economic sovereignty and push all governments towards adopting more financially prudent and market-friendly economic strategies.

By contrast the sceptics consider such views as 'globaloney', pointing to the centrality of states – especially the great powers – in engineering global markets. Moreover, far from contemporary economic trends leading to the end of the welfare state and effective national economic strategies, both have become increasingly more important. This is because most economic activity is still rooted in nation-states; multinationals remain essentially national companies with international operations; and national economic policies are still central to the creation of wealth and prosperity. Rather than a single global economy in the making, the world is breaking up into three major regional blocs in which states remain in control, competing for economic advantage. There is no new global capitalist order. Indeed, the world, the sceptics argue, was considerably more economically integrated at the beginning of the twentieth century than it was at its close.

Central to the debate about contemporary globalization is the question of economic power: namely, whether the transnational organization of finance, production and commerce is creating a borderless world economy. For the globalists, such as Dicken and Castells, the shifting geography of the world economy and the growing integration of economic activity across national borders represent the development of a 'single, planetary scale worldwide economy'. The existence today of global (real-time) markets, manifest most clearly in the cyberspace of twenty-four-hour a day trading across world financial centres, embeds national production, financial and commercial activity within worldwide networks of economic organization. Multinational corporations and global production networks, in fields as diverse as computer chips and apparel, are reorganizing economic activity on a global scale, creating a new global economy which operates according to a different logic than the international economy of the *belle époque* or the imperial economies of earlier centuries.

A heated and intense exchange of views has developed concerning the accuracy and validity of this characterization of the world economy. The contributions by Hirst and Thompson, and Perraton et al. represent different positions in what is a continuing debate. Of the two contributions, Hirst and Thompson mount a powerful case, conceptually and empirically, against the new global economy thesis. Making a careful analytical distinction between the idea of an international economy (links between separate national economies) and a universal global economy (economic organization without borders), they dismiss the central claims of the economic globalists. But this sceptical interpretation is itself open to critical scrutiny as Perraton et al. seek to show. They argue, in contrast to Castells and Dicken, that while economic globalization may not amount to a new form of global capitalism, it is nevertheless transforming the location and distribution of economic and productive power in the world economy. Moreover, the existence of even incomplete global markets imposes significant constraints upon the economic strategies and power of national governments. At issue here is the question of whether there has been a decline in national economic sovereignty and the power of the modern state to regulate economic activity for the national good.

For Garrett, growing international economic independence has not eroded or compromised national economic sovereignty in any significant way. States and national politics still matter, and, somewhat curiously perhaps, more than ever before. As economies become more open to global market forces, their workers seek greater social protection from the consequences of foreign competition. In the light of this, there has not been a notable end to 'progressive politics' but, on the contrary, a strengthening or revival of social democracy as governments seek to respond to their citizens' demands. Global markets have not triumphed over states and remain subject to strong national intervention and regulation. Furthermore, the welfare state, as Rieger and Leibfried contend, has not been a victim of globalization but, on the contrary, has consistently been one of its essential building blocks and chief beneficiaries.

Such propositions are disputed – although for differing reasons – by Yergin and Stanislaw, Rodrik and Gray. These contributors consider that contemporary patterns of economic globalization have shifted power away from democratically elected governments towards unaccountable global market forces. Since capital is increasingly mobile, significant constraints are created on the power of national governments to pursue progressive economic policies or redistributive social policies. It is not that all capital is necessarily 'footloose', but it is the fact that capital and plant could be moved to alternative investment opportunities that creates strong pressures to market appeasing and supporting policies. For Gray, globalization spells the end of social democracy, traditionally conceived as a redistributive political project, and its replacement by a more market-friendly Third Way. By comparison, Rodrik, Yergin and Stanislaw consider that, while economic globalization may have imposed new constraints upon welfare regimes, it has at the same time generated new demands which invite, not the extinction of the welfare state, but its continuing reform. In their account, globalization is redefining the role and functions of national government, emphasizing its potential strategic coordinating role – the intelligent state or the competition state – as opposed to the interventionist, redistributive state of the postwar era. In this respect, economic globalization does not spell the demise of the welfare state but, rather, the end of traditional approaches to welfare, as is evident in the emphasis in the social programmes of the Neue Mitte, the Third Way, and the New Democrats. These programmes stress investment in human capital and technical skills – to make national economies more competitive – as against the provision of 'passive' welfare benefits.

22

A New Geo-economy

Peter Dicken

Something is Happening Out There

[. . .]

The most significant development in the world economy during the past few decades has been the *increasing internationalization – and, arguably, the increasing globalization – of economic activities*. The internationalization of economic activities is nothing new. Some commodities have had an international character for centuries; an obvious example being the long-established trading patterns in spices and other exotic goods. Such internationalization was much enhanced by the spread of industrialization from the eighteenth century onwards in Europe. Nevertheless until very recently the production process itself 'was primarily organized *within* national economies or parts of them. International trade . . . developed primarily as an exchange of raw materials and foodstuffs . . . [with] . . . products manufactured and finished in single national economies . . . *In terms of production, plant, firm and industry were essentially national phenomena*' (Hobsbawm 1979: 313, emphasis added).

The nature of the world economy has changed dramatically, however, especially since the 1950s. National boundaries no longer act as 'watertight' containers of the production process. Rather, they are more like sieves through which extensive leakage occurs. The implications are far-reaching. Each one of us is now more fully involved in a global economic system than were our parents and grandparents. Few, if any, industries now have much 'natural protection' from international competition whereas in the past, of course, geographical distance created a strong insulating effect. Today, in contrast, fewer and fewer industries are oriented towards local, regional or even national markets. A growing number of economic activities have meaning only in a global context. Thus, whereas a hundred or more years ago only rare and exotic products and some basic raw materials were involved in truly international trade, today virtually everything one can think of is involved in long-distance movement. And because of the increasingly complex ways in which production is organized across national boundaries, rather than contained within them, the actual origin of individual products may be very difficult to ascertain.

[. . .]

What these developments imply is the emergence of a *new global division of labour* which reflects a change in the geographical pattern of specialization at the global scale. Originally, as defined by the eighteenth-century political economist Adam Smith, the 'division of labour' referred simply to the specialization of workers in different parts of the production process. It had no explicitly geographical connotations at all. But quite early in the evolution of industrial economies the division of labour took on a geographical dimension. Some areas came to specialize in particular types of economic activity. Within the rapidly evolving industrial nations of Europe and the United States regional specialization – in iron and steel, shipbuilding, textiles, engineering and so on – became a characteristic feature. At the global scale the broad division of labour was between the industrial countries on the one hand, producing manufactured goods, and the non-industrialized countries on the other, whose major international function was to supply raw materials and agricultural products to the industrial nations and to act as a market for some manufactured goods. Such geographical specialization – structured around a *core*, a *semi-periphery* and a *periphery* – formed the underlying basis of much of the world's trade for many years.

This relatively simple pattern (although it was never quite as simple as the description above suggests) no longer applies. During the past few decades trade flows have become far more complex. The straightforward exchange between core and peripheral areas, based upon a broad division of labour, is being transformed into a highly complex, kaleidoscopic structure involving the *fragmentation* of many production processes and their *geographical relocation* on a global scale in ways which slice through national boundaries. In addition, we have seen the emergence of new centres of industrial production in the newly industrializing economies (NIEs). Both old and new industries are involved in this re-sorting of the global jigsaw puzzle in ways which also reflect the development of technologies of transport and communications, of corporate organization and of the production process. The technology of production itself is undergoing substantial and far-reaching change as the emphasis on large-scale, mass-production, assembly-line techniques is shifting to a more flexible production technology. And just as we can identify a new international division of labour in production so, too, we can identify a 'new international financial system', based on rapidly emerging twenty-four-hour global transactions concentrated primarily in the three major financial centres of New York, London and Tokyo.

A 'New' Geo-economy? The Globalization Debate

So, something is undoubtedly happening 'out there'. But precisely what that 'something' might be – and whether it really represents something new – is a subject of enormous controversy amongst academics, politicians, popular writers and journalists alike. [. . .]

[O]n the one hand, we have the view that we do, indeed, live in a new – *globalized* – world economy in which our lives are dominated by global forces. On the other hand, we have the view that not all that much has changed; that we still inhabit an *international*, rather than a globalized, world economy in which national forces remain highly significant. The truth, it seems to me, lies in neither of these two polarized positions. Although in quantitative terms the world economy was perhaps at least as integrated economically before 1913 as it is today – in some respects, even more so – the nature of that integration was *qualitatively* very different (UNCTAD 1993: 113):

- International economic integration before 1913 – and, in fact, until only about three decades ago – was essentially *shallow integration* manifested largely through arm's length *trade* in goods and services between independent firms and through international movements of portfolio capital.

- Today, we live in a world in which *deep integration*, organized primarily by trans-national corporations (TNCs), is becoming increasingly pervasive. ' "Deep" integration extends to the level of the *production* of goods and services and, in addition, increases visible and invisible trade. Linkages between national economies are there-fore increasingly influenced by the cross-border value adding activities within . . . TNCs and within networks established by TNCs' (UNCTAD 1993: 113).

However, although there are undoubtedly global*izing* forces at work we do not have a fully global*ized* world economy. Globalization tendencies can be at work without this resulting in the all-encompassing end-state – the globalized economy – in which all uneven-ness and difference are ironed out, market forces are rampant and uncontrollable, and the nation-state merely passive and supine. [. . .] The position taken in this [article] is that globalization is a complex of inter-related *processes*, rather than an end-state. Such tendencies are highly uneven in time and space. In taking such a process-oriented approach it is important to distinguish between processes of *internationalization* and processes of *globalization*:

- *Internationalization processes* involve the simple extension of economic activities across national boundaries. It is, essentially, a *quantitative* process which leads to a more extensive geographical pattern of economic activity.
- *Globalization processes* are *qualitatively* different from internationalization processes. They involve not merely the geographical extension of economic activity across national boundaries but also – and more importantly – the *functional integration* of such internationally dispersed activities.

Both processes – internationalization and globalization – coexist. In some cases, what we are seeing is no more than the continuation of long-established international disper-sion of activities. In others, however, we are undoubtedly seeing an increasing dispersion and integration of activities across national boundaries. The pervasive internationalization, and growing globalization, of economic life ensure that changes originating in one part of the world are rapidly diffused to others. We live in a world of increasing complex-ity, interconnectedness and volatility; a world in which the lives and livelihoods of every one of us are bound up with processes operating at a global scale.
[. . .]

A New Geo-economy: Unravelling the Complexity

We *are* witnessing the emergence of a new geo-economy which is qualitatively differ-ent from the past but in which both processes of internationalization and globaliza-tion and of shallow and deep integration continue to coexist. However, they do so in ways which are highly uneven in space, in time and across economic sectors. Very few industries are truly and completely global although many display some globalizing tendencies. The question is: how can we begin to unravel the dynamic, kaleidoscopic complexity of this geo-economy?

The conventional unit of analysis in studies of the world economy is the nation-state. Virtually all the statistical data on production, trade, investment and the like are aggregated into national 'boxes'. Such a level of aggregation is less and less useful, given the nature of the changes occurring in the organization of economic activity. This is not to imply that the national level is unimportant. On the contrary, one of the major themes of this book is that nation-states continue to be key players in the contemporary global economy [. . .]. In any case, we shall have to rely heavily on national level data to explore the changing maps of production trade and investment [. . .]. But, as we noted earlier, national boundaries no longer 'contain' production processes in the way they once did. Such processes slice through national boundaries and transcend them in a bewildering array of relationships that operate at different geographical and organizational scales. We need to be able to get both below and above the national scale to understand what is going on.

Production chains: a basic building block

One especially useful conceptual point of entry is the *production chain* [. . .] which can be defined as

> *a transactionally linked sequence of functions in which each stage adds value to the process of production of goods or services.*

[. . .]
Two aspects of production chains are especially important from our point of view [. . .]:

- their *co-ordination and regulation*
- their *geographical configuration.*

Co-ordination and regulation of production chains

Production chains are co-ordinated and regulated at two levels. First and foremost, they are co-ordinated by business firms, through the multifarious forms of intra- and interorganizational relationships that make up an economic system. [. . .] [E]conomies are made up of different types of business organization – transnational and domestic, large and small, public and private – in varying combinations and inter-relationships. [F]irms [. . .] operate over widely varying geographical ranges and perform rather different roles in the economic system.

One of the major themes of this book is that it is increasingly the *transnational corporation* (TNC) which plays the key role in co-ordinating production chains and, therefore, in shaping the new geo-economy [. . .]. However, we need to use a broad definition of the TNC – one which goes beyond the conventional definition based upon levels of ownership of internationally based assets – to capture the diversity and complexity of transnational networks. Thus, a TNC will be defined as

> *a firm which has the power to co-ordinate and control operations in more than one country, even if it does not own them.*

This definition implies that it is not essential for a firm to *own* productive assets in different countries in order to be able to control how such assets are used. TNCs generally do own such assets but they are also typically involved in a spider's web of collaborative relationships with other legally independent firms across the globe. [...]

In this regard, Gereffi [...] makes a useful distinction between two types of 'driver':

- *Producer-driven chains*:

    refer to those industries in which transnational corporations (TNCs) or other large integrated industrial enterprises play the central role in controlling the production system (including its backward and forward linkages). This is most characteristic of capital- and technology-intensive industries like automobiles, computers, aircraft, and electrical machinery . . . What distinguishes 'producer-driven' production systems is the control exercised by the administrative headquarters of the TNCs.

- *Buyer-driven chains*:

    'refer to those industries in which large retailers, brand-named merchandisers, and trading companies play the pivotal role in setting up decentralized production networks in a variety of exporting countries.' (It is important to emphasize that, in terms of the definition introduced above, such firms are also TNCs.) [Gereffi and Korzeniewicz 1994: 97]

[...]

The second level at which production chains are regulated is that of the *state*. Contrary to those who argue that the state is either dead or dying as a viable force in the contemporary global economy, the position taken here is that the state remains a fundamentally significant influence. All the elements in the production chain are regulated within some kind of political structure whose basic unit is the nation-state but which also includes such supranational institutions as the International Monetary Fund or the World Trade Organization, as well as regional economic groupings such as the European Union or the North American Free Trade Agreement. All markets are socially constructed. Even supposedly 'deregulated' markets are still subject to some kind of political regulation. All states operate a battery of economic policies whose objective is to enhance national welfare. However, the particular policy orientation and policy mix varies according to the political, social and cultural complexion of the individual state. Hence, just as there is great diversity in TNC behaviour so, too, states vary in their behaviour depending upon their position along the ideological spectrum.

Consequently, all business organizations – even the most global TNC – have to operate within national and international regulatory systems. They have to conform to national business legislation. It is true, of course, that TNCs attempt to take advantage of national differences in regulatory regimes while states attempt to minimize such 'regulatory arbitrage'. The result is a very complex situation in which firms and states are engaged in various kinds of power play; what Stopford and Strange [1991] call a *triangular nexus* of interactions comprising firm–firm, state–state and firm–state relationships . . . In other words, the new geo-economy is essentially being structured and restructured not by the actions of either firms or states alone but by complex, dynamic interactions between the two sets of institutions [...].

Geographical configuration of production chains

[...] Just as we can identify a spectrum of organizational arrangements for co-ordinating a particular production chain so, too, we can identify a geographical spectrum of possibilities. [...] [P]roduction functions may be *geographically dispersed* at one end of the spectrum or *geographically concentrated* at the other along a continuum from the global through to the local scale. One obvious influence on the geographical configuration of production chains is technological – primarily the technologies of transport and communications which transform the meaning of geographical distance. In general, therefore, there has been a tendency for the geographical extensiveness of virtually all production chains to increase. However, different types of production chain may be configured geographically in very different ways.

Even in a Globalizing World, All Economic Activities are Geographically Localized

'The end of geography'; 'the death of distance'. These two phrases resonate, either explicitly or implicitly, throughout much of the globalization literature. According to this view, dramatic developments in the technologies of transport and communication have made capital – and the firms controlling it – 'hyper-mobile', freed from the 'tyranny of distance' and no longer tied to 'place'. In other words, it implies that economic activity is becoming 'deterritorialized'. The sociologist Manuel Castells argues that the forces of globalization, especially those driven by the new information technologies, are replacing this 'space of places' with a 'space of flows' [Castells 1989, 1996]. Anything can be located anywhere and, if that does not work out, can be moved somewhere else with ease [...]. Seductive as such ideas might be, a moment's thought will show just how misleading they are. Although transport and communications technologies have indeed been revolutionized [...] both geographical distance and, especially, *place* remain fundamental. Every component in the production chain, every firm, every economic activity is, quite literally, 'grounded' in specific locations. Such grounding is both physical, in the form of sunk costs [...] and less tangible in the form of localized social relationships.

Geographical clustering of economic activities is the norm

Not only does every economic activity have to be located somewhere; more significantly, there is also a very strong propensity for economic activities to form *localized geographical clusters* or *agglomerations*. In fact, the geographical concentration of economic activities, at a local or subnational scale, is the norm not the exception. The pervasiveness and the significance of geographical clustering has recently been recognized – and has come to occupy a central position – in the writings of some leading economists and management theorists, notably Paul Krugman, Michael Porter and Kenichi Ohmae. [...] However, economic geographers and location theorists have been pointing to the pervasiveness of this phenomenon of geographical concentration for decades. [...]

In a whole variety of ways, therefore, once established a localized economic cluster or agglomeration will tend to grow through a process of cumulative, self-reinforcing development [. . .].

The cumulative nature of these processes of localized economic development emphasizes the significance of historical trajectory. It has become common to use terminology from evolutionary economics [. . .] to describe the process as being *path dependent*. Thus, a region's (or a nation's) economy becomes 'locked in' to a pattern which is strongly influenced by its particular history. This may be either a source of continued strength or, if it embodies too much organizational rigidity, a source of weakness. However, even for 'successful' regions, such path dependency does not imply the absolute inevitability of continued success. [. . .] A central argument, then, is that *place* matters; that 'territorialization' remains a significant component in the organization of economic activity.

Scales of Activity; Scales of Analysis

The geo-economy, therefore, can be pictured as a geographically uneven, highly complex and dynamic web of production chains, economic spaces and places connected together through threads of flows. But the spatial *scale* at which these processes operate is, itself, variable. So, too, is the meaning which different scales have for different actors within the global economic system. The tendency is to collapse the scale dimension to just two: the global and the local, and much has been written about the *global–local tension* at the interface between the two. Firms, states, local communities, it is argued, are each faced with the problem of resolving that tension.

There is no doubt that this is a real problem. However, it is not always the case that the terms 'global' and, especially, 'local' mean the same thing in different contexts. In the international business literature, for example, the term 'local' generally refers to the national, or even the larger regional, scale (i.e. at the level of Europe, Asia, North America). But for most people, 'local' refers to a very much smaller spatial scale: that of the local community in which they live. However, it is a mistake to focus only on the two extremes of the scale – the global and the local – at which economic activities occur. It is more realistic to think in terms of inter-related scales of activity and of analysis: for example, the local, the national, the regional (i.e. supranational) and the global. These have meaning both as activity spaces in which economic and political actors operate and also as analytical categories which more accurately capture some of the complexity of the real world.

However, we need to bear in mind that the scales are not independent entities. [. . .] Individual industries (production/commodity chains) can be regarded as vertically organized structures which operate across increasingly extensive geographical scales. Cutting across these vertical structures are the territorially defined political-economic systems which, again, are manifested at different geographical scales. It is at the points of intersection of these dimensions in 'real' geographical space where specific outcomes occur, where the problems of existing within a globalizing economy – whether as a business firm, a government, a local community or as an individual – have to be resolved.

References

Bairoch, P. (1982) International industrialization levels from 1750 to 1980. *Journal of European Economic History* 11.

Bairoch, P. (1993) *Economics and World History*. Brighton: Wheatsheaf.

Braudel, F. (1984) *Civilization and Capitalism*. 3 vols, London: Collins.

Castells, M. (ed.) (1989) *The Informational City*. Oxford: Blackwell.

Castells, M. (1996) *The Rise of the Network Society*, vol. 1 of *The Information Age*. Oxford: Blackwell.

Dunning, J. H. (1983) Changes in the level and structure of international production: the last hundred years. In M. Casson (ed.), *The Growth of International Business*, London: Allen and Unwin.

Dunning, J. H. (1993) *Multinational Enterprises and the Global Economy*. Reading, Mass.: Addison-Wesley.

Gereffi, G. and Korzeniewicz, M. (eds) (1994) *Commodity Chains and Global Capitalism*. Westport: Praeger.

Hobsbawm, E. (1979) The development of the world economy. *Cambridge Journal of Economics* 3.

Kennedy, P. (1987) *The Rise and Fall of the Great Powers*. New York: Random House.

Kitson, M. and Michie, J. (1995) Trade and growth: a historical perspective. In J. Michie and J. Grieve-Smith (eds), *Managing the Global Economy*, Oxford: Oxford University Press.

Kozul-Wright, R. (1995) Transnational corporations and the nation-state. In J. Michie and J. Grieve-Smith (eds), *Managing the Global Economy*, Oxford: Oxford University Press.

Krugman, P. (1991) *Geography and Trade*. Leuven: Leuven University Press.

Krugman, P. (1995) *Development, Geography and Economic Theory*. Cambridge, Mass.: MIT Press.

Krugman, P. (1996) *Pop Internationalism*. Cambridge, Mass.: MIT Press.

MacBean, A. I. and Snowden, P. N. (1981) *International Institutions in Trade and Finance*. London: Allen and Unwin.

McGrew, A. G. (1992) Conceptualising global politics. In A. G. McGrew and P. G. Lewis (eds) *Global Politics: Globalization and the Nation-State*, Cambridge: Polity Press.

Ohmae, E. (1995) *The End of the Nation-State: The Rise of Regional Economies*. New York: Free Press.

Porter, M. E. (1990) *The Competitive Advantage of Nations*. London: Macmillan.

Stopford, J. M. and Strange, S. (1991) *Rival States, Rival Firms: Competition for World Market Shares*. Cambridge: Cambridge University Press.

Stubbs, R. and Underhill, G. R. D. (eds) (1994) *Political Economy and the Changing Global Order*. London: Macmillan.

UNCTAD (1993) *World Investment Report 1993: Transnational Corporations and Integrated International Production*. New York: United Nations Conference on Trade and Development.

23

The Global Economy

Manuel Castells

[...]

The informational economy is global. A global economy is a historically new reality, distinct from a world economy. A world economy, that is an economy in which capital accumulation proceeds throughout the world, has existed in the West at least since the sixteenth century, as Fernand Braudel and Immanuel Wallerstein have taught us.[1] **A global economy is something different: it is an economy with the capacity to work as a unit in real time on a planetary scale.** While the capitalist mode of production is characterized by its relentless expansion, always trying to overcome limits of time and space, it is only in the late twentieth century that the world economy was able to become truly global on the basis of the new infrastructure provided by information and communication technologies. This globality concerns the core processes and elements of the economic system.

Capital is managed around the clock in globally integrated financial markets working in real time for the first time in history:[2] billion dollars-worth of transactions take place in seconds in the electronic circuits throughout the globe. [...] New technologies allow capital to be shuttled back and forth between economies in very short time, so that capital, and therefore savings and investment, are interconnected worldwide, from banks to pension funds, stock exchange markets, and currency exchange. Since currencies are interdependent, so are economies everywhere. Although major corporate centers provide the human resources and facilities necessary to manage an increasingly complex financial network,[3] it is in the information networks connecting such centers that the actual operations of capital take place. Capital flows become at the same time global and increasingly autonomous *vis-à-vis* the actual performance of economies.[4]

Labor markets are not truly global, except for a small but growing segment of professionals and scientists [...], but labor is a global resource at least in three ways:[5] firms may choose to locate in a variety of places worldwide to find the labor supply they need, be it in terms of skills, costs, or social control; firms everywhere may also solicit highly skilled labor from everywhere, and they will obtain it provided they offer the right remuneration and working conditions; and labor will enter any market on its own initiative, coming from anywhere, when human beings are pushed from their homes by poverty and war or pulled towards a new life by hope for their children. Immigrant labor from all over the planet may flow to wherever jobs are, but its mobility is increasingly restricted by xenophobic movements leading to much stricter immigration controls. Indeed, citizens and politicians of affluent societies seem to be determined to keep barbarians of impoverished areas off their world, protected behind the walls of immigration authorities.[6]

Science, technology, and information are also organized in global flows, albeit in an asymmetrical structure. Proprietary technological information plays a major role in creating competitive advantage, and R&D centers are heavily concentrated in certain areas and in some companies and institutions.[7] However, the characteristics of new productive knowledge favor its diffusion. Innovation centers cannot live in secrecy without drying up their innovative capacity. Communication of knowledge in a global network of interaction is at the same time the condition to keep up with fast advancement of knowledge and the obstacle to its proprietary control.[8] In addition, the capacity to innovate is fundamentally stored in human brains, which makes possible the diffusion of innovation by the movement of scientists, engineers, and managers between organizations and production systems.

In spite of the persistence of protectionism and restrictions to free trade, markets for goods and services are becoming increasingly globalized.[9] This does not mean that all firms sell worldwide. But it does mean that the strategic aim of firms, large and small, is to sell wherever they can throughout the world, either directly or via their linkage with networks that operate in the world market. And there are indeed, to a large extent thanks to new communication and transportation technologies, channels and opportunities to sell everywhere. This statement must be qualified, however, by the fact that domestic markets account for the largest share of GDP in most countries, and that in developing countries, informal economies, mainly aimed at local markets, constitute the bulk of urban employment. Also, some major economies, for instance Japan, have important segments (for example, public works, retail trade) sheltered from worldwide competition by government protection and by cultural/institutional insulation.[10] And public services and government institutions throughout the world, accounting for between one-third and over a half of jobs in each country, are, and will be, by and large removed from international competition. Yet, the *dominant segments and firms, the strategic cores* of all economies are deeply connected to the world market, and their fate is a function of their performance in such a market. The dynamism of domestic markets depends ultimately on the capacity of domestic firms and networks of firms to compete globally.[11] Here again, the globalization of markets has only been made possible in the late twentieth century by dramatic changes in transportation and communication technologies, for information, people, goods, and services.

However, the most important transformation underlying the emergence of a global economy concerns the management of production and distribution, and of the production process itself.[12] The dominant segments of most economic sectors (either for goods or for services) are organized worldwide in their actual operating procedures, forming what Robert Reich has labeled "the global web." The production process incorporates components produced in many different locations by different firms, and assembled for specific purposes and specific markets in a new form of production and commercialization: high-volume, flexible, customized production. Such a web does not correspond only to the vision of a global corporation obtaining its supplies from different units around the world. The new production system relies on a combination of strategic alliances and ad hoc cooperation projects between corporations, decentralized units of each major corporation, and networks of small and medium enterprises connecting among themselves and/or with large corporations or networks of corporations. These transborder production networks operate under two main configurations: in Gereffi's terminology, producer-driven commodity chains (in industries such as automobiles, computers, aircraft, electrical machinery), and buyer-driven commodity chains (in industries such as garment, footwear, toys, housewares). What is fundamental in this web-like industrial structure it that it is territorially spread throughout the world, and its geometry keeps changing, as a whole and for each individual unit. In such a structure, the most important element for a successful managerial strategy is to position a firm (or a given industrial project) in the web in such a way as to gain competitive advantage for its relative position. Thus, the structure tends to reproduce itself and to keep expanding as competition goes on, so deepening the global character of the economy. For the firm to operate in such a variable geometry of production and distribution a very flexible form of management is required, a form that is dependent on the flexibility of the firm itself and on the access to communication and production technologies suited to such flexibility [. . .]. For instance, to be able to assemble parts produced from very distant sources, it is necessary to have, on the one hand, a microelectronics-based precision quality in the fabrication process, so that the parts are compatible to the smallest detail of specification;[13] on the other hand, a computer-based flexibility enabling the factory to program production runs according to the volume and customized characteristics required by each order.[14] In addition, the management of inventories will depend on the existence of an adequate network of trained suppliers, whose performance was enhanced in the last decade by new technological capability to adjust demand and supply on-line.[15]

The limits to globalization

After reviewing the operation of current economic processes, it appears that the new, informational economy works on a global scale. Yet the notion of globalization has come under spirited attack, particularly from Stephen Cohen.[16] Some of the criticism is based on a commonsense, often forgotten observation: the international economy is not global *yet*. Markets, even for strategic industries and major firms, are still far away from being fully integrated; capital flows are restricted by currency and banking regulations (although the offshoring of financial centers and the prevalence of computer transactions tend to increasingly circumvent such regulations);[17] the mobility of labor is undermined by immigration controls and people's xenophobia; and multinational corporations still keep most of their assets and their strategic command centers in their historically defined "home" nations.[18] However, this is a very important objection only when dealing with economic policy issues [. . .]. If the argument is simply that the trends toward globalization are not yet fully realized, it would be only a matter of time down the historical sequence to observe in all clarity the profile of the new, global economy.

But there is something else in the critical appraisal of the notion of globalization: in its simplistic version[19] the globalization thesis ignores the persistence of the nation state and the crucial role of government in influencing the structure and dynamics of the new economy [. . .]. Evidence shows that government regulation and policies affect the international boundaries and structure of the global economy.[20] There is not, and there will not be in the foreseeable future, a *fully integrated*, open world market for labor, technology, goods, and services, as long as nation states (or associations of nation states, such as the European Union) exist, and as long as governments are there to foster the interests of their citizens and of firms in the territories under their jurisdiction, in the global competition. Furthermore, corporate nationality is not irrelevant to corporate behavior, as is shown by the stream of research produced by the United Nations Center on Transnational Corporations. [. . .] European multinationals have been the object of systematic support by their own governments, as well as by the European Union, both in technology and in market protection. German multinationals (such as Volkswagen) have disinvested in West European countries to undertake financially risky investments in East Germany to fulfill the national ideal of German unification.[21] American multinationals (for example, IBM) have followed the instructions of their Government, sometimes reluctantly, when it came to withholding technology or restraining trade with countries at odds with US foreign policy. Accordingly, the US Government has supported technology projects for American corporations or intervened in business transactions in the name of national security interests. [...]

Furthermore, it is rightly claimed that market penetration is not reciprocal. While the American and, to a lesser extent, European economies are relatively open markets (for trade and for foreign direct investment), the Japanese economy, as well as the Chinese, Korean, Taiwanese, Indian, or Russian economies, remain highly protected. For instance, in 1989–91 Japanese direct investment in the US amounted to 46 percent of total Japanese direct investment abroad, and in the European Union, to 23 percent. However, both US and European direct investment in Japan amounted to only about 1 percent of their total direct investment abroad.[22] Because the mentioned Asian economies represented over one-fifth of world markets in the early 1990s this "exception" to the formation of a world market is significant.[23]

Nevertheless, the overall, dominant trend points toward the increasing interpenetration of markets, particularly after the reasonably successful Uruguay Round of GATT, the birth of the World Trade Organization, the slow but steady progress in European unification, the signing of the North American Free Trade Agreement, the intensification of economic exchanges within Asia, the gradual incorporation of Eastern Europe and Russia into the global economy, and the growing role played by trade and foreign investment in economic growth everywhere. Furthermore, the quasi-total integration of capital markets makes all economies globally interdependent. Yet, because of the persistence of nations and national governments, and because of the role of governments in using economic competition as a tool of political strategy, boundaries and cleavages between major economic regions are likely to remain for a long period, establishing a regional differentiation of the global economy.

The regional differentiation of the global economy

The global economy is internally diversified into three major regions and their areas of influence: North America (including Canada and Mexico, after NAFTA); the European Union (particularly after some revised version of the Maastricht Treaty trickles down into policy-making); and the Asian Pacific region, centered around Japan, but with the increasing weight of South Korea, Indonesia, Taiwan, Singapore, Overseas Chinese, and, most of all, China itself, in the region's economic potential.
[...]
Around this triangle of wealth, power, and technology, the rest of the world becomes organized in a hierarchical and asymmetrically interdependent web, as different countries and regions compete to attract capital, human skills, and technology to their shores.
[...]
The notion of a regionalized, global economy is not a contradiction in terms. There is indeed a global economy because economic agents do operate in a global network

of interaction that transcends national and geographic boundaries. But such an economy is not politically undifferentiated, and national governments play a major role in influencing economic processes. Yet the economic accounting unit is the global economy, because it is at such a global scale that strategic production and trade activities take place, as well as capital accumulation, knowledge generation, and information management. The political differentiation of this global system defines economic processes and shapes the strategies of competing agents. In this sense, **I consider internal regionalization to be a systemic attribute of the informational/global economy.** This is because states are the expression of societies, not of economies. **What becomes crucial, in the informational economy, is the complex interaction between historically rooted political institutions and increasingly globalized economic agents.**

The segmentation of the global economy

An additional qualification is essential in defining the contours of the global economy: *it is not a planetary economy*. In other words, the global economy does not embrace all economic processes in the planet, it does not include all territories, and it does not include all people in its workings, although it does affect directly or indirectly the livelihood of the entire humankind. While its effects reach out to the whole planet, **its actual operation and structure concern only segments of economic structures, countries, and regions, in proportions that vary according to the particular position of a country or region in the international division of labor.**[24] Furthermore, such a position can be transformed over time, placing countries, regions, and populations constantly on the move, which is tantamount to structurally induced instability. Thus, the new, global economic system is at the same time highly dynamic, highly exclusionary, and highly unstable in its boundaries. While dominant segments of all national economies are linked into the global web, segments of countries, regions, economic sectors, and local societies are disconnected from the processes of accumulation and consumption that characterize the informational/global economy. I do not pretend that these "marginal" sectors are not socially connected to the rest of the system, since there is no such thing as a social vacuum. But their social and economic logic is based upon mechanisms clearly distinct from those of the informational economy.[25] Thus, while the informational economy shapes the entire planet, and in this sense it is indeed global, most people in the planet do not work for or buy from the informational/global economy. Yet all economic and social processes do relate to the structurally dominant logic of such an economy. How and why such a connection is operated, and who and what is connected and disconnected over time is a fundamental feature of our societies that requires specific, careful analysis [...].

The sources of competitiveness in the global economy

The structure of the global economy is produced by the dynamics of competition between economic agents and between the locales (countries, regions, economic areas) where they are situated. Such competition is played out on the basis of factors that are specific to the new, informational economy, in a global system articulated by a network based on information technologies. Four main processes determine the form and outcome of competition.

The first is *technological capacity*. [...][26] It refers to the appropriate articulation of science, technology, management, and production in a system of complementaries, each level being provided, by the educational system, with the necessary human resources in skills and quantity. The excellence of a given element in a given economic unit, for instance a strong science base or a long manufacturing tradition in a country, is not enough to ensure the successful adoption of a new technological paradigm based on information technologies. It is the articulation of different elements that becomes critical. This is why technological capacity can hardly be the attribute of individual firms (even giant global firms such as IBM). It is related to production complexes that tend to have a territorial basis, although they connect to each other once they have established themselves in a given territory, and they diffuse and interact globally via telecommunication/transportation networks.[27]

[...]

Available evidence shows that competitiveness of industrial sectors in OECD countries is largely determined by the technological level of each sector. Similarly, the ability of countries to compete in the international economy is directly related to their technological potential.[28]

The second major factor influencing competitiveness is *access to a large, integrated, affluent market*, such as the European Union, the United States/North American Trade Zone or, to a lesser extent, Japan. The best competitive position is the one that enables firms to operate unchallenged within one of these large markets, and still have the possibility of access to the others with as few restrictions as possible.[29] Thus, the larger and deeper the integration of a given economic area, the greater the chances of spurring productivity and profitability for firms locating in that zone.[30] Therefore, the dynamics of trade and foreign investment between countries and macro-regions affect decisively the performance of individual firms or networks of firms.

The third factor that explains competitive performance in the global market is *the differential between production costs at the production site and prices at the market of destination* – a calculation that is more appropriate than the simplistic formula that focuses only on labor costs, since other cost factors may be as important (for example, land costs, taxes, environmental regulations, and so on).[31] However, this factor can only affect competitiveness if the two preceding factors are integrated positively in the firm's commercial strategy. [...]

Finally, competitiveness in the new global economy, as stated above, seems to be highly dependent on *the political capacity of national and supranational institutions to steer the growth strategy of those countries or areas under their jurisdiction*, including the creation of competitive advantages in the world market for those firms considered to serve the interests of the populations in their territories by generating jobs and income. [...]

The above-mentioned factors jointly determine the dynamics and forms of competition between firms, regions, and countries in the new global economy, thus ushering in a new international division of labor.

The Newest International Division of Labor

The global economy emerging from informational-based production and competition is characterized by its *interdependence*, its *asymmetry*, its *regionalization*, the *increasing diversification within each region*, its *selective inclusiveness*, its *exclusionary segmentation*, and, as a result of all these features, an extraordinarily *variable geometry* that tends to dissolve historical, economic geography.

[...]

Changing patterns of international division of labor in the informational/global economy: triad power, the rise of the Pacific, and the end of the Third World

As mentioned above, the global economy is still far from being a single, undifferentiated system. Yet the interdependence of its processes and agents has advanced at a fast pace in a short period of time. [...]

International trade is concentrated in the exchanges between Western Europe, the United States, and the Asian Pacific, with a clear advantage for the latter region. Thus, as an illustration of the intertwining of trade flows, in 1992 the European Union exported goods and services worth $95 billion to the US and imported from America $111 billion; it exported $96 billion to the Asian Pacific, and imported $153 billion. As for the US, it exported goods and services worth $128 billion to the Pacific Rim and imported from that region a staggering $215 billion.[32] If we add financial interdependence, technology transfer, and alliances, interlockings, and joint ventures between firms, it is obvious that the core of the global economy is a tightly interdependent network between the USA, Japan, and Western Europe that is becoming increasingly so, constituting what Ohmae labeled years ago "Triad Power."[33] Around this core, as argued by Barbara Stallings,[34] all the other areas of the world organize their economies in a multiple dependency relationship. However, patterns are changing. Japan has substantially increased its investments in Asia in recent years, as well as opening its markets to a greater extent to Asian exports, although the bulk of Japanese imports from Asia still originate from Japanese companies offshore.[35] Japan is also investing heavily in Latin America, particularly in Mexico. And South American exports in the mid-1990s are more oriented toward the European Union and the Asian Pacific than toward the United States.

The global economy is deeply asymmetric. But not in the simplistic form of a center, semi-periphery, and a periphery, or following an outright opposition between North and South; because there are several "centers" and several "peripheries," and because both North and South are so internally diversified as to make little analytical sense in using these categories.[36] Still, a group of countries that corresponds, approximately, to the membership of the Organization for Economic Cooperation and Development (OECD), concentrates an overwhelming proportion of technological capacity, capital, markets, and industrial production. If we add to the OECD the four newly industrialized countries of Asia, in 1988 the three major economic regions represented 72.8 percent of the world's manufacturing production, and in 2000 their share should still amount to 69.5 percent, while the population of these three regions in 2000 would only be 15.7 percent of world population. The concentration of resources is even greater at the core of the system, in the G-7 countries, particularly in terms of technology, skills, and informational infrastructure, key determinants of competitiveness. Thus, in 1990 the G-7 countries accounted for 90.5 percent of high-technology manufacturing in the world, and were holding 80.4 percent of global computing power.[37] The differential in human resources is critical: while the world average of scientific and technical manpower in 1985 was 23,442 per million population, the actual figure for developing countries was 8,263; for developed countries, 70,452; and for North America, 126,200, that is more than 15 times the level of developing countries. As for R&D expenditures, while North America accounted for 42.8 percent of the world's total in 1990, Latin America and Africa *together* represented less than 1 percent of the same total.[38]

Thus, the new competitive paradigm, based on technological capacity,[39] while inducing interdependency in the new global economy, has also reinforced dependency in an asymmetrical relationship that, by and large, has reinforced patterns of domination created by previous forms of dependency throughout history.

However, this apparent historical continuity must be corrected by observing processes of diversification taking place both in the so-called "North" and in the so-called "South" [. . .]. First of all, a dramatic realignment in the distribution of capital, technology, and manufacturing capacity has taken place among the three dominant regions in the last third of the century, to the benefit of the Asian Pacific Region [. . .]. Adding the newly industrialized Asian countries to Japan to form the "developed Asia" region, such a region is poised to become the largest industrial region of the world, with 26.9 percent of world manufacturing in the year 2000, against 24.6 percent for Western Europe, and just 18 percent for North America. And this is without counting China, whose rapid growth and technological modernization will make it a major economic power before long. Furthermore, the importance of manufacturing in developed Asia, extrapolating on the basis of current tendencies, would be particularly significant in electronics, the critical sector for the informational economy, and [it] may also take the lead in automobile manufacturing.[40]

In addition, if we include in the picture the growing linkages between Japan and the "four tigers" with China and the South East Asian region, what seems to be emerging at the turn of century is a powerful, semi-integrated Asian Pacific economy that has become a major center of capital accumulation in the world.[41] The Asian Pacific economy is internally differentiated among at least five distinct networks of economic power: the Japanese corporations; the Korean corporations; American multinational corporations, particularly in electronics and finance, established in the area for many years; the powerful networks of ethnic Chinese capital, connecting Hong Kong, Taipei, Singapore, and "overseas" Chinese business groups (often operating through Hong Kong), all of them with direct linkages to China, forming what observers are calling "the China Circle"; the Chinese Government and Chinese provincial and local governments, with their diversified financial and industrial interests.[42]

[. . .]

The economic power accumulated in the Asian Pacific region, even without counting Japan, is staggering. In 1993, East Asian governments had foreign currency reserves of $250 billion, three times those of Japan. In addition, private corporations outside Japan were holding another $600 billion in cash reserves. Savings were expected to increase by $550 billion per year during the 1990s, so that by the year 2000 the gross domestic product of East Asia (including China) could reach $2 trillion, and surpass Japan.[43] [. . .]

Thus, if we consider together the lasting technological and economic power of Japan, the sustained process of economic growth and international integration of China, the explosion of investment by Japanese, ethnic Chinese, and Korean firms in the East and South East Asia region, the meaning of the "North" in the new global economy is definitively blurred. The emergence of Asian Pacific fast-growth capitalism is, with the end of the Soviet Empire and the process of European unification, one of the most important structural changes taking place in the world at the turn of the century. [...]

This process of extreme diversification of development trajectories is also visible at the other end of the global economy, the so-called "South," to the point that Nigel Harris was proven to be correct when announcing "the end of the Third World."[44] To be sure, there is widespread poverty and human suffering throughout the planet, and it will unfortunately continue to be so in the foreseeable future.[45] Indeed, there is a growing polarization of income at the world level [...]. Yet, there is also increasing differentiation of economic growth, technological capacity, and social conditions between areas of the world, between countries, within countries, and even within regions. Thus, South Asia, and particularly some areas of India, in the 1990s started upon a process of fast economic growth and integration into the global economy, improving over the moderate performance of the previous decade: in the 1980s, South Asia's GDP per capita increased at an average annual rate of 3.2 percent (5.5 percent in GDP growth), contrasting to the meager 0.6 percent per capita growth during the 1970s. After the economic crisis of 1990, India went into a new policy of internationalization and liberalization of its economy that induced an economic boom around areas such as Ahmedabad, Bombay, Bangalore (a new node in the world's electronics industry), and New Delhi. However, economic quasi-stagnation continues in most rural areas, as well as in some major metropolitan centers such as Calcutta. Furthermore, social inequality and a new brand of unrestrained capitalism keep the majority of the Indian population, including in the most dynamic urban centers, in miserable living conditions. Sub-Saharan Africa is projected to continue to stagnate at a subhuman level. Latin America as a whole has hardly recovered from the social costs inflicted by the "lost decade" of the 1980s, in spite of its dynamic integration into the global economy in the mid-1990s. Most of the ex-Soviet Empire countries for the remaining years of the century will still be catching up with their standards of living in the 1960s. And even Asia as a whole, while experiencing substantial growth (about 6 percent per year on average during the 1980s, most likely to be improved in the 1990s), will still remain at an abysmal distance from living standards of developed regions, with the obvious exceptions of Japan and the four Asian tigers.

Nevertheless, there is a substantial process of development under way for millions of people in some areas, particularly in China, home of one-fifth of the world's population, but also in most of Asia (over two-thirds of humankind), and in major Latin American countries. By development I mean, for the sake of this analysis, the simultaneous process of improvement in living standards, structural change in the productive system, and growing competitiveness in the global economy. While theorizing on postindustrialism we are experiencing, toward the end of the twentieth century, one of the largest waves of industrialization in history, if we use a simple indicator such as the absolute number of manufacturing workers, at its peak in 1990 [...] and growing: in the Pearl River Delta alone at least 6 million new manufacturing jobs were created in the last decade. On the other hand, some rural regions of China, India, and Latin America, entire countries around the world, and large segments of the population everywhere are becoming irrelevant (*from the perspective of dominant economic interests*) in the new pattern of international division of labor, and thus they are being socially excluded.[46]

[...]

The Architecture and Geometry of
the Informational/Global Economy

I can now sum up the structure and dynamics of the new global economy emerging from the historical interaction between the rise of informationalism and capitalist restructuring.

The structure of this economy is characterized by the combination of an enduring architecture and a variable geometry. The architecture of the global economy features an asymmetrically interdependent world, organized around three major economic regions and increasingly polarized along an axis of opposition between productive, information-rich, affluent areas, and impoverished areas, economically devalued and socially excluded. Between the three dominant regions, Europe, North America, and the Asian Pacific, the latter appears to be the most dynamic yet the most vulnerable because of its dependence upon the openness of the markets of the other regions. However, the intertwining of economic processes between the three regions makes them practically inseparable in their fate. Around each region an economic hinterland has been created, with some countries being gradually incorporated into the global economy, usually through the dominant regions that are their geographic neighbors: North America for Latin America; the European Union for Eastern Europe, Russia, and the South Mediterranean; Japan and the Asian Pacific for the rest of Asia, as well as for Australia and New Zealand, and maybe for the Russian Pacific, Eastern Siberia and Kazakhstan; Africa, while still dependent on ex-colonial economic networks, seems to be increasingly marginalized in the global economy; the Middle East is, by and large, integrated into the global networks of finance and energy supply, although highly dependent on the avatars of the world's geopolitics.
[...]

However, this is not the whole story. Within this visible architecture there are dynamic processes of competition and change that infuse a variable geometry into the global system of economic processes. Indeed, the evolution that I have recalled somewhat schematically in the preceding pages shows the emergence of a new pattern of international division of labor, characteristic of the global economy. What I call the newest international division of labor is constructed around four different positions in the informational/global economy: the producers of high value, based on informational labor; the producers of high volume, based on lower-cost labor; the producers of raw materials, based on natural endowments; and the redundant producers, reduced to devalued labor. The differential location of such different types of labor also determines the affluence of markets, since income generation will depend upon the capacity to create value incorporated in each segment of the global economy. The critical matter is that these different positions do not coincide with countries. *They are organized in networks and flows, using the technological infrastructure of the informational economy.* They feature geographic concentrations in some areas of the planet, so that the global economy is not geographically undifferentiated. Yet the newest international division of labor does not take place between countries but between economic agents placed in the four positions I have indicated along a global structure of networks and flows. In this sense, all countries are penetrated by the four positions indicated because all networks are global in their reality or in their target. Even marginalized economies have a small segment of their directional functions connected to the high-value producers network, at least to ensure the transfer of whatever capital or information is still accumulated in the country. And certainly, the most powerful economies have marginal segments of their population placed in a position of devalued labor, be it in New York,[47] in Osaka,[48] in London,[49] or in Madrid.[50]

Because the position in the international division of labor does not depend, fundamentally, on the characteristics of the country but on the characteristics of its labor (including embodied knowledge) and of its insertion into the global economy, changes may occur, and indeed do, in a short time span. Actions by governments and by entrepreneurial sectors of societies are critical in this matter. The newest international division of labor is organized on the basis of labor and technology, but is enacted and modified by governments and entrepreneurs. The relentlessly variable geometry that results from such processes of innovation and competition struggles with the historically produced architecture of the world economic order, inducing the creative chaos that characterizes the new economy.

[. . .]

Notes

1   Braudel (1967); Wallerstein (1974).
2   Chesnais (1994: 206–48); Shirref (1994); Heavey (1994); *Economist* (1995); Khoury and Ghosh (1987).
3   Sassen (1991).
4   Lee et al. (1994); Chesnais (1994: 206–48).
5   Sengenberger and Campbell (1994).
6   Baldwin-Evans and Schain (1995); Portes and Rumbault (1990); Soysal (1994).
7   Sagasti and Araoz (1988); Soete (1991); Johnston and Sasson (1986).
8   Castells and Hall (1994); Arthur (1985); Hall and Preston (1988); Soete (1991).
9   Andrieu et al. (1992); Daniels (1993); Chesnais (1994: 181–206).
10 Tyson (1992).
11 Chesnais (1994); UNCTAD (1993); Reich (1991); Stallings (1993); Porter (1990).
12 BRIE (1992); Dicken (1992); Reich (1991); Gereffi (1993); Imai (1990).
13 Henderson (1989).
14 Coriat (1990).
15 Gereffi and Wyman (1990); Tetsuro and Steven (1994).
16 Cohen (1990).
17 Bertrand and Noyelle (1988).
18 Carnoy et al. (1993).
19 Ohmae (1990).
20 Johnson et al. (1989); Evans (1995).
21 UNCTAD (1993); Carnoy et al. (1993); Okimoto (1984); Johnson et al. (1989); Abbeglen and Stalk (1985); Van Tulder and Junne (1988); Dunning (1985); Cohen (1990).
22 Stallings (1993).
23 CEPII (1992).
24 Sengenberger and Campbell (1994); UNCTAD (1993); Portes et al. (1989); Carnoy et al. (1993); Sassen (1988); Mingione (1991).
25 I elaborated on the new processes of dualism in a comparative perspective in Castells [1989].
26 Castells et al. (1986).
27 Castells and Hall (1994).
28 Dosi et al. (1988); Dosi and Soete (1983); OECD (1992); Soete (1991); Castells and Tyson (1988); Tyson (1992).
29 Lafay and Herzog (1989).

30 Cecchini (1988); Spence and Hazard (1988).
31 Cohen et al. (1985); Krugman (1986). For an analysis of sources of competitiveness in the new global economy on the basis of experiences in the Asian Pacific, see my monograph, and the economic analyses on which I relied, most of them from Asian scholars, on the sources of economic development of Hong Kong and Singapore: Castells et al. (1990).
32 Sources: for Europe, German Ministry of Economy, for US, US Department of Commerce.
33 Ohmae (1985).
34 Stallings (1993).
35 Doherty (1995); Cohen and Borrus (1995).
36 Coutrot and Husson (1993); Harris (1987).
37 US National Science Board (1991).
38 [UNESCO data.]
39 Foray and Freeman (1992).
40 CEPII (1992); Guerrieri (1991); Mortimore (1992); Bergsten and Noland (1993).
41 Urata, in Bergsten and Noland (1993); Soesastro and Pangestu (1990); Ernst (1994); *Business Week* (1994); Bergsten and Noland (1993); Ernst and O'Connor (1992); Ernst, in Doherty (1995).
42 Sung (1994); Naughton (1994); Hsing (1994).
43 *Business Week* (1993).
44 Harris (1987).
45 Rodgers (1995); Nayyar (1994); Baghwati and Srinivasan (1993); ILO (1993); Lachaud (1994); Lustig (1995); Tchernina (1993); Islam (1995).
46 Rodgers and Van der Hoeven (1995).
47 Mollenkopf and Castells (1991).
48 Sugihara et al. (1988).
49 Lee and Townsend (1993).
50 Leal (1993).

References

Abbeglen, J. C. and Stalk, G. (1985) *Kaisha: The Japanese Corporation.* New York: Basic Books.
Andrieu, Michel, Michalski, Wolfgang, and Stevens, Barrie (eds) (1992) *Long-term Prospects for the World Economy.* Paris: OECD.
Arthur, Brian (1985) Industry Location and the Economics of Agglomeration: Why a Silicon Valley? Economic Policy Research Working Paper, Stanford University.
Baghwati, J. and Srinivasan, T. M. (1993) *Indian Economic Reforms.* New Delhi: Ministry of Finance.
Baldwin-Evans, Martin and Schain, Martin (eds) (1995) *The Politics of Immigration in Western Europe.* London: Frank Cass.
Bergsten, C. Fred and Noland, Marcus (eds) (1993) *Pacific Dynamism and the International Economic System.* Washington DC: Institute for International Economics.
Bertrand, O. and Noyelle, T. J. (1988) *Corporate and Human Resources: Technological Change in Banks and Insurance Companies in Five OECD Countries.* Paris: OECD.
Braudel, Fernand (1967) *Civilisation materielle et capitalisme. XV–XVII siècles*, Paris: Armand Colin.
BRIE (1992) Globalization and Production. Berkeley Roundtable on the International Economy Working Paper 45, University of California at Berkeley.
Business Week (1993) The Horizontal Corporation. Oct. 28.
Business Week (1994) China: Birth of a New Economy. Jan. 31, pp. 42–8.
Carnoy, M. et al. (1993) *The New Global Economy in the Information Age.* University Park: Penn State University Press.
Castells, Manuel (1989) *The Informational City.* Oxford: Blackwell.
Castells, Manuel and Hall, Peter (1994) *Technopoles of the World: The Makings of Twenty-First Century Industrial Complexes.* London: Routledge.

Castells, Manuel and Tyson, Laura D'Andrea (1988) High Technology Choices Ahead: Restructuring Interdependence. In John W. Sewell and Stuart Tucker (eds), *Growth, Exports, and Jobs in a Changing World Economy*, New Brunswick: Transaction Books.

Castells, Manuel, Goh, L. and Kwok, R. Y.-W. (1990) *The Shek Kip Mei Syndrome: Economic Development and Public Housing in Hong Kong and Singapore*. London: Pion.

Castells, Manuel et al. (1986) *Nuevas tecnologias, economia y sociedad en Espana*. 2 vols, Madrid: Alianza Editorial.

Cecchini, Paolo (1988) *The European Challenge, 1992: The Benefits of a Single Market*. Aldershot: Gower.

CEPII (Centre d'Études Prospectives et d'Informations Internationales) (1992) *L'Économie mondiale 1990–2000. L'impératif de la croissance*. Paris: Economica.

Chesnais, François (1994) *La Mondialisation du capital*. Paris: Syros.

Cohen, Stephen (1990) Corporate Nationality can Matter a Lot. Testimony before the US Congress Joint Economic Committee, Sept.

Cohen, Stephen and Borrus, Michael (1995) Networks of Companies in Asia. Berkeley Roundtable on the International Economy Research Paper, University of California at Berkeley.

Cohen, Stephen et al. (1985) *Global Competition: The New Reality*. Vol. 3 of John Young (chair), *Competitiveness: The Report of the President's Commission on Industrial Competitiveness*, Washington DC: Government Printing Office.

Coriat, Benjamin (1990) *L'Atelier et le robot*. Paris: Christian Bourgois Editeur.

Coutrot, T. and Husson, M. (1993) *Les Destins du tiers monde*. Paris: Nathan.

Daniels, P. W. (1993) *Service Industries in the World Economy*. Oxford: Blackwell.

Dicken, Peter (1992) *Global Shift: The Internationalization of Economic Activity*. New York: Guilford Press.

Doherty, Eileen M. (ed.) (1995) *Japanese Investment in Asia: International Production Strategies in a Rapidly Changing World*. Proceedings of a conference organized with Berkeley Roundtable on the International Economy. San Francisco: Asia Foundation.

Dosi, Giovanni and Soete, Luc (1983) Technology, Competitiveness, and International Trade. *Econometrica* 3.

Dosi, Giovanni, Pavitt, K., and Soete, L. (1988) *The Economics of Technical Change and International Trade*. Brighton: Wheatsheaf.

Dunning, John (ed.) (1985) *Multinational Enterprises, Economic Structure and International Competitiveness*. New York: John Wiley.

Economist (1995) Currencies in a Spin. Mar. 11, pp. 69–70.

Ernst, Dieter (1994) Inter-Firm Networks and Market Structure: Driving Forces, Barriers and Patterns of Control. Berkeley Roundtable on the International Economy Research Paper, University of California at Berkeley.

Ernst, Dieter and O'Connor, David (1992) *Competing in the Electronics Industry: The Experience of Newly Industrializing Economies*. Development Centre Studies. Paris: OECD.

Evans, Peter (1995) *Embedded Autonomy: States and Industrial Transformation*. Princeton: Princeton University Press.

Foray, Dominique and Freeman, Christopher (eds) (1992) *Technologie et richesse des nations*. Paris: Economica.

Gereffi, Gary (1993) Global Production Systems and Third World Development. University of Wisconsin Global Studies Research Program, Working Paper Series, Aug.

Gereffi, Gary and Wyman, Donald (eds) (1990) *Manufacturing Miracles: Paths of Industrialization in Latin America and East Asia*. Princeton: Princeton University Press.

Guerrieri, Paolo (1991) Technology and International Trade Performance in the Most Advanced Countries. Berkeley Roundtable on the International Economy Working Paper 49, University of California at Berkeley.

Hall, Peter and Preston, Pascal (1988) *The Carrier Wave: New Information Technology and the Geography of Innovation, 1846–2003*. London: Unwin Hyman.

Harris, Nigel (1987) *The End of the Third World*. Harmondsworth: Penguin.

Heavey, Laurie (1994) Global Integration. *Pension World* 30(7): 24–7.

Henderson, Jeffrey (1989) *The Globalization of High Technology Production: Society, Space and Semiconductors in the Restructuring of the Modern World*. London: Routledge.

Hsing, You-tien (1994) Blood Thicker than Water: Networks of Local Chinese Officials and Taiwanese Investors in Southern China. Paper delivered at the conference on The Economics of the China Circle, sponsored by the University of California Institute on Global Conflict and Cooperation, Hong Kong, Sept. 1–3.

Imai, Ken'ichi (1990) *Jouhon Network Schakai no Tenkai* (The development of information network society). Tokyo: Tikuma Shobou.

ILO (International Labour Organization) (1993) *World Labour Report*. Geneva: International Labour Organization.

Islam, Rizwanul (1995) Rural Institutions and Poverty in Asia. In Gerry Rodgers and Rolph van der Hoeven (eds), *The Poverty Agenda: Trends and Policy Options*, Geneva: International Institute of Labour Studies.

Johnson, Chalmers, Tyson, L., and Zysman, J. (eds) (1989) *Politics and Productivity: How Japan's Development Strategy Works*. New York: Harper Business.

Johnston, Ann and Sasson, Albert (1986) *New Technologies and Development*. Paris: UNESCO.

Khoury, Sarkis and Ghosh, Alo (1987) *Recent Developments in International Banking and Finance*. Lexington: D. C. Heath.

Krugman, Paul (ed.) (1986) *Strategic Trade Policy and the New International Economics*. Cambridge, Mass.: MIT Press.

Kur'yerov, V. G. (1994) Ekonomika Rossii: Obshchiye Tendentsii (Russian economy: general trends). *EKO*, no. 5: 2–7.

Lachaud, Jean-Pierre (1994) *The Labour Market in Africa*. Geneva: International Institute of Labour Studies.

Lafay, Gerard and Herzog, Colette (1989) *Commerce international: la fin des avantages acquis*. Paris: Economica/Centre d'Études Prospectives et d'Informations Internationales.

Leal, Jesus (1993) *La desigualdad social en Espana*. Madrid: Universidad Research Monograph.

Lee, Peter and Townsend, Peter (1993) Trends in Deprivation in the London Labour Market: A Study of Low Incomes and Unemployment in London between 1985 and 1992. International Institute of Labour Studies, Discussion Paper 59/1993, Geneva.

Lee, Peter, King, Paul, Shirref, David, and Dyer, Geof (1994) All Change. *Euromoney* (June): 89–101.

Lustig, Nora (1995) Coping with Austerity: Poverty and Inequality in Latin America. In Rodgers and Van der Hoeven 1995.

Mingione, Enzo (1991) *Fragmented Societies*. Oxford: Blackwell.

Mollenkopf, John and Castells, Manuel (eds) (1991) *Dual City: Restructuring New York*. New York: Russell Sage Foundation.

Mortimore, Michael (1992) A New International Industrial Order. *CEPAL Review*, no. 48: 39–59.

Naughton, Barry (1994) Increasing Economic Integration in the China Circle in the Context of East Asian Growth. Paper delivered at the conference on The Economics of the China Circle, sponsored by the University of California Institute on Global Conflict and Cooperation, Hong Kong, Sept. 1–3.

Nayyar, Deepak (1994) Macroeconomic Adjustment, Liberalization and Growth: The Indian Experience. International Institute of Labour Studies, Discussion Paper 73/1994, Geneva.

OECD (1992) *Globalization of Industrial Activities*. Paris: OECD.

Ohmae, Kenichi (1985) *Triad Power: The Coming Shape of Global Competition*. New York: Free Press.

Ohmae, Kenichi (1990) *The Borderless World: Power and Strategy in the Interlinked Economy*. New York: Harper.

Okimoto, Daniel (1984) Political Context. In Daniel Okimoto, Takuo Sugarno, and Franklin B. Weinstein (eds), *Competitive Edge*, Stanford: Stanford University Press.

Porter, Michael (1990) *The Competitive Advantage of Nations*. New York: Free Press.

Portes, Alejandro and Rumbault, Ruben (1990) *Immigrant America: A Portrait*. Berkeley: University of California Press.

Portes, Alejandro, Castells, Manuel, and Benton, Lauren (eds) (1989) *The Informal Economy: Studies on Advanced and Less Developed Countries*. Baltimore: Johns Hopkins University Press.

Reich, Robert (1991) *The Work of Nations*. New York: Random House.

Rodgers, Gerry (ed.) (1995) *The Poverty Agenda and the ILO: Issues for Research and Action. A Contribution to the World Summit for Social Development*. Geneva: International Institute of Labour Studies.

Rodgers, Gerry and Van der Hoeven (eds) (1995) *The Poverty Agenda: Trends and Policy Options*. Geneva: International Institute of Labour Studies.

Sagasti, Francisco and Araoz, Alberto (eds) (1988) *La planificacion cientifica y tecnologica en los paises en desarrollo. La experiencia del proyecto STPI*. Mexico: Fondo de Cultura Economica.

Sassen, Saskia (1988) *The Mobility of Labour and Capital*. Cambridge: Cambridge University Press.

Sassen, Saskia (1991) *The Global City: New York, London, Tokyo*. Princeton: Princeton University Press.

Sengenberger, Werner and Campbell, Duncan (eds) (1992) *Is the Single Firm Vanishing? Inter-enterprise Networks, Labour, and Labour Institutions*. Geneva: International Institute of Labour Studies.

Sengenberger, Werner and Campbell, Duncan (eds) (1994) *International Labour Standards and Economic Interdependence*. Geneva: International Institute of Labour Studies.

Shirref, David (1994) The Metamorphosis of Finance. *Euromoney* (June): 36–42.

Soesastro, Hadi and Pangestu, Mari (eds) (1990) *Technological Challenge in the Asia-Pacific Economy*. Sydney: Allen and Unwin.

Soete, Luc (1991) Technology and Economy in a Changing World. Background paper prepared for the OECD International Policy Conference on Technology and the Global Economy, Montreal, Feb.

Soysal, Yasemin Nuhoglu (1994) *Limits of Citizenship: Migrants and Postnational Membership in Europe*. Chicago: University of Chicago Press.

Spence, Michael and Hazard, Heather A. (eds) (1988) *International Competitiveness*. Cambridge, Mass.: Ballinger.

Stallings, Barbara (1993) The New International Context of Development. Working Paper Series on the New International Context of Development, no. 1, University of Wisconsin.

Sugihara, Kaoru et al. (1988) *Taisho, Osaka, and the Slum: Another Modern History of Japan*. Tokyo: Shinhyoron.

Sung, Yun-Wing (1994) Hong Kong and the Economic Integration of the China Circle. Paper delivered at the conference on The Economics of the China Circle, sponsored by the University of California Institute on Global Conflict and Cooperation, Hong Kong, Sept. 1–3.

Tchernina, Natalia (1993) Employment, Deprivation, and Poverty: The Ways in which Poverty is Emerging in the Course of Economic Reform in Russia. International Institute of Labour Studies, Discussion Paper 60/1993, Geneva.

Tetsuro, Kato and Steven, Rob (eds) (1994) *Is Japanese Management Post-Fordism?* Tokyo: Madosha.

Tyson, Laura D'Andrea (1992) *Who's Bashing Whom? Trade Conflict in High-Technology Industries*. Washington DC: Institute of International Economics.

UNCTAD (United Nations Conference on Trade and Development) (1993) *World Investment Report 1993: Transnational Corporations and Integrated International Production*. New York: United Nations, Programme on Transnational Corporations.

US National Science Board (1991) *Science and Engineering Indicators: 1991*, 10th edn. Washington DC: US Government Printing Office.

Van Tulder, Rob and Junne, Gerd (1988) *European Multinationals in Core Technologies*. New York: John Wiley.

Wallerstein, Immanuel (1974) *The Modern World System*. New York: Academic Press.

24

Globalization and the History of the International Economy

Paul Hirst and Grahame Thompson

The 'globalization' of economic activity and the governance issues it raises are often thought to have appeared only after the Second World War, and particularly during the 1960s. The post-1960s era saw the emergence of MNC activity on the one hand and the rapid growth of international trade on the other. Subsequently, with the collapse of the Bretton Woods semi-fixed exchange rate regime in the 1971–3 period, the expansion of international securities investment and bank lending began in earnest as capital and particularly money markets rapidly internationalized, adding to the complexity of international economic relations and heralding what is often thought to be the genuine globalization of an integrated and interdependent world economy. In this chapter we scrutinize this popular history and trace the main periods of the internationalization of economic activity, which will be shown to have developed in a cyclical and uneven fashion. The key issue at stake in our assessment is the changing autonomy of national economies in the conduct of their economic activity.[1]

MNCs, TNCs and International Business

The history of the internationalization of business enterprises is a long one, in no way confined just to the period since 1960. Trading activities, for instance, date from the earliest civilizations, but it was the Middle Ages in Europe that marked the initiation of systematic cross-border trading operations carried out by institutions of a private corporate nature (though often with strong state backing and support).
[. . .]

However, it is the development of international manufacturing as the industrial revolution took hold that presents the closest precursor to the modern-day MNC. Here the early pre-eminence of British firms as multinational producers becomes apparent. Initially North and South America presented the most favourable investment opportunities, but these were soon followed by Africa and Australasia. There is some dispute as to whether 'colonial investments' should be considered a true precursor of foreign direct investment, but production abroad for the local market began in this way. Technical and organizational developments after the 1870s allowed a wider variety of similar products to be produced domestically and abroad within the boundaries of the same firm, while the exploration and development of minerals and other raw material products also attracted large amounts of FDI (Dunning 1993: ch. 5).
[. . .]

[It] is generally agreed that manufacturing multinationals appeared in the world economy after the mid-nineteenth century and that they were well established by the First World War. International business activity grew vigorously in the 1920s as the truly diversified and integrated MNC matured, but it slowed down during the depressed 1930s and war-torn 1940s, and began a fluctuating expansion again after 1950.
[. . .]

Trade and International Integration

A better statistical base is available for exploring the trends in international trade. Again the history of this part of international economic activity goes back a long way. [. . .] A similar pattern emerges here as in the case of FDI, though perhaps more pronounced in its features. The volume of world foreign trade expanded at about 3.4 per cent per annum between 1870 and 1913. After 1913 trade was adversely affected by the growth of tariffs, quantitative restrictions, exchange controls and then war, and it expanded by less than 1 per cent per annum on average between 1913 and 1950. After 1950, however, trade really took off to grow at over 9 per cent per annum until 1973. Between 1973 and the mid-1980s the growth rate fell back to nearer the late nineteenth-century levels, with expansion at a rate of only 3.6 per cent [. . .].
[. . .]

The relationship between growth in output and in trade is a central one for international economics analysis. It is not our intention to explore the theoretical links between these here (see Kitson and Michie 1995). However, trade growth from 1853 to 1872 was already faster than the growth in world production, while from 1872 to 1911 it grew at about the same rate. Between 1913 and 1950 there was a devastating decline in both the rate of growth of trade (0.5 per cent per annum) and of output growth (1.9 per cent per annum). Only since 1950 has there been a consistent expansion of trade relative to production, even during the cyclical downturn after 1973 [. . .].

Migration and the International Labour Market

A third broad area of analysis in the context of the history of the international economy concerns migration and its consequences for the integration of the global labour market. It is generally agreed that migration is becoming (or has become) a 'global phenomenon' (see, for instance, Serow et al. 1990: 159; Segal 1993: ch. 7; Castles and Miller 1993: ch. 4). However, by global these authors mean that, since the mid-1970s in particular, many more countries have been affected by migration, that there has been a growing diversity of areas of origin for migrants, and that migrants are of a wider range of socioeconomic statuses than ever before. Thus for these authors globalization registers a quantitative change in the extent and scope of migration rather than a feature of a potentially different socioeconomic order.

There are a number of different kinds of migrants. Clearly the early slave trade was a form of 'involuntary' migration (it is estimated that 15 million slaves were moved from Africa to the Americas before 1850: Castles and Miller 1993: 48). Refugees and asylum seekers can also be considered as migrants. But for the purposes of our analysis we focus on 'voluntary' migration. The period considered extends from the 'mass migration' after 1815 (mainly from Europe) to the emergence and extension of labour migration of the 'guest worker' variety after the Second World War.

It is difficult to judge exactly how many migrants there have been since 1815, so all the following numbers should be treated with some caution. Castles and Miller (1993) report that there could have been as many as 100 million migrants of all kinds in 1992 (including some 20 million refugees and asylum seekers, and 30 million overseas workers). They point out, however, that this represented only about 1.7 percent of the world population. Thus the vast majority of the world's population remain in their country of origin.

The greatest era for recorded voluntary mass migration was the century after 1815 [. . .]. Around 60 million people left Europe for the Americas, Oceania, and South and East Africa. An estimated 10 million voluntarily migrated from Russia to Central Asia and Siberia. A million went from Southern Europe to North Africa. About 12 million Chinese and 6 million Japanese left their homelands and emigrated to East and South Asia. One and a half million left India for South East Asia and South and West Africa (Segal 1993: 16 – the statistics for Indian migration are probably severely underestimated here).

Between the two world wars international migration decreased sharply. To a large extent this was in response to the depressed economic conditions during much of the interwar period, but it was also due to restrictive immigration policies instigated in many of the traditional recipient countries, particularly the United States.

An upsurge in international migration began in the post-1945 period, particularly involving Europe and the United States once again (Livi-Bacci 1993). This was the period, however, of the relative growth of migration from the developing countries to the developed ones [. . .] and the introduction of the 'guest worker' phenomenon. During the 1970s and 1980s global trends favoured the controlled movements of temporary workers on a 'guest' basis, with entry for immigrants restricted to the highly skilled or those with family already in the country of destination.

[. . .]

The Relative Openness and Interdependence of the International System

A key question posed by the preceding analysis is whether the integration of the international system has dramatically changed since the Second World War. Clearly, there has been considerable international economic activity ever since the 1850s, but can we compare different periods in terms of their openness and integration?

One way of doing this is to compare trade to GDP ratios. Table 1 provides information on these for a range of countries. Apart from the dramatic differences in the openness to trade of different economies demonstrated by these figures (compare the US and the Netherlands), the startling feature is that trade to GDP ratios were consistently higher in 1913 than they were in 1973 (with the slight exception of Germany where they were near enough equal). Even in 1995, Japan, the Netherlands and the UK were still less open than they were in 1913, with France and Germany only slightly more open. The US was the only country that was considerably more open than it was in 1913. [. . .]

Table 1 Ratio of merchandise trade to GDP at current prices (exports and imports combined), 1913, 1950, 1973 and 1995

	1913	1950	1973	1995
France	35.4	21.2	29.0	36.6
Germany	35.1	20.1	35.2	38.7
Japan	31.4	16.9	18.3	14.1
Netherlands	103.6	70.2	80.1	83.4
UK	44.7	36.0	39.3	42.6[a]
US	11.2	7.0	10.5	19.0

[a] 1994.
Sources: Figures from 1913 to 1973 derived from Maddison 1987, table A-23, p. 695; figures for 1995 derived from *OECD National Accounts, 1997*, country tables

[...] [C]oncentrating on just the period after the Second World War shows a steady growth in trade openness, with a particularly dramatic entry of the East Asian economies into the international trading system.

Getting back to the longer term trends, however, the evidence also suggests greater openness to capital flows in the pre-First World War period compared to more recent years. Grassman (1980), measuring 'financial openness' in terms of current account balance to GNP ratios, finds no increase in openness between 1875 and 1975: indeed there is a decline in capital movements for his leading six countries (Great Britain, Italy, Sweden, Norway, Denmark and the US). This is even the case for the post-Second World War period, though from the mid-1970s there is some sign of an increasing trend in financial openness. [...]

In addition, Lewis reports that capital exports rose substantially over the thirty years before the First World War, though they were subject to wide fluctuations. But when a comparison is made with the years 1953–73, the order of magnitude of capital exports was much lower in the latter period (Lewis 1981: 21). Finally, in a comprehensive comparison of the pre-1914 Gold Standard period with the 1980s, Turner (1991) also concludes that current account imbalances and capital flows, measured in relation to GNP, were larger before 1914 than in the 1980s.

Thus, using gross figures for ratios of trade and capital flows relative to output confirms that 'openness' was greater during the Gold Standard period than even in the 1990s. But these gross figures could disguise important differences between the periods. [...] [The] composition of output might be important in judging the real extent of interdependence. In the case of financial flows we should also recognize the change in their character and the significance of the financial regimes under which they took place. In the high Gold Standard period long-term capital dominated international capital flows. In the recent period there has been a switch to shorter-term capital. In addition, a wider range of countries have now been included under the international capital movement umbrella. [...]

Moving away from trade and capital flows for the moment, we can now look at the implications of the trends in international migration. First, it must be emphasized that these are contained within the twin considerations of the labour market and governmental policy. A world market for labour just does not exist in the same way that it does for goods and services. Most labour markets continue to be nationally regulated and only marginally accessible to outsiders, whether legal or illegal migrants or professional recruitment. Moving goods and services is infinitely easier than moving labour. Even a rapid and sustained expansion of the world economy is unlikely to significantly reduce the multiple barriers to the movement of labour. Other than in the context of regionally developing free trade agreements of the EU type, freedom of labour movement still remains heavily circumscribed. Even the NAFTA explicitly excludes freedom of movement of persons, though there is *de facto* freedom between Canada and the US, and enormous illegal flows between Mexico and the US. Extraregional migration of all kinds is a small percentage of global labour movements. Most migration is of the country next door variety. During the nineteenth century the mass movement of workers to the sources of capital was accepted and encouraged; now it is rejected except as a temporary expedient.

In as much as there is global international migration for employment, it is concentrated on the Gulf states, North America and Western Europe. A crude estimate of this category gives a figure of about 20 million in 1990 (prior to the Gulf War, which saw a massive return home, particularly of Third World migrant workers, from the Gulf states). This form of international labour force reached its peak in the early 1970s. The worldwide recession and subsequent developments like the Gulf War interrupted the growth of temporary migrant employment. A large proportion of these workers are illegally residing and working abroad. Legal expatriate workers tend to be in the managerial, skilled and technical employment categories.

[...]

Two sets of more general points are worth making in the light of these remarks. The first is that there have been phases of massive international migration over many centuries and there seems nothing unprecedented about movements in the post-Second World War period, or those in more recent decades. The second related point is that in many ways the situation between 1815 and 1914 was much more open than it is today. The supposed era of 'globalization' has not seen the rise of a new unregulated and internationalized market in labour migration. In many ways, the world's underprivileged and poor have fewer international migratory possibilities nowadays than they had in the past. At least in the period of mass migration there was the option to uproot the whole family and move in the quest for better conditions, a possibility that seems to be rapidly shrinking for equivalent sections of the world's population today. They have little choice but to remain in poverty and stick it out. The 'empty lands' available to European and other settlers in the US and Canada, South America, southern Africa and Australia and New Zealand just do not exist today, with a concomitant loss of 'freedom' for the world's poor.

Things look different for the well off and privileged, however. Those with professional qualifications and technical skills still have greater room for manoeuvre and retain the option to move if they wish. The 'club class' with managerial expertise, though relatively few in number in terms of the global population, are the most obvious manifestation of this inequity in long-term migratory opportunities.

Another strong contemporary feature of the international system that is often invoked as an indicator of 'globalization' is the emergence of large discriminatory regional trading blocs like the EU, NAFTA and APEC (Asia-Pacific Economic Cooperation). [...] [H]ere it is worth pointing to the historical precedents for these kinds of bodies. A marked discrimination in trade and investment patterns was produced during the colonial empire period in the nineteenth century. For the French and British empires the biases to trade between the colonial power and its colonies were between two and four times greater than would have been expected given the 'natural' economic fundamentals that determine trade, such as the size of the countries involved, GDP per capita, proximity and common borders. The biases were even higher for Belgium, Italy and Portugal and their overseas dependencies. In fact, the concentration of trade with the countries that made up British and French empires did not peak until 1938; it declined steadily following the independence movements after the Second World War, but did not reach unity until as late as 1984 (Frankel 1997: 126). Trade within the Austro-Hungarian Empire, before it broke up at the end of the First World War, was also four or five times what it would have been if determined simply by the natural fundamentals (Frankel 1997: 119). [...]

Thus it was in the 1930s that regionalism was probably at its height. There was a definite discriminatory sterling bloc, overlapping imperfectly with the British Empire/Commonwealth. Then there was a group of countries that remained on the Gold Standard, and a subsection of central and south-eastern European countries that gravitated towards Germany. The US erected trade barriers, and formed a partial dollar bloc with the Spanish-speaking countries adjacent to North America. According to Frankel, all these were heavily discriminatory – though some more than others – except for the partial dollar bloc (Frankel 1997: 127–8). The differences between the blocs have, however, been emphasized by Eichengreen and Irwin (1995, 1997). Sterling bloc countries traded disproportionately among themselves, and discrimination increased during the 1930s, while those remaining on the Gold Standard were more disparate. In as much as they erected barriers between themselves, this reduced trade discrimination.

There have thus been several earlier periods of regionalization, some of which were more intense than the present period. What is distinctive about the present situation, however, is the formation of larger formal *de jure* free trade area (FTA) blocs, and the extension of their *de facto* influence over a wider range of countries and areas. For the first time there are three almost continent-wide blocs (that is the EU, NAFTA, and Japan plus some of East Asia) either firmly established or in proto-existence.

As a preliminary conclusion, then, we can say that the international economy was in many ways more open in the pre-1914 period than at any time since, including from the late 1970s onwards. International trade and capital flows, both between the rapidly industrializing economies themselves and between these and their various colonial territories, were more important relative to GDP levels before the First World War than they probably are today. Add to this the issue of international migration just explored and we have an extraordinarily developed, open and integrated international economy at the beginning of this century. Thus the present position is by no means unprecedented. [...]

Openness and Integration: What is at Stake?

Returning to the broad issue of integration preliminarily discussed above, the actual measurement of the degree of integration in financial markets is difficult both theoretically and empirically. Economic analysis in this area tends to be driven by the idea of 'efficient (international) financial market' theory; that is, that capital markets operate competitively to allocate (international) savings and investment so as to equalize returns on capital. Thus key indicators of the degree of integration would be measures such as interest rates as between countries or the value of the same shares on domestic and international stock markets: the nearer these are to equality as between different national financial markets, the more integrated the international economy has become. With a fully integrated capital market there would be single international rates of interest on short-term and long-term loans, and a single share or bond price, other things remaining equal.

Of course, the key constraint here is the 'other things remaining equal' one. In reality they just do not, so the task of empirical analysis from within this dominant perspective is to account for, and then adjust for, these 'imperfections' so as to arrive at a proxy measure of the degree of 'true' integration. [. . .] As might be expected, all this requires some formidable assumptions to be made, ones that few other than the truly converted *cognoscenti* might either appreciate or accept. However, despite some scepticism about this underlying approach, it is worth considering its main results. [. . .]

The degree of international financial integration could be analysed in a number of forms and at a number of levels (Frankel 1992; Herring and Litan 1995; Harris 1995). These can be grouped under three overlapping headings: those associated with interest rate differentials; those associated with differential prices of securities; and those associated with real resource flows and capital mobility. We deal with each of these in turn, beginning with a discussion of the relationships between interest rates and exchange rates.

One of the most straightforward indicators of financial integration concerns offshore markets like that for Eurocurrencies. Formally, measures of offshore financial market integration can be established in terms of covered interest rate parities. This implies that depositors can receive the same return on whatever Eurocurrency they hold, taking into account the cost involved in protecting against possible exchange rate changes. Such interest rate parity seems to hold in the Eurocurrency markets. A more developed form of integration would be when offshore and onshore markets are closely linked, but it is here that difficulties begin to arise. Banking regulations and capital controls establish a separation between these two spheres, and these have often been introduced and maintained for public policy reasons. But with the progressive harmonization of banking regulations and the abandonment of capital controls this form of integration was effectively established between the advanced countries by 1993: thus covered interest rate parity between national rates has now also been more or less achieved.

Deeper forms of integration would be signalled by first uncovered interest rate parity and then real interest rate parity between deposits in different currencies. [. . .] While tests to measure the presence of these latter two forms of integration are complex and controversial, real interest rate parity seemed far from established by the mid-1990s, so that the level of international financial integration fell short of what would prevail in a truly integrated system. By contrast, the Gold Standard period was one where short-term interest rates were closely correlated, and there was a strong tendency for real rates of return to be equalized internationally (Turner 1991: 16–17).

The second broad approach is to focus on asset prices in different national financial systems. Here one problem is to distinguish domestic influences on prices from international ones, but there is a *prima facie* case that stock markets are closely linked, with disruption in one being quickly transmitted to others (so-called 'contagion'). In this context it is changes in the 'volatility' of price movements that would represent an indicator of increased globalization, not the existence of links as such, and the evidence on this score remains at best ambiguous (Harris 1995: 204–6). In fact, historically based studies have reinforced the impression of greater financial integration, measured in these terms, in the pre-First World War period. [...] Zevin [1992], in his survey of a wide range of the financial integration literature, reports on a number of measures supporting the highly integrated nature of the pre-First World War international economy. [...] The Gold Standard period was thus also the one displaying the most interdependent and integrated international economy in terms of security markets, the extent of which seems yet to have been repeated.

How did the international financial system adjust so rapidly when technological developments were so primitive? In fact, the idea that the contemporary era of communications technology is unprecedented again needs to be challenged. The coming of the electronic telegraph system after 1870 in effect established more or less instantaneous information communications between all the major international financial and business centres (Standage 1998). By the turn of the century a system of international communications had been established that linked parties together much in the way that the contemporary Internet does. Although the networks were not so developed in terms of individual subscribers, corporate and institutional linkages were dense and extensive. Compared to a reliance on the sailing ship (and even steam propulsion), the telegraph marked a real qualitative leap in communications technology, in many ways more important than the shift into computer technology and telematics after 1970.

A third important related approach in trying to identify the extent of financial integration involves measuring real resource flows: can increased financial integration be implied from increased capital mobility? In this case it is the relationship between national savings and investment that becomes the object of analysis. This approach has generated the most extensive literature, but its results remain controversial.

The more integrated the capital markets, the more mobile capital will become internationally and the more likely it is that domestic savings and investment will diverge. If there were a completely integrated global financial system, domestic investment would not be fundamentally constrained by domestic savings, and the correlation between savings and investment would be broken. Thus national economies will lose their ability to 'regulate' or 'determine' domestic investment. In fact, this is just another way of pointing to the key role of interest rate differentials as a measure of integration and as the determinant of investment. As openness increases, domestic savings become irrelevant to domestic investment since interest rates converge and savings and investment adjust accordingly.

But national savings–investment correlations have not unambiguously declined in the 1980s and 1990s, during the period of capital market liberalization and floating exchange rates. Careful analysis by Bosworth (1993: 98–102) and by Obstfeld (1993, e.g. p. 50) shows this not to be the case [...]. The persistence of the correlation between national savings and investment, first established in 1980 (Feldstein and Horioka 1980), well into a period of financial liberalization, deregulation and supposed global integration, testifies to the continued robust relative autonomy of financial systems, and this despite the (sometimes desperate) attempts by conventional economic analysts to prove otherwise (e.g. Bayoumi 1990).

[...]

So long as governments continue to target their current accounts, retain some sovereignty within their borders (so that at least the threat of government intervention in cross-border capital movements remains) and differentially regulate their financial systems, investors cannot think about domestic and foreign assets in the same way.

Different national financial systems are made up of different institutions and arrangements, with different conceptions of the future and assessments of past experience, and thus operate with different modalities of calculation. All these features factor into a continued diversity of expectations and outlooks which cannot all be reduced to a single global marketplace or logic. What is more, even the most committed of the integrationists who have looked at national savings–investment correlations tend to conclude that the less developed countries (LDCs) and most NICs remain largely out of the frame as far as this form of financial integration is concerned. Thus, even for the integration enthusiasts, there are limits to the extent of the 'globalization' of financial markets.[2]
[. . .]

The importance of this assessment of openness and integration is obvious. It has to do with the ability of distinct national economies to devise and regulate their own economic policies. The fact that the degree of constraint on national economies in the Gold Standard period seems to have been consistently greater than at any time since should not blind us to the problems and issues facing economies because of the level of integration at the present time. It is certainly the case that, on the basis of some of the measures discussed above, the level of economic integration has increased since 1960 – though this is not obvious on just the savings–investment measure, except perhaps for the most recent period. In addition, it would be difficult to accept that the qualitative dimension has been constant over the entire period since 1870. The number and range of financial instruments has changed dramatically since 1960, for instance, and with them new problems of management and regulation have arisen (Turner 1991; Cosh et al. 1992). Before we look at the internationalization of money and short-term capital markets, however, we need to look to the more mundane areas of financial integration to see whether the underlying framework for the operation of capital markets has radically changed in the recent period. Money markets are probably more highly integrated than are capital markets. But it is capital markets that most immediately affect the economic prospects for the long-term growth of national economies.

Recent Developments in International Financial Market Activity

These issues can be first approached by investigating the cross-border transactions and holdings of bonds and equities between countries and in various domestic financial institutions. As a percent of GDP the cross-border *transactions* in bonds and equities have escalated since the mid-1970s [. . .]. But if this is looked at from a slightly different angle, changes may not appear quite so dramatic.
[. . .]

What the figures [. . .] demonstrate, however, is the enormous variation between countries in terms of the importance of foreign holdings. Some financial systems are clearly much more 'open' than others on this measure. Of the G5 countries, the UK and Japan are much more 'open' than are the US, Germany and France.
[. . .]
[W]hat is clear is that there is no obvious convergence of all the advanced countries to a common openness position. By and large the differences between them seem to have been maintained, indicating continued variation in the characteristics and structures of their domestic financial systems. Thus, up to the mid-1990s at least,

the operation of 'globalization' did not seem to have forced the domestic financial institutions of the advanced countries to have fundamentally broken with the historical variation in their character, though there had been some increase in their overall internationalization.

[...]

Similar comments could be made about the operation of commercial banks. An increase in the importance of foreign assets and liabilities in their balance sheets is [...] mainly attributable to a growth between 1960 and 1980, since when the positions have tended to stabilize. [...] But there remains a great variation between [...] economies [...] largely based on entrenched historical differences.

The final point to make here is to look at the 'bottom line', as it were, of the internationalization of financial systems by assessing the importance of foreign assets ultimately owned by households as a proportion of their total financial assets. Thus we are still concentrating on the holdings only of financial assets, but looking at their importance in household wealth. The problem with the figures presented so far is that they do not cover the entire financial system. [...]

[...] A variation between countries similar to the patterns outlined above emerges, and with great diversity among them. But only two countries show a foreign proportion of over 15 per cent. Around 10 per cent and below is the norm. Broadly speaking, then, people's financial wealth still remains a domestic affair: it stays at home.

[...]

Short-term Lending

Broadly speaking, the period since the liberalization moves of the 1970s has seen an upsurge in international financial activity associated with three developments: increased extent of international lending, financial innovation and financial agglomeration. [...]

[...] In 1998 it was anticipated that total loans would be over US$2,000 billion – a 2,000-fold increase on the late 1970s position. A key development is the growth of 'securitization': the displacement of conventional loan business (traditionally conducted by banks) by the issue of marketable bonds and other securities. [...]

[...] Since most of these are derivative of the move towards security lending – they provide borrowers and lenders with the possibility of hedging against the risk of interest rate and exchange rate movements – they are collectively termed 'derivatives'. [...]

[...] By 1991 their worth was larger than that of exchange-traded instruments and was more than 50 per cent that of the total of foreign currency claims of all banks reporting to the Bank for International Settlements (BIS). They have shown spectacular growth during the 1990s. Such instruments are often traded 'off-balance sheet' – they earn a fee income rather than constituting part of a financial institution's asset or liability structure. These developments provide opportunities for intermediaries to engage in risk arbitrage in a lower-cost and less regulated environment, but they thereby raise important new problems of systemic exposure to risk. [...]

Financial innovation continues apace. The latest developments represent a resurgence of bond instruments with so-called 'dragon bonds' and 'global bonds'. 'Dragon bonds' are issued and traded simultaneously just on East Asian markets, while their 'global' counterparts are issued and traded in all major international financial centres on a round-the-clock basis. After the first global bond was marketed by the World Bank in 1989, this market expanded to over US$100 billion by mid-1994, capturing 8 per cent of total external bond issue in that year (OECD 1994: 57, table 1).

This latest development in bond markets testifies to the strength of the trend towards internationalization in the world's financial systems. But as mentioned above, the penetration of foreign assets into domestic institutional investment markets is still relatively light. The US, in particular, remains highly undiversified and autonomous on this score. In as much as global trading of securities and derivatives exists, it still tends to remain within a single region (North America, Europe or Asia-Pacific).

But again there is a trend in the government bond market towards further openness. The average foreign penetration of national government bond markets in advanced countries increased from 10 per cent in 1983 to 15 per cent in 1989 (Turner 1991); for the EU countries, it increased only from 19 per cent in 1987 to 26 per cent in 1993 (European Union 1997: 14, table 13).

The final issue to discuss in this subsection is the development of financial conglomerates. The international financial services industry is increasingly characterized by a small number of highly capitalized securities and banking houses which are global players with diversified activities. In part this is the result of the continuing trend towards predominantly institutional investment. 'Collective saving' is a strengthening feature of all OECD countries, so the institutions managing these funds could become key international players.

Broadly speaking, there is worldwide excess capacity in this industry, leading to intense competitive pressures to which cost-cutting and diversification are the strategic commercial responses. As a result, the financial conglomerates operate through very complex and often opaque corporate structures. Attempts at risk transfer between a shrinking number of players are legion, and even between the different components of the companies themselves. Thus contagion risk, market risk and systemic risk have all increased, presenting new and important regulatory problems for governments and international bodies [. . .].

An important point to note about the present era as compared with the Gold Standard period is that the recent growth of international lending has not just dramatically increased the range of financial instruments: it has changed the whole character of capital flows. As mentioned above, late nineteenth-century lending was mainly long term in nature, going to finance investment in real assets. Even that part of total flows consisting of investment in financial assets was mainly used to finance real investment. This is no longer so. The explosion of aggregate lending had until very recently been made up almost exclusively of financial assets. Only since the mid-1980s has substantial real investment reappeared with the growth of FDI [. . .].

[. . .]

Conclusion

We have striven to argue a number of points [here]. First, that the level of integration, interdependence, openness, or however one wishes to describe it, of national economies in the present era is not unprecedented. Indeed, the level of autonomy under the Gold Standard in the period up to the First World War was much lower for the advanced economies than it is today. This is not to minimize the level of integration now, or to ignore the problems of regulation and management it throws up, but merely to register a certain scepticism over whether we have entered a radically new phase in the internationalization of economic activity.

The second point has been to argue that governance mechanisms for the international economy have been in place over almost the entire twentieth century, in one form or another. This is just as much the case today as it was at the turn of the century. We may not like the particular mechanisms that are established now and how they work, but they are there all the same. The issue then becomes how to devise better or more appropriate ones.

Thirdly, we have argued that there are some new and different issues of economic interdependence in the present era which are particular to it. Our argument is not that things have remained unchanged: quite fundamental reorganizations are going on in the international economy to which an imaginative response is desperately needed. [...]

Finally, we have traced the trajectory of 'national economic autonomy' through the various regimes of governance operating over the twentieth century. This has shown that such autonomy has oscillated between periods of strong and then weak forces, and that it has operated with various degrees of effectiveness. Perhaps the overall trajectory of this assessment is to point to the impossibility of complete national economic autonomy as the twentieth century has progressed. The debacle of the floating rates regime of 1974–85 seems, if nothing else, to have confirmed the demise of this form of governance as a viable long-term objective in the present era. [...]

Notes

1   By the term 'autonomy' we mean the ability of the authorities in a national economy to determine their own economic policy and implement that policy. This is obviously a matter of degree. Autonomy is closely linked to 'openness', 'interdependence' and 'integration', three other categories used in this and subsequent chapters. Openness implies the degree to which national economies are subject to the actions of economic agents located outside their borders and the extent to which their own economic agents are orientated towards external economic activity. This is in turn linked to the degree of interdependence of the economic system in which these agents operate. Thus interdependence expresses the systemic links between all economic activity within a system or regime. Integration is the process by which interdependence is established.

2   Of course this emphasis on the relationship between domestic savings and domestic investment might seem to reinforce the neoclassical view of investment determination. The critique of this from an essentially post-Keynesian perspective is that the constraint on investment is not savings but the ability to raise finance for investment. In an advanced industrial economy with a developed financial system, credit creation is the key to investment; it is the access to 'liquidity' that determines economic activity, and this is endogenously created.

Formally we would agree with this analysis for mature advanced economies with a developed banking system operating efficiently in an essentially stable financial environment. However, we would emphasize that there are two exception to this image. The first is for those societies that remain less developed, that have an *underdeveloped* banking system in particular. The second is for those economies that have an *overdeveloped* financial system typified by speculation and instability. In both these cases, the 'normal' financing system for investment either just does not exist, or breaks down in the face of speculative pressures. In addition, we would argue that it is this second case that increasingly typifies the position faced in the advanced industrial countries. In both of these cases, however, we are thrown back on to a more 'primitive' conception of what determines investment, namely the brute fact of national savings.

References

Banuri, T. and Schor, J. B. (eds) (1992) *Financial Openness and National Autonomy*. Oxford: Clarendon Press.

Bayoumi, T. (1990) Saving–investment correlations: immobile capital, government policy or endogenous behaviour? *IMF Staff Papers* 37(2): 360–87.

Bosworth, B. P. (1993) *Saving and Investment in a Global Economy*. Washington DC: Brookings Institution.

Castles, S. and Miller, M. J. (1993) *The Age of Mass Migration*. Basingstoke: Macmillan.

Cosh, A. D., Hughes, A. and Singh, A. (1992) Openness, financial innovation, changing patterns of ownership, and the structure of financial markets. In Banuri and Schor 1992.

Dunning, J. H. (1993) *Multinational Enterprises and the Global Economy*. Wokingham: Addison-Wesley.

Eichengreen, B. and Irwin, D. A. (1995) Trade blocs, currency blocs and the reorientation of world trade in the 1930s. *Journal of International Economics* 38: 1–24.

Eichengreen, B. and Irwin, D. A. (1997) The role of history in bilateral trade flows. In J. A. Frankel (ed.), *The Regionalization of the World Economy*, Chicago: University of Chicago Press.

European Union (1997) Advancing financial integration. In *European Economy, Supplement A: Economic Trends* 12 (Dec.), EU, Brussels.

Feldstein, M. and Horioka, C. (1980) Domestic savings and international capital flows. *Economic Journal* 90 (June): 314–29.

Frankel, J. A. (1992) Measuring international capital mobility: a review. *American Economic Review* 82(2): 197–202.

Frankel, J. A. (1997) *Regional Trading Blocs in the World Economic System*. Washington DC: Institute for International Economics.

Grassman, S. (1980) Long-term trends in openness of national economies. *Oxford Economic Papers* 32(1): 123–33.

Harris, L. (1995) International financial markets and national transmission mechanisms. In J. Michie and J. Grieve Smith (eds), *Managing the Global Economy*, Oxford: Oxford University Press.

Herring, R. J. and Litan, R. E. (1995) *Financial Regulation in the Global Economy*. Washington DC: Brookings Institution.

Kitson, M. and Michie, J. (1995) Trade and growth: a historical perspective. In J. Michie and J. Grieve Smith (eds), *Managing the Global Economy*, Oxford: Oxford University Press.

Lewis, A. (1981) The rate of growth of world trade, 1830–1973. In S. Grassman and E. Lundberg (eds), *The World Economic Order: Past and Prospects*, Basingstoke: Macmillan.

Livi-Bacci, M. (1993) South–North migration: a comparative approach to North American and European experiences. In *The Changing Course of Migration*, Paris: OECD.

Maddison, A. (1987) Growth and slowdown in advanced capitalist economies: techniques of quantitative assessment. *Journal of Economic Literature* 25(2): 649–98.

Obstfeld, M. (1993) International capital mobility in the 1990s. NBER Working Paper 4534, National Bureau of Economic Research, Cambridge, Mass.

OECD (1992) *International Direct Investment: Policies and Trends in the 1980s*. Paris: OECD.

OECD (1994) *Financial Market Trends*. Paris: OECD.

Segal, A. (1993) *Atlas of International Migration*. London: Hans Zell.

Serow, W. J. et al. (eds) (1990) *Handbook on International Migration*. New York: Greenwood Press.

Standage, T. (1998) *The Victorian Internet: The Remarkable Story of the Telegraph and the Nineteenth Century Online Pioneers*. London: Weidenfeld and Nicolson.

Turner, P. (1991) Capital flows in the 1980s: a survey of major trends. *BIS Economic Papers*, no. 30, Bank for International Settlements, Geneva.

Zevin, R. (1992) Are world financial markets more open? If so, why and with what effects? In Banuri and Schor 1992.

25

Economic Activity in a Globalizing World

Jonathan Perraton, David Goldblatt, David Held and Anthony McGrew

Globalisation has been widely used to refer to recent sharp increases in levels of international activity, particularly, but not exclusively, international economic flows.[1] Using various definitions, authors have typically claimed either that it heralds the demise of the nation-state or that it amounts to nothing new. This article argues that conceptions of globalisation underlying current debates are inadequate and their analysis of empirical evidence consequently misleading. [...] We provide a basic conceptual apparatus and use this to analyse the evidence for globalisation in three key economic areas: trade, international finance and multinational production. We conclude with some general observations on the nature of contemporary economic globalisation and its implications for the power of nation-states.

Current Approaches

Our approach contrasts with both the 'hyper-globalisation' school and those sceptical of globalisation. For the hyper-globalisation school,[2] global markets are now perfectly integrated – even for non-tradable goods and services multinational corporations can enter domestic markets. With consumers able to buy products from around the globe and producers able to locate in or source from any site, the notion of a national economy becomes redundant. National controls have largely been rendered redundant by new technology and widespread evasion. Above all, finance, as the most mobile factor, typically flows rapidly and heavily away from countries pursuing policies unfavourable to global markets and to those pursuing 'market-friendly' policies, effectively determining national economic policy.

By contrast [...] sceptics argue that recent developments fall far short of globalisation.[3] In particular, they make four main claims:

1 Economic activity is significantly more nationally based than would be the case under a model globalised economy.
2 The growth of international flows represents internationalisation, namely, rising interactions between well defined national economies, rather than the emergence of global economic activity. National economic policy therefore at least potentially remains coherent and effective.

3   Current levels of global flows are comparable to, or lower than, those during the classical Gold Standard period (*c.*1870–1914) and, as such, the postwar growth in international transactions is little more than a return to the *status quo ante* after the disruption of the 1930s and the Second World War.
4   Much of the increased international activity reflects the emergence of distinct and increasingly self-contained regional groupings, a case of regionalisation rather than global economic activity.

These approaches both use similar conceptions of economic globalisation in terms of perfectly integrated international markets, the sceptics claiming to test the assertion of the hyper-globalisation school that such markets have emerged. This conception is severely limited as an analytical tool. Globalisation refers to a process, not an end-state, and it is therefore inadequate to start from a hypothetical conception of a fully globalised economy. Historical forms of globalisation – both as a general social phenomenon and in their specific forms – have multiple causes and, given the likelihood of multiple equilibria, are unlikely to have a single implied end-point. In particular, the conception of global markets is often conflated with perfect markets, so that, when international markets do not operate as [such] this is erroneously taken as evidence [for the sceptical case].
[. . .]
 Below we examine the claims of the hyper-globalisation school and the globalisation sceptics against recent empirical evidence [. . .]. We attempt to move beyond this debate by showing that the processes below operate at a global level and by distinguishing between them and their historical forms [. . .].

Empirical Evidence

[. . .]

International trade

International trade links national markets and production for goods and, increasingly, services. All countries trade, and almost all now trade significant proportions of their output as the postwar growth of trade has led to national markets for goods and services becoming increasingly enmeshed and to global ones emerging. For the hyper-globalisation school production and consumption in national economies have become separated as consumers can now buy from around the globe. With heightened competition increasingly based on technological advantage, countries can no longer rely on natural comparative advantage and have to generate continuous technological advances to maintain their trading position. The effect is to render national economies as firms in the global economy. For the [. . .] sceptics this wildly overstates the growth of trade. They claim that world trade relative to output has only recently returned to classical Gold Standard levels, that it is regionally biased and that its growth is restricted by rising protectionism. National economies thus remain important.
 An extensive trading system has developed since the Second World War. Nierop estimated the trading links between countries as a percentage of the maximum possible (every

country trading with every other one): for a constant sample of 68 countries, the figure rose from 64.4 per cent in 1950 to 95.3 per cent in 1990; the figure for a larger but non-constant sample was lower (66.2 per cent in 1990), but rising: the majority of countries trade with the majority of others.[4] Thus extensive trading networks have been created between continents. This interconnectedness was lower in earlier periods.[5] Although there are some regional patterns to trade, interregional trade has grown alongside intra-regional trade and indicators of the relative intensities of intraregional and interregional trade do not reveal a trend towards increasing regional concentration.[6] The EU and NAFTA do not generally operate aggressive trade policies, nor are they likely to gain by doing so, while Pacific Asian countries have not formed a comprehensive trading arrangement and are acutely aware of the importance of open markets for their own trade.

Falling transport costs and protectionist barriers have created open world markets for goods and services. [...] [T]ransport costs for goods fell at least until the 1970s, and telecommunications costs have fallen continuously since the 1930s, reducing the costs of trade and making a range of goods and especially services newly tradable and thus subject to international competition. Services trade has more than doubled in the past decade to over US$1 trillion annually, more than 20 per cent of total trade, and this is probably a significant underestimate.[7] The postwar period saw tariffs among developed countries reduced to negligible levels and, although non-tariff barriers may have risen in their level and coverage, they do not affect the majority of world trade.[8] Recent liberalisations among developing countries have increased the proportion of the world operating open trade policies from around a quarter by population in the 1970s to over half, a proportion that would rise still further with the inclusion of China.[9] Since the collapse of the Comecon system East European economies have liberalised their trade regimes and their trade–GDP ratios have now typically risen above 50 per cent, largely from trade with Western nations. These countries are now incorporated into global markets for traded goods and services.

The intensity of trade has increased as trade has risen faster than income so that the world export–GDP ratio has risen from below 10 per cent in the 1950s to 15–20 per cent today. There are marked country variations within this trend, notably the shift from virtually autarchic trade ratios to extensive participation by the USA and China. At first sight, the ratios at country and global levels seem little greater than during the classical Gold Standard: trade grew rapidly through the 'long nineteenth century' up to the First World War as tariffs and transport costs fell. Exports played a key role in industrialisation and the rising demand for raw materials brought various developing areas into the world trading system. Increased trade led to partial convergence in wages and profits, as predicted by trade theory.[10] Nevertheless, even on current price figures the 1913 world trade–GDP ratio had been overtaken by the 1980s, if not earlier.[11] Moreover, these figures tend to underestimate the relative growth of trade: traded goods prices typically rise more slowly than non-traded because producers of traded goods face greater competition and their methods of production often possess greater potential for technical progress. Measured in constant prices the classical Gold Standard ratios had been surpassed by the 1970s and ratios are now significantly higher [...] for advanced countries. Further, much of postwar GDP growth has been in non-tradable services, particularly public services: ratios of trade to private sector GDP (as a proxy for tradable GDP) had surpassed classical Gold Standard levels by the 1970s and are now typically around one-third for developed economies. [...] Although developing country participation in trade rose dramatically up to the First World War, this only incorporated some countries into world trade and the marked variations in the development of market relations within developing countries also often limited its intensity.[12] A global trading system emerged at the end of the 19th century, but it was less extensive than today and was often less enmeshed with national markets and production.

The dense network of trading relations that form the infrastructure of contemporary global markets for traded goods and services has been created by trading firms.[13] The institutional framework for classical Gold Standard trade emerged from bilateral trade treaties and a series of international agreements governing the conduct and standards of trade.[14] The legal infrastructure for the postwar growth of trade was provided by an extensive but low intensity legal framework, incorporating most countries into a global set of rules.[15] The GATT provided an effective skeletal framework for reducing tariffs on manufactured goods. During the Uruguay Round non-OECD countries for the first time played an active role in the negotiation of trading arrangements, as opposed to simply being subject to GATT rules, reflecting their increasing importance in global trade. The GATT framework was inadequate for dealing with issues raised by contemporary trade, notably trade in services and intellectual property rights, as this entails moving beyond the minimum common legislation necessary to permit trade in goods to questions of deeper legal harmonisation. Beside direct protectionist measures, differences in national legal systems affect competitive advantage in these new trade areas and are consequently a source of trade friction. The emergence of such issues in the Uruguay Round highlighted the GATT's inadequacies and has led to the establishment of a qualitatively new institution in the World Trade Organization.

Both the hyper-globalisation and sceptical approaches see the postwar expansion of trade as driven by falling protection and transport costs, but this misses how trade has grown through the emergence of global markets and the nature of its impact on national economies. [. . .] Trade has continued to grow relative to income and has continued to be concentrated between industrialised countries, in contrast to the classical Gold Standard era when exchange of products between developed and developing countries accounted for around half of total trade. Adapting recent theories of trade to explain this, intra-industry trade led to relative growth in industries with scale economies and technological dynamism, while rising income levels increased demand for variety so that demand for imported differentiated products rose, largely between industrialised countries.[16] Firms are increasingly able to divide the production process into different stages and locate them according to comparative advantage – 'slicing up the value chain'[17] – thus increasing trade in inputs and semi-finished manufactures. [. . .] [T]his has significantly increased the import content of manufactured goods in developed countries, except Japan. Intra-industry trade has both transformed national markets for manufactured goods into global ones and led to the development of interdependent production processes across countries. It has done so on the basis of competition in differentiated products, which face less than perfectly elastic demand. Global markets do not, therefore, imply that any price increase will eliminate sales.

The other major transformation in postwar trade has been the rapid growth of manufactured exports from a range of developing countries, which have risen from less than 5 per cent of world trade in these products in the mid-1960s to over 15 per cent today. The opening up of trade regimes in the exporting countries, together with reduced protection by developed countries, falls in transport costs and the acquisition of manufacturing capability by these countries through the global spread of technologies, has led to growth in exports, predominantly to OECD markets. Export growth through [...] incorporation into the world economy has been central to the development of these newly industrialising economies (NIEs). The growth of NIEs has led to increased differentiation between developing countries in terms of income levels, wages and the products they export, so that the richest NIEs have now reached income and wage levels comparable to poorer West European levels and it is no longer possible to consider developing countries as a homogeneous bloc in income or trading terms.

[...] Rather than indicating a blanket loss of competitiveness by industrialised countries to lower-wage economies elsewhere, this growth can be explained by trade theory. The opening up of trade has led to increased specialisation in production so that, as industrialised countries have lost markets for low-skill-intensive products, demand for their high-skill-intensive products has risen. This has led to major shifts in the distribution of world industry, with wholesale shifts of industry away from OECD countries. This in turn has led to large falls in, particularly, male manufacturing employment in OECD countries, increasing unemployment and/or falling real wages where a wage floor is not provided by unions or minimum wages. Conversely, wages for skilled workers have tended to rise and differentials to widen. The reverse trends can be seen in NIEs. With trade leading to demand for products operating at the global level, fortunes in national labour markets are increasingly determined at the global level with some convergence in wages for labour of similar skill levels.[18] The most advanced NIEs now compete with established industrial countries in a range of sectors, but no longer on the basis of low wages. Trade pressure implies structural adjustment in economies and the need to transfer resources, particularly labour, from declining to expanding industries, rather than a general loss of competitiveness requiring an overall fall in wages and conditions.

Trade has reached unprecedented levels relative to output, leading to global goods and services markets and the transformation of production and labour markets. Interregional trade has continued to grow with the dense network of trading relations between countries, so that global markets have emerged for tradable goods and services. Thus the [...] sceptics underestimate the quantitative and qualitative changes in global trade. Trade growth was driven not simply by falling barriers, but by the nature of the growth process in developed and developing countries. However, the vision of the hyper-globalisation school remains inaccurate: non-tradables remain a significant proportion of economies and because of intra-industry trade countries typically face less than perfectly elastic demand for their exports. [...] Recent changes do not provide theoretical or empirical grounds for rejecting the principle of comparative advantage: countries still cannot be competitive in everything or nothing and loss of competitiveness in any one product is not fatal to national economies. The rise of manufactured exports from NIEs points to the continued relevance of national comparative advantage, but also to the fragility of existing advantages. The costs of adjustment to shifting advantages can be considerable.

International finance

From negligible levels in the 1950s international finance grew rapidly, more rapidly than world trade or income. The total size of the international capital market is now around US$6 trillion in outstanding loans. Turnover in the foreign exchange markets has risen astronomically to over US$[1.5] trillion every day; already over 10 times trade levels in 1979, it is now over [60] times levels of world trade.[19] For the hyper-globalisation approach these are the ultimate perfect global markets – in particular, through continuous trading of currencies and government bonds, financial markets effectively dictate macroeconomic policy. The [...] sceptics argue that national capital markets remain predominant, as evidenced by low levels of net capital mobility. Compared to the classical Gold Standard, net capital mobility appears low and the room for national policy autonomy greater. Although they acknowledge that international financial markets can precipitate crises, sceptics argue that such crises would be inevitable because of policy inconsistencies, while variations in government spending, taxation and general macroeconomic policy point to a [...] range of national policy options.

The Bretton Woods system was designed for limited international financial flows: capital controls were instituted to enable national policy autonomy, while developing countries were expected to have little or no access to private financial markets. Private international finance developed in the 1960s primarily through the Eurocurrency markets as clients, often multinational corporations, sought to avoid national restrictions. Following the collapse of the Bretton Woods system, floating exchange rates led both to increased demand for instruments to hedge foreign exchange risk and to increased speculative demand. The recycling of 'petrodollars' through private international financial markets after the 1973 oil price rises sharply increased activity in these markets. As this activity rose, lending to a range of developing and Comecon countries brought them into the international financial system as borrowers – savers in developing countries were often able to deposit hard currency with international banks whatever the controls formally in place. Their access to these markets was sharply curtailed after the 1982 debt crisis, but has partially revived in the 1990s.

Although the extent of private international finance thus grew through the 1970s, the intensity of international finance varied. National financial markets remained partially insulated from the growing international financial system by national controls, although these became increasingly ineffective. As demand for international finance increased, global financial flows became more and more important in relation to economic activity [...]. [F]oreign assets and liabilities have risen from negligible to significant levels in the balance sheets of national commercial banks since the 1960s. This growth has been facilitated by the development of a range of instruments that have increased liquidity and the ability to raise funds: the growing reach and intensity of global finance were often closely linked as external liberalisation was accompanied or preceded by decisions to permit the trading of such instruments. OECD countries eliminated most or all capital controls in the 1980s. There has since been some liberalisation of [controls] among middle income countries, and recently too among some East European economies, under pressure from international agencies and in an attempt to attract private finance. As financial [markets] have developed within countries, this has acted to increase the impact of a country's international financial transactions on the national economy as a whole.

A key impact of domestic financial markets having become enmeshed with international ones is that interest rates are now largely determined globally, even for economies effectively unable to borrow on international markets. However, while rates are primarily determined globally, they have not converged between all countries. Among developed countries interest rates are converging when expressed in a common currency – differences between national rates being offset by movements in the relative exchange rate. Specifically, when currency can be sold forward any difference between rates is exactly offset by the difference between the current and forward exchange rate for the period the asset is held so that returns are equalised when expressed in a common currency (covered interest rate parity holds). Outside of this condition returns are not equalised, so that exchange rates do not exactly move to offset differences in interest rates (uncovered interest rate parity does not hold). This failure of exchange rates to move to offset differences in interest rates is the result both of variations over time in the premium over standard interest rates that the markets demand for holding assets denominated in particular currencies and of operational features of the foreign exchange markets.[20] [. . .] Over the longer term there is evidence of interest rate parity, including evidence of convergence of real interest rates among the leading economies, implying some convergence in the costs of capital.[21]

Although most developing countries retain capital controls, these have become increasingly ineffective at insulating their economies from international financial markets, as demonstrated by periodic episodes of capital flight. [. . .] Since debtors continue to repay past loans at interest rates determined in global markets and agents within them can move funds to international markets, developing countries remain part of global financial markets. Interest rates are now determined in global markets with differentials caused by irreducible uncertainty, market features and risk assessment, not lack of globalisation.

Beyond the trading of government assets, rising international issuing and trading of private bonds and equities points to the emergence of global capital markets. Although retail finance remains largely national and corporate finance is typically raised at the national or regional level, these markets are linked by financial flows that respond to differences in rates of return, and markets for more sophisticated financial instruments are often global. Although investors still tend to hold domestic bonds and equities, there were clear trends towards global diversification of their portfolios and convergence of returns in the 1980s and 1990s.[22] Against this [. . .] sceptics cite the close correlations between national savings and investment rates as evidence of the continued importance of national capital markets. On examination this proves little. National savings–investment correlations declined in the 1980s, with the emergence of significant balance of payments surpluses and deficits, and high correlations can arise even with perfect capital mobility if investment and savings are jointly determined by common factors or governments target the current account. Net capital flows are driven by differences in rates of return between countries and these are now low, in part because of past capital flows. Gross capital flows remain high, consistent with a high degree of enmeshment between national capital markets. Much of this activity has been speculative; thus a study of the variance of national current accounts since 1975 found gross flows to be excessive for four out of five major developed countries.[23] Improvements in technology and new instruments have made high levels of transactions possible, while the turbulence since the demise of Bretton Woods continues to present large, potentially profitable, opportunities for trading, often speculatively. Although national financial systems still differ [. . .] the fact that base interest rates are determined in global markets and larger firms are able to borrow and save on global markets means that their influence is limited. Thus the impact of global finance is to diminish sharply the influence of national financial markets on their economy's performance and consequently to reduce the ability of governments to direct national finance to their economic priorities.

The growth of multinational banks and other financial institutions enabled this growth of global finance, but has also posed major regulatory challenges for national authorities. A global system of regulation of international transactions has developed from cooperation among central banks and also between other financial authorities, with clear geographic demarcation of national responsibilities within an agreed multilateral framework.[24] The innovation of new instruments has made regulation significantly more difficult. Banks remain dependent on national central banks to act as crisis managers and lenders of last resort. Thus the 1982 Third World debt crisis saw national authorities – especially the US administration – effectively take over and manage a private financial crisis.

Contemporary global finance stands comparison with earlier periods. An international financial market can emerge in the absence of restrictions on trading once a communications infrastructure is established between national markets. Asset prices converged between the London and Amsterdam financial markets during the 18th century and a global financial market emerged towards the end of the 19th century with the laying of intercontinental telegraph cables;[25] this was institutionalised by the Gold Standard of international payments. Although for most of the pre-1914 period only advanced economies were on this Standard, its stability provided the basis for massive financial flows from surplus to some deficit countries to take advantage of the persistently higher returns there. These flows mainly took the form of bond finance to natural resource-rich developing countries. As such, it was concentrated on a small number of countries and many developing countries effectively remained outside the international financial system. Domestic financial institutions, particularly in the borrowing countries, were often not directly limited to this international finance. For some lending and borrowing countries net financial flows were higher relative to their national incomes than during any period since. Nevertheless, overall the classical Gold Standard was both less extensive and less intensive than contemporary global finance, and its impact varied widely between countries.

Contemporary financial globalisation has transformed the framework for national economic policy. Global market evaluations of national economic policy are reflected in risk premia on national interest rates and, in the case of developing countries, credit rationing. Standard economic analysis since Mundell–Fleming indicates that, in the absence of capital controls, countries can choose between fixing their exchange rate or pursuing an independent monetary policy. However, this is ceasing to be an accurate representation of the policy choices available to national authorities. Financial globalisation has rendered fixed exchange rate systems unsustainable over the longer term: a fixed exchange rate must be capable of acting as a disciplinary device, implying that rates will sometimes appear misaligned. This invites speculative attacks from agents with massive funds, thus raising the cost of maintaining parities to intolerable levels. The end result is devaluation and thus an expansion of the country's money supply, the opposite effect to the widespread belief that global financial markets maintain low inflation. The logic of this is that countries' choices are now limited to floating rates or monetary union.[26] However, globalisation has also weakened countries' abilities to pursue independent monetary policies with floating exchange rates. Market activity leads to exchange rates diverging from values consistent with either interest rate differentials or the relative costs of producing goods and services, so that exchange rates only partially reflect differentials in national money supplies and are no longer a reliable tool of monetary management. Financial innovations and global flows have weakened both national authorities' control over monetary aggregates and their ultimate relationship to the inflation rate. The nature of these markets may provide some room for manoeuvre: when speculative activity has driven exchange rates out of line with fundamentals, piecemeal intervention by governments can be effective, as analysis of G5 intervention between the 1985 Plaza Agreement and 1987 Louvre Accord suggests.[27] To this extent a piecemeal international regime has been constructed by the major economic powers which provides some control over international financial activity, but it is far more limited than under Bretton Woods.

The speculative nature of global financial markets fits neither the hyper-globalisation view that they dictate government policy according to simple criteria, nor the sceptics' view that their power is limited to precipitating inevitable crises. Markets' response to government policies depends on their assessment of the economic credibility of the government; as such, there is no set market response to particular policies. However, the short-term and speculative nature of these markets can lead to sudden and sharp re-evaluations of the sustainability of policies. In the past this has allowed countries to pursue unsustainable policies for years followed by rapid changes in assessment leading to speculative attacks on the currency, such as with the large inflows of capital and subsequent crisis in Mexico over the period 1991–94, and Britain's experience with the Exchange Rate Mechanism (ERM) between 1990 and 1992.

Rather than global financial markets imposing specific policies on national governments, they have significantly changed the costs associated with particular policies and instruments through their effects on interest rate risk premia and exchange rate movements; at times these costs may be so high as to make the policy prohibitively expensive. These costs vary over time and between countries according to their level of economic development and the political stance of their government. Developing countries may face credit rationing [. . .]. At the other end of the spectrum the richest states, particularly where their currency is used as an international reserve currency, can often pursue a range of policies with limited consequences, as with the US budget and trade deficits of the 1980s. Even here shifts in market sentiments can significantly change the costs of such policies. The political make-up of a government affects the opportunity cost of policies: governments of the left can pursue financially orthodox policies with paltry gains in terms of declining risk premia, while, conversely, governments of the right can sometimes pursue relatively loose policies without being penalised. This can partially be rationalised if markets believe that governments of the right implement positive supply-side measures, implying a looser appropriate macroeconomic stance, but that governments of the left do not, or do so less effectively.[28] Shifts in market opinion may then partly be traced to reassessments of supply-side developments. Governments pursue policy packages and markets impose opportunity costs on the package as a whole. During the 1980s governments of the right were often perceived by the markets to be pursuing effective supply-side policies and were able to pursue a loose fiscal policy with a tight monetary policy or vice versa (the USA and Britain respectively) with limited adverse consequences. Governments then do not face clear policy rules, but uncertainty over market reactions.

There is no simple way to compare the impact of contemporary financial globalisation on policy with the classical Gold Standard, partly because of the much more limited concept of national economic policy then. In principle, national economies were expected to adjust automatically to payments imbalances not covered by long-term borrowing as gold flows from deficit to surplus countries led to contraction in the former and expansion in the latter; in practice, adjustment was not automatic nor did it necessarily take this form, and thus a range of macroeconomic policies was pursued under the classical Gold Standard too.[29]

By starting from a conception of a perfect international capital market under which there would be few, if any, speculative flows, both the hyper-globalisation and sceptical views miss key features of contemporary financial globalisation and its differences from earlier episodes. Interest rates are now determined globally, and although national differences remain in other financial markets they are increasingly affected by global developments. Above all, the speculative nature of many of these flows does not merely severely limit government freedom for manoeuvre, but does so in a manner that is unpredictable.

Multinational corporations and foreign direct investment

Throughout the postwar period foreign direct investment rose rapidly as multinational corporations (MNCs) expanded across the globe. The FDI figures understate the growth of MNCs, since much of their growth is financed internally or from capital markets. Multinationals' turnover has grown faster than world income, except during the mid-1970s, and they now account for up to a third of world output and two-thirds of world trade, with around a quarter of world trade being between branches of the same company.[30] As major international borrowers and savers they have been central to the development of global finance.

For the hyper-globalisation school MNCs are global companies able to shift production around the globe easily in response to differences in conditions. Governments are forced into a 'beauty contest' of offering increasing incentives for MNCs to locate in their country. [. . .] [S]ceptics emphasise that even the largest MNCs often have the majority of their sales and assets in their home country, along with their core operations, and argue that they remain essentially national companies with international operations but subject to national controls.

MNCs have operated for centuries, although FDI was not significant in the world economy until the high foreign investment of the classical Gold Standard, of which around a third was FDI.[31] The interwar years saw both expansion and disruption, the postwar period almost continuous expansion. Initially, this expansion was driven by the growth of US firms abroad, but since the 1960s European and East Asian MNCs have expanded their overseas operations rapidly. As MNCs have developed, their managements have evolved a range of more complex strategies for managing international production.

Multinationals' activity is as extensive as trade or finance: the great majority of countries now have trading links with MNCs and some FDI. Developing countries have made strenuous efforts to attract foreign investment, while following economic liberalisation FDI in the emerging market economies has often accounted for a significant proportion of their national investment levels. The regional bias of FDI stocks and flows appears to be even less than for trade,[32] partly because some FDI has been undertaken to circumvent actual or potential protectionist barriers. For example, US, European and East Asian MNCs invested heavily in each others' regions during the 1980s, partly to ensure market access.

Multinationals' postwar expansion increased the intensity of their operations in national economies, at least in developed countries, both directly as they have expanded their share of output and indirectly through their linkages as purchasers and suppliers.

This conceals wide variations in levels of MNC production in national economies between countries and over time, and the balance between inflows and outflows of FDI.[33] For many developing countries the intensity of MNC production is unprecedented, but for some, classical Gold Standard levels have not since been exceeded. Like trade and finance, although MNC activity is world-wide it is concentrated in developed countries, a postwar process related to the decline of FDI in primary industries and the rise of FDI in manufacturing and services, services now accounting for half of all FDI stocks. Around three-quarters of FDI stocks are located in developed countries and the majority of FDI elsewhere is concentrated in the NIEs.[34] MNCs obviously produce where cost and demand conditions are appropriate and the unevenness of this affects the intensity of their activity [in] national economies.

[. . .] Increasingly, MNCs cannot rely solely on their domestic base for generating technological advantage and have responded by diversifying their innovatory capacity internationally.[35] Rising costs of innovation and the need to tap into overseas innovation networks have led to increasing numbers of joint ventures and strategic alliances between MNCs for the generation and diffusion of technology. Such developments are particularly common in industries with high levels of recurrent R&D expenditure.

Although the extent of overseas production varies between companies, the impact of MNCs producing and selling abroad has been to create global competition, in non-tradables as well as tradables. The degree of global competition varies between industries, but trade and multinational production have forced national firms across a range of industries to reach the world productivity frontier.[36] MNCs both created and were subject to global competition: they sought to take advantage of its opportunities, but they also faced its competitive pressures. This forced MNCs to take a global perspective. Many firms responded in the 1980s with substantial intercontinental FDI to establish and consolidate their bases in the major world markets, often using mergers and acquisitions to do so. MNCs are not homogeneous and vary in the strategies they adopt and their success. Broadly, multinationals' global strategies can be distinguished in terms of both the degree of geographical dispersion of their operations and the degree of international coordination of them.[37] [. . .]

Past studies have often defined globalisation as dispersed production with strong coordination so that MNCs are able to shift production easily within the firm in response to changing national conditions. But globalisation cannot be reduced to one strategy [. . .]. While individual MNCs vary in their capacity and strategy for shifting production, overall they have increased the responsiveness of output to changes in national conditions. The hyper-globalisation vision of MNCs shifting production virtually costlessly around the globe is misleading, if only because of the sunk costs of investment. More fundamentally, since overseas production is undertaken precisely because there are significant differences in production conditions between countries, small cost changes usually do not eliminate that advantage.

These global strategies increase the exit options of MNCs without necessarily making them footloose. This creates a hierarchy of countries and products in terms of the ease of shifting production, and therefore a hierarchy of national power relative to MNCs. With the predominance of higher value production few processes are highly footloose. Conversely, few production advantages are unique to one country or location, so that global competition and multinational production have increased the vulnerability of national production to changes in costs. Multinationals' ability to transfer technology abroad and the ability of foreign MNCs to tap into domestic innovation structures limit the effectiveness of national industry and technology strategies. Since technological advantage is necessarily temporary, these developments do not necessarily make such strategies ineffective; indeed, by attracting FDI it may enhance them. Nevertheless, multi-nationalisation appears to have led to a shift in industrial policy away from national industrial development strategies and towards an emphasis on offering inducements for inward FDI.

[. . .]

Conclusions

Economic globalisation has been interpreted here as both a rise in economic activity that is world-wide in scope and a growing intensification of economic flows and activities across societies and between people, a process of both growing extent and intensity. World trade has not simply become an unprecedented proportion of output, it has linked developing market relations within countries to growing global markets for goods and services as a greater proportion of these has become tradable. The development of financial institutions means that the determination of key variables in global markets has a direct impact on domestic asset values and financial conditions. MNCs have created structures of global competition and global production: individual companies vary in both their ability to operate on such a scale and the appropriateness of such a strategy for them, but the aggregate effect is to produce global competition and global organisation of production. The multilateral regulation of these flows is limited [. . .]. The structure of economic flows and access to economic resources has been hierarchical and uneven; however, rather than being fixed, there have been significant changes in the relative positions of specific countries within these structures.

We have argued here that the hyper-globalisation and sceptical approaches miss key aspects of these processes by focusing on an ideal-type model of a globalised economy. The hyper-globalisation school confuses globalisation with costless adjustment. Its vision of easy movement of activity around the globe abstracts from the key differences between countries that make international transactions profitable in the first place. Returning to the [. . .] sceptics' claims, the world does fall short of perfect globalised markets, but this misses the significance of global processes. Global economic activity is significantly greater relative to domestically-based economic activity than in previous historical periods and impinges directly or indirectly on a greater proportion of national economic activity than ever before. Rather than rising regional activity being contradictory to globalisation, as the sceptics claim, it appears to be part of a more general rise in international economic activity.

[. . .]

Sceptics are correct in noting that national economies retain boundaries and, insofar as tools of macroeconomic and microeconomic policy are ever effective, national policy does still operate. But this still radically understates the shift in structural power to global markets and firms. Some economic policy options now appear foreclosed, as many sceptics acknowledge, while, importantly for many states, the costs of pursuing many other options have changed sharply as a result of globalisation. These costs and possibilities, moreover, vary significantly between countries and over time.

State location in the global power hierarchy remains important. Yet even for the most powerful states the pursuit of 'autonomous' policy paradoxically sometimes requires the active cooperation of other national authorities, such as with supporting exchange rate parities. Power is a relative concept. Thus, although states, at least in advanced countries, have access to large resources and have increased many of their powers in the last 30 years, the power of some social actors has increased still further. The exit options of capital have increased strongly and global competition has emerged, marking state power over national production and finance correspondingly weaker. [. . .]

The late twentieth century has seen the emergence of global economic processes of an unprecedented scale becoming deeply enmeshed with national and local economic processes. The nature of these processes has radically changed the costs and benefits of particular economic activities and national economic strategies. Global economic forces may increasingly determine national fortunes, but not in accordance with existing theoretical accounts of globalisation. The task of political economy in an era of globalisation is to adapt existing theoretical tools to explain these developments and to suggest what policy tools may be effective for managing them.

Notes

1 This paper is based on work for the Globalization and the Advanced Industrial State Project at the Open University, funded by ESRC Research Grant R000233391.
2 Kenichi Ohmae, *The Borderless World* (Collins, 1990); and Robert Reich, *The Work of Nations* (Simon and Schuster, 1991).
3 Paul Hirst and Grahame Thompson, *Globalization in Question: The International Economy and the Possibilities of Governance* (Polity Press, 1996).
4 Tom Nierop, *Systems and Regions in Global Politics* (John Wiley, 1994), ch. 3.
5 Estimating the same variable for 54 territories, from League of Nations, *The Network of World Trade* (1942), gave 55.4 percent in 1928 and 53.5 percent for 1938. See also Douglas Irwin, 'Multilateral and bilateral trade liberalisation in the world trade system: an historical perspective', in J. de Melo and A. Panagariya (eds), *New Dimensions in Regional Integration* (Cambridge University Press, 1993).
6 K. Anderson and H. Norheim, 'Is world trade becoming more regionalized?', *Review of International Economics* 1(2) (1993): 91–109.
7 World Trade Organization, *International Trade Yearbook*.
8 Sam Laird and Alexander Yeats, *Quantitative Methods for Trade Barrier Analysis* (Macmillan, 1990), ch. 3.
9 J. Sachs and A. Warner, 'Economic reform and the process of global integration', *Brookings Papers on Economic Activity*, no. 1 (1995): 1–118. The figures were less than half to around two-thirds in terms of world GDP.
10 K. O'Rourke, A. Taylor and J. Williamson, 'Factor price convergence in the late nineteenth century', *International Economic Review* 37(3) (1996): 499–530.
11 See also Paul Krugman, 'Growing world trade: causes and consequences', *Brookings Papers on Economic Activity*, no. 1 (1995): 327–77.
12 Cynthia Morris and Irma Adelman, *Comparative Patterns of Economic Development, 1850–1914* (Johns Hopkins University Press, 1988), chs 3 and 6.
13 Jonathan Perraton, 'What are global markets? The significance of networks of trade', in Randall Germain (ed.), *Globalization and its Critics* (Macmillan, 1999).
14 Craig Murphy, *International Organization and Industrial Change: Global Governance since 1850* (Polity Press, 1994), chs 2–4.
15 Signatories to the GATT accounted for around two-thirds of the world's population and over 80 per cent of its GDP in 1990.
16 Elhanan Helpman and Paul Krugman, *Market Structure and Foreign Trade* (MIT Press, 1985); and L. Hunter and J. Markusen, 'Per-capita income as a determinant of trade', in R. Feenstra (ed.), *Empirical Methods for International Trade* (MIT Press, 1988).

17 Krugman, 'Growing world trade'.
18 Adrian Wood, *North–South Trade, Employment and Inequality: Changing Fortunes in a Skill-Driven World* (Oxford University Press, 1994); Wood, 'How trade hurt unskilled workers', *Journal of Economic Perspectives* 9(3) (1995): 59–80; and World Bank, *World Development Report 1995: Workers in an Integrating World* (Oxford University Press, 1995).
19 Bank for International Settlements, annual reports.
20 Richard Marston, *International Financial Integration: A Study of Interest Differentials between the Major Industrial Countries* (Cambridge University Press, 1995); and Jeffrey Frankel, *On Exchange Rates* (MIT Press, 1993), parts 3–4.
21 J. Gagnon and M. Unferth, 'Is there a world real interest rate?', *Journal of International Money and Finance* 14(6) (1995): 845–55.
22 Haluk Akdogan, *The Integration of International Capital Markets* (Edward Elgar, 1995); and S. Golub, 'International capital mobility: net versus gross stocks and flows', *Journal of International Money and Finance* 9(4) (1990): 424–39.
23 A. Ghosh, 'International capital mobility amongst the major industrialised countries: too little or too much?', *Economic Journal* 105 (1995): 107–28.
24 Tony Porter, *States, Markets and Regimes in Global Finance* (Macmillan, 1993); and Ethan Kapstein, *Governing the Global Economy* (Harvard University Press, 1994).
25 Robert Zevin, 'Are world financial markets more open? If so, why, and with what effects?', in T. Banuri and J. Schor (eds), *Financial Openness and National Autonomy* (Oxford University Press, 1992).
26 Cf. Barry Eichengreen, *International Monetary Arrangements for the 21st Century* (Brookings Institution, 1994).
27 Kathryn Dominguez and Jeffrey Frankel, *Does Foreign Exchange Intervention Work?* (Institute for International Economics, 1993); and Pietro Catte et al., 'Concerted interventions and the dollar', in Peter Kenen et al. (eds), *The International Monetary System* (Cambridge University Press, 1994).
28 M. Bleaney, 'Politics and the exchange rate', *Economic Notes* 22(3) (1993): 420–9.
29 Mica Panic, *European Monetary Union: Lessons from the Classical Gold Standard* (Macmillan, 1992).
30 UNCTAD, *World Investment Report 1994*.
31 John Dunning, 'Changes in the level and structure of international production: the last one hundred years', in Dunning, *Explaining International Production* (Unwin Hyman, 1988).
32 UNCTAD, *World Investment Report 1993*, pp. 169–70; and N. de Jong and R. Vos, 'Regional blocs or global markets? A world accounting approach to analyze trade and financial linkages', *Weltwirtschaftliches Archiv* 131(4) (1995): 748–73.
33 M. Wilkins, 'Comparative hosts', *Business History* 36(1) (1994): 17–50.
34 UNCTAD, *World Investment Report 1994*.
35 Robert Pearce and Satwinder Singh, *Globalizing Research and Development* (Macmillan, 1992).
36 M. Baily and H. Gersbach, 'Efficiency in manufacturing and the need for global competition', *Brookings Papers on Economic Activity*, Microeconomics Issue (1995): 307–58.
37 Winfried Ruigrok and Rob van Tulder, *The Logic of International Restructuring* (Routledge, 1995), ch. 8.

26

Global Markets and National Politics

Geoffrey Garrett

[...]

This article puts under the analytic microscope the proposition that global markets trump national politics as social forces. I focus on the relationships between three dimensions of integration into international markets – trade in goods and services, the multinationalization of production, and financial capital mobility – and the macroeconomic policy choices of the advanced industrial countries up until the mid-1990s.

One can certainly point to examples where globalization constraints on national policy choices are readily apparent. The mobility of financial capital, for example, has tended to put downward pressure on budget deficits because of the interest rate premiums the capital markets attach to them. But it is hard to make the case that globalization constraints are pervasive, or even the norm. Indeed, there are numerous instances in which various facets of market integration have been associated with both more interventionist government policies and greater divergence in national trajectories over a range of policy areas – without precipitating damaging capital flight in countries that have eschewed the neoliberal path.

Trade and government spending is the classic relationship that goes against simplistic conceptions of the lowest common denominator effects of market integration – not only in the Organization for Economic Cooperation and Development (OECD)[1] but also in the developing world.[2] Other globalization myths, however, should also be exposed. For example, increasing liquid capital mobility has been associated with faster growth in government spending and even with increases in effective rates of capital taxation – without resulting in capital flight or higher interest rates. Moreover, there is no evidence that the multinationalization of production has reduced macroeconomic policy autonomy.

There are two basic reasons why globalization constraints on policy choice are weaker than much contemporary rhetoric suggests. First, market integration has not only increased the exit options of producers and investors; it has also heightened feelings of economic insecurity among broader segments of society. This situation has strengthened political incentives for governments to use the policy instruments of the state to mitigate market dislocations by redistributing wealth and risk.

Second, although there are costs associated with interventionist government (the familiar refrain of neoclassical economics about tax distortions, crowding out, and regulatory rigidities), numerous government programs generate economic benefits that are attractive to mobile finance and production. Today it is not controversial to argue that good government entails protecting property rights and increasing human capital and physical infrastructure. But the logic should be extended further. Some economists have argued that reducing inequality stimulates growth by increasing social stability.[3] Prominent political scientists contend that economic policies redistributing wealth and risk also maintain popular support for the market.[4]

It should be a central objective of globalization research to see how these two sets of dynamics – capital's exit threats versus popular demands for redistribution, and the economic costs and benefits of interventionist government – play out in different contexts. In this article I point to two sources of variation. The first concerns differences among various facets of market integration and aspects of government policy choice (see the preceding examples). The second source of variation concerns domestic political conditions. Countries in which the balance of political power is tilted to the left continue to be more responsive to redistributive demands than those dominated by center-right parties. The existence of strong and centralized organizations of labor and business that coordinate economic activity reduces the economic costs of interventionist government by mitigating free-rider problems.

In summary, I do not believe that "collision course" is the correct metaphor to apply to the panoply of relationships between interventionist national economic policies and global markets. Peaceful coexistence is probably a better general image, as all agree it was during the golden age of capitalist democracy after World War II. One might go further to argue that, even in a world of capital mobility, there is still a virtuous circle between activist government and international openness. The government interventions emblematic of the modern welfare state provide buffers against the kinds of social and political backlashes that undermined openness in the first half of the twentieth century – protectionism, nationalism, and international conflict. At a time when Ethan Kapstein and others voice fears of the 1930s all over again [Kapstein 1996: 37], it is important that the economic benefits of government activism be better understood.
[...]

Globalization Constraints

Three globalization mechanisms

Market integration is thought to affect national policy autonomy through three basic mechanisms. These are trade competitiveness pressures, the multinationalization of production, and the integration of financial markets.

Increasing trade competition is the first component of the conventional globalization thesis. According to this view, big government is by definition uncompetitive.[5] Government spending crowds out private investment, is less efficient than market allocations, and cushions market disciplines on prices and wages. In turn, spending must be funded either by borrowing or by higher taxes. Taxes cut into firms' profits and depress entrepreneurial activity. Government borrowing increases interest rates. As a result of these effects, output and employment suffer from public sector expansion. Since no government can afford these consequences, trade competition must result in a rolling back of the public economy.

The second globalization mechanism concerns the multinationalization of production and the attendant credibility of firms' threats to move production from one country to another in search of higher rates of return. This was the "giant sucking sound" Ross Perot predicted the North American Free Trade Agreement would produce.

Multinational exit has also been at the forefront of European debates in the 1990s. Indeed, for some, software engineers telecommuting from Bangalore to Seattle and Silicon Valley are the harbingers of the New World of the twenty-first century.[6] Robert Reich, for example, proclaimed in influential articles in the *Harvard Business Review* that the distinction between "us" and "them" in the global economy is not between countries, but rather between a nation's citizens and multinational firms operating in it, irrespective of where they are owned.[7]

As with trade, conventional arguments about the policy consequences of the multinationalization of production focus on the costs to business of interventionist government. The difference is that firms with production facilities in more than one country can evade these costs by exiting the national economy. Governments must thus embrace the free market if they are to compete for the investment and jobs provided by multinational firms.

The final argument made about globalization constraints focuses on the international integration of financial markets. Traders operating twenty-four hours a day can move mind-boggling amounts of money around the globe more or less instantaneously in ceaseless efforts to arbitrage profits. The potential for massive capital flight acts as the ultimate discipline on governments. In an already infamous aside, Clinton political strategist James Carville is said to have uttered "I used to think that if there was reincarnation, I wanted to come back as the president or the pope. But now I want to be the bond market: you can intimidate everyone."[8]

Scholarly analyses of the domestic effects of the integration of financial markets often are almost as strident, replete with evocative images such as "casino capitalism,"[9] "quicksilver capital,"[10] and "who elected the bankers?"[11] The central logic underpinning this research program is the power conferred on financial capital by the credibility of its exit threats. Governments are held to ransom by the markets, the price is high, and punishment for noncompliance is swift.[12] If the policies and institutions of which the markets approve are not found in a country, money will hemorrhage until they are.
[...]

Reassessing the Policy Consequences of Globalization

Trade, compensation, and embedded liberalism

Arguments about the constraining effects of market integration on economic policy choice have a long and distinguished history. There is, however, a very different approach to the globalization–domestic politics relationship that also has an impressive pedigree. Karl Polanyi's analysis of the emergence of industrial democracy in the nineteenth century emphasized a "double movement" with two components.

> One component was the principle of economic liberalism, aiming at the establishment of a self-regulating market, relying on the support of the trading classes, and using largely laissez faire and free trade as its methods; the other was the principle of social protection, aiming at the conservation of man and nature as well as productive organization, relying on the varying support of those most immediately affected by the deleterious action of the market, and using instruments of intervention as its methods.[13]

Forty years later, John Gerard Ruggie made a similar argument about the post–World War II reconstruction of open markets and democratic politics.[14] He characterized the Bretton Woods system as sustaining an "embedded liberalism" compromise that coupled trade liberalization with domestic policies that cushioned market dislocations. At about the same time, Peter Katzenstein argued that the distinctive feature of the small European democracies was their willingness to adjust and adapt to international markets while compensating those adversely affected by this process.[15] Most recently, Dani Rodrik showed that the trade openness–domestic compensation nexus continues to hold throughout the world, not just in the industrial democracies.[16]

The embedded liberalism perspective did not question the core proposition of trade theory that liberalization, in the long run, is good for all segments of society. The distinctive feature of this scholarship was the recognition that the short-run political dynamics of exposure to trade (and to other international markets) are very different. Openness increases social dislocations and inequality and hence heightens political pressures for dampening these effects. If protectionism (and the disastrous spiral of economic decline, nationalism, and conflict with which it was associated in the 1930s) is to be averted, government must redistribute market allocations of wealth and risk.

Bretton Woods facilitated the twin goals of trade liberalization and domestic compensation by combining fixed exchange rates with capital controls.[17] Fixed rates promoted trade by stabilizing expectations about future price movements. Capital controls gave governments the macroeconomic autonomy to smooth business cycles through countercyclical demand management.

[...]

Strategies of domestic compensation in response to trade liberalization, however, were not limited to demand management. Rather, analysts describe the domestic policy regimes that emerged during the Bretton Woods era as the "Keynesian welfare state." In addition to the Keynesianism described earlier, the term also implied the public provision of social insurance (through pensions, unemployment benefits, and other income transfer programs) and social services (most notably education and health care), all paid for by relatively high and progressive systems of taxation.[18]

It is easy to see why the welfare state component served the political purposes of embedded liberalism. Social insurance directly supports those adversely affected by market risk. The public provision of social services not only provides benefits to consumers irrespective of their ability to pay but also generates a source of employment that is less vulnerable to the vicissitudes of market competition. Progressive taxes take into account the ability of different segments of society to pay for government programs. The welfare state redistributes wealth and risk, thereby dampening popular opposition to free markets.

But what about the economic effects of the welfare state (that is, assuming spending and taxation are in balance)? [...] The contending arguments mirror closed economy analyses from public finance, made all the more important by trade liberalization, which renders national economies price takers in international markets. Claims about the uncompetitiveness of the welfare state concentrate on the costs of government provision of social insurance and social services. The welfare state lessens market disciplines and crowds out private sector entrepreneurship; taxes distort investment decisions in ways that reduce efficiency.

On the other hand, many people argue that interventionist government generates numerous economic benefits that may at least offset these costs. The key notion here is the public provision of collective goods that are undersupplied by markets. Even economists in the Chicago school tradition consider some government services to be essential to capitalism: the rule of law and securing of property rights.[19] For new growth theorists, public education and the government provision of human capital and physical infrastructure are also important drivers of development.[20]

The logic of politically correctable market failures can, however, be applied more broadly. For example, it is well established in development economics that material inequality is bad for growth. Alberto Alesina and Roberto Perotti have argued that this is because inequality leads to social conflict, which stability-seeking investors do not like.[21] Since the welfare state mitigates conflict by reducing market-generated inequalities of risk and wealth, it may have beneficial rather than deleterious consequences for business.[22] Government spending may thus stimulate investment via two channels – increasing productivity through improvements in human and physical capital and increasing stability through maintaining support for market openness.

In summary, the embedded liberalism compromise of the Bretton Woods period combined an international regime of trade openness, fixed exchange rates, and capital controls with the domestic political economy of the Keynesian welfare state. The final observation that should be made about this combination is that many analysts believe that embedded liberalism was most prominent and worked best in countries characterized by strong and centralized (corporatist) labor movements and powerful social democratic parties. Center-left parties are more likely to be sensitive to the political demands of short-term market losers. Corporatist labor movements have incentives to tailor wage growth to benefit the economy as a whole and hence not to take advantage of government compensation (in the form either of Keynesian demand management or welfare state expansion) with demands for less work at higher pay.[23]

The crisis of embedded liberalism?

Notwithstanding the manifest successes of embedded liberalism in the Bretton Woods period, it is widely believed today that the open markets–domestic compensation compromise is no longer viable. The most prominent causal agent in its purported demise is heightened mobility of productive and financial capital and the decline of restrictions on international flows with which it has been associated.[24] No one suggests that political demands for compensation or the need for government to mitigate anti-international pressures have declined.[25] Rather, the conventional view is that the ability of government to deliver its side of the embedded liberalism compromise has been dramatically reduced.

There are two different mechanisms by which increased capital mobility is thought to render domestic compensation infeasible.[26] The first concerns financial market integration and traditional Keynesianism. Ruggie and others argue that financial integration makes fixed exchange rates imperative, to increase the markets' confidence about the stability of national economic policy.[27] But [. . .] fixing the exchange rate under capital mobility vitiates macroeconomic policy autonomy.

The second mechanism concerns the multinationalization of production and the nature of the public economy. Rodrik argues that governments can no longer maintain, let alone expand, the generous welfare state–progressive taxation mix.[28] Mobile firms are deemed unwilling to pay the taxes to fund government programs. Rodrik claims that the future of the welfare state can only be secured by shifting the tax burden from mobile (firms and financiers) to immobile (labor) asset holders, emasculating its redistributive effects.

Thus, two of the most perceptive students of the contemporary international political economy both accept the core proposition of the conventional wisdom on globalization. A quantum leap in the exit threats of mobile producers and investors has tilted the balance of power strongly in favor of the market over politics at the national level. The following two subsections question this argument by exploring in more detail the domestic effects of the multinationalization of production and financial market integration.

The multinationalization of production and the collective goods of government

Embedded liberalism, Bretton Woods style, comprised three elements – fixed exchange rates and capital controls, Keynesian demand management, and extensive government spending and redistributive taxation. How might we expect these to be affected by the multinationalization of production?

One could argue that multinationals favor fixed exchange rates because these lessen uncertainty about the consequences of internationally diversified production regimes.[29] If this were the case in a world of liquid capital mobility, governments that acceded to the demands of multinationals would also be giving up their monetary autonomy. But today there is arguably a better way than pressing for fixed exchange rates for multinational producers to insure against international price movements: hedging using financial instruments. The range of derivatives options available to investors is limited only by the imagination of market makers. And multinationals would probably prefer to control their own risk portfolios than to cede this right to governments. This is all the more likely given the difficulty of running stable pegged exchange rates in the contemporary era (see the next subsection). As a result, it seems unlikely that the multinationalization of production should significantly increase the incentives for governments to fix their exchange rates and hence tie their hands with respect to monetary policy.

The primary concern of the globalization literature with respect to the multinationalization of production, however, is the reaction of mobile producers to high levels of government spending and taxation (and to other production costs, most notably wages). The conventional view is that the decisional calculus of multinationals is simple: produce in the lowest cost location. If this were correct, increased exit options for firms would put considerable downward pressures on the size and scope of the public economy.

For those who study FDI decisions and corporate alliance strategies for a living, however, the behavior of multinational producers is more complex. First, the right metric of costs controls for productivity, and on this score small government–low-wage economies do not look nearly so attractive.[30] Second, the literature on international corporate strategy focuses primarily on accessing new technology, new distribution channels, and new markets as the drivers of FDI and strategic alliances.[31] Third, if a firm opens, acquires, or allies with a production facility in a foreign country, this does not necessarily imply that it reduces activity in its home country. Under many circumstances new foreign activities will go hand in hand with increased activity and employment at home – "upstream" – in portions of the productive, marketing, and distributive processes where more of the final value is added. Finally, international diversification provides another way for firms to hedge against currency risk. Taken together, these considerations belie the notion of a lowest cost mantra in the location decisions of multinational producers.[32]

Why might multinationalized producers be willing to locate in countries with large public economies and high taxes? My answer is the same as that for trade. Multinational producers care about the real economy, and factors such as productivity and stability heavily influence their investment decisions. Activist governments can do something positive to influence these decisions, by increasing human and physical capital stocks and by promoting public support for open markets. Indeed, these collective goods may be even more important than was the case for trade as a result of the heightened feelings of economic insecurity among citizens generated by multinationalization.

There is an important objection to my argument, however, that was not germane to the trade discussion – tax competition among governments for mobile producers. Rodrik rightly argues that even if multinational producers benefit from government interventionism in the ways I have suggested, they nonetheless have incentives to try to free ride on these collective goods by not paying the taxes to fund them.[33] Multinationals can use threats of exit to force governments to shift the tax burden away from capital and onto labor. But before making such threats, firms must weight the costs and benefits of helping finance the provision of collective goods from which they benefit in one country versus paying lower taxes but receiving fewer benefits in another.[34] It is an empirical, not a theoretical, matter whether the costs of big government outweigh the benefits I have outlined and hence whether multinationalization should put downward pressures on capital taxation.

In summary, there is little reason to expect that the multinationalization of production produces strong pressures for fixed exchange rates or constrains macroeconomic policy autonomy in the classical Keynesian sense. A better argument can be made about constraints on the spending, and particularly the taxing, policies of governments. But these constraints will be much less apparent if, as I argue in this case, large public economies generate numerous outcomes that are attractive to multinationals.

The mobility of financial capital, exchange rate regimes, and fiscal policy

Even if I am right to question common assumptions about the behavior of multinationalized producers, the debate could simply shift to policy constraints generated by the integration of financial markets. Here again, I wish to argue that the strictures imposed by global capital are not nearly so tight as is often presumed. Unpacking the likely policy effects of the international integration of financial markets should begin with its implications for the choice of exchange-rate regimes.

There is only one clear case where financial integration vitiates macroeconomic policy autonomy – monetary policy where there are no barriers to cross-border capital movements and where a country's exchange rate is fixed.[35] But this only raises the questions: Why do countries choose to fix their exchange rates? How important is globalization to this choice?[36] European Union officials in the context of the monetary union debate have revived old arguments from Bretton Woods about the importance of currency stability to trade.[37] Empirical work, however, fails to show any strong positive impact of fixed rates on trade expansion, presumably because of the effectiveness of currency-hedging instruments under floating rate regimes.[38] The more common argument these days concerns the policy credibility of governments with the financial markets. By fixing the exchange rate, governments are supposed to be able to mitigate the damaging effects of capital flight or other policies that would be required to stop it.

Unlike exporters and multinational producers, financial market actors care much less about productivity and the real economy than they do about monetary phenomena that affect day-to-day returns on financial transactions. Inflation is the key variable. If the markets expect inflation to increase in the future, the price they are willing to pay for a national currency will decrease, and the interest rates they charge on loans will be higher. Thus, governments have incentives to establish reputations for price stability because inflationary expectations lead the financial markets to behave in ways that harm the real economy.

Few economists dispute the argument that inflation-fighting credibility is important to macroeconomic performance.[39] There is much less support, however, for the notion that fixing the exchange rate is a good way to achieve credibility under conditions of financial integration. The evidence is at best mixed as to whether participation in fixed exchange-rate regimes lowers inflation rates.[40] There may be better domestic ways to gain credibility with the financial markets, such as making the central bank more independent or enacting balanced budget laws.[41] Moreover, one should expect financial market actors to prefer floating exchange rates to fixed ones since they make money from arbitrage and commissions.[42]

On the other side of the equation, the costs of fixed exchange rates are often high. Although fiscal policy may be quite effective in a country that pegs its exchange rate, it cannot use monetary policy to adjust to any economic shock that affects it differently from the object of the peg (gold, a single currency, or a basket of currencies). Depreciating the nominal value of a currency remains a very effective way to increase the real competitiveness of an economy in recession – because domestic prices do not rise immediately in response to nominal depreciations.[43] But smooth depreciations are not possible for countries seeking to defend currency pegs. Rather, governments typically engage in desperate efforts to maintain a given exchange rate and are often vanquished by the markets in damaging waves of speculative attacks. In this context it should be noted that the headline currency crises of the 1990s – in Europe, Mexico, and East Asia – all involved countries seeking to sustain pegs that the markets deemed untenable.

For these reasons many economists today recommend that fixed exchange-rate regimes under conditions of financial integration should only extend to countries that constitute optimal currency areas. These areas comprise only those countries for whom there is little need to maintain domestic monetary autonomy – because their business cycles move together, wages adjust quickly to asymmetric shocks, labor is mobile across national borders, or fiscal arrangements transfer funds from boom to bust regions.

In the headline case of European monetary union, for example, most analysts believe that Europe's optimal currency area extends only to Austria, the Benelux countries, Germany, and perhaps France – but certainly not to Italy.[44] [...]

In summary, the arguments in favor of the common globalization proposition that the integration of financial markets creates irresistible pressures for government to fix their exchange rates to increase market credibility are far from convincing. Fixed exchange rates may make sense for some highly interdependent economies. Countries that cannot gain market credibility with domestic policies (for example, some unstable developing nations) may have little choice but to fix their exchange rates. But for many countries, and probably the bulk of the OECD, floating the exchange rate makes more sense under conditions of financial capital mobility.

Moving to fiscal policy, increasing public sector deficits clearly puts upward pressure on interest rates in a world of capital mobility (particularly if the exchange rate floats). But how large is this interest-rate premium? Financial integration reduces the costs of fiscal expansion by making available an immense size of potential lenders.[45] At some point, of course, higher debt burdens may trigger fears of governments' defaulting on their loans – resulting in dramatic reductions in the availability of credit and skyrocketing interest rates. This was the case during the Latin American debt crises of the 1980s, but this limit seems not yet to have been reached in any industrial democracy.[46]

Belgium is the clearest instance of the weakness of fiscal constraints under capital mobility. The Belgian franc has long been stably pegged against the deutsche mark, with very small interest-rate differentials between the two countries. This is despite the fact that Belgian public debt has been the highest in the OECD for most of the last decade, and more than twice as large as Germany's. To take a harder European case, public debt is also very high in Italy. Italian interest rates have sometimes during the past twenty years been as much as three or four points higher than German rates. But if this is the most brutal fiscal repression wrought by global finance among the industrial countries, the proclamations of many commentators would seem somewhat hyperbolic.

I have now discussed two conventional parts of macroeconomic policy – exchange-rate regime choice and the running of fiscal deficits – in the context of global finance. What about constraints on the size of government itself? Here a distinction should be drawn between the preferences of financial markets actors and those of multinationalized producers. The latter can and should pay predominant attention to the effect of government policy on productivity and real aggregates – and hence ask whether the costs of big government outweigh the benefits (as discussed in the previous subsection). Financial market participants, in contrast, focus almost exclusively on the effect of government policy on the supply of and demand for money.

The financial markets must ask a simple question: will a government raise new taxes to pay for higher spending, or will it seek to borrow money? If the answer is "tax," one should expect the markets to be relatively unconcerned – even if some of these revenues are raised by capital taxation. But if the answer is "borrow," the markets know that the government will have an incentive to inflate in the future to try to reduce the real cost of their debt. Higher interest rates must be charged if bond yields are to be maintained, the currency must depreciate if real exchange rates are to remain stable. Thus, the financial markets care much less about the size and scope of government interventions than about how they are paid for.

[. . .]

Macroeconomic Policy

In this section I examine the relationships between market integration and macroeconomic policy. I concentrate on three policy indicators: total government spending, public sector deficits, and capital taxation. Spending is a simple summary indicator of government involvement in the economy. Deficits measure overall budgetary stances.

Capital taxation is the single part of tax systems that many believe to be most vulnerable to globalization constraints.[47]

Over-time trends

[. . .] Average [OECD] government spending basically doubled as a portion of GDP from 1960 to the mid-1990s, when it comprised over half of total output. As might be expected, spending increased most during the deep recessions of the mid-1970s, early 1980s, and early 1990s. But the size of the public economy only decreased as a portion of GDP during one upturn in the business cycle – the mid-1980s. Given that this is the period on which many influential analyses of globalization constraints are based, this may explain the prominence of assertions about public sector rollback. Nonetheless, the history of government spending in the postwar OECD is predominantly one of sustained growth.

The expansion of the public economy has not been wholly matched by increased taxes. Budget deficits increased by about seven points from 1960 to 1994. It is often assumed that this revenue shortfall reflects the declining ability of governments to tax increasingly mobile capital. Changes in marginal rates of corporate income taxation are consistent with this view – they have declined considerably in most OECD countries in the past fifteen years.[48] But from the perspective of revenue-hungry governments, these marginal rates are not the whole story. Governments certainly have incentives to reduce taxes that impede growth-creating investment, of which marginal corporate tax rates are a clear example. But most cuts in marginal rates in the OECD have been accompanied by other reforms that have increased the tax base – reductions in investment incentives, depreciation allowances, and other loopholes that pertain to capital taxation.[49]

[. . .] [T]he overall trend in effective rates of capital taxation has been upward, quite strongly so. Rates in the early 1990s averaged almost 40 percent, up from around 30 percent in the early 1970s. This is a long way from predictions of a free fall in capital taxation resulting from the exit threats of multinational firms and financial speculators.

In summary, the trends [. . .] are hard to square with the notion of pervasive globalization constraints on national economic policy autonomy. Does one get a different picture by examining economic policy data on a country-by-country basis?

Variations across countries and market segments

In this subsection I explore cross-national variations in economic policy and their relationships with globalization. Three indicators of market integration are used – total trade (a simple proxy for competitiveness pressures),[50] FDI flows (for the multinationalization of production),[51] and the financial openness index and covered interest-rate differentials (the integration of financial markets). These relationships are also compared with the associations between economic policy and a simple partisan politics variable (the combined power of left-wing parties and organized labor movements) that historically has had a marked impact on economic policy choice.
[. . .]
The coefficient of variation for total government spending since 1985 is quite small. One could debate whether OECD public economies have become "about the same size."

After all, Switzerland's public economy is still only half the size of Sweden's. What is more interesting, however, is that national trajectories diverged considerably from historical averages (1960–84) to the post-1985 period. Taking the extreme cases, spending grew six times as much in Spain as in the United Kingdom. This divergence is precisely the opposite of the conventional wisdom about the effects of globalized markets.

The deficits data are even less supportive of the conventional view. There was considerable dispersion in budgetary stances in the post-1985 period as well as in terms of changes from historical averages. Some of the cross-national differences are dramatic. Switzerland ran surpluses of over 2 percent of GDP after the 1985 period, whereas deficits in neighboring Italy were over 10 percent. Deficits in Greece increased by more than six points from the pre- to post-1985 periods, but they declined by almost two points in Japan.

Perhaps most surprisingly of all, the capital tax coefficients of variation do not look much different from the spending and deficits numbers. In the post-1985 period, considerable dispersion in capital tax rates remained. But the divergence from pre- to post-1985 rates of capital taxation was even more marked. Capital tax rates declined by 2.7 points in the United States, but they increased by more than 10 points in Finland, Japan, and Sweden.

These descriptive data can only support one conclusion: fiscal policies among the OECD countries have not converged in recent years. Is there any more evidence of globalization constraints when one breaks market integration down into its components?

[. . .]

On the one hand, and consistent with my arguments, exposure to trade, FDI flows, and left-labor power were all associated with greater spending after 1985. On the other hand, the covered interest rate–spending correlation implies a constraining effect of capital mobility on the public economy. One way to reconcile these findings would be to endogenize capital mobility, hypothesizing that strong left-labor regimes have chosen to protect their public economies by retaining significant controls on the mobility of capital.[52] This may have been the case in the past, but the correlation between the power of the left and the strength of trade unions and capital mobility all but evaporated by the latter half of the 1980s.[53]

An alternate explanation is that countries have reacted in very different ways to increasing capital mobility, based on the balance of partisan power within their borders. I have presented elsewhere more sophisticated analyses – using panel regressions with multiplicative interactions between globalization and partisan politics – that support this view.[54] Strong left-labor regimes responded to financial market integration with ever-higher levels of public spending, whereas governments in countries with much weaker left parties and trade unions cut back the public economy.

Now consider the correlations for public sector deficits after 1985. Contra standard assumptions about left-labor power, deficits historically have been smaller in strong left-labor regimes than elsewhere.[55] Nonetheless, one should expect globalization – especially financial market integration – to have put downward pressures on deficits. The bivariate correlations do not strongly support this expectation. Financial openness and total trade were somewhat correlated with smaller deficits. But this was not the case for FDI or interest-rate differentials.

Finally and perhaps most surprisingly, the capital tax correlations for the post-1985 period were no more supportive of globalization conventional wisdom. Lower tax rates were correlated with greater exposure to trade, financial openness, and covered interest-rate differentials, but none of these associations was at all strong. In contrast, FDI flows were weakly associated with higher capital taxes. Finally, the association between left-labor power and capital tax rates was positive and larger than any of the globalization–taxation correlations were.

No great weight can be attached to these simple bivariate correlations. But even the most sophisticated existing research on taxation and globalization does not strongly support a race-to-the-bottom interpretation. Rodrik finds that capital mobility constrains capital taxation but only in countries with high levels of trade dependence and trade volatility.[56] Quinn and Swank report little or no relationship between capital mobility and corporate taxation.[57] Garrett argues that the effects of globalization on capital taxes, as was the case for spending, are contingent on the partisan balance of power.[58] Hallerberg and Basinger demonstrate that the number of veto players, not capital mobility, best explains changes in marginal corporate tax rates in the latter 1980s.[59]

Let us now turn to correlations based on changes in economic policy pre- and post-1985 [. . .]. These data are no more indicative of a policy race to the bottom. Both measures of financial integration were quite strongly associated with faster increases in government spending (as was left-labor power). The financial integration–deficit correlations were much weaker and of contradictory signs.

Consistent with the over-time analysis, the bivariate correlations presented in this subsection belie common notions about strong and pervasive globalization constraints on national autonomy. These analyses are certainly not definitive, but they should prompt further research into what are undoubtedly complicated relationships between globalization and policy choice.

Capital Flight

If the OECD countries have not converged around a less interventionist macroeconomic policy regime in recent years, have countries with larger public economies or bigger budget deficits suffered from debilitating capital flight? If the answer is "yes," one might reasonably suspect that globalization-induced convergence would soon become the norm. If not, continuing cross-national variations in policy regimes would seem more likely. This section examines the policy–capital flight relationship with respect to multinational exit, interest rate premiums, and currency depreciation.

[. . .] Larger public sector deficits were associated with smaller, not larger, net outflows of FDI – reflecting the need for domestic debt to be funded by infusions of foreign capital. These correlations should give pause to purveyors of conventional globalization parables, for whom the loss of multinational investment as a result of interventionist government is a central theme.

Things were different, however, with respect to the behavior of the financial markets, measured by the long-term interest rates charged on government debt and the strength of currencies in foreign exchange markets. There was a clear correlation between a country's budgetary stance and the reaction of the financial markets. Bigger deficits were associated with higher interest rates and with greater depreciations against the dollar. Furthermore, interest rates were higher in countries with larger public economies, and depreciations were associated with higher rates of capital taxation. [. . .]

In summary, there is some evidence supporting the view that governments that have persisted with activist fiscal stances in recent years have paid a price in global capital markets. The causal pathways between fiscal policy and the propensity for capital flight, however, are quite diffuse. It is possible, of course, that the absence of globalization constraints on government spending and taxation only shows that financial markets are not yet sufficiently integrated for these effects to be apparent. There may be a threshold – not yet reached in the OECD – beyond which the policy race to the bottom will ensue. One preliminary way to test this argument is to examine the political economy of fiscally decentralized countries, where there are effectively no barriers to movement across state lines. The United States is a good example.

[. . .] The relevant comparison with respect to the OECD is not overall tax rates (given the size of the federal government in the United States), but rather the dispersion of tax rates. The coefficient of variation for state taxes is .32. This is higher than the comparable OECD-wide coefficients for both capital taxation and government spending [. . .]. The complete integration of the US market has not resulted in convergence of tax rates around a minimal mean. Nor is it the case that the low-tax states are the best macroeconomic performers – Louisiana, North Dakota, and Wyoming are quite poor. Texas and Alaska can afford low taxes because of their wealth of natural resources. The data should give pause to those who believe that it is only a matter of time before market pressures force fiscal convergence on the OECD.

Governing in the Global Economy

In this article I have sought to paint in broad brush strokes the relationship between the globalization of markets and national autonomy in the OECD. I have made two basic points. First, there are strong parallels between recent arguments about the constraining effects of globalization on national autonomy and those all the way back to the eighteenth century about the domestic effects of market integration. With hindsight, we know that past predictions of the effective demise of the nation-state were unfounded. Are there signs that things will be different in the contemporary epoch?

My second point is that, up until the mid-1990s, globalization has not prompted a pervasive policy race to the neoliberal bottom among the OECD countries, nor have governments that have persisted with interventionist policies invariably been hamstrung by damaging capital flight. Governments wishing to expand the public economy for political reasons may do so (including increasing taxes on capital to pay for new spending) without adversely affecting their trade competitiveness or prompting multinational producers to exit. The reason is that governments provide economically important collective goods – ranging from the accumulation of human and physical capital, to social stability under conditions of high market uncertainty, to popular support for the market economy itself – that are undersupplied by markets and valued by actors who are interested in productivity. This is particularly the case in corporatist political economies where the potential costs of interventionist government are mitigated by coordination among business, government, and labor.

This is not to say, however, that no facet of globalization significantly constrains national policy options. In particular, the integration of financial markets is more constraining than either trade or the multinationalization of production. But even here, one must be very careful to differentiate among various potential causal mechanisms.

Talk of lost monetary autonomy only makes sense if one believes that the integration of financial markets forces governments to peg their exchange rates to external anchors of stability. On recent evidence, the credibility gains of doing so are far from overwhelming; indeed, noncredible pegs (that is, those not consistent with other political and economic conditions) have promoted the most debilitating cases of financial speculation and instability. On the other hand, the costs of giving up the exchange rate as a tool of economic adjustment are great, and economies that allow their currencies to float freely seem to benefit as a result. Governments simply should not feel any compunction to give up monetary autonomy in the era of global financial markets.

But even if countries float their exchange rates, the financial markets – fearing inflation – do impose interest-rate premiums on governments that persistently run large budget deficits. Some governments have been willing to pay this price in the name of other objectives. Others have sought domestic solutions to credibility problems in the markets, such as central banking reforms. Still others (especially in the developing world) apparently have been unable to attain reputations for fiscal responsibility. For these countries, fixing the exchange rate may be the only option, but there can be no guarantee that this will not just fuel even more financial speculation.

Finally, there is no evidence that the financial markets attach interest-rate premiums to the expansion of the public economy per se – that is, provided new tax revenues balance increased spending. This is even true if the taxation of capital is one source of new revenues. Moreover, the empirical connections between expansion of the public economy and deficits are quite weak and heavily mediated by domestic political conditions. Strong left-labor regimes, for example, have historically been able to increase government spending without incurring large debts. The financial markets are essentially disinterested in the size and scope of government. Their primary concern is whether the government balances its books.

My analysis is thus considerably more bullish about the future of the embedded liberalism compromise than some of its earlier advocates suggest. As a result, I do not believe that supporters of interventionist government must call for a dose of protectionism or the reimposition of capital controls to maintain the domestic balance between equity and efficiency. Nor must advocates look to international cooperation and institutions as the only attractive option for the future. As has been the case for more than two hundred years, the coupling of openness with domestic compensation remains a robust and desirable solution to the problem of reaping the efficiency benefits of capitalism while mitigating its costs in terms of social dislocations and inequality.

Notes

1   Cameron 1978.
2   Rodrik 1997.
3   Alesina and Perotti 1996.
4   See Katzenstein 1985; Przeworski and Wallerstein 1982; and Ruggie 1983.
5   See C. Pierson 1991; and Pfaller et al. 1991.
6   Greider 1997.
7   Reich 1990 and 1991.
8   "A Survey of the World Economy: Who's in the Driving Seat?" *The Economist*, Oct. 7, 1995, p. 3.
9   Strange 1986.
10 McKenzie and Lee 1991.
11 Pauly 1997.

12   For review article, see Cohen 1996.
13   Polanyi [1944] 1957: 132.
14   Ruggie 1983.
15   Katzenstein 1985.
16   Rodrik 1997.
17   The Bretton Woods system also allowed for consensually agreed adjustments in exchange-rate parities to correct fundamental disequilibrium in the balance of payments and IMF lending to support exchange rates during temporary crises. For an excellent analytic history of Bretton Woods, see Eichengreen 1996.
18   The seminal study is Shonfield 1965. Other important examples include Esping-Andersen 1985; Goldthorpe 1984; and Lindberg and Maier 1985.
19   [. . .] It has also become a central component of official development policy; World Bank 1997.
20   See Aschauer 1991; and Barro and Sala-I-Martin 1995.
21   Alesina and Perotti 1996.
22   Garrett 1998a. For an alternative view, see Persson and Tabellini 1994.
23   See Alvarez et al. 1991; Garrett 1998a; and Lange and Garrett 1985. Some scholars argue that the successes of this regime type had as much to do with the organization of business as the organization of labor; see Soskice 1990; and Swenson 1991.
24   Some scholars suggest that financial integration has been driven by developments in information technology over which governments have had little control; see Bryant 1987; and Goodman and Pauly 1993. Others argue that the removal of capital controls was an ideological choice that could be reversed; see Sobel 1994; and Banuri and Schor 1992. I take the intermediate position of Frieden and Rogowski that, even if theoretically still effective, the opportunities costs associated with capital controls have increased greatly in recent decades; Frieden and Rogowski 1996.
25   P. Pierson 1996.
26   Scholars often argue that corporatist labor market institutions have eroded over time, particularly in Scandinavia. Iversen 1996; and Pontusson and Swenson 1996. But more broadly based studies suggest that the structure of organized labor movements has been remarkably stable; see Golden 1998; Lange and Scruggs 1997; and Lange et al. 1995.
27   Ruggie 1996. See also Scharpf 1991.
28   Rodrik 1997. For a similar argument, see Steinmo 1993.
29   Moravcsik makes this argument, for example, with respect to European efforts to fix exchange rates since the end of Bretton Woods; Moravcsik 1998.
30   Krugman 1996. Nonetheless, many fear that the rapid dissemination of technology will soon dramatically reduce productivity differences among countries.
31   See Cantwell 1989; Caves 1996; Dunning 1988; and IMF 1991.
32   This is not to claim, however, that production costs are irrelevant. There are some sectors, such as textiles and apparel, where labor costs have a large bearing on location decisions; Leamer 1996. Moreover, there are temptations for governments to try to attract FDI by offering specific tax concessions and other monetary inducements; see Hines 1997.
33   Rodrik 1997.
34   Of course, multinational firms could still try to free ride on government services through tax evasion or accounting tricks.
35   Mundell 1962.
36   For a good precis of the various arguments about the determinants of exchange-rate regime choice, see Eichengreen 1994.
37   Commission of the European Communities 1990.
38   IMF 1983.
39   This is the core of the rational expectations revolution in macroeconomics. See Friedman 1968; and Lucas 1972.
40   Collins was the first to question the inflation-fighting properties of the EMS; Collins 1988.
41   Fratianni and von Hagen 1992.
42   Frieden 1991.

43   Obstfeld 1997.
44   If this is correct, why would Germany want irrevocably to fix its exchange rate against Italy? Analyses of Germany's EMU position typically involve politics, specifically Helmut Kohl's ambitions concerning political union in Europe. For an accessible survey of the contending arguments and evidence, see Garrett 1998b.
45   Corsetti and Roubini 1995.
46   Corsetti and Roubini 1991.
47   These indicators exclude important facets of microeconomic reform that arguably have been driven by globalization in recent decades – deregulation and privatization, for example. The qualitative evidence on microeconomic reform, however, is not conclusive. For insightful analyses, see Berger and Dore 1996; and Vogel 1995.
48   Cummins et al. 1995.
49   Swank 1998.
50   Garrett and Mitchell show that the effects of total trade on welfare state expenditures are not significantly different from those of trade volatility or imports from low-wage economies; Garrett and Mitchell 1998.
51   Note that these flow numbers do not take into account the stock of foreign investment in a country, nor strategic alliances among multinational firms from different countries.
52   Quinn and Inclan 1997.
53   Garrett 1998a.
54   Garrett 1995.
55   Garrett and Lange 1991.
56   Rodrik 1997.
57   See Quinn 1997; and Swank 1998.
58   Garrett 1998c.
59   Hallerberg and Basinger 1998.

References

Alesina, A. and Perotti, R. (1996) Income Distribution, Political Instability and Investment. *Quarterly Journal of Economics* 94.

Alvarez, R., Garrett. G., and Lange, P. (1991) Government Partisanship, Labor Organization and Macroeconomic Performance. *American Political Science Review* 85.

Aschauer, D. (1991) *Public Investment and Private Sector Growth*. Washington DC: Economic Policy Institute.

Banuri, T. and Schor, J. (1992) *Financial Openness and National Autonomy*. New York: Oxford University Press.

Barro, R. and Sala-I-Martin, X. (1995) *Economic Growth*. New York: Macmillan.

Berger, S. and Dore, R. (1996) *National Diversity and Global Capitalism*. Ithaca: Cornell University Press.

Bryant, R. (1987) *International Financial Integration*. Washington DC: Brookings Institution.

Cameron, D. R. (1978) The Expansion of the Public Economy. *American Political Science Review* 72.

Cantwell, J. (1989) *Technical Innovations in MNCs*. Oxford: Blackwell.

Caves, R. (1996) *Multinational Enterprise and Economic Analysis*, 2nd edn. New York: Cambridge University Press.

Cohen, B. J. (1996) Phoenix risen: the resurrection of global finance. *World Politics* 48: 268–96.

Collins, S. (1988) Inflation and the European Monetary System. In F. Giavazzi, S. Milosia, and M. Miller (eds), *The European Monetary System*, New York: Cambridge University Press.

Commission of the European Communities (1990) One Market, One Money. *European Economy* 44.

Corsetti, G. and Roubini, N. (1991) Fiscal Deficits, Public Debt and Government Insolvency. *Journal of Japanese and International Economies* 5.

Corsetti, G. and Roubini, M. (1995) Political Biases in Fiscal Policy. In B. Eichengreen, J. Frieden, and J. Von Hagen (eds), *Monetary and Fiscal Policy in an Integrated Europe*, New York: Springer.

Cummins, J., Hassett, K., and Hubbard, R. (1995) Tax Reforms and Investment: A Cross-Country Comparison. NBER Working Paper 5232, National Bureau of Economic Research, Cambridge, Mass.

Dunning, J. (1988) *Multinationals, Technology and Competitiveness*. Boston: Unwin Hyman.

Eichengreen, B. (1994) The Endogeneity of Exchange Rate Regimes. In P. Kenen (ed.), *Understanding Interdependence*, Princeton: Princeton University Press.

Eichengreen, B. (1996) *Globalizing Capital: A History of the International Monetary System*. Princeton: Princeton University Press.

Esping-Andersen, G. (1985) *States against Markets*. Princeton: Princeton University Press.

Fratianni, M. and Von Hagen, J. (1992) *The European Monetary System and European Monetary Union*. Boulder: Westview Press.

Frieden, J. (1991) Invested Interests: The Politics of National Economic Policies in a World of Global Finance. *International Organization* 45.

Frieden, J. and Rogowski, R. (1996) The Impact of the International Economy on National Policies in Internationalization and Domestic Policies. In R. Keohane and H. Milner (eds), *Internationalization and Domestic Politics*, New York: Cambridge University Press.

Friedman, M. (1968) The Role of Monetary Policy. *American Economic Review* 58: 1–17.

Garrett, G. (1995) Capital Mobility, Trade and the Domestic Politics of Economic Policy. *International Organization* 49.

Garrett, G. (1998a) *Partisan Politics in the Global Economy*. New York: Cambridge University Press.

Garrett, G. (1998b) The Transition to Economic and Monetary Union. In B. Eichengreen and J. Frieden (eds), *Forging an Integrated Europe*, Ann Arbor: University of Michigan Press.

Garrett, G. (1998c) Capital Flows, Capital Mobility and Capital Taxation. MS, Yale University.

Garrett, G. and Lange, P. (1991) Political Responses to Interdependence, What's Left for the Left? *International Organization* 45.

Garrett, G. and Mitchell, D. (1998) External Risk and Social Insurance: Reassessing the Globalization–Welfare State Nexus. MS, Yale University.

Golden, M. (1998) Economic Integration and Industrial Relations. MS, University of California at Los Angeles.

Goldthorpe, J. (1984) *Order and Conflict in Contemporary Capitalism*. New York: Oxford University Press.

Goodman, J. and Pauly, L. (1993) The Obsolescence of Capital Controls. *World Politics* 46.

Greider, W. (1997) *One World, Ready or Not*. New York: Simon and Schuster.

Hallerberg, M. and Basinger, S. (1998) Internationalization and Changes in Tax Policy in OECD Countries. *Comparative Political Studies* 31.

Hines, J. (1997) Altered States: Taxes and the Location of FDI in America. *American Economic Review* 87.

IMF (1983) Exchange Rate Volatility and World Trade. MS, IMF, Washington DC.

IMF (1991) Determinants and Systemic Consequences of International Capital Flows. MS, IMF, Washington DC.

Iverson, T. (1996) Power Flexibility and the Breakdown of Centralized Wage Bargaining. *Comparative Politics* 28.

Kapstein, E. B. (1996) Workers and the World Economy? *Foreign Affairs* 75: 16–37.

Katzenstein, P. (1985) *Small States in World Markets: Industrial Policy in Europe*. Ithaca: Cornell University Press.

Krugman, P. (1996) *Pop Internationalism*. Cambridge, Mass.: MIT Press.

Lange, P. and Garrett, G. (1985) The Politics of Growth. *Journal of Politics* 47.

Lange, P. and Scruggs, L. (1997) Where Have All the Members Gone? Paper presented at the 93rd Annual Meeting of the American Political Science Association, Washington DC, Aug.

Lange, P., Wallerstein, M., and Golden, M. (1995) The End of Corporatism? Wage Setting in the Nordic and Germanic Countries. In S. Jacoby (ed.), *The Workers of Nations*, New York: Oxford University Press.

Leamer, E. (1996) Wage Inequality from International Competition and Technological Change. *American Economic Review* 86.

Lindberg, L. and Maier, C. (1985) *The Politics of Inflation and Economic Stagnation.* Washington DC: Brookings Institution.

Lucas, R. (1972) Expectations and the Neutrality of Money. *Journal of Economic Theory* 4.

McKenzie, R. and Lee, D. (1991) *Quicksilver Capital; How the Rapid Movement of Wealth Has Changed the World.* New York: Free Press.

Moravcsik, A. (1998) *The Choice for Europe: Social Purpose and State Power From Messina to Maastricht.* Ithaca: Cornell University Press.

Mundell, R. (1962) A Theory of Optimal Currency Areas. *American Economic Review* 51.

Obstfeld, M. (1997) Open Economy, Macroeconomics, Developments in Theory and Policy. NBER Working Paper 6319, National Bureau of Economic Research, Cambridge, Mass.

Pauly, L. (1997) *Who Elected the Bankers?* Ithaca: Cornell University Press.

Persson, T. and Tabellini, G. (1994) Is Inequality Harmful for Growth? *American Economic Review* 86.

Pfaller, A. et al. (1991) *Can the Welfare State Compete?* London: Macmillan.

Pierson, C. (1991) *Beyond the Welfare State?* Cambridge: Polity Press.

Pierson, P. (1996) The Politics of the Welfare State. *World Politics* 48.

Polanyi, K. (1957) *The Great Transformation,* first publ. 1944. New York: Farrar and Rinehart.

Pontusson, J. and Swenson, P. (1996) Labor Markets, Production Strategies and Wage Bargaining Institutions. *Comparative Political Studies* 29.

Przeworski, A. and Wallerstein. M. (1982) The Structure of Class Conflict in Democratic Capitalist Societies. *American Political Science Review* 76.

Quinn, D. (1997) The Correlation of Changes in International Financial Regulation. *American Political Science Review* 91.

Quinn, D. and Inclan, L. (1997) The Origins of Financial Openness. *American Journal of Political Science* 41.

Reich, R. (1990) Who Is Us? *Harvard Business Review* 68.

Reich, R. (1991) Who Is Them? *Harvard Business Review* 69.

Rodrik, D. (1997) *Has Globalization Gone Too Far?* Washington DC: Institute for International Economics.

Ruggie, J. (1983) International Regimes, Transactions and Change: Embedded Liberalism in the New Post War Economic Order. In S. Krasner (ed.), *International Regimes,* Ithaca: Cornell University Press.

Ruggie, J. (1996) Globalization and the Embedded Liberalism Compromise. Working Paper 97/1, Max Planck Institute for Gesellschaftforschung, Cologne.

Scharpf, F. (1991) *Crisis and Choice in European Social Democracy.* Ithaca: Cornell University Press.

Shonfield, A. (1965) *Modern Capitalism.* New York: Oxford University Press.

Sobel, A. (1994) *Domestic Choices, International Markets.* Ann Arbor: University of Michigan Press.

Soskice, D. (1990) Wage Determination: The Changing Role of Institutions in Advanced Industrialised Countries. *Oxford Review of Economic Policy* 6.

Steinmo, S. (1993) *Taxation and Democracy.* New Haven: Yale University Press.

Strange, S. (1986) *States versus Markets.* Cambridge: Cambridge University Press.

Swank, D. (1998) Funding the Welfare State. *Political Studies* 46(4).

Swenson, P. (1991) Bringing Capital Back In, or Social Democracy Reconsidered. *World Politics* 45.

Vogel, D. (1995) *Trading Up: Consumer and Environmental Regulation in a Global Economy.* Cambridge, Mass.: Harvard University Press.

World Bank (1997) *World Development Report 1997.* New York: Oxford University Press.

27

The Woven World

Daniel A. Yergin and Joseph Stanislaw

Today, there is a resumption – a relinking – of a global economy after the disruptions of world wars, revolutions, and depression. As the steam engine and the telegraph shrank the dimensions of the nineteenth-century world, so technology today is once again eroding distance and borders. But this time the effects are much more comprehensive, for they leave virtually no country or community untouched. The pattern is evident in a host of measures. The number of international air passengers rose from 75 million in 1970 to 409 million in 1996. Between 1976 and 1996, the cost of a three-minute phone call from the United States to England dropped in real terms from about eight dollars to as low as thirty-six cents – and the number of transborder calls has increased from 3.2 billion in 1985 to 20.2 billion in 1996. Today, the world shares the same images from film and entertainment; the same news and information bounces down from satellites, instantaneously creating a common vocabulary for events.

Amid all this, the decisive new force is computers: Information technology is creating a woven world of distant encounters and instant connections. Knowledge and information do not have to wait. Within, outside, and across organizations and national boundaries, people are tied together, sharing information and points of view, working in virtual teams, bartering goods and services, swapping bonds and currencies, exchanging chatter and banalities, and passing the time. Information of every kind is available. With the establishment of the US government data Web site in 1997, a ten-year-old could gain access to more and better data than a senior official could have done just five years earlier. Libraries are open for business on the Internet. Researchers share their results in real time. Activists band together to promote their causes. Would-be terrorists surf for weapon designs. All this is increasingly heedless of the nation-state and outside the traditional structure of organizations. If the Internet is the new commanding heights, it is also beyond the reach of the state. While governments can promote the Internet, they cannot control it.

The hallmark of this new globality is the mobile economy. Capital sweeps across countries at electron speed; manufacturing and the generation of services move flexibly among countries and are networked across borders; markets are supplied from a continually shifting set of sources. Ideas, insights, techniques all disperse among countries with increasing ease. Access to technology across national boundaries continues to grow. Borders – fundamental to the exercise of national power – are eroded as markets are integrated. International trade between 1989 and 1997 grew at an annual rate of 5.3 percent – nearly four times faster than global output (1.4 percent). Over the same years, foreign direct investment rose even faster – at a rate of 11.5 percent per year. One indicator of the rapidity of change is the transformation of more and more firms into multinationals that provide the world market with goods and services that are conceived, produced, and assembled in several countries. The criterion of "national origin" has given way to "local content," which in turn is becoming harder and harder to pin down. The spread of fast, reliable information and communications technology pushes companies to draw on people and resources the world over.

As the barriers fall, private capital seeks new markets in what had once been the special preserve of state investment: energy, communications, and infrastructure. And governments, anxious to reduce deficits and shift spending to social needs, increasingly welcome this investment. In another telling reminder of a hundred years ago, private firms are taking on an increasing share of new investment, as well as responsibility for management, in telecommunications, waterworks, power utilities, and road construction worldwide. Most countries today have one or several mobile phone operators. A growing number have private electric power providers. Even the remaining large state monopolies are behaving like private companies – and their managers as businessmen – as they compete for major contracts beyond their own national borders in both developed and developing countries.

The integration of financial markets is particularly significant. Information and communications technology has, of course, provided the architecture for globally connected capital markets, but that is only part of the explanation. The big British privatizations in the mid-1980s were the first true global offerings of equity, and they changed the orientation and widened the ken of investment managers throughout the world. Not long after, European companies began to offer their shares. Increasingly, investors around the globe are using the same approach and criteria to make their decisions, and they are looking at the same pool of companies. The distinctions among national markets have become lost. In not so many years, a few national stock exchanges could well become global exchanges, opening for business not long after the sun rises and not closing until well after dark – all in order to deal in the equity of world-class companies, irrespective of their domicile. In turn, shares of leading firms will be traded on a twenty-four-hour basis.

When Harold Wilson was Britain's prime minister in the 1960s, he would blame the "gnomes of Zurich" for the pound's recurrent weakness, suggesting a cabal of a few hard-faced Swiss bankers cynically betting against the British currency. Conspiracy theories die hard: no less colorful allegations – against the "rogues" and "highwaymen" of the international economy – surfaced with the 1997 currency crisis in Southeast Asia. But, in fact, today thousands and thousands of traders drive a foreign-exchange market that has grown from a daily turnover of $190 billion in 1986 to an estimated $1.3 trillion in 1997. Analysts and brokers and strategists see the same information at the same moment and compete in their response time. Performance – whether it is a company's quarterly earnings or a country's inflation or trade balance data or the outcome of a national election – sets off an immediate chain reaction. While the publics vote only every few years, the markets vote every minute. And it is private capital – the pensions and accumulated retirement savings of the first world – that is being courted and lured by what used to be called the third world. But this financial integration comes with a price. National governments, whether in developed or developing countries, must increasingly heed the market's vote – as harsh as it sometimes can be.[1]

"Open capital markets create tremendous opportunity and benefits," observed US Secretary of the Treasury Robert Rubin. "But they create risks as well. World trade is growing, but trading in currency is growing at a much steeper rate. There is a greater risk of these markets causing instability because they are so large, and so much money is moving around in them. If it all moves in one direction, the size of the flows can be destabilizing, and the impact could be substantial."

[. . .]

What Government Does

One of the characteristics of the new global marketplace is the apparent precedence of economics over politics. But that means precedence only over traditional ideological politics. A firm would make a terrible mistake if it worked on the assumption that eroding borders meant the end of national politics, national identity, and economic nationalism. These forces will continue to express an amalgam of aspirations and ambitions. Politics within each country will still be shaped by its history, its culture, and its definition of national objectives – a reality that the firm can ignore only at its peril. This is not the end of the nation-state, and even less the end of government. If money and goods travel more freely now than at any time in living memory, individual life continues to be shaped by rules, customs, incentives, and constraints that are fundamentally national and political – the province of government. Personal access to the woven world still remains restricted to a minority of the world's population. The vast majority still get their signals not from global financial markets, let alone cyberspace, but from the national capital.

This leaves governments with a daunting challenge: to figure ways to reduce their intervention in some areas, and to retool and refocus their intervention in others, while preserving the public trust. It is a challenge of imagination. It requires buying into the idea of fundamental global change and taking on the task of translating that change into policies that accord with national culture, history, and temperament.

What will be the new role of government? After all, there is no market without government to define the rules and the context. The state creates and maintains the parameters within which the market operates. And that is the new direction. The state accepts the discipline of the market; government moves away from being producer, controller, and intervenor, whether through state ownership or heavy-handed regulation. The state as manager is an increasing laggard in the competitive, mobile economy. Instead, government shifts toward becoming a referee, setting the rules of the game to ensure, among other things, competition.

Economic imperatives and political interests will also force a reconsideration of the government's role in dealing with the range of social programs that make up the welfare state. For governments do spend a great deal of money. Among industrial countries, public expenditure rose from 28 percent of GDP in 1960 to 46 percent in 1996 – a surge driven, most of all, by rapid growth in subsidies, transfer payments, and social spending. But government's performance in these roles will move more clearly into the spotlight as it withdraws from the commanding heights of industry and planning. For the shift of role entails also a shift of resources and the way they are applied. The public money and human skills freed up through privatization and deregulation will be partly invested, in many countries, in "human infrastructure" – health, education, the environment – with, it is hoped, the creativity and success that can come from a clearer and better-focused role. What this means, then, is that for all the erosion of boundaries and fundamental technological change, governments still matter – and, most of all, political leadership matters. It also means that even if change in the direction of "more market" and "less state" is a pervasive global phenomenon, it does not lead to a single, common result.[2]

The World after Reform

The move to the market is beyond doubt a truly global phenomenon. It draws on a stock of ideas and recent experience shared around the world. The processes of change – particularly privatization, deregulation, and trade liberalization – are largely common ones, refined over time to a professional craft by their political champions and expert practitioners. As countries anchor themselves in a world of open and connected markets, they are to a significant degree transferring control of the commanding heights from the traditional state apparatus to the dispersed intelligence of the market. And the extraordinarily fast flow of information, made possible by the rapid diffusion of accessible technologies, has helped reinforce the sense of common momentum. Yet that feeling should not be overstated. For despite the common features, each country and region is executing its move to the market according to its own political and economic history and perception of the national interest. In the postreform world that is now emerging, each major region faces specific challenges in reconciling the increasingly complex demands of global participation with the realities of its own history, politics, economics, and culture – all the things that make up the experience and living memory of individuals and nations.

Each area, then, will grapple in this world after reform with its own agenda for the new century. As the withdrawal of the state from the commanding heights opens new perspectives and opportunities, it also conditions success on understanding the regional dynamics. Indeed, the growing connection of markets means that these regional agendas will feed back ever more directly into the workings of the world economy. The future of the postreform world, and certainly the future health and credibility of markets, will thus be shaped not only by technology and global forces but also by how different regions come to grips with their particular challenges.
[. . .]

Notes

1   Interviews with Robert Rubin and Eric Dobkin. [. . .]
2   Interview with John Browne. On BP's transformation, see Steven E. Prokesch, "Unleashing the Power of Learning," *Harvard Business Review* (Sept.–Oct. 1997); Vito Tanzi and Ludger Schuknecht, "The Growth of Government and the Reform of the State in Industrial Countries," IMF Working Paper W/95/130, Dec. 1995; Clive Crook (ed.), "The Future of the State: A Survey of the World Economy," *The Economist*, Sept. 20–26, 1997.

28

Has Globalization Gone Too Far?

Dani Rodrik

[...]

The process that has come to be called "globalization" is exposing a deep fault line between groups who have the skills and mobility to flourish in global markets and those who either don't have these advantages or perceive the expansion of unregulated markets as inimical to social stability and deeply held norms. The result is severe tension between the market and social groups such as workers, pensioners, and environmentalists, with governments stuck in the middle.[1]

This book argues that the most serious challenge for the world economy in the years ahead lies in making globalization compatible with domestic social and political stability – or to put it even more directly, in ensuring that international economic integration does not contribute to domestic social *dis*integration.

[...]

Sources of Tension

I focus on three sources of tension between the global market and social stability and offer a brief overview of them here.

First, reduced barriers to trade and investment accentuate the asymmetry between groups that can cross international borders (either directly or indirectly, say through outsourcing[2]) and those that cannot. In the first category are owners of capital, highly skilled workers, and many professionals, who are free to take their resources where they are most in demand. Unskilled and semiskilled workers and most middle managers belong in the second category. Putting the same point in more technical terms, globalization makes the demand for the services of individuals in the second category *more elastic* – that is, the services of large segments of the working population can be more easily substituted by the services of other people across national boundaries. Globalization therefore fundamentally transforms the employment relationship.

The fact that "workers" can be more easily substituted for each other across national boundaries undermines what many conceive to be a postwar social bargain between workers and employers, under which the former would receive a steady increase in wages and benefits in return for labor peace. This is because increased substitutability results in the following concrete consequences:

- Workers now have to pay a larger share of the cost of improvements in work conditions and benefits (that is, they bear a greater incidence of nonwage costs).
- They have to incur greater instability in earnings and hours worked in response to shocks to labor demand or labor productivity (that is, volatility and insecurity increase).

- Their bargaining power erodes, so they receive lower wages and benefits whenever bargaining is an element in setting the terms of employment.

These considerations have received insufficient attention in the recent academic literature on trade and wages, which has focused on the downward shift in demand for unskilled workers rather than the increase in the elasticity of that demand.

Second, globalization engenders conflicts within and between nations over domestic norms and the social institutions that embody them. As the technology for manufactured goods becomes standardized and diffused internationally, nations with very different sets of values, norms, institutions, and collective preferences begin to compete head on in markets for similar goods. And the spread of globalization creates opportunities for trade between countries at very different levels of development.

This is of no consequence under the traditional multilateral trade policy of the WTO and the General Agreement on Tariffs and Trade (GATT): the "process" or "technology" through which goods are produced is immaterial, and so are the social institutions of the trading partners. Differences in national practices are treated just like differences in factor endowments or any other determinant of comparative advantage. However, introspection and empirical evidence both reveal that most people attach values to processes as well as outcomes. This is reflected in the norms that shape and constrain the domestic environment in which goods and services are produced – for example, workplace practices, legal rules, and social safety nets.

Trade becomes contentious when it unleashes forces that undermine the norms implicit in domestic practices. Many residents of advanced industrial countries are uncomfortable with the weakening of domestic institutions through the forces of trade, as when, for example, child labor in Honduras displaces workers in South Carolina or when pension benefits are cut in Europe in response to the requirements of the Maastricht treaty. This sense of unease is one way of interpreting the demands for "fair trade." Much of the discussion surrounding the "new" issues in trade policy – that is, labor standards, environment, competition policy, corruption – can be cast in this light of procedural fairness.

We cannot understand what is happening in these new areas until we take individual preferences for processes and the social arrangements that embody them seriously. In particular, by doing so we can start to make sense of people's uneasiness about the consequences of international economic integration and avoid the trap of automatically branding all concerned groups as self-interested protectionists. Indeed, since trade policy almost always has redistributive consequences (among sectors, income groups, and individuals), one cannot produce a principled defense of free trade without confronting the question of the fairness and legitimacy of the practices that generate these consequences. By the same token, one should not expect broad popular support for trade when trade involves exchanges that clash with (and erode) prevailing domestic social arrangements.

Third, globalization has made it exceedingly difficult for governments to provide social insurance – one of their central functions and one that has helped maintain social cohesion and domestic political support for ongoing liberalization throughout the postwar period. In essence, governments have used their fiscal powers to insulate domestic groups from excessive market risks, particularly those having an external origin. In fact, there is a striking correlation between an economy's exposure to foreign trade and the size of its welfare state. It is in the most open countries, such as Sweden, Denmark, and the Netherlands, that spending on income transfers has expanded the most. This is not to say that the government is the sole, or the best, provider of social insurance. The extended family, religious groups, and local communities often play similar roles. My point is that it is a hallmark of the postwar period that governments in the advanced countries have been expected to provide such insurance.

At the present, however, international economic integration is taking place against the background of receding governments and diminished social obligations. The welfare state has been under attack for two decades. Moreover, the increasing mobility of capital has rendered an important segment of the tax base footloose, leaving governments with the unappetizing option of increasing tax rates disproportionately on labor income. Yet the need for social insurance for the vast majority of the population that remains internationally immobile has not diminished. If anything, this need has become greater as a consequence of increased integration. The question therefore is how the tension between globalization and the pressures for socialization of risk can be eased. If the tension is not managed intelligently and creatively, the danger is that the domestic consensus in favor of open markets will ultimately erode to the point where a generalized resurgence of protectionism becomes a serious possibility.

Each of these arguments points to an important weakness in the manner in which advanced societies are handling – or are equipped to handle – the consequences of globalization. Collectively, they point to what is perhaps the greatest risk of all, namely that the cumulative consequence of the tensions mentioned above will be the solidifying of a new set of class divisions – between those who prosper in the globalized economy and those who do not, between those who share its values and those who would rather not, and between those who can diversify away its risks and those who cannot. This is not a pleasing prospect, even for individuals on the winning side of the divide who have little empathy for the other side. Social disintegration is not a spectator sport – those on the sidelines also get splashed with mud from the field. Ultimately, the deepening of social fissures can harm all.

Globalization: Now and Then

This is not the first time we have experienced a truly global market. By many measures, the world economy was possibly even more integrated at the height of the gold standard in the late 19th century than it is now. [. . .] In the United States and Europe, trade volumes peaked before World War I and then collapsed during the interwar years. Trade surged again after 1950, but none of the three regions is significantly more open by this measure now than it was under the late gold standard. Japan, in fact, has a lower share of exports in GDP now than it did during the interwar period.

Other measures of global economic integration tell a similar story. As railways and steamships lowered transport costs and Europe moved toward free trade during the late 19th century, a dramatic convergence in commodity prices took place (Williamson 1996). Labor flows were considerably higher then as well, as millions of immigrants made their way from the old world to the new. In the United States, immigration was responsible for 24 percent of the expansion of the labor force during the 40 years before World War I (Williamson 1996: appendix table 1). As for capital mobility, the share of net capital outflows in GNP was much higher in the United Kingdom during the classical gold standard than it has been since.

Does this earlier period of globalization hold any lessons for our current situation? It well might. There is some evidence, for example, that trade and migration had significant consequences for income distribution. According to Jeffrey Williamson, "[G]lobalization . . . accounted for more than half of the rising inequality in rich, labor-scarce countries [e.g., the United States, Argentina, and Australia] and for a little more than a quarter of the falling inequality in poor, labor-abundant countries [e.g., Sweden, Denmark, and Ireland]" in the period before World War I (1996: 19). Equally to the point are the political consequences of these changes:

> There is a literature almost a century old that argues that immigration hurt American labor and accounted for much of the rise in inequality from the 1890s to World War I, so much so that a labor-sympathetic Congress passed immigration quotas. There is a literature even older that argues that a New World grain invasion eroded land rents in Europe, so much so that landowner-dominated Continental Parliaments raised tariffs to help protect them from the impact of globalization. (Williamson 1996: 1)

Williamson (1996: 20) concludes that "the inequality trends which globalization produced are at least partly responsible for the interwar retreat from globalization [which appeared] first in the rich industrial trading partners."

Moreover, there are some key differences that make today's global economy more contentious. First, restrictions on immigration were not as common during the 19th century, and consequently labor's international mobility was more comparable to that of capital. Consequently, the asymmetry between mobile capital (physical and human) and immobile "natural" labor, which characterizes the present situation, is a relatively recent phenomenon. Second, there was little head-on international competition in identical or similar products during the previous century, and most trade consisted of the exchange of noncompeting products, such as primary products for manufactured goods. The aggregate trade ratios do not reflect the "vast increase in the exposure of tradable goods industries to international competition" that is now taking place compared with the situation in the 1890s (Irwin 1996: 42). Third, and perhaps most important, governments had not yet been called on to perform social-welfare functions on a large scale, such as ensuring adequate levels of employment, establishing social safety nets, providing medical and social insurance, and caring for the poor. This shift in the perceived role of government is also a relatively recent transformation, one that makes life in an interdependent economy considerably more difficult for today's policymakers.

At any rate, the lesson from history seems to be that continued globalization cannot be taken for granted. If its consequences are not managed wisely and creatively, a retreat from openness becomes a distinct possibility.

Implications

[. . .]

We need to be upfront about the irreversibility of the many changes that have occurred in the global economy. Advances in communications and transportation mean that large segments of national economies are much more exposed to international trade and capital flows than they have ever been, regardless of what policymakers choose to do. There is only limited scope for government policy to make a difference. In addition, a serious retreat into protectionism would hurt the many groups that benefit from trade and would result in the same kind of social conflicts that globalization itself generates. We have to recognize that erecting trade barriers will help in only a limited set of circumstances and that trade policies will rarely be the best response to the problems that will be discussed here. Transfer and social insurance programs will generally dominate. In short, the genie cannot be stuffed back into the bottle, even if it were desirable to do so. We will need more imaginative and more subtle responses.

[...]

Notes

1   See also Kapstein (1996) and Vernon (n.d.). Kapstein argues that a backlash from labor is likely unless policymakers take a more active role in managing their economies. Vernon argues that we might be at the threshold of a global reaction against the pervasive role of multinational enterprises.
2   Outsourcing refers to companies' practice of subcontracting part of the production process – typically the most labor-intensive and least skill-intensive parts – to firms in other countries with lower costs.

References

Irwin, Douglas (1996) The US in a New Global Economy? A Century's Perspective. *American Economic Review, Papers and Proceedings* 86(2) (May).

Kapstein, Ethan (1996) Workers and the World Economy. *Foreign Affairs* 75(3) (May–June).

Vernon, Raymond (n.d.) In the Hurricane's Eye: Multinational Enterprises in the Next Century. MS, Harvard University.

Williamson, Jeffrey (1996) Globalization and Inequality Then and Now: The Late Nineteenth and Late Twentieth Centuries Compared. NBER Working Paper 5491, National Bureau of Economic Research, Cambridge, Mass.

29

The Passing of Social Democracy

John Gray

[. . .]

Social democrats in Britain and other European countries who imagine that the social market economies with which they are familiar can be reconciled with a global free market have not understood the new circumstances in which advanced industrial societies find themselves.

Social market economies developed in a particular economic niche. They are bound to be transformed or destroyed by the industrialization of Asia and the entry into world markets of the post-communist countries.

The effect of competition from countries in which a regime of deregulation, low taxes and a shrinking welfare state has been imposed is to force downwards harmonization of policies on states which retain social market economies. Policies enforcing a deregulated labour market and cuts in welfare provision are adopted as defensive strategies in response to policies implemented in other countries. Tax competition among advanced states works to drain public finances and make a welfare state unaffordable. As a *Financial Times* editorial has noted: 'by eroding the revenue base, tax competition can become too much of a good thing . . . Bidding wars between countries can even undermine the collective revenue base. This increases the tax burden on less mobile industries and on labour, relative to capital.'[1]

Tax rivalry is only one mechanism through which competition among governments for mobile capital and industries works to drive down social provision and raise taxes on labour. The workings of the global bond markets reduce or remove from the world's social markets much of the freedom their governments had in the past to pursue counter-cyclical policies. They force them to return to a pre-Keynesian situation in which they have few effective levers of macroeconomic management. They are condemned to wait out cyclical downturns in economic activity – whatever their social and economic costs.

By penalizing governments which attempt to stimulate economic activity by borrowing or undertaking public works the markets force them back into a pre-Keynesian world in which governments responded to recessions by the disastrous deflationary expedient of expenditure cuts. Thus world bond markets mimic the workings of the Gold Standard. But they do so without replicating its semi-automatic character, which conferred a degree of stability on the economies it governed. They operate in a context of market uncertainties which makes speculative booms and busts (such as the global bond market crash of early 1994) inevitable. The mechanism of the Gold Standard has been replaced by the house rules of a casino.

Global capital markets do more than this. They make social democracy unviable. By social democracy I mean the combination of deficit-financed full employment, a comprehensive welfare state and egalitarian tax policies that existed in Britain until the late 1970s and which survived in Sweden until the early 1990s.

That social democratic regime presupposed a closed economy. Capital movements were limited by fixed or semi-fixed exchange rates. Many of the core policies of social democracy cannot be sustained in open economies. This applies to deficit-financed full employment and the welfare states of the post-war period. It applies equally to social democratic deals of equality. All social democratic theories of justice (such as John Rawls's egalitarian theory) presuppose a closed economy.[2]

It is only within a closed system of distribution that we can know if the principles of justice dictated by such theories are satisfied. More practically, it is only in a closed economy that egalitarian principles can be enforced. In open economies they will be rendered unworkable by the freedom of capital – including 'human capital' – to migrate.

Social democratic regimes presuppose that high levels of public provision could be funded unproblematically from general taxation. That proposition no longer holds. It is not even true of what economic theory understands to be real public goods. The logic of unfettered mobility of capital is that financing public goods becomes harder for all states. In the standard understanding of them, public goods are services enjoyed by all. They cannot be split up or partitioned, and they must be paid for out of taxation if they are not to be under-produced. In the technical literature of economic theory and public administration in which this standard view is found, public goods are such things as law and order, national defence and environmental conservation.

The classic solution to the problems of financing the provision of public goods is mutually agreed coercion. Everyone agrees that they will benefit if public goods are produced. They resolve the classical problem of the public goods trap – freeloaders who seek to enjoy public goods without paying their way – by requiring everyone to contribute through taxation. This classic solution breaks down when taxation is not enforceable on mobile capital and corporations. If sources of revenue – capital, enterprises and people – are free to migrate to low-tax regimes, mutually agreed coercion does not work as a means of paying for public goods. The kinds and levels of taxation levied in order to pay for public goods in any state cannot significantly exceed those found in states that are otherwise comparable.

Global mobility of capital and production in a world of open economies have made the central policies of European social democracy unworkable.[3] By so doing they have made today's mass unemployment a problem without a simple solution.

The monetarist theories that presently dominate the world's central banks and transnational financial institutions deny that any trade-off of price stability with full employment can be achieved. The intellectual credentials of such doctrines are not especially impressive. They appear to presuppose a view of economic life as tending to equilibrium of the sort that Keynes successfully criticized. In our time an equilibrium view of economic life has been anachronistically revived in the 'rational expectations' theories emanating from the University of Chicago. These are controversial theorizings which command no general consensus even among mainstream economists.[4]

Yet these dubious theories have inspired the structural adjustment programmes of the World Bank that, in countries as remote as Mexico and Nigeria, have imposed deep and enduring depressions of real economic activity in the pursuit of fiscal rectitude. Global bond markets simulate these structural adjustment programmes. They impose on the countries of the First World the deflationary disciplines of structural adjustment which have manifestly failed as emergency measures in developing countries.

[...]

By destabilizing any national government that attempts to break with these doctrines – such as that of François Mitterrand in the early 1980s – the world's bond and currency markets can act to make them self-fulfilling. They box in any state which tries to increase employment by a deficit-led expansion in economic activity. [...]

During the 1980s, the largest sovereign nation-state, the United States, was able to deploy Keynesian-style expansionist policies when it engaged in a large arms build-up; but it is doubtful if anything similar could be attempted by the United States in present circumstances. President Clinton's experience early in his first administration, when bond markets inflicted high interest rates as a deterrent against potential fiscal laxity, taught him that even the world's 'borrower of last resort' is vulnerable to the judgement of the global market in government bonds.

The long-standing Swedish experiment in full employment, which by the early 1990s was already in serious difficulties, was brought to an end by the power of the global bond market. [...]

What happened in Sweden has implications for social market economies everywhere. Contrary to many conventional interpretations, the core of Swedish full employment was not the active labour policies pursued by successive Social Democratic governments. It was the willingness of these governments to use the state as the employer of last resort.[5] That was vetoed by the bond markets. The implication for other governments committed to maintaining social cohesion by avoiding mass unemployment is that they cannot do so by any policy which the bond markets judge to be fiscally imprudent.

Bond markets have knocked away the floor from under post-war full employment policies. No western government today has a credible successor to the policies which secured western societies against mass unemployment in the Keynesian era. The numbers of people excluded from access to work have been growing in most western societies for twenty years or more. This has occurred despite strong and nearly continuous economic growth in all advanced countries. The social democratic objective of full employment cannot now be achieved by social democratic policies.

To imagine that the social market economies of the past can renew themselves intact under the forces of downwards harmonization is the most dangerous of the many illusions associated with the global market. Instead, social market systems are being compelled progressively to dismantle themselves, so that they can compete on more equal terms with economies in which environmental, social and labour costs are lowest. The question social market economies face is not whether they can survive with their present institutions and policies – they cannot. It is whether the adjustments that are imperative will be made by a further wave of neo-liberal reforms or by policies which harness markets to the satisfaction of human needs.

[...]

Notes

1 'Living with tax rivalry', *Financial Times*, 14 Jan. 1997.
2 For a criticism of Rawls's theory, see my book, *Liberalisms* (London: Routledge, 1989), ch. 6.
3 I have argued this more systematically in my monograph, *After Social Democracy* (London: Demos, 1996), reprinted as chapter 2 of my book, *Endgames: Questions in Late Modern Political Thought* (Cambridge: Polity Press, 1997).

4   A powerful critique of 'rational expectations' equilibrium theories of economic life is developed in G. Shackle's *Epistemics and Economics* (Cambridge: Cambridge University Press, 1976).

5   The view that it was the willingness of the state to act as employer of last resort, not its active labour policy, which enabled Social Democratic Sweden to avoid mass unemployment is argued for persuasively in R. B. Freeman, B. Swedenborg and R. Topel, *Reforming the Welfare State: Economic Troubles in Sweden's Welfare State*, Occasional Paper 69 (Stockholm: Centre for Business and Policy Studies, 1995).

30

Welfare State Limits to Globalization

Elmar Rieger and Stephan Leibfried

"Globalization" has become a catchword for the encompassing interdependence and the ever deepening division of labor in the world economy. It is seen as one of the grand challenges for the politics and economics of the developed nation-states at the end of the twentieth century.[1] Increasing numbers of people in the Western welfare states seem to perceive globalization as the cause of unexpected trajectories of and an unknown destination for the development of economy and society. Globalization is increasingly perceived as a threat, since some "external force" provokes reactions in all areas of public life, determines policy content, and also sanctions "nondecisions." At the same time, for broad strata of the population, the agents and powers behind this permanent economic restructuring remain rather diffuse and beyond the reach of national politics. [. . .]

Beyond the deepening of already existing cleavages between the "haves" and "have-nots" of the global economy and the social consequences of austerity policies in developing countries, the new imperatives of the world economy seem to press most vigorously on the social policies of the most developed nation-states. Private enterprises in these societies see welfare state institutions – and their industrial relations, which rest mostly on corporatist foundations – not only as the cause for lost ground in international competitiveness but also as shackles in their efforts to adapt to the new competitive challenges.[2] The pressure for rationalization in industry unhinges industrial relations regimes, such as company-financed employee benefits, and forces corporations to look at social security systems and the social regulation of employment mainly in terms of "fiscal effort" and of their effect in immobilizing the labor force and blocking internal restructuring.[3] At the same time, the increasing social and economic consequences of globalization make growing demands on social policies, which nation-states have ever greater difficulties in satisfying as their fiscal capacity declines.

The political conflicts over globalization and the welfare state are myopic in at least two ways. First, the general notion of an inexorable globalization pressure to shrink welfare states is untenable. In fact, at least in Western Europe in general and in Germany in particular, economic globalization has not led to any radical dismantling of welfare states. On the contrary: The stronger the pressure of globalization and the more open a country's economy is, the more difficult it becomes to touch the status quo of the welfare state. Social policies have proven highly resistant to change. On balance, globalization presently tends to function as a *blocking mechanism* vis-à-vis policy reforms deemed necessary from an "internal," domestic perspective; it has *not* become a forcing mechanism for such reforms. [. . .]

Second, today's globalization conflicts are characterized by short-term considerations only. The functions of institutions of the welfare states in achieving and ensuring economic openness are overlooked. The way globalization and the welfare state are discussed makes it seem as if there were a completely new constellation and challenge. But movements toward the internationalization of the economy and national countertrends are recurrent phenomena. The decisive novelty of the current constellation is the existence of the welfare state and its internal transformation. It was the institutionalization of income maintenance programs after World War II that enabled governments to switch to free trade policies. Welfare state systems, however, create their own inequalities and rigidities. Moreover, the privileged strata they produce became powerful defendants of the distributional status quo. With this transformation, perception of the results of economic globalization on internal conditions in developed societies has changed along with the institutions regulating the economy on an international level.

[. . .]

Our general thesis is that the movement toward and the trends in a globalized economy have been triggered, contained, differentiated or modified, weakened or strengthened, and slowed down or speeded up through *national structures of social policy and their developments*, to the degree that these could replace protectionism. The crucial variables are the institutional characteristics of social policy. They are the starting and focusing points for new social groups, varying political mobilization, and structural change in interest mediation in the welfare state. The conditions for action and the capacity to exert power, to veto, and to implement policy have all been changed substantially by the welfare state transformation of the postwar societies. The new social groups – "claimant classes" and "provider classes" – try to monopolize their new income sources and to build up strong lobbying positions. Depending on their institutional and political clout, they embody different potentials for the paralysis or for the adaptability of welfare states; therefore, when these groups are challenged by welfare state reforms and, at the same time, economic insecurity increases due to economic change induced by globalization, we can expect the emergence of new interest coalitions urging protectionism and resisting domestic deregulation that would enhance competitiveness. How salient such developments will be depends mainly on social policy's capacity for reform and adaptation.

[. . .]

The Welfare State Foundations of an Open International Economy

[. . .]

Contrary to the expectations of leading political scientists and economists, the transformation of industrial societies to welfare states did not put an end to economic openness. On the contrary, this transformation became a foundation and guarantee of openness and made feasible a level of international division of labor and integration formerly unimaginable.[4] Decisive were changes in the calculus of interests and security strategies by those groups that had been most exposed to the risks of world market integration. A look at the welfare state's changes in the perception and evaluation of economic risks shows the degree to which economic openness depends on certain domestic social and political preconditions of societies interested in free trade. These preconditions – and their functional equivalence to protectionism – are hard to fulfill and even harder to sustain. Relevant here are three effects of welfare state building: the stabilization of expectations, the organization of nonmarket sources of life chances, and the possibility of compensating those unable to adapt.

[...]

Social wealth-transfer and service policies secure futures. They can create a situation in which the social groups concerned do not perceive the autonomous movements, structural changes, and cycles of an open economy as dangers to their lives, but as increasing opportunities and as an expansion of options. Also, the extension of the time taken to gain occupational qualifications and the earlier exit from the labor force reduce the period in life that is directly exposed to economic cycles and structural change.

But the effects of welfare states are more far-reaching. Democratization of the vote and parliamentarization of politics generally ensured that the politicization of the economy and the distribution of resources did not make economic nationalism a characteristic of all developed industrial societies. The risk of free trade remained, but the institutionalization of social policy made the national welfare more independent of economic developments: "Economic nationalism receives one of its main impulses from this risk, from the fear of entrusting national well-being to factors beyond the nation's control."[5]

[...]

But it took until the welfare state had developed completely before this mechanism for abandoning protectionism revealed its decisive effectiveness. Social policy after World War II, in the 1950s and 1960s, changed structurally from a subsidiary security against emergencies to a comprehensive securing of achieved standards of living. This change in the structure and function of social policy also massively affected national integration into the world market. Social policy changes were augmented by a more extensive and intensive policy of occupational qualification, of upgrading human capital.[6] For the first time, social and educational policy could be used as a general compensation (transfers, qualification) of globalization losers. These policies provided a general, transsectoral, and transbranch mechanism for redistributive adaptation. The expansion of the welfare state to the middle classes, in particular to some of the self-employed, also increased their tolerance for accelerated economic developments and for the higher risks implied in the economic changes brought about by deeper integration into the world market and the increase of competitive pressure from imports.

Welfare State Limits to Globalization

[...]

Instead of guaranteeing dynamic labor markets, compensating the losers of globalization on short notice, and assuring social and geographic mobility in the long term, the welfare state may turn into a platform for defensive coalitions of the status quo. The deeper social policy structures are embedded in interest groups, and the more political parties have internalized the welfare state ambitions of the claimant and provider classes, the higher are the hurdles for efficient welfare state reform. The internal challenges to reform the welfare state – stemming from demographic change and changes in the labor market, in gender relationships, and in the organization of family life[7] – turn into additional, autonomous adaptive problems for national systems vis-à-vis the economy. The domestic formation of distributive coalitions then becomes an independent source of hurdles for economic internationalization and of economic closure: The tax and contribution burdens of the welfare state are not reduced, and the economic and social regulation of the labor markets, jobs, products, and trade remain untouched. This increases the danger that investment capital will move abroad as the domestic market loses its attractiveness for foreign investors.

In addition to the external shocks of globalization, internal blockades of institutional policy in the welfare state have become the second great challenge for national government at the turn of the millennium. This domestic policy produces winners and losers in its own way. As when opening the economy for free trade, the costs of institutional change immediately and concentratedly affect specific social groups, while the benefits of reforms are diffuse and relegated to an uncertain future.[8] The result is political advantages for reform losers. The crucial point is, therefore, that social policy reform can produce its own insecurities and, above all, can provoke resistance against further internationalization of the economy, if those affected directly connect the probable, reform-induced worsening of their position with site policy and international competition.

That the positive relationship between the expansion of the welfare state and the internationalization of trade, production, and investment may have changed due to the autonomous dynamics of social policy can be attributed mainly to two consequences of the institutionalization of the welfare state itself: the development and consolidation of "claimant" as well as "provider classes" and the social policy–induced immobilization and increased cost of labor. The rise of manifest and latent claimant and provider classes – primarily pensioners, long-term benefit-recipients, and public sector employees – has decisively shrunk the social base for an open economy and at the same time sharpened political parties' attention to these new interests at the cost of the free market system. The numerical growth of these "classes" – via broader access to a prolonged education and the institutionalization of the "pension age," but also through welfare and unemployment insurance transfers, which can to a great extent replace market income, and finally through fiscal welfare's vastly complex structures of benefits and systems of "equalizing burdens" – has shifted the lines of social conflict, highly socialized the structures of mediating interests, and thus altered the functional laws of the political market in favor of the welfare state clientele.[9] [...]

For the fate of free trade as the guiding principle of foreign economic policy, this development is ambivalent at best. On one hand, it reduces the social risks of increasing integration in the world market, because the living conditions of large parts of the population are less dependent on the movements of the world market. More important, perhaps, early retirement programs and other means of exiting labor markets help companies to restructure and reorganize internally by removing those people who, because of seniority rules, not only are the most expensive but also have the most incentives to resist change.[10] On the other hand, the social-political situation of groups depending on the welfare state is threatened by the constraints of adaptation that globalization dictates to national budget and finance policy; this expresses itself as resistance to the open economy. As the general increase in the public debt in the welfare states shows, it has been some time since social policy has been able to be financed through current tax and contribution revenues.[11] Over the long term, what may be decisive is that the combination of welfare-state transformation and demographic aging has greatly reduced the social basis for open foreign trade. This development could become the basis for the formation of new redistributive coalitions that find a common interest in resisting the feared redistributive effects of globalization and attendant changes in welfare state policies.

[...]

The more politicians point to international competitive pressures, the EMU, and so on to legitimate and push through changes in structures of social policy, the more they run the risk that potential, putative, and real losers of such policies will turn against globalization, European integration, and other such processes, and demand more control over foreign economic policy – in short, protectionism.

If we shelve the question of how rational and efficient present social policy structures are, we can make a strong argument for the following thesis: With increasing economic openness and international interdependence, social policy orients itself increasingly to the status quo. A comparative look at the United States and West European countries seems to indicate that, with growing external pressures from globalization, the capacity to adapt national social policy shrinks. The radical change in US welfare policy in 1996 – the discontinuation of a federal guarantee of right to welfare, the introduction of time limits for income transfers, the devolution of welfare to the states – indicates how a relatively low level of globalization pressure goes hand in hand with a broad capacity for massive change, while in Western Europe and Germany a high level of external pressure seems almost to prohibit any change in the social policy status quo.[12] Whereas in Germany the stickiness of social policy structures at least up to now assists in sustaining a high level of economic international integration, the United States currently experiences a political backlash against free trade policies. In the framework of our argument it is the fragmentation and downgrading of safety nets which decreases the chances for the installment of free trade policies.

[. . .]

Notes

1   For a first foray into the literature, see Geoffrey Garrett, *Partisan Politics in the Global Economy* (New York: Cambridge University Press, 1998); Robert Z. Lawrence, Albert Bressand, and Takatoshi Ito, *A Vision for the World Economy: Openness, Diversity, and Cohesion* (Washington DC: Brookings Institution Press, 1996); Beate Kohler-Koch, "Politische Unverträglichkeiten von Globalisierung," in Ulrich Steger (ed.), *Globalisierung der Wirtschaft – Konsequenzen für Arbeit, Technik und Umwelt* (Bonn: J. H. W. Dietz, 1995), pp. 83–114; and Michael Zürn, "Jenseits der Staatlichkeit: Über die Folgen der ungleichzeitigen Denationalisierung," *Leviathan* 20 (1992): 490–513. For a bibliography on the welfare state and globalization, see Elmar Rieger and Stephan Leibfried, *Globalization and the Western Welfare State: An Annotated Bibliography* (Bremen: GAAC/SSRC/Wissenschaftskolleg zu Berlin with Centre for Social Policy, Bremen, and Centre for European Social Research, Mannheim, 1995). The pros and cons of globalization discussed among economists are illustrated by a contrast of the work and biography of Lester Thurow and Paul Krugman: "Like Oil and Water: A Tale of Two Economists," *New York Times*, Feb. 16, 1997, sec. 3, pp. 1, 10, 11.
2   For example, Werner Maly, "Die Bedeutung der Sozialpolitik für unternehmerische Standortentscheidungen," in Winfried Schmähl and Herbert Rische (eds), *International-isierung von Wirtschaft und Politik: Handlungsspielräume der nationalen Sozialpolitik* (Baden-Baden: Nomos, 1997), pp. 79–101; and Amity Shlaes, "Germany's Chained Economy," *Foreign Affairs* 73 (1994): 109–24.
3   See Josef Wieland, "Sozialpartnerschaft, betriebliche Sozialpolitik und Unternehmen-skultur: Eine institutionenökonomische Analyse," *Wittener Jahrbuch für ökonomische Literatur* (1996): 143–60; and Michael Hüther, "Umbau der Sozialen Sicherungssysteme im Zeichen der Globalisierung," *Zeitschrift für Wirtschaftspolitik* 46 (1997): 193–214. For a contraposition see Heinz Lampert, "Voraussetzungen einer Sozialstaatsreform – kritische

Anmerkungen zur aktuellen Diskussion über den Umbau des Sozialstaats," *Jahrbücher für Nationalökonmie und Statistik* 214 (1995): 513–31.

4 We do not claim that the politics leading to the expansion of the welfare state after World War II can be explained *in terms of conscious decisions* to provide for an institutional foundation for a closer integration of world markets. We believe that the relationship between social policies and foreign economic policies is much more fruitfully analyzed *in terms of unintended consequences*.

5 A. O. Hirschman, *National Power and the Structure of Foreign Trade* (Berkeley: University of California Press, 1980), p. 79.

6 On the economic-historical context of this "Golden Age" and on the labor and social policy components of the social compact formulated in the 1950s, see Barry Eichengreen, "Institutions and Economic Growth after World War II," in Nicholas Crafts and Gianni Toniolo (eds), *Economic Growth since 1945* (Cambridge: Cambridge University Press, 1996), pp. 38–72.

7 For a comprehensive account of the internal challenges see Franz-Xaver Kaufmann, *Herausforderungen des Sozialstaates* (Frankfurt: Suhrkamp, 1997).

8 For a corresponding study of UK and US social policy developments in the 1980s, see Paul Pierson, *Dismantling the Welfare State? Reagan, Thatcher and the Politics of Retrenchment* (Cambridge: Cambridge University Press, 1994). For an extension of this analysis to additional countries see Pierson, "The New Politics of the Welfare State," *World Politics* 48 (1996): 147–79.

9 See Jens Alber, *Der Sozialstaat in der Bundesrepublik 1950–1983* (Frankfurt: Campus, 1989); Morris Janowitz, *Social Control of the Welfare State* (Chicago: University of Chicago Press, 1976); and M. Rainer Lepsius, "Soziale Ungleichheit und Klassenstrukturen in der Bundesrepublik Deutschland," in Hans-Ulrich Wehler (ed.), *Klassen in der europäischen Sozialgeschichte* (Göttingen: Vandenhoeck und Ruprecht, 1979), pp. 166–209.

10 See Günther Schmid, "Beschäftigungswunder Niederlande? Ein Vergleich der Beschäftigungssysteme in den Niederlanden und in Deutschland," *Leviathan* 25 (1997): 302–37; and Birgitta Wolff, "Incentive-Compatible Change Management in a Welfare State: Asking the Right Questions in the German Standort-Debate," Working Paper Series 6.4, Center for European Studies, Harvard University, 1997.

11 Between 1981 and 1996, the average quotient of government outlays on all levels to the nominal domestic product rose from 47 to 49 percent, while state debt – the quotient of gross obligations of all levels of government to gross domestic product – climbed from 44 to 76 percent. See Paul Bernd Spahn and Wolfgang Föttinger, "Fiskalische Disziplin und institutionelle Budgetkoordinierung: Internationale Erfahrungen und ihre Bedeutung für die Europäische Union," in Thomas König, Elmar Rieger, and Hermann Schmitt (eds), *Europäische Institutionenpolitik* (Frankfurt: Campus, 1997), pp. 140–59.

12 On the United States see Thomas Gebhardt, *Ending Welfare as We Know It: Die US-amerikanische Sozialhilfereform 1993–1996* (Bremen: University of Bremen, Zentrum für Sozialpolitik, 1997); Martin Seeleib-Kaiser, "Sozialpolitik nach dem Ende des Ost-West-Konflikts," in Herbert Dittgen and Michael Minkenberg (eds), *Das amerikanische Dilemma: Die Vereinigten Staaten nach dem Ende des Ost-West-Konflikts* (Paderborn: Schöningh, 1996), pp. 239–68; and Michael Wiseman, "Welfare Reform in the United States: A Background Paper," *Housing Policy Debate* 7 (1996): 1–54. On the contrasting German case, see Herbert Jacobs, *Zwischen Mißbrauch und Arbeitspflicht – Die Diskussion um die Sozialhilfe und die Novellierungen des BSHG 1993* (Bremen: University of Bremen, Zentrum für Sozialpolitik, 1997). In Germany, a "leaning" of the welfare state is discernible with means- and income-tested benefits. Germany's 1996 introduction of old-age nursing-care insurance, however, indicates how well entrenched the welfare state is, since this policy did not consider the imperatives of integration in the global market for German industry. On the failure of the United States's 1995 health insurance reform, proposed as a strategy to expand the welfare state, see Jacob Hacker, *The Road to Nowhere: The Genesis of President Clinton's Plan for Health Security* (Princeton: Princeton University Press, 1997).

Part V
Divided Nations, Unruly World

Global inequality is one of the most critical issues on the contemporary global agenda. The debate about its causes and remedies is complex and does not readily fit into the dichotomy of sceptics versus globalists. Nevertheless, the sceptics are, for the most part, cautious about placing the sole responsibility for growing global inequality on world markets or international capital. They consider national factors to be equally (if not more) important, and the problem of inequality itself to be largely unamenable to international intervention. Globalists tend to disagree with this, arguing that the problem of global inequality can be ameliorated, if not resolved, through concerted global action. They consider neoliberal economic globalization as the primary cause of growing world inequality.

On one issue both globalists and sceptics tend to agree: growing interdependence is associated with a more unequal world. Although the specific causes and remedies of the growing gap between rich and poor in the world economy remain subject to dispute, there is a general agreement that, over the last several decades, the numbers of people in absolute poverty have increased. The 1999 UNDP Report describes the various dimensions of this poverty, and the forms of inequality associated with globalization. Castells links the dynamics of the new 'global informational capitalism' to the growth of poverty and social exclusion within and between the world's states, while Hoogvelt argues that the uneven nature of globalization is creating a new social division which transcends the old core–periphery organization of the world economy. Although the OECD in general benefits most from globalization, all nations are being divided by the forces of global capitalism into a new pattern of winners and losers.

Of course, this is not to deny that global standards of living for the most part have been on the increase, and that more of the world's peoples have better standards of living than fifty or a hundred years ago. Nor is it to suggest that development in a global capitalist economy is impossible, for Fieldhouse disputes the idea that globalization is associated with an intractable North–South divide. Yet it is evident, from the contribution of Steans as well as Yearley, that the particular form taken by economic globalization in the last two decades – neoliberal economic globalization – has not transcended the old North–South division of the world but superimposed on it new kinds of division along gender, ethnic and ecological lines. Thus, while for some the world may appear increasingly as a shared social and ecological space, for many others globalization is experienced as new forms of poverty (information rich and poor), social exclusion, division and inequality. In other words, our shared planet is marked by the creation of rapidly diverging social worlds and life chances. The implications of these developments for global stability and world order are considered by Woods. Whether globalization, through the combined efforts of the major institutions of global and regional governance, can be given a human face, or whether it will generate a more unruly world, are issues which, suggests Woods, will dominate the global agenda of the new century.

31

Globalization with a Human Face

UNDP Report 1999

[...]

Globalization is not new. Recall the early sixteenth century and the late nineteenth. But this era is different:

- *New markets* – foreign exchange and capital markets linked globally, operating 24 hours a day, with dealings at a distance in real time.
- *New tools* – Internet links, cellular phones, media networks.
- *New actors* – the World Trade Organization (WTO) with authority over national governments, the multinational corporations with more economic power than many states, the global networks of non-governmental organizations (NGOs) and other groups that transcend national boundaries.
- *New rules* – multilateral agreements on trade, services and intellectual property, backed by strong enforcement mechanisms and more binding for national governments, reducing the scope for national policy.

Globalization offers great opportunities for human advance – but only with stronger governance.

This era of globalization is opening many opportunities for millions of people around the world. Increased trade, new technologies, foreign investments, expanding media and Internet connections are fuelling economic growth and human advance. All this offers enormous potential to eradicate poverty in the 21st century – to continue the unprecedented progress in the 20th century. We have more wealth and technology – and more commitment to a global community – than ever before.

Global markets, global technology, global ideas and global solidarity can enrich the lives of people everywhere, greatly expanding their choices. The growing interdependence of people's lives calls for shared values and a shared commitment to the human development of all people.

The post–cold war world of the 1990s has sped progress in defining such values – in adopting human rights and in setting development goals in the United Nations conferences on environment, population, social development, women and human settlements.

But today's globalization is being driven by market expansion – opening national borders to trade, capital, information – outpacing governance of these markets and their repercussions for people. More progress has been made in norms, standards, policies and institutions for open global markets than for people and their rights. And a new commitment is needed to the ethics of universalism set out in the Universal Declaration of Human Rights.

[...]

When the market goes too far in dominating social and political outcomes, the opportunities and rewards of globalization spread unequally and inequitably – concentrating power and wealth in a select group of people, nations and corporations, marginalizing the others. When the market gets out of hand, the instabilities show up in boom and bust economies, as in the financial crisis in East Asia and its worldwide repercussions, cutting global output by an estimated \$2 trillion in 1998–2000. When the profit motives of market players get out of hand, they challenge people's ethics – and sacrifice respect for justice and human rights.

The challenge of globalization in the new century is not to stop the expansion of global markets. The challenge is to find the rules and institutions for stronger governance – local, national, regional and global – to preserve the advantages of global markets and competition, but also to provide enough space for human, community and environmental resources to ensure that globalization works for people – not just for profits. Globalization with:

- *Ethics* – less violation of human rights, not more.
- *Equity* – less disparity within and between nations, not more.
- *Inclusion* – less marginalization of people and countries, not more.
- *Human security* – less instability of societies and less vulnerability of people, not more.
- *Sustainability* – less environmental destruction, not more.
- *Development* – less poverty and deprivation, not more.

The opportunities and benefits of globalization need to be shared much more widely.

Since the 1980s many countries have seized the opportunities of economic and technological globalization. Beyond the industrial countries, the newly industrializing East Asian tigers are joined by Chile, the Dominican Republic, India, Mauritius, Poland, Turkey and many others linking into global markets, attracting foreign investment and taking advantage of technological advance. Their export growth has averaged more than 5 percent a year, diversifying into manufactures.

At the other extreme are the many countries benefiting little from expanding markets and advancing technology – Madagascar, Niger, the Russian Federation, Tajikistan and Venezuela among them.

These countries are becoming even more marginal – ironic, since many of them are highly "integrated", with exports nearly 30 per cent of GDP for Sub-Saharan Africa and only 19 per cent for the OECD. But these countries hang on the vagaries of global markets, with the prices of primary commodities having fallen to their lowest in a century and a half. They have shown little growth in exports and attracted virtually no foreign investment. In sum, today, global opportunities are unevenly distributed – between countries and people [. . .].

If global opportunities are not shared better, the failed growth of the last decades will continue. More than 80 countries still have per capita incomes lower than they were a decade or more ago. While 40 countries have sustained average per capita income growth of more than 3 per cent a year since 1990, 55 countries, mostly in Sub-Saharan Africa and Eastern Europe and the Commonwealth of Independent States (CIS), have had declining per capita incomes.

Many people are also missing out on employment opportunities. The global labour market is increasingly integrated for the highly skilled – corporate executives, scientists, entertainers and the many others who form the global professional elite – with high mobility and wages. But the market for unskilled labour is highly restricted by national barriers.

Inequality has been rising in many countries since the early 1980s. In China disparities are widening between the export-oriented regions of the coast and the interior: the human poverty index is just under 20 per cent in coastal provinces, but more than 50 per cent in inland Guizhou. The countries of Eastern Europe and the CIS have registered some of the largest increases ever in the Gini coefficient, a measure of income inequality. OECD countries also registered big increases in inequality after the 1980s – especially Sweden, the United Kingdom and the United States.

Inequality between countries has also increased. The income gap between the fifth of the world's people living in the richest countries and the fifth in the poorest was 74 to 1 in 1997, up from 60 to 1 in 1990 and 30 to 1 in 1960. In the nineteenth century, too, inequality grew rapidly during the last three decades, in an era of rapid global integration: the income gap between the top and bottom countries increased from 3 to 1 in 1820 to 7 to 1 in 1870 and 11 to 1 in 1913.

By the late 1990s the fifth of the world's people living in the highest-income countries had:

- 86 per cent of world GDP – the bottom fifth just 1 per cent.
- 82 per cent of world export markets – the bottom fifth just 1 per cent.
- 68 per cent of foreign direct investment – the bottom fifth just 1 per cent.
- 74 per cent of world telephone lines, today's basic means of communication – the bottom fifth just 1.5 per cent.

Some have predicted convergence. Yet the past decade has shown increasing concentration of income, resources and wealth among people, corporations and countries:

- OECD countries, with 19 per cent of the global population, have 71 per cent of global trade in goods and services, 58 per cent of foreign direct investment and 91 per cent of all Internet users.
- The world's 200 richest people more than doubled their net worth in the four years to 1998, to more than $1 trillion. The assets of the top three billionaires are more than the combined GNP of all least developed countries and their 600 million people.
- The recent wave of mergers and acquisitions is concentrating industrial power in megacorporations – at the risk of eroding competition. By 1998 the top 10 companies in pesticides controlled 85 per cent of a $31 billion global market – and the top 10 in telecommunications, 86 per cent of a $262 billion market.
- In 1993 just 10 countries accounted for 84 per cent of global research and development expenditures and controlled 95 per cent of the US patents of the past two decades. Moreover, more than 80 per cent of patents granted in developing countries belong to residents of industrial countries.

All these trends are not the inevitable consequences of global economic integration – but they have run ahead of global governance to share the benefits.

Globalization is creating new threats to human security – in rich countries and poor.

One achievement of recent decades has been greater security for people in many countries – more political freedom and stability in Chile, peace in Central America, safer streets in the United States. But in the globalizing world of shrinking time, shrinking space and disappearing borders, people are confronting new threats to human security – sudden and hurtful disruptions in the pattern of daily life.

Financial volatility and economic insecurity

The financial turmoil in East Asia in 1997–99 demonstrates the risks of global financial markets. [. . .] Two important lessons come out of this experience.

First, the human impacts are severe and are likely to persist long after economic recovery.

[. . .]

Second, far from being isolated incidents, financial crises have become increasingly common with the spread and growth of global capital flows. They result from rapid buildups and reversals of short-term capital flows and are likely to recur. More likely when national institutions regulating financial markets are not well developed, they are now recognized as systemic features of global capital markets. No single country can withstand their whims, and global action is needed to prevent and manage them.

Job and income insecurity

In both poor and rich countries dislocations from economic and corporate restructuring, and from dismantling the institutions of social protection, have meant greater insecurity in jobs and incomes. The pressures of global competition have led countries and employers to adopt more flexible labour policies with more precarious work arrangements. Workers without contracts or with new, less secure contracts make up 30 per cent of the total in Chile, 39 per cent in Colombia.

France, Germany, the United Kingdom and other countries have weakened worker dismissal laws. Mergers and acquisitions have come with corporate restructuring and massive layoffs. Sustained economic growth has not reduced unemployment in Europe – leaving it at 11 per cent for a decade, affecting 35 million. In Latin America growth has created jobs, but 85 per cent of them are in the informal sector.

Health insecurity

Growing travel and migration have helped spread HIV/AIDS. More than 33 million people were living with HIV/AIDS in 1998, with almost 6 million new infections in that year. And the epidemic is now spreading rapidly to new locations, such as rural India and Eastern Europe and the CIS. With 95 per cent of the 16,000 infected each day living in developing countries, AIDS has become a poor person's disease, taking a heavy toll on life expectancy, reversing the gains of recent decades. For nine countries in Africa, a loss of 17 years in life expectancy is projected by 2010, back to the level of the 1960s.

Cultural insecurity

Globalization opens people's lives to culture and all its creativity – and to the flow of ideas and knowledge. But the new culture carried by expanding global markets is disquieting. As Mahatma Gandhi expressed so eloquently earlier in the century, "I do not want my house to be walled in on all sides and my windows to be stuffed. I want the cultures of all the lands to be blown about my house as freely as possible. But I refuse to be blown off my feet by any." Today's flow of culture is unbalanced, heavily weighted in one direction, from rich countries to poor.
[. . .]

Personal insecurity

Criminals are reaping the benefits of globalization. Deregulated capital markets, advances in information and communications technology and cheaper transport make flows easier, faster and less restricted not just for medical knowledge but for heroin – not just for books and seeds but for dirty money and weapons.

Illicit trade – in drugs, women, weapons and laundered money – is contributing to the violence and crime that threaten neighbourhoods around the world. Drug-related crimes increased from 4 per 100,000 people in Belarus in 1990 to 28 in 1997, and from 1 per 100,000 to 8 in Estonia. The weapons trade feeds street crime as well as civil strife. In South Africa machine guns are pouring in from Angola and Mozambique. The traffic in women and girls for sexual exploitation – 500,000 a year to Western Europe alone – is one of the most heinous violations of human rights, estimated to be a $7 billion business.
[. . .]

At the root of all this is the growing influence of organized crime, estimated to gross $1.5 trillion a year, rivalling multinational corporations as an economic power. Global crime groups have the power to criminalize politics, business and the police, developing efficient networks, extending their reach deep and wide.

Environmental insecurity

Chronic environmental degradation – today's silent emergency – threatens people worldwide and undercuts the livelihoods of at least half a billion people. Poor people themselves, having little choice, put pressure on the environment, but so does the consumption of the rich. The growing export markets for fish, shrimp, paper and many other products mean depleted stocks, less biodiversity and fewer forests. Most of the costs are borne by the poor – though it is the world's rich who benefit most. The fifth of the world's people living in the richest countries consume 84 per cent of the world's paper.

Political and community insecurity

Closely related to many other forms of insecurity is the rise of social tensions that threaten political stability and community cohesion. Of the 61 major armed conflicts fought between 1989 and 1998, only three were between states – the rest were civil.

Globalization has given new characteristics to conflicts. Feeding these conflicts is the global traffic in weapons, involving new actors and blurring political and business interests. In the power vacuum of the post–cold war era, military companies and mercenary armies began offering training to governments – and corporations. Accountable only to those who pay them, these hired military services pose a severe threat to human security.

New information and communications technologies are driving globalization – but polarizing the world into the connected and the isolated.

With the costs of communications plummeting and innovative tools easier to use, people around the world have burst into conversation using the Internet, mobile phones and fax machines. The fastest-growing communications tool ever, the Internet had more than 140 million users in mid-1998, a number expected to pass 700 million by 2001.

Communications networks can foster great advances in health and education. They can also empower small players. The previously unheard voices of NGOs helped halt the secretive OECD negotiations for the Multilateral Agreement on Investment, called for corporate accountability and created support for marginal communities. Barriers of size, time and distance are coming down for small businesses, for governments of poor countries, for remote academics and specialists.

Information and communications technology can also open a fast track to knowledge-based growth – a track followed by India's software exports, Ireland's computing services and the Eastern Caribbean's data processing.

Despite the potential for development, the Internet poses severe problems of access and exclusion. Who was in the loop in 1998?

- *Geography divides.* Thailand has more cellular phones than Africa. South Asia, home to 23 per cent of the world's people, has less than 1 per cent of Internet users.
- *Education is a ticket to the network high society.* Globally, 30 per cent of users had at least one university degree.
- *Income buys access.* To purchase a computer would cost the average Bangladeshi more than eight years income, the average American, just one month's wage.
- *Men and youth dominate.* Women make up just 17 per cent of the Internet users in Japan, only 7 per cent in China. Most users in China and the United Kingdom are under 30.
- *English talks.* English prevails in almost 80 per cent of all Websites, yet less than one in 10 people worldwide speaks it.

This exclusivity is creating parallel worlds. Those with income, education and – literally – connections have cheap and instantaneous access to information. The rest are left with uncertain, slow and costly access. When people in these two worlds live and compete side by side, the advantage of being connected will overpower the marginal and impoverished, cutting off their voices and concerns from the global conversation. [. . .]

National and global governance have to be reinvented – with human development and equity at their core.

None of these pernicious trends – growing marginalization, growing human insecurity, growing inequality – is inevitable. With political will and commitment in the global community, they can all be reversed. With stronger governance – local, national, regional and global – the benefits of competitive markets can be preserved with clear rules and boundaries, and stronger action can be taken to meet the needs of human development.

Governance does not mean mere government. It means the framework of rules, institutions and established practices that set limits and give incentives for the behaviour of individuals, organizations and firms. Without strong governance, the dangers of global conflicts could be a reality of the 21st century – trade wars promoting national and corporate interests, uncontrolled financial volatility setting off civil conflicts, untamed global crime infecting safe neighbourhoods and criminalizing politics, business and the police. [. . .]

32

The Rise of the Fourth World

Manuel Castells

The rise of [global] informationalism in this end of millennium is intertwined with rising inequality and social exclusion throughout the world. In this chapter I shall try to explain why and how this is so, while displaying some snapshots of the new faces of human suffering. The process of capitalist restructuring, with its hardened logic of economic competitiveness, has much to do with it. But new technological and organizational conditions of the Information Age [...] provide a new, powerful twist to the old pattern of profit-seeking taking over soul-searching.

However, there is contradictory evidence, fueling an ideologically charged debate, on the actual plight of people around the world. After all, the last quarter of the century has seen access to development, industrialization, and consumption for tens of millions of Chinese, Koreans, Indians, Malaysians, Thais, Indonesians, Chileans, Brazilians, Argentinians, and smaller numbers in a variety of countries. The bulk of the population in Western Europe still enjoys the highest living standards in the world, and in the world's history. And in the United States, while average real wages for male workers have stagnated or declined, with the exception of the top of the scale of college graduates, the massive incorporation of women into paid labor, relatively closing their wage gap with men, has maintained decent standards of living, overall, on the condition of being stable enough to keep a two-wage household. Health, education, and income statistics around the world show, on average, considerable improvement over historical standards.[1] In fact, for the population as a whole, only the former Soviet Union, after the collapse of statism, and Sub-Saharan Africa, after its marginalization from capitalism, have experienced a decline in living conditions, and for some countries in vital statistics, in the past ten years (although most of Latin America regressed in the 1980s). Yet, as Stephen Gould entitled a wonderful article years ago, "the median isn't the message."[2] Even without entering into a full discussion of the meaning of the quality of life, including the environmental consequences of the latest round of industrialization, the apparently mixed record of development at the dawn of the Information Age conveys ideologically manipulated bewilderment in the absence of analytical clarity.

This is why it is necessary, in assessing the social dynamics of informationalism, to establish a distinction between several processes of social differentiation: on the one hand, *inequality*, *polarization*, *poverty*, and *misery* all pertain to the domain of relationships of distribution/consumption or differential appropriation of the wealth generated by collective effort. On the other hand, *individualization of work*, *over-exploitation of workers*, *social exclusion*, and *perverse integration* are characteristic of four specific processes *vis à vis* relationships of production.[3]

Inequality refers to the differential appropriation of wealth (income and assets) by different individuals and social groups, relative to each other. *Polarization* is a specific process of inequality that occurs when both the top and the bottom of the scale of income or wealth distribution grow faster than the middle, thus shrinking the middle, and sharpening social differences between two extreme segments of the population. *Poverty* is an institutionally defined norm concerning a level of resources below which it is not possible to reach the living standards considered to be the minimum norm in a given society at a given time (usually, a level of income per a given number of members of household, as defined by governments or authoritative institutions). *Misery*, a term I propose, refers to what social statisticians call "extreme poverty," that is the bottom of the distribution of income/assets, or what some experts conceptualize as "deprivation," introducing a wider range of social/economic disadvantages. In the United States, for instance, extreme poverty refers to those households whose income falls below 50 percent of the income that defines the poverty line. It is obvious that all these definitions (with powerful effects in categorizing populations, and defining social policies and resource allocation) are statistically relative and culturally defined, besides being politically manipulated. Yet, they at least allow us to be precise about what we say when describing/ analyzing social differentiation under informational capitalism.

The second set of processes, and their categorization, pertains to the analysis of relations of production. Thus, when observers criticize "precarious" labor relations, they are usually referring to the process of individualization of work, and to its induced instability on employment patterns. Or else the discourse on social exclusion denotes the observed tendency to permanently exclude from formal labor markets certain categories of the population. These processes do have fundamental consequences for inequality, polarization, poverty, and misery. But the two planes must be analytically and empirically differentiated in order to establish their causal relationships, thus paving the way for understanding the dynamics of social differentiation, exploitation, and exclusion in the network society.

By *individualization of labor* I mean the process by which labor contribution to production is defined specifically for each worker, and for each of his/her contributions, either under the form of self-employment or under individually contracted, largely unregulated, salaried labor. [. . .] [I]ndividualization of labor is the overwhelming practice in the urban informal economy that has become the predominant form of employment in most developing countries, as well as in certain labor markets of advanced economies.[4]

I use the term *over-exploitation*[5] to indicate working arrangements that allow capital to systematically withhold payment/resource allocation, or impose harsher working conditions, on certain types of workers, below what is the norm/regulation in a given formal labor market in a given time and space. This refers to discrimination against immigrants, minorities, women, young people, children, or other categories of discriminated workers, as tolerated, or sanctioned, by regulatory agencies. A particularly meaningful trend in this context is the resurgence of child paid labor throughout the world, in conditions of extreme exploitation, defenselessness, and abuse, reversing the historical pattern of social protection of children existing under late industrial capitalism, as well as in industrial statism and traditional agricultural societies.[6]

Social exclusion is a concept proposed by the social policy think-tanks of the European Union's Commission, and adopted by the United Nation's International Labour Office.[7] According to the European Commission's Observatory on National Policies to Combat Social Exclusion, it refers to "the social rights of citizens . . . to a certain basic standard of living and to participation in the major social and occupational opportunities of the society."[8] Trying to be more precise, I define *social exclusion as the process by which certain individuals and groups are systemically barred from access to positions that would enable them to an autonomous livelihood within the social standards framed by institutions and values in a given context.*[9] Under normal circumstances, in informational capitalism, *such a position is usually associated with the possibility of access to relatively regular, paid labor, for at least one member of a stable household.* Social exclusion is, in fact, the process that disfranchises a person as labor in the context of capitalism. In countries with a well-developed welfare state, inclusion may also encompass generous compensations in case of long-term unemployment or disability, although these conditions are increasingly exceptional. I would consider among the socially excluded the mass of people on long-term welfare assistance under institutionally punitive conditions, such as is the case in the United States. [. . .]

Social exclusion is a process, not a condition. Thus, its boundaries shift, and who is excluded and included may vary over time, depending on education, demographic characteristics, social prejudices, business practices, and public policies. Furthermore, although the lack of regular work as a source of income is ultimately the key mechanism in social exclusion, how and why individuals and groups are placed under structural difficulty/impossibility to provide for themselves follows a wide array of avenues of destitution. [. . .]

Moreover, the process of social exclusion in the network society concerns both people and territories. So that, under certain conditions, entire countries, regions, cities, and neighborhoods become excluded, embracing in this exclusion most, or all, of their populations. This is different from the traditional process of spatial segregation [. . .]. Under the new, dominant logic of the space of flows [. . .] areas that are non-valuable from the perspective of informational capitalism, and that do not have significant political interest for the powers that be, are bypassed by flows of wealth and information, and ultimately deprived of the basic technological infrastructure that allows us to communicate, innovate, produce, consume, and even live, in today's world. This process induces an extremely uneven geography of social/territorial exclusion and inclusion, which disables large segments of people while linking up trans-territorially, through information technology, whatever and whoever may offer value in the global networks accumulating wealth, information, and power.

The process of social exclusion, and the insufficiency of remedial policies of social integration, lead to a fourth, key process characterizing some specific forms of relations of production in informational capitalism: I call it *perverse integration*. It refers to the labor process in the criminal economy. By criminal economy, I mean income-generating activities that are normatively declared to be crime, and accordingly prosecuted, in a given institutional context. [. . .] [I]nformational capitalism is characterized by the formation of a global criminal economy, and by its growing interdependence with the formal economy and political institutions. Segments of the socially excluded population, along with individuals who choose far more profitable, if risky, ways to make a living, constitute an increasingly populated underworld which is becoming an essential feature of social dynamics in most of the planet.

There are systemic relationships between [global] informational capitalism, capitalist restructuring, trends in the relationships of production, and new trends in the relationships of distribution. Or, in a nutshell, between the dynamics of the network society, inequality, and social exclusion. [. . .] [L]et me briefly overview the state of the world concerning inequality, poverty, and social exclusion.

Toward a Polarized World? A Global Overview

"Divergence in output per person across countries is perhaps *the* dominant feature of modern economic history. The ratio of per capita income in the richest versus the poorest country [between 1870 and 1989] has increased by a factor of 6 and the standard deviation of GDP per capita has increased between 60 and 100 percent" writes Pritchett, summarizing the findings of his econometric study for the World Bank.[10] In much of the world, this geographical disparity in the creation/appropriation of wealth has increased in the past two decades, while the differential between OECD countries and the rest of the planet, representing the overwhelming proportion of the population, is still abysmal. Thus, using the historical economic statistics elaborated by Maddison,[11] Benner and I have elaborated [. . .] the evolution of GDP per capita [. . .] for a group of selected countries [. . .] *vis à vis* the United States, between 1950, 1973, and 1992. Japan has succeeded in almost catching up in the past four decades, while Western Europe has improved its relative position, but still trails the US by a considerable margin. During the 1973–92 period, the sample of Latin American, African, and Eastern European countries studied by Maddison have fallen behind even further. As for ten Asian countries, including the economic miracles of South Korea, China, and Taiwan, they have substantially improved their relative position, but in absolute levels, in 1992, they were still poorer than any other region of the world except Africa, representing, as a whole, only 18 percent of the US level of wealth, although this is mainly due to China's population.

However, if the distribution of wealth between countries continues to diverge, overall the average living conditions of the world's population, as measured by the United Nations Human Development Index, have improved steadily over the past three decades. This is due, primarily, to better educational opportunities, and improved health standards, which translate into a dramatic increase in life expectancy, which in developing countries went up from 46 years in the 1960s to 62 years in 1993, particularly for women.[12]

The evolution of income inequality presents a different profile if we take a global view, or if we look at its evolution within specific countries in a comparative perspective. In a global approach, there has been, over the past three decades, increasing inequality and polarization in the distribution of wealth. According to UNDP's 1996 Human Development Report, in 1993 only US$ 5 trillion of the US$ 23 trillion global GDP were from the developing countries even if they accounted for nearly 80 percent of total population. The poorest 20 percent of the world's people have seen their share of global income decline from 2.3 percent to 1.4 percent in the past 30 years. Meanwhile, the share of the richest 20 percent has risen from 70 percent to 85 percent. This doubled the ratio of the share of the richest over the poorest – from 30:1 to 61:1. The assets of the world's 358 billionaires (in US dollars) exceed the combined annual incomes of countries with 45 percent of the world's population. The gap in per capita income between the industrial and the developing worlds tripled, from $5,700 in 1960 to $15,000 in 1993.[13] "Between 1960 and 1991, all but the richest quintile [of the world's people] saw their income share fall, so that by 1991 more than 85 percent of the world's population received only 15 percent of its income – yet another indication of an even more polarized world."[14]

On the other hand, there is considerable disparity in the evolution of *intra-country inequality* in different areas of the world. In the past two decades, income inequality has increased in the United States,[15] United Kingdom,[16] Brazil, Argentina, Venezuela,

Bolivia, Peru, Thailand, and Russia;[17] and, in the 1980s, in Japan,[18] Canada, Sweden, Australia, Germany,[19] and in Mexico,[20] just to cite a few relevant countries. But income inequality *decreased* in the 1960–90 period in India, Malaysia, Hong Kong, Singapore, Taiwan and South Korea.[21] Also, according to data elaborated by Deininger and Squire, if we compare the level of income inequality [. . .] by major regions of the world, between the 1990s and the 1970s, in 1990 it was much higher in Eastern Europe, somewhat higher in Latin America, but lower in all other regions, when analyzed at a highly aggregate level.[22] This disparity in the evolution of inequality between the world's regions is probably associated with two main factors. For developing countries, this is the rate of rural–urban migration, since the main factor in the disparity of income distribution is the abysmal difference in income levels between rural areas and urban agglomerations, even accounting for widespread urban poverty.[23] For industrialized countries, the key issue is the differential development in welfare states, and in the level of wages and social benefits, directly related to the bargaining power of labor unions.[24]

But if the evolution of intra-country inequality varies, *what appears to be a global phenomenon is the growth of poverty, and particularly of extreme poverty*. Indeed, the acceleration of uneven development, and the simultaneous inclusion and exclusion of people in the growth process, which I consider to be a feature of informational capitalism, translates into polarization, and the spread of misery among a growing number of people. [. . .]

In the mid-1990s, taking as the extreme poverty line a consumption equivalent to one US dollar a day, 1.3 billion people, accounting for 33 percent of the developing world's population were in misery. Of these poor people, 550 million lived in South Asia, 215 million in Sub-Saharan Africa, and 150 million in Latin America.[25] In a similar estimate, using the one dollar a day dividing line for extreme poverty, ILO estimated that the percentage of the population below this line increased from 53.5 percent in 1985 to 54.4 percent in 1990 in Sub-Saharan Africa; from 23 percent to 27.8 percent in Latin America; and decreased from 61.1 percent to 59 percent in South Asia, and from 15.7 percent to 14.7 percent in East/South East Asia (without China).[26] The largest concentration of poverty was, by far, in the rural areas: in 1990, the proportion of poor among the rural population was 66 percent in Brazil, 72 percent in Peru, 43 percent in Mexico, 49 percent in India, and 54 percent in the Philippines.[27]

Thus, overall, *the ascent of informational, global capitalism is indeed characterized by simultaneous economic development and underdevelopment, social inclusion and social exclusion*, in a process very roughly reflected in comparative statistics. There is polarization in the distribution of wealth at the global level, differential evolution of intra-country income inequality, and substantial growth of poverty and misery in the world at large, and in most countries, both developed and developing.
[. . .]

Notes

1   UNDP (1996).
2   Gould (1985).
3   For an informed discussion on analyzing poverty and social exclusion in a comparative perspective, see Rodgers et al. (1995); Mingione (1996).
4   Portes et al. (1989).

5   I use the term "over-exploitation" to distinguish it from the concept of exploitation in the Marxian tradition, that, in strict Marxist economics, would be applicable to all salaried labor. Since this categorization would imply accepting the labor theory of value, a matter of belief rather than of research, I prefer to bypass the debate altogether, but avoid creating further confusion by using "exploitation," as I would like to do for cases of systematic discrimination such as the ones I am referring to in my categorization.

6   ILO (1996).

7   Rodgers et al. (1995).

8   Room G. (1992: 14).

9   By "autonomy," in this context, I mean the average margin of individual autonomy/social heteronomy as constructed by society. It is obvious that a worker, or even a self-employed person, is not autonomous *vis à vis* his/her employer, or network of clients. I refer to social conditions that represent the social norm, in contrast with people's inability to organize their own lives even under the constraints of social structure, because of their lack of access to resources that social structure mandates as necessary to construct their limited autonomy. This discussion of socially constrained autonomy is what underlies the conceptualization of inclusion/exclusion as the differential expression of people's social rights.

10 Pritchett (1995: 2–3).

11 Maddison (1995).

12 UNDP (1996: 18–19).

13 UNDP (1996: 2–3).

14 UNDP (1996: 13).

15 Fischer et al. (1996).

16 Townsend (1993).

17 UNDP (1996).

18 Bauer and Mason (1992).

19 Green et al. (1992).

20 Skezely (1995).

21 UNDP (1996).

22 Deininger and Squire (1996: 584).

23 Jazairy et al. (1992).

24 Townsend (1993); Navarro (1997).

25 UNDP (1996: 27).

26 ILO (1995: table 13).

27 ILO (1994).

References

Bauer, John and Mason, Andrew (1992) The Distribution of Income and Wealth in Japan. *Review of Income and Wealth* 38(4).

Deininger, Klaus and Squire, Lyn (1996) A New Data Set Measuring Income Inequality. *World Bank Economic Review* 10(3).

Fischer, Claude et al. (1996) *Inequality by Design*. Princeton: Princeton University Press.

Gould, Stephen Jay (1985) The Median Isn't the Message. *Discover* (June).

Green, Gordon et al. (1992) International Comparisons of Earnings Inequality for Men in the 1980s. *Review of Income and Wealth* 38(1).

ILO (International Labour Organization) (1994) *World Labour Report 1994*. Geneva: ILO.

ILO (International Labour Organization) (1995) *World Employment Report 1995*. Geneva: ILO.

ILO (International Labour Organization) (1996) *Child Labour: Targeting the Intolerable*. Geneva: ILO.

Jazairy, Idriss et al. (1992) *The State of World Rural Poverty: An Inquiry into its Causes and Consequences*. New York: New York University Press.

Maddison, Angus (1995) *Monitoring the World Economy, 1820–1992*. Paris: OECD Development Centre Studies.

Mingione, Enzo (ed.) (1996) *Urban Poverty and the Underclass*. Oxford: Blackwell.

Navarro, Vincente (1997) *Neoliberaliso y estado del bienestar*. Madrid: Alianza Editorial.

Portes, Alejandro, Castells, Manuel, and Benton, Lauren (eds) (1989) *The Informal Economy: Studies on Advanced and Less Developed Countries*. Baltimore: Johns Hopkins University Press.

Pritchett, Lant (1995) *Divergence, Big Time*. Policy Research Working Paper 1522. Washington DC: World Bank.

Rodgers, Gerry, Gore, Charles, and Figueiredo, José B. (eds) (1995) *Social Exclusion: Rhetoric, Reality, Responses*. Geneva: International Institute of Labour Studies.

Room G. (1992) *Observatory on National Policies to Combat Social Exclusion: Second Annual Report*. Brussels: Commission of the European Community.

Skezely, Miguel (1995) Poverty in Mexico during Adjustment. *Review of Income and Wealth* 41(3).

Svedberg, Peter (1993) Trade Compression and Economic Decline in Sub-Saharan Africa. In Magnus Blomstrom and Mats Lundahl (eds), *Economic Crisis in Africa: Perspectives on Policy Responses*, London and New York: Routledge.

Townsend, Peter (1993) *The International Analysis of Poverty*. London: Harvester Wheatsheaf.

UNDP (United Nations Development Programme) (1996) *Human Development Report 1996*. New York: Oxford University Press.

33

Globalization and the Postcolonial World

Ankie Hoogvelt

There are three key economic indicators which are conventionally marshalled to attest to the increasing internationalization of the world economy: world trade figures [. . .]; the growth and spread of foreign direct investments through multinational corporations [. . .]; and the expansion of all international capital flows [. . .]. We shall look at each of these [. . .] in regard to the participation of the periphery in this internationalization. [. . .]

Core and periphery: respective shares of world trade

Given our interest in the core–periphery structure, it is of [. . .] relevance to look at the long-term data in respect of the participation of each of these two subgroups, and the evolution of trade between the two.
[. . .]
According to [. . .] GATT statistics, by 1962 the share of the industrial areas in world trade was 63.6 per cent and that of the non-industrial areas 24.1 per cent. In fact, it is during the immediate postwar period that the share of the non-industrial group reached its peak level of 31.3 per cent (in 1953). Turning to subsequent years, we find a remarkable continuity in the historical long run despite small periodic fluctuations. For example in 1973 the percentage share of the industrial areas had climbed back up to 69 per cent, and that of the non-industrial group had fallen back to 18.1 per cent. By 1990 it was 71.9 per cent and 20.0 per cent respectively.
[. . .]
By far the most revealing statistic is the proportion of world population involved in the respective world trade shares. In the period before 1880, the population of the 'industrial' or 'core' group of countries included north America and western Europe only. Their combined population rose from about 118 million in 1800 to almost 303 million in 1900. That of the 'Rest of the World' rose from 783 million to 1319 million, giving the 'industrial' group a rising share of the world population from 13 per cent in 1800 to 18.7 per cent in 1900. By 1990, even with the inclusion of Japan as belonging to the core, that proportion is just 15.8 per cent [. . .].[1] And, even if we were to add the population (72 million) of the four Asian Tigers to the core group, the combined population of the 'core participants', at 17.1 per cent, remains below the historical bench mark.

The conclusion to be drawn from these figures is that the record of world trade can neither be summoned to testify to 'the increasing interconnectedness which characterizes our world economy', nor to evidence of 'the deepening and widening penetration by the core of the periphery'. Rather, it stands as evidence of a modestly thickening network of economic exchanges within the core, a significant redistribution of trade participation within the core, the graduation of a small number of peripheral nations with a comparatively small population base to 'core' status, but above all to a declining economic interaction between core and periphery, both relative to aggregate world trade and relative to total populations participating in the thickening network.[2]

Foreign Direct Investment (FDI) and the Growth of Multinational Enterprises

Even if world trade is *not*, surely foreign direct investment *is* 'the most important manifestation of transnationalization'?[3] Or is it?

[. . .]

What is both a *new and consistent* feature of postwar foreign direct investment flows is the *geographic redirection* of such flows away from the periphery and into the core of the system. In the colonial period, right up until 1960, the Third World had received half of total direct investment flows; this percentage had declined to one-third in 1966, and to one-quarter in 1974. By 1988–9 it had dropped still further to 16.9 per cent.[4] But over half of this remaining trickle went to the regions of east, south and south-east Asia.[5]

In the data for south-east Asia, China dominates today as the single largest developing host country of inward investment. Because China has a very large population of 1.2 billion, this often distorts the picture on foreign direct investment (FDI) and growth in the developing world. But it is well-known that in China, both investments and growth are concentrated in the eight coastal provinces (mainly in the south) and in Beijing.

In their recent book *Globalization in Question*, Paul Hirst and Grahame Thompson have tried to discount this anomaly by including only the populations of the coastal provinces and Beijing in their summation of all populations in the ten most important developing countries in terms of inward investment. Together with the other nine most important developing countries hosting FDI, they constitute 758,820 million or 14 per cent of the world population; they receive 16.5 per cent of all global direct investment. Hirst and Thompson add to this the percentage of world population in the USA/Canada, EC and EFTA, and Japan who together receive 75 per cent of all direct investment flows, and they come to the staggering conclusion that only 28 per cent of the world's population receives 91.5 per cent of the FDI.

[. . .]

Global Financial Deepening and the Structural Position of the Third World

[. . .]

If we now look at the structural position of the Third World in the financial superbowl [that is, increasingly integrated world financial markets] we encounter a curious paradox. On the one hand [. . .] its share of the total stock of international bank lending has declined to about 11 per cent.[6] Indeed, for most of the 1980s, new bank lending to the developing countries declined to the point of virtual extinction as the debt crisis took its toll and banks refused to lend anew to troubled sovereign debtors. Even the

11 per cent (or $512 billion) is an overestimate since it includes incremental values attributable to arrears; that is, it is not a summation of continuous fresh inflows. On the other hand, we also find an increased participation of Third World élites in the international financial markets. How is that?

Given that much of the Third World is unbankable in the traditional sense of the word, namely offering a safe return on investment, it is more likely that élites in the Third World will buy securities in the global markets rather than in their national markets. Studies by research staff of the International Monetary Fund on the scale of *capital flight* from the developing countries lend credence to this thesis. For example, between 1975 and 1985 an estimated $165–200 billion were placed by individual investors from the Third World in the international financial markets.[7]

This is surely the critical difference between the earlier, expansive, phase of capitalism and today's 'imploding' phase. In the earlier prewar period, when nearly 44 per cent of all international long-term lending (including foreign direct investments) went to the regions of Africa, Asia and Latin America, it found its way into the development of railways, port installations, mines and factories. Capital accumulation and saving in the core of the world system through the financial intermediation of international portfolio lending, converted into fixed investments in the rest of the world laying the foundations for future wealth creation.

Today, however, the regime of privatization and deregulation imposed by the World Bank and IMF structural adjustment programmes, have created a climate of what is euphemistically called 'financial openness' in which the Third World bourgeoisie are less restricted and more enabled than ever before to channel their nation's wealth to the financial markets and institutions of the core countries. In so doing, *they* can participate in the economies of the core of the world system, while their countries cannot. [. . .]

Core–Periphery: From Structural Exploitation to Structural Irrelevance

I have tried in the foregoing analysis to substantiate my thesis of 'imploding' capitalism. By 'implosion' I understand an intensification of trade and capital linkages within the core of the capitalist system, and a relative, selective, withdrawal of such linkages from the periphery. Looking over the longer historical period, we have examined the relationship between the core and the periphery of the world system and found that the linkages between the two in terms of the volume of both trade and capital flows between them, which increased during earlier phases of the period, have since diminished. Moreover, even allowing for the shift in positions of some countries from the periphery to the core, it was also found that the proportionate share of populations in core and periphery has remained surprisingly constant from about 1880 to 1990.

Characterizing the core and the periphery in the manner in which we have done [. . .] namely the core being western Europe, North America and Japan and the periphery covering the entire regions of Africa, Latin America and Asia, there is furthermore evidence that the gap between their respective shares of world income too has widened.

For example, in its 1992 *Human Development Report* the United Nations Development Programme (UNDP) calculated that in 1989 22.9 per cent of the world population estimated to be living in 'industrial' countries had 84.2 per cent of global GNP, compared with 77.1 per cent of the world population in the 'developing countries' who made do with just 15.8 per cent of global GNP. While the share of global GNP of each of these two groups has been practically constant over the period since 1960, their respective share of world populations, in this report, is said to have worsened, with the 'industrial' group of countries comprising a declining share (from 31.5 per cent in 1960 to 22.9 per cent in 1989), while that of the developing countries has risen from 68.5 per cent in 1960 to 77.1 per cent in 1989.[8]

Going back over an even longer period [...] we come up against almost impossible limitations owing to the unavailability of comparable statistics. Economic historians have, however, attempted to *estimate* the GNP level of per capita incomes for 'developed' and 'underdeveloped' countries in earlier periods. [...] Bairoch notes a divergence between per capita income ratios between non-communist underdeveloped countries and the non-communist developed countries rising from 1:5 in 1860, 1:6 in 1900, 1:7 in 1929, 1:8.5 in 1953 to 1:13 in 1970.[9] This compares with the UNDP ratio of income for the same two groups of countries in 1989 of 1:18[10] [...]. Thus, the gap that almost a hundred years ago separated the rich world from the poor world has continuously widened, both during periods of capitalist expansion and during the more recent period of contraction.

Conclusion

[...]
Globalization [...] has rearranged the architecture of world order. Economic, social and power relations have been recast to resemble *not* a pyramid but a three-tier structure of concentric circles. All three circles cut across national and regional boundaries. In the core circle we find the élites of all continents and nations, albeit in different proportions in relation to their respective geographic hinterlands. We may count in this core some 20 per cent of the world population who are 'bankable'. They are encircled by a fluid, larger social layer of between 20 and 30 per cent of the world population (workers and their families) who labour in insecure forms of employment, thrown into cut-thoat competition in the global market. State-of-the-art technology, frenzied capital mobility and neo-liberal policies together ensure both a relentless elimination of jobs by machines, and a driving down of wages and social conditions to the lowest global denominator.

On the first point, a UNDP report in 1993 projected the gap between world output and jobs to grow twice as fast in the 1990s as in the 1980s. On the second point, the distinguished historian Paul Kennedy recently has warned of the 'global gales ahead'.[11] Quoting research by Harvard Business School researchers, Jensen and Fagen, he argues that the move to market-oriented production in South America, Indonesia, India, parts of China and the rest of south-east Asia which is taking place today, is likely to put 1.2 billion Third World workers into world-wide product and labour markets over the next generation. The vast majority of them earn less than $3 per day. As a consequence, wages in the traditional advanced countries are set to fall by as much as 50 per cent. [...]

The third, and largest, concentric circle comprises those who are already effectively excluded from the global system. Performing neither a productive function, nor presenting a potential consumer market in the present stage of high-tech information-driven capitalism, there is, for the moment, neither theory, world view nor moral injunction, let alone a programme of action, to include them in universal progress. Developmentalism is dead, containment and exclusion rule OK!

In the third part of the book, I described a variety of situations and options that are present in different parts of the postcolonial world. I used the term 'postcolonial' to capture the notion that the distinct social formations which have emerged are a result of the way in which the aftermath of colonialism interacts with the forces of globalization and responds to it. I identified four such postcolonial conditions or situations.

A first condition, that of 'exclusion and anarchy', is exemplified in subSaharan Africa, where all too frequently the patrimonial state form emerging after independence proved too weak to weld a viable political unity or civil society out of the mosaic of ethnic fragments bequeathed by colonial administrations. The failure to progress from a juridical state to an empirical state derailed the state-led developmental project. It made countries in Africa especially vulnerable to the deepening dependency characteristic of the neo-colonial period. Globalization, including structural adjustments imposed since the 1980s, has overwhelmed the fragile social and political orders while further peripheralizing their economies. The combined outcome of these external and internal forces manifests itself in a zone of civil collapse, anarchy and instability on the edge of the global system. And, while today there *are* forms of constructive contestations, for example in innovative coping strategies at the micro-level,[12] my own view is that these are not indicative of what is going to happen in the foreseeable future. Rather, *other* forms of contestations, frequently expressed in resource wars, fragmentation into warlordism, banditry and large-scale population displacements are more likely to characterize the region for some time to come. In emerging international practices of conditionality, aid and humanitarian relief, we discern policies of management and containment rather than of incorporation of the region in the global economy.

I sketched a second postcolonial condition in the anti-developmentalism of fundamental Islam. Here the failure of the developmentalist project, coupled with the exclusionary effect of contemporary processes of globalization, has interacted with the spirit of renewal ever-present within Islam *and* with its long history of cultural confrontation with the West, to render a quite different social formation. It is one in which the politics of religious identity and lifestyle has gained pre-eminence in the private sphere without, however, yielding a political project to (re)create civil society and rearrange state–society relations. As long as the state élites continue to be co-opted into the global élite system there is neither much hope for constructive rebellion nor any threat to established geopolitical relations.

In East Asia, the state-led developmentalist project has succeeded in catapulting the economies of a small number of NICs into the heartland of the reconstructed global capitalist sytem. A unique postwar configuration of geostrategic forces has assisted the emergence of a state apparatus relatively autonomous from civil relations, and hence relatively free to steer an export-oriented path to industrialization at a precise historical juncture when the world capitalist system of production underwent transformative change. However, today the gales of globalization threaten the drive to maturity of the developmentalist project (and the social emancipation of the masses) unless this drive becomes anchored in a regional division of labour. There are signs that a resurgent Asianization may provide the glue to just such regionalization.

We encountered a fourth and final postcolonial condition in Latin America. For reasons peculiar to its own colonial history, the continent has a long intellectual tradition of absorption, experimentation and revolt against western models of modernity and progress. This intellectual commitment has helped to politicize the process of impoverishment and exclusion as the counterpart of Latin America's dependent insertion in the world economy. In recent decades, as Latin America has become a testing ground for neo-liberal policies of globalization and privatization, democracy and the strengthening of civil society have become the arena for intellectual and political renewal.

[...]

Notes

1　Note that the reference to 'all other areas' in the narrative . . . embraces Eastern Europe and the Soviet Union.

2　Note that Paul Hirst and Grahame Thompson in their book *Globalization in Question* (London: Polity Press, 1995) come to the same conclusion. Using gross figures of ratios of trade relative to output 'confirms unequivocally that "openness" was greater during the Gold Standard period than even in the 1980s' (p. 28).

3　UNCTC, *Transnational Corporations in World Development: Trends and Prospects* (New York: United Nations, 1988), p. 16.

4　For the 1960 picture, see M. Barratt Brown, *The Economics of Imperialism*, (London: Penguin, 1974), pp. 206–7. For 1966 see L. B. Pearson, *Partners in Development* (London: Pall Mall Press, 1970), p. 100. For 1974 see *Transnational Corporations in World Development*, table 3, p. 242. For 1989 see UNCTC, *World Investment Report* (New York: United Nations, 1991), table 4, p. 11.

5　See UNCTC, *World Investment Report*, table 4, p. 11.

6　UNCTAD, *Trade and Development Report* (New York: United Nations, 1989), table 17, p. 35.

7　Cited in IMF Occasional Paper 7, *Determinants and Systemic Consequences of International Capital Flows* (Mar. 1991), p. 11.

8　UNDP, *Human Development Report 1992* (New York: Oxford University Press, 1992), p. 36. Note that UNDP in this report includes the countries of eastern Europe and the Soviet Union in the industrialized group. For confirmation of the widening gap in incomes between the traditional core and periphery countries, see also P. Sweezy, 'Globalization to what end', part 2, *Monthly Review* 43(10) (Mar. 1992), table 9, p. 10, and G. Arrighi, 'World income inequalities and the future of socialism', *New Left Review*, no. 189 (1991).

9　P. Bairoch, *The Economic Development of the Third World since 1900* (London: Methuen, 1975), p. 193.

10　UNDP, *Human Development Report 1992*, p. 35.

11　P. Kennedy, 'The global gales ahead', *New Statesman and Society*, 3 May 1996, pp. 28–9.

12　Many of such positive grassroots strategies are documented in M. Barratt Brown, *Africa's Choices* (London: Penguin, 1995); and W. Rau, *From Feast to Famine: Official Cures and Grassroots Remedies to Africa's Food Crisis* (London: Zed Books, 1991).

34

The West and the Third World

D. K. Fieldhouse

Two basic questions were posed in the Introduction. Have the Third World countries benefited or suffered from close economic relationships with the more developed countries of the West? Conversely, would they have done better if they had been able to maintain their autonomy and keep the West at arm's length? It was admitted that no definite or universally acceptable answer is possible to either of these questions, and it is not now proposed to attempt to provide one. On the other hand, the evidence surveyed [...] makes it possible at least to suggest on which side the balance of the argument has swung.

Consider first the second of these questions, what may be called the autonomy option. Historically, of course, this was never a genuine possibility. The combined economic and military resources of the West from the sixteenth century can be seen, in retrospect, to have been certain sooner or later to incorporate the rest of the world into a single 'world system', to use Wallerstein's term. [...]

Nevertheless, it was common ground after 1945 [...] that, once a Third World country obtained political freedom, it was in its best interests to cut or restrict its links with the international capitalist economy and develop in its own way. Although reasons for such pessimism varied widely, the common ground was belief that all indigenous societies at some stage possessed the potential to develop successfully, but that this potential had been blocked, arrested or checked by the effects of incorporation into the single 'world system'. Satisfactory development therefore required disengagement from the international system, rejection of capitalism and, for many, adoption of socialism.

It is important that from the 1940s to the 1980s, when most of these arguments were being generated, this socialist alternative did seem both desirable and feasible. The Soviet Union appeared to many, not only in the Third World but also in the West, to provide a far better model of development than capitalism. Moreover, in practical terms, a country which wanted to opt out of the international capitalist economy could, for that half century, rely on the USSR, its east European satellites and also the post-1949 China to substitute for the West by providing the capital, consumer goods and export markets needed in the transition to sustained development. The prescription of socialism for the Third World in much of the more radical development literature of the period after about 1950 commonly assumed that this option existed and that it offered the only route to true development.

By the 1990s, however, it had become clear that this had been a mirage. Hitherto the communist states had given considerable support to nationalist movements and new Third World states, and this aid had encouraged some Third World countries to proclaim their independence of capitalism. But, even at its peak, it had serious limitations.

First, the USSR lacked the economic, and in some respects the technical, ability to fill the role of the far more affluent West.

Secondly, in accepting Third World commodity exports in return for capital and consumer goods, the USSR was merely replicating the role of the western market. In most places it did little or nothing to enable these countries to transform themselves into developed industrial economies. The consequences are difficult to judge, because few of the USSR's Third World clients provided useful information to the World Bank. But in 1994 two of these in West Africa that did so, Guinea and Guinea-Bissau, had clearly not made much progress in this direction. In that year the proportion of Guinea's labour force said to be in agriculture was still 87 per cent, that of Guinea-Bissau 85 per cent. The corresponding shares of manufactures in GDP were 5 and 7 per cent.[1] Both remained among the poorest states of the Third World. One suspects that countries such as Cuba, for which no such statistics are available, would show comparably limited structural change. In short, the shift from dependence on the capitalist West to dependence on the non-capitalist East seems to have made little difference.

Finally, however, the real moment of truth came with the effective collapse of state socialism in the USSR and its European satellites in the late 1980s. Even in China the economy was being rapidly switched towards capitalism. For all practical purposes there was no longer a 'Second World' in which dissenters from the western-dominated international system could take refuge. More importantly, the ideological option of state socialism could no longer be held up as a successful model for Third World countries to adopt.

This meant that the Third World was left to make its way as best it could in the single world system dominated by the capitalist West. That in turn brings us to the central issue. [...] Were the LDCs richer or poorer in the 1990s than they had been a century earlier? Did they do well or badly from the operation of comparative advantage? Should they still concentrate on export-led growth and rely on the principle of comparative advantage?

Any answers must, of course, be heavily qualified; moreover, we have no reliable statistics on national or per capita incomes before the mid-twentieth century for most Third World countries. But, at least on the more reliable evidence of the last half of the twentieth century, there seems no doubt that virtually every Third World country that has not been devastated by war, civil war or crass governmental incompetence is now richer in real terms than it was before its integration. By other standards also there has been very considerable improvement, notably in life expectancy, health and literacy. That progress was not continuous. Adverse trends in international economic conditions in the 1930s, and again in the period after about 1980, may have set it back. But at least there is little evidence to support belief in the general or inevitable immiseration of the Third World as a result of its incorporation into the international division of labour.

What of the role of trade and exporting and the operation of comparative advantage in this economic advance? How much correlation has there been between growth and specialization in export production? What qualifications seem necessary in stating that trade was a generally successful engine of development?

First, the evidence suggests that, in the initial stage at least, the establishment of an export trade was almost invariably the starting point of greater economic growth. This was true of most of Latin America, of North America, Australasia, Asia and Africa. [...]

This, however, leaves the more important question of how far such a strategy enabled these countries to develop. Was there [...] an impassable limit beyond which exporting, particularly of commodities, could not take Third World economies? Was it a dead end, leaving them as a poorly rewarded proletariat in the international division of labour? Alternatively, what factors differentiated countries that were able to maintain the momentum of growth, through commodity exporting to industrialization and sustained development, from those that did not?

The limited evidence [...] seems to suggest that the critical factor was the extent to which a newly established export–import sector was able to permeate and transform the rest of a country's economy. The great success stories of the nineteenth and early twentieth centuries were the settler societies of North America and Australasia. Starting as exporters of natural resources such as timber, skins and easily accessible minerals, they moved to intensive production of agricultural exports, and thence to investment in infrastructure and industry. In the process, virtually all sectors became part of a single capitalist economy, based on high levels of education and skills and relatively high wages. Conversely, average national incomes were not held down by the existence of large numbers of people whose productivity was very much smaller than that of the modern sector: there was never a significant dual economy. In the later twentieth century a comparable pattern can be seen in parts of East and South-East Asia.

It is important also that much of this development was based on foreign technology and capital. None of these countries, nor those of Latin America, hesitated to borrow extensively in their earlier development phase. Heavy borrowing caused serious problems when international recessions reduced foreign-exchange earnings, but none of the anglophone and few of the Latin American countries ever reneged on their liabilities. Direct foreign investment also played an important role in development. Its main advantage, as always, was that it brought with it technology and know-how. Moreover, international transfers were conditional on profitability, whereas other forms of foreign borrowing had to be serviced irrespective of economic conditions. Its concomitant disadvantage was that FDI might take vital sectors of the host economy out of the control of the indigenous society. Over time, however, most foreign enterprises came under local control, either by state action or by purchase of shares.

But, if incorporation of these New World, Australasian and Asian countries into the international economy proved generally beneficial, most Latin American states remain on the margins of the Third World. Furtado and other Latin American analysts, particularly dependency theorists, suggest special reasons for this, including foreign control of key sectors, excessive protectionism for import-substituting industry, and improvident government control of money supply. But a common and probably more fundamental problem was the inability of the modernized, mainly industrial and urban, sector to raise the general level of productivity and incomes in the rural sector. This was often due to archaic landownership and employment patterns. The result was economic dualism, a key factor in much dependency theory. This provides a key to the comparable, though usually far worse problems of Black Africa and other less-developed Third World countries.

[...] [The] fundamental reason for the limited economic growth of the Gold Coast/ Ghana, taken as a model of development based on commodity production in Black Africa both during and after the colonial period, was that a very dynamic, innovatory and largely capitalist sector producing cocoa for the international market failed to transform the economy as a whole: this was in marked contrast with the role of wool and other export commodities in Australia and New Zealand. [...]

Comparable patterns of limited sectoral growth could be described in most other parts of Black Africa and pre-1945 Asia. India, however, differed in one major respect from most African countries. Trade was never a major factor in Indian economic life.

Though there were isolated areas of commodity export production, notably of tea, wheat, cotton and jute, these had a limited effect on the economy as a whole. Yet, paradoxically, India was the first Asian country, apart from Japan, that generated a significant industrial sector, and it did so largely on Indian, not expatriate, initiative. In absolute terms, Indian industry was very large; yet, in common with the exporting commodity sector, it was very small in relation to both the domestic product and the labour force. Moreover, although in the earlier years manufactured textiles, particularly cotton and jute, found important export markets, this did not lead to an export-oriented industrial system. With protection from the 1920s, Indian industry became increasingly import substituting, unable to compete internationally with rivals such as Japan. The Indian example, both before and after independence, therefore, throws little light on the potential of an export-oriented development strategy.

The best modern examples of the potential of such a strategy in the Third World were obviously the states of East and later South-East Asia. All began their modern development by exporting: Japan initially with simple labour-intensive manufactures, leading to the highest technical levels; the others from conventional commodity exports, again leading to simple labour-intensive manufactures and ultimately high technology. All, bar Hong Kong, went through periods of very severe protectionism, but most found means of combining domestic protection with virtual free trade for the export sector. All, in varying degrees, relied on imported technology, foreign loans and FDI. All ran the same risk of over-borrowing, with attendant debt-servicing dangers, which, for example, forced South Korea, Thailand and Indonesia to depend on the IMF help in 1997–8. But basically all had demonstrated the value of exploiting comparative advantage, which in their cases consisted mainly of a supply of increasingly educated and hardworking people who were able to spot where the opportunities lay and move flexibly to exploit them.

What general conclusion should be drawn? [. . .]

1   There is no strong evidence to suggest that the Third World was made poorer by the creation of a single world economy and market, though there may well have been undesirable side effects, particularly in cultures and lifestyles.
2   The concept of 'dependence', though superficially very attractive as a description of the resulting relationship between more and less economically developed trading partners [. . .] has little explanatory power. All economies in a world system are to some extent dependent on others for markets and sources of imports. Any adverse effects of such interdependence must stem from the inability of a particular country to adjust its economic and social structures to the challenge of internal and external markets [. . .].
3   Colonialism played a complex and in some ways paradoxical role. On the one hand, it facilitated the evolution of a world market by opening up territories to trade through improved transport and by integrating regions politically. In some territories it promoted the transition to capitalism by the use of state compulsion to overcome indigenous resistance, though, as in East Africa, the transition was commonly partial, producing 'straddling' or 'articulation' rather than a conventional capitalist bourgeoisie and proletariat. On the other hand, colonialism can be seen as an obstacle to sustained development. The interests of the metropolis were often incompatible with those of the subject people, as over the establishment of local industries. Colonial

governments had conservative attitudes to development, more concerned with political stability than growth. Neither they, nor expatriate private enterprise, provided
much opportunity for indigenous people to gain experience in the higher levels
of administration or the economy. The concept of intra-imperial 'cooperation',
as preached by the French and others, was valid in so far as it reflected a genuine
complementarity between economies, and may have been mutually beneficial in
times of acute recession. But it often concealed selfish imperial stratagems and, in
the longer term, might perpetuate archaic patterns of production in Third World
countries. In short, while colonialism was not an insuperable obstacle to growth, and
may have helped it up to a certain point, it might also become an obstacle to sustained development.

4   Trade, and the concept of development based on the exploitation of comparative
advantage, come well out of this survey. Most Third World societies willingly
adapted to the possibilities offered by international trade because exchange offered
them tangible material benefits. For all the countries considered here, and for many
others, Furtado's critique of Latin America holds good: sustained growth often began
with the establishment of large-scale export–import trades. On the other hand, it is
also clear that, if trade was a necessary starting point, it was not by itself a sufficient
condition for sustained growth or development. This depended on the ability of a
particular society to exploit the gains from trade to the full, which in practice meant
employing the profits from trade to transform the society as a whole. In practice it
also meant that the capitalist relations implicit in the trading sector had to be extended
throughout the economy.

5   The logic of this developmental process, as the development economists correctly
saw, was that commodity production and export must lead to industrialization, since
this alone could break through both the Malthusian obstacle of limited land and the
barrier of an inelastic and unpredictable world commodity market. The first step to
industrialization was almost always ISI. But the evidence everywhere suggests that
this could also prove an economic dead end, since, as early Marxists predicted, highly
protected industries will eventually come up against the limits of a domestic market, sooner in small states, such as those of Black Africa, later in large countries
such as the United States or even India. In the long run, therefore, industrialization
will lead to sustained growth only if a substantial part of the manufacturing sector
becomes internationally competitive. Exporting was as critical for manufactures as
for commodities.

My conclusion, therefore, must be that, in principle, Adam Smith, Ricardo and their
later disciples were right. Trade, specialization and comparative advantage have always
led to growth, not to underdevelopment or immiseration. But trade alone has not been
sufficient for sustained development. This depended on the ability of a society to exploit
and invest the benefits of trade, so that each stage of specialized production led to higher
technical levels and to the ability to compete in international markets.

Note

1   World Bank, *World Development Report 1996: From Plan to Market* (Oxford, 1996), table 1,
p. 188; table 12, p. 210.

35

The Gender Dimension

Jill Steans

[...]

Global Political Economy

Critical interventions

The study of global political economy has become a dynamic and expanding area within the study of International Relations in recent years. From an initial narrow focus on the relationship between state power and decision-making in the context of the constraints imposed by the economic environment, global political economy has expanded to include the activities of multinational corporations, the influence on state policy of 'military industrial complexes', the role of international organizations in the global economy and the problems of debt and development.

In part the conceptual shift from *international* to *global* political economy is a response to the phenomenon of *globalization*. Global 'restructuring', the increasing influence of transnational corporations, the complex global division of labour, and the intimate relationship between debt, 'development' and environmental degradation, are all integral parts of the ongoing process of interconnectedness characteristic of globalization.[1] While the nature of globalization has been disputed, and its impact is undoubtedly uneven, it can nevertheless be usefully understood as a reordering of time and distance in our lives.[2] Critical approaches to [global political economy] recognize that global processes shape and transform economic activity and that a number of 'actors', both governmental and non-governmental, are agents of economic, social and political change. Political economy can no longer be viewed as an entirely 'internal affair'; it is necessary, therefore, to explore its global dimension while recognizing the specificity of some areas. Furthermore [...] globalization has encouraged new forms of identification and expressions of solidarity which cut across state boundaries. This concern with the global dimension of social and economic activity has led to considerable criticism of the statecentric assumptions of the orthodoxy in *international* political economy.
[...]

Gender and global restructuring

Since the 1970s, the global economy has been undergoing a process of restructuring. The first phase of global restructuring can be traced to the 1973 oil crisis when big companies in the West resorted to international subcontracting to survive. Initially the knowledge-intensive parts of the production process went to the West, while transnational corporations shifted the labour-intensive parts of the production process to developing countries where cheap female labour was abundant. In the 1980s as big business emphasized the importance of managerial flexibility and decentralized production, corporate strategies in the West sought a more flexible workforce to undermine the power of trade unions.[3]

Global restructuring and the many resistances that it has generated have given rise to profound challenges to the orthodoxy, notably its statecentric predilections. However, neither neorealist, liberal interdependence, nor Marxist-inspired dependency models seem to be able fully to capture this phenomenon, and none are able to elucidate the gender-specific effects of restructuring. Mitter claims that restructuring in the 1980s had a profound effect on the composition of the workforce.[4] The process encouraged the growth of a 'new proletariat' in both the North and South, with women ghettoized in assembly-line work with poor pay and prospects. The 'feminization' of the workforce was a significant phenomenon in many regions of the North previously characterized by heavy industry. Mitter argues that in areas where traditionally unionized industries such as coal and steel had previously thrived, the male workforce frequently had a reputation for radicalism. Employers in growth industries thus preferred to employ the wives and daughters of, for example, ex-miners and ex-steelworkers.

In the 1980s big business also invested more and more in hitech research, automation and computer-integrated manufacturing systems. This investment was aimed at replacing skilled labour. However, where labour-intensive and skilled-work aspects of production predominated, it was not always cost-effective to invest heavily in machinery. This was particularly the case where there was a supply of cheap female labour, because women made the most flexible robots of all.[5] In both Europe and North America, in the garment industry, for example, employers who felt threatened by the restructuring of the global economy but who could not relocate abroad moved to feminize their workforce and this resulted in the re-emergence of sweatshops and home-working.[6] This phenomenon was replicated in a number of other industries, including electronics, toy-manufacturing and food-processing. In the West, the official reasons given for preferring women were similar to those offered in the Third World. Employers stressed the 'natural dexterity' and 'nimble fingers' of women workers. However, because women's skills were thus defined in an ideologically biased way – that is, as natural rather than learnt – they were not rewarded.

Furthermore, 'masculinity' continued to be identified with the claims of 'breadwinner' status, and this also provided a justification for paying women less, even though male unemployment was actually increasing. Women were frequently paid between 20 and 50 percent less than men in comparable jobs.[7] This was justified both by the idea that women and men had innate capabilities and personality traits and on the grounds that men needed to support families but women did not. A further significant aspect of global restructuring in the 1980s was the increasing numbers of part-time and home-workers. The rise in home-working in the West was also a direct manifestation of 'flexible-manning' business strategies. Mitter and van Luijken claim that women constituted and continue to constitute the majority of home-workers, because everywhere women constitute the poorest sections of society.[8] They claim that there is a marked similarity between home-work and housework – both are done by women and both remain invisible. Calling home-working the 'informal sector' of the economy misrepresents the numbers involved. It is not outside or parallel to the formal sector. It is an integral part of the global market economy.[9]

As the least unionized and poorest paid of all workers, women have been particularly vulnerable to the market policies which have continued to characterize global economic restructuring in the 1990s. Where women are encouraged to take up roles in the paid sector – and women now make up some 41 per cent of paid workers in developed countries and 34 per cent worldwide,[10] – it is still the case that on average they earn 30–40 per cent less than men for comparable work. Women in general work longer hours than men and make up a disproportionate number of those working in the informal sector, though much of this work is unrecorded and so invisible. Women are concentrated in low-paid jobs. In the developing world, women are still heavily concentrated in Export Production Zones. The centrepiece of recent IMF strategies in the 1980s and 1990s has been export-led growth and structural adjustment. Indebted governments set aside territory specifically for the use of factories producing goods for the global market. In Asia, in the 1980s, women made up 85 per cent of workers in Export Production Zones. In other areas, the figure for women workers was typically around 75 per cent.[11] While there is some evidence that the 1990s have seen a 'remasculinization' of the workplace, women remain concentrated in the lowest-paid jobs.

Elson and Pearson claimed that the provision of women into such jobs was encouraged because it could be viewed as a way of involving women in the development process.[12] World-market factories producing components for the electronics industry, for example, are usually owned or partially owned by subsidiaries of Japanese, North American and European multinationals. These have been particularly important in the development of the global trade in consumer goods. A number of large US and European retailing firms are continuing to place large contracts with world-market factories. When deciding where to locate, a crucial factor remains the availability of a suitable labour force, which is defined in terms of low cost and high productivity. It seems that, as in the 1980s, in the 1990s women remain the cheapest and most productive of all workers. Women's attempts to translate paid employment into financial independence, however, are often thwarted by lack of access to capital, inadequate education and training and because women carry an unequal burden of family responsibilities.

A further aspect of global political economy which has attracted the interest of feminist scholars, is the rapid growth of sex tourism, or prostitution, which is linked to the expansion of the tourist industry. In a number of countries tourism has become an important earner of foreign currency. In Thailand, the Philippines, the Caribbean, West Africa and Brazil, the growing sex industry is linked closely with the expansion of tourism and is inextricably linked to the problems of debt and development strategies.[13] Sex tourism does not just involve women, although it is overwhelmingly women who are drawn into this particular form of prostitution – frequently women who have been displaced as a direct consequence of 'development' strategies. Nor can prostitution be viewed solely from the perspective of tourism. Nevertheless it is conditioned by the demands of a stratified global market and the impact of development policies which are themselves conditioned by global economic processes.[14] Thahn Dan has suggested that prostitution is itself becoming a globally traded commodity. The growing integration of the tourist industry which links countries, hotel chains and package-holiday firms is a crucial enabling factor which allows spare capacity in airline seats and hotel beds to be matched with the demand for esoteric sexual services. With the growing globalization of capital, one finds the spread of prostitution. It is, Thahn Dan claims, no accident that Bangkok and Manila, both major cities which have experienced massive growth in prostitution in recent years, are also both major centres for multinational corporations and regional centres for global organizations. Increasingly the issue of prostitution needs a global analysis.[15] Enloe argues that sex tourism is both a part of the global political system and the global economy and the fact 'that it is not taken seriously says more about the ideological construction of seriousness than the politics of tourism'.[16] [. . .]

The UN Decade for Women

From its inception, the United Nations (UN) has seen itself as having a role to play in promoting development. Similarly the UN has a long history of promoting the status of women throughout the world. Until quite recently most of the UN's work in this area had concentrated on promoting women's status through the development process. In 1973 the United States Foreign Assistance Act led to the setting up of USAID. This act required women to be involved in decision-making bodies which dealt with aid and development issues. This measure prompted UN agencies, including the International Bank for Reconstruction and Development, UNESCO, the ILO and FAO to set up special offices that concentrated on women's role in the development process. Shortly afterwards, in 1975, the First United Nations Conference on Women was held in Mexico to mark the beginning of International Women's Year. At the Mexico conference, delegates adopted a Plan of Action which aimed to improve the status of women, and 1976–85 was duly designated as the United Nations Decade for the Advancement of Women. In 1976 INSTRAW[17] and the Voluntary Fund for the UN Decade for Women (UNIFEM) were set up. The midway point in the UN Decade for Women was marked by the Second United Nations Conference on Women, held in Copenhagen in 1980.

In some respects the very existence of the UN Decade for Women was an important step forward. Up until that point, women had not really figured in debates about development at all. For the first time attempts were made to assess women's contribution to development, particularly in the crucial area of subsistence agriculture. The UN initiative required the attention of governments and gave women some access to policy-making by insisting that women's offices were set up within development agencies. It also led to the first real attempts to look at how technologies could be developed and applied which would help to reduce the drudgery characteristic of much women's work. In addition, it also helped to legitimize the women's movement as an international actor.[18] The so-called 'Women in Development' (WID) approach that underpinned various initiatives was also important in terms of facilitating the inclusion of women in workshops and seminars, by facilitating networking amongst women and by disseminating information through the WIDlink newsletter. The WID literature produced in the 1970s put the issue of women firmly on the political agenda, highlighted the inequalities of opportunity and the disproportionate contribution which women made to the development process. Furthermore, while the special offices set up to deal with women and development were often poorly funded, they did at least allow women to travel and meet and challenged the idea that men were the bread-winners in all societies.[19]

However, since 1985, the WID approach has been subjected to considerable criticism. At the end of the UN Decade for Women, surveys suggested the relative status and position of women throughout the world had declined in the previous ten years.[20] To some extent, the failure of the UN Decade can be explained by the failure on the part of many states to implement UN recommendations. In the 1980s a survey conducted by INSTRAW found that out of ninety-six countries, only six included women's issues as central issues in their development plans.[21] However, the failure was also attributed to the underlying assumptions of the WID approach. During the UN Decade, development policies were based on the underlying belief that the problems of Third World women were related to insufficient participation in the process of development. It has been argued that WID rested on a liberal feminist view that the problems of sexual inequality could be largely overcome if women were integrated into the public sphere. The aim of WID was to 'bring in' women, but women were already involved in the development process. According to Ashworth and Allison, the WID idea also contained the seeds of its own failure, because it recognized as visible producers only those whose commodities could be traded. The economic role of women as subsistence farmers, providers and full-time carers, which is the cornerstone of economic life, remained uncounted and unrewarded.[22]

Furthermore, the possibility that increasing poverty amongst women, and the relative decline of women to men during the decade, were the direct result of previous development policies was not considered. However [...] many development strategies which made reform and restructuring of agriculture production a priority had led directly to the displacement of women from the land that they had traditionally farmed. Critics argued that WID policy documents avoided and obscured issues of inequalities and power by presenting the issue of assistance to women as a purely technical exercise. It did not address the broader redistributional issues that assisting women raised. The WID approach ignored the broader context in which women-specific projects were inscribed. Increases in the productivity of women were not matched by relief from reproductive tasks. Women were too often regarded as 'victims' in need of assistance, rather than farmers, workers, investors and trade unionists. Ashworth, Allison and Redcliffe have argued that the central issue of gender inequalities in development policies ignored the fact that men and women could not benefit equally from aid and development initiatives if they had different political rights, burdens of time, and expectations and if the laws of inheritance and ownership discriminated against women and they could not get access to credit.[23]

Criticisms of the assumptions that guided the WID approach led to widespread calls for a different approach, which placed less emphasis on access and more on recognition of the degree to which women were already involved in the development process. The term 'gender and development' (GAD) was coined to describe an approach which was sensitive to the specificity of gender relations in particular countries and localities, rather than simply centred on women. Here 'the technical project of access, as numerical inclusion' was seen as insufficient to challenge the unequal allocation of values which sustained oppressive gender relations.[24] The stress on gender, rather than women, was a reminder that men must also be the target of attempts to redress gender inequalities and that their interests are also socially constructed and amenable to change.[25]

Gender and development approaches also highlighted the degree to which the neutrality and autonomy of the state, the focus of the liberal feminist strategies typical of WID, could not simply be taken for granted. As feminists have long argued, 'part of the definition of the state and the delimitation of the state's proper sphere involves the active codification and policing of the boundaries of the public and the private.[26] Furthermore, 'in many states those boundaries also 'delineate gendered spheres of activity, where the paradigmatic subject of the public and economic arena is male and that of the private and domestic is female'.[27] In this way, according to Goetz, by confirming and institutionalizing the arrangements that distinguish the public from the private, states are involved in the social and political institutionalization of gendered power differences. For example, states set the parameters for women's structurally unequal position in families and markets by condoning gender-differential terms in inheritance rights and legal adulthood, by tacitly condoning domestic and sexual violence, or by sanctioning differential wages for equal or comparable work.[28]

[. . .]

'Mainstreaming' gender issues

Since the UN Decade for Women, there have been calls to 'mainstream' gender issues in development strategies. Mainstreaming means incorporating gender concerns into development strategies and policies as a matter of course rather than as 'add ons'. Although, as debates about gender and development have shifted from an emphasis on bringing women in, to an analysis of gender relations, to understanding the gender dimension of environmental concerns, 'mainstreaming' in common usage has also come to mean highlighting gender issues in other areas within the remit of the UN, such as human rights provision.

The Third UN Conference on Women, held in Nairobi in 1985 at the end of the UN Decade for Women, produced an important document called *Forward Looking Strategies for the Advancement of Women to the Year 2000* (FLSAW). The strategies outlined in the document aimed to promote women's interests in health, employment, family life, political life, and also promote women's human rights. Since the UN Decade for Women in 1976, UN development agencies have included sections that are specifically charged to advance the interests of women. These sections have pushed for a greater degree of gender sensitivity in government policies, for awareness of the problems of women's double burden, for equal access to and control over land and property, and for equal access to credit. The United Nations has long recognized the need to include the contribution which women make to the economy in order to undertake effective planning and estimate potential output. More accurate data enables more effective policies to be formulated in areas ranging from employment and income distribution to social security provision and welfare. Thus, the FLSAW document pressed for the inclusion of unpaid work in national accounts and in social and economic indicators. It also pressed for the allocation of social and economic benefits to take into account this broader definition of work. Redefining work in the global economy effectively means recognizing both waged and unwaged work as essential to the social and economic well-being of countries.

The Fourth UN Conference on Women, held in Beijing in 1995, took place after the Commission on the Status of Women had met in 1990 to review the progress of the FLSAW since 1985. The Commission decided that not enough progress had been made. The Fourth UN Conference on Women was the largest UN conference to date. The Draft Platform for Action which was negotiated at Beijing echoed many of the key themes and objectives of the FLSAW, identifying eleven specific areas of concern: poverty, access to education, inequality in health-care provision, violence against women, the needs of women refugees, access to participation in economic decision-making structures, greater participation in public life and the political process, improvements in monitoring mechanisms, improvements in the awareness on the part of women of the commitments made by member states, the representation of women in the media, and, finally, women's contribution to managing natural resources and safeguarding the environment. The conference 'Platform of Action' made explicit linkages between the empowerment of women, access to reproductive health care, equality and women's human rights.

[...]

Gender issues in global perspective

[...]

In much contemporary feminist analysis the still striking disparities between North and South, rural and urban and rich and poor are emphasized. Western feminists acknowledge explicitly that concern with gender inequalities has to be seen in the context of broad inequalities not only between states and regions, but between women of colour and women of different social groups. For example, the 'expert report' on the ECE region, in preparation for Beijing,[29] explicitly recognized that issues of women's rights and sustainable development could not be seriously addressed unless the consumption and production patterns in the ECE region changed. Significantly European feminists have also cited the problems of racism in Europe, noting that women of colour in the region are particularly affected by global restructuring processes and make a particular contribution to unwaged and low-waged work. Women in Europe have, therefore, joined women in Latin America and in the Asia Pacific region in rejecting dominant economic paradigms and arguing that the deep contradictions in economic policies of restructuring and globalization are resulting in economic and social policies which are detrimental to the rights of women.

[...]

Notes

1   A. Giddens, *The Consequences of Modernity* (Cambridge: Polity Press, 1990).
2   Ibid.
3   S. Mitter, *Common Fate, Common Bond: Women in the Global Economy* (London: Pluto, 1986).
4   Ibid.
5   Ibid.
6   S. Mitter and A. Luijken, *The Unseen Phenomenon: The Rise of Homeworking* (London: Change Publications, 1989).
7   See discussion in G. Ashworth and N. May, *Of Conjuring and Caring* (London: Change Publications, 1990).
8   Mitter and Luijken, *The Unseen Phenomenon*.
9   Ibid.
10 E. Hooper, *Report on the UN ECE Regional Preparatory Meeting for the Fourth World Conference on Women* (Geneva, 1994).
11 See Mitter, *Common Fate*, and D. Elson and R. Pearson, 'The situation of women and the internationalisation of factory production', in K. Young, C. Wolkowitz and R. McCullagh, *Of Marriage and the Market: The Subordination of Women Internationally and its Lessons* (London: Routledge, 1991).
12 Elson and Pearson, 'Situation of women'.
13 M. Umfreville, *$£XONOMIC$: An Introduction to the Political Economy of Sex, Time and Gender* (London: Change Publications, 1990).

14   T. Thahn Dan, 'The dynamics of sex tourism: the case of South East Asia', *Development and Change*, 14: 533–53.

15   Ibid.

16   C. Enloe, *Bananas, Beaches and Bases: Making Feminist Sense of International Politics* (London: Pandora, 1989), p. 40.

17   The United Nations' international research and training institute for the advancement of women.

18   For a fuller discussion see I. Tinker and J. Jaquette, 'UN Decade for Women: its impact and legacy', *World Development*, 15(3) (1987): 419–27; J. Vickers *Women in the World Economic Crisis* (London: Zed Books, 1991).

19   Tinker and Jaquette, 'UN Decade'.

20   Ibid.

21   Ibid.

22   E. Boserup, *Women's Role in Economic Development* (London: Earthscan, 1989).

23   H. Allison, G. Ashworth and N. Redcliffe, *Hardcash: Man Made Development and its Consequences: A Feminist Perspective on Aid* (London: Change Publications, 1980).

24   Ibid.

25   Ibid.

26   A. M. Goetz, *The Politics of Integrating Gender to State Development Processes: Trends, Opportunities and Constraints in Bangladesh, Chile, Jamaica, Mali, Morocco and Uganda* (Geneva: United Nations Research Institute for Social Development, 1995), p. 8.

27   Ibid.

28   Ibid., p. 3.

29   E. Hooper, *Report on the UN ECE Regional Preparatory Meeting for the Fourth World Conference on Women* (Geneva, 1994).

36

Environmental Issues and the Compression of the Globe

Steven Yearley

Introduction

[...] [T]here are reasons for thinking that environmental threats and environmental awareness ought to display the logic of globalization. After all, we commonly hear that environmental problems threaten the globe. Such a threat to the planet, even more than world-wide cultural homogeneity, should perhaps lead us to shift our thinking, analysis and policy-making onto a global level. Some ecological problems, such as global warming, actually carry claims to globality in the very names by which they are known, while other problems, such as acid rain, lend themselves to depiction in terms of threats to the well-being of the planet. At the same time, many environmental organizations make much of their global character, claiming [...] to be Friends of the *Earth* (FoE), *Earth*First! or the *World Wide* Fund for Nature. [...]

Eating away the world's ozone layer

In the late 1980s unprecedented anxiety was displayed by members of the public in several European countries about the ozone-depleting chemicals (chlorofluorocarbons or CFCs) which were to be found in the majority of aerosol spray cans. Through the awareness-raising activities of groups such as Friends of the Earth [...] and through the response of the media, some manufacturers and a number of retail outlets, the public came to accept that whenever they squirted deodorant sprays or many polishes and spray foams, polluting chemical gases escaped into the atmosphere. These gases are dangerous because they encourage the breakdown of the earth's protective ozone-layer – a stratum of the atmosphere in which naturally occurring molecules of the gas ozone, a gas which filters out harmful ultraviolet radiation, are particularly numerous.

The striking thing about this form of pollution threat was that the geographical connection between the release of the pollutant and the damage it caused was extremely remote. CFCs sprayed in Edinburgh were not likely to affect the ozone layer over the city, or indeed over London or even Great Britain. The CFCs were carried by winds and only gradually worked their way into the upper atmosphere. The most extreme loss of ozone in fact occurs at the two poles, where presumably there is less call for deodorant. So, pollution emitted in Britain, or Japan, or Brazil could end up causing a problem across the other side of the globe.

People had long got used to the idea that private citizens or companies could pollute their local environment, with loud noise, smelly industry or whatever. But here was a startling example that showed that modern substances and modern technology [...] could cause pollution on a global scale. Such pollution compresses the world radically, allowing us to despoil the environment of our 'neighbours', thousands of kilometres away on the planet.

[...]

Dumping out of sight

Kassa Island lies just off the coast of Guinea, a former French colony in the west of Africa, a little north of the Equator. In 1988, the thirtieth anniversary of the country's independence, it was discovered that a large quantity (the Guinean authorities estimated around 15,000 tonnes) of incinerator ash from Philadelphia had been dumped on the island. According to the US Environmental Protection Agency, the ash from such incinerators includes dangerous materials such as heavy metals (the general term for various toxic metals, for example, cadmium) and poisonous organic compounds known as dioxins. The people of North America are increasingly aware of the potential dangers from such materials and do not wish to have them disposed of in their own locality. Hence they were shipped over five thousand kilometres to Guinea and, just to make sure that local people did not object too much, they were redescribed as 'building materials' (*The Independent*, 17 June 1988, p. 8). Of course this ash could be used in the construction business but it is safe to assume that it would not be a popular building material. To add to the international flavour of the incident, the material was transported on a Norwegian-owned ship. Following the discovery of the nature of the ash, the Guinean authorities arrested the Norwegian consul. Norway subsequently undertook to remove the waste.

In this second case too it is clear that people are capable of polluting the other side of the globe. But in this instance it is international trade rather than the transnational dispersion of molecules which links the world. From these two examples we can see that (a) certain modern pollutants can contaminate the global environment while (b) the transnational nature of modern trade allows the waste from industrialized regions and countries to pollute every region of the world.

[...]

How Environmental Problems Can Compress the World

The cases of ozone-depleting pollution and the international voyages undertaken by American incinerator rubbish symbolize in a striking way [...] that the world's growing environmental problems are connecting the lives of people in very different societies. And while individuals can try to minimize the impact on their own lives, it is ultimately impossible to hide oneself away from these phenomena altogether. No humans and virtually no plants or animals are exempted from these problems. That is not to say that all forms of pollution and environmental hazard are now global in scale. They are not. A good deal of pollution, for example, is still local or restricted to a region. Moreover, the impact of any given pollutant is liable to be modified by the details of the local geology and geography. But [...] most forms of pollution and other environmental problems have increased markedly in the last third of the twentieth century and continue to grow. Also, more and more of that pollution has an international spread so that in the closing years of the twentieth century no one is immune from all of it.

But while the experience of *suffering* from pollution and certain kinds of environmental degradation are nowadays almost universal, the rest of the story displays far greater inequalities. Some of the world's people make far more of a contribution to causing pollution and loss of environmental value than do others – and of course wild animals and plants which suffer from pollution cannot really be said to create any. Of the people causing pollution, some derive more personal benefit from each unit of pollution caused than do others. For example, Europeans typically create more pollution than Africans because more of them can afford cars, washing machines, goods with masses of packaging and so on. In other words, the wealthier society tends also to be the more polluting society. But, for every kilometre they drive, car owners in the former Soviet Union and Eastern Europe are likely to cause more pollution than their Western European counterparts because their cars are dirtier and less efficient. The same is true of power stations in the former state socialist countries: on average, for every useful unit of electrical power they generate, they cause more pollution. So, though wealth and pollution-generation are usually connected, they are not completely bound to each other.
[…]
Overall, then, while pollution and environmental despoliation are very widespread experiences, their origins are far less uniformly distributed, and sometimes those who cause such problems and benefit from them are rich and powerful enough to try to limit the impact on themselves by imposing it on others. We can therefore anticipate that there will be many dimensions to the globalization of environmental problems, depending on how and why environmental harm is spread.
[…]
As we have seen with the issue of ozone depletion, some pollution problems can plausibly be presented as global by their very nature. At least on the face of it, it is in virtually everyone's interest to oppose such forms of pollution. And this is the message that some environmentalists try to draw from the fact that we are all 'space crew' on our global spaceship. A sense of global identity is supposed to promote the idea that we face environmental hazards *together*. Yet many other 'global' forms of pollution and environmental harm get to have global effects because they are dispersed through trade and the spread of industrialization, not because they are inherently global. It would be wrong therefore to assume that responses to pollution problems are globally harmonious. There may be some common threats, but other environmental hazards result from people in one part of the globe displacing their problems on to other parts. Furthermore, certain kinds of pollution and ecological damage are diminishing in the North (because of tighter regulations or because of technological advances) even while they are on the increase in the underdeveloped world, because of the growth of industrialization. Different parts of the globe may thus be experiencing markedly different environmental-quality trends.
[…]

How Do Environmental Problems Get to be World-wide in Scale?

On the face of it, one might expect the answer to this question to be an ecological or physical science one. For example, one might anticipate answers such as that ozone-depleting chemicals constitute a global problem because of their world-wide dispersal by air currents. Without wishing to downplay the significance of this type of consideration, it is important to realize this type of answer is never the whole reason, and sometimes hardly a part of the reason for the world-wide scale of ecological problems at all. Thus [earlier] we reviewed the chief types of pollution and the principal threats to resource depletion, but we have not yet asked what determines where and whether pollutants are produced, and in what quantities and combinations resources get used. A simple, yet still quite informative answer to this line of questioning is that the types and extent of pollution and of other forms of environmental harm are influenced by the political economy of present-day production, trade and regulation – in other words by developments in economic activity and by the outcomes of political contests. Thus, it is clear that the vast majority of pollution and environmental despoliation arise from economic activities themselves, from power generation, from the operation of chemical plants, from mining operations, from travelling to and at work, and from agricultural enterprises.

[. . .]

Where industries locate

There has always been controversy over the location of industry because of the effluent it produces. In the nineteenth century aristocrats and large landowners in Britain complained that emissions from the soap and allied chemicals business were poisoning their livestock (less consideration was given to workers' health). Planning laws have since been tightened to ensure that consideration is given to the consequences of location. But another factor has worked in the contrary direction. Industry has spelt jobs and the prospect of wealth. Accordingly, there has generally been a trade-off between wanting the benefits that industry brings and wishing to avoid the pollution. Many working-class communities have simply had to put up with high levels of pollution in order to keep jobs in the local economy. It was not that the businesses could not be cleaner; it was that rather than pay the costs of cleaning up, they would have located elsewhere.

[. . .]

This problem has been internationalized in two ways. First the effluent has itself been dispersed internationally. As the scale of industry has grown, there have been more wastes and these have led, for example, to the pollution of large rivers such as the Rhine and Danube which pass through many countries, bearing Swiss wastes to the Netherlands or Austrian wastes to Hungary and Romania. Similarly, air pollution has been 'handled' by building higher chimneys. For a long while, firms (notably in the smelting industry and in electrical generation) tended to respond to complaints about emissions not by reducing the production of pollutants so much as by trying to spread them more thinly. [. . .] In all cases, pumping the effluents higher into the air reduced local contamination but meant that they landed over a wider area and further away, leading to pollution of neighbouring territories.

The second path of internationalization has been the decision to locate businesses away from the Northern countries in areas desperate for jobs, investment and economic development. In the most well known examples, from the 1970s US companies started moving away from the pioneering domestic environmental legislation to Southern countries with laxer laws.

There is a push and a pull effect here. The push is the urge to escape tightening regulations which would mean increased costs or limitations on productivity. For example, new laws which demand cleaner emissions to the atmosphere or which impose charges on the dumping of wastes into sewers drive up production costs. Firms also face tougher planning controls on the development of new plant. If these companies can find overseas locations which are keen to get investment and with less demanding laws, they are able to make the same products more cheaply. On the face of it this urge to escape regulation looks morally dubious. If a substance is harmful in the USA or France, then one can only suppose that it is harmful elsewhere too. In other words, by relocating these firms are imposing risks on the host country which are deemed unacceptable in their home state. [. . .]

The complementary pull comes from the governments and development authorities of countries eager for investment. [. . .] Stott cites the example of a brochure designed to persuade companies to locate in an industrial complex in Trinidad. The text informs companies that '*In the absence* of legislation dealing with the discharge of effluents and other forms of pollution' (1984: 30, my italics) intending investors have to convince the development authorities that the environmental impact of the proposed factory has been properly assessed. What this means is that at the time Trinidad itself had no legislation covering the discharge of likely pollution; the only obligation on incoming firms was to convince the economic development agency that an assessment had been made of the environmental impact of the development. Given that this agency's job was to stimulate investment, one can only assume that they would have been sympathetic to investors' claims about the cleanliness of their operations. [. . .]

Through the 1970s and 1980s more and more attention was focused on these reasons for relocation and on the possibility that dirty industry from the North was spreading pollution around the globe [. . .]. Michalowski and Kramer's study noted that as Northern companies exported 'their industrial operations to developing nations, many of the hazards of industrial production and the associated possibilities for corporate crime are relocated from developed to developing countries' (1987: 35). As these authors go on to note, a dispute arose over 'whether pollution control costs actually play a significant role in location decisions'. In other words, there are many economic factors which incline Northern companies to move to the underdeveloped world, including cheaper labour, fewer legal benefits and rights for employees, more lenient tax laws and direct financial inducements such as subsidies for building factories. Where the avoidance of pollution control costs comes in any hierarchy of benefits is hard to specify. Leonard carried out a comparative study of this issue, published at the end of the 1980s, and he concluded that the story varied greatly from one industrial sector to another. In some businesses environmental protection measures are very costly; in others they are more or less negligible (1988: 86–93).

All the same, and this is Michalowski and Kramer's chief point, even if it is some factor other than the avoidance of pollution control costs which directs TNCs to the Third World, once located there they 'remain legally free to expose the water, air, soil and bodies of workers to hazardous substances at rates higher than those allowed in their home countries' (1987: 37). Even if they did not move to the South in order to pollute, companies may be tempted to pollute once they get there. To install pollution abatement equipment which is not required by law would only cut into one's profits.

Where wastes end up

It is clear that the countries of the South can face environmental damage if dirty industries relocate there. Given the low standards of environmental control which often prevail, local firms are also likely to pollute. But, as the example of Kassa Island vividly shows, the South can sometimes end up with the pollution without even the benefit of hosting the industrial processes which cause it. Some countries are so poor, so in need of earnings of foreign currencies (to pay for necessary imports and so on) and so lacking in resources [...] that they will consider any trade that is likely to generate an income. In the 1980s, as citizens of Northern countries became more aware of environmental threats, there was a growing problem of hazardous waste disposal. Such wastes were either very expensive to dispose of because the authorities insisted on special treatment, or impossible to dispose of because no community would tolerate having the waste dumped near their town. Local politicians tended to side with the outraged citizens of their constituencies so it became difficult for governments to impose a solution in the face of parliamentary protest. The obvious answer was to export the wastes to countries which were so desperate for income that they would overlook the risks. Such deals were easier when the receiving country had a non-democratic government. They were easier still when the recipients were misled about the nature of the wastes or when local officials were offered bribes.

The double standards in this trade are, however, immediately apparent and disclosures in the late 1980s led to protests in the receiving countries as well as in the North. Through bodies such as the Organization of African Unity, the receiving countries (many of which, like Guinea, were in western Africa) were able to cooperate in pushing up standards and in 1989 the United Nations Environment Programme agreed an international convention regulating the trade in wastes, namely The Basel Convention on the Control of Transboundary Movements of Hazardous Wastes and their Disposal (Susskind 1994: 172–5). However, as Susskind and Ozawa point out (1992: 147), this Treaty allowed the significant loophole of admitting bilateral trade arrangements between individual signatories and non-signatory nations. In other words, one could sign up to the Treaty but still off-load or receive waste from a non-signatory nation which could – in turn – pass one's waste on to another Treaty-member (see Birnie and Boyle 1992: 332–43).

The European Union subsequently developed more demanding policies for its member nations, measures which – in essence – were adopted by the OECD nations (with the exception of the USA) in 1994 (Seager 1995: 61). In a complementary move, the great majority of African countries adopted the Bamako Convention in 1991, banning the importation of hazardous wastes (Susskind 1994: 175). Such measures may have halted the most glaring waste-dumping practices, but they have not stopped it entirely. Countries can still trade hazardous waste and, as with any UN agreement, there are always countries which refuse to be signatories and which, with the assistance of unscrupulous operators, can act as routes for avoiding controls.

Two further factors have led to the perpetuation of this trade. The first – ironically enough – is the continuing rise in environmental standards within Northern countries. For example, Germany has recently introduced demanding regulations on recycling. Picking through waste to sort and recycle the various components is labour intensive work and can only be made economically attractive if it is subsidized or if wage rates are very low. Consequently, an attractive approach to recycling policy is to collect the waste of wealthy people and send it to poor countries with low wage rates. [. . .] [S]ome commentators fear that 'international recycling' could become a way of bypassing some of the provisions of the Basel Convention (Edwards 1995: 5).

The second factor is rather more complicated and demands a section to itself.

International debt, monetary institutions and transnational environmental problems

Countries seeking to develop industrially usually suffer from a lack of capital. They want modern factories, for example, but before the factories ever generate any profit the countries will need to make a large investment. As we have seen, one way to overcome this problem is to attract foreign investors by making one's country a cheap or convenient place to set up business. An alternative approach is to try to get loans or aid (in the form of grants or 'concessionary', that is reduced-rate, loans) to assist with the initial investment costs. In the 1970s the sources of such loans were revolutionized when Northern commercial banks began to seek new business in the South. [. . .]

The banks, notably US ones, lent enthusiastically and loans accumulated so that by the 1980s several South American countries had debts around $100 billion and so that the total indebtedness of the Third World came close to $1000 billion. [. . .] In their eagerness to lend, the banks had backed some very poor investments. They even lent to corrupt states where much of the money simply disappeared. Very little of it generated enough profits to pay the interest on the loans, though the banks still demanded their repayments. In the worst cases, countries were having to use all their export earnings just to service their debts and their populations were therefore not benefiting at all from trade or from the loans.

Through the 1980s this complex and distressing story unfolded. Three consequences are of particular importance to the present discussion. The first and pivotal consequence was the growing importance of [. . .] the World Bank and the International Monetary Fund (IMF). As the commercial banks fretted over the extent of their bad debts and the indebted countries tried to work out a strategy for survival, these two bodies assumed a powerful advisory and brokerage role. [. . .]

The second and third consequences followed from the strategy advocated by the World Bank and IMF. Their view was that debtor countries should try to meet repayments by increasing their export earnings. They should thus do more to attract investment even if that meant accepting dirty industry or building incinerators to deal with the wastes of the North, and they should be willing to increase the rate of exploitation of their natural resources, even if that entailed poorly-regulated mining and increases in logging. These institutions' advice thus made pollution, resource depletion and biodiversity loss in the underdeveloped world more likely. This focus on increasing earnings was to be coupled with decreases in government spending, a policy which hit expenditure on such government tasks as maintaining sewerage systems, reserve maintenance, pollution monitoring and abatement measures. At the same time as environmental harm was likely to be on the increase, spending on environmental management was reduced.

[. . .]

In her studies of special export-orientated industrial developments in Mexico (known as the 'maquiladora' zone) George has sought to document how the free-market solutions proposed for overcoming the debt aggravate environmental problems. As she observes, 'there are few environmental regulations in this zone . . . and virtually none that Mexico can now afford to enforce . . . [local officials say] that "the red tape and the expense" of American environmental law is a powerful motivation for firms to come to Mexico' (1992: 25). But George goes on to make the additional point that environmental problems arising from countries' responses to debt are not confined to those countries themselves. In the case of the maquiladora zone, the consequences spill over into the United States. For example untreated sewage from the growing cities in northern Mexico has already forced sporadic closures of Californian beaches while 'The maquiladoras themselves generate huge quantities of toxic wastes, many of which end up in California via the New River which flows northward' (1992: 26). In other words, their 'developed' neighbour has to suffer the air pollution from Mexican factories, the waste from industrial areas which is disposed of through the sewerage system, marine pollution from poorly treated human sewage and contaminated foodstuffs from Mexican agriculture. For the USA, the most important source of Third-World lending and the dominant voice in the World Bank, there is certainly an irony: the environmental costs of Mexico's debt are rebounding on US citizens too.
[. . .]

Just How Global Are 'Global' Environmental Problems?

As we have seen there are good physical grounds for regarding some environmental problems as global. Some processes genuinely do have global reach and global impact. If the sea level rises, it will rise everywhere; a radiation cloud from a nuclear accident could travel for thousands of kilometres in any direction. There are also grounds for accepting that the globalization of production and commerce tends to spread even local environmental problems until they are global in scale. Third, there are philosophical and principled reasons for accepting that the green message has a global flavour. All over the globe, humans are threatening the well-being of other species, by disturbing or removing their habitats. Some form of coordinated response will be required if the Earth's other inhabitants are to get a chance to prosper. Equally, it is clear that – one way or another – energy and mineral resources are limited. For the sake of long-term survival, lifestyles which do not recognize these limits need to be altered world-wide. However [. . .] many pressure groups and certain companies may benefit from propagating the idea that all environmental problems are truly global. We must accordingly be cautious about accepting claims about 'globality' at face value, and when people make such claims we should examine their arguments carefully. In this section we shall take a critical look at claims about globality.

Global heterogeneity

There are two major issues at stake here. The first point is straightforward, but no less significant for that. Even literally global phenomena have different impacts at different places on the globe depending on geographical and economic differences. Thus, ozone depletion is one of the best candidates for the status as a 'global' problem but physical processes ensure that, in fact, the ozone layer is most depleted at the poles. In many respects, equatorial countries have less to worry about (at least in terms of immediate impacts on personal health) than near-polar ones, a fact reflected in the leadership role in ozone-protection negotiations adopted by the Nordic countries. Global warming demonstrates the same variability. In this case the uncertainty of the consequences of atmospheric warming means that it is harder to pick winners and losers, but if sea-level rise is a leading anxiety the Swiss clearly have less to worry about than the Dutch. Other geographical variables can exert an influence too. Thus, acid precipitation causes less of a problem where soils and bedrock are slightly alkaline and can therefore neutralize the impact of the acid than in areas, such as large tracts of Scandinavia, where the earth's surface is already neutral or mildly acidic.

But in addition to variations in geography and the earth's physical processes, there are variations due to wealth. Large areas of the Netherlands are already below sea level; clearly the Dutch have learnt to cope with this problem. Further sea-level rises will cause great expense but engineers can envisage ways of managing them. Countries of the Third World which are faced with the same threat cannot feel so sanguine. Bangladesh is already subject to frequent flooding; the Maldive Islands stand only a few metres above sea level at their highest point. Both lack the financial resources and the decades of engineering experience needed to counter the effects of global warming. A supposedly global process will impact very differently even among the low-lying countries of the world.

Given the significance of these differences in geography and, particularly, in wealth, talk of global 'challenges' and calls for united, global responses can be seen as misleading and tendentious. The emphasis on the global nature of current environmental problems tends to imply that there is much more of a common interest in combating them than is, in fact, the case.

[. . .]

Questioning the global interest

The first major difficulty confronting the idea that globally unified responses will flow from common global problems stems from the disunifying influences of differences in geography and wealth. The second possibility is that the very claims to globality will come to be interpreted as expressions of special interest. It now appears that in many instances 'global' policies have been perceived as attempts by First-World governments to solve their own problems at the expense of the Third-World's development potential. This accusation is made by, for example, Middleton et al. (1993: 5) who argue that at the Earth Summit, by giving priority to 'an environmental agenda [that is, not a poverty or redistribution agenda] the North has once more concentrated on its own interests and has called them "globalism"'. This issue has particularly come to the fore over the management of global warming. [. . .] [T]he gas principally responsible for global warming is carbon dioxide (CO_2), produced by fossil-fuel burning power stations, furnaces, boilers, vehicles and fires. The most appropriate policy for combating global warming appears to be limiting and then reducing overall CO_2 emissions. But limiting emissions is far from easy since the gas is a direct product of such key economic activities as generating power and running factories. If the countries of the Third World are to increase their economic production using roughly the technologies employed in the

North, overall world CO_2 emissions will rise rapidly. From the perspective of the South, proposals to limit these emissions threaten to impose a brake on their economic development prospects.

Accordingly, when official agencies and campaign groups in the North propose that overall CO_2 production must be stabilized and then cut, the key question in the South is, how is that 'cut' to be divided up? Proposals to limit CO_2 emissions from the Third World which are not matched by drastic reductions in the First-World's output are seen as merely hypocritical. Voices from the South argue that the industrialized world has enjoyed 200 years of wealth based on carbon emissions. Now, they say, it is the South's turn. Officials in the North are more inclined to favour pollution limits based on current emission levels. But any such proposal tends to reinforce today's economic inequalities by restricting industrialization in the South. This is because it is hard to see how underdeveloped countries could advance their industries and raise living standards without at least coming somewhere near the per capita emission levels of the industrialized world.

[...]

Furthermore national policy responses to these international environmental issues may get blocked or grind to a halt in the light of suspicions about the vested interests which may be smuggled in behind appeals to 'global needs'. [...] [T]hough the great majority of governments – indeed of politicians of virtually all persuasions – may be prepared to admit in principle that climate change and enhanced global warming amount to a world-wide environmental problem, this recognition of itself does not lead them to act in a globally coherent way. Seeing a threat as a 'global' threat does not necessarily make it more likely that policy-makers will respond. Persistent differences in ideas about who is responsible for causing the 'global' problem may lead to unwillingness to act, thus allowing the problem to intensify.

[...]

The question of which environmental problems are 'global' ones is further complicated by the possibility of disagreement about which issues are global *environmental* matters. Even where policy-makers appear to be in agreement about a desire to take action on global environmental problems, difficulties have arisen over the interpretation or definition of the term 'environmental' itself. The first question asked has been, what is to count as an 'environmental' issue in which we all, supposedly, have a common interest. Certain issues, such as air pollution, biodiversity and water pollution have come to occupy the centre ground of the environmental agenda. But other items are more often on the fringes. [...] [For] some officials and campaigners in the North, population is taken as an environmental issue. Others see population per se as a comparatively marginal issue; it is resource use not population itself that matters. Similarly, campaigners in the South have often tried to argue that poverty itself is an environmental problem. Officials in the North have resisted this definition. Since politicians and policy-makers appear unable to agree about what is properly an environmental problem, it seems unrealistic to believe that they will come to find agreement over humanity's supposed common environmental interests.

A second, closely related issue concerns the relationship between environmental topics and other social and economic priorities. All the time – for example – that people demand cars, that companies benefit from selling them, that the motor lobby campaigns on their behalf and national fortunes depend [on them], environmental policies will not be assessed in their own right but in relation to the value people place on cars, and so on. There are few areas of environmental concern which can be considered in relative isolation. Energy policy might be one. If people can light and heat/cool their houses equally well with energy-saving methods, then they are able to adopt them without significantly altering their lives and their values. But most other aspects of environmental policy impact in a broader sense on the way people live their lives, organize their work and conduct their personal relationships. Even if all environmental problems were straightforwardly global (in the way that ozone depletion almost is), people in different regions and countries would still have other priorities which interacted in differential ways with those common environmental problems. The difficulty is that environmental protection measures cut directly across so many political and economic policy areas.

Finally [...] there is one last issue to be taken into account when asking just what it means for global problems to be 'global'. [...] The significance of this link stems from the central role that scientific reasoning and expertise play in the diagnosis and management of environmental problems. It is only through science that we can know of the potentially harmful effects of ozone depletion or work out whether global warming is likely to occur. Given the centrality of science to the diagnosis and analysis of these global environmental issues, it is understandable that the discourse of science will affect the way that environmental problems are conceptualized. Typically, science aspires to universal generalizations. Unless there are powerful reasons to the contrary, scientists assume that natural processes are consistent throughout the natural world. The very term 'biodiversity' [...] displays this universalism. The notion of biodiversity takes for granted the idea that all living beings are based on related genetic materials and that there can therefore be a measure of genetic variability which is applicable across the globe.

To say that science has a 'universal' orientation is not necessarily to imply that scientists are always internationally minded or that there is good scientific collaboration around the globe (though these things are often true). Rather, the point is that science typically aspires to universally valid truths, truths which apply the world over. Accordingly, spokespersons for science proclaim the unique utility of science for addressing global environmental issues, while policy-makers in search of objective, universalistic methods are attracted to science and to the other universalizing discourses including microeconomics. This orientation has left its stamp on the overall international discourse of environmental management.

However the impartiality and universalistic objectivity of many of these discourses have also been called into question. Suspicions about the way the North interprets 'global' interests have spilled over into misgivings about the use of the (alleged) universalistic discourse of science (including economics) to diagnose the globe's problems. [...]

To summarize this whole section, it is increasingly the case that international environmental hazards are being described and treated as 'global environmental problems'. In some cases, their globality arises from the nature of the problem itself (for example, the globe has a protective ozone layer which is suffering depletion). In other cases, environmental problems rise to global significance because – like habitat loss – they are repeated the world over or because one region's problems are distributed or displaced elsewhere. However, the status of 'global' problems is far from straightforward. Being global, one might suspect that everyone should worry about them equally. But, in fact, global problems turn out to have different impacts and implications, depending on geographical and socioeconomic factors. Even the most inherently global hazards, such as 'global warming', turn out to have differential impacts. Because of climate, altitude and other geographical factors, their impacts will be greater in some areas than in others. Furthermore, on average, wealthier societies and the wealthier and more powerful groups within societies will be better placed to withstand their impacts than will other groups.

Accordingly, the label 'global' has itself come to be disputed. Organizations come to refer to a problem as global when they want it to be taken especially seriously and when they want to present its solution as in the 'common interest'. In some cases, spokespersons from underdeveloped countries have argued that the North's identification of 'global' environmental problems is very selective. On this view, the North has tried to give priority to its concerns by implying that these problems are the most urgent for the *globe as a whole*.

Lastly, scientific analysis has been central to the identification and measurement of global environmental problems, such as ozone depletion and biodiversity loss. However, even the universalistic status of scientific claims has met with suspicion, with critics of the North's policies arguing that putatively universal discourses can conceal partiality, and that the assumptions associated with scientific analysis are not always conducive to the just interpretation of international environmental problems.
[. . .]

Concluding Discussion

[. . .] At one level I have argued that certain environmental issues can plausibly be seen as inherently global. Others have been rendered global by the transnational expansion of production, trade and communication. Partly in response to this trend (and also partly promoting awareness of it), there have been increased international collaboration and coordinated action on environmental themes. Many policies have had to be formulated cross-nationally; campaign organizations have internationalized; there have been new UN bodies established in the environmental field; and there have been innovations in international science.

However, the globality or universality of global environmental issues is also susceptible to a certain degree of deconstruction. Even the most strongly global problems turn out to have differentiated impacts. The identity of 'global' problems has been contested and even the definition of what is to count as an 'environmental' issue has not proved unproblematic [. . .]. Furthermore, the appeal to common interests in global environmental management actually appears rather fragile. The potential for exploitation and injustice keep reappearing through the talk of universal values, even though many officials and some commentators propose that there are common human interests in environmental protection. This idea is even encapsulated in the title of the UN Brundtland Report (World Commission on Environment and Development 1987): *Our Common Future*.

The unevenness of development and the inequalities of power and wealth associated with globalization indicate how idealistic [. . .] the notion of a 'common future' is. The majority of transnational environmental problems – most notably the need to abate carbon dioxide emissions – are easier to read as displays of conflicting interests than as instances of people shaping a future in common. [. . .]

References

Birnie, Patricia and Boyle, Alan E. (1992) *International Law and the Environment*. Oxford: Oxford University Press.

Edwards, Rob (1995) Danes defend ban on toxic trade. *New Scientist*, 25 Mar.

George, Susan (1992) *The Debt Boomerang: How Third World Debt Harms Us All*. London: Pluto.

Leonard, H. Jeffrey (1988) *Pollution and the Struggle for the World Product*. Cambridge: Cambridge University Press.

Michalowski, R. J. and Kramer, R. C. (1987) The space between laws: the problem of corporate crime in a transnational context. *Social Problems* 34(1).

Middleton, Neil, O'Keefe, Phil and Moyo, Sam (1993) *Tears of a Crocodile: From Rio to Reality in the Developing World*. London: Pluto.

Seager, Joni (1995) *The New State of the Earth Atlas*. New York: Simon and Schuster.

Stott, Martin (1984) Industrial pollution in the Third World. *Links* 19.

Susskind, Lawrence E. (1994) *Environmental Diplomacy: Negotiating More Effective Global Agreements*. Oxford: Oxford University Press.

Susskind, Lawrence E. and Ozawa, Connie (1992) Negotiating more effective international environmental agreements. In Andrew Hurrell and Benedict Kingsbury (eds), *The International Politics of the Environment*, Oxford: Oxford University Press.

World Commission on Environment and Development (1987) *Our Common Future* (The Brundtland Report). Oxford: Oxford University Press.

37

Order, Globalization and Inequality in World Politics

Ngaire Woods

Why Investigate Inequality?

Traditional investigations into world order have tended to neglect the issue of inequality. They have confined themselves to questions such as: how relations are ordered among states?; who comprises the 'society of states'?; who makes the rules?; and what kinds of leverage and coercion are available to enforce the rules? In other words, they have eschewed investigating the role that equality and inequality have played in promulgating and influencing international order.[1] Yet there are powerful reasons for investigating inequality in any discussion of order in international relations today. Although traditionally great powers or super-powers have provided stability and order through leadership or the balance of power, today these rudimentary institutions will not suffice. Processes of globalization are challenging the bases of order in profound ways: first, [. . .] by exacerbating inequalities both within and among states; and second, by eroding the capacity of traditional institutions to manage the new threats.

[. . .] Globalization [. . .] transforms the processes, the actors and capabilities, and the agenda of world politics, necessitating more effective international institutions of management. Today institutions need to probe deeply into domestic politics, ensuring compliance with agreements on issues ranging from the environment to trade and arms control. To do this effectively, they need full participation and commitment from a wide range of members. Yet [. . .] existing multilateral organizations are still hierarchically arranged. Their authority and effectiveness depends upon the will and actions of their most powerful members and, as the most powerful states balance up the advantages of stronger and more effective institutions against possible losses in their own control and sovereignty, they repeatedly come down on the side of the latter. This means [. . .] that international institutions are committing themselves to maintaining the old hierarchical order, even in the face of its ineffectiveness in dealing with new challenges and problems.

Inequality and the Traditional View of International Order

Order in international relations carries many meanings and many interpretations. At a conference on 'Conditions of World Order' thirty years ago, several leading academic lights in international relations were brought together in Bellagio, Italy. They defined 'order' as 'the minimum conditions for coexistence',[2] eschewing any wider definition of order which would open up discussions of necessary conditions for a 'good life' or any other set of deeper values. And indeed, this is a traditional vision of international order. It begins with a European conception of the 'Westphalian system',[3] the key actors within which are sovereign states who are in a formal sense equal – each is accorded an equal 'formal' sovereignty. However, order among these states is traditionally understood to be a product of *hierarchy*. A balance of power among the major states, such as that prescribed in the Treaty of Utrecht (1713), prevents any one state from predominating or extinguishing the sovereignty of all others.

Inequality within the traditional conception of world order is a positive, restraining, and ordering force. It permits the operation of a balance of power as a substitute for the centralized authority of a Hobbesian Leviathan in domestic politics. At the same time, hierarchy in the international system, or the imbalance of power, has never meant a strict imposition of the absolute will of the most powerful state or states. Rather, within the hierarchical system institutions have emerged which permit limited accommodation and change. The Concert of Europe, for example, or the League of Nations, were institutions which reflected the need of the most powerful to accommodate those directly beneath them – to ensure that they have a stake in the system so that they will assist in preserving the status quo. However, the scope of this type of accommodation within traditional realist views of international relations has been strictly limited.[4]

Similarly, in contemporary accounts of international relations the comfortable relationship between power and accommodation is continued in theories that assume that 'hierarchy' breeds order. In the realist tradition, inequality simply describes the status quo in international relations and not a deeper set of normative concerns.[5] Order is provided by a powerful state which sets up institutions and rules in the international system.[6] The real debate within the recent literature has been about whether or not a hegemon is required to maintain and enforce the rules. It has certainly not focused on the degree to which a particular regime will cement or alleviate inequalities. Neo-realists argue that a hegemon is essential.[7] The institutionalist critics of neo-realism argue that a hegemon is not required for the institutions to acquire a driving force of their own.[8] However, even within the institutionalist view, the role of norms and institutions can only be explained *after* a power-political framework has been ascertained.[9] Hierarchy and inequality are thus asserted as a precondition for subsequent kinds of order. [. . .]

Yet the experience of the 1990s suggests that traditional hierarchy does not maintain order in the face of new challenges. Although immediately after the end of the Cold War there was a brief euphoric period during which a 'New World Order' led by the United States was trumpeted,[10] the idea was short-lived. The United States and its close allies soon found that a global agenda of democratization, liberalization, peace, and self-determination would often be self-contradictory. In transition or democratizing countries, difficult choices had to be made between either economic liberalization or democratization, with governments often forced to give priority to one or the other.[11] Self-determination, on the other hand, often seemed to lead to civil war and conflict, nowhere as starkly as in the former Yugoslavia.[12] A clearer hierarchy of power in the international system – the new 'leadership' of the United States – did not offer solutions to these problems. Rather, a second wave of policy since the end of the Cold War has highlighted the shortcomings of existing international institutions [. . .].

Today, in order for countries to achieve the myriad goals of wealth, environmental protection, and a wide range of forms of security [. . .] a more sophisticated order is

required. Yet while the most powerful states in the system resist any reform of the institutions they dominate, it is difficult to imagine any such new order evolving.
[. . .]

The Impact of Globalization

In the market-based economists' account, globalization opens up opportunities and advantages to all states. Yet the existing evidence highlights that the process is a much more uneven one than the theory suggests. Globalization describes dramatic changes in the transactions and interactions taking place among states, firms, and peoples in the world. It describes both an increase in cross-border transactions of goods and services, and an increase in the flow of images, ideas, people, and behaviour. Economistic views treat the process as technologically driven. Yet globalization has also been driven by deregulation, privatization, and political choices made by governments. Whilst flows of goods, services, people, and capital are increasing, they are, at the same time, often barred or blocked by regulations. In other words, the impact of globalization has been strongly shaped by those with the power to make and enforce the rules of the global economy.[13] At the same time, however, to create rules which are enforceable, rule-makers are increasingly having to rely upon a wider group of actors and a wider range of institutions. This creates a real tension between increases in inequality caused by processes of globalization and the necessary increase in participation required to regulate the processes. In this section, the key elements of globalization are analysed to highlight these tensions.

A first core aspect of globalization is technological change, which has transformed the possibilities of global economic activity. Firms can now organize production globally using new means of communication, and new, more flexible techniques of production. This has led to what Charles Oman [. . .] calls 'global localization'. Increasingly, multinational firms (MNCs) produce goods as close to their markets as they can. This means they have a presence in several regions or areas of the world economy. The political implications are manifold and, importantly for our purposes, they do not all point to deregulation and an opening up of possibilities. Rather, those who benefited first (and most) from technological change have also been very quick in seeking to protect their position, pushing for international rules which may well hinder others wishing to emulate them.

Where once MNCs were a force for liberalization and the opening up of trade barriers (so that they could trade into regions and countries), today, having situated themselves within regions or countries in which they wish to trade, they no longer need to press for the opening up of borders. Life inside a 'fortress' Europe or NAFTA might be quite comfortable. Furthermore, rather than diffusing technological advances worldwide, leading companies have pushed for increasingly strict international rules on intellectual property.[14] Competition today is not just for a competitive edge in technological or economic terms. Rather, firms also compete for control of the rules of the game at international and at regional levels. Yet, for the rules to have an impact they must be enforced by governments not all of whom firms can influence. Globalization is cementing old economic inequalities between 'haves' and 'have-nots' – not just in the sense of having technology or not, but also in the sense of having the capacity to make rules or not. Yet at the same time, globalization is creating a new set of requirements for regulation and enforcement which requires the cooperation of the so-called 'have-nots'. This cannot be achieved through the hierarchical arrangements of old.

International trade is another aspect of globalization which has had highly uneven consequences. While there is a dispute as to how much world trade has increased,[15] there is clear evidence that high levels of trade in today's world economy are strongly concentrated in trade among industrialized countries.[16] For this reason, although globalization suggests that world markets are opened up and the flow of transactions among all states is thereby increased, in fact we find that the effects of change are vastly unequal. Although many developing countries have liberalized their trade policies, some are being marginalized. [. . .] In brief, trade liberalization has cemented inequalities among states. Yet it has also resulted in increasing demands for regulation, for example from industrialized countries who argue that where countries flout international labour, environmental, and safety standards, they present 'unfair' competition. The demand for an 'even playing field' requires greater regulation and enforcement at a global level.

Yet greater demands for regulation do not translate solely into efforts to strengthen global institutions. On the contrary, globalization has been accompanied by a surge of new regional and bilateral arrangements.[17] In some ways regionalism cements the old hierarchy, yet in others it loosens it. In theory, regional organizations offer small and less powerful states a way to unite and exercise more influence in setting trade rules and in enjoying open access to a wider market than their national market.[18] Furthermore, the prospect of regional trade arrangements and integration offers a useful lever to governments who need to dismantle powerful domestic vested interests: new policies offer both the carrot of wider markets and the stick of stiffer regional competition.[19] In these ways, the 'new regionalism' could well be seen as an even and powerful way of opening up trade. However, increasing regionalism may also cement inequalities by marginalizing less powerful states – for example, by excluding developing countries from the 'fortresses' mentioned above. Furthermore, regional institutions can provide powerful states with excuses for not using global institutions: they might, for example, choose to take their disputes to the forum in which they feel they have the most power to ensure a particular outcome.[20]

International finance is a further arena of globalization which has powerful implications for traditional notions of hierarchy and order. Technology and US policies in the post-war period[21] have unleashed powerful forces in financial markets, as international banks and investment funds expand their global operations. Today financial markets and investment funds shift capital so fast that governments in both industrialized and developing countries fear capital flight and speculative attacks by the market. In some ways this has a levelling effect: all governments live in some fear of the markets and all are susceptible to a speculative attack. Yet the tendency of capital markets to punish governments occurs in an uneven way which highlights both weaknesses and vulnerabilities in developing countries as well as in the institutions upon which they rely for assistance.[22] Industrialized countries in the more global economy can borrow to ease the monetary costs of fiscal expansion[23] and the evidence suggests that this does not necessarily heighten the risks of capital flight and market fear of default.[24] By contrast, in developing countries, high public debt, and indeed even high private debt (as in Mexico in 1994, and South Korea in 1997) can trigger markets into withdrawing, leading to a run on both investment and the currency.[25] Yet paradoxically, the threat of this kind of crisis means that previously less significant countries can now pose a systemic threat to international economic stability: the tail can now wag the dog. So whilst financial globalization reinforces old inequalities, at the same time it creates new challenges and crises which the old unequal order cannot deal with particularly effectively.

Finally, globalization has included the spread of policy ideas. Global economic order is not founded on state power and rules alone, but also on sets of policy ideas and beliefs. These are promulgated both formally through international organizations [...] and informally through networks of education and research which 'globalize' particular orthodoxies. Both the 1980s and the 1990s provide powerful examples of this. In the 1980s 'structural adjustment' was urged on developing countries the world over,[26] and in the 1990s a similar set of liberalizing policies were urged on the former Eastern bloc countries – the so-called 'transition economies'. The impact of these policy changes was mostly to increase income inequality within these countries.[27] In the late 1990s, there have been some changes in the prescriptions being written in Washington. The reform of the economy is now being followed up with second and third phases of reform, described as 'modernizing the state'. Good governance, transparency, accountability, and participation are now being advocated by the international financial institutions.[28] In theory, of course, if these ideas were applied to these institutions themselves, the result might well be a more egalitarian and participatory international economic order.[29] In reality, however, their application is being strictly limited.[30] Nevertheless, for the international institutions the new agenda reflects a recognition that to succeed, their reforms need greater commitment and participation by recipient governments – a top-down model of incentives and leverage exercised from Washington will not succeed.

Globalization, it has been argued, is changing both competition among, and policies within, countries. It is also affecting the nature of actors and institutions in world politics. In a system created for 51 countries, 193 states now enjoy a sovereignty which is becoming ever more diffuse. Control over policy in certain areas is increasingly passing either 'down' to local bodies, or 'up' to regional or international bodies.[31] Alongside states, new actors are striding the stage of world politics: the 'stateless' multinational in the 'borderless world';[32] national groups without a state (such as Quebec, Scotland, Chiapas, Palestine, and Chechnya); rebels and terrorists enjoying a greater capacity to publicize themselves and gain an audience.[33] These new actors cut across the traditional structures of state sovereignty and inter-state order, challenging governments and demanding access to the inter-state organizations charged with global governance.[34] Indeed, the very principles on which sovereignty is recognized and respected are changing, so that, in the words of an international law scholar, we are faced with an 'impossibility of reconciling the notions of sovereignty which prevailed even as recently as fifty or sixty years ago with the contemporary state of global interdependence'.[35] [...]

Particularly noticeable in their demands for a status in international organizations are the non-governmental organizations (NGOs) claiming a transnational or sub-national constituency.[36] NGOs have carved out a role for themselves in many multilateral organizations,[37] not to mention taken a lead in international relations on some issues such as the environment.[38] It is now the case that NGOs can participate within some international fora, such as the World Bank's Panel of Inspection hearings on environmental issues.[39] Yet, before heralding the rise of a 'transnational civil society', the limitations on NGO claims to greater legitimacy or accountability must also be recognized.[40]

Traditional conceptions of order not only fail to take new actors into account in portraying international order, they also fail to explain how and why these actors have emerged onto the stage of world politics. It is assumed that actors change as the configuration of power changes. Yet the new actors and the changing authority of old actors also reflects a shift in beliefs and understandings about representation and legitimacy, as we will see in the following section.

In summary, globalization is challenging the traditional state-centred and hierarchical world order.[41] Yet few of the forces analysed here have altered the structure of institutions of management. Rather, technological change, trade liberalization, regionalism, the globalization of international finance, and policy ideas are all proceeding within the rules and institutions which reflect the traditional hierarchy of power. However, that hierarchical order is becoming less effective as new 'global' issues, such as environmental problems, trade rules, and concerns about transnational crime or movements of people, demand greater levels of cooperation among states.

International Institutions and the Management of Order

The above discussion of globalization underlines that inequality is not just about starting positions and outcomes in international relations. It is also, crucially, about 'meta-power' or who gets to make the rules within which international relations proceed and who decides how and where to enforce them. During the 1970s North–South debate, the South pressed for more of a say in the rules governing international economic order and, for the most part, they failed. The rules governing trade, investment, finance, and monetary order continued largely to be written by Northern countries. Today, this top-down approach to making and enforcing rules is being questioned even within the North. The question being posed is: what makes international institutions effective?
[. . .]

International trade

Until 1992, international trade was regulated globally under the auspices of the GATT, a very loose institution whose rules and procedures were developed in an ad hoc way.[42] Within this arrangement there was a clear inequality of power, with the 'Quad' (the US, the European Union, Japan, and Canada) able to work behind the scenes to shape most decisions. The results were trading rules which had a very uneven impact on countries [. . .]. Importantly, these results reflected a process which magnified inequalities among members. The GATT operated as a club with a core membership empowered to decide who to admit and on what conditions.[43] Several attempts were made to change the structure of representation and decision-making within the GATT: developing countries tried unsuccessfully in the 1970s to create a powerful Executive Committee within which they would have a voice; and in the other direction, the United States tried to push the idea of an IMF-style Executive Board with weighted voting during the Uruguay Round.

Yet the unequal 'club' approach of the GATT has become unsatisfactory as globalization, or more specifically trade liberalization, proceeds apace. Trading nations both large and small require an institution which can regulate in areas such as non-tariff barriers and domestic practices, and which can deal with a raft of new issues, including services, intellectual property, trade-related investment, and labour and environmental standards.[44] For these reasons, even the United States needs a multilateral organization, for its strongest regional arrangement – NAFTA – accounts for less than a third of its trade.[45] In a globalizing world, compliance with an international trade regime requires a high level of participation, commitment, and confidence from all members. Hence, the decentralized framework of the GATT was inadequate: the resolution of disputes, for example, was held hostage to the consensus required of panels making decisions. Yet the replacement for the GATT, the World Trade Organization (WTO), has not resolved the problem of participation and compliance.[46]

The new organization has a structure and enforcement mechanisms which transform it into a more powerful international institution. The WTO is now the administrator of all multilateral trade agreements, an overseer of national trade policies, and has a disputes settlement procedure which, unlike that of the GATT, can make rulings on disputes which are automatically accepted by the organization unless there is a consensus *against* acceptance. At least in theory, developing countries are better served by this step towards more legalized and institutionalized procedures, since it restrains the capacity of large trading countries to veto Panel decisions. Certainly, developing countries seem already to be using the new WTO processes more: whereas the GATT mechanisms tended to be used mainly by the 'Quad', about half the requests before the WTO in mid-1996 were from developing countries.[47]

However, for the WTO to be effective in upholding an international rule of law, it needs compliance from its largest and most powerful member. Yet the United States had the worst record of compliance with GATT panel judgements of any country,[48] and further 'retreated from multilateralism' in the 1980s, adopting policies which were 'increasingly aggressive and bilateral'.[49] The trend towards unilateral trade policy was reflected in Congress during its debate on ratifying the Uruguay Round results (and the new WTO),[50] and yet more obviously since then, as the US has boycotted the WTO dispute settlement proceedings triggered by the Helms–Burton Act's penalties on other countries' dealings with Cuba.[51] [. . .]

The World Trade Organization has been created in recognition of the need for powerful rule-based institutions to facilitate global trade. Yet alongside the WTO, unilateral and bilateral actions are continuing, such as those of the US. This means that the credibility and effectiveness of the new system is being constantly undermined by assertions of the old power-political hierarchy as the basis for order in international trade. Yet that power-political order, which had been so clearly reflected in the GATT, simply cannot deal effectively with the new issues mentioned above. The tension is a simple one. Although a strong rule-based international regime is increasingly in the interests of the US in a global world economy, it remains to be seen whether the US is prepared to give up the rights of its special position as *primus inter pares* in order to reap the benefits of a multilateral regime.

The international financial system

The international financial and monetary system has changed dramatically with the emergence of ever-larger global capital markets, investment funds, and floating exchange rates. From the end of the Second World War, the rules of the system were very much set by the United States, conferring at various stages with Western Europe and Japan.[52] The fora within which decisions have been taken include the G7, the Bank for International Settlements (BIS), and the IMF (within which the United States is the largest voter and shareholder). During the 1970s developing countries made repeated attempts to increase their voice on the international financial and monetary system, with very limited success.[53] However, over the past two decades, the success and ongoing stability of the international financial and monetary system had come to rely much more heavily on the behaviour of less powerful countries, who have traditionally been marginalized.

Recent crises show the vulnerabilities of an increasingly globalized international financial and monetary system. At the end of 1994, the Mexican currency collapsed, sending reverberations through the system which have been dwarfed by the more recent crises in East Asia 1996–7 and in Russia 1998. Overall, all actors now agree that international financial and monetary stability requires a much deeper and broader level of cooperation than ever before – in order to deal with issues of capital account liberalization, financial sector reforms, exchange rate policies, and sound banking regulation and supervision. The costs of inadequate cooperation are clear. When financial crisis erupted in East Asia, the International Monetary Fund provided some US$36 billion in financial support, and mobilized a further US$77 billion from multilateral and bilateral sources. In Russia, the IMF provided US$11.2 billion in financial support and likewise coordinated an even larger relief package. The policies associated with both 'resources' have subsequently been heavily criticized.[54]

[. . .]

Politically, the depth of conditions being required of East Asian countries has caused many commentators to ask fundamental questions about how legitimate it is for the IMF to do this. For example, Marty Feldstein recently wrote in *Foreign Affairs*: 'The legitimate political institutions of the country should determine the nation's economic structure and the nature of its institutions. A nation's desperate need for short-term financial help does not give the IMF the moral right to substitute its technical judgements for the outcomes of the nation's political process.'[55]

The issue here is a difficult one. The IMF is charged with the role of safeguarding the stability of the international monetary system. Yet in a globalizing world, this is difficult to do without incursion into the domestic policies of countries. An alternative approach is to accept that stability requires deeper international standards and to ask how the Fund might bolster its legitimacy in entering into this new terrain. The answer here surely lies in rethinking the representation and participation of those whose compliance is required – so as to lessen the sense of unequal 'imposition' or the impingement on democratic processes.[56] Already the IMF has made some effort to open up its way of working, such as by publishing an increasing number of background papers to bilateral negotiations, by rethinking the role 'external evaluation' might play in its work, and by opening up the issue of 'governance' in its dealings with member countries. These changes, however, do not alter the representation and ownership structure which underpins the Board of the organization, and as a result do not imbue the organization with any greater degree of legitimacy in propounding 'deep' interventions and reforms such as we have seen in East Asia.

[. . .]

International financial institutions have been undergoing some changes in the 1990s. However, for the most part, these have been refinements on 'work as usual' in these organizations. It is doubtless useful for the institutions to open themselves up to greater scrutiny and wider membership. However, decision-making processes have remained the same and rely on a hierarchy which reflects fifty-year-old inequalities. Yet the evidence suggests that effectively to manage a globalizing world economy, these institutions need greater legitimacy, and a greater degree of representation and participation. This requires change of a more fundamental kind, which is unlikely given the persistence of the old hierarchy.

The United Nations Security Council

Finally, the United Nations Security Council has sprung into action since the end of the Cold War.[57] Yet its membership today seems anachronistic with respect to the work it is trying to do. The victors of the Second World War took permanent seats on the Council in an attempt to institute a system of collective security managed by the Great Powers. Those original five members still have permanent seats, and their concurring vote is still required for the Council to pass any substantive resolution. This gives each of China, Russia, the US, France, and the UK a veto over Security Council decisions. The other ten seats on the Council rotate around different groupings of countries. Like other institutions this chapter has analysed, the Security Council institutionalized a hierarchy of states which existed at the end of the Second World War. Yet the Council remained virtually inactive during the Cold War, marginalized by balance-of-power politics between the super-powers. This has now changed.

Between August 1990 and May 1995 the Council adopted 325 resolutions (as well as some 82 'Presidential statements'), giving an average of 80 resolutions per year. This compares with an average of 14 per year over the preceding 44 years. The new high level of Security Council activity brings prominently to the fore several issues of governance. Developing countries have been quick to point out that the Council's new level of activity involves intervention in an unprecedented way into the affairs of (almost exclusively) developing countries. This has focused attention sharply on the core inequality of the institution. The power inequality was amply demonstrated in the 1980s, when the United States bullied the UN as a whole into de facto altering its Constitution so as to give the US a veto over critical budget decisions.[58]

In the 1990s, some very modest changes have occurred in the United Nations Security Council.[59] Beyond this, many members have accepted that the membership of the Council should be enlarged, to include at least Germany and Japan as permanent members and probably also representatives of developing countries.[60] However, there is great unwillingness on the part of the existing permanent members to permit any dilution of their rights in the institution. Leading the opposition but not alone is the United States.[61] [...]

Concluding Thoughts

Inequality and effective institutions in a globalizing world

Although the traditional view of international order placed great weight on the hierarchy of power, when modern international institutions were created fifty years ago it was appreciated that a balance had to be struck between 'efficiency' wrought through great-power management, and 'legitimacy', which was necessary to ensure the cooperation of the rest. The latter required that some basic notion of 'equality' be respected. Within the United Nations the balance was felt to be struck by a General Assembly in which all states would have an equal vote, and a Security Council in which the most powerful states would have a veto. Even in the IMF, where most voting power was apportioned according to economic power, 'basic votes' were apportioned to symbolize the equality of member states. As Joseph Gold explains, 'the authors of the plans for the Fund and the negotiators felt that the bold step of weighting the voting power . . . should be combined with the political consideration of the traditional equality of states in international law. The basic votes were to serve the function of recognizing the doctrine of the equality of states.'[62] What theorists have referred to as the 'trappings of universality'[63] have been vital to the place and role of international organizations.

In the 1990s, for international institutions to be effective they will have to reflect more than ever a wide range of members and to embody commitments that all members are prepared to implement. On some issues, this has already been recognized. Although many believed the era of global summitry to be over at the end of the 1970s, in fact the 1990s has seen North–South Summits on issues including: the environment and development (Rio de Janeiro 1992); population and development (Cairo 1994); women (Beijing 1995); and global climate change (Kyoto 1997). These summits reflect a recognition that effective action in these areas will depend vitally upon commitments from a range of governments – rich, poor, weak, and strong – and that compliance is unlikely to be forthcoming unless parties each have a stake in the final agreement and a clear stake in abiding by it. Yet outside of these summits, in the organizations and institutions which are needed to regulate and facilitate international issues, there is little indication that powerful member states have any intention of altering the hierarchical basis on which order has traditionally been maintained, even though that hierarchy will not serve to meet the more complex challenges of order in a globalizing world.

Notes

1 Stanley Hoffmann (ed.), *Conditions of World Order* (New York, 1968).
2 Raymond Aron, chairing the meeting, argued that world order could mean any one of five things: an arrangement of reality; relations among the parts of world politics; the minimum conditions for existence; the minimum conditions for *co*existence; or the conditions for the good life. Yet Stanley Hoffmann notes that the fifth meaning was instantly ruled out on the grounds that it could lead members only 'to platitudes or to an acrimonious reproduction of the conflicts of values that exist in the world' (ibid., p. 2). Instead, the Conference chose to focus on the fourth definition, defining order as the 'conditions under which men might live together relatively well in one planet' (ibid.).
3 Although one might equally quote a plethora of other non-European systems – Asian, African, and pre-Columbian American – each of which were also ordered by hierarchically structured suzerain systems of considerable longevity.
4 Hedley Bull, *The Anarchical Society: A Study of Order in World Politics*, 2nd edn (London, 1995); Martin Wight, *Power Politics*, 2nd edn, ed. Hedley Bull and Carsten Holbraad (London, 1986); Hans J. Morgenthau, *Politics among Nations: The Struggle for Power and Peace* (New York, 1985).
5 Kenneth N. Waltz, *Theory of International Politics* (New York, 1979); and see the critiques by Robert Cox and Richard Ashley in Robert O. Keohane (ed.), *Neorealism and its Critics* (New York, 1986).
6 Barry Buzan, Charles Jones and Richard Little, *The Logic of Anarchy: Neorealism to Structural Realism* (New York, 1993); David A. Baldwin, *Neorealism and Neoliberalism: The Contemporary Debate* (New York, 1993).
7 Joseph M. Grieco, *Cooperation among Nations: Europe, America, and Non-tariff Barriers to Trade* (Ithaca, 1990).

8   Robert O. Keohane, *After Hegemony: Cooperation and Discord in the World Political Economy* (Princeton, 1984).

9   Robert Keohane, Joseph Nye and Stanley Hoffmann, *After the Cold War: International Institutions and State Strategies in Europe, 1989–1991* (Cambridge, Mass., 1993).

10 George Bush, 'New World Order', in *Public Papers of the Presidents, Administration of George Bush*, vol. 2 (1990), pp. 1218–22.

11 B. Grosh and S. Orvis, 'Democracy, confusion, or chaos: political conditionality in Kenya', *Studies in Comparative International Development* 31(4) (1997): 46–65; Luiz Carlos Bresser Pereira, Adam Przeworski and José María Maravall, *Economic Reforms in New Democracies: A Social-Democratic Approach* (Cambridge, 1993); Stephan Haggard and Robert R. Kaufman, *The Political Economy of Democratic Transitions* (Princeton, 1995); Laurence Whitehead, *Economic Liberalization and Democratization: Explorations of the Linkages* (London, 1993); Adam Przeworski, *Democracy and the Market: Political and Economic Reforms in Eastern Europe and Latin America* (Cambridge, 1991).

12 Michael Ignatieff, *Blood and Belonging: Journeys into the New Nationalism* (London, 1994).

13 Thomas Franck, *Fairness in International Law and Institutions* (Oxford, 1995).

14 Frederick Abbott and David Gerber, *Public Policy and Global Technological Integration* (The Hague, 1997); Michael Blakeney, *Trade-Related Aspects of Intellectual Property Rights: A Concise Guide to the TRIPs Agreement* (London, 1996); Carlos Correa, *Intellectual Property Rights and Foreign Direct Investment* (New York, 1993).

15 UNDP, *Human Development Report* (New York, 1997) takes 17 countries for which there are data and shows that exports as a share of GDP in 1913 were 12.9 percent compared to 14.5 percent in 1993.

16 Indeed, the least developed countries, which account for 10 percent of the world's people, have seen their share of world trade drop to 0.3 percent – half of what it was two decades ago: UNDP, *Human Development Report*, p. 84.

17 See Diana Tussie, 'From multilateralism to regionalism', in *Oxford Development Studies Special Issue on Globalization* (Oxford, 1998).

18 Vincent Cable (ed.), *Trade Blocs? The Future of Regional Integration* (London, 1994); Till Geiger, *Regional Trade Blocs, Multilateralism and the GATT: Complementary Paths to Free Trade?* (London, 1996); Andrew Gamble and Anthony Payne, *Regionalism and World Order* (London, 1996).

19 John Whalley, *Why Do Countries Seek Regional Trade Agreements?* (Cambridge, 1996); Haggard and Kaufman, *The Political Economy of Democratic Transitions*; Joan Nelson (ed.), *Economic Crisis and Policy Choice: The Politics of Adjustment in the Third World* (Princeton, 1990).

20 Robert Z. Lawrence and Charles Oman, *Scenarios for the World Trading System and their Implications for Developing Countries* (Paris, 1991). For a more general statement about international institutions, see Stephen Krasner, *Structural Conflict: The Third World against Global Liberalism* (Berkeley, 1985).

21 Eric Helleiner, *States and the Reemergence of Global Finance: From Bretton Woods to the 1990s* (Ithaca, 1994).

22 Ricardo Ffrench-Davis, 'The Tequila effect: its origins and its widespread impact', *Desarrollo Económico: Revista de Ciencias Sociales* 37 (1997): 195–214.

23 G. Corsetti and N. Roubini, 'Political biases in fiscal policy', in Barry Eichengreen, Jeffrey Frieden and J. von Hagen (eds), *Monetary and Fiscal Policy in an Integrated Europe* (New York, 1995).

24 Geoffrey Garrett, 'Shrinking states? Globalization and national autonomy in the OECD', in *Oxford Development Studies Special Issue on Globalization*; G. Corsetti and N. Roubini, 'Fiscal deficits, public debt and government insolvency', *Journal of Japanese and International Economies* 5 (1991): 354–80.

25 Ffrench-Davis, 'The Tequila effect'.

26 John Williamson (ed.), *Latin American Adjustment: How Much Has Happened?* (Washington DC, 1990).

27   See A. Hurrell and N. Woods (eds), *Inequality, Globalization and World Politics* (Oxford, 1999), ch. 6, and A. B. Atkinson and John Micklewright, *Economic Transformation in Eastern Europe and the Distribution of Income* (Cambridge, 1992).

28   World Bank, *Governance: The World Bank's Experience* (Washington DC, 1994); IMF, *Good Governance: The IMF's Role* (Washington DC, 1997).

29   Ngaire Woods, 'Governance in international organizations: the case for reform in the Bretton Woods institutions', in UNCTAD (ed.), *International Monetary and Financial Issues for the 1990s*, vol. 9 (New York, 1998), pp. 81–106.

30   For critiques of this agenda, see P. Blunt, 'Cultural relativism, good governance, and sustainable human development', *Public Administration and Development* 15 (1995): 1–9; A. Goetz and D. O'Brien, 'Governing for the common wealth: the World Bank's approach to poverty and governance', *IDS Bulletin* 26 (1995): 17–26.

31   Thomas J. Biersteker and Cynthia Weber, *State Sovereignty as Social Construct* (Cambridge, 1996); Joseph Camilleri and Jim Falk, *The End of Sovereignty? The Politics of a Shrinking and Fragmenting World* (Aldershot, 1992).

32   Kenichi, Ohmae, *The Borderless World: Power and Strategy in the Interlinked Economy* (London, 1994).

33   Adrian Guelke, *The Age of Terrorism and the International Political System* (London, 1995).

34   Thomas George Weiss and Leon Gordenker, *NGOs, the UN and Global Governance* (Boulder, 1996).

35   Franck, *Fairness in International Law*, p. 4.

36   L. MacDonald, 'Globalizing civil society: interpreting international NGOs in Central America', *Millennium* 23(2) (1994): 267–85; Thomas Princen, *Environmental NGOs in World Politics: Linking the Local and the Global* (London, 1994).

37   Weiss and Gordenker, *NGOs, the UN and Global Governance*; Nick Wheeler, 'Guardian angel or global gangster: a review of the ethical claims of international society', *Political Studies* 44 (1996): 123–35.

38   John Meyer, David Frank, Ann Hironaka, Evan Schoefer and Nancy Tuma, 'The structuring of a world environmental regime 1870–1990', *International Organization* 51 (1997): 623–52.

39   R. Bisell, 'Recent practice of the Inspection Panel of the World Bank', *American Journal of International Law* 91 (1997): 741–4; Ibrahim Shihata, *The World Bank Inspection Panel* (Oxford, 1994).

40   See the views expressed by IMF Executive Directors as to the non-accountability of NGOs, reported in Anne Bichsel, 'The World Bank and the International Monetary Fund from the perspective of the Executive Directors from developing countries', *Journal of World Trade* 28 (1994): 141–67; and M. Edwards and D. Hulme, 'Too close for comfort: the impact of official aid on non-governmental organizations', *World Development* 24 (1996): 961–73.

41   This point is not new to the 1990s. See Richard N. Cooper, *The Economics of Interdependence: Economic Policy in the Atlantic Community* (New York, 1968); Robert O. Keohane and Joseph S. Nye, *Power and Interdependence*, 2nd edn (London, 1989); Joseph Nye, *Bound to Lead: The Changing Nature of American Power* (New York, 1990); James N. Rosenau and Ernst-Otto Czempiel (eds), *Governance without Government: Order and Change in World Politics* (Cambridge, 1992).

42   The GATT was originally a temporary measure and little provision was made for procedures, voting structure, and decision-making rules. These arose subsequently by evolution – the Council, for example, was created by a resolution of GATT contracting parties in 1960.

43   Vincent Cable, 'The new trade agenda: universal rules amid cultural diversity', *International Affairs* 72 (1996): 227–46, at 232.

44   Jeffrey Schott and John Buurman, *The Uruguay Round: An Assessment* (Washington DC, 1994); Carl Hamilton and John Whalley, 'Evaluation of the Uruguay Round results on developing countries', *World Economy* 18 (1995): 31–49; World Bank, *The Uruguay Round: Winners and Winners* (Washington DC, 1995).

45   John Odell and Barry Eichengreen, 'The United States, the ITO, and the WTO: exit options, agent slack and presidential leadership', in Anne Krueger (ed.), *The WTO as an International Organization* (Chicago, 1998), pp. 181–209, at p. 206.

46   On the background to this, see John Jackson, *Restructuring the GATT System* (London, 1990).

47   Information from the WTO Legal Office.

48   Robert Hudec, *Enforcing International Trade Law: The Evolution of the Modern GATT Legal System* (Salem, Mass., 1993).

49   Anne Krueger, 'Introduction', in Krueger, *The WTO as an International Organization*.

50   John Jackson, 'The great 1994 sovereignty debate: US acceptance and implementation of the Uruguay Round results', *Columbia Journal of Transnational Law* 36 (1997): 157–88.

51   Odell and Eichengreen, 'The United States, the ITO, and the WTO'.

52   Benjamin Cohen, *In Whose Interest? International Banking and American Foreign Policy* (New Haven, 1986); Andrew Walter, *World Power and World Money: The Role of Hegemony and International Monetary Order* (New York, 1993); Helleiner, *States and the Reemergence of Global Finance*.

53   C. Randall Henning, 'The Group of Twenty-Four: two decades of monetary and financial cooperation among developing countries', in UNCTAD (ed.), *International Monetary and Financial Issues for the 1990s*, vol. 1 (New York, 1992), pp. 137–54.

54   A Supplemental Reserve Facility has been created.

55   Marty Feldstein, 'Refocusing the IMF', *Foreign Affairs* 77 (1998): 20–33; Nigel Gould-Davies and Ngaire Woods, 'Russia and the IMF', International Affairs 75 (Jan. 1999): 23–42.

56   See Woods, 'Governance in international organizations'.

57   James Mayall (ed.), *The New Interventionism 1991–1994: United Nations Experience in Cambodia, Former Yugoslavia and Somalia* (Cambridge, 1996).

58   Articles 17(1) and 18(2) of the UN Charter require that the UN budget be approved by a two-thirds majority of the General Assembly. US demands for a change in this requirement led to a compromise whereby critical budget decisions would be adopted by consensus at the stage of the Committee for Programme and Coordination – hence giving the United States a de facto veto over the UN budget: Gene M. Lyons, 'Competing visions: proposals for UN reform', in Chadwick Alger et al. (eds), *The United Nations System: The Policies of Member States* (Tokyo, 1995).

59   Michael Wood, 'Security Council: procedural developments', *International and Comparative Law Quarterly* 45 (1996): 150–61.

60   Bruce Russett, Barry O'Neill and James Sutterlin, 'Breaking the Security Council restructuring logjam', *Global Governance* 2 (1996): 65–80. Note that among the developing countries' regions there are competing contenders for a permanent seat: India vs Pakistan or Indonesia; Brazil vs Mexico or Argentina; Nigeria vs South Africa or Egypt.

61   Benjamin Rivlin, 'UN reform from the standpoint of the United States', in *UN University Lectures: 11* (Tokyo, 1996).

62   Joseph Gold, *Voting and Decisions in the International Monetary Fund* (Washington DC, 1972), p. 18; and William N. Gianaris, 'Weighted voting in the International Monetary Fund and the World Bank', *Fordham International Law Journal* 14 (1990–1): 910–45, at 919.

63   Friedrich Kratochwil and John Gerard Ruggie, 'International organization: a state of the art on an art of the state', *International Organization* 40 (1986): 753–5.

Part VI
World Orders, Normative Futures

The debate between globalists and sceptics involves fundamental considerations about the nature of world order – as it is and as it might be. Disagreements can range over at least three separate dimensions: first, the philosophical – concerned, above all, with conceptual and normative tools for analysing world order; second, the empirical-analytical – concerned, above all, with the problems of understanding and explaining world order; and, third, the strategic – concerned, above all, with an assessment of the feasibility of moving from where we are to where we might like to be.

On the one hand, globalists take the view that the progressive emergence of a global economy, the expansion of transnational links which generate new forms of collective decision-making, the development of intergovernmental and quasi-supranational institutions, the intensification of transnational communication systems, and the development of new regional and global military orders – all raise fundamental questions about the fate of the modern state and about the appropriate locus for the articulation of the political good. Globalists seek to rethink the nature and meaning of the modern polity in its global setting. They reject the assumption that one can understand the nature and possibilities of political life by referring primarily to national structures and processes.

The transnational and global scale of contemporary economic and social problems presents, globalists contend, a unique challenge to the modern state. This challenge involves, in the first instance, the recognition of the way globalization generates a serious 'political deficit' – a deficit which encompasses democracy, regulation and justice. As regional and global forces escape the reach of territorially based polities, they erode the capacity of national states to pursue programmes of regulation, accountability and social justice in many spheres. Second, re-examining the changing context of the modern state entails recognizing the way globalization stimulates new political energies and forces which are providing an impetus to the reconfiguration of political power. These include the numerous transnational movements, agencies and NGOs pursuing greater coordination and accountability in regional and global settings. Third, globalists affirm that a shift is, and ought to be, taking place between political and ethical frameworks based on the national political community and those based on a wider set of considerations. In this account, national viewpoints are highly partial and particular and can be juxtaposed with a cosmopolitan outlook. Such an outlook is preoccupied with the claims of each person as an individual or as a member of humanity as a whole. It defends the idea that human beings are in a fundamental sense equal, and that they deserve impartial political treatment – that is, treatment based on principles upon which all people could act. Cosmopolitanism is a moral frame of reference for specifying principles that can be universally shared; and, concomitantly, it rejects as unjust all those practices, rules and institutions anchored in principles not all could adopt. Weighing the claims of each person equally and considering principles which each person could accept implies that the particular boundaries between states and other communities have no deep (over-riding) moral significance.

Globalists often link their moral cosmopolitanism to a fourth consideration: the advo-cacy of institutional cosmopolitanism; that is, the extension of global governance and the creation of political institutions and mechanisms which would provide a framework of political regulation across the globe. Although globalists often differ with each other over the precise form and nature of such a framework, they are generally committed to the view that a cosmopolitan institutional framework means that states should have a somewhat, if not markedly, diminished role in comparison with institutions and organizations of regional and global governance. Accordingly, states would no longer be regarded as the sole centre of legitimate power within their own borders. States would need to be rearticulated with, and relocated within, an overarching political framework which would strip away the idea of sovereignty from fixed borders and territories, and rearticulate it as a form of legitimate political authority which could be embedded or entrenched in diverse realms, from local associations and cities to states, regions and, eventually, the global order.

In stark contrast, sceptics hold that the modern theory of the state presupposes a community which rightly governs itself. The modern theory of the sovereign democratic state, they contend, upholds the idea of a national community of fate – a community which properly governs itself and determines its own future. This idea is not challenged by the nature of the pattern of global interconnections and the issues that have to be confronted by a modern state. For the sceptics, particularly those who subscribe to a communitarian outlook, the values of the community take precedence over all uni-versal requirements. The national political good trumps universal principles of right. The boundaries of political community stipulate the proper boundaries for theories of democracy and justice. The modern political community remains the fundamental unit of world order, the key basis of contemporary politics, the proper locus of rights and duties, and the key focus for all regulatory activity. Even if particular regional or global problems escape the immediate capacities of states, it is only by states collaborating together, that is through various forms of intergovernmentalism, that such issues and problems can be actually – and legitimately – tackled.

In the first contribution to this part of the book, Anthony McGrew critically reviews the normative debates about the meaning of democracy and the prospects for the demo-cratic project under conditions of contemporary regionalization and globalization. He argues that globalization presents modern democratic theory 'with a daunting task: how to reconcile the principle of rule by the people with a world in which power is exer-cised increasingly on a transnational, or even global scale'. In addressing this problem he considers a number of leading theoretical approaches – liberal internationalism, rad-ical communitarianism and cosmopolitan democracy – and their attempts to rethink the nature of democracy. McGrew sets out a new agenda for democratic theory and prac-tice, one which seeks to break with conventional accounts of democracy in which the nation-state is conceived as the only proper site of democratic processes and outcomes.

Held explores similar themes in his concern to unravel how globalization might be regulated given that the collective fortunes of peoples are determined increasingly by processes that stretch across their borders. Exploring changing forms of political and economic power, Held seeks to argue both against the thesis that the intensification of globalization has diminished the powers of the state and against the view that the state is as robust and as integrated as it ever was. He seeks to show that a new regime of government and governance is emerging which is displacing traditional conceptions of state power as an indivisible, territorially exclusive form of public power. The key challenge, he argues, is how to embed these newly emerging regimes of government and governance within effective systems of openness, transparency and accountability. Examining the ways in which contemporary globalization has contributed to the transformation of the nature and prospects of democratic political community, Held sets out and advocates a cosmopolitan response: in essence, the principles and institutional arrangements for making accountable those sites and forms of power that presently operate beyond the scope of democratic control. He adds, however, that it would be wholly fallacious to conclude that the politics of national democratic communities will or should be wholly eclipsed by new forms of regional and global governance. Rather, he thinks, democracy must become multilayered and operate at many levels if it is to prosper in the century ahead.

Halliday focuses on the prospects and problems posed by the development of global governance. He accepts that the task of promoting global governance is very important but he also wants to stress that it is immensely difficult. For beyond the identification and evaluation of problems, and the elaboration of hypothetical solutions to them, the pursuit of global governance today 'involves confronting some deep resistances in the international system and some obstacles that have arisen in the very process of global change over recent years'. Testing this thesis, Halliday explores five contentious issues around which arguments about global governance have developed – these include the nature and role of the great powers; dilemmas of peacekeeping (the Yugoslav case); economic nationalism; the changing nature and loss of innocence of non-governmental organizations; and the role of global values. He accepts that without the development and expansion of the institutions of global governance, international political order or prosperity will be hard to sustain, but he also recognizes that the modern state has had an essential role in managing and regulating the economy and promoting welfare within and between countries over the last one hundred years. Arguments about global governance should not be carried to the point where the essential role of the state in regulating order and prosperity is eclipsed from view. Nor should arguments in favour of global governance ignore the role that most central institutions of the state can play, and that no other institutions are able to play at the present time – for no other political institution has the resources, capabilities and legitimacy of the modern state. Arguments for cosmopolitanism would be all the stronger if they understood this better, and grasped the sheer complexity of many of the issues they must confront.

The fourth contribution to this section concerns international distributive justice. In the words of the author, this topic is both 'new and messy'. O'Neill argues that the topic 'is new because global distribution is a fairly new possibility. It is messy because principles of distributive justice are contentious, and because it is unclear to whom arguments about international distributive justice should be addressed.' O'Neill begins by arguing that any attempt to restrict a theory of justice to the nation-state is doomed to failure. For we live in a world that is not one of closed communities within impenetrable ways of thought, self-sufficient economies and ideally sovereign states. The communities we all live in now are already highly intermeshed. O'Neill sets out the argument for international justice based on Kantian principles. For Kant, justice is a matter of acting only on principles on which everyone could act. A Kantian approach aims to identify fundamental principles which may be used to govern the lives and institutions of all. Elaborating these thoughts, O'Neill presents a forceful case for re-thinking the nature and meaning of international distributive justice. She hopes that her programme offers 'a procedure for identifying certain principles of justice, and arguments to show why their institutionalization and implementation should take account of relationships of power and vulnerability'.

The penultimate article by Brown defends the central importance of the national political community. Accordingly, he expresses severe scepticism about all arguments which favour a form of moral and/or institutional cosmopolitanism. Brown critically evaluates the idea of an emerging world community. He rejects all suggestions that there is a cultural, historical or ethical basis for the emergence of a common framework for humanity. He finds such an idea implausible. There is no global community in the making; no global common interests which can be identified; and there is no basis for the emergence of a global common identity. Moreover, the ideal of a universal principle of justice or of an ideal world community with its own substantive ends is, he suggests, far less attractive and desirable than the recognition of 'the ideal of a plurality of morally autonomous, just communities relating to one another in a framework of peace and law'. Such an ideal, according to Brown, is closer to the empirical reality of today's world and far more appropriate to it than the cosmopolitan alternative.

Finally, in the closing piece Bull explores various arguments about developmental tendencies which might take one beyond the states system. His contribution appraises different forms of universal political organization which might arise. He focuses on some of the classical arguments for world government; and he finds that they rest on an assumed priority of order over liberty or human justice. He defends the idea of a states system as a better prospect than world government. But there are other tendencies that he explores, notably the tendency to what he has called 'a new mediaevalism'. A new medieval order would be one in which individuals were no longer simply loyal to one centre of political authority. Political life would be marked by overlapping authority and criss-crossing loyalties, without necessary allegiance to one form of concentrated political power. Bull concedes that such a development is not beyond our imagination, and might already exist in germ in communities such as the European Union, but he doubts it would prove more durable than the states system. However, his essential contention is that the states order has, despite its many limitations, served us well, and that the most likely alternatives to it carry not only serious risks of failure but also questions about their desirability and feasibility. He warns against the proliferation of alternative schemes to the states system which do not take account of our inability to transcend past experience, and of the limits of our knowledge and political imagination.

38

Democracy beyond Borders?

Anthony McGrew

Globalization presents modern democratic theory with a daunting task: how to reconcile the principle of rule by the people with a world in which power is exercised increasingly on a transnational, or even global scale. Since classical times the history of democratic thought has been a story of the successive re-thinking and re-grounding of the idea of democracy in contemporary historical conditions. Today the fate of democratic communities across the globe is becoming ever more tightly interwoven by patterns of contemporary globalization with the result that established territorial models of liberal democracy appear increasingly hollow. This invites a serious re-examination of the meaning of democracy to confront an epoch in which the scale of human social organization no longer appears to coincide with national territorial boundaries. What is, and what should be, the meaning of democracy under contemporary conditions of globalization are questions of the utmost importance to democratic theory and practice. A new agenda for democratic theory is called for: one which breaks with conventional accounts of democracy in which the nation-state is conceived as the only proper incubator of democratic political life. Central to this new agenda is a critical enquiry into the necessity, desirability, and possibility of 'global democracy' – that is, of democracy beyond borders.

The Argument Previewed

During the Enlightenment the great philosophers, amongst them Rousseau and Kant, sought to design the ideal form of international order – 'perpetual peace' – conducive to the entrenchment of republican (democratic) government. However, for much of the twentieth century, this tradition of normative thinking was wantonly abandoned as the academic study of politics embraced a form of 'intellectual apartheid', separating the analysis of modern political life into the domestic and the international spheres; into politics within and politics between states; into politics as government and politics between governments respectively. As a consequence normative thinking about the 'good political community' became divorced almost totally from theorizing about the 'global human condition', and vice versa. This is especially true of modern democratic theory which, despite its enlightenment heritage, for the most part, has bracketed the international in its elaboration and advocacy of the democratic project. But, in the late twentieth century, the international diffusion of liberal democracy and the globalization of social life have provoked a revival of normative theorizing, cutting across the disciplinary boundaries of political theory and international relations, concerning the nature of the 'good (democratic) political community' and the form of world order necessary to its cultivation.

Paradoxically, just as liberal democracy has become the 'universal political standard of civilization', democratic theorists are beginning to engage in a critical reinterpretation of the meaning of democracy in the context of late twentieth-century patterns of globalization. This rethinking of democracy, of democratic ideas and practices, is animated by a strong normative attachment to the 'democratic good' and to the conviction that, in an epoch of intense globalization, the vitality of democracy within nation-states is intimately connected to the democratization of world order, to an ideal of 'democracy beyond borders'. But such an 'ideal' is subversive of the existing international order; an order in which the struggle for power and security amongst sovereign states defines an amoral, anarchic system in which force is the final arbiter of the good.

[. . .] this chapter will argue that contemporary globalization invites a significant rethinking of democratic theory, most especially in respect of traditional accounts of liberal democracy (qua national or territorial democracy). Accordingly [. . .] the chapter offers an explication, and critical assessment, of the challenges posed by globalization to the principles and institutional forms of liberal democracy. This culminates in a review of the argument that, under conditions of contemporary globalization, the realization of substantive, as opposed to simply procedural, democracy – that is, a polity cultivating the active citizen as opposed to the passive voter – demands the extension of democracy beyond the nation-state to bring to account those global and transnational forces which presently escape effective democratic control. But the argument for global democracy provokes a series of important analytical and normative questions, including amongst others: How would a democratic world order be constituted? Can democracy be 'transplanted' to the global domain? Is global democracy desirable? What kinds of normative principles would underpin a democratic world order?
[. . .]

Liberal democracy today confronts an era of global organization. The contemporary scale of human social and economic organization is transforming the institutional conditions under which liberal democratic states operate. As Walker [argues]: 'Although it is with respect to the state that we have come to understand what is meant by democracy, states are caught up in processes that make democracy more and more difficult to achieve' (Walker 1988: 83). However, democracy's predicament, suggests Sandel, is not entirely without historical precedent, for 'the challenge to self-government in the global economy resembles the predicament American politics faced in the early decades of the twentieth century' (Sandel 1996: 339). By the turn of the twentieth century, industrialization had transformed the scale of economic organization in the USA and created huge new concentrations of power. A significant disjuncture therefore existed between the 'nationalization' of economic activity and the capacity of local democratic political institutions to regulate it. For the progressive politicians of the era the solution lay in centralizing political power within the federal (national) government, creating a strong national state, and encouraging a potent sense of national identity and solidarity. Transposed to liberal democracy's present predicament this suggests a solution lies in the direction of formal world government. But the historical record also confirms that world government is neither a politically attainable nor a desirable arrangement. Instead we must acknowledge that 'contemporary conditions call for a radical rethinking of what democracy must involve' (Walker 1991).

Rethinking Democracy: Models of Global Democracy

If the aspiration for substantive democracy is to be realized under contemporary conditions then liberal democracy must embrace those global and transnational spheres of modern life which presently escape its territorial jurisdiction. In this respect the democratization of world order and global governance promise not only a means to reclaim and regenerate the ethic of self-governance, which is at the heart of democratic politics, but also to harness the democratic energies of those progressive social forces which increasingly operate across, below, and above the nation-state. But such a project requires, in the first instance, a normative vision of 'democracy beyond borders', an account of what democracy might be or could become; a cogent rethinking of democracy. In this section we explore three quite different normative accounts or 'models' of global democracy: the liberal-internationalist; the radical communitarian; and the cosmopolitan.

Before elaborating these accounts a word of clarification is necessary concerning the nature of normative theory and these three models. Although normative theory is concerned primarily with explicating and analysing what is desirable, the principles underlying what ought to be or should be the case, it is neither necessarily wildly utopian in nature nor divorced from an understanding of contemporary historical circumstances. On the contrary it derives its intellectual credibility from an understanding of both 'where we are – the existing pattern of political relations and processes – and from an analysis of what might be: desirable political forms and principles' (Held 1995: 286). To discount normative theory simply on the grounds that it trades in ideas or projects which, under existing historical conditions, may appear politically infeasible is to accept a deterministic view of history. But '1989 and all that', completely unanticipated as it was, is a solemn reminder that prevailing assumptions about what appears politically feasible are often a feeble guide to history's possibilities. The ideals of eighteenth-century political theorists, often at the time treated with great disdain, are embedded in many of the routines of modern political life, from the language of rights to the institutions of liberal democracy, such that it is no exaggeration to claim that 'we live some [normative] theory – all the time' (Sandel 1996: ix). As the accounts of global democracy discussed here exemplify, normative theory justifiably is concerned above all with the limits to and the possibilities of the politically desirable.

Although they offer different prescriptions for global democracy, the following accounts share a number of features in common. Firstly, an acknowledgement that globalization is transforming the conditions of liberal democracy. Secondly, a commitment to the widening and deepening of democratic politics. Thirdly, a rejection of the idea of world government. Fourthly, a belief that new democratic arrangements for global governance are necessary. Fifthly, and lastly, a conviction that political ideas and ideals can, and do, shape political practice. However, each account embodies a distinctive democratic ethic and reflects a unique inheritance of ideas from different democratic traditions. Together they represent diverse interpretations of the central questions of democracy: How is the demos to be conceived? How is rule to be conceived? What is the purpose of democracy? In the exegesis which follows the discussion will examine, in each case, a specific prescriptive account of global democracy which is representative of that normative approach, its underlying normative principles, its democratic heritage, and its limitations. This analysis seeks to identify the normative theory which underpins each account and thus establish the basis for comparing the democratic principles and general features of each 'model' of global democracy. In this context the concept of 'model' refers to a simplified and ideal-type construction of a specific normative theory.

Liberal-democratic internationalism: 'neighbourhood democracy'

In late 1995 the Commission on Global Governance, an independent international committee of senior statespersons, published its report *Our Global Neighbourhood* (Governance 1995). The report recognizes the profound political impact of globalization: 'The shortening of distance, the multiplying of links, the deepening of interdependence: all these factors, and their interplay, have been transforming the world into a neighbourhood' (p. 43). Its main purpose is to address the problem of democratic governance in this new 'global neighbourhood', acknowledging that the fate of national democracy, in an interdependent world, is intimately tied to the prospects for the democratization of world order. As the report asserts:

> It is fundamentally important that governance should be underpinned by democracy at all levels and ultimately by the rule of enforceable law . . . As at the national level, so in the global neighbourhood: the democratic principle must be ascendant. The need for greater democracy arises out of the close linkage between legitimacy and effectiveness . . . as the role of international institutions in global governance grows, the need to ensure that they are democratic also increases. (pp. 48, 66)

But the report is emphatic that global governance 'does not imply world government or world federalism' (p. 336). Rather it understands global governance as a set of pluralistic arrangements by which states, international organizations, international regimes, non-governmental organizations, citizen movements and markets combine to regulate or govern aspects of global affairs. In this sense there 'is no single model or form of global governance, nor is there a single structure or set of structures. It is a broad, dynamic, complex process of interactive decision-making that is constantly evolving and responding to changing circumstances' (p. 4).

To achieve a more secure, just and democratic world order the report proposes a multi-faceted strategy of international institutional reform and the nurturing of a new global civic ethic. Central to its proposals is a reformed United Nations system buttressed by the strengthening, or creation, of regional forms of international governance, such as the EU. Through the establishment of a peoples' assembly and a Forum of [Global] Civil Society, both associated with the UN General Assembly, the world's peoples are to be represented directly and indirectly in the institutions of global governance. Moreover, it proposes that individuals and groups be given a right of petition to the UN through a Council of Petitions, which will recommend action to the appropriate agency. Combined with the deeper entrenchment of a common set of global rights and responsibilities the aim is to strengthen notions of global citizenship. An Economic Security Council is proposed to co-ordinate global economic governance, making it more open and accountable. Democratic forms of governance within states are to be nurtured and strengthened through international support mechanisms whilst the principles of sovereignty and non-intervention are to be adapted 'in ways that recognize the need to balance the rights of states with the rights of people, and the interests of nations with the interests of the global neighbourhood' (p. 337). Binding all these reforms together is a commitment to the nurturing of a new global civic ethic based upon 'core values that all humanity could uphold: respect for life, liberty, justice and equity, mutual respect, caring, and integrity' (p. 336). Central to this global civic ethic is the principle of participation in governance at all levels from the local to the global. As a serious, as well as systematic, attempt to 're-think' the conditions of democracy and to establish a set of normative principles and institutional arrangements by which to entrench democratic politics within all levels of governance the Commission's report represents a remarkable achievement.

Richard Falk has referred to the Commission as the 'last of the great liberal commissions', since underlying its carefully argued report is a normative theory of global governance which is rooted in liberal-internationalist approaches to world order and liberal models of democracy (Falk 1995). Liberal-internationalism has its origins in the thinking of enlightenment philosophers. Given their faith in progress and human rationality, liberal-internationalists, since the last century, have argued that creating a peaceful and democratic world order is far from a utopian project but, on the contrary, a necessity in a world of growing interdependence. As a normative theory of world order it is concerned with how to *reform* the system of states with the aim of abolishing power politics and war (D. Long 1996).

Three factors are absolutely central to this theory: growing interdependence, democracy and global governance. Cobden and Bright, leading liberal-internationalists of the nineteenth century, argued that economic interdependence generates propitious conditions for international co-operation between governments and peoples (Hinsley 1967). Since their destinies are bound together, states, as rational actors, come to recognize that international co-operation is essential to managing their common fate. In turn international co-operation to deal with collective problems, alongside the international diffusion of prosperity brought about by global commerce, makes war both increasingly irrational as a means to achieving political goals and increasingly unnecessary (Mueller 1989). Secondly, democracies are constrained in their actions by the principles of openness and accountability to their electorates. In these conditions rational governments are less likely to engage in war (Howard 1981). Accordingly, the spread of democracy establishes a framework for international peace. Thirdly, through the creation of international law and institutions to regulate international interdependencies, world harmony can be maintained. Moreover, in an increasingly interdependent world the political authority and jurisdiction of these international institutions has a natural tendency to expand, at the expense of state sovereignty, as the welfare and security of domestic society becomes increasingly bound up with the welfare and security of global society. Although a simplification of liberal-internationalist theory, this summary sheds light on its underlying utilitarian logic.

In the twentieth century, liberal-internationalist ideology has played a critical role in the design of historical world orders, specifically under US hegemony, in the aftermath of both the First and Second World Wars. The creation of the League of Nations, and a 'world safe for democracy', was infused with such ideology, as was the UN system. In the context of the post-Cold War New World Order, liberal-internationalist ideas have acquired renewed vitality but adapted to fit 'new times' (P. Long 1995). Whilst still remaining faithful to the liberal 'emancipatory' ideal – 'to subject the rule of

arbitrary power . . . to the rule of law within global society' (Governance 1995: 5) –
contemporary thinking, as reflected in the Commission on Global Governance report,
is decidedly reformist rather than radical.

Reformist in this context refers to incremental adaptation of the institutions and practices of global governance, as opposed to reconstructing or abolishing them. Thus the
Commission proposes reform of traditional geo-political forms of international governance by means of a more representative and democratic UN system. But even in this
arrangement the great powers and states are to retain their primacy in systems of global
governance. The proposed Peoples' Assembly is to be constituted in the first instance
by an assembly of national parliamentarians. This tension between state sovereignty
and popular sovereignty, which is evident in liberal theories of national democracy, is
more explicit in liberal-internationalist thinking about the democratization of world order.
So too is the liberal fascination with constitutional and legal solutions to problems which
are essentially political in nature. Moreover, as might be expected, whilst the Commission's report documents a host of reforms to the political arrangements for global
governance it is more circumspect with regard to reform of the global economy – 'In
some cases, governance will rely primarily on markets and market instruments, perhaps with some institutional oversight' (Governance 1995: 5). Yet, as noted previously,
economic globalization is deeply implicated in the transformation of modern liberal democracy. This ambivalence reflects conventional liberal thinking, which separates the
economic from the political and restricts democracy to the political sphere.

Implicit in liberal-internationalist discourse is an assumption that political necessity
will drive forward the democratization of global governance. Avoiding global ecological crisis and managing the pervasive social, economic and political dislocation arising
from contemporary processes of globalization 'will require the articulation of a collaborative ethos based upon the principles of consultation, transparency, and accountability.
. . . There is no alternative to working together and using collective power to create a
better [democratic] world' (Governance 1995: 2, 5). But this ignores the central fact
that growing interdependence is also a significant source of global conflict.

In key respects liberal-internationalism is a normative theory which seeks to transpose a weaker form of domestic liberal-democracy into a model of democratic world
order (Clark 1989: 215). Its contemporary proponents are seeking to construct an ideal
of 'democracy beyond borders' upon the theoretical foundations of modern liberal-
democratic thinking, including the developmental democracy of J. S. Mill and the pluralist democracy of R. A. Dahl (Held 1996). But there is a real paradox here: for just at
the historical moment when liberal democracy is being transformed by the forces of
globalization it is proposed to erect a version of it at the global level.

Radical communitarianism: demarchy

Whereas liberal-internationalism emphasizes the *reform* of existing structures of global
governance, the radical project stresses the creation of *alternative* forms of global social,
economic and political organization based generally upon communitarian principles: that
is principles which emerge from the life and conditions of particular communities, from
local communities to communities of interest or affection e.g. environmental, religious,
gender. It combines a commitment to direct forms of democracy and self-governance
together with new structures of functional governance. It rejects existing structures of

global governance since they are conceived as privileging the interests of the wealthy and powerful and excluding the possibilities of more humane and democratic forms of governance. As Burnheim states, 'Democracy hardly exists at the international level, and it is difficult to see how it could in the context of existing institutions and practices' (1986: 218). The radical project is therefore concerned with establishing the necessary conditions which will empower people to take control of their own lives and to create 'good communities' based upon ideas of equality, the common good, and harmony with the natural environment. Unlike liberal-internationalism this necessarily involves the transformation of existing forms of social and economic organization to ensure a correspondence with democratic principles of governance. In this regard the radical project does not seek to transpose domestic democracy into the global domain but rather to transcend it. It is animated by a rethinking of existing 'political categories through which political practice is constituted' (Walker 1988: 136).

Radical thinking is reluctant to prescribe substantive constitutional or institutional blueprints for a more democratic world order since this represents the centralized, modern 'top down', statist approach to political life which it rejects. Accordingly, the emphasis is upon identifying the normative principles upon which 'democracy beyond borders' might be constructed irrespective of the particular institutional forms it might take. One significant attempt to identify such principles is Burnheim's normative theory of 'demarchy' (Burnheim 1985). Central to this model of global democracy is the principle that democratic governance should be organized along functional (e.g. trade, environment, health), as opposed to territorial lines, and that such functional authorities should be directly accountable to the communities and citizens whose interests are directly affected by their actions. Thus 'democracy and democratic legitimacy are not to be sought in geographically-bounded entities like nation-states, but rather in functional authorities of varying geographical scope run by individuals selected by lot from among those with a material interest in the issue in question' (Dryzek 1995). The spatial jurisdiction of these authorities would reflect the spatial scope of the problems and activities they seek to regulate or promote. According to Dryzek, 'The point is that the reach of public spheres [authorities] is entirely variable and not limited by formal boundaries or jurisdictions, or obsolete notions of national sovereignty. And they can come into existence, grow and die along with the importance of particular issues' (Dryzek 1995).

Each authority would be managed by a committee, chosen on the basis of a statistically representative sample of those citizens and communities whose interests are implicated in its decision making. This would ensure that those with a stake in the decisions of each authority would have a voice in the governance of that functional domain of social life 'to the degree that they are materially and directly affected by decisions in that domain' (Burnheim 1995). Thus, for instance, global environmental problems would be dealt with by one set of authorities whilst specific regional, national and local ecological problems would be regulated by other authorities. But each authority would be governed by representatives of the relevant political communities affected by its decisions. The co-ordination of decision making between these various authorities would be managed by committees organized on the same principle of representation so ensuring that they 'are not representative of states but of the kinds of people affected by their decisions' (Burnheim 1995). Demarchy, as a principle of global governance, seeks to facilitate and encourage 'the active participation of people in decision making, sometimes as representatives of specific interests they themselves have, but often too as the trustees of interests that cannot speak for themselves' (Burnheim 1995).

Demarchy is subversive of existing forms of global governance since its objective 'is to chip away and ultimately destroy sovereignty at all levels of social life' (Burnheim 1995). Its radical agenda is influenced by a political philosophy which asserts that one of the 'great fallacies of political theory is the assumption that a centralized management of power . . . is necessary to assure political order' (Burnheim 1986). It ultimately aspires to the 'end of the nation-state' as a liberation from power politics and the inadequacies of territorial forms of liberal democracy. In its place it offers a vision of a proliferation of diverse, overlapping and spatially differentiated self-governing 'communities of fate' in which there would be multiple sites of power but no 'sovereign' or centralized structures of authority of any kind. Such a vision entertains the possibility of a 'massive shift in power in favour of the disadvantaged, which would eventually result in radical change in the overall pattern of [global] society' (Burnheim 1986: 238).

But how is such a radical re-structuring of global power relations to be achieved? For many radicals the agents of change are to be found in existing (critical) social movements, such as the environmental, women's and peace movements, which challenge the authority of states and international agencies as well as orthodox definitions of the 'political'. Through a politics of resistance and empowerment these new social movements are conceived as playing a crucial role in global democratization similar to the role of the (old) social movements, such as organized labour, in the struggle for national democracy. In 'politicizing' social activities and eroding the conventional boundaries of political life (the foreign/domestic, public/private, society/nature) social movements are defining a 'new progressive politics' which involves 'explorations of new ways of acting, new ways of knowing and being in the world, and new ways of acting together through emerging solidarities' (Walker 1988: 147–8). As Walker suggests, 'one lesson of critical social movements is that people are not as powerless as they are made to feel. The grand structures that seem so distant and so immovable are clearly identifiable and resistible on an everyday basis. Not to act is to act. Everyone can change habits and expectations or refuse to accept that the problems are out there in someone else's backyard' (Walker 1988: 159–60). These new social movements are engaged in mobilizing transnational communities of resistance and solidarity whose activity, according to Falk, 'may remain largely "underground" until it erupts at an opportune moment to reshape the relationship of forces in many parts of the world' (Falk 1987). Those opportune moments tend, in radical accounts, to be associated with impending global ecological and economic crisis (Chase-Dunn 1986; Deudney 1994).

Underlying the radical model of global democracy is an attachment to normative theories of direct democracy and participatory democracy (Held 1996). There are echoes here of Rousseau's 'general will' and New Left ideals of community politics and participatory democracy. But the radical model also draws upon neo-Marxist critiques of liberal democracy, as is evident in the language of equality, solidarity, emancipation and transformation of existing power relations. Democracy is conceived as inseparable from the achievement of social and economic equality, the establishment of the necessary conditions for self-development, and the creation of self-governing communities. In this regard the radical model connects with the civic republican tradition of democratic thinking which conceives 'individual freedom is embedded within and sustained by a [strong] sense of political community and of the common good' (Barns 1995). Encouraging and developing in citizens a sense of simultaneous belonging to overlapping (local and global) communities of interest and affection is central to the politics of new social movements as well as the search for new models and forms of social, political and economic organization consonant with the principle of self-government. As Sandel concludes:

> Since the days of Aristotle's polis, the republican tradition has viewed self-government as an activity rooted in a particular place, carried out by citizens loyal to that place and the way of life it embodies. Self-government today, however, requires a politics that plays itself out in a multiplicity of settings, from neighbourhoods to nations to the world as a whole. Such a politics requires citizens who can think and act as multiply-situated selves. (Sandel 1996: 351)

The radical model of 'democracy beyond borders' is a 'bottom up' theory of the democratization of world order. It represents a normative theory of 'humane governance' which is grounded in the existence of a multiplicity of 'communities of fate' and social movements as opposed to the individualism of liberal-internationalism [. . .].

Cosmopolitanism: 'cosmopolitan democracy'

Recent years have witnessed what Linklater calls the 'cosmopolitan turn' in thinking about democracy (Linklater 1996b). Its resurgence, in part, arises out of a conviction that, 'Today the territorial/security state forms the space of democratic liberation and imprisonment. It liberates because it organizes democratic accountability through electoral institutions. It imprisons because it confines and conceals democratic energies flowing over and through its dykes' (Connolly 1991). Cosmopolitan thinking has a heritage stretching back to the Greek stoics and reflects a faith in the idea that humankind is bound together morally, if not materially, in a politics of 'spaceship earth'. Immanuel Kant, the eighteenth-century German philosopher, was a powerful advocate of the cosmopolitan ideal, observing that the 'greatest problem for the human species, whose solution nature compels it to seek, is to achieve a universal civil society administered in accord with the right' (Kant 1784: 33). For Kant the solution to this problem lay in the development of republican states – 'democratic' government – and their association within a peaceful union of states, and civil societies, operating under the rule of a cosmopolitan law (Kant 1795). Inspired by Kant's cosmopolitan thinking and commitment to democratic ideals, the 'cosmopolitan turn' has generated a distinctive normative approach to the contemporary problems of liberal democracy under conditions of globalization. David Held's model of 'cosmopolitan democracy' speaks to these problems directly (Held 1995).

　At the core of this model is a belief that contemporary patterns of globalization and regionalization are undermining existing national forms of liberal democracy. In this context 'national democracies require an international cosmopolitan democracy if they are to be sustained and developed in the contemporary era' (Held 1995: 23). The cosmopolitan model of democracy attempts to specify the principles and the institutional basis upon which democratic governance within, between and across states is to be expanded. This model is underpinned by an ethic of democratic autonomy which Held distinguishes from the self-interest of liberal individualism since it refers to 'a structural principle of self-determination where the "self" is part of the collectivity or "majority" enabled and constrained by the rules and procedures of democratic life . . . Hence, this form of autonomy can be referred to as "democratic autonomy" – an entitlement to autonomy within the constraints of community' (p. 156). To achieve this, under contemporary conditions, requires the embedding of democratic practices more deeply 'within communities and civil associations by elaborating and reinforcing democracy from "outside" through a network of regional and international agencies and assemblies that cut across spatially delimited locales' (p. 237). By such means those global sites and transnational networks of power which presently operate beyond the scope of territorial democratic control will be brought to account, so establishing the political conditions befitting the realization of democratic autonomy.

Central to the achievement of democratic autonomy is the necessity for a cosmopolitan democratic law, that is, law which 'transcends the particular claims of nations and states and extends to all in the "universal community"' (p. 228). Although this idea of law comes close to existing notions of international law, such as that concerning universal human rights, it involves a more powerful and radical notion of legal authority which 'allows international society, including individuals, to interfere in the internal affairs of each state in order to protect certain rights' (Archibugi 1995). Accordingly, the principle of democratic autonomy depends upon 'the establishment of an international community of democratic states and societies committed to upholding a democratic public law both within and across their own boundaries: a cosmopolitan democratic community' (Held 1995: 229). This does not require the creation of world government, nor a federal super-state, but rather the establishment of a 'transnational, common structure of political action' – a transnational structure embracing all levels of, and participants in, global governance, from states, multinational corporations, international institutions, social movements, to individuals. In this way the cosmopolitan model builds upon the post-Westphalian conception of global order as 'a global and divided authority system – a system of diverse and overlapping power centres shaped and delimited by democratic law' (p. 234). It defines a complex structure of political authority which lies between federalism (as in the USA) and, the much looser arrangements implied by the notion of, confederalism. For it requires 'the subordination of regional, national and local "sovereignties" to an overarching legal framework, but within this framework associations may be self-governing at diverse levels' (p. 234). The realization of 'cosmopolitan democracy' would thus deliver the ultimate triumph of democracy, as the global 'political good', for it seeks 'the recovery of an intensive and participatory model of democracy at local levels as a complement to the public assemblies of the wider global order: that is, a political order of democratic associations, cities and nations as well as of regions and global networks' (p. 234).

The implications of this model for the nation-state and individual citizenship are profound. It proposes the end of sovereign statehood and national citizenship as conventionally understood and their re-articulation within a framework of cosmopolitan democratic law. Nation-states would 'wither away' only in the sense that they would clearly 'no longer be regarded as the sole centres of legitimate power within their own borders' (p. 233); but they would not be redundant. Whilst, as Linklater argues, citizenship would involve a recognition that individuals 'can fall within the jurisdiction of several authorities; they can have multiple identities and they need not be united by [national] social bonds which make them indifferent to, or enemies of, the rest of the human race' (Linklater 1996b).

The entrenchment of 'cosmopolitan democracy' within the global system requires, in the first instance, a process of *reconstructing* the existing framework of global governance. This is to involve both short- and long-term measures in the conviction that, through a process of incremental change, geo-political forces will come to be socialized into democratic practices. These measures require that international organizations and the UN system be made both more representative and accountable. Thus functional international institutions, such as the WTO or the World Bank, would have elected supervisory boards whilst the UN General Assembly would be complemented by a directly elected 'assembly of peoples' which would form a 'second chamber'. Referenda would reinforce the voices of the world's peoples in these structures as would the exploitation of new communication technologies such as the Internet. Alongside these global structures regional forms of governance, with associated regional parliaments and executive authorities, would be expanded or developed. Moreover, the incorporation of cosmopolitan democratic law into the constitutional and legal frameworks of governance at all levels is central to this process of reconstructing global governance. An International Human Rights Court would dispense justice, in relation to human rights abuses, on a global scale. In addition, the cosmopolitan law would require the backing of coercive force at all levels of governance through the creation of new internationalized and accountable military structures. Finally, the institutions and operation of the global economy would be subject to democratic intervention to embed the principle of democratic autonomy in the structures and functioning of global market capitalism.

'Cosmopolitan democracy' proposes an enormously ambitious agenda for the institutional and political reconstruction of global governance. Nevertheless, its utopian vision is reflected in a variety of contemporary developments, from the 'big' structural shift towards a post-Westphalian international order, to the 'micro' level development of 'European citizenship' in the context of the EU. Crawford, too, identifies in international law a formal commitment to democracy 'which a generation or even a decade ago would have been regarded as political or extra-legal' and which more importantly is 'entering into the justification of legal decision making in a new way' (Crawford 1994: 14). Over the last half-century the number of national referenda on foreign and international issues has grown considerably in all regions of the globe (Rourke et al. 1992). Linklater, moreover, argues that cosmopolitan democracy 'expresses important if challenged trends within Europe which favour the greater democratization of international life' (Linklater 1996b).

Such trends, by themselves, do not necessarily portend dramatic change. Advocates of cosmopolitan democracy remain extremely aware of the fact that 'it is precisely because our current social and political institutions are a reflection of political values and preferences that ideas of the future can be instrumental in bringing about qualitative change' (Clark 1989: 52). Normative thinking, in this view, is not simply an analytical account of the 'good political community' but also an intellectual activity which identifies the political possibilities inherent in the present. In this sense it is both a reflection upon the contemporary historical condition and also constitutive of it, promoting the 'theorist as advocate, seeking to advance an interpretation of politics against countervailing positions . . . [creating] . . . the possibility of a new political understanding' (Held 1995: 286).

In comparison with the radical and 'neighbourhood' models of global democracy the cosmopolitan model reflects an eclectic democratic heritage, in that it has strong links to a variety of traditions of democratic thought. Whilst it draws considerable inspiration from modern theories of liberal democracy, it is also influenced by the thinking of contemporary theorists of direct democracy and civic (republican) democracy. This is reflected in the emphasis upon the principle of democratic autonomy and participatory democracy. In some respects it combines aspects of both radical communitarianism and liberal-internationalism. However, unlike liberal-internationalist theory it is not concerned with the *reform* of global governance *per se* but rather with its *reconstruction*. It seeks to replace the primacy of power politics in the conduct of global governance with the primacy of democratic decision making. It also seeks to address the democratization of global economic relations and forms of governance. It embraces a stronger commitment to self-governance in comparison with the top-down model proposed by the Commission on Global Governance. Moreover, it distinguishes itself from radical models of global democracy with its recognition of the centrality of law and public authorities as necessary conditions for the establishment of a more democratic world order. But the idea of cosmopolitan democracy is not without its critics.

Sandel argues that, 'Despite its merits . . . the cosmopolitan ideal is flawed, both as a moral ideal and as a public philosophy for self-government in our time' (1996: 342). This, he argues, is because at the core of cosmopolitanism is a liberal conception of the individual which neglects the ways in which individuals, their interests and values, are 'constructed' by the communities of which they are members. Accordingly, democracy can only thrive by first creating a democratic community with a common civic identity. Whilst globalization does create a sense of universal connectedness it does not, in Brown's view, generate an equivalent sense of community based upon shared values and beliefs (Brown 1995). Thus cosmopolitan democracy, as global democracy, lacks the normative and moral foundations for its effective realization. The model is also criticized for its emphasis upon a constitutional-legal approach to the democratization of world order which fails to specify a convincing rationale for how cosmopolitan democratic law can be institutionalized in the absence of a global authority or without resort to coercion. Finally, it might be argued that without stronger mechanisms for taming the power of global capital the idea of cosmopolitan democracy remains seriously deficient.

This section has explored three normative accounts, or models, of global democracy. These are summarized in table 1. There are significant differences, as well as similarities, between these three models of global democracy. Moreover, they are the product of quite distinct combinations of democratic traditions and reflect the influence of different schools of international relations theory (see figure 1). All three offer a vision of a more democratic world order, although based upon quite different normative principles. [. . .]

Can any general conclusions be derived from this analysis? Two, in particular, appear incontrovertible. Firstly, contemporary democratic theory has to continue to explore the consequences of globalization and the dissolution of the historical identity between democracy and the sovereign nation-state. If it fails to do so, it is in danger of encouraging

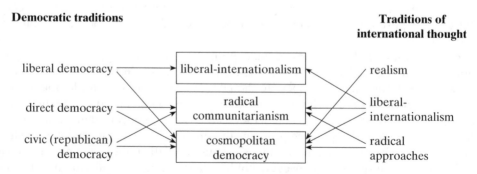

Figure 1   Models of global democracy: an intellectual genealogy

Table 1 Models of global democracy: a summary and comparison

	Liberal internationalism	Radical communitarianism	Cosmopolitan democracy
Who should govern?	The people through governments, accountable international regimes and organizations.	The people through self-governing communities.	The people through states, associations, international organizations, all subject to cosmopolitan law.
Form of global governance?	*Polyarchy* – pluralistic fragmented system, sharing of sovereignty.	*Demarchy* – functional democratic governance, devoid of sovereignty.	*Heterarchy* – divided authority system subject to cosmopolitan democratic law.
Key agents/ instruments, processes of democratization	Accelerating interdependence, self-interest of key agencies of power in creating more democratic/co-operative forms of global governance.	New social movements, impending global ecological and economic crises.	Constitutional and institutional reconstruction, intensification of globalization and regionalization, new social movements, impending global crises.
Traditions of democratic thought	Liberal democratic theory – pluralism and protective democracy, social democracy, reformism.	Direct democracy, participatory democracy, civic republicanism, socialist democracy.	Liberal democratic theory, pluralism and developmental democracy, participatory democracy, civic republicanism.
Ethic of global governance	'Common rights and shared responsibilities.'	'Humane governance.'	'Democratic autonomy.'
Mode of political transformation	*Reform* of global governance.	*Alternative structures* of global governance.	*Reconstruction* of global governance.

what Connolly calls a 'homesickness' or 'a nostalgia for a time when a coherent politics of place could be imagined as a real possibility for the future' (Connolly 1991). This 'homesickness' pervades world politics today and its more extreme, rather than benign, consequences are articulated in the horrors of ethnic cleansing, virulent nationalism and genocide. Democratic theorists must continue to avoid such nostalgia through continuing to reconstruct accounts of democracy to accord with the historical conditions of globalization and an expanded vision of the 'good community'. A theory of global democracy today also requires a theory of global politics. In this respect, democratic theory has begun to reconnect with its past and thus to overcome the modern separation of political theory from international political theory, the separation of a theory of the good life within the state from a theory of the good life for humankind. [. . .]

Secondly, democratic theory and democratic practice are organically connected. The reconstruction of democratic theory is inseparable from the rejuvenation of democratic political life and vice versa. In this sense democratic theory is a form of 'transformative political practice'. As Walker comments, 'if we are all democrats today . . . then we are all engaged in a problematic, in an ongoing struggle, rather than a finished condition' (Walker 1991). [. . .]

References

Angell, N. (1933) *The Great Illusion*. London: Heinemann.

Archibugi, D. (1995) Immanuel Kant, cosmopolitan law and peace. *European Journal of International Relations* 1(4): 429–56.

Barns, I. (1995) Environment, democracy and community. *Environment and Politics* 4(4): 101–33.

Bradshaw, Y. W. and Wallace, M. (1996) *Global Inequalities*. London: Pine Forge Press/Sage.

Brown, C. (1995) International political theory and the idea of world community. In K. Booth and S. Smith (eds), *International Relations Theory Today*, Cambridge: Polity Press.

Burnheim, J. (1985) *Is Democracy Possible?* Cambridge: Cambridge University Press.

Burnheim, J. (1986) Democracy, nation-states, and the world system. In D. Held and C. Pollitt (eds), *New Forms of Democracy*, London: Sage.

Burnheim, J. (1995) Power-trading and the environment. *Environmental Politics* 4(4): 49–65.

Chase-Dunn, C. (1986) Comparing world-systems. Mimeo.

Clark, I. (1989) *The Hierarchy of States: Reform and Resistance in the International Order*. Cambridge: Cambridge University Press.

Coates, R. A. (1996) The UN and civil society. *Alternatives*, no. 21: 93–133.

Connolly, W. E. (1991) Democracy and territoriality. *Millennium* 20(3): 463–84.

Cox, R. (1981) Social forces, states and world orders. *Millennium* 10(2): 126–55.

Cox, R. (1996) Globalization, multilateralism and democracy. In R. Cox (ed.), *Approaches to World Order*, Cambridge: Cambridge University Press.

Crawford, J. (1994) *Democracy in International Law*. Cambridge: Cambridge University Press.

Deudney, D. (1994) Global environmental rescue and the emergence of world domestic politics. In R. D. Lipschutz and K. Conca (eds), *The State and Social Power in Global Environmental Politics*, New York: Columbia University Press.

Dryzek, J. S. (1995) Political and ecological communication. *Environmental Politics* 4(4): 13–30.

Falk, R. (1987) The global promise of social movements: explorations at the edge of time. *Alternatives* 12(2): 173–96.

Falk, R. (1995) Liberalism at the global level: the last of the independent commissions? *Millennium* 24(3): 563–78.

Gill, S. (1995) Globalization, market civilization, and disciplinary neoliberalism. *Millennium* 24(3): 399–424.

Governance, Commission on Global (1995) *Our Global Neighbourhood*. Oxford: Oxford University Press.

Held, D. (1991) Democracy, the nation-state, and the global system. In D. Held (ed.), *Political Theory Today*, Cambridge: Polity Press.

Held, D. (1995) *Democracy and the Global Order*. Cambridge: Polity Press.

Held, D. (1996) *Models of Democracy*, 2nd edn. Cambridge: Polity Press.

Hinsley, F. H. (1967) *Power and the Pursuit of Peace*. Cambridge: Cambridge University Press.

Howard, M. (1981) *War and the Liberal Conscience*. Oxford: Oxford University Press.

Kant, I. (1784) Idea for a universal history with a cosmopolitan intent. In *Perpetual Peace and Other Essays*, Indianapolis: Hackett.

Kant, I. (1795) To perpetual peace: a philosophical sketch. In *Perpetual Peace and Other Essays*, Indianapolis: Hackett.

Linklater, A. (1996a) The achievements of critical theory. In S. Smith, K. Booth and M. Zalewski (eds), *International Theory; Positivism and Beyond*, Cambridge: Cambridge University Press.

Linklater, A. (1996b) Citizenship and sovereignty in the post-Westphalian state. *European Journal of International Relations* 2(1): 77–103.

Long, D. (1996) *Towards a New Liberal Internationalism*. Cambridge: Cambridge University Press.

Long, P. (1995) The Harvard School of Liberal International Theory: the case for closure. *Millennium* 24(3): 489–505.

Mitrany, D. (1975) A war-time submission (1941). In P. Taylor (ed.), *A Functional Theory of Politics*, London: LSE/Martin Robertson.

Modelski, G. (1972) *Principles of World Politics*. New York: Free Press.

Mueller, J. (1989) *Retreat from Doomsday: The Obsolescence of Major War*. New York: Basic Books.

Rourke, J. T., Hiskes, R. P. and Zirakzedh, C. E. (1992) *Direct Democracy and International Politics*. Boulder: Lynne Rienner.

Sandel, M. (1996) *Democracy's Discontent*, Cambridge, Mass.: Harvard University Press.

Scholte, J. (1993) *International Relations of Social Change*. Buckingham: Open University Press.

Spruyt, H. (1994) *The Sovereign State and its Competitors*. Princeton: Princeton University Press.

UNDP (1996) *Human Development Report 1996*. Oxford: Oxford University Press.

Walker, R. B. J. (1988) *One World, Many Worlds: Struggles for a Just World Peace*. Boulder: Lynne Rienner.

Walker, R. B. J. (1991) On the spatio-temporal conditions of democratic practice. *Alternatives* 16(2): 243–62.

Walker, R. B. J. (1994) *Inside/Outside*. Cambridge: Cambridge University Press.

Wapner, P. (1995) Politics beyond the state: environmental activism and world civic politics. *World Politics*, no. 47 (Apr.): 311–40.

39

Regulating Globalization?

David Held

Political communities are in the process of change. Of course, change is nothing new in this domain. The history of political communities is replete with developing (and decomposing) forms and structures – from empires to nation-states to emerging regional structures and organizations of global governance. But only one set of transformations is of concern in this paper: the significant, albeit uneven, enmeshment of human communities over time with each other, and the way in which the collective fortunes and fate of peoples are determined increasingly by complex processes which stretch across their borders. It is against this backdrop that I wish to pose the question: can globalization be regulated?

To put the question in this way is already to risk misunderstanding. Globalization connotes the stretching and intensification of social, economic and political relations across regions and continents. It is a multidimensional phenomenon embracing many different processes and operating on many different time scales (see Held et al. 1999). Some of these processes – for example, the expansion and development of trade across diverse countries, or the spread and diffusion of weapons of mass destruction among the world's major regimes – already involve intensive political surveillance, supervision and regulation. Public and private bodies, operating at national, regional and global levels, are deeply enmeshed in decision-making and regulatory activities in these and many other domains. Thus, the question this paper addresses needs from the outset to be refined further. At the very least, it needs to be sensitive to shifting forms of regulation and the changing balance between private and public power, authority and governance. Another way to express the concerns of this paper is to ask: what are prospects of public regulation and democratic accountability in the context of the intensification of regional and global interconnectedness, and of changes in the balance between public and private power, and in local, national, regional and global regulatory mechanisms?

Conventional maps of the political world disclose a very particular conception of the geography of political power. With their clear-cut boundary lines and unambiguous colour patches, they demarcate territorial areas within which there is assumed to be an indivisible, illimitable and exclusive sovereign state with internationally recognized borders. Only the polar regions appear to stand outside of this jigsaw, though some maps highlight the claims of some states to these as well. It is worth recalling that at the beginning of the second millennium, this cartography would have appeared practically incomprehensible. A cursory inspection of the limited cartographic knowledge of the time shows how even the most well-travelled civilizations would have been able to make little sense of the details of the known world today. At the turn of the first millennium the most deeply rooted ancient civilizations, particularly the Chinese, Japanese and Islamic, were quite 'discrete worlds' (Fernández-Armesto 1995: 15–51). While they were highly sophisticated and complex worlds, they had relatively little contact with one another. There were some forms of direct interchange; for example, trade flowed across cultures and civilizations, linking the economic fortunes of different societies together as well as acting as a conduit for ideas and technological practices (Mann 1986; Watson 1992; Fernández-Armesto 1995; Ferro 1997). Yet, the ancient civilizations developed largely as a result of 'internal' forces and pressures; they were separate and to a large extent autonomous civilizations, shaped by imperial systems which stretched over scattered populations and territories.

Changing forms of political rule were accompanied by a slow and largely haphazard development of territorial politics. The emergence of the modern nation-state and the incorporation of all civilizations within the interstate system changed all this; for they created a world organized and divided into domestic and foreign realms – the 'inner world' of territorially bounded national politics and the 'outer world' of diplomatic, military and security affairs. While these realms were by no means hermetically sealed, they were the basis on which modern nation-states built political, legal and social institutions. Modern cartographers recorded and affirmed these developments. From the early twentieth century (although the exact dating is open to dispute), this division became more fragile, and increasingly mediated by regional and global flows and processes.

In the contemporary period there have been changes across different social and economic realms which have combined to create forms of regional and global interconnectedness which are unique, which are more extensive and intensive than ever before, and which are challenging and reshaping our political communities and, in particular, aspects of the modern state. These changes involve a number of developments which can be thought of as deep, indicative, structural transformations. These include the development of such phenomena as human rights regimes, which have ensured that sovereignty alone is less and less a guarantee of state legitimacy in international law; the internationalization of security and the transnationalization of a great many defence and procurement programmes, which means, for example, that some key weapons systems rely upon components from many countries; environmental shifts, above all ozone depletion and global warming, which highlight the growing limits to a purely state-centric politics; the revolution in communications and information technology, which has increased massively the stretch and intensity of all manner of socio-political networks within and across the borders of states; and the deregulation of capital markets, which has altered the power of capital by creating a greater number of 'exit' options in relation to both labour and the state.

The broad implications of such developments for the regulative capacity of states have been much debated. It is frequently alleged that the intensification of globalization has diminished the powers of states. According to this view, social and economic processes operate predominantly at the global level and national states have largely become 'decision-takers' (see, for instance, Ohmae 1990; Gray 1998). On the other hand, there are those who are highly critical of this position and argue that the national state, particularly in the advanced economies, is as robust and as integrated as it ever was (see, for example, Hirst and Thompson 1996). How has state power altered in the face of globalization? Has political power been reconfigured?

Changing Forms of Political and Economic Power

Contemporary globalization is transforming state power and the nature of political community, but any description of this as a simple loss or diminution of national powers distorts what has happened. For although globalization is changing the relationship between states and markets, this is not straightforwardly at the expense of states. States and public authorities initiated many of the fundamental changes – for example, the deregulation of capital in the 1980s and early 1990s. In other spheres of activity as well, states have become central in initiating new kinds of transnational collaboration, from the emergence of different forms of military alliances to the advancement of human rights regimes.

The fact of the matter is that on many fundamental measures of state power – from the capacity to raise taxes and revenue to the ability to hurl concentrated force at enemies – states are, at least throughout most of the OECD world, as powerful if not more powerful than their predecessors (Mann 1997). On the other hand, the pressures upon them have grown massively as well. In this context, it makes more sense to talk about the transformation of state power in the context of globalization – rather than simply to refer to what has happened as a decline (Held et al. 1999: Conclusion). The power, authority and operations of national governments are changing but not all in one direction. The entitlement of states to rule within circumscribed territories (sovereignty) is far from on the edge of collapse, although the practical nature of this entitlement – the actual capacity of states to rule – is changing its shape. A new regime of government and governance is emerging which is displacing traditional conceptions of state power as an indivisible, territorially exclusive form of public power. Far from globalization leading to 'the end of the state', it is stimulating a range of government and governance strategies and, in some fundamental respects, a more activist state.

Nowhere is this better seen than in the political context of economic globalization. Alongside global economic change there has been a parallel but distinct set of political changes, shifting the reach of political power and the forms of rule. Although governments and states remain powerful actors, they have helped create, and now share the global arena with, an array of other agencies and organizations. The state is confronted by an enormous number of intergovernmental organizations, international agencies and regimes which operate across different spatial reaches, and by quasi-supranational institutions like the European Union (Held 1995: chs 5 and 6). Non-state actors or transnational bodies also participate intensively in global politics. These developments challenge the conventional state-based accounts of world order, generating a much more complex picture of regional and global governance. In this more complex world, states deploy their sovereignty and autonomy as bargaining chips in negotiations involving coordination and collaboration across shifting transnational and international networks (Keohane 1995).

What developments in domains such as politics, law and the economy suggest is that globalization is far from being a singular process. While it is, as previously noted, a multi-dimensional phenomenon, depicting a general shift in the organization of human activity and the deployment of power towards transcontinental or interregional patterns, this shift can take different forms and follow different types of trajectory across economic, political and other domains. It can also generate conflicting as well as complementary tendencies in the determination of relations of power and authority.

For example, the global economy is more open, fluid and volatile than ever before; economies are less protected and international markets react rapidly to changing political and economic signals (see Perraton et al. 1997). It is harder to buck international economic trends than it was in the earlier decades of the postwar years. Because markets are more liquid, they are an enhanced source of instability. Financial and industrial capital enjoy increased exit options from political communities, altering the economic context of national labour markets. Moreover, in a 'wired world' disturbances rapidly transfer across markets and societies, ramifying the effects of change. Accordingly, the costs and benefits of pursuing certain policies become fuzzier, and this encourages political caution, 'adaptive politics' and precautionary supply-side economic measures.

Nonetheless, there has been a massive growth in regional and global governance which increasingly surveys, mediates and manages these developments. Moreover, demands for increased levels of international regulation are growing – from George Soros to the World Trade Organization (WTO) and the UN. More and more people recognize the need for enhanced political accountability, for transparency and openness of decision-making, in international, social and economic domains; although the proper form and place for such initiatives, it has to be said, is far from clear.

The Transformation of Democracy

Contemporary globalization has contributed to the transformation of the nature and prospects of democratic political community in a number of distinctive ways. It is worth dwelling on these for a moment. First, the locus of effective political power can no longer be assumed to be national governments – effective power is shared and bartered by diverse forces and agencies at national, regional and international levels. Second, the idea of a political community of fate – of a self-determining collectivity – can no longer be meaningfully located within the boundaries of a single nation-state alone, as it could more reasonably be when nation-states were being forged. Some of the most fundamental forces and processes that determine the nature of life chances within and across political communities are now beyond the reach of individual nation-states. The system of national political communities remains, of course, but it is articulated today with complex economic, organizational, administrative, legal and cultural networks and processes that limit and check its efficacy. If these processes and structures are not acknowledged and brought into the political process themselves, they may bypass or circumvent the democratic state system (see Sassen 1998).

Third, national sovereignty today, even in regions with intensive overlapping and divided political structures, has not been wholly undermined – far from it. However, the operations of states in increasingly complex global and regional systems affect both their autonomy (by changing the balance between the costs and benefits of policies) and aspects of their sovereignty (by altering the balance between national, regional, and international legal frameworks and administrative practices). While massive concentrations of power remain features of many states, these are frequently embedded in, and articulated with, other domains of political authority – regional, international and transnational.

Fourth, the late twentieth century is marked by a significant series of new types of 'boundary problem', which challenge the distinctions between domestic and foreign affairs, internal political issues and external questions, the sovereign concerns of the nation-state and international considerations. States and governments face issues like BSE (Bovine Spongiform Encephalopathy), the spread of malaria, the use of non-renewable resources, the management of nuclear waste and the proliferation of weapons of mass destruction, which cannot easily be categorized in traditional political terms as domestic or international. Moreover, issues like the location and investment strategy of multinational corporations, the regulation of global financial markets, the development of EMU, the threat to the tax base of individual countries which arises from the global division of labour and the absence of capital controls, all pose questions about the continued effectiveness of some of the traditional instruments of national economic policy. In fact, in all major areas of government policy, the enmeshment of national political communities in regional and global processes involves them in intensive issues of transboundary coordination and control. Political space for the development and pursuit of effective government and the accountability of political power is no longer coterminous with a delimited national territory.

The growth of transboundary problems creates what I like to refer to as 'overlapping communities of fate'; that is, a state of affairs in which the fortunes and prospects of individual political communities are increasingly bound together (see Held 1995, 1996; and see also Archibugi et al. 1998). Political communities are locked into a diversity of processes and structures which range in and through them, linking and fragmenting them into complex constellations. Moreover, national communities themselves by no means make and determine decisions and policies exclusively for themselves when they decide on such issues as the regulation of sexuality, health and the environment; national governments by no means simply determine what is right or appropriate exclusively for their own citizens. The assumption that one can understand the nature and possibilities of political community by referring merely to national structures and mechanisms of political power is clearly anachronistic. Accordingly, questions are raised both about the fate of the idea of the political community and about the appropriate locus for the articulation of the political good. If the agent at the heart of modern political discourse, be it a person, group or government, is locked into a variety of overlapping communities and jurisdictions, then the proper 'home' of politics and democracy becomes difficult to locate.

This matter is most apparent in Europe, where the development of the EU has created intensive discussion about the future of sovereignty and autonomy within individual nation-states. But the issues are important not just for Europe and the West, but for countries in other parts of the world, for example, in East Asia. The countries of East Asia must recognize emerging problems – for instance, problems concerning AIDS, migration and new challenges to peace, security and economic prosperity – which spill over the boundaries of nation-states. Moreover, they are developing within the context of growing interconnectedness across the world's major regions, with few better illustrations than the economic crisis of 1997–8 (see Held and McGrew 1998, and below). This interconnectedness is marked in a whole range of areas, from the environment and human rights, to issues of international crime. In other words, East Asia is necessarily part of a more global order and is locked into a diversity of sites of power which shape and determine its collective fortunes.

Global transformations have affected our concept of the political community and, in particular, our concept of the democratic political community. It is too rarely acknowledged that the proper nature and form of political communities are clouded by the multiplying interconnections among them. How so exactly?

Electoral politics and the ballot box are at the heart of the process whereby consent and legitimacy are bestowed upon government in liberal democracies. However, the notions that consent legitimates government, and that the national vote is the appropriate mechanism by which authority is periodically conferred on government, become problematic as soon as the nature of a 'relevant community' is examined (Held 1995). What is the proper constituency, and proper realm of jurisdiction, for developing and carrying out policy in relation to issues such as the policing and prosecution of paedophilia, the maintenance of military security, the harvesting of rainforests, the use of non-renewable resources, the instability of global financial markets, the pursuit of those who have committed crimes against humanity, and the management and control of genetic engineering in animals and humans? It has been taken for granted for the best part of the last two hundred years that national boundaries are the proper basis to demarcate which individuals are included and excluded from participation in decisions affecting their lives; but if many socio-economic processes, and the outcomes of decisions about them, stretch beyond national frontiers, then the implications of this are serious, not only for the categories of consent and legitimacy but for all the key ideas of democracy. At issue is the nature of a political community and how the boundaries of a political community might be drawn; the meaning of representation and the problem of who should represent whom and on what basis; and the proper form of political participation – who should participate in which domains and in what ways. As fundamental processes of governance escape the categories of the nation-state, the traditional national resolutions of the key questions of democratic theory and practice look increasingly threadbare.

The idea of government or of the state, democratic or otherwise, can no longer be simply defended as an idea suitable to a particular closed political community or nation-state. The idea of a political community of fate – of a self-determining collectivity – can no longer meaningfully be located within the boundaries of a single nation-state alone. We are compelled to recognize that the extensity, intensity and impact of economic, political and environmental processes raises questions about where they are most appropriately addressed. If the most powerful geopolitical and economic forces are not to settle many pressing matters simply in terms of their own objectives and by virtue of their power, then the current institutions and mechanisms of accountability need to be reconsidered. In my writings over the last few years, I have sought to offer such a reconsideration, by setting out a cosmopolitan conception of democratic governance.

The Cosmopolitan Project

In essence, the cosmopolitan project attempts to specify the principles and the institutional arrangements for making accountable those sites and forms of power which presently operate beyond the scope of democratic control (see Held 1995; Archibugi et al. 1998; and cf. Linklater 1998). It argues that in the millennium ahead each citizen of a state will have to learn to become a 'cosmopolitan citizen' as well: that is, a person capable of mediating between national traditions, communities of fate and alternative styles of life. Citizenship in a democratic polity of the future is likely to involve a growing mediating role: a role which encompasses dialogue with the traditions and discourses of others with the aim of expanding the horizons of one's own framework of meaning and prejudice. Political agents who can 'reason from the point of view of others' might be better equipped to resolve, and resolve fairly, the new and challenging trans-boundary issues and processes that create overlapping communities of fate. In addition, the cosmopolitan project contends that, if many contemporary forms of power are to become accountable and if many of the complex issues that affect us all – locally, nationally, regionally and globally – are to be democratically regulated, people will have to have access to, and membership in, *diverse* political communities. Put differently, a democratic political community for the new millennium necessarily describes a world where citizens enjoy multiple citizenships. Faced with overlapping communities of fate they need to be not only citizens of their own communities, but also of the wider regions in which they live, and of the wider global order. Institutions will certainly need to develop that reflect the multiple issues, questions and problems that link people together regardless of the particular nation-states in which they were born or brought up.

With this in mind, the cosmopolitan position maintains that democracy needs to be rethought as a 'double-sided process'. By a double-sided process – or process of double democratization – is meant the deepening of democracy within a national community, involving the democratization of states and civil societies over time, combined with the extension of democratic forms and processes across territorial borders (Held 1996). Democracy for the new millennium must allow cosmopolitan citizens to gain access to, mediate between, and render accountable the social, economic and political processes and flows which cut across and transform their traditional community boundaries. The core of this project involves reconceiving legitimate political authority in a manner which disconnects it from its traditional anchor in fixed borders and delimited territories and, instead, articulates it as an attribute of basic democratic arrangements or basic democratic law which can, in principle, be entrenched and drawn upon in diverse self-regulating associations – from cities and subnational regions, to nation-states, regions and wider global networks. It is clear that the process of disconnection has already begun as political authority and legitimate forms of governance are diffused 'below', 'above' and 'alongside' the nation-state.

Recent history embraces many different forms of globalization. There is the rise of neoliberal deregulation so much emphasized from the mid-1970s. But there is also the growth of major global and regional institutions from the UN to the EU. The latter are remarkable political innovations in the context of state history. The UN remains a creature of the interstate system; however, it has, despite all its limitations, developed an innovative system of global governance which delivers significant international public goods – from air traffic control and the management of telecommunications to the control of contagious diseases, humanitarian relief for refugees and some protection of the environmental commons. The EU, in remarkably little time, has taken Europe from the disarray of the post-Second World War era to a world in which sovereignty is pooled across a growing number of areas of common concern. Again, despite its many limitations, the EU represents a highly innovative form of governance which creates a framework of collaboration for addressing transborder issues.

In addition, it is important to reflect upon the growth in recent times of the scope and content of international law. Twentieth-century forms of international law – from the law governing war, to that concerning crimes against humanity, environmental issues and human rights – have created the basis of what can be thought of as an emerging framework of cosmopolitan law, law which circumscribes and delimits the political power of individual states. In principle, states are no longer able to treat their citizens as they think fit; for the values embedded in these laws qualify in fundamental ways the nature and form of political power; and they set down basic standards and boundaries which no agent (political or economic) should be able to cross.

Moreover, the twentieth century has seen the beginnings of significant efforts to reframe markets – to use legislation to alter the background conditions and operations of firms in the marketplace. While efforts in this direction failed in respect to the NAFTA agreement, the Social Chapter of the Maastricht agreement, for instance, embodies principles and rules which are compatible with the idea of restructuring aspects of markets. If implemented, the Social Chapter could, in principle, alter working conditions – for example, with respect to the provision of information and patterns of employee consultation – in a number of distinctive ways. While the provisions of the Maastricht agreement fall far short of what is ultimately necessary if judged by the standards of a cosmopolitan conception of democracy, they set down new forms of regulation which can be built upon (Held 1995: 239–66).

These examples of changes in global politics and regulation suggest that, while globalization is a highly contested phenomenon, it has embraced important collaborative initiatives in politics, law and the economy in the twentieth century. Together, these create an anchor on which to build a more accountable form of globalization. The cosmopolitan project is in favour of a radical extension of this development so long as it is circumscribed by democratic public law, that is, by the entrenchment of a far-reaching cluster of democratic rights and duties. Democratic public law sets down standards – entitlements and constraints – which specify an equality of status with respect to the basic institutions and organizations of a community, and of overlapping communities of fate. The cosmopolitan project advocates its entrenchment via a series of short- and long-term measures in the conviction that, through a process of progressive, incremental change, geopolitical forces will come to be embedded in, and socialized into, democratic rules and practices (see Held 1995: part 3).

What does this vision mean in the context of the kind of economic crisis which engulfed Indonesia, Russia and many other countries in 1997–8? I would like to address this briefly by considering some of the underlying economic and political issues involved in the crisis and some of the questions they raise about political regulation and the proper site of democratic accountability. The aim of this will be to show that cosmopolitanism, as I understand it, has policy implications – in the here and now, and not just in the there and then!

The explosive growth of global financial activity and the expansion of global financial markets since the 1980s has transformed the context of national economies (see Held et al. 1999: chs 3–5). Contemporary global finance is, as already noted, marked by high extensity, intensity and volatility in exchange rates, interest rates and other financial asset prices. As a result, national macroeconomic policy becomes vulnerable to changes in global financial conditions. Speculative flows can have rapid and dramatic domestic economic consequences; and financial difficulties faced by a single institution or sector in one country can have major implications for the rest of the global financial sphere. The collapse of the Thai currency in 1997 contributed to dramatic falls in currency values across East Asia and affected currency values in other emerging markets. The rapid flow of short-term capital out of these economies also affected stock markets around the world. Given the volatile nature of financial markets, and the instantaneous diffusion of financial information between the world's major financial centres, risks were generated with implications for the entire global financial system, and which no government alone could either defuse or insulate itself from (Held and McGrew 1998: 229–30).

A cosmopolitan political approach to economic and financial crises distinguishes itself from both liberal market solutions, with their constant emphasis on unburdening or deregulating markets in the hope that they might function better in the future, and national interventionist strategies, which champion the primacy of national economic management without giving due attention to regional and global policy options and initiatives. What are the targets that a cosmopolitan approach could pursue?

First, the extension of legislation to reframe markets is necessary in order to counter their indeterminacy and the massive social and environmental costs they sometimes generate. The ground rules of the free-market and trade system have to be altered in subtle and less subtle ways. Ultimately, this necessitates entrenching new regulatory terms – about child labour, trade union activity, social matters (such as child care and leave for parenting) and environmental protection – into the articles of association and terms of reference of economic organizations and trading agencies. Only by introducing new terms of empowerment and accountability throughout the global economic system, as a supplement and complement to collective agreements and welfare measures in national and regional contexts, can a new settlement be created between economic power and democracy.

Second, new forms of economic coordination are indispensable. Organizations like the IMF, the World Bank, the OECD and G7 all operate with separate agendas. Policy-making is fragmented. A new coordinating economic agency, working at both regional and global levels, needs to be created. This is not as fanciful as it might at first seem, especially in the light of the establishment of new multilateral bodies after the Second World War, and most recently the WTO. Where exactly a new economic coordinating agency should be located (at the UN, or elsewhere?) is a matter for debate. But the primary issue is to recognize the need for a new transnational economic authority capable of deliberating about emergency economic situations, the dynamics of international capital markets, and the broad balance of public investment priorities and expenditure patterns. The brief of such a body would be to fill a vacuum; that is, to become a coordinator for economic policy that is set at global or regional levels or is not set at all, at least not by public authorities.

Third, it is important to develop measures to regulate the volatility of international financial markets, and their speculative pursuit of short-term gains. Taxes on turnover in foreign exchange markets, the retention of capital controls as a policy option and a substantial increase in the regulation and transparency of bank accounting and of other financial institutions are necessary measures if international short-term capital markets are to be amenable to democratic intervention.

Such initiatives must be thought of as steps towards a new 'Bretton Woods' system – a system which would introduce accountability and regulation into institutional mechanisms for the coordination of investment, production and trade. If linked, fourth, to measures aimed at alleviating the most pressing cases of avoidable economic suffering – by radically reducing the debt of many developing countries, by generating new economic facilities at organizations like the IMF and World Bank for development purposes, and perhaps (as George Soros has suggested) by creating new international credit insurance funds – then the basis would be created for entrenching capitalism in a set of democratic mechanisms and procedures.

But none of these developments alone will create the foundations for adequate democratic regulation unless they are, fifth, firmly linked to measures to extend democratic forms and processes across territorial borders. Such a positive policy of democratization might begin in key regions by creating greater transparency and accountability in leading decision-making centres. In Europe this would involve enhancing the power of the European Parliament and reducing the democratic deficit across all EU institutions. Elsewhere it would include restructuring the UN Security Council to give developing countries a significant voice in decision-making; deepening the mechanisms of accountability of the leading international and transnational public agencies; strengthening the enforcement capacity of human rights regimes (socio-economic as well as political), and creating, in due course, a new democratic UN second chamber. Such targets point the way towards laying the foundations for forms of accountability at the global level. In short, they are necessary elements of what I earlier referred to as a cosmopolitan conception of democracy. Faced with overlapping communities of fate, citizens in the future must become not just active citizens of their own communities, but also of the regions in which they live, and of the wider global order.

Conclusion

If globalization refers to those processes which underpin a transformation in the organization of human affairs, linking together and expanding human activity such that it encompasses frameworks of interregional and intercontinental change and development, then many of our most cherished political ideas – which formerly centred on nation-states – need to be recast. It is beyond the brief of this paper to pursue these issues at any length. But if we live in a world marked by enhanced forms of global politics and multilayered governance, then the efficacy of national democratic traditions and national legal traditions is challenged fundamentally. However this challenge is specified precisely, it is based upon the recognition that the nature and quality of democracy within a particular community and the nature and quality of democratic relations among communities are interconnected, and that new legal and organizational mechanisms must be created if democracy and political communities themselves are to prosper.

It would be wholly fallacious to conclude from this that the politics of local communities, or national democratic communities, will be (or should be) wholly eclipsed by the new forces of political globalization. To assume this would be to misunderstand the very complex, variable and uneven impact of regional and global processes on political life. Of course, certain problems and policies will remain properly the responsibility of local governments and national states; but others will be recognized as appropriate for specific regions, and still others – such as elements of the environment, global security concerns, world health questions and economic regulation – will be seen to need new institutional arrangements to address them. Tests of extensiveness, intensity and comparative efficiency can be used to help filter and guide policy issues to different levels of governance (see Held 1995: 236–7). But however such issues are precisely filtered, the agenda facing political theory in the face of regional and global shifts is now clearly defined.

The history of democratic political thought and practice has been marked by two great transitions. The first led to the establishment of greater participation and accountability in cities during antiquity and, again, in Renaissance Italy; and the second led to the entrenchment of democracy over great territories and timespans through the invention of representative democracy. From the early modern period to the late nineteenth century geography could, in principle, be neatly meshed with sites of political power and authority. Today, we are on the cusp of a third great transition (cf. Dahl 1989). Democracy could become entrenched in cities, nation-states and wider regional and global fora, or else it might come to be thought of as that form of national government which became progressively more anachronistic in the twenty-first century. Fortunately, the choice remains ours.

References

Abu-Lughod, J. (1989) *Before European Hegemony*. Oxford: Oxford University Press.

Archibugi, D., Held, D. and Köhler, M. (eds) (1998) *Re-imagining Political Community: Studies in Cosmopolitan Democracy*. Cambridge: Polity Press.

Dahl, R. A. (1989) *Democracy and its Critics*. New Haven: Yale University Press.

Fernández-Armesto, F. (1995) *Millennium*. London: Bantam.

Ferro, M. (1997) *Colonization: A Global History*. London: Routledge.

Goldblatt, D., Held, D., McGrew, A. G. and Perraton, J. (1997) Economic globalization and the nation-state: shifting balances of power. *Soundings* 7: 61–77.

Gray, J. (1998) *False Dawn*. London: Granta.

Held, D. (1995) *Democracy and the Global Order: From the Modern State to Cosmopolitan Governance*. Cambridge: Polity Press.

Held, D. (1996) *Models of Democracy*, 2nd edn. Cambridge: Polity Press.

Held, D. and McGrew, A. G. (1998) The end of the old order? *Review of International Studies*, Special Issue: 219–42.

Held, D. and McGrew, A. G., Goldblatt, D. and Perraton, J. (1999) *Global Transformations: Politics, Economics and Culture*. Cambridge: Polity Press.

Hirst, P. and Thompson, G. (1996) *Globalization in Question*. Cambridge: Polity Press.

Keohane, R. (1995) Hobbes's dilemma and institutional change in world politics: sovereignty in international society. In H. H. Holm and G. Sørensen (eds), *Whose World Order?* Boulder: Westview Press.

Linklater, A. (1998) *The Transformation of Political Community*. Cambridge: Polity Press.

Mann, M. (1986) *The Sources of Social Power*, vol. 1. Cambridge: Cambridge University Press.

Mann, M. (1997) Has globalization ended the rise and rise of the nation-state? *Review of International Political Economy* 4(3): 472–96.

Ohmae, K. (1990) *The Borderless World*. London: Collins.

Perraton, J., Goldblatt, D., Held, D. and McGrew, A. (1997) The globalization of economic activity. *New Political Economy* 2(2): 257–77.

Sassen, S. (1998) *Globalization and its Discontents*. New York: New Press.

Watson, A. (1992) *The Evolution of International Society*. London: Routledge.

40

Global Governance: Prospects and Problems

Fred Halliday

Introduction: Global Governance

In the 1990s special attention is being paid to the question of 'global governance'. This is a term almost no one used a decade ago, but which is now generally held to refer to the institutions for managing relations between states across a range of issues, from security to human rights and the environment. 'Governance' in its simplest sense refers to the art of governing, to ensuring that it is morally defensible and efficient.[1] It does not imply that there should be any one institution, but rather, in the present context, refers to a set of interlocking but separate bodies which share a common purpose. Thus it covers the activities of states, but also those of inter-governmental organisations, most notably the UN, and the role of non-governmental organisations (NGOs) and transnational movements: all of these combine, not least through influencing each other, to produce the system of global governance. The argument is not whether such a system is desirable or not: we already have a many-layered global governance system, and indeed one of the central issues is to overcome, through reform, the defaults of a system that has been up and running for several decades. The question is how to make this governance system more effective, more just, and more responsive to the changing international situation.
[...]

The discussion on global governance has [...] acquired an importance and an urgency [...]. The case being made is clear and powerful: that the problems facing the contemporary world cannot be solved either by leaving everything to the actions of individual states, or to the workings of the market, and that the existing mechanisms are insufficient to deal with them. Some proposals do suggest that existing institutions be wound up: the Economic and Social Council of the UN (ECOSOC), and the UN Conference on Trade and Development (UNCTAD), being favourite candidates. But the majority of proposals speak of developing existing institutions and, where appropriate, adding on new ones. [...]

The proposals for reform also tend to reflect ways in which the philosophies of global governance, and the concerns uppermost in the minds of the drafters, have shifted over the past fifty years [since the UN was established]. This is evident above all in three respects: first, there is much greater awareness of the importance of unspecific, 'global', problems, of which defence of the environment, an issue almost ignored up to the mid-1980s, is one; secondly, many recognise the importance, for social and economic reasons as much as for reasons of equity, of promoting the interests of women; thirdly, there is a shift from the overwhelmingly state-centred approach of the UN Charter to a recognition of the rights of individuals and communities who may be in conflict with states [. . .].

Contentious Issues: Five Examples

These [points] present a powerful case [. . .]. What is more difficult is to match these calls for change, in institutions but also in values, against the world as we know it, and to come up with approaches that meet the challenge, and also have a chance of being implemented. That such reforms can work should not be doubted: few, before they were set up, could have believed that either the UN or the European Union would get as far as they did.

Yet assertion of the need for strengthening governance may not be sufficient: the difficulties involve not only the obstacles that currently exist to such a process, but also something less often discussed, the very inherent complexity of these questions, the conflicts that are necessarily tied up with managing the world and building institutions of governance. These conflicts are not the products of chance or political ill-will, but are also inherent ones, and will require difficult choices. Some obvious examples of such inherent problems are raised in the current public debate – that between the world-wide demand for economic growth and the need to protect the environment is an obvious one, as is that between human rights and the sovereignty of states. In what follows here I want to take five such issues pertaining to global governance and address their implications for the growth of global governance. These are intended both to illustrate the possibilities of global governance, and to underline the need for realistic thinking in regard to it.

(i) The role of the great powers

It is the assumption of most writing on global governance, and on growing international cooperation, that this will take place on a shared, multilateral, basis. Proposals for the reform of the Security Council embody such a perspective. Yet international relations has rarely been conducted on this basis, but rather on a mixture of such shared policy-making and of leadership by the more powerful members. In the UN system, for example, the General Assembly is counterposed to the, much more effective, Security Council, in which powerful states have a special place. In the field of security one could contrast the international response to the Kuwait crisis, in which one power did play a leading role, and that to the Yugoslav crisis, in which, until the NATO bombing attacks of late August 1995, this spectacularly failed to occur. In the literature on managing the world economy there is a strong current that argues for 'hegemonic stability', i.e. for the view that unless one country is willing and able to play a leading role, to set the rules and punish wrong-doers, the system will not work. The classic case is the collapse of 1929.[2] More recently the argument is that the Bretton Woods system did not 'fail' – it was destroyed by Richard Nixon in 1971. The lack of any such hegemonic system thereafter has been the source of the world's financial and economic instability. In the ecological debate, there is little point in having agreements if the richest, and most pollution-producing, states do not sign and observe them. The argument can, therefore, be made that the pursuit of international goals – peace, prosperity, safety from ecological collapse, etc. – requires that some states play a leading role and ensure that others follow the rules. This need not necessarily take the form of traditional, imperial, coercion, but can involve a range of pressures and inducements. Indeed, the evidence suggests that as prosperity is diffused, and as democratic institutions grow, then the room for peaceful, negotiated, agreements between states increases and the need for coercion and enforcement decreases.

The difficulties with this argument are many. The most obvious is that it is unjust and that the awareness of this injustice will provoke revolt: any such system will go the way of the colonial empires.[3] It is not easy to argue in favour of a hegemonic system of global governance and few of this year's sets of proposals try to do so. Even when the UN does act effectively this issue tends to be avoided: one of the most repeated arguments *against* the UN role in Kuwait was that the Security Council was 'manipulated' by the USA into taking military action, the assumption being that this in itself was sufficient reason to invalidate the result. Yet one can argue that this is the only way in which such institutions can, realistically, be supposed to operate and that it is better to recognise this. The same would apply, with obvious variations, to the international economic system: the US no doubt gains from having its currency used for three-quarters of world trade, but if this leads the US to maintain a relatively free trading system and to support some stability in world financial and currency systems, it is, arguably, a price worth paying.

There is, however, another problem with this argument, and that is that it presupposes that the great powers, their governments and populations, *actively want* to play an appropriate international role, to reap the benefits and to assume the burdens. It can be argued that a major challenge facing the international system today is that the one power capable of playing such a role shows very little interest in so doing: the US has been the dominant power in the world economy since 1945 and was handed victory in the political and military conflict with the USSR in 1991 – its response has been to draw back from those victories. Many in the USA seem to doubt whether, in any meaningful sense, they won the cold war at all, and there is scant enthusiasm in Congress for an activist US foreign policy, be this in the economic or security fields. If there is little enthusiasm for the advantages, there is, less surprisingly, little enthusiasm for paying the costs. US foreign economic aid is much smaller, as a percentage of GNP, than that of most other developed countries. When it comes to the ecological issue, the US is a reluctant participant in any policy that inhibits its own population: no one will run for office proposing that US taxes on gasoline prices, currently a third or less of European levels, are raised to international levels. The US is, as Secretary-Generals have not tired of telling us, the largest debtor to the UN. One might conclude that the one significant obstacle to the development of global governance is the reluctance of the world's leading power to assume the role that the consolidation and development of that system requires. Yet there is no obvious reason why the US 'ought' to perform these roles, whatever the rest of the world may think.

(ii) Dilemmas of peace-keeping: the Yugoslav case

Reform of peace-keeping activities is, along with reform of the Security Council and Secretariat itself, a favoured theme of writers on the UN and global governance. The current sets of proposals are no exception: while few favour a revival of the Charter's own mechanism as originally conceived, the Military Staff Committee, composed of senior officers of the permanent members' armed forces, many see a stronger peace-keeping role as desirable and possible. Suggestions are many: more effort should go into anticipating crises and into pre-emptive diplomacy; there should be a permanent UN force, capable of rapid reaction and intervention; the member states should put up more money for peace-keeping; all should contribute forces; mandates should be clear; the 'integrity' of the UN command should be respected.

Yet of all the shadows cast over the fiftieth anniversary of the UN, that of the war in ex-Yugoslavia was perhaps the greatest.[4] Here is a war in which the UN played an active role, in the humanitarian, diplomatic and peace-keeping fields, in which the Security Council maintained an active involvement, passing many resolutions, and yet where the organisation's ability to reduce conflict was apparently little. Yugoslavia represented a crisis not just of the UN itself, not least in the organisation's failure to deliver on threats or protect those who sought refuge with it in the 'safe havens', but of international institutions and internationalist values in general: far from the 'integrity' of the UN command being respected, it is an open secret that interested states time and again sought to influence the activities of UN officials, military and civilian, in the field. At times it was unclear which international body – the UN or NATO – was in charge: certainly the bombing of Serb positions in late August 1995 was ordered by NATO, not the UN. Yugoslavia has involved a crisis for the many other organisations – NATO, EU – that have tried to play a role, for the many non-governmental organisations involved, for any belief in restraint in the conduct of war towards combatants and non-combatants alike and, not least, for any idea that the world is moving away from a situation in which ethnic communities resort to hatred and killing to resolve problems that could, on any objective calculation, be settled by peaceful means. Whatever else can be said of the period before war broke out, it cannot be claimed that pre-emptive diplomacy was not tried. The wars of former Yugoslavia seem therefore to defy much that is subsumed in the term 'global governance'.

There are, of course, some very important qualifications to be made to this judgement. In the first place, it is pure coincidence, if an unhappy one, that this conflict should have flared up in the fiftieth year of the UN: in a broader perspective, the UN's record in peace-keeping is a quite substantial one, and above all in the years since the end of the cold war. In a range of countries – El Salvador, Namibia, Cambodia to name but some – the UN has been central to the attainment of peace. In many other parts of the world – South Africa, the Israel/Palestine conflict, Ireland, Russo-Ukrainian relations – diplomatic breakthroughs have taken place, in which the UN may have been secondary, but where the institutions of global governance, NGOs included, played an important role. There is much in that achievement to build on, and for the UN to be proud of. Secondly, much of the criticism of the UN in former Yugoslavia ignores what it did achieve: the saving of hundreds of thousands of lives, the insulation of Macedonia. Above all, criticism of the UN rests upon an illusion, namely that the UN can in some way impose peace. In fact, as the UN learnt long ago, you cannot keep peace in a situation where the combatants do not want peace, and where, as they have done so spectacularly in former Yugoslavia, they use and abuse the UN, manipulating cease-fires, diplomatic initiatives and humanitarian issues for their own purposes. The first result of what has happened to the UN in the Balkans should be not to criticise it, but to identify those in every camp who have prevented peace, and, at the same time, to *reduce our expectations* of what the UN can actually do. There have certainly been failures in the UN operation, and not a little mismanagement and corruption too:[5] but the main responsibility for what has occurred there does not lie with the UN.

Beyond these qualifications, there are, however, other issues of a more general kind, that are inherent in the present debate on global governance and which pertain to peacekeeping in general. Three of these can be mentioned here. The first concerns that of recognition of states, and of the right of groups to secede from existing states: the fighting in Yugoslavia was precipitated by the decisions of Slovenia, Croatia and Bosnia to leave the Yugoslav federation, and by the decision of key states in the international community to recognise them. The argument for this course of action is clear enough: the leaderships who declared independence had the support of the majority of their peoples, they were exercising their right to self-determination under the UN Charter, and those who recognise them were acting in accordance with international law and practice. But this is to ignore the contrary arguments, concerning the rights of the ethnic minorities within Croatia and Bosnia and, more broadly, the predictable international consequences of such an action. For all that the text of the UN Charter allows secession, the international community has, until the collapse of Soviet communism, been very cautious about recognising it, for obvious reasons.[6] Yet some resolution of this issue, some sense of when secession is and is not possible, is a necessary part of any system of global equity and security.

The second issue underlying the Balkan case is the relation between different forms of intervention: human rights, humanitarian, diplomatic, peace-keeping, peace-enforcement (i.e. coercive). The UN has been involved in all of these, yet they are, in many respects, incompatible: humanitarian intervention (i.e. saving lives) can conflict with the human rights approach (i.e. identifying and prosecuting war criminals) and with enforcement; diplomatic efforts may involve working with those responsible for ethnic cleansing, and may, at times, lead negotiators to accept the results of such forcible expulsions; most obviously of all, peace-keeping, with white vehicles and with a presumption of neutrality, conflicts with peace-enforcement, which involves bombing violators of cease-fires and safe havens. Behind all of these problems, and indeed behind the whole Yugoslav story, lies another problem, namely that of the international response: if there has been an international failure, including a failure of global governance, it lies not in external manipulation of one party or the other, or in the indecisiveness of Boutros-Ghali, his representative Yasuko Akashi and others, but in the lack of support *from public opinion in the developed world* for a stronger military commitment. The question of *why* the armies of France, Britain, the US or anywhere else should be actively involved with the risk of serious casualties has not been resolved: in the actions of late August 1995 NATO forces intervened, but with air power and long-range artillery. There was no commitment of combat troops on the ground, and not a little suspicion that this show of force was a prelude to a withdrawal of forces in the event of negotiations breaking down. The subsequent Dayton agreement did lead to deployment of a Stabilisation Force on the ground, but it set a timetable for withdrawal and remained restrained, to say the least, in implementing contentious parts of the Dayton programme. The issue of weak public support for peace-enforcement is the one that is most avoided, yet it is the central one in the wars of former Yugoslavia, if not in the whole future of global governance.

(iii)   Economic nationalism

This discussion of the challenges to international peace and security is parallel to another issue, one that both underlies the need for global governance but also highlights the difficulties involved, namely what is termed 'globalisation'. By 'globalisation' is meant that breaking down of national barriers and the creation of a new single, world-wide, entity: this is most obviously the case in the field of finance, with the spread of a global currency market, and the attendant mobility of investment capital. But it is increasingly so with regard to trade, as national barriers come down, and production, with the rise of multinational corporations. In other areas too – in culture, fashion, information technology – globalisation is on the increase.

The globalisation issue itself has provoked an enormous amount of controversy, both as to what is actually occurring and as to what is desirable. Each of these arguments has implications for the debate on global governance. Those who argue that globalisation *is* indeed occurring would conclude that the nation state, as historically constituted, is increasingly unable to fulfil its traditional roles – of managing the economy, defending the living standards of its population, ensuring equity within its own frontiers, and even of defending security interests. The conclusion they would draw is that these functions have to be transferred to international bodies that can now manage the world economy and international welfare across frontiers: some existing institutions can be developed for this purpose – the World Bank, the IMF, the Bank of International Settlements, the Group of Seven Economic Summits, the OECD, the General Agreement on Tariffs and Trade and now the World Trade Organization, founded on 1 January 1995 – but, they would argue, more are needed. Yet there are two obvious problems with this line of argument: the first, long made by critics from the Third World, is that international bodies reflect not the general interest of their members, but the interests of the powerful minority of rich states, and that any proposals for extending their powers or creating a new UN Economic Council would serve to protect the privileges of the rich; the second, inherent in the globalisation argument itself, is that these bodies can only function if their constituent members, nation states, are themselves strong – yet the very reason for having such bodies is said to be that nation states are now in a weaker situation than hitherto.

There is little doubt that such globalisation has produced a growing process of global economic interdependence. While the EU states have decided at their Intergovernmental Conference to take further steps towards integration (whatever the British may decide to do or not do), the other two global trading blocs – NAFTA and a yen bloc in the Far East – are being consolidated, while in South America a range of countries have created MERCOSUR. *Our Global Neighbourhood*, the report of the Commission on Global Governance, suggests a range of ways in which the promotion of interdependence and the management of the world economy may be enhanced, including the setting up of an Economic Security Council, a renewed effort to get donor states to meet the target of 0.7 per cent of GDP for official development assistance, co-operation on migration and the financing of 'global purposes' through charges on the use of common global resources.[7] The Ford Foundation proposes that the Economic Council become, in effect, a global equivalent of the European Union: it 'would promote the harmonisation of the fiscal, monetary and trade policies of the Member States and encourage international cooperation on issues such as transfers of technology and resources, indebtedness, and the functioning of commodity markets'.[8] Here the two distinct currents of thought – global governance in the institutional sense and globalisation in the economic and financial spheres – seem to meet.

There are, however, questions that can be raised about this line of argument. They suggest that all may not go as expected in this sphere, and that matters could indeed go into reverse: universities could, in a decade or two, be offering courses on the break-up of trading blocs, just as they now study decolonisation or the end of the cold war, two equally unanticipated transformations. Equally, and even if we do not see an outright retreat from interdependence and multilateralism, there are difficult, and inevitable, choices that will have to be made and which cannot be resolved by goodwill and political effort alone.

In the first place, it is far from obvious that all countries, or even the richer OECD states, would really be prepared to cede their economic sovereignty to a world body. There are tensions enough in the EU, and the kind of global planning body proposed by Ford may be a long way off. In the same vein, it is not clear that even the major states are committed to a full system of free trade. Within months of the establishment of the WTO we have seen conflicts involving the USA and Japan over automobile imports, and over US reluctance to extend the WTO's multilateral regime to cover banking, insurance and securities. The EU is committed to freeing trade within its frontiers, but has institutionalised a set of barriers to free trade in agricultural and industrial goods between its members and the rest of the world: the Common Agricultural Policy is a protectionist policy on a grandiose scale. When it comes to less developed countries, not least those with strong state sectors, then the record is even more mixed.

This reluctance on free trade reflects a growing concern in the developed world with employment levels: this is as true in Europe as it is in the USA and has led to a growing respectability for what is broadly termed 'protectionism'. Since this can take many forms – tariffs, but also a range of obstacles politely termed 'non-tariff barriers' – it remains within the range of options open to many countries. What is striking is that over the past year or two calls for protectionism have become more common in the developed world, a response both to the opening of markets and to the enduring effects of the recession. We heard a lot about it in the French elections of 1995, and more, not least from Pat Buchanan, in the US elections of 1996. At the same time, this has been as much a concern of the traditional parties of the left, influenced by trade unions, as of the right.

Interlocked with this issue is a topic that is becoming of greater and greater concern throughout the developed world, namely migration. At a time when other factors of production – capital, technology, productive capacity – are becoming more mobile, the most traditional factor of production, labour, is becoming less so. In many countries a combination of trade union defence of jobs and the rise of new right-wing parties is pushing towards a strong nationalist restriction of immigration. The old liberal regime, assuming relatively free movement of labour across frontiers, one that lasted from the early nineteenth century through to the 1960s, has collapsed: yet no one is sure what can, or should, replace it. Many individuals still hold to a presumption in favour of free movement, but no government in the world is willing to implement it. There are obvious conflicts here of economic need and political sensitivity, of universalist moral obligation and nationalist interest. One only has to look at the passions aroused in Germany by limits on the admission of refugees, or in French debates on the Muslim immigrant population, to see how difficult it is to discuss this question in a reasonable way. Is there some means of managing, even planning, migration through instruments of global governance? This issue is not going to go away. *Our Global Neighbourhood* talks of the need to respect international conventions on migrant workers, and of the need 'to develop more comprehensive institutionalised co-operation regarding migration'. These are, of course, different things: the former is relatively easy to envisage, involving the proper treatment of people who have already migrated; the latter involves the much thornier question of freedom of movement and open labour markets.

(iv)   The loss of innocence of NGOs

One of the distinguishing features of the current debate on global governance is the emphasis put on the role of non-governmental organisations. They are seen as part of a growing international civil society, and are, in various ways, incorporated into the formal, state-to-state, processes of the UN. On many issues – political prisoners, the environment, landmines to name but three – it is NGOs which have, within countries and internationally, developed the policies of global institutions.

This growth of NGOs and of the recognition of their work is in broad terms positive, but it is accompanied by several difficulties, ones that have become clearer as the initial, first, generation of NGO activity has given way to the more complex world of the 1990s. In the first place, it is often an illusion to see NGOs as an alternative to, or substitute for, states. What NGOs seek to do is, in many cases, to influence states, to get them to keep to their promises or conform in greater degree to international norms. NGOs are, moreover, often working not to fill a role but to get the state to do so – be this in the realm of welfare provision, or providing food, or maintaining order. In this sense NGOs are not a replacement for states, or a solution to attempts to reduce the role of the state: they are part of the broader support *for* the role of states. In some cases, of course, states deliberately support NGOs in work that the state itself supports but would prefer not to organise directly: British aid agencies, for example, acquire a considerable percentage of their income from the state, in the form of 'matching funds' that combine with monies received from private sources. Increasingly, moreover, and very much parallel with the growth in awareness of NGOs, states have come to influence or even control NGOs: many of the supposedly 'independent' bodies that attend international conferences on particular issues are what are termed 'GONGOs' – government-controlled NGOs, sponsored, more or less overtly, by states. They use the appearance of independence to promote the goals of their state.

This loss of innocence of NGOs has, however, been compounded by two other developments which qualify, even if they do not contradict, the initial liberal view of such bodies as constituents of international civil society. On the one hand there is the very diversity of the programmes of NGOs themselves: some, arguably most, are participants in 'international civil society' and can be said, in broad terms, to reinforce the system of global governance; but some most certainly are not – be this in movements against immigration in developed countries, fundamentalist religious groups in north and south, criminal and terrorist organisations. Not all that is 'non-governmental' is civil. On the other hand, NGOs are themselves becoming increasingly involved in controversy and becoming the objects of political hostility: in the 1980s this involved, for example, disputes on the provision of humanitarian aid to guerrilla movements in Ethiopia or South Africa; in the 1990s NGO representatives have become targets of attack – murder, kidnapping and extortion, while the issue of humanitarian aid to refugees becoming embroiled with assistance to armed, criminal, groups was highlighted in the case of eastern Zaire. The killing of six Red Cross nurses in Chechnya in December 1996 and the kidnapping of NGO officials in Cambodia are examples of this trend.

For NGOs themselves the shifting contours of global governance, and the changed circumstances of the post-cold war world, have also involved questioning of their role, general and specific, that has affected their morale and performance. The Director of Amnesty International, for example, shocked many of his fellow workers in saying that Amnesty was a creation of the cold war: what this meant, in terms of mission, the focus on political prisoners and the commitment to universality, was less clear. The Red Cross has found its role, of mediating between states in war, made far more complex by the spreading of wars in which states are not the main actors, and in which traditional conceptions of military discipline, and indeed the military/civilian distinction, are less relevant.[9] The largest British aid-giving NGO, Oxfam, has been confronted with a shift in public attitudes away from charitable North–South transfers, and a questioning, by public and specialist alike, of the earlier conception of aid. At the same time it has come under increasing pressure to promote its activities in support of the needy not only in the Third World, but in developed countries. For NGOs in general, this loss of certainty and clarity from within has compounded the increase in pressures from without.

(v)   Global values

Much is made, in the literature on 'globalisation' and in the report of the Commission on Global Governance, of the emergence of 'global' values, of a commitment to humanity as a whole rather than to individual states and/or nations. The Report talks of a 'Global Civic Ethic' and, in particular, argues for a strengthened interpretation of the right of humanitarian intervention, undercutting where necessary the traditional concept of state sovereignty. There is much validity in these arguments: the lawyers have made considerable headway in showing how we can talk of values that transcend individual states or peoples; there are plenty of areas – international law, signature of human rights conventions, the very language and practice of international relations – where such a common culture exists. There is also evidence to suggest that amongst younger elites the world over there is a more shared culture, of value and aspiration, and an easier interaction than would have been the case in earlier times: a brief tour of the student cafeteria at LSE will illustrate this. *Le Monde Diplomatique* has talked of the new 'cosmocratie' produced by globalised educational opportunity.

There are, however, reasons to be cautious about this perspective of continued progress towards a common humanity. First of all, the philosophers, for all their progress on some issues, are very much not of one mind about the existence of universal, or global, values. On the one hand, in contrast to the lawyers, many doubt whether it is ever possible to talk of a common, or universal, interest – differences of interest will almost always prevail, and cannot be dissolved by identifying some chimerical, harmonious, shared concern. Secondly, the main trend in moral philosophy today is away from belief in universal, rationally justified, values towards a stress on the inevitable link between values and particular, historically formed and separate, 'communities'. These communities may debate with each other, and engage in more or less civilised interaction, but they cannot dissolve their differences.[10]

Outside the world of philosophy the picture is even less sanguine. For a variety of reasons, there has, over the past two decades or so, been an explosion in nationalist movements, proclamations of new identities, and demands for the recognition of new ethnic and communal rights. This long predated the collapse of communism but has, most spectacularly in former Yugoslavia, been stimulated by the disintegration of multi-ethnic communist states. Within many societies, not least those of western Europe and the USA, there has also been a growing assertion of diversity, of difference, in rejection of hitherto prevailing common norms. Among the majority populations of developed countries there has also, as already noted in regard to hostility to migration, been a growing resort to nationalism and intolerance. For many regions of the world, the trend is towards more difference, and more rejection of universal or common values. At the same time, with the rise of movements of both ethnic and religious character, there has been a growing rejection of the universal aspirations associated with the west – in the rhetoric of non-western states, be they China or Iran, and in that of many movements, there is a denial that any values, especially those associated with the former imperialist countries, can have universal application. One of the most common terms of derogation is to say that something is 'ethnocentric' or 'eurocentric', as if this origin is, in itself, a source of invalidity. This goes, among other things, for any attempt to establish common norms on human rights, on the position of women, or on democracy. Even amongst educated and much-travelled elites it is an open question how deep the new internationalism goes: people who work in multinational corporations or international institutions may feel some commitment to international values, but they can, at the same time, remain very much committed to their own countries of origin. More and more people may speak English, but they do not cease to speak their own languages, and they may resent the way in which globalisation of communications, through the media and information technology, has been dominated by one language. If there is much truth in the saying that 'Travel broadens the mind', the opposite has also been known to occur.

Conclusion: Democracy and Global Governance

The task of promoting global governance is, therefore, both a necessary and a daunting one: beyond the identification or evaluation of problems, and the elaboration of proposals, it involves confronting some deep resistances in the international system and some obstacles that have arisen in the very process of global change over recent years. We can see this in a range of contexts: the success of peace-keeping, for example, continues to run up against the reluctance of sovereign states to commit their forces to combat, and of states criticised by the international community to yield to UN pressure; growing awareness of the ecological crisis threatening us goes together with contention and evasion, in north and south; the rising recognition of the importance of women's position in society has produced outright rejection of change in some states, in the name of sovereignty and national tradition, and adaptive manipulation in others – there was lots of this at Beijing; a greater stress on the rights of individuals produces denunciation of international, and specifically 'western', interference from others. [...]
For much of the middle of this century it was held that the state had a necessary role to play in managing the economy and promoting welfare within countries: the concept

of 'global governance' is, broadly speaking, a translation to the international sphere of this argument. The Commission on Global Governance and Ford Foundation reports are, although they avoid saying so too explicitly, Keynesianism on a global scale. Despite the success of neo-liberal thinking over the past decade or two, the argument is much more evenly balanced than might at first sight appear. There are many, not least the governments of the successful countries of the Far East, who insist that without state direction there can be no attainment of order or prosperity. That is, in a nutshell, the argument for global governance, an argument that may be made all the more forcefully if the obstacles, and difficult choices involved, are clearly recognised.

Notes

1 *The Shorter Oxford English Dictionary* (1973) defines 'governance' as 'the action or manner of government . . . the office, function or power of governing . . . method of management, system of regulations'.
2 Charles Kindelberger, *The World in Depression, 1929–39* (Berkeley: University of California Press, 1980).
3 This is, in essence, the argument of Robert Harvey's *The Return of the Strong: The Drift to Global Disorder* (London: Macmillan, 1995).
4 On the record of post-1989 peace-keeping see James Mayall (ed.), *The New Interventionism 1991–1994* (Cambridge: Cambridge University Press, 1996).
5 One of the less publicised downsides of global governance is the opportunities it provides for making money through fraud. The means favoured by UN division commanders in the Balkans peace-keeping operations has been to sell off fuel to the combatants and present UN headquarters with fake invoices: it is reckoned that this could earn the commanders several million dollars a year.
6 The collapse of Soviet communism has produced the fragmentation of four multi-ethnic states (the USSR, Yugoslavia, Czechoslovakia, Ethiopia) and has led to the emergence of twenty-two new sovereign states. Yet from 1945 to 1989 only one state, Bangladesh, was created through secession.
7 *Our Global Neighbourhood*, Report of the Commission on Global Governance (Oxford: Oxford University Press, 1995).
8 Ford Foundation, *The United Nations in its Second Half-Century* (New York: Ford Foundation, 1995).
9 The ICRC is, technically, *not* an NGO but an intergovernmental organisation. It is included here because of its independent status.
10 Note e.g. Michael Walzer, *Thick and Thin Moral Argument at Home and Abroad* (London: University of Notre Dame Press, 1994).

41

Transnational Justice

Onora O'Neill

Justice across Boundaries

The discussion of international distributive justice is both new and messy. It is new because global distribution is a fairly new possibility. It is messy because principles of distributive justice are contentious, and because it is unclear to whom arguments about international distributive justice should be addressed. Neither the agents of change nor its beneficiaries (or victims) are easily identified.

The novelty of discussing global distribution and redistribution has both technical and historical aspects. Evidently wealth and entitlements,[1] poverty and hunger, have always been unevenly distributed; but traditional societies could do little to change this. Without modern technologies and institutions it is hard or impossible to use a surplus in one region to redress deficit in another. Within the great empires of the past, grain distribution was sometimes well controlled from the centre, but the boundaries of empire were also the boundaries of redistribution. Transport of grain or goods even within those boundaries was problem enough; global transport simply impossible. Global distributive justice was hardly imaginable.

This being the case, traditional codes said little about economic justice to those who lived beyond the frontiers – whether of tribe, community or empire. There might be limited advice on the right treatment of the 'stranger', but strangers were thought of only as outsiders (travellers, refugees), present for a limited time and in limited numbers, who had some claim to share resources. The duties of hospitality and the claims of strangers cannot offer an adequate model for the distribution of resources in a world in which goods can be shifted and trade regulated; where development can be planned across vast distances and can affect vast numbers.

It is not obvious that better models for thinking about international distributive justice will be found within Western political philosophy. In early modern European thought and politics 'outsiders' were often denied moral standing. Their occupation of land was not recognized as ownership; their customs and institutions were condemned and often destroyed. The European colonial expansion, which has shaped the present international economic order, was achieved in part by invasion, genocide, expropriation, transportation, slavery and proselytising that Europeans would have condemned as unjust in dealings with those whose standing they acknowledged.

Today questions of global distributive justice will arise whether or not we can find the theoretical resources to handle them. Modern technical and institutional possibilities make far wider intervention not only possible but unavoidable. We can now hardly avoid asking how individuals, institutions and societies may change (exacerbate, alleviate) distant poverty and distress. Current answers range from the *laissez-faire* view that it is permissible, or even obligatory, to do nothing, to claims that global redistribution is mandatory and even that it is obligatory to use any surplus to alleviate distress wherever it may be.

These answers are not only contentious but often ill-focused. To make them more precise we would have to establish *who* is (or is not) obliged to take *which* sorts of action for *whom*. Here the messiness begins. The agents and agencies whose action and operation constitute and achieve distributions of resources are not only numerous but heterogeneous. They include not only individual actors, but also states (and their various government agencies), international organizations (e.g. the World Bank, the UN and regional organizations), and both corporations and other non-governmental organizations (NGOs), some of which are confined within national frontiers while others operate transnationally (e.g. BP and Oxfam). Even those corporations and NGOs which operate only within state frontiers often have intimate links with and a degree of dependence on others that operate transnationally, and those that operate transnationally also operate within frameworks that are defined and constituted both by state law and by international agreements. Equally, those who may be wronged by the present international economic order are scattered through many regions and jurisdictions, and have a vast array of differing forms of involvement with and dependence on the international economic order. The very transformations that have made an international economic order a reality and international distributive justice a possibility have vastly expanded the web of actions, practices and institutions that might be challenged by judgements about international distributive justice.

This suggests that any discussion of international distributive justice needs to take account of the diversity of capacities and scope for action of these various agents and agencies, and of the possibility and limits of their transformation. In practice discussions of principles of distributive justice have mainly been conducted on the basis of very incomplete views of agency. Some writers assume that the only relevant agents are individuals; others allow for the agency of states as well as individuals; most are vague about the agency or ethical responsibilities of corporations, government and international agencies and charities. While economists and development specialists are quite ready to use the vocabulary of action, obligation and responsibility when speaking of a wide variety of agencies and institutions, discussions of the ethical issues lag behind for lack of any general and convincing account of the responsibilities of collectivities.[2] Sometimes the issue is bracketed and an abstract account of ethical requirements offered without allocating particular obligations to specified agents and agencies.

Such abstraction may be all that can readily be achieved: but it makes it hard to question or investigate the justice of present institutional structures. It fails to identify where the obligations of justice should fall, and for whom the benefits or rights that justice might achieve should be secured. If agents of change are not identified, discussions of international distributive justice will lack focus, and may proceed in terms that seem irrelevant to those whose practice is challenged. If recipients of change are not identified, the changes sought may neither find advocates nor meet the most urgent injustices. In particular, it may prove hard to connect demands for economic justice directly to claims of need and poverty.

Much modern ethical thought makes no use of the category of needs. In utilitarian thinking needs can be considered only if reflected in desires or preferences; and this is an imperfect reflection. Discussions of human rights often take no account of needs at all; and where they try to do so, strains are placed on the basic structure of rights theory, and the identification of needs is sketchy. A full account of international distributive justice would require a complete theory of human needs, which I shall not provide. This is partly a matter of prudence and ignorance, but is perhaps defensible in discussions that must take hunger and poverty seriously. It is not controversial that human beings need adequate food, shelter and clothing appropriate to their climate, clean water and sanitation, and some parental and health care. When these basic needs are not met they become ill and often die prematurely. It is controversial whether human beings need companionship, education, politics and culture, or food for the spirit – for at least some long and not evidently stunted lives have been lived without these goods. But these issues do not have to be settled for a discussion of hunger and destitution to proceed; discussion of international distributive justice can at least begin with a rudimentary account of needs.

Given the complexity and intractability of questions about agency and need, most writing on international distributive justice has understandably bracketed both topics and has concentrated on working out the implications various ethical positions would have for international distribution *if* there were agents and recipients for whom these implications were pertinent. In what follows I shall sketch and criticize a number of these positions, propose an alternative and then consider how far it can illuminate questions of agency and need. I begin with a consideration of positions that have least to say about international justice; for if these positions are convincing there will be little need to go further.

Community and Cosmopolis

The deepest disagreement about international justice is between those who think that there is at least something to be said about duties beyond borders, and those who think that ethical concern cannot cross boundaries.[3] Liberal and socialist thinkers view justice as universal in scope, and *a fortiori* as having cosmopolitan implications. No doubt both liberal and socialist practice has usually subordinated these to the demands of nation and state; but this has been seen as a practical and temporary rather than a fundamental concession. However, various forms of relativism and historicism deny that the category of justice has implications or even makes sense beyond the boundaries of nation-state or communities. Burke's critique of the *Rights of Man*, and his insistence that the revolutionaries of France would have done better to appeal to the traditional rights of Frenchmen, is a classical version of this thought. Contemporary communitarian critics of 'abstract' liberal justice repeat and develop many points raised by early critics of rights.[4]

One frequently made criticism of liberal, and particularly rights-based, accounts of justice is that they are too abstract.[5] However, abstraction taken strictly is neither objectionable nor avoidable. We abstract as soon as we make claims whose truth does not depend on the satisfaction or non-satisfaction of some predicate. Abstraction, in this sense, is essential to all language and reasoning; it is the basis for bringing any plurality of cases under a single principle. The critics of 'abstract liberalism' themselves do not and cannot avoid abstraction. Even if we think that justice differs in Athens and in Sparta, the justice of Athens will be formulated in principles that apply to Athenians who differ in any number of ways, from which Athenian justice abstracts.

If abstraction in itself is unavoidable, critics of 'abstract liberalism' probably have something else in mind. One point that many make is that abstract principles do not merely have universal scope but mandate mindlessly uniform treatment of differing cases. This would be true if abstract principles were algorithms that fully determine action; but if they are side constraints that regulate but do not wholly determine action, as most liberals hold, there is no reason why they should mandate uniform treatment of differing cases. In fact, abstract principles sometimes mandate differentiated treatment. A principle of proportioning taxation to ability to pay uses an abstract account of taxpayers and is universal in scope; but it mandates uniform treatment only when everyone has the same ability to pay. Even abstract principles that do not prescribe differentiated treatment may require differentiated applications. The actions required of those who are committed to such abstract aims as relieving poverty or combating imperialism or maximizing profit vary greatly depending on context. Universal principles can guide highly differentiated practice: applying abstract principles to varying cases needs painstaking adjudication rather than mechanical implementation.

A second and more serious objection to 'abstraction' complains of ethical and political reasoning that assumes enhanced, 'idealized' accounts of individual rationality and independence and of national sovereignty. This is a serious objection, but what it objects to is not strictly abstraction. Idealized reasoning does not simply *omit* predicates that are true of the objects and agents to which it is applied; it applies only to hypothetical agents who satisfy predicates that actual agents or agencies do not (fully) satisfy. Speaking strictly, idealized reasoning applies only in those ideal worlds inhabited (for example) by rational economic men with perfect information, fully transitive preferences and unlimited capacities to calculate. By contrast, merely abstract reasoning applies to agents whether or not they satisfy the predicates from which it abstracts. Since much liberal and socialist thought uses idealized models of the human agent, and of other agents such as classes and states, objections to idealized reasoning have a serious point.

Communitarians have positive as well as negative things to say about justice. Many of them contend that the categories, the sense or at least the authority of any ethical discourse is anchored within a specific community or tradition, and that attempts to apply such reasoning universally detach it from the forms of life and thought on which it depends. On this account, international justice is illusory, because it assumes that everyone shares categories and principles, whereas, as Michael Walzer put it, the largest sphere of justice is the political community. Walzer does not wholly dismiss international justice, for he allows that the admission of individual aliens to membership of the community and conflicts between states raise issues of justice. Other communitarian critics of 'abstract liberalism' see the boundaries of justice as coterminous with those of community. For example, MacIntyre argues that ethical reasoning must be internal to a particular tradition, which it seeks to further, and sees an irresolvable tension between the demands of liberalism and of nationalism. Rawls, in his most nearly communitarian writing,[6] anchors his principles of justice in the outlook of citizens of a modern liberal democratic polity, and offers no reasons why others should accept them.

If communitarians are correct, international distributive justice is not an issue: compatriots have legitimate priority.[7] International distributive justice would indeed be unthinkable if the boundaries between states, and between modes of discourse and ideologies, were total and impervious. This, however, is the very respect in which the modern world is different from its predecessors. It is not a world of closed communities with mutually impenetrable ways of thought, self-sufficient economies and ideally sovereign states. What is more, communitarians acknowledge this in practice as much as anyone else. Like the rest of us they expect to interact with foreigners, and rely on practices of translation, negotiation and trade that cross boundaries. If complex, reasoned communication and association breach boundaries, why should not principles of justice do so too? Although the internationalist images of a 'world community' or 'global village' may be sentimental slogans, the view that boundaries of actual communities are impervious is sheer nostalgia; and often it is self-serving nostalgia. Questions of international distributive justice cannot now be ruled out of order.

[. . .]

Universal Obligations and International Justice

Theories of rights come close to providing a framework for thinking about international distributive justice. What is missing from the positions [. . .] is a way of combining an account of the allocation of obligations with acknowledgement of the claims of need and poverty. Libertarians allocate obligations, but overlook need; other liberals acknowledge need but fail to allocate some obligations. I shall try to meet both demands by sketching an account of obligations among finite, needy beings.

Those who make rights basic to their account of justice start with the thought that all have equal rights. An analogous approach to identifying obligations of justice would look for principles of action that can be universally adopted. As is well known, this is the basic move of the Kantian ethical enterprise.[8] Kant identifies principles of obligation as those which must be adopted if principles that cannot be universally held are rejected. Injustice on this account is a matter of adopting fundamental principles which not all can adopt. To make non-universalizable principles fundamental, to institutions or to lives, presumes status and privilege that cannot be open to all. Justice on such accounts is a matter of acting only on principles on which all *could act* (not either *would* or *should* act, as in many quasi-Kantian approaches).

A Kantian construction of principles of obligation is in one crucial way less ambitious than the constructions of human rights [. . .]. Those constructions aim to determine the greatest possible liberty, or the best set of liberty and welfare rights. At some stage in these constructions an *optimum* or *maximal* arrangement must be identified. Just as the poles of a wigwam cannot stand in isolation, so these constructions of rights are all-or-nothing affairs: if one component right of 'the most extensive liberty' is identified, so are all the rest; if less than the full set is established, none is established. When principles of obligations are constructed on Kantian lines they are identified *seriatim*. The construction uses a procedure for checking whether any proposed principle could be fundamental for all institutions and lives. A Kantian construction of obligations can identify *some* principles of obligation without establishing *all* of them.

Discovering which principles must be adopted if non-universalizable principles are rejected is not a matter of finding out which specific types of action ought to be done. Act descriptions which refer to particular times, places, persons or scarce resources cannot be universally satisfied, yet clearly acts, including permissible and obligatory acts, must fall under such descriptions. Superficial and detailed act descriptions need not and cannot be universalizable. We cannot all of us eat the same grain, nor share the same roof. A Kantian approach aims to identify *fundamental* principles (Kant's maxims) which may be used to govern lives and institutions. Justice on this account is a matter of not basing actions, lives or institutions on principles that cannot be universally shared; it is not a matter of uniform action.[9]

Two examples of obligations that can be identified by the Kantian method of construction are those of rejecting reliance on fundamental principles either of coercion or of deception. The background arguments here show that it is impossible for a principle of coercion to be universally shared – for those who are coerced are (at least temporarily) denied agency and so *cannot* (in principle) share their coercers' principles of action, and those who are deceived are denied knowledge of their deceiver's underlying principle (if they knew, the deception would be discredited, so ineffective) so again *cannot* share the plan to deceive. Such arguments do not show that all coercion or deception is unjust: they show only that actions, institutions and lives which make coercion or deception fundamental are unjust.[10]

So far it may seem that a Kantian construction would identify as principles of obligation only those which correspond to the rights libertarians identify. If a construction of obligations could only proceed in this way, it could not take account of needs. However, this less ambitious approach can go beyond theories of rights in two important respects. Both follow from Kant's insistence that obligations are relevant to *finite* rational beings. (On Kant's account, idealized rational beings would in any case find principles of obligation redundant.)

Justice and the Virtues

The first way in which a Kantian approach via obligations yields more than theories of rights can provide is that it can offer an account of virtue as well as of justice. It allows for the construction both of imperfect obligations, whose performance is not allocated to right-holders, and of perfect obligations, whose performance can be claimed as a right. Principles of imperfect obligation, on a Kantian account, reflect human finitude. Finite beings are inescapably needy, and their obligations cannot be based on denying this. The principles of imperfect obligation for which Kant argued are ones that must be adopted if non-universalizable principles are rejected by beings of limited capacities. Two (slightly adapted) examples are the following. First, beings who (like human beings) find that their individual abilities are not adequate to achieve their ends must (if rational) be committed to relying (to some extent) on others' help; hence, if they reject non-universalizable principles, they must be committed to a principle of offering (at least some) help to others. This commitment is a matter of rejecting principled non-beneficence rather than commitment to a determinate level of beneficence. Secondly, beings who have to develop their abilities, rather than relying on instinct or maturation, know that they will have ends that require various abilities, so will, if rational, be committed to developing some range of abilities in themselves and in others.

This construction of principles of imperfect obligation is not subjective: it does not refer to actual ends or desires. It does take the needs of finite beings into account. The line of thought can be paraphrased as follows. Rational beings whose desires, unlike those of creatures of instinct, standardly outrun both their own resources and those of their fellows will (regardless of the specific content of their desires) discover that they cannot universally act on principles of neglecting needs. They cannot rationally will that they should be part of a world in which either a principle of refusing needed help or a principle of refusing to develop abilities and resources is universally adopted. Hence their fundamental principles must include some commitment to helping others and to developing human (and other) potential. However, the non-universalizability of

neglecting to help or to develop human potential does not entail that there are obligations to help all others in all their projects or to develop all possible potentials: indeed,
these are impossible commitments. Nor does this account of the social virtues determine required levels of help or commitment to development. However, those who do
nothing reveal that their underlying principle is to neglect both virtues. They act
wrongly even if their victims cannot be identified.

In distinguishing the demands of perfect and imperfect obligations a Kantian construction respects the asymmetry of obligations to refrain and obligations to intervene.
The advantage of an account of imperfect obligations is that it neither insists that what
have traditionally been thought of as imperfect duties have corresponding rights nor
treats them as in no way obligatory. In short, the approach leaves room, as rights-based
approaches do not, for a non-trivializing account of the social and institutional virtues.
Yet, unlike most contemporary accounts of the virtues, it does not rely on historicist
or communitarian claims, and still allows us to talk about rights, considered as the reciprocal of perfect obligations. When it is either relevant or politic to adopt the perspective of recipience, the idiom of rights can be used to discuss and demand justice.

Justice, Abilities and Needs

All of this, however, does not show how an account of the claimable, perfect obligations of justice can take account of need. If perfect duties, and specifically matters
of justice, are a matter of non-interference, how could meeting needs be a matter of
justice? And if the allocation of help to those who need it is undetermined by fundamental ethical considerations, may we not allocate it capriciously among the needy? If
so, what advantage does a Kantian approach offer for considering international distributive
justice, where a guaranteed and reliable allocation of help and of the development of
human resources is crucial? No doubt a capacity to offer a serious, non-relativist
account of social and institutional virtues is an advantage, but Kantian justice still looks
like an obligation-based analogue of libertarian justice.

A Kantian construction can, however, guide a non-selective approach to basic human
needs within a theory of justice; and herein lies its second advantage over rights-based
theories. Kant stresses repeatedly that *all* principles of obligation are principles for *finite*
rational beings, and in particular that human beings are finite not only in rationality but
in many other ways. In deliberating about what it takes to apply and institutionalize
fundamental principles of rejecting coercion or deception, human finitude, need and
vulnerability must be taken into account.

We cannot interpret what it is to reject a principle of coercion without an account
of what constitutes coercion in the human condition. It is generally agreed that physical force is coercive for human agents: when A pushes B, B's movement does not reflect
B's agency, which is pre-empted. However, it is also generally thought that threat and
duress constitute coercion, and the notion of a threat cannot be explicated without reference to context. What constitutes a threat depends on what powers a threatener has
to harm particular victims – hence also on the reciprocal of power, i.e. on the vulnerability of those threatened. It is impossible to determine what constitutes a threat in
abstraction from an account of the respective capacities of those who threaten and are
threatened. Human finitude can take many shapes: each shape constitutes a specific
configuration of need and vulnerability, which others can exploit or respect.

Here the task cannot be to judge particular cases, but only to suggest which considerations would be relevant in deciding how to ensure that lives and institutions eschew fundamental principles and practices of coercion and deception. Marx's slogan, 'From each according to his abilities; to each according to his needs', is a suggestive way into this topic. The slogan gestures towards a vision of social relations in which antagonisms are overcome. This victim was of the far future. For the present, Marx acknowledged, progress would be marked by forms of bourgeois right and law; many of his followers thought, in particular, that Marxism could bracket internationalist commitments and pursue socialism in one country. Socialist practice, like liberal practice, has long subordinated underlying cosmopolitan commitments to the sovereignty of nation-states. It is only in a distant future, in which states would have withered away, that justice – or rather, the full human emancipation that would succeed justice – would not be confined by state boundaries. These reminders might suggest that socialist thought has little to contribute to present issues of international justice, except perhaps by way of its influence on theories of economic development. However, Marx's slogan brings together the two issues that other theories so often sever. I shall sketch a way of reading a joint emphasis on *abilities* and *needs* into the construction of principles of justice just attempted.

Principles of obligation are relevant only for agents (perhaps some individual and others institutional). Agents must have at least some abilities or capacities for independent action: they must combine some cognitive and some executive abilities. Without these they could not act, and practical reasoning would be irrelevant for them; in short, they would not be agents. The agents and agencies who affect international distributions of goods are highly diverse. However, all of them have fairly limited abilities. This is evidently true of human agents, whose abilities are reciprocal to their needs. It is also true of the many agents and agencies and even of those supposedly sovereign bodies, the nation-states. Even superpowers are limited powers; so, of course, are those new global operators, the transnational corporations. The steps that this motley range of finite agents must take if they are to reject fundamental principles and policies of coercing or deceiving others are clearly enormously diverse. However, two aspects of their action can be clearly distinguished.

To reject principled coercion is a matter of not relying on any policy or practice of treating others in ways to which they *could not* consent. (The claim is modal; it does not invoke actual preferences.) This may seem too weak a claim: surely overriding others' actual dissent, even when they could have consented, is already coercive. However, provided action is tailored to make others' dissent *possible*, actual dissent will be registered by refusing or renegotiating others' proposals. It is action that is pushed through in the face of dissent, and makes refusal impossible, that coerces: such 'offers' cannot be refused.

Relations between the powerful and the powerless are often governed by principles of coercion. This is evident in relations between developed and underdeveloped states, agencies and enterprises. Those who are weak cannot refuse or renegotiate the 'offers' of the strong, unless the strong adjust these offers to the actual lack of abilities and weakness of those to whom they are made. Poor and powerless states and institutions, like poor and powerless individuals, may make dismal bargains, trading their only resources for inadequate returns, 'agreeing' to damaging terms of trade and taking out loans that they cannot service. Poor states may agree to accept dirty manufacturing and to offer massive tax concessions for foreign investors. All of this reflects their vulnerability and need. Miscalculation apart, neither individuals nor institutions would accept such arrangements unless they were vulnerable.

For just transactions with vulnerable others it is not enough to meet standards that would not coerce or deceive others of equal or greater power. To act justly, the rich and powerful must adopt policies that are not based on coercing or deceiving those with whom they interact. It is not enough to observe outward forms of contract, bargain and negotiation (as libertarians might think), or to secure others from destitution (as advocates of welfare rights would insist). It is necessary to reject fundamental policies, principles or practices which deny those on the receiving end, with their specific vulnerabilities and needs, the possibility of refusing or renegotiating. Just agents and agencies allow others, including those most vulnerable to them, the space to refuse and to renegotiate offers.

A commitment not to take advantage of others' weakness is in itself frail. The strong are easily tempted – and, after all, they are not that strong; most of them live amid many competitors and stronger powers. It is hardly realistic to demand that institutions and agents, who will be squeezed by others, if they do not pursue their own advantage, not lean on the weak, unless the demand is given 'teeth'. Hence a genuine, action-guiding commitment to enacting principles of justice in a world of disparate agents, many of them vulnerable to others' powers, cannot be *only* a demand for justice in transactions. It must also, and crucially, be a commitment to transform the structure of institutions and the characters and powers of individual agents, i.e. the presuppositions of transactions, so as to reduce powerlessness and vulnerability.

More specifically, international markets, transactions and relations will require as much regulation as internal markets and transactions and domestic social relations, if differentials of power are not to undercut the lives and plans of the weak. This point does not impugn or challenge the presumed performance of *ideal* markets, or the *realpolitik* of *ideally* sovereign states, or the decision-making of *idealized* rational choosers. It does recognize the vast gap between the idealized agents and agencies modelled by social scientists and their actual prototypes. Without regulation, actual markets may magnify rather than minimize the implications of disparities in power and vulnerability, actual states may oppress their own and other peoples, and ruthless individuals may dominate others. Powerlessness and vulnerability are the reciprocals of others' power: a commitment to control the coercive potential of differentials of power is a commitment to reduce or restrain the capacities of the most powerful agents and to increase those of the most vulnerable. A commitment to lessen both economic and political inequality therefore follows from a serious, action-guiding commitment to justice among unequals.

Which forms of regulation would best achieve these results is a vast and selectively discussed matter. The stock antithesis between 'state regulation' and 'non-interference', which structures many discussions, may itself be obsolete, and there may be as much reason to look at the social and discursive practices that discipline and foster certain types of agent and institution as at the legal and administrative frameworks that constrain them. Questions of good practice may be as vital as questions of legal limits.

The present international economic order is the product of a vast and interlocking range of institutional changes and transformations. Many of the actors on this stage did not exist at the end of the Second World War. There were then no transnational corporations of the modern sort; there were few independent ex-colonies other than those whose population was of European descent. The international bodies, development agencies and NGOs that operate transnationally are new types of agencies. Some of them may have exacerbated international distributive injustice; others may have reduced it. Such a process of institution-building and transformation, including the education and transformation of human capacities, is endlessly extendable. A full commitment to international distributive justice would be a matter of seeking to transform the present institutional structure into one better able to ensure that the powers and abilities it constructs and fosters serve rather than exploit actual needs and reduce vulnerabilities.

At this point the initial question of audience can be raised again. For whom are these discussions of justice relevant? By the very arguments pursued, there is no unique locus of responsibility. But it does not follow that there are agents or agencies who have no responsibilities. The fact that nobody and no agency can do *everything* does not entail that they can do nothing. This is true not only of rich but of poor individuals, not only of governments and institutions in the North, but of those in the South; and it is true of the manifold international, multinational and transnational agencies that have proliferated in the global economy.

An account of principles of obligation among finite and mutually vulnerable beings has powerful and complex implications for issues of development and international justice. Many steps are needed for effective institutionalization of the principles defended here. The salient contrasts with other accounts of justice show some of the strengths and limitations of approaching questions of international justice by relying on a constructivist account of obligations. First some limits: the approach does not yield algorithms either for identifying principles of justice, or for their implementation. Then some strengths: the programme offers a procedure for identifying certain principles of justice, and arguments to show why their institutionalization and implementation should take account of relationships of power and vulnerability. [. . .]

Notes

1 For the concept of entitlement see A. K. Sen, *Poverty and Famines: An Essay on Entitlement and Deprivation* (Oxford: Clarendon, 1981), and *Gender and Cooperative Conflicts*, working paper, World Institute for Development Economics Research (Helsinki: United Nations University, 1987); and Barbara Harriss, 'Intrafamily distribution of hunger in South Asia', in J. Drèze and A. K. Sen (eds), *Hunger: Economics and Policy* (Oxford: Clarendon, forthcoming).

2 For recent discussions of corporate responsibilities see Peter French, *Collective and Corporate Responsibility* (New York: Columbia University Press, 1984); Norman Bowie, 'The moral obligations of multinational corporations', in Stephen Luper-Foy (ed.), *Problems of International Justice* (Boulder: Westview, 1988), pp. 97–113; and Larry May, *The Morality of Groups: Collective Responsibilities, Group-Based Harm and Corporate Rights* (Notre Dame: University of Notre Dame Press, 1987).

3 For discussions of problems of duties that cross borders see Charles Beitz, *Political Theory and International Relations* (Princeton: Princeton University Press, 1979), and 'Cosmopolitan ideals and national sentiments', *Journal of Philosophy* (1983): 591–600; Robert Goodin, 'What is so special about our fellow countrymen?', *Ethics* (1988): 663–86; Stanley Hoffman, *Duties beyond Borders: On the Limits and Possibilities of Ethical International Politics* (Syracuse: Syracuse University Press, 1981); Luper-Foy, *Problems of International Justice*; Alasdair MacIntyre, 'Is patriotism a virtue?', paper, University of Kansas Department of Philosophy, 1984; David Miller, 'The ethical significance of nationality', *Ethics* (1988): 647–62; Onora O'Neill, *Faces of Hunger: An Essay on Poverty, Development and Justice* (London, Allen and Unwin, 1986), and 'Ethical reasoning and ideological pluralism', *Ethics* 98 (1988): 705–22; Henry Shue, 'Mediating duties', *Ethics* 98 (1988): 687–704; and Michael

Walzer, *Spheres of Justice: A Defence of Pluralism and Equality* (Oxford: Martin Robertson, 1983).

4   On the communitarian critique of liberalism see Michael Sandel, *Liberalism and the Limits of Justice* (Cambridge: Cambridge University Press, 1982); Alasdair MacIntyre, *After Virtue* (London: Duckworth, 1981), 'Is patriotism a virtue?', and *Whose Justice? Which Rationality?* (London: Duckworth, 1988); and Walzer, *Spheres of Justice*; as well as the discussion and bibliographical essay in Jeremy Waldron, *Nonsense upon Stilts: Bentham, Burke and Marx on the Rights of Man* (London: Methuen, 1987).

5   For fuller discussion of the contrasts between abstraction and idealization, and their relevance to international issues, see Onora O'Neill 'Abstraction, idealization and ideology', in J. G. D. Evans (ed.), *Ethical Theories and Contemporary Problems* (Cambridge: Cambridge University Press, 1988), 'Ethical reasoning and ideological pluralism', and 'Gender, justice and international boundaries', *British Journal of Political Science* 20 (1990): 439–59.

6   John Rawls, 'Justice as fairness; political not metaphysical', *Philosophy and Public Affairs* 14 (1985): 223–51.

7   On the question of priority for compatriots see Goodin, 'What is so special about our fellow countrymen?' and Miller 'The ethical significance of nationality'.

8   The Kantian texts that lie behind this are mainly *Groundwork of the Metaphysic of Morals* and *The Critique of Practical Reason*; for a reading which applies them to problems of international distributive justice see O'Neill, *Faces of Hunger*, chs 7 and 8.

9   The level of description that is important – that of the Kantian maxim of action – is that of the principle which is *fundamental* to a given action. The maxim is the guiding or controlling principle of an action, the principle that makes sense of and orchestrates ancillary aspects of action. On Kant's account neither agents nor others have privileged knowledge of maxims. Although we cannot judge either others' actions or our own definitively, deliberation can identify action which would not express a non-universalizable action. Agents can strive to avoid acting on non-universalizable principles even if they cannot guarantee that they have succeeded. See O. O'Neill, *Constructions of Reason* (Cambridge: Cambridge University Press, 1989).

10 Some coercion and deception may even be needed for justice. For example, state power, or less centralized forms of social coercion, may be essential to establish the rule of law and to prevent the endemic coercion of conditions of insecurity which threaten all agency.

42

The Idea of World Community

Chris Brown

'Community' is a deceptive and [difficult] notion to employ. It is one of Raymond Williams's *Keywords*. Having noted its reference to a sense of common interests and common identity – and the classical contrast with 'society' formalized by Tönnies (1963) as a contrast between *Gemeinschaft* and *Gesellschaft* – he remarks that it is a 'warmly persuasive' word, whether used to describe an existing or alternative set of relationships: 'What is more important, perhaps, is that unlike all other terms of social organization (state, nation, society, etc.) it never seems to be used unfavourably, and never to be given any positive opposing or distinguishing term' (Williams 1976: 66). Much the same could be said of the use of the term 'world community' – it is never employed with pejorative connotations. It may not be entirely clear what is, or should be, meant by the term, but it is clear that those who use it believe that the world would be a better place if it could be described as a community. As with the diplomatic use of 'international community' – a related but, in contrast to world community, essentially state-centric term – it is always employed persuasively.
[. . .]

With these points in mind, it is now possible to turn to [. . .] a critical examination of the prospects for the emergence of a world community. The existence of such a community would be signalled by the development not just of global common interests but also of a worldwide consciousness of common identity. A number of countervailing forces in the modern world – in the realms of ideas, or of technology broadly defined, or of social and political action – appear to act either to promote or to hinder this development but, crucially, behind the struggle between these forces it is, I suggest, generally assumed that there is an underlying trend guaranteeing, or at least making very likely, a victory for the promoters of community. The assumption that universal norms and values will triumph over those based on particular local contexts is a feature of contemporary liberalism in almost all its forms – indeed is termed the 'liberal expectancy' by Milton Gordon (cited from Moynihan 1993: 27) – but draws support equally from Christian, eschatological, Enlightenment, Marxist and Western progressivist thinking in general. The premise is that the world is moving in the direction of community, albeit with a faltering step because of the contest between forces representing common interests and common identity and those representing the old, particularistic, order. In what follows these claims will be set out in greater detail and, in the process, subjected to criticism. [. . .]

The Underlying Trend

On what basis can it be argued that there is a trend towards the development of ever-wider common interests and a deepening sense of common identity? Clearly, it is important at the outset to make a distinction between a trend towards the creation of *community*, and trends which, simply, point towards the emergence of 'one world' [the notion that the world is becoming more closely linked or integrated by common forces or practices] – failure to make this distinction bedevils a great deal of thought on the subject of world community.

[...]

For community to begin to emerge there has to be a growing awareness of common interests and identity; the creation of 'one-world' is a necessary condition for the emergence of a world community but it is not, of itself, sufficient. This is clearly so with regard to the unifying forces of global economic interdependence but, perhaps less intuitively obviously, the point also applies when it comes to other unifying forces, including material factors such as common consumer goals and non-material factors such as the global spread of common notions of scientific method and, possibly, common standards of rationality. The fact that young people everywhere desire the same jeans, trainers and electronic games, or that contemporary technology seems to work better when based on Western science rather than, say, the Hindu scriptures is, obviously, something that it is useful to know about the world, but something further is needed if an essentially *empirical* account of an increasingly unified world is to be accompanied by an essentially *normative* account of the emergence of a world community.

Returning to square one, the 'something further' required is the moral impulse which creates a sense of common interests and identity. [...] [T]his is not something that can be expected to emerge simply as a result of individuals and peoples coming to have more contact with one another, because such contact need not generate the essentially moral consciousness of common identity that is required. It could, instead, generate incomprehension or hatred – as seems to have been the case with initial contacts between Europeans and Aztecs (Todorov 1987). The question is, are there good reasons for thinking that the gradual, recently quite rapid, widening of the range and scope of contacts between individuals, groups and peoples has been accompanied by some kind of corresponding recognition of common interests and a common identity?

As a first approximation, it would seem that there is good reason to answer this question in the affirmative. *Prima facie* it does seem that there has been an 'expanding circle' of concern (Singer 1981) and that the extension of the range and scope of political reference groups from kin to tribe to city to state *has* been accompanied by something like an equivalent extension of moral concern. Within the scope of this chapter such a proposition cannot be defended, only illustrated: thus, Greeks of the age of Pericles identified with their kin, tribe and city, to a lesser extent with Hellas but not at all with 'barbarians' – those who did not speak Greek. Roman thinking was politically universalist, but morally orientated only to fellow citizens. Christendom offered a wide moral identity, but one explicitly achieved by the exclusion of Slavs, Saracens, Jews and 'others' generally. In contrast, in the world today, modern nation-states involve tens, even hundreds, of millions of people who believe one another, in principle at least, to be fellow citizens and are prepared to accept obligations to one another – through, for example, redistributive taxation – which give substance to this belief. Moreover, the growth of voluntary aid organizations such as Oxfam and human rights groups such as Amnesty International suggests that some concern for the interests and rights of citizens of other states is quite widely accepted. This loosely delineated temporal sequence – which could be replicated for other cultures – supports the view that on the whole, and so far, a widening sense of identity has accompanied the growth of ever larger networks of interdependence. It is not totally implausible to hypothesize that this process will continue until a worldwide community becomes a reality.

Of course, the fact that the circle of concern has expanded in the past does not mean that it will continue to do so in the future. Certainly there are forces working towards both the expansion and the contraction of common identity in the modern world, and it is quite possible that the latter will prove more effective than the former. These are issues that will be examined in the next section of this chapter, but before taking this step it is necessary to address some ways in which the idea of a trend towards world community might be damagingly misunderstood.

First, it should be stressed that the notion of a secular trend implies movement in a particular direction, but not necessarily on a smooth, untroubled curve. There are always likely to be setbacks as well as advances [. . .].

A more important point concerns the competing claims of different kinds of community. Some writers of a cosmopolitan disposition seem to assume that an emerging world community would require of its members an implausibly high level of loyalty, overriding all other obligations.

[. . .]

But this is not how the world works nor is there any reason that it should work in this way. In practice, and quite sensibly, we recognize degrees of obligation towards family, friends, acquaintances, fellow citizens, and so on, and as long as this recognition does not lead us to disregard the interests of those in the outer circles of our concern there is no reason to see this as immoral. Priority to fellow nationals becomes contrary to the requirements of world community only if it is pushed beyond the bounds of the quite defensible view that those nearest to us have the first, but not an exclusive, call on our sympathies.

So, perhaps fortunately, a belief that world community is emerging need entail neither adherence to a facile progressivism of the 'ever onwards, ever upwards' variety, nor the belief that a saintly, self-sacrificing altruism is, will be, or should be rife among the peoples of the world. The sense of common identity that *is* required is more down to earth and practical, closer to Nagel's (1986) requirement that we should not be indifferent to the suffering of others than to Singer's [1985] or Beitz's [1983] requirement that we give the interests of others equal weight with our own. However, even in this less ambitious form, there are still reasons to doubt whether this sentiment will, or could, come to dominate – and it is to this issue that we now turn.

Immovable Objects, Irresistible Forces

Assuming for the sake of argument that there is a trend towards the emergence of world community, which are the forces in the modern world that promote and enhance this trend, and which are those that obstruct or block its operation? And can a judgement be reached on the relative strength of these forces? As at the beginning of the previous section – but here the point can be made more simply – it must be stressed at the outset that forces which simply promote or obstruct the integration of the world as a system are not, taken on their own terms, critical to these judgements. At least as a first approximation, what is of interest is the clash between forces articulating global solidarities and forces expressing particularistic loyalties – although these normative positions may be related to empirical trends they are clearly distinguishable from them, and should be so distinguished.

Global solidarities clash with particularistic loyalties in a number of different contexts, but at the heart of each such clash is a contest between differently based normative claims on the individual, often reaching to critical questions concerning his or her sense of identity. Ought women in countries where Islamic law is in force see themselves as victims of discrimination – as the international women's movement would have it – or as participants in a living and sacred culture, as their co-religionists see the matter? How is a Brazilian environmentalist to reconcile within his or her own mind the claims of national development with the need to protect the common heritage of humanity? What is the mechanism by which those who seek social justice in the advanced industrial world choose between the claims of their disadvantaged fellow nationals and the usually greater, but always more distant, poverty of the dispossessed of the less developed countries? In each case, the real question is not so much 'What should I do?' but, rather, 'Who am I?' – because what I do will depend on who I think I am.

As the examples above suggest, the contest here is often cast in terms of an opposition between the different conceptions of moral identity [. . .]. The problem is that this way of setting up the issue is based on the assumption that these different packages of ideas are internally consistent, which often they are not.

Thus, some of the new social movements have particularistic as well as global implications. For example, it is a matter of some debate among different wings of the feminist movement as to whether gender should be seen as the basis of a new division of the world or, alternatively, as a force which overcomes divisions and creates, for the first time, the basis for a genuine worldwide common identity – on which see classifications of feminist thought such as Zalewski (1993) [. . .]. This situation is similar in structure and in its general implications to one that appears with some regularity in all variants of Marxism, with, of course, gender replacing class. [. . .] Thus, even on the assumption that the new social movements such as feminism aim eventually to promote global solidarity, they may do so via the indirect route of increased tension and a heightened sense of disunity.

In much the same, rather confusing, way, some of the forces which appear to have the effect of promoting particularistic loyalties do so from a basis that can plausibly claim to offer an alternative conception of global solidarity. Some, but not all, world religions can be seen in this light. For example, the occasionally quite virulent clash between Islam and the West (often in this case represented by the new social movements, or by human rights pressure groups such as Amnesty International) is generally seen by the latter as a clash between the universal values of enlightenment, science and rationality and the mores generated by a particularistic, culture-specific vision of the world. Unsurprisingly, this is not how radical Islam sees itself. This proselytizing religion regards its message as of universal import for humanity, and its goal is a world community in which all have submitted to this message – in this respect resembling Christianity in contrast to, say, Hinduism, where, in principle, the only way to possess a caste identity is to be born to it.

The purpose of this discussion is to suggest that setting up the issue of world community in terms of a contrast between the forces of globalism and localism, solidarity and particularism, may be less helpful than, at first glance, it seems to be. Clearly there *are* circumstances where this way of seeing things does approximate to reality. Secularists in India who oppose Hindu 'fundamentalism' can reasonably see themselves as representing a global solidarity as opposed to local particularism – although whether this status conveys moral superiority will, of course, be a matter of opinion.

Nationalism and racism are self-evidently not dead forces in the modern world, and those who oppose their local manifestations in the name of universal human values are not misleading themselves or others – there is a real struggle here which is not lightly to be explained away. However, some of the most interesting of contemporary contests are *not* of this form: instead of pitting local norms against global, universal values, they take the form of a contest between different conceptions of what is or should be universal. What is at issue in these cases is not whether or not there should be a world community but, rather, which of several possible world communities will emerge.

For this reason it is difficult, if not impossible, to see which way the wind is blowing when it comes to assessing the prospective growth of common interests and identities in the world today. In most parts of the world genuinely local forces such as nationalism and ethnicity may be under pressure but they are fighting back and, in any event, their opponents are as varied as they are and engaged in equally fierce contests with one another. This complex, multidimensional reality cannot be simplified into a straightforward contest between world community and its opponents: in different concrete contexts, apparently particularistic 'immovable objects' can become 'irresistible forces' based on universal values, as witness the role of Islam, anti-secularist in its relations with the West, but aligned with secularism in India in opposition to Hindu particularism.
[. . .]

If these judgements approach in some measure the truth – and, obviously, in a chapter of this length approximation is all that can be expected – it would seem that there is very little that can be said about the probability that some kind of world community is emerging: the complex interplay of forces in the modern world simply do not readily sort themselves into those supporting and those opposing such a development. This degree of indeterminacy is not exactly unusual in contemporary political theory and it may be that there is not much else to be said on this matter – the hypothetical trend towards world community identified in the previous section will simply have to be left, as it were, in the air. However, there is another possibility, namely that the indeterminacy of this issue has a direct bearing on the very idea that there could be a secular trend towards world community – a reexamination of the root idea of community seems called for.

The Limits of Community

It was suggested above, first, that a trend towards the emergence of an ever wider sense of community could be identified as a complement to the development of larger political units, and, second, that it is reasonable to hypothesize that this trend would continue – that the sequence 'kin, tribe, city, state' would, eventually, be completed by 'world'. However, the burden of the previous section of this chapter is that it is difficult to read the contemporary world in this light – the signs are simply too confusing to convey any clear sense of which way the world is going. It seems possible that something has gone wrong with the argument somewhere along the line – and there are at least two points at which error might have crept in.

First, it might be that the very idea of a historical trend towards *anything*, much less an ever widening sense of community, is mistaken. The idea that it is possible to find patterns of meaning in history has a very long heritage in Western thought and not simply in the Enlightenment and post-Enlightenment eras – the biblical and Christian roots of this idea are brilliantly reviewed by Karl Löwith in his *Meaning in History* (1949) – but has been put under question from a number of directions in recent years. The radical approach to the history of ideas associated with Quentin Skinner (Tully 1988) denies the existence of a common set of 'problems of politics' persisting over time in different contexts; such a denial necessarily undermines the idea that trend lines can be identified on any long-term cross-cultural basis. The postmodern 'turn' in social thought offers an even more radical 'scepticism towards metanarratives' (Lyotard 1986: xxiv) such as the metanarrative of 'community'. Moreover, outside the academy, the obvious failures of Marxism–Leninism – and, less dramatically, of the sort of programmatic liberalism associated with Hayek (1960) – seem to have led to a widespread public mood of disillusionment with grand political ideas, a position which endorses this postmodern scepticism, albeit not in so many words.

However, on closer inspection, this pervasive scepticism seems overblown. Clearly it is good to get away from the sort of facile Victorian progressivism which portrays the history of ideas in such a way that our predecessors are seen as inadequately addressing our agenda rather than doing their best to cope with their own, and, equally clearly, it is good that the spirit of the age is unwilling to allow itself to be conscripted into the armies of the oversimplifiers, but these healthy tendencies should not be allowed to underwrite a self-destructive nihilism. To suggest that the political problems of the past have *nothing* to do with modern man, or that *all* ideologies and general perspectives on life are equally distorted would be to turn a serious point of view into an affront to common sense. It is perfectly possible to defend the idea that we have today a wider sense of political community than that of our forebears without falling into irredeemable naivety. Modern states clearly have not solved the problems of community but to recognize that this is so need not involve a denial that considerable progress has been made or a refusal to recognize the real virtues possessed by contemporary liberal democratic states.

There is, then, no good *a priori* reason to deny that within the sequence 'kin, tribe, city, state' can be found a widening and deepening of community, but a second possibility – namely, that there are good and substantial reasons that this sequence cannot be completed by 'world' – is less easily disposed of. At its simplest, it might be the case that a sense of common identity actually *requires* the existence of 'others' with whom one does not identify. This is a commonplace and seductive point of view, nicely expressed in 1972 by Daniel Bell: 'It is always possible to bind together a considerable number of people in love, so long as there are other people left over to receive the manifestations of their aggressiveness' (cited from Moynihan 1993: 61). But, although seductive, such an argument is ultimately unconvincing, not just because it offers such a bleak view of human nature, but also because it denies without good reason the possibility that this nature might change. More plausible are those arguments for pluralism which rest upon a specific idea of community, one rather less loosely defined than that upon which this chapter has, so far, rested. The *locus classicus* for such an idea is to be found in the writings of the communitarian tradition [. . .] and particularly, but not exclusively, in the work of modern neo-Hegelians such as Charvet (1981), Sandel (1982) and Frost (1986).

In order to understand this position it is necessary to backtrack somewhat, and ask *why* the growth of a sense of community has, apparently, accompanied the growth of networks of communication and interdependence signalled by the sequence from kinship group to state referred to above. From some perspectives, this is not a very interesting question. If, for example, in the best liberal tradition, society is a 'co-operative venture for mutual advantage' (Rawls 1971: 4) then a degree of identification with fellow co-operators is unsurprising, and, equally, there is no reason to look for a deep explanation to account for the fact that as the scope of the venture becomes more extensive so the number of co-operators who identify with one another is also likely to increase. By the same token, as this co-operative venture becomes worldwide in scope, so one might expect the emergence of a worldwide sense of community – hence the attempts by Beitz (1979) and Pogge (1989) to apply Rawlsian notions of social justice to a global definition of society.

But from a communitarian perspective, this account of the growth of society and community is highly misleading because it rests on the characteristically liberal assumption that the individual co-operators who venture together for mutual advantage have a pre-social existence, and pre-social interests and values, that they bring with them to the process. By contrast, the communitarian perspective suggests, first, that human beings become 'individuals' only by the process of relating to one another in societies and, second, that, by extension, the kind of individuals they become will be a product of the kind of society within which this takes place. Thus, the sense of community that emerges from kinship group or tribe is not simply quantitatively different from that which is shaped by the modern state. There is a qualitative difference here. By situating the family within the context of civil society – a location within which the individual learns to make his or her way in the world – and by situating civil society within a constitutional context wherein law is seen as ultimately self-created rather than an external, alien force, the modern state makes possible the creation of individuals whose potentiality is far greater than that possessed by those whose individuality is constituted by societies in which these institutions are not differentiated – such at least is the position of communitarians of a Hegelian disposition.

From this perspective the sequence 'kin, tribe, city, state' is not simply a sequence of ever larger political and social units: it is a sequence of progressively differentiated entities, each adding something to the constitution of human beings that its predecessor could not offer. At this point, the obvious next step is to ask whether a *world* community would continue this process by providing something that the modern state does not – and the classic communitarian answer, given by Hegel and Rorty [. . .] is that it would not. From the communitarian perspective, the modern state could already provide the individual with the basis for a life lived in freedom, dealing justly with all, and there is, thus, no necessity to go beyond this to any allegedly higher form of community, even if such a move were possible. World community cannot be seen as a *necessary* step, because it could not provide any resource for the creation of individuality and personality on top of those already to hand in the modern state. [. . .]

Thus, communitarians of this Hegelian or neo-Hegelian persuasion have no difficulty in explaining the indeterminate nature of the struggle between the forces of global solidarity and those of local particularism. This global struggle has no obvious shape and is leading in no clearly defined direction because the underlying logic which created community at 'lower' levels of social organization does not operate on this terrain. Local struggles *can* be understood in communitarian terms, and neo-Hegelians *do* believe that the modern state is a superior form of social organization to its alternatives but even here, without the metaphysical assurance provided to their predecessors by the notion of *Geist*, there can be no guarantee that the good will in the end drive out the bad. In any event many modern communitarians would be less willing than the neo-Hegelians to make this kind of comparative judgement, believing that different political forms will be appropriate to different communities (Walzer 1983).

[. . .]

Conclusion – International Society and World Community

The line of argument espoused here clearly flies in the face of a great deal of conventional rhetoric, and seems in particular to contradict socialist, communist and (some) liberal hopes for the emergence of a universal commonwealth, a solidarity which encompasses the whole of humanity. However, it needs to be asked whether the values articulated by such aspirations might not find expression in different forms, and, indeed, a refusal to think in universalist terms opens up the possibilities of a pluralistic conception of world order, an openness to the recognition and acceptance of difference, which may actually signal a more practical and less ethnocentric understanding of human solidarity than conventional radicalism has to offer – such, at least, is the promise of late modernist thinkers such as Connolly (1991).

It is here that the notion of international society becomes important, because it is plausible to suggest that many of the positive features that a putative world community might provide could be found within the scope of an association of communities founded on the rule of law but not united in any global project – international society as a practical association, in the terminology of Nardin (1983). Such an association could be based on the recognition of a general duty to relieve suffering by mutual aid and assistance and, thus, would mandate substantial redistributions of income and wealth, but the basic premise would be that the pursuit of social justice and a deeper sense of community is something that makes more sense locally than on a global scale – that the most important 'spheres of justice' are those which are internal to particular societies rather than cross-cultural in aspiration (Walzer 1983). The goal would be an association of socially just communities which was, itself, constructed on socially just lines. In so far as this notion involves the setting of standards that can serve as goals of political change in a non-ideal world it is as much a product of 'ideal theory' (Beitz 1979: 156) as the notion of a world community with its own substantive ends – but the ideal of a plurality of morally autonomous, just communities relating to one another in a framework of peace and law seems rather more appropriate to today's world than does its alternative.

References

Beitz, C. R. (1979) *Political Theory and International Relations*. Princeton: Princeton University Press.

Beitz, C. R. (1983) Cosmopolitan ideals and national sentiment. *Journal of Philosophy* 80: 591–600.

Charvet, J. (1981) *A Critique of Freedom and Equality*: Cambridge: Cambridge University Press.

Connolly, W. E. (1991) *Identity/Difference: Democratic Negotiations of Political Paradox*. Ithaca: Cornell University Press.

Frost, M. (1986) *Towards a Normative Theory of International Relations*. Cambridge: Cambridge University Press.

Hayek, F. A. (1960) *The Constitution of Liberty*. London: Routledge and Kegan Paul.

Hegel, G. W. F. (1991) *Elements of the Philosophy of Right* (first published 1821), trans. H. B. Nisbet, ed. A. Wood. Cambridge: Cambridge University Press.

Löwith, K. (1949) *Meaning in History*. Chicago: University of Chicago Press.

Lyotard, J.-F. (1986) *The Postmodern Condition: A Report on Knowledge*, trans. G. Bennington and B. Massumi. Manchester: Manchester University Press.

Moynihan, D. P. (1993) *Pandemonium: Ethnicity in International Politics*. New York: Oxford University Press.

Nagel, T. (1986) *The View from Nowhere*. New York: Oxford University Press.

Nardin, T. (1983) *Law, Morality and the Relations of States*. Princeton: Princeton University Press.

Pogge, T. (1989) *Realizing Rawls*. Ithaca: Cornell University Press.

Rawls, J. (1971) *A Theory of Justice*. Oxford: Oxford University Press.

Rorty, R. (1989) *Contingency, Irony and Solidarity*. Cambridge: Cambridge University Press.

Sandel, M. (1982) *Liberalism and the Limits of Justice*. Cambridge: Cambridge University Press.

Singer, P. (1981) *The Expanding Circle: Ethics and Sociobiology*. Oxford: Clarendon Press.

Singer, P. (1985) Famine, affluence and morality. In C. R. Beitz et al. (eds), *International Ethics*, Princeton: Princeton University Press.

Todorov, T. (1987) *The Conquest of America*, trans. R. Howard. New York: Harper Torchbooks.

Tönnies, F. (1963) *Community and Association*, trans. C. P. Loomis. New York: Harper and Row.

Tully, J. (ed.) (1988) *Meaning and Context: Quentin Skinner and his Critics*. Cambridge: Polity Press.

Walzer, M. (1983) *Spheres of Justice: A Defence of Pluralism and Equality*. Oxford: Martin Robertson.

Williams, R. (1976) *Keywords: A Vocabulary of Culture and Society*. Glasgow: Fontana.

Zalewski, M. (1993) Feminist theory and international relations. In M. Bowker and R. Brown (eds), *From Cold War to Collapse: Theory and World Politics in the 1980s*, Cambridge: Cambridge University Press.

43

Beyond the States System?

Hedley Bull

If an alternative form of universal political order were to emerge that did not merely constitute a change from one phase or condition of the states system to another, but led beyond the states system, it would have to involve the demise of one or another of the latter's essential attributes: sovereign states, interaction among them, such that they form a system; and a degree of acceptance of common rules and institutions, in respect of which they form a society.

A System But Not a Society

It is conceivable that a form of universal political organisation might arise which would possess the first and the second of these attributes but not the third. We may imagine, that is to say, that there might exist a plurality of sovereign states, forming a system, which did not, however, constitute an international society. Such a state of affairs would represent the demise of *the* states system, which, it has been argued here, is an international society as well as an international system. There would be states, and interaction among them on a global basis, but the element of acceptance of common interests or values, and, on the basis of them, of common rules and institutions, would have disappeared. There would be communications and negotiations among these states, but no commitment to a network of diplomatic institutions; agreements, but no acceptance of a structure of international legal obligation; violent encounters among them that were limited by the capacity of the belligerents to make war, but not by their will to observe restraints as to when, how and by whom it was conducted; balances of power that arose fortuitously, but not balances that were the product of conscious attempts to preserve them; powers that were greater than others, but no agreed conception of a great power in the sense of a power with special rights and duties.

Whether or not the states system, at some point in the future, has ceased to be an international society, it might well be difficult to determine. There may be acceptance of common rules and institutions by some states, but not by others: how many states have to have contracted out of international society before we can say that it has ceased to exist? Some rules and institutions may continue to find acceptance, but others not: which rules and institutions are essential? Acceptance of rules and institutions may be difficult to determine: does it lie in verbal assent to these rules, in behaviour that conforms strictly to them, or in willingness to defer to them even while evading them? Granted these difficulties [...] there is ample historical precedent for an international system that is not an international society [...].

An international system that is not an international society might nevertheless contain some elements of order. Particular states might be able to achieve a degree of domestic order, despite the absence of rules and institutions in their relations with one another. Some degree of international order might also be sustained by fortuitous balances of power or relationships of mutual nuclear deterrence, by great power spheres of preponderance unilaterally imposed, by limitations in war that were the consequence of self-restraint or limitations of capacity. But an international system of this kind would be disorderly in the extreme, and would in fact exemplify the Hobbesian state of nature.

States But Not a System

It is also conceivable that a form of universal political organisation might emerge which possessed the first of the essential attributes that have been mentioned but not the second. We may imagine that there are still sovereign states, but that they are not in contact or interaction with each other, or at all events do not interact sufficiently to cause them to behave as component parts of a system. States might be linked with each other so as to form systems of states in particular regions, but there would not be any global system of states. Throughout the world as a whole there might be mutual awareness among states, and even contact and interaction on a limited scale, but it would no longer be the case that states in all parts of the world were a vital factor in one another's calculations.

It might be difficult to determine how much decline in the global interaction of states would have to have taken place before we could say that they had ceased to form a system. If there is a high degree of interaction throughout the world at the economic and social levels, but not at the strategic level, can we say that there is a global system? Does a global states system cease to exist merely because there are some societies that are excluded from it? Even today in the jungles of Brazil or in the highlands of Papua/New Guinea there are societies scarcely touched by what we nevertheless call the global states system.

Once again, there is ample historical precedent for an alternative to the states system of this kind; [. . .] it was not before the nineteenth century that there arose any states system that was global in dimension. Does such an alternative represent a superior path to world order?

It has often been maintained that it does. A series of isolated or semi-isolated states or other kinds of community might each achieve a tolerable form of social order within its own confines, and a form of world order would exist that was simply the sum of the order that derived from each of these communities. At the same time the classic sources of disorder that arise in a situation of interaction between states would be avoided because interaction itself would be avoided or kept to a minimum.

This was the substance of Rousseau's vision of a world of small self-sufficient states, each achieving order within its own confines through the operation of the general will of its community, and achieving order in their relations with one another by minimising contact.[1] It also entered into the prescription that Washington laid down for the United States in his Farewell Address: 'The great rule of conduct for us in regard to foreign relations is, in extending our commercial relations, to have with them as little *political* connection as possible.'[2] This for Washington was a maxim only for the United States, which was in a position of actual physical isolation from the powers that might threaten her. Cobden later transformed it into a general prescription for all states in his dictum: 'As little intercourse as possible betwixt the governments, as much connection as possible between the nations of the world.'[3]

Cobden believed in non-intervention in the most rigid and absolute sense. He opposed intervention in international conflicts as well as civil ones; for ideological causes (such as liberalism and nationalism on the European continent) of which he approved, as well as for causes of which he disapproved (such as the interventionism of the Holy Alliance); and for reasons of national interest such as the preservation of the balance of power or the protection of commerce. He rejected the distinctions John Stuart Mill drew between intervention in the affairs of civilised countries and intervention in a barbarian country, and between intervention as such and intervention to uphold the principle of non-intervention against a power that had violated it.[4] He even opposed the attempt to influence the affairs of another country by moral suasion, and declined to sanction the formation of any organisation in England for the purpose of interfering in another country, such as the organisations formed to agitate against slavery in the United States. However, in Cobden's vision the promotion of the maximum systematic inter-action at the economic and social levels was just as important as the promotion of minimum interaction at the strategic and political levels. Assuming as he did the desir-ability of universal pursuit by governments of *laissez-faire* policies in relation to the eco-nomy, he was able to imagine that the strategic and political isolation of states from one another might coexist with their economic interdependence.[5]

A form of universal political organisation based on the absolute or relative isolation of communities from one another, supposing it to be a possible development, would have certain drawbacks. If systematic interaction among states has in the past involved certain costs (international disorder, the subjection of the weak to the strong, the exploita-tion by the rich of the poor), so also has it brought certain gains (assistance to the weak and the poor by the strong and the rich, the international division of labour, the intel-lectual enrichment of countries by each other). The prescription of universal isolationism, even in the limited form Cobden gave it of political and strategic non-interventionism, implies that the opportunities arising from human interaction on a global scale will be lost, as well as that the dangers to which it gives rise will be avoided.

World Government

It is conceivable also that a form of universal political organisation might arise lacking the first of the above essential attributes, namely sovereign states. One way in which this might occur is through the emergence of a world government.

We may imagine that a world government would come about by conquest, as the result of what John Strachey has called a 'knock-out tournament' among the great powers, and in this case it would be a universal empire based upon the domination of the conquering power;[6] or we may imagine that it would arise as the consequence of a social contract among states, and thus that it would be a universal republic or cosmopolis founded upon some form of consent or consensus. In the latter case it may be ima-gined that a world government would arise suddenly, perhaps as the result of a crash programme induced by some catastrophe such as global war or ecological breakdown (as envisaged by a succession of futurologists from Kant to Herman Kahn), or it may be thought of as arising gradually, perhaps through accretion of the powers of the United

Nations. It may be seen as coming about as the result of a direct, frontal assault on the political task of bringing states to agree to relinquish their sovereignty, or, as on some 'functionalist' theories, it may be seen as the indirect result of inroads made on the sovereignty of states in non-political areas.

There has never been a government of the world, but there has often been a government supreme over much of what for those subjected to it was the known world. Throughout the history of the modern states system there has been an undercurrent of awareness of the alternative of a universal government, and of argument on behalf of it: either in the form of the backward-looking doctrine calling for a return to Roman unity, or in the form of a forward-looking doctrine that sees a world state as the consequence of inevitable progress. In the twentieth century there has been a revival of world government doctrine in response to the two World Wars.

The classical argument for world government is that order among states is best established by the same means whereby it is established among individual men within the state, that is by a supreme authority. This argument most commonly relates to the goal of minimum order, and especially the avoidance of war, which is said to be an inevitable consequence of the states system. But it is also sometimes advanced in relation to goals of optimum order; it is often argued today, for example, that a world government could best achieve the goal of economic justice for all individual men, or the goal of sound management of the human environment.

The classical argument against world government has been that, while it may achieve order, it is destructive of liberty or freedom: it infringes the liberties of states and nations (as argued by the ideologists of the successful grand alliances that fought against universal monarchy); and also checks the liberties of individuals who, if the world government is tyrannical, cannot seek political asylum under an alternative government.

The case for world government may thus appear to rest on an assumed priority of order over international or human justice or liberty. It may be argued, however, that the states system affords a better prospect than world government of achieving the goal of order also [. . .].

A New Mediaevalism

It is also conceivable that sovereign states might disappear and be replaced not by a world government but by a modern and secular equivalent of the kind of universal political organisation that existed in Western Christendom in the Middle Ages. In that system no ruler or state was sovereign in the sense of being supreme over a given territory and a given segment of the Christian population; each had to share authority with vassals beneath, and with the Pope and (in Germany and Italy) the Holy Roman Emperor above. The universal political order of Western Christendom represents an alternative to the system of states which does not yet embody universal government.

All authority in mediaeval Christendom was thought to derive ultimately from God and the political system was basically theocratic. It might therefore seem fanciful to contemplate a return to the mediaeval model, but it is not fanciful to imagine that there might develop a modern and secular counterpart of it that embodies its central characteristic: a system of overlapping authority and multiple loyalty.

It is familiar that sovereign states today share the stage of world politics with 'other actors' just as in mediaeval times the state had to share the stage with 'other associations' (to use the mediaevalists' phrase). If modern states were to come to share their authority over their citizens, and their ability to command their loyalties, on the one hand with regional and world authorities, and on the other hand with sub-state or sub-national authorities, to such an extent that the concept of sovereignty ceased to be applicable, then a neo-mediaeval form of universal political order might be said to have emerged.

We might imagine, for example, that the government of the United Kingdom had to share its authority on the one hand with authorities in Scotland, Wales, Wessex and elsewhere, and on the other hand with a European authority in Brussels and world authorities in New York and Geneva, to such an extent that the notion of its supremacy over the territory and people of the United Kingdom had no force. We might imagine that the authorities in Scotland and Wales, as well as those in Brussels, New York and Geneva, enjoyed standing as actors in world politics, recognised as having rights and duties in world law, conducting negotiations and perhaps able to command armed forces. We might imagine that the political loyalties of the inhabitants of, say, Glasgow, were so uncertain as between the authorities in Edinburgh, London, Brussels and New York that the government of the United Kingdom could not be assumed to enjoy any kind of primacy over the others, such as it possesses now. If such a state of affairs prevailed all over the globe, this is what we may call, for want of a better term, a neo-mediaeval order.

The case for regarding this form of universal political organisation as representing a superior path to world order to that embodied in the states system would be that it promises to avoid the classic dangers of the system of sovereign states by a structure of overlapping authorities and criss-crossing loyalties that hold all peoples together in a universal society, while at the same time avoiding the concentration of power inherent in a world government. The case for doubting whether the neo-mediaeval model is superior is that there is no assurance that it would prove more orderly than the states system, rather than less. It is conceivable that a universal society of this kind might be constructed that would provide a firm basis for the realisation of elementary goals of social life. But if it were anything like the precedent of Western Christendom, it would contain more ubiquitous and continuous violence and insecurity than does the modern states system.

Non-historical Alternatives

We must finally note the possibility that an alternative will develop to the states system which, unlike the four that have just been considered, does not conform to any previous pattern of universal political organisation.

Of course, any future form of universal political organisation will be different from previous historical experience, in the sense that it will have certain features that are unique and will not exactly resemble any previous system. My point is not this trivial one but the more serious one that a universal political system may develop which does not resemble any of the four historically derived alternatives even in broad comparison. The basic terms in which we now consider the question of universal political organisation could be altered decisively by the progress of technology, or equally by its decay or retrogression, by revolutions in moral and political, or in scientific and philosophical ideas, or by military or economic or ecological catastrophes, foreseeable and unforeseeable.

I do not propose to speculate as to what these non-historical alternatives might be. It is clearly not possible to confine the varieties of possible future forms within any finite list of possible political systems, and for this reason one cannot take seriously attempts to spell out the laws of transformation of one kind of universal political system to another. It is not possible, by definition, to foresee political forms that are not foreseeable, and attempts to define non-historical political forms are found in fact to depend upon appeals to historical experience. But our view of possible alternatives to the states system should take into account the limitations of our own imagination and our own inability to transcend past experience.

Notes

1 See 'Rousseau on war and peace', in Stanley Hoffman, *The State of War: Essays in the Theory and Practice of International Politics* (London: Pall Mall Press, 1965).
2 This is quoted by Richard Cobden at the beginning of 'England, Ireland and America': see *The Political Writings of Richard Cobden* (London: Cassell, 1886), p. 3.
3 Ibid, p. 216.
4 John Stuart Mill, 'A few words on non-intervention', in *Dissertations and Discussions*, vol. 3 (London: Longmans, Green, 1867).
5 See, especially, Cobden, 'England, Ireland and America' and 'Russia, 1836', in *Political Writings*.
6 John Strachey, *On the Prevention of War* (London: Macmillan, 1962).

Index

Abuja summit 160–1
Acheson, Dean 110
aesthetics of place 82, 89–90
Africa 121n15, 135n15, 162, 165–6n6,
  168, 267, 342, 359, 362, 363, 375, 379,
  438
Ahmed, Akbar 199, 200
aid 438, 439
Alesina, Alberto 305
Allison, H. 370
American Convention on Human Rights
  168
Amnesty International 18, 439, 454, 456
anarchy: Hobbesian 110–11, 112; institutional
  change 117; international relations 121n26,
  148; nation-states 128; neorealists 115;
  predation 119; regions 158; world politics
  184
Anderson, Benedict 231, 246n2
Appadurai, Arjun 192
Arab states 133
arbitrage 303, 308
Arendt, Hannah 66n6
Argentina 65n3
Aristotle 413
arms trade 346
Ashworth, G. 370
Asia, East 3, 12, 20, 22, 23–4, 28, 30, 141–2,
  150, 262, 266–7, 342, 344, 359, 364, 394,
  424, 427, 441
asset prices 280–1
asylum seekers 275
autarchy 110
authority 117, 126, 148, 185–6, 465; see also
  legitimacy of state; sovereignty
automobile industry 266, 437
autonomy 285n1, 353n9; compromised 64,
  124, 125, 129–31; democracy 414;
  macroeconomics 301; nation-state 11, 132,
  285, 313–14; sovereignty 115; Westphalian
  model 127

Back, Les 199
Balkans 132, 133
Bamako Convention 379
Bank of England 62
banking: electronic 82; EU 177; interest rates
  280; legislation 177; multinational 25, 294;
  North/South 380; see also finance
Basinger, S. 312
Basle accord 127, 134n6, 379, 380
Basque nationalism 200
Beitz, C. R. 455, 459, 460
Belgium 85, 279, 309
Bell, Daniel 458
belle époque 4–5, 19, 20, 22, 23, 24, 71
beneficence 447–8
Benetton 198–9
Berlin Treaty 132
Bernstein, Lisa 176
Bertelsmann group 208, 217, 218, 220
Beyer, Peter 200
bilateralism 117
Billen, Andrew 197
biodiversity 384
biological weapons 145–6
BIS 283, 393
Bodin, Jean 113
bonds 283–4, 328, 330
book publishing 217
boundaries: cross-border issues 172–3, 177–8,
  179n14, 282–3; permeable 251; TNCs 249;
  transborder flows 12, 126, 127, 423–4;
  transcended 17–18, 24, 38
Boyer, R. 86
Braudel, Fernand 6, 259
Breton identity 200
Bretton Woods 22, 70–1, 86, 274, 292, 293,
  304, 305, 315n17, 428, 432
Bright, John 409
Britain 10, 16, 50–1, 70, 102, 114, 163, 196,
  199, 279, 438
Brown, Chris 404, 416

Brundtland Report 385
Bull, Hedley 113–14, 404
bureaucracy 51, 149
Burke, Edmund 444
Burnheim, J. 411–12
Bush, George 109, 163
Buzan, Barry 164

cable services 195, 209
Cambodia 439
capital: controls 293, 294; exports 277; flight 303, 312–13, 357; flows 19, 293; footloose 19, 20–1, 72; global integration 259; global markets 78–9, 328–9; high-technology firms 78; international 291–2; labour 79; mobility 13, 69, 250, 256, 281, 301, 307–9, 311, 312, 319, 325; national markets 292; private 320; taxation 309–10, 311, 312, 314
Capital Group Companies 223
capitalism 1, 5, 20, 62; disorganized 74, 231, 236; global 20, 25, 136, 137, 139; implosion 357–8; networks 76–7, 137; post-industrial 25; power 94; space 89–90; threats 139–43, 146; trilateral 139
car ownership 383
Castells, Manuel 249, 250, 256, 339
Castles, S. 275
Catholic Church 125, 126, 134n1, 137
CENTO 157
Cerny, Philip G. 123n41
Chechnya 439
chemical weapons 145–6
Chicago school of economics 305
child labour 324, 349, 428
China 49, 78, 212–13, 266, 267, 356
Christendom 454, 465
CIS 133, 161, 342
citizenship: commonsense 148; cosmopolitan 425–9; EU 167–8, 415; multiple 426; national 414; power 32; rights/obligations 167
civil society 11; global 144; international 438; regional 158; transnational 26, 136; universal 413
class differences 89, 225, 278, 333, 335
Clausewitz, K. M. von 96, 98n6
Clinton, Bill 330
clustering 256–7
Cobden, Richard 409, 464
coercion 125–6, 130–1, 133, 448–9, 452n10
Cohen, Stephen 261
Cold War 11, 25, 109–10, 163, 185, 341–2

colonialism 9, 114, 274, 279, 364–5, 442
Commission on Global Governance 408–9, 410, 436, 438, 439, 441
commodity production 83, 325, 342
common heritage of mankind 170, 456
common identity 453, 454, 455, 458
communications 14, 58, 151–2, 191, 256, 319, 320, 326; capital mobility 256; elites 233; globalization 202–7; Internet 17; media 14; private capital 320; technological innovations 151–2, 191, 202, 260, 319, 326; unevenness 208–9
communications and information technology 15–16, 71, 97, 281, 421
communism 361–2
communitarianism 31–2, 410–13, 445, 459
community 84, 425, 453; ethnicity 14; global 404; imagined 14, 32, 230, 235–6, 240, 246n2; and institutions 32; limits 457–60; as metanarrative 458; national 32, 35, 404; political 14, 32, 35–6, 415; working-class 89; world 453, 454, 457, 459, 460
community of fate: nation-state 31, 32, 33, 423; overlapping 33, 423–6, 424, 426, 429
comparative advantages 140, 362, 365
competitiveness 21, 25, 263–4, 328
conflict: interdependence 116, 410; local/global 96; political 345–6; WTO 324; zones 118–19
conglomerates: financial 284; media 208–9, 214n12, 220, 222–3
Connolly, W. E. 417, 460
constitutionalism 112–15
consumption 53n6, 83, 142–3
contracts 125–6, 130, 133, 134n5
control mechanisms 133, 135n10, 181–2, 184, 186–8
conventions 125–6, 129, 133, 173
cooperation 158, 159–60, 409
core–periphery 20, 30–1, 355–6, 357–8
corporations 17, 53n4, 78, 261–2; see also MNCs; TNCs
corporatism 86
corruption 186, 441n5
cosmopolitanism 401–2, 407, 413–16, 425–9
Crawford, J. 415
credit: insurance 428; rationing 295
crime 186, 345
cross-border issues 172–3, 177–8, 179n14, 282–3
Cuba 362
cultural flows 18, 197, 231–4

cultural identity 100
cultural imperialisms 239–40
cultural politics 235–6, 243–5
culture: conflicts 196–7; contamination 197,
    212; difference 16, 237; entertainment 225;
    food 88; globalization 16–18, 191–3, 200,
    237, 239–40, 241–2, 245–6; homogenization/
    heterogenization 192, 198, 230, 237; identity
    198, 241; imports/exports 17; indigenized
    230; indigenous 62, 230; insecurity 345;
    local 13–14, 16; national 14–16, 192–3,
    240–1; technology 240; third cultures
    175–7, 196
currencies 87, 259, 280, 292, 308, 320–1, 427;
    see also exchange rates
Czechoslovakia 128

Dayton agreement 435
debt: Asia 364; developing economies 363;
    Latin America 309, 380; markets 390;
    Third World 294, 356–7; US 86
deception 448–9, 452n10
decolonization 9, 10, 139
deindustrialization 21, 97
demarchy 410–13, 417
democracy 429–30; accountability 409, 429;
    autonomy 414; Enlightenment world-view
    233; global 405, 407–17; as ideoscape
    233–4; nation-state 416; normative theory
    402, 407–8; transformed 406, 423–5, 426,
    429–30; types 403, 405, 412–16; see also
    liberal democracy
dependency theory 363, 364
deregulation 219–20, 224–5, 426
de-skilling 82
deterritorialization 234–6
developing economies: capital controls 293,
    294; comparative advantages 362; credit
    rationing 295; debt 363; environmental
    issues 380; exports 24, 290–1, 362–3, 380;
    FDI 24, 296; living standards 362–3;
    Montreal Protocol 118; trade 289–90;
    see also Third World
development 365, 382–3, 456
Dezalay, Yves 174
Dicken, Peter 249, 250
difference 16, 85, 237
disaggregation 183–4
Disney 217, 218, 220, 221–2
distance: social 80–1; symbolic 212–13
distributive justice 403–4, 442, 443–4, 451
domination 61, 65–6n3

Dryzek, J. S. 411
duties 32, 36; see also obligations

EAEC 159, 161
Earth Summit 170, 382
EC 115, 116
ecological dangers 103
economic blocs: see trading blocs
economic crisis: cosmopolitanism 427–8; East
    Asia 3, 22, 23–4, 30, 342, 344, 394
economic nationalism 436–8
economy: globalized 18–19, 68, 71–4, 99,
    185–6, 249; inter-national 70–1, 74–5;
    internationalized 20, 30, 68, 69–71, 250,
    251, 285, 292; openness 333–4; policies
    160, 264; politicized 321, 331, 334; power
    249; security 344; TNCs 94–5; women's
    contribution 371; world 22–3, 94; see also
    global economy; national economies
ECOSOC 431
ECOWAS 165–6n6
education 14, 222, 346
egalitarian theory 329
Eichengreen, B. 279
elites 14–15, 233, 240
EMI 218
employment: bond markets 330; global
    labour market 343; globalization 323, 358;
    relocation 29; security of 344
energy policies 384
English language 3, 17, 220, 346, 440
Enlightenment world-view 233, 237, 405, 409,
    456
entrepreneurs 78
environmental issues: developing economies
    380; globality 374, 381, 383–5, 411; impact
    variations 381–2, 385; insecurity 103, 345;
    North/South gap 377–8, 382–3; policies
    385; pressures 143–4; protection 377–8,
    381, 428, 431; World Bank 391
environmentalism 143–4, 374, 456
ethics: global 29, 33–6, 409, 439; universalism
    341
Ethiopia 121n15, 438
ethnicity 14–15, 88, 144–5, 149–50
ethno-history 242–3, 244
ethnoscapes 231, 236
EU: banking 177; citizenship 167–8, 415;
    ERM 295; governance 34, 142, 426; Hague
    Conventions 173; hazardous waste 379;
    Intergovernmental Conference 436;
    Maastricht Treaty 115, 168, 324, 427;

media deregulation 219; monetary union
307–8; pensions 324; post-militarism
145–6; production chains 255;
protectionism 437; racism 372; regionalism
12, 22, 159; regionalization 12, 160–1;
social market 156; trade 20, 72, 262, 437;
see also triadization
Europe: expansion 50, 52, 61–2; modern
states 8–10; *see also* EU
Europe, Eastern 117, 127, 132, 292, 342
European Convention for the Protection of
Human Rights and Fundamental Freedoms
167–8, 169
European Court of Human Rights 168
European Court of Justice 174
exchange rates: current/forward 293; ERM
295; financial integration 305–6; fixed 294,
306, 308–9; floating 86–7, 292, 308, 309;
macroeconomics 305; pegged 313–14;
see also Bretton Woods; foreign exchange
markets
exploitation 345, 349, 353n5
exports 24, 277, 290–1, 362–3, 380

Falk, Richard 162, 409
family 64, 84, 182
FDI: capital taxes 312; China 356;
colonialism 274; developing economies 24,
296; distribution 69, 296–7, 356; growth
310, 319–20; MNCs 296–7, 306–7, 356;
TNCs 73
Feldstein, Marty 394
feminism 137, 144, 370, 456
Fieldhouse, D. K. 339
film industry 217, 218–19, 235; *see also*
media
finance: conglomerates 284; cross-border
282–3; globalization 259; international 252,
291–6, 390, 393–5; multinational banks 25;
national 282, 295, 298; technological
innovation 82, 152–3, 283–4
financial integration 307–8; exchange rates
305–6; Gold Standard 281, 284–5; left-
wing politics 312; openness 277, 279–83,
310; public spending 312
financial markets: arbitrage 303; Eastern
Europe 292; global 13, 34, 97, 295, 427–8;
Gold Standard 294; hyper-globalization
school 292; sceptics 292; state intervention
309; technology 390
finanscapes 231, 232, 236
fiscal policy 309; *see also* taxation

flexibility: accumulation 82, 85; workforce 83,
367
flows: capital 3, 19; cultural 18, 197, 231–4;
globalization 55; information 322;
population 3, 64, 195–6; resources 35–6;
space of 256; technology 231–2; trade 3;
transborder 12, 126, 127, 423–4; *see also*
mobility
food market 88, 195, 222
Ford Foundation 436, 441
Fordism 82
foreign exchange markets 23, 291–2, 320
Fortress Europe 159, 161, 389
Forum of Civil Society 408
France 10, 50–1, 197, 279
Frankel, J. A. 279
free trade: blocs 72, 157, 279; challenged 165;
liberalism 303; as risk 334; US 336
Frick, Klaus 176–7
Friends of the Earth 18, 374
fundamentalism 200, 234, 359
futures markets 83

G-3 countries 69
G-5 countries 282
G-7 countries 26, 30, 265–6
Gandhi, Mahatma 345
Garrett, Geoffrey 250, 312
Garth, Bryant 174
Gates, Bill 20
GATT 116–17, 142, 197, 262, 290, 324, 392–3,
398n42; *see also* WTO
GDP: country comparisons 351; Gold
Standard 289–90; public spending 310, 321;
trade 276–7, 289–90
gender: global governance 431; inequalities
367, 368, 371, 372; Internet use 346; labour
costs 79, 367–8; Marxism 456; poverty
370; religion 456; UN agencies 369
gender and development approach 370
genetically modified food 38
geo-economy 253–4, 257
geopolitics 1, 138; hard 136, 137–8, 145,
146; power blocs 157; power shifts 10;
soft 144, 146; time–space compression
82, 90
George, Susan 381
Gereffi, G. 255, 260–1
Germany 24, 112, 121n14, 145, 336, 379–80
Gessner, Volkmar 107–8
global culture 192–3, 239–40, 241–2, 245–6
global democracy 405, 407–18

global economy 23–7; asymmetries 265; capitalism 25; competitiveness 263–4; globalists 24, 249; informational 259, 268; national autonomy 313–14; openness 423; regional differentiation 262–3; regulation 140; restructuring 366–7; sceptics 249

global governance 181; command systems 181–2; control mechanisms 184, 186–7; corruption 441n5; demarchy 410–13, 417; democratization 407; dynamics 183–4, 403, 409, 431–2; gender 431; and globalization 341–2; hegemony 432–3; heterarchy 417; human development 346–7; interdependence 182–3; NGOs 431; obligations 443; polyarchy 417; sovereignty 391; UN 181; welfare 441; women 431

global–local tensions 257

global markets: capital 78–9; commodities 342; disintegration 72; and domestic 260; financial 13, 34, 97, 295, 427–8; globalists 28–9; Gold Standard 325; hyper-globalization school 287; national politics 301, 302–3; regulations 26, 428; sceptics 249, 298

global media 195, 219, 220–1, 224–5

global networks 137–8, 146

global products 195

global village 84, 195, 198

global warming 382, 385

globalism 100–1, 139, 142, 143

globalists 2; global economy 24, 249; global inequality 339; globalization 6–8, 16–18, 33–6, 37, 38; nation-state 27, 107; neoliberal 28–9; political community 35–6; political good 401; political power 105–6; social democracy 29

globality 100; environmental issues 374, 381, 383–5, 411; irreversible 101–2; labour markets 259; local organization 64

globalization 2, 3–4, 52–3, 95, 101–2, 341; capitalism 20, 25, 136, 137, 139; communications 202–7; culture 16–18, 191–3, 200, 237, 239–40, 241–2, 245–6; economic 18–19, 68, 71–4, 99, 185–6, 249; employment 323, 358; ethics of care 29, 33–6; financial sector 259; globalists 6–8, 16–18, 33–6, 37, 38; history of 1, 49, 51–2, 56–9; impacts 57–8; industrial development 96–7; international relations 93–4, 109, 366; internationalization 55, 253; liberal democracy 413; limits 55–6, 102, 261–2, 302–3; localization 92, 186; media 192,

210–11, 216–19; nation-state 8, 34, 92–3, 106, 137; politics 401; regulation 420; religion 6–7, 49–50; sceptics 4–5, 37–8, 68–9, 191–2, 287–8; taxation 305–6, 328–9; technological capability 290–1; tensions 323–5; threat 332, 344; trade 51; unevenness 4, 28, 93, 198; welfare state 27, 250, 332–4; winners/losers 29, 35, 52, 77, 100, 119–20, 332, 342, 389

GNP 277, 358

Goetz, A. M. 370–1

Gold, Joseph 396

Gold Standard 70, 277, 279, 280, 281, 282, 284–5, 289–90, 294, 325

Goldblatt, David 250

Gould, Stephen 348

governance: EU 34, 142, 426; IMF 394; international 38, 285; world economy 21–2; see also global governance

Gowa, Joanne 109

Gramsci, Antonio 163

Grassman, S. 277

Gray, John 250

Greenpeace 18, 143

guest workers 196, 234, 275

Guinea 362, 375

Guinea-Bissau 362

Gulf War 195

Habermas, Jürgen 103n3

Hague Conventions 173

Hallerberg, M. 312

Halliday, Fred 403

Harris, Nigel 267

Havas, Charles 205

Hayek, F. A. 458

hazardous waste 375, 379

health 141, 344

Hegel, G. W. F. 459

Held, David 107, 250, 402–3, 413–14

Helsinki accords 127, 134n8, 166n7

Helsinki Conference on Security and Cooperation in Europe (CSCE) 169

Herman, Edward 192

Herz, John 112

heterarchy 417

heterogenization, cultural 192, 230

Hettne, Björn 107

hierarchy 388, 392

high-technology firms 78, 265–6

Hinduism 234, 456, 457

Hirst, Paul 250, 356, 360n2

history and tradition 89
HIV/AIDS 344
Hobbes, Thomas 32, 106, 110, 111–12
Hobbes's dilemma 112–15, 118, 119, 120
Hobsbawm, Eric 66n5
home-workers 367
homogeneity 86, 159, 237
homogenization: culture 192, 198, 230;
    economic policies 160
Hoogvelt, Ankie 339
housework 151–2
human capital 301–2, 334
human development 346–7
human needs 443–4, 448
human rights 168, 345, 401, 421, 443–5, 454;
    accords 129, 167; groups 456
humanitarianism 167, 439
hybridization 196, 199
hyper-globalization school 287, 290, 291, 292,
    296

identity 454–5; caste 456, 457; common 453,
    454, 455, 458; culture 198, 241; global 376;
    local 89; moral 456; multilayered 35–6;
    national 14–15, 16–17, 18, 65n3, 140;
    personal/collective 89, 241; place 89;
    political 33; religion 200; socio-cultural 32
identity politics 136, 144–5
ideoscapes 231, 232–3, 236–7
IGOs 11, 144, 422, 431
imagined community 14, 32, 230, 235–6, 240,
    246n2
imagined worlds 231, 233
IMF: capital flight 357; conditionality 125;
    credit monopoly 160, 380; East Asia 394;
    governance 393, 394; media 219–20;
    production chains 255; Russia 394;
    structural adjustment programmes 29, 30;
    voting power 393, 395–6
immigration: class differences 278; food
    market 88; labour market 259, 325, 437–8;
    nationalism 440; restrictions 326
imperialism 5, 30, 62, 278–9
import substitution 364
income inequality 268, 351–2, 358, 360n8,
    367, 368, 391
income per capita 342, 351, 358
independence, postcolonial 15
India 49, 225, 235, 267, 363–4, 456, 457
indigenous culture 62, 230
individual rights/obligations 167, 432, 459
individualization of work 77, 79–80, 348, 349

industrialization 96–7, 267, 376–7, 406
industry and location 377–8
inequality 348; global 27–8, 339;
    international order 387–9; intra-country
    351–2; migration opportunities 278–9;
    sceptics 30–1, 339; social conflict 305;
    social stability 301–2; see also income
    inequality
inflation 308
informal sector 235, 344
information technology 209, 322; access 321;
    capitalism 77–8, 320, 350; financial 315n24;
    networks 16, 76, 319; polarization 346;
    research 319
informational economy 259, 263, 268
informationalism 268, 348
INGOs 11
institutionalism: Hobbes's dilemma 112–15,
    118, 120; neoliberal 127, 128; neorealism
    388; new 189n3
institutionalization 58–9, 187, 188, 335
institutions: anarchy 117; domestic/
    geopolitical 136; global governance 35–6,
    172–8; Gold Standard 290; international
    114, 396; multilateral 26; nation-states 15;
    political community 32
integration: economic 252–3; global 3, 62,
    259; market 309–12; NAFTA 72, 159, 389,
    436; openness 277, 279–83, 310; perverse
    350; see also financial integration
intellectual property rights 389
intelligentsia 244, 245; see also elites
interaction 3, 58, 59, 137–8, 146
interconnectedness: East Asia 424; economic
    38; global 3; impact propensity 56–7;
    intensification 54; interdependence 202;
    military hardware 421; political 12; social
    movements 18
interdependence 409; accelerating 3, 54–5,
    60n1; asymmetrical 268, 339; autonomy
    285n1; complex 106, 111, 117; conflict 116,
    410; currencies 259; disintegration 72;
    global governance 182–3; interconnectedness
    202; international 5; laissez-faire policies
    464; OECD states 20, 118; problems
    134n10; technology/information 78;
    triadization 24; world system theory 1
interest rates 280, 292–3, 307–8
intergovernmental organizations 11, 144, 422,
    431
International Covenant on Civil and Political
Rights 169

international law 107, 168, 170–1, 173–4, 175, 426–7
inter-national networks 137–8
international order 387–9, 405
international relations: anarchy 121n26, 148; Cold War 109; English school 113, 128; globalization 93–4, 109, 366; nation-states 10, 70, 93; neorealism 148–9, 388; Westphalian model 127–9
international society 148, 462–3
International Telecommunication Union 207
international trade: Asia-Pacific 277; GATT 116–17, 290, 392–3; history of 274–5, 288–9; intensity 289–90; manufacturing 290–1; technological innovations 319; triad 265–7; unevenness 390; WTO 393
internationalization 4–5; economic 20, 30, 68, 69–71, 250, 251, 285, 292; globalization 55, 253; India 267
Internet 17, 25, 58, 319, 346, 415
investment 281, 285n2, 293, 378; see also FDI
Iran 196, 197, 212
Irwin, D. A. 279
Islam 49–50; fundamentalism 200, 234, 359; globalization 63; Hinduism 457; Western states 196, 456; women 456
isolationism 463, 464
Italy 51, 85, 279, 309

Jameson, F. 8
Japan 73, 78, 109, 141–2, 145, 265; see also triadization
Jefferson, Thomas 113
joint ventures 223
Julius, D. 73
justice: international 403–4; liberalism 444; obligations 446–7; social 456, 459; universalism 444; vulnerability 450; see also distributive justice

Kant, Immanuel 403–4, 413, 446–7, 448, 452n9
Kapstein, Ethan 302, 327n1
Katzenstein, Peter 304
Kennedy, Paul 358
Keohane, Robert O. 106
Keynes, J. M. 165, 304
'Khalistan' 234
knowledge-based growth 346
Kramer, R. C. 378
Krasner, Stephen D. 106–7, 113
Kuwait crisis 432, 433

labour: bargaining power 73–4, 342, 352; and capital 79, 261; control 85; exits 335; exploitation 349; flexible hiring 83; generic 80; global 343; globality 259; immigration 259, 325, 437–8; informational 268; left-wing politics 310, 311, 314; migration 275–6, 277–8, 303; MNCs 327n1; mobility 261, 278; production 79; see also employment; work; workers
labour costs 79, 268, 367–8
labour division: geographical 252; global 62–3, 96–7; international 70; new global 25, 26, 251–2; new international 21, 264–7, 269; world economy 332
labour movements 315n26
laissez-faire policies 464
Lando, Ole 173, 174
Lash, S. 74, 231
Latin America 28, 127, 265, 267, 309, 359–60, 380
Law of the Sea Convention 170
League of Nations 115, 167, 388, 409
left-wing politics 310, 311, 312, 314; see also socialism
legislation 174–5; authority 117; banking 177; cross-border exchanges 172–3; environment 377–8, 381; global uncertainty 178–9; third cultures 175–7
legitimacy of state 9, 14, 62, 138, 425
Leibfried, Stephan 250
leisure 196
lending 130, 283–4, 284; see also debt
Leonard, H. Jeff 378
Lewis, A. 277
Lewis, Flora 166n7
lex mercatoria 173–4, 176
liberal democracy 10, 31–2, 134n5, 405–6, 412, 413
liberal interdependence approach 126, 127
liberal internationalism 407, 408–10
liberalism 2, 112, 303, 304, 305–6, 444–5, 453; see also neoliberalism
Linklater, A. 413, 414, 415
List, Friedrich 165
living standards 348, 362–3
local networks 137–8
localization 6, 55, 73–4, 92, 186, 389
location: industry 377–8; MNCs 84, 389, 424
Locke, John 32, 113
Louvre Accord 295
Löwith, Karl 458

loyalty 455, 456, 465
Lull, James 212–13

Maastricht Treaty 115, 168, 324, 427
McChesney, Robert 192
McGrew, Anthony 250, 402
McHale, B. 89
McLuhan, Marshall 84, 93, 195
McNeill, William 50
macroeconomics: autonomy 301; exchange
    rates 305; global finance 427–8; market
    integration 309–12; nation-states 138, 141
macroregions 137, 144, 156–7
Maddison, Angus 351
Madison, James 113
Mann, Michael 107
manufacturing 265, 275, 290–1
Marcos, Imelda and Ferdinand 168–9
marginalization 29, 30–1, 342
market economy 148, 156, 166n9, 306, 328,
    341–2
market failures 305, 342
market integration 309–12
markets 152, 255; debt 390; nation-state 13,
    149, 320; national 292; politics 153–4, 306;
    power 164–5; world 100–1, 149; see also
    financial markets; global markets
Marx, Karl 21, 99, 449
Marxism 5, 30–1, 456
Massey, Doreen 197–8, 199–200
media: appropriation 211–13; commercialization
    225–6; commodification 225, 230;
    competition 223–4; conglomerates 208–9,
    214n12, 220, 222–3; cultural imports/exports
    17; deregulation 219–20; educational
    sponsorship 222; food industry 222;
    globalization 192, 210–11, 216–19; local/
    national firms 221; marketing spin-offs
    221–2; politics 80; technology 14; US 210,
    220–4, 230; WTO 220; see also global media
mediascapes 231, 232–3, 234, 236–7
MERCOSUR 436
metanarratives 458
Mexico 52, 278, 295, 381, 394
Michalowski, R. J. 378
Middleton, Neil 382
migrant workers 197, 275–6, 277–8
migration: cross-border legislation 179n14;
    from Europe 52; globalization 23; HIV/
    AIDS 344; labour 275–6, 277–8, 303;
    from Mexico 278; restrictions 437–8;
    rural–urban 352; see also immigration

Milan Chamber of Commerce 178, 180n19
military hardware 12, 141, 151, 421
military power 12, 62, 96, 145
Mill, John Stuart 464
Miller, M. J. 275
minority rights 132, 133
Mitter, S. 367
Mitterrand, François 330
MNCs 274; European 261–2; FDI 296–7,
    306–7, 356; fixed exchange rates 306;
    GATT 142; global production 23; home
    nations 19, 261–2; labour backlash 327n1;
    labour costs 367; locational advantages 84,
    389, 424; manufacturing 275; nation-states
    21; production 23, 249; scale of operations
    17, 25; sceptics 296; taxation 307;
    technological innovation 297–8, 389; and
    TNCs 72–3, 74, 75n1
mobile phones 320, 346
mobility: capital 13, 69, 250, 281, 301, 307–9,
    311, 312, 319, 325; cross-border 195;
    geographical 84–5; labour 261, 278; people
    64, 197–8; resources 64
mobilization, vernacular 243–5
modernity 1, 92, 100–1, 103n3
money 79, 86–7; see also finance
money laundering 38, 78
Montesquieu, Charles de Secondat 113
Montreal Protocol 118
Moon and Other Celestial Bodies
    Convention 170
Morgenthau, Hans J. 95, 113
MTV 195, 217
Multilateral Agreement on Investment 346
multilateral trade agreements 346, 393
multinationalization of production 302–3,
    305
Murdoch, Rupert 208–9, 224
museum culture 89
music: cultural forms 196, 199
music industry 216–18
mutual assured destruction 151

NAFTA 72, 109, 159, 255, 262, 302, 389,
    392–3, 427, 436
Nagel, T. 455
Nair, Mira 235
Nardin, T. 460
national economies 19–23; autonomy 285;
    financial policies 295, 298; inter-national
    70–1; sceptics 19–23, 288–9
national incomes 363

nationalism: citizen 138; economic 436–8;
  ethno-history 242–3; extended 157;
  immigration 440; local 92–3; racism 457
nationalist movements 391, 440
nationalization 55
nation-building 240, 244
nationhood 14, 235–6, 240–1, 242, 246n2
nation-state 10–11, 57, 138; anarchy 128;
  autonomy 11, 132, 285, 313–14; community
  of fate 31, 32, 33, 423; democracy 416;
  global governance 181; globalists 27, 107;
  globalization 8, 34, 92–3, 106, 137;
  hollowed-out 34, 150; international
  relations 10, 70, 93; isolated 463–4;
  legitimacy 9, 14, 138, 425; markets 13,
  149, 320; MNCs 21; multi-ethnicity 15;
  political/economic power 9, 105, 138, 141,
  422–3; political good 33–4; public policy
  138; redistributive taxation 454; sceptics
  10, 105, 402; social organization 459–60;
  sovereignty 9, 11, 13, 93, 95–6, 117–18,
  121n15, 414, 422, 423; strong/weak 132,
  133, 154, 449; territory 9, 15, 95, 105, 132,
  152; TNCs 74; violence 95; welfare 440–1;
  see also welfare state
NATO 34, 434, 435
navies 51
Nederveen Pierterse, Jan 196
needs 443–4, 448, 449–50
neo-Hegelians 458, 459–60
neoliberal institutionalism 127, 128
neoliberalism 20; deregulation 426; economic
  globalization 339; global free market 5,
  100–1; globalists 28–9, 100–1
neo-Marxism 412
neo-mediaevalism 466
neo-mercantilism 164–5
neo-nationalism 200
neorealism: anarchy 115; institutionalism
  388; international relations 148–9, 388;
  self-help 115; Westphalian model 127–8
network society 76, 77, 81
networks: capitalism 76–7, 137; Chinese
  business 78; exchange 64; family 64;
  global 137–8, 146; information age 76;
  infrastructures 58; institutionalization
  58–9; national 137–8; NGOs 341;
  transnational 137–8, 144
new social movements: *see* social movements
New World Information and Communication
  Order 206, 214n6
news agencies 204–6

News Corporation 208–9, 217, 218, 220, 224
NGOs: accountability 391; environmental
  143; global governance 431; growth of 183,
  341; problems with 438–9
NICs: development 97, 252, 342; FDI 297;
  global exports 25; manufacturing
  production 265; OECD investment 24;
  wage levels 291
Nierop, Tom 288–9
Nordenstreng, Kaarle 210
North/South gap: banking 380; comparative
  advantages 140; distributive justice 451;
  environmental problems 377–8, 382–3;
  feminism 372; interdependence 21; labour
  division 26; marginalization 20, 30, 339
nuclear radiation 381
nuclear states 145–6
nuclear war 96, 151
Nuremberg Tribunal 167, 171n1

OAU 161, 168, 379
obligations: agents 449; beneficence 447–8;
  citizenship 167; degrees of 455; global
  governance 443; individual 167, 432,
  459; justice 446–7; Kant 446–7, 448;
  vulnerability 449–50, 451
OECD states 10, 20, 24, 28, 117, 118, 264,
  265, 301, 310
Ohmae, K. 73, 265
Oman, Charles 389
O'Neill, Onora 403–4
output 275, 291
Oxfam 439, 454
Ozawa, Connie 379
ozone layer 374–5, 381–2

Palestinian state 133
Panama 133
Parr, Martin 196
paternalism 85
pax americana 63
pax britannica 63, 70
People's Assembly 408, 410
Perot, Ross 302
Perotti, Roberto 305
Perraton, Jonathan 250
Peru 52
Philippines 169
place 8, 103; aesthetics 82, 89–90;
  differentiation 85–6; hybridity 199–200;
  production 257; space 85–6, 89; *see also*
  location

Plaza Agreement 295
pluralism 122–3n40
Pogge, T. 459
Polanyi, Karl 163, 164, 165, 166n9, 303
polarization 348–9; income/wealth 29, 267,
    351–2; information technology 346;
    rich/poor 99; workers 323
policy choices 12–13, 60n3
political community 14, 32, 35–6, 415
political good 31, 32, 33–4, 401
politics: adaptation 423; charismatic 84, 90;
    conflict 345–6; economics 321, 334; global
    11–13; globalization 401; of identity 136,
    144–5; interconnectedness 12; international
    74; left-wing 310, 311, 312, 314; limits 148;
    markets 153–4, 306; media 80; national
    11, 301, 302–3; power 105–6, 148, 162,
    420–1; territorial 32, 421; transnational
    414; universalism 404, 465, 466–7; world
    11, 109–10, 123n41, 184
pollution 374–8, 381, 382–3
polyarchy 417
PolyGram 217, 220
population: ageing 335; flows 64, 195–6;
    global 53n5; growth 143; power 32, 412;
    world trade shares 355–6
Portugal 50–1, 179n14, 279
postcolonialism 66n4, 359–60
post-hegemony 24, 165
post-militarism 145–6
poverty 349; gender 370; global 28, 29;
    growth 267, 352
power 7, 8, 58–9; asymmetries 133; balance
    388; capitalism 94; citizenship 32;
    concentrations 14, 62, 406; hegemonic
    157; nation-state 9, 105, 138, 141, 422–3;
    people 32, 412; politics 105–6, 162; society
    148
predation 119
pressure groups 11, 143–4
printing 203
Pritchett, Lant 351
private enterprise 78, 320
production 260, 290; acceleration 82;
    clustering 256–7; commodity 83, 325, 342;
    fragmented 252; global 23, 195; labour 79;
    manufacturing 275, 290–1; MNCs 23, 249;
    multinationalization 302–3, 305; social
    relationships 79, 80, 349; TNCs 254–5
production chains 254–5, 256, 260–1, 290
production costs 264, 315n32
professions: legal roles 174–5

profit-making 77, 221
property rights 112, 140, 301–2, 305
prostitution 368
protectionism 101; *belle époque* 24; degrees
    of 260, 262, 326–7; East Asia 364;
    embedded liberalism 304; EU 437;
    regional 161; sceptics 288
public sector deficits 309–10
public spending 301, 302, 306, 309–10, 312,
    314, 321

Quinn, D. 312

racism 62–3, 66n6, 372, 457
radio 206–8, 211
rational expectations theory 329, 331n4
Rawls, John 329, 330n2, 445, 459
R&D 73, 297
realism 5, 112, 128, 148–9; *see also*
    neorealism
reciprocity 121n25, 202
recycling of waste 379–80
Red Cross 439, 441n9
Redcliffe, N. 370
redistributive taxation 454
refugees 197, 231, 275, 439
region-state 158–9, 164–5
regional groupings 26, 60n2, 157–8, 255,
    262–3, 278–9
regionalism 156–9, 390; EU 12, 22, 159; Gold
    Standard 279; hegemonic 157, 160–1,
    162–3; new 158–9, 160–1, 163, 164; security
    12, 159–60, 161, 162
regionalization 5, 6, 55, 157, 279; black-hole
    syndrome 161–2; East Asia 12, 262, 266;
    EU 12, 160–1; homogeneity 159; and
    liberal democracy 413
regulation: coordination 72; global market
    26, 428; globalization 420; international
    450; NAFTA 427; WTO 423
Reich, Robert 260, 303
reinsurance 177, 180n17
religion 6–7, 49–50, 83–4, 200, 456; *see also*
    Christendom; Hinduism; Islam
re-skilling 82
resources 53n6, 64, 169–70
Reuters 205–6, 214n5
Rieger, Elmar 250
rights 32, 36, 446, 447
Rio Declaration on Environment and
    Development 170, 171n3, 396
risk society 99, 136, 143

Robins, Kevin 191–2
Rodrik, Dani 250, 304, 305, 312
Romans 49, 203, 454
Rome, Council of 181
Rorty, R. 459
Rosenau, James N. 107–8
Rousseau, Jean Jacques 412, 463
Ruggie, John Gerard 304, 305
Rushdie, Salman 16, 102, 196, 199
Russia 78, 133, 394

SAARC 158, 160
SADC 161
Salamon, L. M. 189n6
sanctions 131
Sandel, M. 406, 413, 416
satellite communications 84, 195, 207, 209–10
savings and investments 281, 285n2, 293
sceptics 2; financial markets 292; global
    economy 249; globalization 4–5, 37–8,
    68–9, 191–2, 287–8; inequality 30–1, 339;
    metanarratives 458; MNCs 296; nation-
    state 10, 105, 402; national culture 14–16;
    national economies 19–23, 288–9; political
    community 32; savings/investments 293;
    trade 290, 291; world economy 22
Schattschneider, E. F. 57
science: universalism 384
Scotland 200
sea levels 381, 382
Seagram 223
SEATO 157
securities 280, 283
security 118–19; economic 344; global 12,
    119–20, 436; regional 12, 159–60, 161, 162
self-determination 388
self-government 413, 416
self-interest 114, 115
self-organization 184
settler societies 363
sex tourism 368, 369
sexual exploitation 345
Shapiro, Michael 198–9
Shaw, Martin 145
Shell 144
Simmel, Georg 83
Singer, P. 455
skills 29, 185, 291
Skinner, Quentin 458
slave trade 275
Smith, Adam 151, 154, 251
Smith, Anthony D. 192–3, 200

social democracy 27, 29, 328–9
social distance 80–1
social exclusion 267, 349–50, 358–9
social movements 11, 18, 136, 144–5, 412, 456
social policy 303, 321, 336
social relationships 79, 80
socialism 1, 2, 10, 30, 89, 144, 361, 362, 444,
    449
society 459; and community 453; globalization
    6, 181; interaction 3, 137–8; international
    460; market economy 166n9; power 148;
    world 101; see also civil society
solidarity 29, 455, 456
Somalia 121n15, 162
Sony 218, 220
Sørensen, Georg 115
Soros, George 20, 423, 428
South Africa 135n15, 438
South Korea 28
sovereignty 112–15; demarchy 412; global
    governance 391; Hobbes 110–11;
    international agreements 126; international
    law 168; Morgenthau 113; nation-state 9,
    11, 13, 93, 95–6, 117–18, 121n15, 414, 422,
    423; national leaders 168–9; public
    authority 126; reciprocity 121n25;
    resources 169–70; territorial 119;
    transborder 126; transformed 106, 115–18;
    Westphalian model 124, 126–9, 388; world
    economy 22–3
Soviet Union 109, 128, 139, 362
space: capitalism 89–90; globalization 102;
    place 85–6, 89; socio-economic/political
    7–8; and time 82, 87; transformed 80
space of flows 256
Spain 50–1
stability 301–2, 432
Stallings, Barbara 265
Stammel, Christine 177
Stanislaw, Joseph 250
state 8–11, 62, 149–50, 441; collective goods
    306; gender inequalities 371; intervention
    149, 301–2, 303, 304–5, 309; legitimacy 14,
    62, 425; modernization 391; non-
    interference 450, 464; power 422–3;
    predatory 106, 112; production chains 255;
    role 321; see also nation-state
Steans, Jill 339
Stopford, John 152
Stott, Martin 378
Strachey, John 464–5
Strange, Susan 107

structural adjustment programmes 29, 329, 359, 391
subcontracting 82, 83, 366–7
subordination 61, 65–6n3
Sub-Saharan Africa 267, 342, 359
supranational institutions 255
Susskind, L. E. 379
Swank, D. 312
Sweden 330, 331n5

tariffs 289
taxation: capital 309–10, 311, 312, 314; and financial markets 309, 422; MNCs 307; progressive 305–6; public goods 329; redistributive 302, 306, 454; US 313; welfare 328; welfare state 305–6, 328–9
TCI 220, 223, 224
technological innovation 82, 152–3, 191, 202, 260, 283–4, 297–8, 319, 326, 389
technology 78, 231–2, 240, 264, 265, 290–1, 390, 466–7
technoscapes 231–2, 236
telecommunications 209–10, 289
Telecommunications Act (US) 219
telecommuting 303
telegraph technology 71, 151, 203–4, 281
television 84, 88–9, 195, 210, 212–13, 216
territoriality 7, 8, 9, 15, 32, 95, 105, 119, 124, 129–31, 132, 152, 421
Thahn Dan, T. 368–9
theocracy 465
third cultures 175–7, 196
Third World 28, 96, 174, 267, 294, 356–7, 361–2, 365, 378, 436; see also developing economies
Thirty Years' War 9, 112, 121n14, 124
Thompson, Grahame 250, 356, 360n2
Thompson, John B. 192
time concepts 80, 82, 87, 102
time–space compression 3, 54, 82, 90
Time Warner 208, 217, 218, 220, 222
TNCs 69; borderless economy 249; economic integration 253; economic power 94–5, 249; FDI 73; and MNCs 72–3, 74, 75n1; nation-states 74; pollution/location 378; production 254–5; innovation 152–3
Toffler, A. 83
tourism 196, 368, 369
trade 274–5, 365; barriers 140, 437; developing economies 289–90; EU 70, 72, 262, 437; GDP 276–7, 289–90; globalization 51; Gold Standard 277;

hyper-globalization school 290; illicit 345; intensity 279, 289–90, 357–8; interest rates 307–8; intra-industry 290; liberalization 140, 289, 304, 390; market integration 310; multilateral agreements 346, 393; output 275, 291; public spending 301; sceptics 290, 291; wages 324; world 355–6; see also free trade; international trade
trade unions 85, 310, 352, 428, 437–8
trading blocs 20, 72, 157, 266–7, 279
transborder flows 12, 126, 127, 423–4
transnational movements 235–6, 431
transnationality 103
transport 51, 84, 191, 256, 289, 319, 326
triadization 5, 24, 69, 139, 265–7, 289
tribalism 200

UN 10, 138, 396, 409, 415, 433–5; corruption 441n5; Covenants on Rights 167; ECOSOC 431; global governance 181; human rights 129, 167; International Covenant on Civil and Political Rights 169; Iraq 115; Law of the Sea Convention 170; membership 154, 183; Moon and Other Celestial Bodies Convention 170; reforms 408; Rio Declaration on Environment and Development 170, 171n3; Third World 436; Universal Declaration of Human Rights 167; and US 399n58, 433; women's role 369–72
UN Brundtland Report 385
UN Decade for Women 369–72
UN Economic Council 436
UN Environment Programme 379
UN Human Development Index 351
UN Security Council 395, 429, 432
UNCITRAL Arbitration Conventions 173
UNCTAD 431
UNCTC 261–2
UNDP report 27, 339, 351, 357–8, 360n8
unemployment 291, 329
UNESCO 206, 214n6
Universal 218, 220, 222
Universal Declaration of Human Rights 167, 169, 341
universal human rights 10, 129, 167
universalism: abstract principles 444–5; civil society 413; ethics 341; justice 444; liberalism 453; political organization 404, 465, 466–7; science 384; values 439, 453, 456
Urry, J. 74, 231

Uruguay Round: GATT 116–17, 197, 262, 290, 392, 393
US 70, 78, 86, 109, 114, 133, 141, 143, 145, 163, 184, 210, 220–4, 230, 278, 295, 313, 336, 348, 349, 380, 381, 388, 392–3, 399n58, 409–10, 433, 463–4; *see also* triadization
US Environmental Protection Agency 375
USAID 369
Utrecht Treaty 388

van Luijken, A. 367
Varis, Tapio 210
vernacular mobilization 243–5
Versailles Treaty 132
Viacom 217, 218, 220, 221
video market 218
violence 12, 50, 95, 219
Virilio, P. 84, 87
Voltaire, F. M. A. de 109
vulnerability 449–50, 451

wage levels 291, 352, 358, 367, 379–80
wages 323–4, 348
Walker, R. B. J. 406, 412, 418
Wallerstein, Immanuel 93–4, 259, 361
Waltz, Kenneth N. 110, 115
Walzer, Michael 445, 460
war 74, 145, 151, 409
Washington, George 463
waste recycling 379–80
wealth distribution: economic justice 302, 442; globalization 27, 29, 57; inter-country 343, 351
Weber, Max 243
welfare: claimants/providers of benefit 333, 335; competition 328; global governance 441; globalists 36; institutions 10, 332; nation-state 440–1; social insurance 304, 324–5; taxation 328
welfare state: country comparisons 352; globalization 27, 250, 332–4; institutionalization 335; Keynes 304; taxation 305–6, 328–9; wealth gap 99
Wendt, Alexander 115
Western hegemony 62, 63
Westphalia, Peace Treaties 9, 106–7, 113, 124, 125–6

Westphalian model 124, 131–2; autonomy 127; compromised 125–6, 129, 130–1, 133, 134n5; EU 127; international relations 127–9; neorealism 127, 128; sovereignty 124, 126–9, 388; violated 128–9, 133
Wight, Martin 111, 113, 114, 121n25
Williams, Raymond 453
Williamson, Jeffrey 326
Winchester, Simon 196
Wolff, Bernard 205
women: economic contribution 371; global governance 431; Islam 456; paid work 79, 367–8; UN agencies 369; *see also* gender; gender inequalities
Women in Development 369–70
Woods, Ngaire 339
work: individualized 77, 79–80, 348, 349; job security 344; *see also* employment; labour
workers: bargaining power 73–4, 324, 352; children as 324, 349, 428; job security 344; migrant 197, 275–6, 277–8; polarization 323; wages/working conditions 323–4
workforce: feminization 367; segmentation 29
World Administrative Radio Conference 207
World Bank: credit monopoly 160, 380; elected boards 415; environmental issues 391; global bonds 283–4; structural adjustment programmes 29, 30, 329
world community 453, 454, 457, 459, 460
world government 464–5, 466; *see also* global governance
world markets 100–1, 149
world order 119–20, 387–92, 396n2, 409
world politics 11, 109–10, 123n41, 184
world system 66n5, 93–4, 361, 455
WTO 7, 22, 34, 220, 255, 262, 290, 324, 341, 393, 415, 423, 437

xenophobia 4, 261

Yearley, Steven 339
Yergin, Daniel A. 250
Yugoslavia 162, 200, 388, 432, 433–5

Zaire 439
Zalewski, M. 456
Zevin, R. 280–1